NATIVE AMERICAN RESOURCES SERIES

Advisory Board

1. *Handbook of the American Frontier: Four Centuries of Indian-White Relationships,* by J. Norman Heard
   Volume I: *Southeastern Woodlands.* 1987
   Volume II: *Northeastern Woodlands.* 1990

HANDBOOK OF THE AMERICAN FRONTIER:

Four Centuries of Indian-White Relationships

VOLUME II:
The Northeastern Woodlands

by
J. NORMAN HEARD

Native American Resources Series, No. 1

The Scarecrow Press, Inc.
Metuchen, N.J., & London
1990

British Library Cataloguing-in-Publication data available

Library of Congress Cataloging-in-Publication Data
(Revised for volume 2)

Heard, J. Norman (Joseph Norman), 1922-
    Handbook of the American frontier.

    (Native American resources series ; 1)
    Contents: v. 1. The southeastern woodlands -- v. 2.
The northeastern woodlands.
    1. Indians of North America--History--Dictionaries and
encyclopedias. 2. Frontier and pioneer life--United
States--Dictionaries. 3. United States--History--
Dictionaries. I. Title. II. Series.
E76.2.H43 1987   973'.03   86-20326
ISBN 0-8108-1931-7 (v. 1)
ISBN 0-8108-2324-1 (v. 2)

Dedicated to Elizabeth Hull Heard, a seventeenth-century New Hampshire housewife, who saved the life of an Indian boy in 1676 during King Philip's War and was spared, as a result, more than a decade later during the destruction of Dover in King William's War.

EDITOR'S FOREWORD

It is fitting that the first volume in the Native American Resources Series is Norman Heard's Handbook of the American
Frontier. The Handbook brings together reference material
on American Indian and non-Indian relationships that can
usually only be found after painstaking research in a number
of historical, ethnological, and biographical sources. The
book contains such topics as American Indian tribes, Indian
leaders, frontier settlers, captives, explorers, missionaries,
mountain men. The scope is from the time of earliest contact
into the twentieth century.

As Professor Heard describes in detail in his preface,
the Handbook will contain five volumes when completed.
Volume I covers the area of the Southeastern Woodlands following the definition of these in John R. Swanton's The Indians of the Southeastern United States, Bureau of American
Ethnology Bulletin, 137 (1946). Volume II on the area of
the Northeast includes materials north of the area covered
in Volume I and west to the plains. Volume III will be on the
Plains, patterned on the delineation of the area of Walter Prescott Webb's The Great Plains (1931). It will cover the plains
from the Canadian border to Texas. Volume IV will cover
the Southwest and the Pacific Coast. Volume V will consist
of a comprehensive index, a chronology, and a bibliography.

When completed, the Handbook of the American Frontier
will contain the widest coverage of the frontier activities of
the American Indians and white settlers. The entries are
balanced and objective. Professor Heard has eliminated the
anti-Indian bias that occurs in almost all of the early accounts
of Indian/non-Indian relationships.

Norman Heard has spent his career as a librarian and
researcher. Early in his career he contributed twenty articles

v

to Walter Prescott Webb's Handbook of Texas (1952), and he
has written the article on Indian captivities for a revised
edition of this work (not yet published). He is the author
of The Black Frontiersmen (1969) and White into Red (1973).
With Charles F. Hamsa, he is the author of the ninth edition
of Bookman's Guide to Americana (1986).

Jack W. Marken
English Department, Emeritus
South Dakota State University
Brookings, South Dakota

PREFACE

The subject of Indian-white relationships during the exploration and settlement of our nation has been of great interest for centuries to students of history and ethnology, as well as to armchair adventurers. Much information on the Indian side of the question is available in the venerable Handbook of American Indians North of Mexico (Washington, 1912-13), and a new Handbook of North American Indians (twenty volumes projected) is in the process of publication by the Smithsonian Institution. Experiences of prominent white frontiersmen are included in the Dictionary of American Biography and the Dictionary of American History, as well as in a multitude of historical monographs and articles. Indeed such a mass of material has been published about Indian warfare that it is exceeded by few other topics in American history. Many of the primary source materials are out-of-print and scarce, however, and some secondary works should be used with caution.

A need exists for works of first reference that provide insights into both sides of the Indian-white relationship. It is hoped that the Handbook of the American Frontier will help to fill this need and that it will guide the reader to reliable sources of additional information. It is the Handbook's objective to provide a series of brief articles in dictionary arrangement about American Indian tribes and leaders, explorers, traders, frontier settlers, soldiers, missionaries, mountain men, captives, battles, massacres, forts, treaties, and other topics of importance or interest in the history of the first forty-eight United States, from the arrival of the earliest seafarers to the end of the Indian wars, four centuries later.

This study will emphasize the frontier aspects of the careers of prominent subjects, and it will present articles on many people and events excluded or mentioned only in passing in general reference sources. As it is intended as ethnohistory it will exclude frontier topics that are irrelevant to Indian-white relationships. Subjects are gleaned from ethnological studies, tribal histories, state or regional histories, narratives of captivity, compilations of incidents of border warfare, military histories, and other biographical and historical studies readily available only to readers with access to research libraries. The reader may find that the author has devoted a disproportionate amount of attention to the experiences of frontier women, blacks, and captives. These subjects represent lifelong interests which led to a doctoral dissertation and two books, The Black Frontiersmen (New York, 1969), and White into Red, a Study of the Assimilation of White Persons Captured by Indians (Metuchen, 1973).

The work will be divided regionally, roughly corresponding to major Indian culture areas. Volume I will cover the southeastern woodlands, substantially as delineated by John R. Swanton in his monumental study, The Indians of the Southeastern United States (Washington, 1946). This area includes the Atlantic coastal states from Chesapeake Bay to the tip of Florida, the Gulf Coast states from Florida to southwestern Louisiana, eastern Texas, most of Arkansas, southeastern Missouri, Kentucky, West Virginia, and Tennessee. It excludes Pennsylvania and most of Maryland. Volume II will be devoted to the Northeast, north of Swanton's line and east of the range of the Plains Indians. Volume III will cover the vast region roamed by the Plains tribes from the Canadian border to Texas as depicted in Walter Prescott Webb's enduring study, The Great Plains (Boston, 1931). The scope of Volume IV will be the Rocky Mountains, southwestern deserts, and the Pacific Coast. Volume V will provide a general index, chronology, and list of readings.

This geographical arrangement presents difficulties, as a number of Indian nations ranged or resided between Swanton's southeastern tribes and Webb's Great Plains. Coastal tribes of southwestern Louisiana and eastern Texas will be included in Volume I unless they were characterized by Webb as marginal Plains Indians. Southern Texas was raided by Plains Indians but inhabited by peoples with culture traits ranging from the southeastern woodlands to the southwestern deserts, and these tribes will be discussed in Volumes I and IV respectively. At the northern boundary of Swanton's Southeast, the Shawnees, classed by him as a southeastern tribe, lived north of the Ohio River during later frontier times. White men first encountered them in the South, however, and the principal article on the tribe will be included in Volume I. After the Treaty of Greenville in 1795, Shawnee warfare shifted northward, and later leaders and events will be included in Volume II. The Tuscaroras lived in North Carolina and moved to New York after their defeat by the Carolinians in 1713 to become the Sixth Nation of the Iroquois. They will be included in Volume I because of their importance in the southern Indian wars and their somewhat subordinate role in Iroquois affairs.

Pennsylvania traders operated both north and south of the Ohio, and some of them were notorious for leading Indian raids into Kentucky and western Virginia. As northerners, they will be included in Volume II, while southern captives held by northern tribes will be assigned to the Southeast. Farther west, explorers and traders transversed the Plains and Rocky Mountains and some, such as Cabeza de Vaca, traveled from coast to coast. Inevitably the author had to choose which volume should contain an article relative to more than one area. Occasionally this problem was resolved by separate articles, such as a division of the Seminole campaigns of Army officers from their later experiences in the West. More often, however, it was decided that a subject's career in one region predominated over that in another, and the volume assignment was made on that basis. The reader should be advised, therefore, that until the general index appears it may be necessary to consult more than one volume to locate the principal article on such a frontier figure as Simon Girty, a "white savage" who led northern and southern Indians in raids both above and below the Ohio River. Like other Pennsylvania "Indian diplomats" he will be found in the volume on the Northeast. His Virginia and Kentucky exploits will be described in Volume I, however, in articles on battles, captivities, and forts.

A problem of nomenclature faces a researcher dealing with frontier topics. Names of tribes differ so greatly in primary sources that it sometimes is difficult to identify the Indians described. Even eminent ethnologists differ as to the spelling of tribal names. In this regard it is helpful to consult the synonymy in F. W. Hodge, ed., Handbook of American Indians North of Mexico, II, to work one's way through the maze. Name difficulties abound regarding individual Indians as well. A chief may have been known by one Indian

name to his own people, and by another to other Indians, as
well as by a European name to the whites. Settlers' names,
too, are spelled so differently in some early chronicles that it
is difficult to determine identity. Usually the subject is
readily identified, but a question remains as to the spelling
to be adopted. The author has attempted to compensate for
varying names and spellings by the use of cross-references.

The most formidable problem to be faced by the student
of frontier history is credibility of sources. It quickly be-
comes evident that many frontiersmen and early chroniclers
of the Indian wars were prone to exaggeration ("to draw the
long bow" as R. W. G. Vail described it in his invaluable Voice
of the Old Frontier, Philadelphia, 1949). Others, particularly
persons claiming to be redeemed captives, published entirely
fictitious narratives. Some narratives, while based upon real
captivities, deliberately distorted events to increase sales, to
foster hatred of Indians, or to promote a religious perspec-
tive. (See Richard Van Der Beets, Held Captive by Indians,
Knoxville, 1973, for an enlightening introduciton to this topic.)

It is not surprising that editors who interviewed Indian
fighters in later life found that faulty memories led to numerous contradictions. Even nineteenth-century frontier historians who sifted accounts of battles and raids have come to
conflicting conclusions, and several of them have taken pains
to point out errors in the interpretations of others. Accounts
of attacks on Wheeling are a case in point, with reputable
scholars in disagreement as to the number of sieges, the names
of leaders of war parties, and even the identity of the girl
who ran through Indian lines to obtain gun powder for the
defenders.

Few studies of racial conflicts reflect the Indian point
of view, and the narratives of most white frontiersmen reveal
a strong anti-Indian bias. The same tendency is evident in
the works of earlier editors who interviewed survivors and
published their narratives. It is difficult, therefore, to au-
thenticate details of incidents that took place more than a
century ago when confronted by irreconcilable primary sources.
Fortunately the studies of twentieth-century scholars are of
tremendous assistance in this regard, particularly those of
ethnologists and historians who published or edited volumes
in the Bulletins of the Bureau of American Ethnology, in the
University of Oklahoma's "Civilization of the American Indian

Series," and in works of other university presses. Even there, however, problems persist: scholarly works disagree in regard to whether or not the Cherokee chief, Bowles, was the son of the white "Creek Emperor," William Augustus Bowles; an eminent ethnologist states in one standard work that the Chowanoc Indians supported the colonists in the Tuscarora War, while asserting in another that they fought on the side of the Tuscaroras. When conflicting accounts could not be otherwise reconciled, final reliance in this study is placed whenever possible on the Dictionary of American History.

The Handbook of the American Frontier is based upon hundreds of published sources, both primary and secondary. It would have been a more comprehensive study if the author had delved into governmental reports, newspaper files, unpublished letters of frontier people, and other archival materials. Beginning his research at age 60, however, it seemed prudent to embark upon a project of more manageable proportions.

Included in this Handbook, therefore, are experiences and events, believed to be representative of those of frontier peoples--red, white, and black--some famous, some forgotten. It is hoped that the casual reader will be interested in these incidents and that the student will gain an insight into what life was like when Europeans and their descendants strove for mastery over this magnificent continent, and Indian nations fought courageously to preserve their country and culture.

J. Norman Heard
Curator, Mississippi Valley
Missionary Museum
Lafayette, Louisiana

HANDBOOK OF THE AMERICAN FRONTIER:

Four Centuries of Indian-White Relationships

THE NORTHEASTERN WOODLANDS

ABABCO INDIANS. The Ababco Indians, an Algonquian people, resided in the Choptank River region (present Dorchester County, Maryland) during the colonial period. James Mooney surmised that they constituted a division of the Choptank tribe, while John R. Swanton identified them as a Choptank village or subtribe of the Nanticokes. In 1741 colonial officials confirmed them in the possession of their lands. The Ababco population decreased rapidly as a result of contact with other races, and by 1837 only a few mixed-bloods remained.

 (Frederick Webb Hodge, ed., Handbook of American Indians, I; John R. Swanton, Indian Tribes of North America.)

ABBIGADASSET, ABNAKI CHIEF. Abbigadasset, a seventeenth-century Abnaki sachem, was more important in Maine history for selling land to settlers than for waging war against them. Among his several land deals with Englishmen was the sale of Swans Island to the colonist Humphrey Davy in 1667.

 (Dictionary of Indians of North America, I.)

ABBOTT, EDWARD. Captain Edward Abbott of the British Royal Artillery fought in Pontiac's War, helping to defend Detroit against the forces of that formidable chief. During 1777-78 he served as British lieutenant governor of Vincennes, where he constructed Fort Sackville to replace the dilapidated stockade that had protected the French community.

 Abbott disagreed strongly with his fellow lieutenant governor, Henry Hamilton of Detroit, regarding the use of Indians against the American frontier settlers. In that regard he wrote the following to Sir Guy Carleton, governor of Canada:

> Your excellency will plainly perceive the employing Indians on the Rebel frontiers has been of great hurt to the cause, for many hundreds would have put themselves under His Majesty's protection was there a possibility; that not being the case, these poor, unhappy people are forced to take up arms against their Sovereign, or be pillaged & left to starve: cruel alternative. This is too shocking a subject to dwell upon: Your Excellency's known humanity will certainly put a stop to such proceedings, as it is not people in arms that Indians will ever daringly attack, but the poor inoffensive families who fly to the deserts to be out of trouble & who are being inhumanely butchered, sparing neither woman

nor children. It may be said it is necessary to employ Indians to prevent their serving our enemies, I will be bold to
say their keeping a neutrality will be equally (if not more)
serviceable to us, as their going to war.

Unfortunately, Abbott's view did not prevail, and he retired
to Canada in February 1778. Hamilton's employment of war parties
against the settlements strengthened American determination to resist the British.

(Louise Phelps Kellogg, The British Régime in Wisconsin and
the Northwest.)

ABEEL, JOHN. John Abeel (O'Bail, O'Beal), a Dutch trader, had a
white family in Albany and an Indian family among the Senecas. His
Seneca wife was the daughter of a chief, and their son became the
famous Iroquois sachem known to the whites as Cornplanter. Abeel
had little to do with the child, and Cornplanter grew up as a complete Indian.

Abeel was one of the foremost sellers of rum to the Senecas,
and he acquired a considerable fortune in the Indian trade. He reputedly boasted that his liquor sales realized a profit of 1,000 percent.
Although English authorities detested Abeel, he did them a good turn
in 1756 when he warned that Indian friends of the French were waiting to murder their envoys if they entered the Seneca country.

In 1780 Cornplanter and four hundred warriors attacked Canajoharie, burning Abeel's home and taking him prisoner. When Cornplanter discovered that his father had been made destitute, he apologized to the aged trader and offered to take care of him in his own
home. But Abeel opted to return to his white family, and Cornplanter sent several of his followers to escort him to safety at Albany.

(Barbara Graymont, The Iroquois in the American Revolution;
Arthur Pound, Johnson of the Mohawks; Frank H. Severance, An
Old Frontier of France; Paul A. W. Wallace, Indians in Pennsylvania;
William L. Stone, Border Wars of the American Revolution.)

ABENAKI INDIANS see ABNAKI INDIANS

ABENQUID, ABNAKI CHIEF. Abenquid was a prominent Abnaki war
chief, feared for his ferocity by the settlers of northern New England.
In February 1696, accompanied by Chiefs Egeremet and Moxus and a
large war party, he surrounded the fort at Pemaquid and sought a
parley with the commanding officer Capt. Pascho Chubb. When the
Indians displayed a flag of truce, Chubb and several officers met
them outside the gate. It is believed that the Indians wanted to exchange prisoners, but the parley never reached that stage. The
New England historian Samuel Adams Drake related that "the English
suddenly fell upon the Indians, that weapons were drawn, and that
in the melee Egeremet and Abenquid, two as untamed spirits as ever
lifted the war-hatchet, were killed on the spot."

(Samuel Adams Drake, Border Wars of New England.)

ABNAKI INDIANS. The Abnaki (Abenaki, Wabanaki, Tarrateen) Indians, an important Algonquian confederacy, lived in the present state of Maine at the time of first European contact. In 1524 they met Giovanni da Verrazzano at Casco Bay in a manner that convinced the mariner that they had traded with Europeans at an even earlier time. One year later the Spanish sea captain Esteban Gómez seized 58 Abnakis and abducted them to Spain. In 1604 Samuel de Champlain sailed up the Kennebec River and conferred with Abnaki sachems near the present site of Bangor, offering trade and his good offices to restore peace with enemy tribes. The following year Capt. George Waymouth kidnapped 5 members of the tribe and took them to England, 2 of whom returned with George Popham to help establish a short-lived colony on the Maine coast. (See SAGADAHOC.) The Abnakis, finding the French more to their liking, killed 11 Englishmen and broke up the colony.

Between 1616 and 1619 an epidemic, probably caused by European contacts, swept through the coastal Abnaki villages. The English offered better trade goods than the French and used that advantage to establish posts in Abnaki territory. The Plymouth colonists, whose patent included the Abnaki country, traded corn to them for furs in 1625 and wampum for furs shortly thereafter. But the French contended that their province of Acadia extended westward to the Kennebec, and they were determined to defend it with Abnaki assistance. The result was a series of bloody colonial wars, and, in Parkman's opinion, the French "constantly spurred the Abnakis against New England, in order to avert the dreaded event of their making peace with her." The Abnakis "were continually drawn to New England by the cheapness and excellence of English goods; and the only sure means to prevent trading with the enemy was to incite them to kill him."

If left alone to pursue their own interests the Abnakis would have preferred to follow a neutral course, but they could not avoid involvement, stimulated by large scalp bounties offered by both nations. They were tied ideologically to the French, especially through the influence of such missionaries as Gabriel Druillettes, Pierre Biard, and especially Sebastian Rasles. In 1670 French-Abnaki ties were strengthened by the marriage of Chief Madockawando's daughter to the French officer and trader Jean-Vincent D'Abbadie de Saint-Castin.

After the close of King Philip's War the English expanded settlement into Abnaki territory, and many of the Indians withdrew to Canada, settling with their missionaries at Bécancour, Sillery, and St. Francis. From these sanctuaries they dispatched raids on New England settlements, returning with hundreds of captives that they adopted or sold to the French. But the English won the colonial wars, and in 1762 the Abnakis capitulated to the victorious power. During the American Revolution the Abnakis that remained in Maine, principally the Penobscots, took the part of the colonies; nevertheless, the victorious Americans deprived them of most of their lands. The Abnakis in Canada supported the English in the War of 1812.

(See PENOBSCOT INDIANS; PEQUAWKET INDIANS; NORRIDGE-WOCK INDIANS; MOSELEY, SAMUEL; ROGERS, ROBERT; LOVEWELL, JOHN; CHURCH, BENJAMIN.)

(Francis Parkman, The Jesuits in North America; Neal Salisbury, Manitou and Providence; Herbert Milton Sylvester, Indian Wars of New England, II-III; William C. Sturtevant, ed., Handbook of American Indians, XV.)

ABOITE RIVER MASSACRE. In the fall of 1780 Col. Augustin Mottin de la Balme, a French officer and land speculator who had come to America with Lafayette, determined to attack the British at Detroit and their Indian allies. At the head of more than a hundred French settlers from Kaskaskia and Vincennes, he captured Kekionga, the principal Miami village, driving the Indians out and plundering their possessions. Afterward he camped on the Aboite River to await reinforcements before continuing the march to Detroit.

Led by Little Turtle, a Miami war party surrounded La Balme's camp during the night and struck before dawn. The Indians killed La Balme and all of his men except one who was captured and turned over to the British. This attack was Little Turtle's first victory.

(Calvin M. Young, Little Turtle; Dale Van Every, A Company of Heroes; Clarence Walworth Alvord, The Illinois Country; Louise Phelps Kellogg, The British Régime in Wisconsin and the Northwest.)

ABOMAZINE, ABNAKI CHIEF. Abomazine (Bomazeen), one of the most formidable foes of the northern New England settlers, was born about 1675 near Kennebec, Maine, and became an Abnaki war chief before he was 20. On July 18, 1694, he led an attack on the New Hampshire settlers on the south side of the Oyster River. Four months later he appeared outside the fort at Pemaquid under a flag of truce, was invited to enter, and was immediately seized and sent to Boston for imprisonment. Frederick J. Dockstader, Indian historian and biographer, asserts that "Abomazine swore vengeance for the treachery," and raided English settlements for the next 20 years.

When Queen Anne's War broke out in America in 1703, Abomazine conferred with Gov. Joseph Dudley of Massachusetts and agreed that the Abnakis would remain neutral. Apparently, says Parkman, this was not his real intention, however, for he led several forays against the English soon afterward. In 1707 he struck Chelmsford and Sudbury. In 1710 he attacked Saco, and he kept up hostilities until 1713, when he signed a peace treaty at Portsmouth, New Hampshire. The peace was soon interrupted, however, and raids by both Indians and whites kept the New England frontier in turmoil for many more years.

Finally, in 1724, a force of 208 frontiersmen led by Captain Jeremiah Moulton caught up with Abomazine at Taconnet, Maine, and shot him to death as he attempted to swim the river to safety. Then they killed his daughter near Taconnet Falls and captured his wife, compelling her to guide them to their village. (See NORRIDGEWOCK INDIANS.)

(Frederick J. Dockstader, Great North American Indians; Samuel Adams Drake, Border Wars of New England; Francis Parkman, A Half-Century of Conflict, I; Herbert Milton Sylvester, Indian Wars of New England, III.)

ABRAHAM, MAHICAN CHIEF. Abraham, the first Moravian convert
to Christianity in the northern colonies, was a resident of the Mahican village of Shecomeco, New York, until the mission there was
removed to Friedenshutten, and afterwards to Gnadenhutten, Pennsylvania. In 1745, he was appointed chief of the Mahican remnant.
In 1754 he helped Chief Tedyuscung establish a Delaware-Mahican
village in the Wyoming Valley. He attempted to prevent the Delawares from attacking the Pennsylvania settlements during the French
and Indian War.

    (Anthony F. C. Wallace, King of the Delawares: Teedyuscung.)

ABRAHAM, MOHAWK CHIEF. Abraham, also known as Little Abraham, was a prominent Mohawk chief and the father of Sir William Johnson's first Iroquois wife, Caroline. A noted orator, he spoke for the
Six Nations at the Albany Conference of 1775, assuring the Americans of neutrality in the conflict with Britain and urging them to
fight their battles outside the Indian country. A few months later,
however, when the Americans attempted to arrest Sir John Johnson
(son of Sir William Johnson), Abraham scolded them for breaking the
treaty and threatened to intervene with his warriors if they persisted.

    Abraham succeeded Hendrick as chief of the Mohawks when the
latter was killed at the Battle of Lake George. He was disposed toward peace, but his friendship for the Johnsons led him to sym-
pathize with the British during the American Revolution.

    (Barbara Graymont, The Iroquois in the American Revolution;
Arthur Pound, Johnson of the Mohawks.)

ACCOMINTA INDIANS see PENNACOOK INDIANS

ADAQUARANDE, ONONDAGA CHIEF see SADEKANAKTIE, ONONDAGA
CHIEF

ADARIO, HURON CHIEF. Adario (Kondiaronk, The Rat) was a noted
Huron chief and orator who played a curious and important role in
Indian-French relations during the latter part of the seventeenth
century. At various times the French referred to him as the most
noble red man of his time and as a savage Machiavelli. His machina-
tions led to the murders of hundreds of Montreal settlers, yet he was
buried with honors in that community a few years afterward.

    In 1688, having a reputation for valor and wisdom, Adario was
employed by the French to lead an expedition against the Iroquois.
He recruited a large war party and set out on his mission, but before reaching the Iroquois country he received instructions to stay
his hand, for the French had received an unexpected opportunity to
negotiate peace with the Five Nations. This turn of events infuriated
Adario, for he believed that a French-Five Nations rapprochement
would result in Huron destruction by the Iroquois.

    Determined to disrupt the proposed treaty, Adario intercepted
the Iroquois envoys en route to Montreal and took them prisoner.
He informed them that the French had instructed him to massacre

the entire party. The ensuing deception was described by Cadwallader Colden:

> The Ambassadors being much surpris'd with the French Perfidy, told Adario the Design of their Journey, who, the better to play his part, seem'd to grow Mad and Furious, declaiming against Mr. De Nonville, and said, He would, some Time or other be Revenged of him for making a Tool of him to commit such horrid Treachery. Then looking stedfastly on the Prisoners (among whom Dekanesora was the Principal Ambassador) Adario said to them, Go my Brethren, I Unty your Bonds, and send you Home again, tho our Nations be at War; The French Governor has made me commit so black an Action, that I shall never be easy after it till you Five Nations shall have taken full Vengeance.

Enraged by what they perceived to be "French perfidy," the Iroquois assembled their forces for a massive assault on Montreal. Governor Denonville attempted to disown Adario's actions, but the Iroquois refused to believe him. On August 25, 1689, more than a thousand warriors attacked Montreal and all of the settlements along the St. Lawrence and massacred many Canadians. At Lachine alone 120 settlers were captured, many of them destined to suffer death at the stake.

But, strange as it seems, this wily chief soon regained the goodwill of the Canadian officials. T. J. Campbell, biographer of the Jesuit fathers, noted that "this wretch, though his treachery was commonly known, was afterward admitted to the confidence of the French, and promoted to the rank of captain in the army. He was even admitted to the Governor's table. His wit was so keen, and his power of repartee, in which no one was a match for him but the Governor, so remarkable, that these unusual distinctions were willingly accorded to him."

Adario became a Christian in later life and he used his skill as an orator to preach to his people and to urge Indian tribes to live in peace with each other and with the French. On August 1, 1701, he died at Montreal in the midst of an appeal for peace to a thousand Indians of several tribes. His body, clothed in a French officer's uniform, lay in state at the Hôtel Dieu, and he was buried with military honors.

(T. J. Campbell, Pioneer Priests of North America; Francis Parkman, Count Frontenac and New France Under Louis XIV; Cadwallader Colden, The History of the Five Indian Nations; Frederick Webb Hodge, ed., Handbook of American Indians, I.)

ADRIAENSEN, MARYN, MASSACRE. Maryn Adriaensen, characterized by E. B. O'Callaghan as "a noted freebooter," instigated a group of New Amsterdam citizens to attack a band of peaceful Wecquaesgeek Indians who were camped at Corlaer's Hook seeking Dutch protection from their Mohawk enemies. The participants, asserting that they sought retaliation for murders committed by other Indians during recent years, obtained the approval of Director Kieft and other officials. Adriaensen and his cohorts fell upon the sleeping Indians during the night of February 25-26, 1643, massacring 30 men, women, and children. The victims, having been kindly treated by the Dutch until the night of the massacre, believed the attackers to be Mohawks. At the same time a second Indian encampment was assaulted at Pavonia. (See PAVONIA MASSACRE.)

The massacres resulted in increased Indian hostilities near New Amsterdam, and the settlers condemned Adriaensen as the cause. Confronted by citizen anger, Kieft conveniently forgot that he had accepted a gift of Indian heads from Adriaensen and condemned the man as a murderer. In retaliation, Adriaensen attempted to assassinate Kieft, but was overpowered and imprisoned. Kieft, lacking the courage to conduct the trial, sent the prisoner to Holland. Apparently Adriaensen escaped severe punishment, however, for three years later he returned to New Amsterdam and received a land grant from Kieft.

(E. B. O'Callaghan, History of New Netherland, I; Allen W. Trelease, Indian Affairs in Colonial New York.)

AGARIATA, MOHAWK CHIEF, EXECUTION OF. A peace conference was held between the French and the Iroquois at Quebec on August 31, 1666. As a gesture of goodwill, Gov. Alexandre de Prouville, Marquis de Tracy, invited Agariata and another chief to dinner. During the meal the governor asked them whether they knew who had murdered his nephew a few months earlier. Insolently, Agariata raised his right arm and boasted, "This is the hand that split the head of that young man!" Tracy's astonishment at the rash admission gave way to fury and he shouted that the assassin would not live to murder again. Agariata was seized, dragged from the table, and summarily hanged.

The execution brought an end to peace negotiations. The governor determined to muster French fighting men from throughout Canada and to lead them himself against the Mohawk villages.

(Francis Parkman, The Old Régime in Canada.)

AGWRONDOUGWAS, PETER, ONEIDA CHIEF. Peter Agwrondougwas (Good Peter), chief of the Oneida Indians, was one of the most outstanding orators among the Six Nations. About 1750 he was converted to Christianity by the Rev. Elihu Spencer, a Protestant missionary. He assisted several white preachers in the Susquehanna River region, and after whites were compelled to withdraw during the French and Indian War he carried on their missionary labors. In 1762 when the Rev. Eli Forbes went to Oquaga to reestablish missionary work in the area he found Good Peter preaching there and in neighboring villages. Forbes considered him to be "the equal of any Englishman he knew in his Christian virtues and abilities."

(Francis Whiting Halsey, The Old New York Frontier.)

AHNYERO, ONEIDA CHIEF see SPENCER, THOMAS, ONEIDA CHIEF

ALBANY, NEW YORK, INDIAN TRADE AND DIPLOMACY. The present city of Albany had its beginnings in 1624 when Fort Orange was built by the Dutch West India Company. About a decade later a village was established near the fort by Dutch colonists of the patroon, Kiliaen Van Rensselaer. The settlement became known as Beverwyck in 1642. Located not far from the Mohawk villages, it developed immediately into a major center of Indian commerce as a result of Dutch traders competing successfully with the French of Montreal for pelts acquired by the Iroquois from western tribes. This association resulted in generally amicable Dutch-Iroquois relations, and some of the settlers became highly influential Indian diplomats. (See VAN CURLER, ARENT.)

In 1664 the English seized the settlement and renamed it Albany. They inherited the Iroquois trade relationship, continuing in many instances to rely on the Dutch as Indian managers, and improving the quality of trade goods. This development was seriously detrimental to Montreal interests, and, after a time, even some of the Caughnawaga Indians of Canada began trading at Albany, obtaining goods which they sold to French traders for use in bartering with western tribes. The Albany trade remained a major source of conflict throughout the colonial wars. During King Philip's War, New England officials accused Albany traders of selling guns to the Indians attacking their settlements, a charge angrily denied.

In addition to its importance in trade, Albany became a center of colonial Indian diplomacy during the last decade of the seventeenth century. In 1689 delegates from Massachusetts and Connecticut conferred there with the Iroquois and convinced them to continue their attacks on the French. From that time forward, annual conferences were held at Albany, sometimes lasting as long as a week and creating a financial burden for officials who provided large numbers of Indians with presents and food. Sometimes these conferences led to important diplomatic results, as in 1722 when warfare between the Iroquois and the southern Indians was brought to an end.

In 1754 the famous Albany Congress was conducted under the leadership of Benjamin Franklin. Sydney G. Fisher has characterized it as "an attempt on the part of the British Government to settle all Indian affairs in a general agreement and to prevent separate treaties by the different colonies; but the Pennsylvania delegates, by various devices of compass courses which the Indians did not understand and by failing to notify and secure the consent of certain tribes, obtained a grant of pretty much the whole of Pennsylvania west of the Susquehanna," land claimed by the Iroquois but occupied by other tribes. This fraud, he asserted, was a major factor in influencing the Pennsylvania Indians to go over to the French and to begin "scalping men, women and children among the Pennsylvania colonists."

While Franklin failed to gain united colonial action on Indian affairs and other matters of mutual concern, this attempt to foster intercolonial cooperation led to an increased awareness of the threat of the French and their Indian allies. It served as a model 20 years later when the colonies were forced to cooperate at the onset of the Revolution.

In 1775 American commissioners met at Albany with the Six Nations and urged them to remain neutral in the impending conflict. The Indians agreed, while insisting that the combatants keep out of the Iroquois country. By 1777, however, most tribes had decided to fight for the British, and the Americans returned to Albany to seek Indian allies of their own. Upon presentation of war belts, hundreds of Iroquois, chiefly Oneidas and Tuscaroras, accepted, and the League of the Iroquois burst asunder.

(Cadwallader Colden, The History of the Five Indian Nations; Sydney G. Fisher, The Quaker Colonies; Barbara Graymont, The Iroquois in the American Revolution; Allen W. Trelease, Indian Affairs of Colonial New York; Dale Van Every, Forth to the Wilderness; E. B. O'Callaghan, ed., Documentary History of the State of New York.)

ALDEN, ICHABOD. Col. Ichabod Alden, a Massachusetts officer more noted for political connections than military prowess, was placed in command of the fort at Cherry Valley, New York, in the spring of 1778. His forces consisted of 200 regular troops and 150 militiamen, but they were poorly prepared to protect the settlers who feared a massive invasion by Indians and Tories.

The fort had been built by the settlers, but Alden denied them permission to stay in it, asserting that his scouts would provide ample warning if enemies entered the area. To show his lack of concern he and his officers were quartered in private homes outside the stockade. On November 8 he ignored a warning by Oneida Indians of an impending attack.

When Cherry Valley was invaded on November 11 by 200 Loyalist Rangers commanded by Walter Butler and 600 Indians led by Joseph Brant, Alden was a quarter mile from the fort at the home of Robert Wells holding a meeting with his officers. When Indians suddenly attacked the house, Alden took time to put on his boots while his subordinates fled safely to the fort. The delay cost him his life. When he ran out of the house, an Indian, believed to have been Brant, pursued and downed him with a tomahawk throw. As Alden was being scalped the Indians attacked the homes of the settlers. (See CHERRY VALLEY MASSACRE.)

"It was part of the tragedy of Cherry Valley to be at the mercy of a criminally incompetent commander."--Barbara Graymont.

(Barbara Graymont, The Iroquois in the American Revolution; Francis Whiting Halsey, The Old New York Frontier; T. Wood Clark, The Bloody Mohawk.)

ALIQUIPPA, QUEEN see ALLIQUIPPA, QUEEN, IROQUOIS CHIEF

ALLEN, FORT, PENNSYLVANIA. Fort Allen was built in Carbon County, Pennsylvania, in January, 1756, as a result of an Indian attack on the Moravian mission of Gnadenhutten. Benjamin Franklin supervised construction of the stockade which was garrisoned by provincial soldiers for the next four years. The fort, which served also as a trading post, was the scene of several Indian conferences.

(William A. Hunter, Forts on the Pennsylvania Frontier.)

ALLERTON, ISAAC. Isaac Allerton was a Plymouth settler and one of the eight leaders who formed a partnership to manage the Indian trade for six years in exchange for insuring that the colony's debts were paid. Sent to England to obtain trade goods for the colony, he purchased a supply for personal profit. Falling into disfavor with the other undertakers, he established a trade partnership with Edward Ashley, a "white savage" who had been living for some time among the Indians on the Penobscot River. They monopolized the Indian trade in that area until Ashley was arrested for selling guns to the Indians.

Allerton left Plymouth about 1631, managing business affairs in Marblehead, New Amsterdam, and New Haven. He continued his ventures, largely by means of a trading vessel, for many years. He died a rich man in 1659.

(William Bradford, Of Plimoth Plantation; Charles M. Andrews, The Colonial Period of American History, I; Neal Salisbury, Manitou and Providence.)

ALLIQUIPPA, QUEEN, IROQUOIS CHIEF. Queen Alliquippa, a female chief frequently mentioned in colonial chronicles, is variously described as a Delaware, a Mohawk, or a Conestoga. Paul A. W. Wallace, historian of the Indians of Pennsylvania, believes that she was a Seneca, and other writers assert that "Queen Alliquippa's Town" was principally inhabited by members of that nation.

She came to public notice in 1701 by accompanying her husband, a Seneca or Conestoga chief, to Newcastle, Delaware, to call upon William Penn. After the death of her husband she established a village on the Ohio River, a few miles below the forks, before 1731. In 1749 Pierre Joseph de Céleron's expedition visited her on its way down the Ohio to warn English traders to leave the area. Céleron reported that "the Iroquois inhabit this place, and it is an old woman of this nation who governs it. She regards herself as sovereign; she is entirely devoted to the English."

It was her attachment to the English that forced Alliquippa to leave the Ohio at the onset of the French and Indian War. George Washington visited her at the mouth of the Youghiogheny in December 1753, and the following June she and her people joined him at Fort Necessity. After the surrender of that post to the French she removed to Aughwick, where she was living when last brought to public notice at a meeting of the Pennsylvania Council in 1755.

(Charles A. Hanna, The Wilderness Trail; Paul A. W. Wallace, Indians in Pennsylvania; Carolyn Thomas Foreman, Indian Women Chiefs.)

ALLOUEZ, CLAUDE. Father Claude Allouez, one of the foremost Jesuit missionaries of the Great Lakes region, was born at St. Didier, France, on June 6, 1622. Educated at Toulouse, he was sent to Canada in 1658. After serving the St. Lawrence settlements for 7 years, he set out in 1665 to convert the Ottawas on Lake Superior, where he established the Mission of St. Esprit at Chequamegon Bay.

The Ottawas rejected his teachings and broke down his chapel walls, but visiting Illinois Indians described the majesty of the Mississippi River and aroused his zeal to labor among them. In 1669 he established a mission at Green Bay, and for the next 10 years, as related in Early Narratives of the Northwest, "heedless of fatigue or hunger, cold or heat, he travelled over snow and ice, swollen streams, or dangerous rapids, seeking distant Indian villages, counting it all joy if by any means he could win a few savages for a heavenly future."

About 1672 Father Allouez established the Mission St. Francis at De Pere. Soon afterward, replaced by other priests, he left the Green Bay missions to seek converts among the fierce Fox and Mascouten Indians. In 1674 he took charge of the Illinois missions, remaining in that field until his death in 1689 at the Miami Indian village on the St. Joseph River.

"A second St. Xavier, Allouez is said during his 24 years of service to have instructed a hundred thousand Western savages and baptized at least 20,000."--Clarence Walworth Alvord.

(Clarence Walworth Alvord, The Illinois Country; Louise Phelps Kellogg, ed., Early Narratives of the Northwest; The French Régime in Wisconsin and the Northwest; Edna Kenton, ed., Black Gown and Redskins; John Gilmary Shea, Discovery and Exploration of the Mississippi Valley; Jesuit Relations and Allied Documents; John Anthony Caruso, The Mississippi Valley Frontier.)

ALLUMAPEES, DELAWARE CHIEF   see   SASSOONAN, DELAWARE CHIEF

AMASECONTI INDIANS. The Amaseconti Indians, one of the less numerous members of the Abnaki confederacy, lived in or near Franklin County, Maine. They participated in Abnaki attacks on the New England settlements and joined the tribe's exodus to Canada. By 1797 the last of them left Maine and settled at St. Francis.
(F. W. Hodge, ed., Handbook of American Indians, I.)

ANDERSON, WILLIAM, DELAWARE CHIEF. William Anderson (Kithtuwheland) was the son of a Delaware woman and a white man who operated a ferry across the Susquehanna River near Harrisburg, Pennsylvania, before the American Revolution. During the War of 1812 he and the members of his band lived at Piqua, Ohio, where he attained great influence over the Indians. He signed the treaties of the Rapids of the Ohio and St. Marys (1817-1818) in which the Delawares ceded their lands, and he eagerly awaited the move west of the Mississippi. In 1820, so ill he believed that only his desire to see his people safely settled at their new home kept him alive, he finally managed to move them to the Arkansas River. But still he was unable to die in peace, for new pressures were applied for further removal. In 1830 Anderson led his people to a large reservation in Kansas. Soon afterward, believing that at last they had reached their permanent home, the aged chief died.

"This chief was a very dignified man ... of great benevolence and ... greatly beloved by his people."--Grant Foreman.

(Grant Foreman, The Last Trek of the Indians; George A. Shultz, An Indian Canaan.)

ANDRE, LOUIS. Louis André, a young Jesuit priest, sailed from France to Canada in 1670 to serve as a missionary to the Indians. After a short stay with the tribes on the Lake Huron islands, he went to Wisconsin to assist Father Claude Allouez. There he earned the title "Apostle to the Menominees," for, ignoring increasingly poor health, he remained with the Indians 14 years, leading them toward conversion through music, art, and his own firm faith. Finally, in 1684, barely able to hobble about, he was recalled to Quebec to teach at the college.

(Louise Phelps Kellogg, The French Régime in Wisconsin and the Northwest; Jesuit Relations and Allied Documents.)

ANDREWS, WILLIAM. The Rev. William Andrews, an Anglican missionary, served the Mohawk and Oneida Indians for six years beginning in 1712. The Indians built a school at Fort Hunter for his use in instructing their children, and at times as many as 20 children enrolled and 150 adults attended religious services.

Andrews concluded that his labors would have little lasting effect. He considered the Iroquois to be a "sordid, mercenary, beggardly people, having but little sense of religion, honor or goodness among them.... Heathen they are and heathen they will still be." He returned to England in 1718.

(Francis Whiting Halsey, The Old New York Frontier.)

ANDREW'S TOWN, NEW YORK, RAID see ANDRUSTOWN, NEW YORK, RAID

ANDROS, EDMUND, INDIAN RELATIONS. Sir Edmund Andros, a British soldier and a favorite of the Duke of York, served as governor of New York from 1674 until 1681 and added New Jersey to his jurisdiction in 1680. His initial Indian policy, based upon rivalry with the French of Canada, was to include Iroquois lands as portions of his province and to protect the Five Nations if necessary. In 1675 he visited the Mohawks, declared his eternal friendship, and persuaded several chiefs to concede English sovereignty.

At the onset of King Philip's War, Andros disarmed the Indians on Long Island and instructed the militia to keep a close watch on their movements. Although he persuaded New York and New Jersey Indians to avoid involvement in the bloody war that began in New England, Massachusetts and Connecticut officials charged that Philip's followers were obtaining firearms at Albany, an accusation that Andros denied. When Philip camped near Albany during the winter of 1675-76, Andros instructed the Mohawks to drive them out of New York. Later in the war, in response to a plea from New England for armed assistance against the Abnakis of Maine, he sent a small army that recaptured Pemaquid from the hostiles. This victory was instrumental in forcing the Indians of that area to the peace table.

Andros again became at odds with the New England governors, however, over the issue of treatment of Indian refugees. In order to increase trade he wanted more Indians to live in New York, and near the end of the war he offered asylum to refugees that agreed to move to lands under his jurisdiction. Some New England Indians accepted the proposal and settled near Albany. When Connecticut and Massachusetts officials demanded that they be punished for participation in attacks on New England settlements, Andros turned a few of the most notorious raiders over to the Mohawks, but he rejected demands to discipline the others. In March 1677 he proclaimed that Indians entering New York would be permitted to join local tribes and would receive his protection.

During 1677 and 1678 Andros was active in promoting peace between the New York Indians and the colonies to the east and south. He persuaded the Senecas, Oneidas, and Onondagas to make peace with both whites and Indians in New England, Maryland, and Virginia and to release prisoners they had captured in those provinces.

In 1686 Andros was appointed governor of all northern colonies, including New England. Establishing his headquarters at Boston, he immediately notified the French that he would protect the Iroquois against invasion from Canada. Because a truce was then in effect, however, he recommended to the Iroquois that they release Canadian captives and make peace with tribes allied to the French.

Convinced that his jurisdiction extended into Acadia, in 1688 Andros invaded Pentegoet and seized the property of the French officer and trader, Jean Vincent d'Abbadie Saint-Castin. Unfortunately this Frenchman, married to the daughter of Chief Madockawando, was a favorite of the Indians, and the plundering of his post infuriated the Abnakis and led to renewed hostilities.

The overthrow of James II (the former Duke of York) and the unpopularity of Andros with the people of New England resulted in his being deposed in April 1689. Sent back to England, he was fortunate to escape trial. By 1692, however, he was back in America, serving as governor of Virginia.

(Allen W. Trelease, Indian Affairs in Colonial New York.)

ANDROSCOGGINS INDIANS see AROSAGUNTACOOK INDIANS

ANDRUSTOWN, NEW YORK, RAID. Andrustown, a village located several miles south of German Flats, was attacked on July 18, 1778, by hundreds of Indians allied with the British. Four men died attempting to defend their families, and all of the surviving citizens were carried into captivity. Every house in the community was destroyed. The German Flats militia pursued the war party but failed to rescue the captives.

(T. Wood Clark, The Bloody Mohawk; Francis Whiting Halsey, The Old New York Frontier.)

ANNAWAN, WAMPANOAG CHIEF. Annawan was one of the foremost Wampanoag warriors during King Philip's War. As one of Philip's most brilliant tacticians he is credited with planning most of the attacks that cost so many New England settlers their lives.

When King Philip was killed by the colonists, Annawan escaped the ambush and fled into the wilderness. Soon afterward he assumed command of the survivors and resumed raiding in the vicinity of

Plymouth and Swansea. Benjamin Church and his forces kept on his trail, but by his superior skill in woodcraft and his intimate knowledge of the terrain he managed to escape time after time. Several of his warriors were captured, however, and one of them agreed to lead Church to his quarry, camped in a swamp near Taunton, Massachusetts.

During the night, Church approached the camp unobserved, lowered himself down a cliff, seized the warriors' guns, and crept up to the sleeping Annawan with an uplifted tomahawk. Suddenly the chief awoke, realized that resistance was futile, and gave a sign of surrender. When awakened the other warriors followed suit.

While marching his captives to Plymouth for trial, Church developed a sincere friendship for the formidable chief and determined to try to save him from execution. His wishes had little influence with colonists bent on revenge, however, and a mob seized the chief and beheaded him. "The greatness of the Wampanoags died with him."--Douglas Edward Leach.

(Thomas Church, The History of the Great Indian War of 1675 and 1676; Frederick J. Dockstader, Great North American Indians; Douglas Edward Leach, Flintlock and Tomahawk.)

AONTARISATI, MOHAWK CHIEF. In 1653 a prominent Mohawk chief named Aontarisati fell into the hands of Indian allies of the French. The Jesuit missionary, François Joseph Le Mercier, described his fate as follows: "On the day of the Visitation of the Holy Virgin, the chief, Aontarisati, so regretted by the Iroquois, was taken prisoner by our Indians, instructed by our fathers, and baptized, and on the same day, being put to death, he ascended to heaven. I doubt not that he thanked the Virgin for his misfortune and the blessing that followed, and that he prayed to God for his countrymen."

(Francis Parkman, The Old Régime in Canada.)

APPLE RIVER, ILLINOIS, RAID. In response to a dream, the famous Sauk chief Black Hawk attacked the fort at Apple River on June 24, 1832. The settlers inside the poorly constructed stockade milled about in terror while the Sauks fired their rifles with little effect. Finally a courageous, tobacco-chewing woman "drove round the fort like a fury, cursing and swearing like a pirate," and compelling the settlers to put up a fight. She pulled one coward out of a barrel and dragged him to a loophole. The battle lasted less than three hours. Black Hawk, in dictating his autobiography, described it as follows:

> I told my warriors my dream in the morning, and we all started for Mos-co-ho-co-y-nak. When we arrived in the vicinity of a fort the white people had built there ... we attacked the fort. One of their braves, who seemed more valiant than the rest, raised his head above the picketing to fire at us, when one of my braves, with a well-directed shot, put an end to his bravery! Finding that these people could

not all be killed, without setting fire to their houses and fort, I thought it more prudent to be content with what flour, provisions, cattle and horses we could find, than to set fire to their buildings, as the light would be seen at a distance, and the army might suppose that we were in the neighborhood, and come upon us with a force too strong.

(Black Hawk, Black Hawk, An Autobiography; Cecil Eby, That Disgraceful Affair, The Black Hawk War.)

ARMSTRONG, FORT, TREATIES OF. Fort Armstrong, built during 1817-1818 at the foot of Rock Island to control the Sauk and Fox Indians, was the scene of several United States conferences and treaties with Indian tribes. On September 3, 1822, Thomas Forsyth negotiated a treaty there with the Sauk and Fox Indians, agreeing to pay the united tribes $1,000 in return for release from an agreement to build a trading post in their territory. On September 5, 1831, Maj. John Bliss, commanding two companies of regulars, summoned the Sauks and Foxes to the fort to demand the surrender of warriors accused of murdering Menominee Indians, but Chief Keokuk responded that he lacked the necessary authority.

On September 15, 1832, Winfield Scott and John Reynolds negotiated a treaty with the Winnebago Indians, providing an annuity of $10,000 in exchange for the tribe's agreement to cede their lands and move west of the Mississippi. Six days later the same commissioners negotiated a treaty with the Sauk and Fox Indians requiring them to cede 6 million acres as a result of depredations committed during the Black Hawk War. The tribes acquiesced when offered a $20,000 annuity.

(William T. Hagan, The Sac and Fox Indians; Charles J. Kappler, ed., Indian Affairs: Laws and Treaties, II.)

ARMSTRONG, JACK, MURDER OF. Jack Armstrong, a pioneer Pennsylvania Indian trader, operated at various times at Shamokin, Frankstown and Ohesson. In April 1744 he and two of his employees seized a horse belonging to a Delaware warrior, Mussemeleen, who owed him a debt. When the Indian paid the debt, Armstrong refused to return the horse. Thereupon, Mussemeleen followed the three traders to a remote gorge on the Juniata River and killed them from ambush.

(Charles A. Hanna, The Wilderness Trail.)

ARMSTRONG, JOHN. Col. John Armstrong was born in Ireland in 1717 and emigrated as a youth to the Cumberland district of Pennsylvania. He became a surveyor, laid out the frontier community of Carlisle in 1751, and served as militia captain of that Scotch-Irish strong point at the foot of the mountains. He was among the few Pennsylvanians disposed to take aggressive action against the Delaware Indians for attacking settlers at the onset of the French and Indian War. In 1755 he was responsible for building a chain of forts to protect Pennsylvania from Delaware attacks. The following year, after the loss of his brother Edward at the fall of Fort Granville, he led an attack on the Indian stronghold of Kittanning, burning the town and killing about forty warriors. White casualties, also, were heavy, and Armstrong was wounded. (See KITTANNING EXPEDITION.)

In 1758 Armstrong helped build the Forbes Road, facilitating the destruction of Fort Duquesne. After the fall of New France, he fought in Pontiac's War and the American Revolution.

(Solon J. Buck, The Planting of Civilization in Western Pennsylvania; William A. Hunter, Forts on the Pennsylvania Frontier; Francis Parkman, Montcalm and Wolfe, II.)

ARMSTRONG, ROBERT, CAPTIVITY OF. Robert Armstrong was captured at the age of five near Pittsburgh, Pennsylvania, in 1786. His captors, Wyandot Indians, adopted him and treated him kindly. Easily assimilated, he became a warrior and married a Wyandot woman. After the close of the Indian wars he lived on the Wyandot reservation, where he acted as interpreter for missionaries. In time he became a devout Christian and preached to his adopted people. His second wife was the daughter of the famous captive Isaac Zane.

(James B. Finley, Life Among the Indians.)

ARMSTRONG, THOMAS, CAPTIVITY OF. Thomas Armstrong, aged two, was captured in Pennsylvania by the Seneca Indians during the American Revolution. In 1779 John Sullivan's army defeated the Senecas and, as a result, most of their captives were released. But Thomas insisted upon remaining with the Indians. He married a white girl who had been captured in infancy and who was so completely assimilated that an observer described her as "essentially Indian in all save blood."

Armstrong lived on a reservation where he frequently came into contact with whites and acquired some use of the English language. He retained little memory of his white family, but he gradually developed a longing to meet his relatives. The Indians informed him of the place where he had been captured, and he learned that one of his sisters still lived there. Soon afterward he went to Pennsylvania and located the home of his sister. Although she did not recognize him she invited him into her home and treated him kindly. Thomas was too ill at ease to identify himself as her brother, and after a short visit he returned to the reservation to continue his life as an Indian.

(J. Norman Heard, White into Red.)

AROSAGUNTACOOK INDIANS. The Arosaguntacook Indians, an Abnaki tribe, lived near the present site of Lewiston, Maine, during the colonial wars. In 1690 Col. Benjamin Church destroyed their village and crops and recovered several white women and children from captivity. Afterward, members of the tribe removed to St. Francis in Canada.

(Thomas Church, The History of the Great Indian War of 1675 and 1676; Frederick Webb Hodge, ed., Handbook of American Indians, I.)

ASHLEY, EDWARD. Edward Ashley was one of the earliest New England traders to become adapted to Indian civilization. During the 1620's he obtained a patent from the Council of New England to trade with the Abnakis on the Penobscot River. William Bradford described him as "a very profane yonge man; and he had for sometime lived among ye Indeans as a savage, & wente naked amongst them, and used their maners (in wch time he got their language) ...." With the assistance of Isaac Allerton he formed a business connection with the Plymouth colony. For a time he monopolized the Abnaki trade until he was arrested for selling firearms to the Indians and sent to England in chains. After his release from prison, English merchants employed him to engage in the Russian fur trade. While returning from Russia he was lost at sea.

(William Bradford, Of Plimoth Plantation; Neal Salisbury, Manitou and Providence.)

ASHUELOT, NEW HAMPSHIRE, RAID. On April 23, 1746, a war party of about eighty Indians surrounded a small settlement on the Ashuelot River, near the present site of Keene, New Hampshire. They captured Ephraim Dorman, but he broke loose and ran to the palisaded fort to give the alarm. The men in the stockade sallied forth and fought the warriors until most of the settlers had the opportunity to escape. The Indians killed two settlers and captured a third, but they were unable to break into the fort. After suffering heavy losses they burned the houses outside the stockade and withdrew. Two days later they returned, but a sentry shot the chief, and the raiders gave up the attempt.

(Francis Parkman, A Half-Century of Conflict.)

ASPENQUID, ABNAKI CHIEF. Aspenquid, an Abnaki sachem who lived at Agamenticus, Maine, was one of the first American Indians to accept Christianity. This conversion occurred near the end of the sixteenth century, and afterward he went from tribe to tribe in northern New England and eastern Canada preaching about the road to salvation. He died in Maine about 1682, having attained the age of 100.

(Frederick Webb Hodge, ed., Handbook of American Indians, I.)

ASPINET, NAUSET CHIEF. Aspinet, a Nauset chief who lived at Cape Cod, Massachusetts, was a firm friend of the earliest English colonists. In 1621 he found a small English boy lost in the wilderness and brought him safely to the Plymouth settlement. During the winter of 1622 he brought food to the starving colonists. He maintained peace with the Pilgrims in spite of the threats by Miles Standish to attack his village. Finally forced to hide in the swamps in fear for his life, he sickened and died there about 1623.

(Frederick Webb Hodge, ed., Handbook of American Indians, I.)

ASSACOMBUIT, ABNAKI CHIEF. Assacombuit, an Abnaki chief of

Pigwacket, was one of the fiercest enemies of the New England colonies and a firm ally of the French in Canada. In 1696 he assisted Iberville to destroy Fort St. Johns, New Brunswick. He attacked the settlers of Casco, Maine, in 1703 and joined the French in attempting to drive the English from Newfoundland the following year. In 1706 he was taken to France and received a saber from King Louis XIV as a mark of favor for having slain, by his own account, 150 enemies of France. After being knighted he returned to America in 1707 and renewed his attacks on the settlements. He was wounded in the bloody attack on Haverhill, Massachusetts, in 1708, doubtlessly after adding several notches to his famous war club, for more than thirty Englishmen were killed. He died in 1727.

(Samuel Adams Drake, Border Wars of New England; Frederick Webb Hodge, ed., Handbook of American Indians, I.)

ATTUCKS, CRISPUS. Crispus Attucks, son of a black father and a Massachuset Indian mother, was the first man killed by British troops in the American Revolution. A giant 47-year-old sailor at the time of his death, he was born at Natick (possibly Framingham), Massachusetts, in 1723 and escaped from slavery at Framingham to go to sea in 1750. Most accounts of the Boston Massacre assert that he led the crowd of taunting Americans that defied British troops on March 5, 1770, in front of the Boston customhouse, and that he was the first man shot by the soldiers.

(Dictionary of Indians of North America; John R. Swanton, Indian Tribes of North America.)

AUBRY, CHARLES PHILIPPE. Charles Philippe Aubry, a French military officer and Indian diplomat, was one of the most active wilderness commanders during the French and Indian War. Appointed commandant of the Illinois country, he built Fort Ascension (later known as Fort Massac) in 1757 and repelled a Cherokee attempt to capture that post. On September 14, 1758, he led a sortie from Fort Duquesne that crushed Maj. James Grant's premature attempt to capture that stronghold. On October 12, 1758, he led an attack on Loyalhannon, killing 60 English soldiers. (See LIGONIER, FORT.)

In July 1759, Aubry mustered 600 Indians and 300 Frenchmen to march to the defense of Fort Niagara, threatened by the English forces of Sir William Johnson. They were defeated at the Battle of La Belle Famille, near Niagara, and Aubry survived a severe head wound. He and most of his officers surrendered to the English to save themselves from the Iroquois. (See LA BELLE FAMILLE, BATTLE OF.)

After being exchanged he was appointed governor of Louisiana, and it was he who surrendered that French colony to Spanish authorities in 1766. He died in a shipwreck in 1770.

"His American employment had been hazardous, typical of the French partisan of the time, who relied on savages and employed their methods."--Frank H. Severance.

(Clarence W. Alvord, The Illinois Country; Frank H. Severance, An Old Frontier of France; Dale Van Every, Forth to the Wilderness.)

AU GLAIZE COUNCIL. The Au Glaize council, a meeting of 28 Indian tribes with the British agent Alexander McKee, was held at the confluence of the Auglaize and Maumee rivers in September 1792. Among tribes participating were the Iroquois, Shawnee, Miami, Ottawa, Chippewa, Wyandot, Delaware, Creek, and Cherokee nations. The Indians were in a belligerent mood, aroused by recent victories over the Americans, and determined to continue their attacks on frontier settlements. McKee, on the other hand, had been instructed by his superiors in Canada to encourage the Indians to insist upon maintaining the Ohio River as the boundary of the Indian country, while at the same time offering British mediation of Indian-United States hostilities, thus forestalling an anticipated Indian request for the assistance of British troops. McKee was supported by the Iroquois, and after much deliberation the council agreed to negotiate with the Americans only if the British were represented.

(Randolph C. Downes, Council Fires on the Upper Ohio; Dale Van Every, Ark of Empire; William L. Stone, Border Wars of the American Revolution.)

AUGUSTA, FORT, PENNSYLVANIA. Fort Augusta was built by Pennsylvania troops at Shamokin on the Susquehanna River in July 1756. A large fort and trading post, it was garrisoned by 200 to 400 soldiers. Its strategic location near a confluence of Indian trails facilitated the safeguarding of settlements downstream against surprise attacks. The fort was besieged on February 26, June 9, and June 23, 1757. Seven sentries and guards were killed, but the Indians dared not assault the formidable stockade. Afterward it served as the site of negotiations with several Indian nations before its abandonment about 1780.

(William A. Hunter, Forts on the Pennsylvania Frontier.)

AWASHONKS, WAMPANOAG CHIEF. Awashonks, a woman chief of the Wampanoags, lived in Rhode Island with her husband, Tolomy. She supported the Indians at the outbreak of King Philip's War, but she soon made peace with the English and provided warriors to scout for Benjamin Church's army in his campaign against her own people.

(Thomas Church, The History of the Great Indian War of 1675 and 1676; Carolyn Thomas Foreman, Indian Women Chiefs.)

-B-

BAD AXE, BATTLE OF. The Battle of Bad Axe, bloody conclusion to the Black Hawk War, was fought on the Mississippi River bank, at the mouth of the Bad Axe River, a few miles below La Crosse, Wisconsin, on August 3, 1832. Black Hawk, a Sauk chief who had attempted to reclaim tribal lands east of the Mississippi, was cornered with his back to the broad river by Gen. Henry Atkinson's army of 1,300 men. To make his position even more precarious, the steamboat Warrior, armed with a six-pound cannon, barred the way to escape across the river.

Realizing that he was trapped, and hoping to save his starving women and children, Black Hawk sent a delegation forward with a flag of truce, but soldiers ignored it and opened fire. The Indians returned the fire, and a battle, which William T. Hagan calls "little more than a massacre," lasted eight hours. Women and children were shot as they attempted to hide in the willows along the bank. Warriors climbed trees on two islands and attempted to retaliate, but the steamboat raked them with cannon fire and riflemen picked them off as they attempted to swim to safety. One witness reported that the river was tinged red by their blood.

The soldiers killed more than 200 Indians and captured 39 women and children. Some 200 Sauks escaped across the river, but most of them were killed by the Sioux who were waiting on the western bank. Atkinson lost less than twenty of his men. (See BLACK HAWK WAR.)

(William T. Hagan, The Sac and Fox Indians; John Tebbel and Keith Jennison, The American Indian Wars; Robert M. Utley and Wilcomb E. Washburn, The Indian Wars; Black Hawk, Black Hawk, An Autobiography; Cecil Eby, That Disgraceful Affair, The Black Hawk War.)

BAGNALL, WALTER. Walter Bagnall established a trading post on Richmond's Island, Maine, a few years after the settlement of Plymouth. He sold liquor to the Indians and cheated them of their furs at every opportunity. Finally, about 1630, the Indians became so enraged by his conduct that they murdered him and burned his trading post.

(Herbert Milton Sylvester, Indian Wars of New England, I.)

BARCLAY, HENRY. The Reverend Henry Barclay, an Episcopalian missionary, was assigned to serve the Mohawk Indians at Fort Hunter in 1731. By 1743 he had baptized almost all of the Indians there. Two years later the border raids associated with King George's War compelled him to withdraw from the area.

(Francis Whiting Halsey, The Old New York Frontier.)

BARROW, SAM. Sam Barrow, an early New England outlaw, lived with the Narraganset Indians for many years prior to 1676. He married an Indian woman and was the father of the Narraganset chief Totoson. He was captured and executed by Benjamin Church during King Philip's War.

(Thomas Church, The History of the Great Indian War of 1675 and 1676.)

BASHABA, ABNAKI CHIEF. Bashaba, a powerful Penobscot Abnaki sachem, traded furs to Champlain in 1604 in exchange for a promise by the French to teach the tribe agriculture and to negotiate peace with the hostile Micmac and Montagnais Indians. The French failed to follow up their advantage, however, and Bashaba attempted unsuccessfully to establish trade with the English in 1605 and 1607. He was killed in a war with the Micmacs about 1615.

(Neal Salisbury, Manitou and Providence.)

BAYNTON, WHARTON, AND MORGAN, ILLINOIS TRADE. Baynton, Wharton, and Morgan, Philadelphia merchants, became the dominant firm in the western Indian trade at the close of Pontiac's War. In 1765 they dispatched a pack train of goods intended for the Illinois Indians, but it was seized by Pennsylvania frontiersmen. (See BLACK BOYS; CROGHAN, GEORGE; MORGAN, GEORGE.) The following year, however, they sent goods worth £50,000 to Pittsburgh for the western trade. Their profits declined in 1767, as the Illinois Indians preferred to trade with New Orleans merchants, and the company withdrew from the area in 1772.

(A. T. Volwiler, George Croghan and the Westward Movement.)

BEAUBASSIN, LENEUF DE see LENEUF DE LA VALLIERE DE BEAU-BASSIN, ALEXANDRE, RAID

BEAUJEU, DANIEL HYACINTH MARY see LIENARD DE BEAUJEU, DANIEL-HYACINTHE-MARIE

BEAVER, DELAWARE CHIEF see TAMAQUE, DELAWARE CHIEF

BEDFORD, FORT. Fort Bedford (originally known as Fort Raystown), was constructed in the Pennsylvania mountains 100 miles east of Pittsburgh by Col. John Armstrong in 1750. There Capt. Lewis Ourry and his small garrison guarded the Juniata settlements against Indian raids. In 1757 the fort was strengthened by Col. Henry Bouquet, and it served as an important supply post during the construction of the Forbes Road.

During Pontiac's War several settlers were killed near Fort Bedford. In expectation of an attack on the fort, some of the most experienced frontiersmen dressed and painted like Indians. When a party besieged the fort, the disguised defenders managed to infiltrate the Indian positions, then attacked with such fury that the startled braves fled from the scene.

Fort Bedford was abandoned by 1775.

(Solon J. Buck, The Planting of Civilization in Western Pennsylvania; Francis Parkman, The Conspiracy of Pontiac; Dale Van Every, Forth to the Wilderness.)

BEERS, RICHARD, AMBUSH. Northfield, Massachusetts, was one of the frontier settlements most exposed to Indian attacks during King Philip's War. When 8 men were killed by a war party in September 1675, colonial authorities decided to abandon the village. Accordingly, on September 4, Capt. Richard Beers led 36 men to evacuate the settlement. They were only two miles from Northfield when they fell into an ambush. Beers and half of his men were killed, and their severed heads were displayed on poles by the Indians. Two days later a force led by Maj. Robert Treat successfully evacuated Northfield.

(Douglas Edward Leach, Flintlock and Tomahawk.)

BENJAMIN FAMILY, LYCOMING COUNTY, PENNSYLVANIA. In the

autumn of 1777, Indians attacked the Benjamin family of Lycoming County, killing the parents and capturing the children--William, Nathan, Ezekiel, and their little sister. The boys were redeemed after the close of the American Revolution, but the girl grew up among the Indians, married a warrior, and bore him several children. In later life William located his sister and brought her to live at his home in Williamsport. There she remained for a brief time, miserable and longing for her Indian companions. Finally William relented and permitted her to return to her home in the wilderness.

(C. Hale Sipe, Indian Wars of Pennsylvania.)

BENNINGTON, VERMONT, BATTLE OF. In 1777 British Gen. John Burgoyne directed 500 Indians to terrify frontier settlers during his invasion of the Mohawk Valley. On August 16 some 150 of these warriors accompanied Col. Frederick Baum in an attempt to seize the Patriot supply depot at Bennington, Vermont. The Indians moved in advance of Baum's 500 Germans and Tories, looting cabins and killing livestock. But at Bennington Col. John Stark attacked the invaders with more than 2,500 militiamen. At the first fire the Indians fled and Baum's forces were overwhelmed. After the battle most of Burgoyne's Indians, including those who had not accompanied Baum, deserted the British.

(Barbara Graymont, The Iroquois in the American Revolution; Jack M. Sosin, The Revolutionary Frontier.)

BEUKENDAAL, NEW YORK, BATTLE OF. Beukendaal, a village a few miles west of Schenectady, was attacked by 100 Indians and Frenchmen on July 18, 1748. Only 1 citizen was killed at Beukendaal, but troops sent from Schenectady to relieve the settlers were ambushed with the loss of 20 men killed and 13 taken captive.

(T. Wood Clarke, The Bloody Mohawk.)

BIG BOTTOM MASSACRE see MARIETTA, OHIO, RAID

BIG COVE MASSACRE see GREAT COVE MASSACRE

BIG TREE, TREATY OF. By the Treaty of Big Tree, negotiated in 1797, the Seneca Indians ceded most of their lands in western New York, retaining only eleven reservations. All of their territory west of the Genesee River was purchased by the U.S. Government for $100,000.

(William C. Sturtevant, ed., Handbook of North American Indians, XV.)

BIGHAM'S FORT, PENNSYLVANIA. Bigham's Fort, a small stockade in Juniata County, Pennsylvania, was attacked on June 11, 1756, by 27 Indians and Frenchmen led by Ensign Niverville de Montizambert. The fort was destroyed, 5 of the defenders killed, and 18 others carried into captivity.

(William A. Hunter, Forts on the Pennsylvania Frontier; U. J. Jones, History of the Early Settlement of the Juniata Valley.)

BIGOT, JACQUES AND VINCENT. Jacques and Vincent Bigot, brothers and Jesuit priests, were active missionaries and Indian managers during the last quarter of the seventeenth century. Jacques served at Norridgewock and Vincent at Kennebec, Maine, both succeeding in Christianizing Abnaki Indians. They were highly instrumental in removing many Abnakis from Maine to Sillery and St. Francis in Canada and in employing them in the border warfare with New England.

"The most prominent among the apostles of carnage, at this time (1690-97), are the Jesuit Bigot on the Kennebec, and the seminary priest Thury on the Penobscot."--Francis Parkman.

(Samuel Adams Drake, Border Wars of New England; Edna Kenton, ed., Black Gown and Redskins; Francis Parkman, Count Frontenac and New France Under Louis XIV; Jesuit Relations and Allied Documents.)

BLACK BIRD, POTAWATOMI CHIEF see BLACKBIRD, POTAWATOMI CHIEF

BLACK BOYS. In March 1765, Indian Agent George Croghan assembled a large quantity of government trade goods for use in persuading the Indians of the Illinois and Wabash to permit British occupation of western posts recently won in the war with France. In addition, the pack train conveyed goods belonging to Baynton, Wharton, and Morgan, which were intended to open a profitable, but illegal, trade for that Philadelphia firm.

Pennsylvania frontiersmen, led by James Smith (a justice of the peace) were determined to prevent the goods, particularly liquor and ammunition, from reaching Indians who had raided their settlements. Painting their faces black, they attacked the packhorse train at Sideling Hill, not far from Fort Loudoun. They shot horses, confiscated goods, and burned what they could not carry away. Only 17 of the 81 horseloads managed to escape to Fort Loudoun. The Black Boys continued to patrol the trails for the next three years, inspecting packs to prevent firearms from reaching the Indians.

(Dale Van Every, Forth to the Wilderness; Albert T. Volwiler, George Croghan and the Westward Movement.)

BLACK BUFFALO, KICKAPOO CHIEF. Black Buffalo, a young Kickapoo chief, was the scourge of Missouri Territory during the War of 1812. Leading 50 mounted warriors, he murdered settlers and stole their horses and household belongings. By 1832 his band was active in the Indian Territory, and some of his followers were involved in the Cordova Rebellion in Texas in 1838-39.

(A. M. Gibson, The Kickapoos.)

BLACK HAWK, SAUK CHIEF. Black Hawk (Makataimeshekiakiak) was born in the Sauk homeland near Rock Island, Illinois, in 1767. He became a warrior at the age of 15 when he took the scalp of an Indian enemy, and while still a youth he led attacks on the Cherokees and Osages. Twenty years of tribal warfare reached a climax in 1802 when he slew 13 Osage Indians.

In 1804 three Sauk and Fox chiefs signed the Treaty of St. Louis, providing for the cession of lands east of the Mississippi considered by Black Hawk to be sacred tribal territory. This cession so infuriated Black Hawk that he shifted the focus of his warfare from enemy Indians to American soldiers and settlers.

In 1808 American soldiers built Fort Madison, angering the Sauks to the point that Black Hawk asserted that "I am of opinion now, had our party got into the fort, all the whites would have been killed...." The following year Black Hawk participated in an attack on the fort: "... I took my rifle, and shot in two the cord by which they hoisted their flag, and prevented them from raising it again. We continued firing until all our ammunition was expended; and finding we could not take the fort, returned home...."

At the onset of the War of 1812 the British trader Robert Dickson persuaded Black Hawk to fight on the side of the British. He participated in Gen. Henry Proctor's unsuccessful attacks on Forts Meigs and Stephenson, and he captured American supply boats on the Mississippi. When Britain signed the peace treaty, Black Hawk threatened to continue his war on Americans, and, on May 24, 1815, he and his followers killed 4 soldiers near Green Bay. (See SINK-HOLE, BATTLE OF THE.)

In May 1816 Black Hawk, not realizing that he was agreeing to the cession of his village of Saukenuk, signed a confirmation of the hated Treaty of St. Louis. But when his rival, Chief Keokuk, moved the Sauks west of the Mississippi, Black Hawk and his followers refused to accompany them. They continued to trade with the British in Canada and became known as the British band. He devised a plan to unite the Indian tribes of the upper Mississippi and the Great Lakes to fight the Americans, and he schemed to gain the support of the British.

In 1830 when Black Hawk learned that the Saukenuk region would be sold to settlers he determined to defend it. His attempts to obtain allies among other tribes met with little success, however, and a brief war ended in defeat. (See BLACK HAWK WAR; BAD AXE, BATTLE OF.)

Black Hawk was captured by the Winnebago Indians and turned over to the Army. He was imprisoned for a short time at Jefferson Barracks, then taken to Washington to talk with President Jackson in 1833. Afterward he dictated his autobiography and was given a tour of several cities to convince him of the futility of fighting United States forces. Assigned to the custody of Keokuk, he rejoined his people in Iowa and died there in 1838.

(Black Hawk, Black Hawk, An Autobiography; Albert Britt, Great Indian Chiefs; Frederick J. Dockstader, Great North American Indians; William T. Hagan, The Sac and Fox Indians; Cecil Eby, That Disgraceful Affair, The Black Hawk War.)

BLACK HAWK WAR. The Black Hawk War began in the spring of 1832 when the Sauk chief Black Hawk and his 400 warriors and their families known as the British band, crossed the Mississippi River and reoccupied their former homeland on the Rock River in Illinois. As this move violated the treaties of 1804 and 1816, Gen. Henry Atkinson regarded it as an invasion of U.S. territory and called up the militia to expel them. Isaiah Stillman and his militiamen followed the Indians as they moved up the Rock River, attacking settlers and desperately seeking help from other tribes that had encouraged the uprising.

At last, realizing that he could not count on reinforcements, Black Hawk sought a means to end hostilities. He sent peace envoys to Stillman's camp, and 3 of them were killed under a flag of truce. This act so enraged Black Hawk that he ordered an attack and put the militia to flight. (See STILLMAN'S RUN.)

Afterward, the Sauks retreated into Wisconsin, attacking settlements, while pursued by a large force of regulars as well as the militia. (See APPLE RIVER, ILLINOIS, RAID; WISCONSIN HEIGHTS, BATTLE OF; KELLOGG'S GROVE, BATTLES OF.) On July 28 they suffered a devastating defeat by Gen. James D. Henry, and on August 3 many of them were massacred attempting to cross the Mississippi to Iowa. (See BAD AXE, BATTLE OF.) Black Hawk escaped the massacre, but he was captured a short time later. The war resulted in the loss by Sauks of 400 square miles of their Iowa lands.

(Black Hawk, Black Hawk: An Autobiography; William T. Hagan, The Sac and Fox Indians; Cecil Eby, That Disgraceful Affair, The Black Hawk War.)

BLACK KETTLE, ONONDAGA CHIEF. Black Kettle (Chaudière Noire) was the foremost Iroquois war chief fighting the French in Canada during the late seventeenth century. In 1688 he sent several war parties to harass the French settlements. In 1691 he attacked Indians transporting furs to the French. The following year he led hundreds of warriors against Montreal and its environs, desolating the countryside and taking a large number of captives. Four hundred French soldiers pursued, and although he had only 200 warriors he gave battle and broke through their lines after killing a considerable number of soldiers. In 1697 he made peace with the French, and soon afterward he was killed by an Algonquian warrior.

(F. W. Hodge, ed., Handbook of American Indians, I; B. B. Thatcher, Indian Biography; Cadwallader Colden, The History of the Five Indian Nations.)

BLACK PARTRIDGE, POTAWATOMI CHIEF. Black Partridge (Mahkah-ta-pa-ke) was a friend of the troops at Fort Dearborn. When the onset of the War of 1812 led to Indian attacks on American forts, he opposed a Potawatomi assault on the garrison. Failing to prevail in council, he warned Capt. Nathan Heald to beware, and he sorrowfully surrendered his peace medal. During the ensuing uprising (see DEARBORN, FORT, MASSACRE) he saved the life of Mrs. Margaret Helm by pretending to drown her. The captives were assigned to various Indian bands, and he brought a white woman and her baby to his village. When the baby became ill he took them to a French trader for medicine. The Frenchman cured the child and ransomed the mother.

Black Partridge's village on the Illinois River was burned by Gov. Ninian Edwards late in 1812. He signed treaties with U.S. negotiators on July 18, 1815, and August 24, 1816.

(Dictionary of Indians of North America; Milo M. Quaife, Checagou.)

BLACK POINT, MAINE, MASSACRE. On October 6, 1713, Capt. Richard Hunnewell led 19 men of the Black Point garrison to work in the fields nearby. A large war party lay in ambush and killed or captured all of them except 1. "The spot where this affair occurred is on Prout's Neck, in Scarborough, and has ever since been known as Massacre Pond."—S. A. Drake.

(Samuel Adams Drake, The Border Wars of New England.)

BLACKBIRD, POTAWATOMI CHIEF. Blackbird (Makahta-penashe) of the Milwaukee village was the chief instigator of the Fort Dearborn Massacre on August 15, 1812. He was a fiery supporter of Tecumseh and an ally of the British during the War of 1812.

(Louise Phelps Kellogg, The British Régime in Wisconsin and the Northwest.)

BLACKSNAKE, SENECA CHIEF. Blacksnake (Thaonawyuthe) was an important Iroquois chief during and after the American Revolution. Born about 1760, he was a nephew of Cornplanter and Handsome Lake and a follower of the latter's teaching about the evils of white men's ways, particularly the abuse of alcohol. During the Revolution he fought against the Americans at the Battle of Oriskany, and he is believed to have participated in the Wyoming Massacre.

After the close of the Revolution, Blacksnake devoted his time to securing better treatment of the Indians by the new government. He fought on the U.S. side in the War of 1812, participating in the Battle of Fort George on August 17, 1813. Soon afterward he became principal chief of the Senecas. He was a strong advocate of education and improved agricultural practices. He died in 1859 at the age of 99.

(Frederick J. Dockstader, Great North American Indians.)

BLANCHE, MARIE, CAPTIVITY OF. Marie Blanche (Mary White) was captured in 1757 by a Delaware Indian chief near Esopus, New York, and brought to the French at Niagara in accordance with the instructions of the commandant François Pouchot to secure English captives. The Delaware had set fire to her cabin during the night, killed a man as he rushed outside, and seized the woman as she attempted to flee. Other settlers were burned to death in the cabin.

Frank H. Severance has pointed out that "here ... is the tale of an 'Indian atrocity,' told by the ... Indian himself. For two centuries or so, American history and romance have been recording attacks on the American pioneer's cabin, and all the dreadful work of the Indian's torch, gun, tomahawk, and scalping-knife. Here we have the same sad picture from the other side, the statement of the savage who explains his bloody deeds as having been accomplished

at the wish of the white man at Fort Niagara."
(Frank H. Severance, An Old Frontier of France.)

BLOCK, ADRIAEN. In 1614 the Dutch explorer, Adriaen Block, charted the New York and New England coast lines and sailed up the Connecticut River, contacting the Indians to extend the trade of the New Netherlands Company. Most of the Indians met by Block had never traded with Europeans, and they were markedly timorous. Block's report of his experiences provides a valuable portrait of Indian life before modification by extensive contact with Europeans.
(Neal Salisbury, Manitou and Providence.)

BLOODY BROOK, BATTLE OF. In 1675, soon after the beginning of King Philip's War, Deerfield, Massachusetts, was attacked by Indians. The settlers fled, leaving their grain unthreshed. A few days later a force of 80 men, led by Capt. Thomas Lathrop, set out from Ipswich to recover the crop. After threshing the grain they loaded it into 18 wagons and began their return march. Unfortunately they halted near a brook to drink and pick grapes, and while they were off guard a Nipmuc war party (700 Indians) attacked them, wiping out all except 7 of the Ipswich men.

Capt. Samuel Moseley heard the firing and rushed to the rescue with a small force of volunteers. They surprised the Nipmucs engaged in scalping their victims and, though badly outnumbered, fought with great courage until reinforcements led by Maj. Robert Treat arrived and drove the Indians from the field. The stream where the battle began is called Bloody Brook to this day.
(Albert Britt, Great Indian Chiefs; John Tebbel and Keith Jennison, The American Indian Wars.)

BLOODY POND, BATTLE OF. The Battle of Bloody Pond was fought on September 8, 1755, when Sir William Johnson, having reached Lake George on his march to attack the French at Crown Point, New York, sent an advance detachment of 500 militiamen and an equal number of Indians to attack the forces of Baron Ludwig Dieskau. The party, led by Col. Ephraim Williams and Hendrick (a Mohawk chief) blundered into an ambush and lost 200 men. The survivors fled back to Johnson's main camp, which they helped to defend when Dieskau attacked it. (See LAKE GEORGE, BATTLE OF.) Afterward some Canadians and Indians returned to the site of the ambush to see what plunder they could find, and there they were attacked by the Americans and driven away. After this bloody encounter the bodies were thrown into the water and the site was designated "Bloody Pond."
(Arthur Pound, Johnson of the Mohawks; Dale Van Every, Forth to the Wilderness.)

BLOODY RUN, BATTLE OF. During Pontiac's siege of Detroit in 1763, Gen. Jeffrey Amherst sent Capt. James Dalyell with 200 men to reinforce Maj. Henry Gladwin's beleaguered garrison. Dalyell, against the advice of Gladwin and other officers, advocated an attack on the Indian villages, and, because he represented Amherst, his argument prevailed.

At 2:30 a.m. on July 31, Dalyell led 280 men in a sortie intended to surprise Pontiac. The Indians had been informed of his plan by French settlers, and 150 warriors were waiting in ambush at a bridge that spanned Parent's Creek. Another 250 Indians were deployed to block Dalyell's retreat. The first platoon to start across the bridge was struck by such heavy fire that dead and wounded soldiers lay piled in the center of the span. Survivors forced their way across the creek and scattered their assailants, but, at the same time, the Indians to the rear of the main column opened fire with devastating effect. Dalyell, wounded in the thigh, recognized the trap and ordered a retreat. Maj. Robert Rogers and Capt. James Grant stationed troops in houses along the retreat route and kept the way open except for one Indian stronghold. Dalyell was killed leading a charge on the stronghold, but his troops cleared the way, and soon after daylight the survivors scrambled into the fort.

Pontiac had won a major victory. Only about 7 Indians were killed, while 20 soldiers had lost their lives, 37 were wounded, and several were captured. The creek where the battle began has been called Bloody Run since that time.

(Howard H. Peckham, Pontiac and the Indian Uprising; Dale Van Every, Forth to the Wilderness.)

BLUE JACKET, SHAWNEE CHIEF. Blue Jacket (Weyapiersenwah) was a powerful Shawnee chief and a fierce opponent of white encroachment on Indian lands north of the Ohio River. He joined Little Turtle in leading the Indians to victory over Gen. Josiah Harmar's army in 1790. When Gen. Anthony Wayne invaded the Indian country in 1794, Blue Jacket refused to accept Little Turtle's advice to make peace. After an unsuccessful appeal to the British for help, he led the Indians during their decisive defeat at Fallen Timbers. Afterward, realizing that the red men could not prevail, he signed the Treaty of Greenville, bringing peace to the region. In 1805 he signed the Treaty of Fort Industry ceding millions of acres of Indian land. On September 12, 1807, shortly before his death, he informed American envoys that he would not fight for the British because the Redcoats had refused admission to their fort to Indians fleeing from Fallen Timbers.

(R. David Edmunds, The Shawnee Prophet; F. W. Hodge, ed., Handbook of American Indians, I.)

BOMAZEEN, ABNAKI CHIEF see ABOMAZINE, ABNAKI CHIEF

BOUCHER, PIERRE, EXPEDITION. Pierre Boucher, a French military officer, was sent to Lake Pepin in Minnesota in 1727 to construct a fort and a trading post to facilitate purchase of furs from the Sioux. He was accompanied by Father Michel Guignas, a Jesuit missionary who felt called to Christianize the tribe.

Not long after the completion of Fort Beauharnois, Boucher

and his 16 companions were compelled to retreat toward the Illinois country because the Fox Indians prevented them from obtaining supplies. On the Mississippi they were captured by Kickapoo Indians, allies of the Foxes, and conveyed to a village a few miles west of the river. There they were treated kindly by the Kickapoos who refused Fox demands that they be burned at the stake. After six months of captivity they were released to the French at Fort Chartres in exchange for Kickapoo prisoners. This exchange infuriated the Foxes and resulted in a Kickapoo alliance with the French.

(A. M. Gibson, The Kickapoos.)

BOUQUET, HENRY. Col. Henry Bouquet, a Swiss mercenary soldier and master of European military tactics, became one of the most successful Indian fighters of the North American wilderness. During the French and Indian War he assisted Gen. John Forbes in the campaign leading to the capture of Fort Duquesne, and he constructed British posts at Venango and Presque Isle. In 1758, assigned the task of preventing settlers from encroaching on Indian land, he established his headquarters at Bedford, Pennsylvania. The Ohio Company offered 25,000 acres as a bribe if he would permit them to occupy land west of the mountains, but he refused. In 1761, aware that the tribes were infuriated by violations of the Treaty of Easton, he issued a proclamation prohibiting both hunting and settling on lands reserved for the Indians. His orders were evaded, however, until a major Indian war drove out the squatters.

At the outbreak of Pontiac's War he received orders from Gen. Jeffrey Amherst to attack the Indians of the Upper Ohio. To carry out this formidable assignment he had only his regiment of Royal Americans—less than 500 men, many of them ill, but every one supremely confident that the wisdom and experience of their leader would enable them to defeat the powerful Indian nations. Bouquet marched from Carlisle in July 1763, to break the siege of Fort Pitt by Pontiac's followers. On August 5-6, 1763, he won a major victory (see BUSHY RUN, BATTLE OF) and he relieved Fort Pitt on August 10.

In October 1764 Bouquet resumed his advance toward the Indian towns beyond the Ohio. At the head of 500 regulars and a force of frontiersmen he marched less than ten miles each day, deliberately affording the Shawnees and Delawares time to appreciate his ability to destroy their homes and crops, leaving them destitute at the onset of winter. When he crossed the Muskingum the Indians sent a delegation of chiefs to negotiate terms. Bouquet demanded that they surrender all of their white captives before he would even consider their request for peace. As a result they brought in 206 captives, many of whom had been with the Indians so long that they regarded restoration to white families as a new captivity.

After taking hostages as a guarantee that captives hiding from redemption would be surrendered the following spring, he led his troops back to Fort Pitt in November 1764. "He had been the first white commander, and for the next 30 years was to remain the only white commander, capable of completely outmaneuvering and outgeneraling Indians in the depth of the wilderness."--Dale Van Every.

In April 1765, Bouquet was promoted to brigadier general and assigned to command the Southern Department. Sick with a fever soon after his arrival at Pensacola, he expired on September 2 at the age of 44.

(Solon J. Buck, The Planting of Civilization in Western Pennsylvania; Howard H. Peckham, Pontiac and the Indian Uprising; Dale Van Every, Forth to the Wilderness.)

BOYD, JOHN, FAMILY OF. The John Boyd family, Scotch-Irish immigrants, settled in western Pennsylvania before the beginning of the French and Indian War. On February 10, 1756, while John was away from home, a Delaware Indian war party captured his wife and children--David, John, Sallie, Rhoda, and an infant son. Because the mother was ill and unable to travel, the Indians tomahawked her and the infant and compelled Sallie and David to carry the scalps to their village. There the survivors were separated and sent to different tribes. David, aged 13, was adopted by the leader of the war party. Kindly treated, he soon became attached to his Indian family. He saw his elder sister, Sallie, the following year but was not permitted to speak to her. He never saw 6-year-old John, Jr., again, and the child's fate is unknown.

Sallie and Rhoda were among the captives released to Col. Henry Bouquet in 1764 when he invaded the Indian country north of the Ohio. But the younger girl, Rhoda, had become completely assimilated during eight years of captivity. During Bouquet's return march to Fort Pitt she fled from the soldiers to rejoin the Indians.

David remained with the Delawares until 1760. At that time his Indian father, feeling remorse for having stolen the boy, sold all of his horses and furs, gave the money to David, and returned him to the settlements. David rejoined his father at Shippensburg, but he tried several times to run away to the Indians.

(J. Norman Heard, White into Red.)

BOYD, THOMAS. Lt. Thomas Boyd, a young Pennsylvania officer of Morgan's Rifles, was assigned reconnaissance duties by Gen. John Sullivan during the expedition against the Six Nations in 1779. At the Battle of Newtown he led an advance patrol that discovered an enemy ambush. His skill as a scout so impressed Sullivan that, on September 12, 1779, he was selected to reconnoiter the Seneca stronghold called the Geneseo Castle.

Taking 25 men, Boyd set out for Geneseo at night, lost his way in the darkness, and came to the deserted village of Gathtsegwarohare. At daylight the scouts fired on three warriors seen at the edge of the woods. One was killed, scalped, and mutilated, but the others escaped to give the alarm. Boyd decided to abort the mission and return to Sullivan's army, but en route they blundered into an ambush set by Maj. John Butler and his Iroquois allies. Boyd and several of his men were captured while most of the others were killed. Eight soldiers fled into a ravine and escaped.

Butler sent Boyd and Sgt. Michael Parker under guard to Geneseo Castle, intending that they should be forwarded to the British forces at Niagara as prisoners of war. But the Senecas overpowered the guards and tortured both captives to death. When Sullivan's army destroyed the town soon afterward they found the decapitated bodies.

(Barbara Graymont, The Iroquois in the American Revolution; Dale Van Every, A Company of Heroes.)

BRADDOCK'S DEFEAT. When the French built Fort Duquesne in 1754 on British claimed territory, Gen. Edward Braddock was sent to America to dislodge them. At the head of two regiments of British regulars and a colonial militia force, a total of almost 2,500 men, he marched into the wilderness in June 1755. George Washington was his aide-de-camp. Realizing that Indians were needed to serve as scouts, Braddock recruited some 50 Iroquois, led by Chief Scarouady, at Fort Cumberland. But when he refused to permit their families to accompany the expedition, all except 8 warriors withdrew.

Braddock's advance was impeded by the need to improve the road and by a lack of teams to transport artillery over the mountains. On June 16 he divided his forces, pushing forward more rapidly with 1,200 men, and assigning Col. William Dunbar to follow with the rest of the troops and most of the artillery. His Indian scouts kept him informed of developments around Fort Duquesne, 1 of them showing him a French officer's scalp that he had lifted within a mile of their destination.

On July 9, as Braddock's forces forded the Monongahela, there were fewer than 300 French soldiers at Fort Duquesne. Almost 1,000 Indians from the Great Lakes and the Ohio were camped outside the walls, but they were apprehensive about attacking so large an army. The commandant, Capt. Pierre de Contrecoeur, considered surrendering, but his fiery subordinate Capt. Daniel-Hyacinthe-Marie Liénard de Beaujeu, begged for the chance to strike a blow for France. Contrecoeur permitted him to take 200 soldiers and to recruit as many of the Indians as he could, a feat which he accomplished by asserting that he would go to meet the enemy alone if necessary. Stung by the implication, some 600 warriors rushed forward to join him.

Beaujeu had hoped to confront the British at the Monongahela, but he encountered them unexpectedly after they had already crossed. Undaunted by British cannon fire, he deployed his men in ravines and on hills commanding the trail. Skilled in wilderness warfare, they fired at Braddock's advance detachment from behind trees. The British recoiled from the deadly assault by unseen enemies and collided with the main body of troops rushing forward. Platoons became scattered and abandoned their standard procedure of firing by volleys. After Beaujeu was killed by cannon fire, Lt. Jean-Daniel Dumas assumed command and kept the British at bay for three hours. Braddock was mortally wounded while attempting to rally the troops into formation, and he ordered a retreat as he was carried from the field. When his men fled across the Monongahela the Indians declined pursuit choosing instead to seek plunder on the battlefield.

The British lost 456 men in the battle, among them Braddock himself who died during the retreat. An additional 421 soldiers were wounded, some of them abandoned at the scene of the battle. The French and Indian losses were limited to 30 men killed and a small number wounded.

When the British survivors reached Dunbar's camp, no effort was made to regroup and return to the field. The entire force retreated rapidly to Fort Cumberland, leaving the way open for the Indians to destroy the settlements of western Virginia and Pennsylvania.

(Solon J. Buck, The Planting of Civilization in Western Pennsylvania; Howard H. Peckham, Pontiac and the Indian Uprising; Dale Van Every, Forth to the Wilderness.)

BRADLEY, HANNAH, CAPTIVITY OF. Hannah Bradley of Haverhill, Massachusetts, was captured two times in different centuries by marauding Indians. In March 1697, during a massive attack on the village, she was carried away along with the famous captive, Hannah Dustin and a dozen others. Twenty-seven settlers were killed in the attack. Little is known of her experiences during her first captivity, but she was back in Haverhill with her husband, Joseph Bradley, a few years later.

Her second captivity occurred on February 8, 1703, and she was redeemed in Canada, along with 54 other captives in May 1706, by her husband, John Sheldon, and John Wells. Francis Parkman has described Bradley's experiences as follows:

> ... seeing the gate open and nobody on the watch, they rushed in. The woman of the house was boiling soap, and in her desperation she snatched up the kettle and threw the contents over them with such effect that one of them ... was scalded to death. The man who should have been on watch was killed, and several persons were captured, including the woman.... Half starved and bearing a heavy load, she followed her captors in their hasty retreat towards Canada. After a time she was safely delivered of an infant in the midst of the winter forest; but the child pined for want of sustenance, and the Indians hastened its death by throwing hot coals into its mouth when it cried. The astonishing vitality of the woman carried her to the end of her frightful journey. A Frenchman bought her from the Indians, and she was finally ransomed by her husband.

(Francis Parkman, A Half Century of Conflict; Samuel Adams Drake, The Border Wars of New England.)

BRADLEY, ISAAC, CAPTIVITY OF. Isaac Bradley, aged 16, was captured at Haverhill, Massachusetts, in 1695 by the Abnaki Indians of Pigwacket and marched to their village on the Saco River. For two years he lived the life of an Indian. Then he escaped into the night, accompanied by 11-year-old William Whittaker. They fled down the bank of the Saco, and when the Whittaker boy became exhausted Bradley carried him on his back to safety.

Bradley had had 13 members of his family killed by Indians. In retaliation he exacted a terrible toll. He led a band of scalp hunters on raids against the Abnakis, killing or capturing 15 Indians, 1 for each lost relative and for the two years he had spent in captivity.

(George Hill Evans, Pigwacket.)

BRADSTREET, JOHN. John Bradstreet was born in England in 1711 and came to America as a small boy. He decided at an early age to pursue a military career. In 1745 he served as a lieutenant-colonel in Sir William Pepperell's capture of Louisburg, and during the following year he acted as lieutenant-governor of Nova Scotia. Afterward he became a resident of Albany.

During the French and Indian War, Bradstreet played an important role in the fighting around Lakes Erie and Ontario. In 1755 he built boats at Oswego to transport Gov. William Shirley's forces during the Niagara campaign. The following year he made an extraordinary expedition to bring supplies to the English post of Oswego, cut off by Canadians and Indians and threatened by starvation. Commanding 300 boats, he set out with enough provisions to accommodate 5,000 men for half a year. His exploit has received high praise by Arthur Pound: "Though frequently challenged, the Americans fought their way through the woods and over the portages, outwitting and outfighting superior numbers.... Bradstreet's progress was a campaign at close quarters with small forces, in which mere handfuls marched and countermarched this way and that with infinite courage, and dozens held off hundreds."

After this expedition, Bradstreet returned to Albany with reliable information that a powerful French force was poised to capture Oswego. Gen. James Abercrombie delayed taking appropriate action, however, and the beleaguered post fell to the Marquis de Montcalm on August 13-14, 1756.

Bradstreet's most important achievement occurred in August 1758, when he led 2,600 provincial troops and 40 Iroquois Indians to capture Fort Frontenac on the north side of Lake Ontario. He knocked down a section of the bastion with a cannon bombardment, and the French surrendered to his superior forces on August 27. He took 150 prisoners, seized a vast store of munitions intended for the French forts on the western lakes, and destroyed all of the French ships on Lake Ontario. T. Wood Clarke asserts that Bradstreet's exploit "marked the turning point in the French and Indian War. Not only did it hearten the colonists and bring the wavering Indians back into the alliance, but it gave the English complete control over Lake Ontario and broke the French line of communication with Niagara and the western forts. They soon abandoned Fort Duquesne."

While Bradstreet's exploits during the French and Indian War gained for him a high place in American history, his role in Pontiac's War somewhat tarnished his image. After Pontiac was defeated,

Bradstreet was sent to Lake Erie to cooperate with Colonel Bouquet in subduing the Delawares and Shawnees. He was outwitted by Indians who claimed to be authorized to make peace for these tribes, and he signed a preliminary peace treaty agreeing not to attack them if they surrendered their captives within 25 days. This unauthorized treaty was ignored by Bouquet, who was still fighting the Indians, and repudiated by his superior officers. Next, Bradstreet proceeded to Detroit where he negotiated treaties with six western Indian nations. These treaties angered Sir William Johnson, who believed that they had not been properly explained to the Indians, but they were allowed to stand.

Bradstreet died in New York City in 1774.

(T. Wood Clarke, The Bloody Mohawk; Arthur Pound, Johnson of the Mohawks; Dale Van Every, Forth to the Wilderness.)

BRADY, SAMUEL. Capt. Samuel Brady was born at Shippensburg, Pennsylvania, in 1756 and moved to the Susquehanna Valley at an early age. In 1776 he was commissioned captain in the American army, fighting in several battles against the British and serving in Col. Daniel Brodhead's expedition against the Seneca Indians. Both his father and brother were killed by Indians during the Revolution, and Samuel "swore vengeance against the whole race."--Wills De Hass.

There are so many legends about Brady's exploits that it is impossible to separate the factual from the fantastic. It is well authenticated, however, that he spied on the Indians north of the Ohio for Brodhead, boldly entering villages dressed and painted like a warrior. At times he was recognized and had to run for his life. Once he escaped by jumping the Cuyahoga River, 25 feet across, and clawing his way up the bank. The Indians opened fire from the opposite bank, wounding him in the leg, but he was able to evade them by hiding in a swamp. On another occasion he and three of his rangers helped a settler, Albert Gray, recover Gray's wife and children from captivity by crawling among the sleeping warriors, tomahawking four, and shooting the others as they tried to flee from the camp. Brady himself was captured by Indians near the Beaver River. When about to be tied to a stake near a fire, he seized an Indian boy, threw him into the flames, and burst through his captors when they rushed to rescue the child.

"For a dozen years after the Revolution," wrote Theodore Roosevelt, "Brady continued to be a power of strength to the frontier settlers of Pennsylvania and Virginia. At the head of his rangers he harassed the Indians greatly, interfering with and assailing their war-parties, and raiding their villages and home camps." One of his victims was the fearsome war chief Bald Eagle, the same raider charged with killing James Brady, Samuel's younger brother.

Brady's health declined as a result of years of hardship spent in the wilderness, and he suffered greatly from his leg wound. He spent his final years in western Virginia, expiring at West Liberty about 1800.

(Wills De Hass, History of the Early Settlement and Indian Wars of Western Virginia; Charles McKnight, Our Western Border; Theodore Roosevelt, The Winning of the West, II, IV.)

BRAINERD, DAVID. David Brainerd, one of the most famous
Protestant missionaries to the northeastern Indians, was born at
Haddam, Connecticut, on April 20, 1718. He had contracted tuberculosis by the time he entered Yale University to study for the ministry, and his health was much too delicate to embark on a missionary
career. Nevertheless, he turned down offers of churches amid comfortable surroundings to accept a missionary assignment among the
Delaware Indians at the request of the Correspondents of the Society
in Scotland for the Propagation of Christian Knowledge.

Because of unrest among the Delawares, Brainerd began his missionary labors at Kaunaumeek, in the wilderness between Albany and
Stockbridge, on April 1, 1743. After a year he persuaded the Indians
to join the mission of Rev. John Sergeant at Stockbridge. On June
12, 1744, newly ordained by the Presbytery of New York, he began
work with the Delawares near the present site of Easton, Pennsylvania. He labored, also, among the Indians on the Susquehanna before his most successful mission at the Delaware village of Cross-
weeksung, near the present site of Freehold, New Jersey, in 1745.
In May 1746, he removed with his Delaware followers about 15 miles
to Cranberry. There, early in 1747, illness compelled him to abandon
his mission. He died on October 9, 1747, at the home of Jonathan
Edwards, whose daughter Jerusha was his fiancée.

During his mission Brainerd rode horseback thousands of
miles in all kinds of weather, stopping to rest briefly when beset
by hemorrhages. Ola Winslow has surmised that he sought sainthood
and glorified in the suffering that led to the grave at the age of 29.

Brainerd kept a diary that inspired other Protestant ministers
to become missionaries. In regard to the difficulty of converting Indians to Christianity he wrote as follows:

> This aversion to Christianity arises partly from a view
> of the immorality and vicious behaviour of many who are
> called Christians. They observe that horrid wickedness in
> nominal Christians, which the light of nature condemns in
> themselves; and ... are ready to look upon all the white
> people alike, for the abominable practices of some. -- Hence,
> when I have attempted to treat with them about Christianity,
> they have frequently objected the scandalous practices of
> Christians. They have observed to me, that the white people
> lie, defraud, steal, and drink worse than the Indians; that
> they have taught the Indians these things, especially the lat-
> ter of them; who before the coming of the English, knew of
> no such thing as strong drink; that the English have, by
> these means, made them quarrel and kill one another; and,
> in a word, brought them to the practice of all those vices
> which now prevail among them. So that they are now vastly
> more vicious, as well as much more miserable, than they
> were before the coming of the white people into the country.
> — These, and such like objections, they frequently make
> against Christianity, which are not easily answered to their
> satisfaction; many of them being facts too notoriously true.

(Jonathan Edwards, Memoirs of the Rev. David Brainerd; Ola
Elizabeth Winslow, Jonathan Edwards.)

BRANT, JOSEPH, MOHAWK CHIEF. Joseph Brant (Thayendanegea),
one of the most remarkable Indians who ever lived, was born in the
wilderness near the Ohio River in 1742. His mother was a Mohawk,
and according to his biographer William L. Stone, his father was
Tehowaghwengaraghkwin, a member of the same tribe. He assumed
the name Brant because his mother married Nichaus Brant, also a
Mohawk, after his father's death. A widespread belief that his real
father was Sir William Johnson has been rejected by most historians,
but Dale Van Every has noted that it was logical "inasmuch as during
his ardent wooing of the Iroquois nation Sir William was reputed to
have fathered upwards of a hundred children." In any event, Joseph's
sister Molly Brant married Johnson, and soon afterward Joseph was
taken into the household.

Joseph's boyhood was similar to that of other Indian children
at Canajoharie, in the Mohawk Valley. When he moved into the Johnson mansion he adjusted with amazing alacrity to the new way of life,
and this dual upbringing enabled him to function equally well conferring with the king of England or leading an Indian raid on the
frontier settlements.

Brant's career as a warrior began at the age of 13 when he
fought in Johnson's victory over the French at Lake George in 1755,
and four years later he participated in the capture of Niagara. Soon
afterward he embarked on a scholarly career, attending classes at
an Anglican mission and at Eleazer Wheelock's academy for Indians
at Lebanon, Connecticut. Wheelock converted him to Christianity and
helped him to translate the Acts of the Apostles and the Gospel of
St. Mark into his native language. After leaving school he served
missionaries as a translator and acted as secretary for the Johnson
family.

In 1763 Brant resumed his warrior role. He served the British
well during Pontiac's War. He married the daughter of an Oneida
chief in 1765, developed a prosperous farm at Canajoharie, and became
a leader in the Iroquois League. When Sir William Johnson died during
the summer of 1774 and was succeeded by Guy Johnson, Brant proved
to be of tremendous service in helping the new superintendent of
northern Indian affairs to maintain the English influence over the Iroquois.

In 1775, at the onset of the American Revolution, Brant accompanied Guy Johnson on a voyage to London. Undecided upon
which side to support, he wanted to determine whether the British
would act favorably in response to Iroquois grievances regarding loss
of their lands. In London he was lionized by British officials and by
literary masters. He reached an agreement with the colonial secretary Lord George Germain to preserve the British alliance in exchange
for a guarantee of Iroquois boundaries. On the voyage back to New
York the ship was attacked by American privateers and Brant proved
his determination to fight for the crown by climbing the rigging and
shooting several enemy officers.

Brant was appointed colonel in the British army, and soon after his arrival at New York City in July 1776, he fought against the Americans in the Battle of Long Island. In November he slipped through the Patriot lines and traveled throughout the Iroquois villages, urging all of the nations to actively support the British. The result was the sundering of the League of the Six Nations, with four Iroquois tribes agreeing with Brant and the other two determined to preserve their neutrality.

During the spring of 1777 Brant established his headquarters at Oquaga. There his band of more than a hundred warriors was poised to strike the New York and Pennsylvania settlements. The Patriot leader, Gen. Nicholas Herkimer, tried to persuade him to remain neutral, but Brant asserted that he would stand by his British allies. Soon afterward Brant supported Gen. Barry St. Leger's forces in the siege of Fort Stanwix, and he led the ambush of Herkimer's army at the Battle of Oriskany. (See ORISKANY, BATTLE OF.)

From 1778 to 1781 Brant led a series of raids that devastated the Mohawk and Schoharie valleys, and he attacked settlements from Kentucky to the New Jersey border. (See CHERRY VALLEY MAS-SACRE; COBLESKILL, NEW YORK, RAIDS; MINISINK, NEW YORK, RAIDS; GERMAN FLATS, NEW YORK; ANDRUSTOWN, NEW YORK, RAIDS; SPRINGFIELD, NEW YORK, RAID; SCHOHARIE VALLEY, NEW YORK, RAIDS.) In 1778 alone he killed or captured 294 people, releasing many of the captives after berating them for disloyalty to their king.

After the Revolution, Brant obtained for the Iroquois a grant of land 100 miles long on the Grand River in Ontario as a reward for faithful service. Determined to preserve Indian lands north of the Ohio, he strove to organize a tribal confederation so that all would have to agree before any nation could cede lands to the whites. His plan came to naught, however, because of the inability of the Indians to maintain a united front. In 1785 he went to London and Paris seeking support for Indian rights, and although he was entertained by the king and queen of England and received an equally warm reception in France, he failed to obtain assurances he sought. Realizing that the Indians could no longer defeat the increasingly numerous Americans by force of arms, he attempted to lead them toward an acceptance of the beneficial aspects of white civilization. He built a school and church on the Grand River reservation and rekindled his interest in Bible translation. Married to a daughter of the trader and diplomat George Croghan, he lived in a substantial home near the present Hamilton, Ontario, until his death on November 24, 1807.

(Albert Britt, Great Indian Chiefs; Frederick J. Dockstader, Great North American Indians; R. David Edmunds, ed., American Indian Leaders; Barbara Graymont, The Iroquois in the American Revolution: T. Wood Clarke, The Bloody Mohawk; Dale Van Every, A Company of Heroes; Harvey Chalmers, Joseph Brant, Mohawk; William L. Stone, Life of Joseph Brant.)

BRANT, MOLLY. Molly Brant was the second Indian wife of Sir William Johnson and the sister of the famous Mohawk chief Joseph

Brant. A beautiful young girl and a member of an important Mohawk family, she first met Johnson in 1753 when he was attracted by her riding ability during a militia drill. They were married according to Indian custom (although he referred to her as his housekeeper), and she bore him at least eight children before his death in 1774.

During the American Revolution, as one of the Mohawk female clan leaders, she played an important role in maintaining the British-Iroquois alliance. When chiefs spoke in favor of making peace with the Americans she rebuked them in council. Before the Battle of Oriskany she sent warning to the British that Gen. Nicholas Herkimer was on his way to relieve Fort Stanwix, and, states Barbara Graymont, "she more than anyone else was responsible for the outcome of the battle." Afterward the Oneida Indians, allies of the Americans, threatened her and she and her children had to flee from her home at Canajoharie. She lived with the Cayugas for a short time and then went to Niagara where her influence was needed to encourage the Indians to keep fighting. In 1786 she moved to Canada, where the British rewarded her services with a generous pension.

(Barbara Graymont, The Iroquois in the American Revolution; Arthur Pound, Johnson of the Mohawks.)

BRESSANI, FRANCESCO GIOSEPPE. Father Francesco Gioseppe Bressani, an Italian Jesuit, was born at Rome in 1612. He studied theology there and at Clermont and went to Canada as a missionary in 1642. He labored among the Algonquians for two years before departing for the land of the Hurons with seven companions in April 1644. Near Fort Richelieu they were captured by Iroquois Indians, and Father Bressani was taken to their village near the Mohawk River and compelled to run the gantlet. Afterward they stabbed him repeatedly with sharp sticks and burned him with torches: "They made me walk around the fire on the burning cinders, under which they had placed sharp-pointed sticks," he reported. "Then they slowly burned off a nail and a finger, taking a quarter of an hour to do it. I have only one complete finger now, and they tore out the nail of that one with their teeth. One night they would tear out a nail; the following day the first joint; and the next day a second. I had to sing during the torture...."

After being tortured for a week while touring seven villages, the priest was sold by his captors to an old Iroquois woman for a few beads of wampum. She kept him a short time and then sold him to the Dutch at Fort Orange. He returned to Europe in 1644 to recover his health, but one year later he sailed back to Canada to resume his mission among the Hurons. During an Iroquois attack he was wounded three times by arrows so seriously that he had to return to Italy in 1650. He died there in 1672.

(T. J. Campbell, Pioneer Priests of North America; T. Wood Clarke, The Bloody Mohawk.)

BRIGEAC, CLAUDE DE, CAPTIVITY OF. Claude de Brigeac, a French soldier, and Father Guillaume de Vignal were attacked by an Iroquois war party near Montreal in 1657. Vignal was seriously wounded and Brigeac had his arm shattered while attempting to protect the priest. Then they and two other soldiers were taken prisoner. As Father Vignal was unable to travel, the warriors killed him and made a meal of his flesh.

Francis Parkman has described the fate of the devout French soldier as follows: "Brigeac and his fellows in misfortune spent a woeful night in the den of wolves; and in the morning their captors, having breakfasted on the remains of Vignal, took up their homeward march, dragging the Frenchmen with them. On reaching Oneida, Brigeac was tortured to death.... They could wring from him no cry of pain, but ... throughout he ceased not to pray for their conversion."

(Francis Parkman, The Old Régime in Canada.)

BRISAY, JACQUES RENE DE, MARQUIS DE DENONVILLE, EXPEDITION. Jacques René de Brisay, marquis de Denonville, governor of Canada and colonel of the Queen's Dragoons, was ordered in 1687 by his superiors in France to attack the Iroquois. He assembled an army of 1,600 soldiers, coureurs de bois, and Christian Indians for a campaign against the powerful Seneca nation.

On July 13 the Senecas, 800 strong, ambushed Denonville's forces in the wilderness near the present site of Victor, New York. Parkman described the action as follows:

> So dense was the forest that the advancing battalions could see neither the enemy nor one another. Appalled by the din of whoops and firing, redoubled by the echoes of the narrow valley, the whole army was seized with something like a panic. Some of the officers, it is said, threw themselves on the ground in their fright. There were a few moments of intense bewilderment. The various corps became broken and confused, and moved hither and thither without knowing why. Denonville behaved with great courage. He ran, sword in hand, to where the uproar was the greatest, ordered the drums to beat the charge, turned back the militia ... who were trying to escape, and commanded them and all others whom he met to fire on whatever looked like an enemy.... The Christian Iroquois fought well from the start, leaping from tree to tree, and exchanging shots and defiance with their heathen countrymen; till the Senecas, seeing themselves confronted by numbers that seemed endless, abandoned the field....

Denonville sent 36 Iroquois prisoners to France to serve as galley slaves. His forces had 40 men killed and more than 50 wounded during the fray. They burned three villages and destroyed the Indians' crops, but the expedition failed in its attempt to destroy the Seneca nation, and Canadian settlers suffered severely from continuing raids by the Iroquois.

(William J. Eccles, The Canadian Frontier; Francis Parkman, Count Frontenac and New France Under Louis XIV; Frank H. Severance, An Old Frontier of France.)

BRODHEAD, DANIEL, INDIAN CAMPAIGNS. Col. James Brodhead, a
Pennsylvania frontiersman, persuaded George Washington in 1779 to
permit him to lead an expedition against the Seneca Indians at the
same time that Gen. John Sullivan was attacking the more eastern
Iroquois. He marched from Fort Pitt on August 11 at the head of
600 men and met the Indians in battle for the first and only time
near Connewango (present Warren, Pennsylvania), killing several
warriors and destroying the village. Afterward the Indians retreated
before he could attack them, but he destroyed several Seneca and
Delaware villages on the Allegheny River as well as 500 acres of
corn and beans. He led his men back to Fort Pitt, arriving on September 14, without having lost a man.

Brodhead's exploit and Sullivan's expedition seriously weakened
the Six Nations, but by the spring of 1780 the Senecas had recovered
sufficiently to renew their raids on the Pennsylvania settlements.
Brodhead was prevented from retaliating by a lack of supplies.

Brodhead negotiated a treaty with the Delaware Indians that
kept them peaceful for a time, but in February 1781 he was warned
by Moravian missionaries that a war faction of the tribe planned to
attack the Pennsylvania settlements. He determined to forestall the
invasion by striking their villages. Assembling 300 men, half of
them regulars, he destroyed Coshocton and Lichtenau, capturing
many of the inhabitants. Theodore Roosevelt reported that "sixteen
noted warriors and marauders were singled out and put to death"
while "the remainder fared little better, for, while marching back
to Fort Pitt, the militia fell on them and murdered all the men, leaving only the women and children." The friendly Moravian Indians
would have been attacked, also, had Brodhead not prevented it. The
expedition caused such fury among the Delawares that they burned
9 white captives to death, 1 each day for nine days in succession.

(Solon J. Buck, The Planting of Civilization in Western Pennsylvania; Randolph C. Downes, Council Fires on the Upper Ohio; Theodore Roosevelt, The Winning of the West, III; Dale Van Every, A
Company of Heroes.)

BROOKFIELD, MASSACHUSETTS, RAIDS. Brookfield (Quabaug), a
village of 20 families, was located in an exposed position at the outbreak of King Philip's War in 1675. The citizens believed that the
neighboring Nipmuc Indians were friendly, but on August 2, when
Capt. Edward Hutchinson led a troop of soldiers and settlers to confer with them, the Nipmucs attacked, killing or wounding 8 men.
The survivors fled back to Brookfield and some 80 men, women, and
children "forted up" in a large house.

The Nipmucs laid siege to the house, firing repeatedly into the
walls, while the women and children lay prone behind the furniture
and the men held their assailants at bay. After capturing and de-
capitating a settler, the Indians set fire to the roof repeatedly with
flaming arrows, but the defenders climbed through holes and extinguished the flames. On the third day of the siege, the Nipmucs
loaded a wagon with burning hay and pushed it against the house.
Having no way to extinguish the fire, the defenders dropped to their

knees and appealed to heaven for help. Apparently in response a
rainstorm put out the fire.

Finally a scout, Henry Young, slipped through the besiegers
and ran thirty miles for help. On August 4, Maj. Simon Willard
arrived at the head of 50 fighting men, attacked the Indians, and
drove them away. The Nipmucs left 80 dead warriors littering the
ground.

Indians raided Brookfield once more on July 22, 1692, killing
6 settlers and carrying 4 others into captivity. They were overtaken
and attacked by Capt. Thomas Colton's company. Some 15 warriors
were killed and 2 of the captives recovered.

In June 1710 Brookfield was attacked by Indians for the third
time. Six settlers died that day at Brookfield and neighboring Marlborough.

(Samuel Adams Drake, Border Wars of New England; Douglas
Edward Leach, Flintlock and Tomahawk; John Tebbel and Keith Jennison, The American Indian Wars.)

BROTHERTON INDIANS. The Brotherton Indians were remnants of
several eastern tribes (Mahicans, Wappingers, Mohegans, Pequots,
Narragansets, and Montauks) who settled at Brotherton, New York,
in 1788, under the leadership of Samson Occom and Joseph Johnson.
They had been invited to settle there by the Oneida Indians, and
their objective was to remove themselves from the pressure of white
encroachment. In 1802 they were joined by bands of Raritan and
Delaware Indians from the Brotherton Reservation in New Jersey.
There was no escape from the spreading white settlements, however,
and in 1833 they removed with the Oneida and Stockbridge Indians
to Lake Winnebago in Wisconsin. Subsequently they became United
States citizens.

(F. W. Hodge, ed., Handbook of American Indians, I; William
C. Sturtevant, ed., Handbook of North American Indians, XV.)

BROWNSTOWN, MICHIGAN, TREATY OF. The Treaty of Brownstown
was negotiated on November 25, 1808, by William Hull with several
Michigan tribes. The Indians ceded a 120-foot-wide roadway, facilitating travel to Detroit. It extended from Maumee Rapids to Lower
Sandusky and south from that point to a line established earlier by
the Treaty of Greenville.

(Charles J. Kappler, ed., Indian Affairs: Laws and Treaties,
II.)

BRULE, ETIENNE. Etienne Brulé a French youth, was sent by
Champlain in 1612 to live a year with the Hurons in order to learn
their language. In 1615 he served as Champlain's interpreter during
negotiations with that nation. Later that year Champlain sent him
to recruit the Susquehanna Indians to assist the French in attacking
the Iroquois. He remained with the Susquehannas three years, becoming greatly assimiliated, and exploring a large area of North
America with warriors of that powerful tribe. It is believed that he
was the first European to see Lakes Erie, Huron, Ontario, and Superior,

that he visited Niagara, and that he descended the Susquehanna to the sea.

While attempting to return to the French in Canada, Brulé became lost. At the point of starvation, he found himself near an Iroquois village and surrendered to his enemies. The Iroquois warriors burned his arms and hands with torches and tore out his beard (making him the first European to experience Indian torture). He was saved from death when he claimed to possess power to exterminate the tribe if they continued to torture him. When his warning was followed immediately by a severe storm, a frightened chief conveyed him to the longhouse and took care of him until he recovered. He remained with the Iroquois for some time, taking part in all of the village activities. Then, at his request to return to the French, they provided guides, and he was reunited with Champlain in the summer of 1618.

But Brulé enjoyed his association with Indians so much that he spent most of the remainder of his life in their villages. In 1633 he was murdered and eaten by the Hurons, apparently for violating their moral standards.

"He was the first Frenchman, but by no means the last, to be completely assimilated by the Indians."--William J. Eccles.

(William J. Eccles, The Canadian Frontier; Francis Parkman, Pioneers of France in the New World; Frank H. Severance, An Old Frontier of France.)

BRUNSWICK, MAINE, RAID. The village of Brunswick, site of Fort George, was attacked by 60 Indians on June 13, 1722. Nine families of settlers were captured and every house was destroyed before cannon shots from the fort forced the raiders to retire. A hastily assembled force from neighboring towns overtook the Indians, killing 18 warriors. Five of the captives were taken to Canada, but the others were released.

"This destruction of Brunswick was in retaliation for the attack made on Norridgewock the year proceeding."--Herbert Milton Sylvester.

(Herbert Milton Sylvester, Indian Wars of New England, II.)

BRUYAS, JAMES. Father James Bruyas, a Jesuit, was one of the most successful missionaries to serve among the Iroquois Indians. He sailed to Canada from France in 1666 and was sent to the Iroquois the following year. After a brief stay with the Mohawks he established a mission among the Oneidas, a nation he characterized as "the most cruel of the Iroquois," so warlike that "they will travel 300 leagues and more to remove one scalp." He managed to attract many of them to the Mission St. Francis Xavier of the Oneida, however, where they listened intently to his religous instructions.

After a year at Oneida, Bruyas returned to the Mohawks. There he encountered hostility because many of the Mohawks had gone to live with the Christian Indians in Canada, and those who remained accused him of weakening the fighting ability of the tribe. He responded by blaming their weakness on "drunkenness and debauchery."

As Superior of the Iroquois missions he traveled from tribe to tribe until 1679. Then he went to Caughnawaga in Canada, serving among the Christian Mohawks until 1691.

In 1693 Bruyas became Superior General, a responsibility which required him to function as an Indian diplomat until 1699. Not only did he succeed in improving Indian relations, but he served France as an envoy to New England to establish peace in accordance with the Treaty of Ryswick. He redeemed ten Frenchmen from Iroquois captivity and persuaded the Five Nations to permit reestablishment of missions in their territory. He died at Quebec in 1712.

(T. J. Campbell, Pioneer Priests of North America.)

BUCKONGAHELAS, DELAWARE CHIEF. Buckongahelas, born in Ohio about 1750, rose as a result of his abilities to become the leading war chief of the western Delawares. In 1781, alarmed by the advance of white settlers along the Ohio, he persuaded many of his people to move to the upper Miami River. The Moravian Indians (mainly Christian Delawares) declined the invitation, convinced that white people would not harm them, only to be massacred the following year by the Pennsylvania militia.

Influenced by the British, Buckongahelas played a prominent part in the Indian wars against the Americans during the early 1790's. Never known to be cruel to noncombatants, he was respected by the whites as a worthy and humane enemy. After the Battle of Fallen Timbers, furious at the British refusal to admit the defeated Indians to their fort, he turned against them and became a friend of the United States. He signed the Treaties of Greenville in 1795, Fort Wayne in 1803, and Vincennes in 1804. He is believed to have died near the present Muncie, Indiana, in 1804 or 1805.

"All writers agree in representing him as fearless, frank, and magnanimous."--B. B. Thatcher.

(F. W. Hodge, ed., Handbook of American Indians, I; B. B. Thatcher, Indian Biography, I.)

BUFFALO CREEK, TREATIES OF. On June 30, 1802, John Taylor negotiated the first treaty of Buffalo Creek with the Seneca Indians. They ceded lands in western New York to the Holland Land Company.

The second treaty of Buffalo Creek was negotiated on January 15, 1838, with the Iroquois Indians by Ransom H. Gillet, representing the United States. The Indians agreed to cede their lands in New York and Wisconsin and to remove within five years to Kansas Territory. One Iroquois nation, the Oneidas, refused to remove.

(Charles J. Kappler, ed., Indian Affairs: Laws and Treaties, II; William C. Sturtevant, ed., Handbook of North American Indians, XV.)

BUFFALO, NEW YORK, RAID. Buffalo, New York, was a small village during the War of 1812. On December 31, 1813, British and Indians led by Gen. Phineas Riall burned every building to the ground. The settlers returned soon afterward and rebuilt the town which developed into New York's second largest city.

(Lloyd Graham, Niagara Country.)

BULL, FORT, NEW YORK. Fort Bull was built in 1755 at the head
of navigation on Wood Creek to guard the portage between the Mohawk River and Oneida Lake. Its location was near the present site
of Rome, New York. In March 1756, an army of 300 Frenchmen from
Montreal and 400 Indians attacked Fort Bull. Led by Joseph De Lery,
the French forces stormed the fort, tore down the gate, and captured
the 30 defenders. Meanwhile the Indians guarded the road from Fort
Williams and ambushed a relief force rushing to the assistance of
Fort Bull. Seventeen soldiers were killed and the survivors fled
back to Fort Williams. The French and Indians lost only 3 men. Before returning to Montreal they destroyed Fort Bull and it was never
rebuilt.

    (T. Wood Clarke, The Bloody Mohawk; Arthur Pound, Johnson
of the Mohawks.)

BULL, TOM. Tom Bull, an Indian, served as a spy for the English
during the French and Indian War. He traveled frequently from Fort
Pitt to Niagara, visiting Indian allies of the French and returning
with information about enemy movements and defenses. In 1759 he
watched the French garrisons at Presque Isle, Venango, and Fort Le
Boeuf and reported their strengths and weaknesses to the English.

    (Frank H. Severance, An Old Frontier of France.)

BURD, JAMES. Col. James Burd of the Pennsylvania militia played
an important role as a road and fort builder during the French and
Indian War. He was building a road from eastern Pennsylvania to
Fort Duquesne to provide supplies for Braddock's army at the time
that British general was defeated by the French and Indians. He
built Fort Morris at Shippensburg in 1755. In January 1756 he commanded Fort Granville, but he was transferred before that stockade
surrendered to the Indians. In October 1758 while building a road
to Fort Duquesne for Gen. John Forbes, he was in command at Fort
Ligonier, Pennsylvania, when 600 French and Indians attacked his
army of 1,500 men. Burd lost 60 men in a battle that lasted a day
and a night, but he compelled the enemy to retreat. In 1759 he
built Fort Burd at Redstone which protected settlers from Indian attacks until the end of the American Revolution.

    (Solon J. Buck, The Planting of Civilization in Western Penn-
sylvania; William A. Hunter, Forts on the Pennsylvania Frontier.)

BUSHY RUN, BATTLE OF. The Battle of Bushy Run was fought on
August 5-6, 1763 at Edge Hill, twenty five miles east of Pittsburgh.
Col. Henry Bouquet was leading 400 British Regulars, Royal Americans, and rangers to relieve Fort Pitt when he was attacked by a
large war party of Shawnees, Delawares, Senecas, and Hurons, led
by Chiefs Custaloga and Kiasutha. The Indians surrounded the
column, firing from the protection of the forest, and Bouquet was
compelled to fall back from Bushy Run to Edge Hill in order to save
his pack train, 340 horse loads of flour intended for the garrison at
besieged Fort Pitt.

    Deployed in a circle at the hill top, the British fought from

behind piles of flour sacks until dark. After the Indians stopped
firing, confident of victory on the morrow, Bouquet devised a plan
to surprise them with a flanking movement. He withdrew two companies from the circle and placed them in the center, giving an appearance that one segment of his line was weakly defended. On the
morning of August 6 the Indians charged that side of the hill, only
to be attacked with bayonets by the two concealed companies. The
warriors hastily retreated toward the woods, pursued by soldiers firing
with such accuracy that the enemy was unable to make a stand.

Bouquet led his men a mile to Bushy Run, where the Indians
fired a final volley before abandoning the fight. The troops relieved
Fort Pitt on August 10. Bouquet had sustained heavy losses--50 men
killed and 60 wounded. The Indian losses were equally as severe.

"At Bushy Run, the matching of red warrior against white
soldier was nearly even, longer in duration, and more gallantly and
stubbornly fought than in any other battle in which they ever
met."--Dale Van Every.

(Howard H. Peckham, Pontiac and the Indian Uprising; Dale
Van Every, Forth to the Wilderness; Paul A. W. Wallace, Indians in
Pennsylvania.)

BUTLER, JOHN. John Butler was born at New London, Connecticut,
in 1728. During his youth he assisted his father, Walter Butler, Sr.,
as an interpreter at Oswego, New York, before embarking on a military career. He held the rank of captain while serving with the Indian contingent at the Battle of Crown Point. Afterward he assisted
Sir William Johnson in managing Indian affairs and became almost as
skillful in tribal diplomacy as his mentor. In the Niagara campaign
of 1759 he took charge of the Indians after Johnson assumed command of the expedition, and he planned the ambush that resulted in
the surrender of the French fort. In 1760 he and Johnson led the
Indians during Amherst's capture of Montreal.

After the close of the French and Indian War, Butler was appointed deputy superintendent of Indian affairs. After Sir William
Johnson's death he continued in that post, serving under the direc-
tion of Col. Guy Johnson. At the onset of the American Revolution
he withdrew to Canada with Johnson, and there he was appointed
major of Indian auxiliaries. At his new post at Niagara he attempted
at first to keep the Indians neutral, but after he received orders
to employ them against the New York and Pennsylvania frontiers he
organized a Tory contingent called Butler's Rangers and recruited
Iroquois war parties to attack his old neighbors in the Mohawk Valley. He and the Mohawk chief Joseph Brant led the ambush of Herkimer's forces at Oriskany (see ORISKANY, BATTLE OF), and he commanded the Indians and rangers at the Battle of Wyoming. (See
WYOMING MASSACRES.) Although much reviled for permitting atrocities at Wyoming, all of those slain were soldiers, and Butler was
praised by his superiors for preventing the Indians from harming
civilians.

In 1779 Butler was assigned to oppose Gen. John Sullivan's
invasion of the Iroquois country. He was greatly outnumbered,

however, and failed to find the right opportunity for an ambush.
(See NEWTOWN, BATTLE OF.) Afterward he went to Niagara and
did his best to provide for the displaced Indians. Appointed British
Superintendent of Indian Affairs, he held that post until his death
on May 14, 1796.

"Of long military experience, careful in planning his campaigns,
meticulous in perfecting the details to cover every contingent, with
marvelous control over his Indian allies, indefatigable and inexhaus-
tible when on the march, thoughtful and considerate of the men under him and ever-alert to prevent injury to non-combatants, Col.
John Butler was probably the most competent and efficient commander
in the British army in America."--T. Wood Clarke.

(T. Wood Clarke, The Bloody Mohawk; Barbara Graymont,
The Iroquois in the American Revolution; Dale Van Every, A Company
of Heroes.)

BUTLER, RICHARD. Gen. Richard Butler was born in Dublin, Ireland, on April 1, 1743. His family moved to Lancaster, Pennsylvania,
during his childhood and he grew up in a frontier environment.
After serving in Henry Bouquet's expedition of 1764, he and his
brother William engaged in the Ohio River region fur trade. He was
one of the traders brought safely through hostile Indian country by
the Shawnees at the outbreak of Dunmore's War.

In July 1775 Butler, then the most important trader at Fort
Pitt, was appointed Indian agent by the Continental Congress for
the area beyond the Alleghenies. He kept close watch on Alexander
McKee, British Indian Agent, and insisted upon being informed of all
of McKee's contacts with the tribes. In 1776 he resigned that post
to accept a commission in Morgan's Rifles. During the Revolution he
served as lieutenant-colonel in the battles of Saratoga and Stony
Point.

In 1783 Butler was appointed Indian Commissioner. He negotiated treaties with the Iroquois in 1784; the Wyandots, Delawares,
Chippewas and Ottawas in 1785; and the Shawnees (compelling them
to cede a large tract of land) in 1786. When the Shawnees objected
to the cession, Butler bent them to his will by threatening the lives
of their women and children. In 1786 he became superintendent of
Indian affairs for the Northern District.

In 1791 Butler was appointed second in command to Gen. Arthur
St. Clair during the campaign against the northwestern Indians.
Neither officer proved to be a competent commander, they refused to
speak to each other, and the campaign ended in disastrous defeat.
Mortally wounded, Butler insisted that rescuers save his less severely
injured brother Thomas instead of himself.

(Randolph C. Downes, Council Fires on the Upper Ohio; R.
David Edmunds, The Shawnee Prophet; Charles A. Hanna, The
Wilderness Trail, II; Dale Van Every, Ark of Empire; John Anthony
Caruso, The Great Lakes Frontier.)

BUTLER, WALTER. Walter Butler, eldest son of Col. John Butler,
was born about 1752 at Butlersbury, New York. At the age of 16

he served as an ensign in his father's militia regiment. Two years later he entered law school at Albany, and at the end of his studies he became a successful attorney.

At the onset of the American Revolution, Butler, who was intensely loyal to the king, left the Mohawk Valley with Indian Agent Guy Johnson, withdrawing with other Tories to Canada. In September 1775 he served in the defense force by which Ethan Allen was captured while attempting to seize Montreal. Two months later he sailed to England with Guy Johnson and Joseph Brant.

When Butler returned to America, Gen. Barry St. Leger assigned him to persuade Mohawk Valley settlers to join the British army. During this mission he was captured at German Flats and imprisoned at Albany. In April 1778 he escaped from prison and rejoined his father in Canada, serving as a captain in Butler's Rangers.

In November 1778 young Butler was given command of a force of 150 rangers, 50 regulars, and 321 Indians and ordered to attack Fort Alden at Cherry Valley, New York. He was unable to capture the fort, but his Indians massacred 32 settlers and captured at least 70. Widely condemned for the atrocities committed at Cherry Valley, he insisted that he had done everything possible to prevent them, but he could not control his Indians. (See CHERRY VALLEY MASSACRE.) The following year he served under his father at the Battle of Newtown, failing to stop Gen. John Sullivan's invasion of the Iroquois country.

In 1781 Butler made his last foray into the Mohawk Valley. He was second in command to Maj. John Ross at the Battle of Johnstown, and retreated before the American forces commanded by Martinus Willett. On November 20, Butler was serving as rear guard at a river crossing. He was in the act of taunting the Americans when one of their guides, an Oneida Indian, shot him from the saddle, forded the river, and tomahawked him to death.

"There was more rejoicing in Tryon County over his death than over the coincidental news from Yorktown."--Dale Van Every.

(T. Wood Clarke, The Bloody Mohawk; Francis Whiting Halsey, The Old New York Frontier; Barbara Graymont, The Iroquois in the American Revolution; Dale Van Every, A Company of Heroes.)

BUTLER, WILLIAM, EXPEDITION. Col. William Butler was ordered in August 1778 to lead his regiment and four companies of Morgan's Riflemen to Schoharie to protect the settlers, threatened by Tories and Indians. Soon afterward it was determined that Butler should take the offensive, destroying Tory and Indian strongholds on the Susquehanna and Unadilla rivers. In October he led 260 men to Unadilla and Oquaga, found that both had been abandoned, and burned them. He destroyed the crops along the Susquehanna and Unadilla, seized several Tories, and burned their homes. By destroying Oquaga he deprived Joseph Brant of his principal store of supplies.

(T. Wood Clarke, The Bloody Mohawk; Francis Whiting Halsey, The Old New York Frontier.)

BUTTE DES MORTS. Butte des Morts, near Lake Winnebago, Wisconsin, was the scene of several Indian battles, conferences, and treaties. In 1716 the French, assisted by the Potawatomi Indians, attacked a Fox stronghold at Butte des Morts. The French commandant Louis de la Porte de Louvigny besieged them, recovered some prisoners, and called off the Potawatomis after the Foxes promised to live in peace.

In 1728 and 1730 the French and their Indian allies defeated the Foxes and inflicted so many casualties on them that they took refuge with the Sauk Indians. In 1733, Nicolas-Antoine Coulon de Villiers and a large force of French and Indians demanded that the Sauks surrender the Foxes for punishment, but the host tribe refused. Villiers led an attack on the palisaded village and was killed trying to force his way inside. The allied Sauks and Foxes fled to Little Butte des Morts, where the French, led by Villiers' son Louis, attacked them once more. A battle lasted an entire day with many men killed on both sides.

On August 11, 1827, Lewis Cass and Thomas L. McKenney negotiated a treaty with the Winnebago, Chippewa, and Menominee Indians at Butte des Morts. Boundaries were established between the various tribes inhabiting or moving to Wisconsin.

(James A. Clifton, The Prairie People; Louis Phelps Kellogg, The French Régime in Wisconsin and the Northwest; Charles J. Kappler, ed., Indian Affairs: Laws and Treaties, II.)

-C-

CADOTTE, JEAN BAPTISTE, FAMILY OF. Jean Baptiste Cadotte (Cadeau), a trader associated with Alexander Henry, married Anastasia, Christian daughter of a prominent Chippewa chief named Nipissing, on October 28, 1756. Anastasia, through force of character and the favor of powerful Chippewa chiefs, assisted her husband to negotiate trade agreements with several tribes, and he and Henry established a profitable business on St. Michel's Island after the French and Indian War. In 1767 he enhanced his favored position, presenting gifts to Indians while exploring Lake Superior in search of copper, and he eventually became a giant of the fur trade.

Jean Baptiste and Anastasia Cadotte became parents of two sons, Jean Baptiste, Jr., and Michel, during the early 1760's. Both boys received a good education at Montreal, and afterward they followed their father's example as prominent fur traders. Jean Baptiste, Jr., established his headquarters at Chequamegon Bay, Wisconsin, while Michel remained at his father's post on St. Michel's Island. Michel married a Christian Chippewa girl named Madeline, and her father, Chief White Crane, renamed the site (near the present La Pointe, Wisconsin) Madeline Island in her honor.

Jean Baptiste, Jr., upon completing college, became associated with the Northwestern Fur Company, and he dispatched huge loads of furs to the Montreal market. He spent more money than he made, however, and eventually lost a fortune. Refinanced by Alexander

Henry, he employed a large contingent of coureurs de bois and established a flourishing fur trade along the waterways from Fond du Lac to Sault Ste. Marie to Cass Lake. He sided with the British during the American Revolution and, in 1784, he served as their interpreter at Sault Ste. Marie.

Michel Cadotte established a post at Lac Courte Oreilles and he traded extensively on the Chippewa River and Superior Bay. Later he extended his trade territory as far north as Winnepeg and westward almost to the present North Dakota boundary. During the American Revolution he served in the British Indian Service, scouting the Lake Superior region and recruiting Sioux warriors to cooperate with the Redcoats in operations along the Mississippi.

Michel's sons, Jean Baptiste and Michel, Jr., were compelled to lead Chippewa warriors who fought for the British in the War of 1812. His daughters, Mary and Charlotte, married the Massachusetts traders Lyman and Truman Warren about 1818, and these wealthy brothers conducted the family fur trade in Wisconsin and Michigan as long as it remained a profitable enterprise.

(Louise Phelps Kellogg, The British Regime in Wisconsin and the North-West; Carolissa Levi, Chippewa Indians of Yesterday and Today.)

CAHOKIA INDIANS. The Cahokia Indians, members of the Illinois confederacy, were gathered with the closely associated Tamaroas in a Jesuit mission near the present site of Cahokia, Illinois, in 1699. Attracted by the accessibility to larger tribes to the south and west, a considerable number of soldiers, traders, and coureurs de bois formed a French community near the Mission of the Holy Family and, as a result of European diseases and vices, the Indian population of 2,000 declined rapidly. A small number of survivors, together with remnants of other Illinois tribes, removed to the West about 1820. Their descendants are now included among the Peoria Indians.

(Clarence Walworth Alvord, The Illinois Country; F. W. Hodge, ed., Handbook of American Indians, I.)

CALDWELL, BILLY see SAGAUNASH, POTAWATOMI CHIEF

CALDWELL, WILLIAM. Capt. William Caldwell, an officer in the Tory Rangers, led or took part in several of the fiercest attacks on American settlements during the Revolutionary War. Born in Ireland, he settled in Pennsylvania at an early age, married a Mohawk woman, and entered the British Indian Service. With Chief Brant, Walter Butler, Alexander McKee, Simon Girty, Matthew Elliott and other partisans, he managed Indian recruiting and raiding in bloody forays from New York to Kentucky.

Caldwell first received recognition as a dangerous leader of Indians on July 3, 1778, during the Wyoming Valley Massacre. In September 1778 he participated in the destruction of German Flats, New York. On November 11, 1778, he led a ranger detachment that accompanied Brant's Indians in the Cherry Valley Massacre. In June 1782 he organized the Indians of the Sandusky region to retaliate against the Americans for a massacre of Moravian Indians. On June 6 they defeated the army of Col. William Crawford, capturing several soldiers and burning Crawford to death. In August 1782 he and Simon Girty led the Indians in the siege of Bryan's Station, Kentucky, and, on August 19, he planned the ambush that killed so many Kentuckians at the Battle of Blue Licks.

After the Revolution, Caldwell and Matthew Elliott became partners in the Indian trade and in land speculation near Detroit. They went bankrupt in 1787. Little is heard of Caldwell thereafter until August 1794 when he led the Detroit militia to assist the Indians in opposing Gen. Anthony Wayne's invasion. After Wayne's victory at Fallen Timbers, Caldwell led a valiant rear guard action that assisted the surviving Indians to escape from the field. Afterward he supplied the British troops at Amherstburg with wagons and teams. He continued to serve in the British Indian Department for many years.

(Barbara Graymont, The Iroquois in the American Revolution; John Bakeless, Daniel Boone; Reginald Horsman, Matthew Elliott; Louise Phelps Kellogg, The British Régime in Wisconsin and the Northwest.)

CAMPANIUS, JOHAN. Johan Campanius, a Swedish Lutheran clergyman, came to America in 1642 to attempt to convert the Indians of the Delaware River region to Christianity. He remained five years, serving Indians and Swedish settlers at Christina, Tinicum, and elsewhere. He mastered the Delaware language so completely that he was able to compile the first vocabulary of that important tribe and to write a catechism for Indian use. In 1647 he requested recall, stating that he had served "with great danger of death night and day in a heathenish country."

(John E. Pomfret, The Province of West New Jersey.)

CAMPBELL, DONALD. Capt. Donald Campbell of the Royal Americans was sent to Fort Detroit in 1760, where he served as second in command to Maj. Henry Gladwin. A Scotsman who had arrived in America in 1756, he held command of the post while Gladwin went to England on leave. He cultivated the goodwill of the French settlers and neighboring Indians, becoming especially friendly with Chief Pontiac. During the summer of 1761, discovering that the Seneca Indians were attempting to organize a conspiracy to attack the British posts, he courageously conferred with the hostiles and convinced them to abandon their attempt to take Fort Detroit.

In September 1761 Gladwin returned and Campbell remained at Detroit in a subordinate role. The following year he attempted to assuage Indian anger over the British lack of adequate trade goods by making them presents of tobacco and rum. By May 1763, however, Pontiac's conspiracy resulted in the siege of Detroit, and Campbell, accompanied by Lt. George McDougall, volunteered to call upon the chief and attempt to make peace. Pontiac seized them as hostages and compelled Campbell to write Gladwin that they would be tortured to death unless the British surrendered the fort. On July 2 McDougall escaped, but Campbell remained in captivity.

Shortly after McDougall's escape, members of the garrison slew the nephew of the Chippewa chief Wasson during a sortie, and Wasson insisted upon taking revenge on the captive. With Pontiac's concurrence, the Chippewa chief tomahawked and scalped Campbell, ate his heart, and dumped his body in the river.

(Howard H. Peckham, Pontiac and the Indian Uprising.)

CAMPBELL, JOHN, FLOTILLA. In 1814 Maj. John Campbell commanded five boats that ascended the Mississippi to bring troops and supplies to Fort Shelby at Prairie du Chien. Unaware that the British were attacking Fort Shelby and that they had incited the Indians to waylay American boats on the river, Campbell unwisely allowed women and children to accompany his 60 regulars and 64 rangers to their new assignment.

On July 21, 1814, with boats bearing contractor's and sutler's supplies in the lead, the flotilla set out through the Mississippi rapids during a gale. Four boats negotiated the rapids successfully, but Campbell's craft went aground on an island. Suddenly a large number of canoes appeared, bringing Sauk, Fox, and Kickapoo Indians to attack the stranded soldiers and their families.

Almost half of the 33 men on board Campbell's craft died in the first exchange of fire. Chief Black Hawk struck the sail with fire arrows, setting it ablaze, and warriors fired through the portholes while Indian women attacked wives and children with hoes. The other boats had proceeded several miles upstream before soldiers saw the smoke of battle, and two of them turned back to investigate. One went aground, but the other, commanded by Lt. Stephen Rector raked the Indians with such heavy fire that they turned their attack away from Campbell's burning boat. Rector sailed through a hail of bullets and rescued the survivors. Campbell had lost 16 men, one woman and one child. Indian losses were limited to two warriors and one woman.

(William T. Hagan, The Sac and Fox Indians.)

CANADASAGA, SENECA TOWN. Canadasaga was an important Seneca Indian town near the present city of Geneva, New York. In 1756 the British Indian Agent Sir William Johnson built a strong stockade around the town to protect the inhabitants. During the American Revolution Gen. John Sullivan's army destroyed Canadasaga in 1779.

(F. W. Hodge, ed., Handbook of American Indians, I.)

CANAJOHARIE, MOHAWK TOWN. Canajoharie, the Upper Mohawk Castle, was located near the present site of Fort Plain, New York. A few years before the outbreak of the American Revolution white settlers infiltrated the area, and they occupied the town itself when the Mohawks evacuated it after hostilities began. On August 2, 1780, the Mohawk chief Brant attacked the settlers, killing 14, taking 60 prisoners, and destroying more than a hundred houses, barns, and mills.

(Dale Van Every, A Company of Heroes.)

CANANDAIGUA, SENECA TOWN. Canandaigua, an important Seneca
Indian town, was located at the present site of Canandaigua, New
York. It was destroyed by Gen. John Sullivan's army during his
invasion of the lands of the Six Nations in 1779.

Reoccupied after the close of the American Revolution, Canandaigua was the site of a treaty negotiated by Timothy Pickering with
the Six Nations on November 11, 1794. The treaty restored peace,
defined Seneca boundaries, and confirmed Iroquois possession of remaining lands.

(F. W. Hodge, ed., Handbook of American Indians, I; Charles
J. Kappler, ed., Indian Affairs: Laws and Treaties, II.)

CANARSEE INDIANS. The Canarsee Indians, a Delaware tribe closely connected to the Munsees, lived on Long Island, Jamaica Bay, and
the present site of Brooklyn, New York. During early colonial times
the tribe played an important part in the Indian-white relationships
of the area. Allen W. Trelease believes that it was a Canarsee band
that attacked one of Henry Hudson's boats on September 6, 1609.
Although the Canarsees did not own Manhattan Island they sold it
to Peter Minuit, representing the Dutch West India Company, in 1626
for some $24 worth of trade goods.

The Canarsees were active against the Dutch settlers during
the seventeenth-century Indian wars. Having been decimated by the
Dutch and Mohawks, they sent their chief to Fort Amsterdam to negotiate peace on March 4, 1643. At that time they reported that
many mixed Dutch-Canarsee children had been slain during recent
raids by Europeans on Indian villages. In February 1644 the Dutch
and English resumed their attacks against the Indians of western
Long Island, inflicting heavy casualties. Of the 120 Indians killed,
a considerable number were Canarsees. Tribal numbers dwindled
rapidly as a result of war and disease, and the last Canarsee died
about 1800.

(E. B. O'Callaghan, History of New Netherland, I; Allen W.
Trelease, Indian Affairs in Colonial New York.)

CANASATEGO, ONONDAGA CHIEF. Canasatego, a member of the
Great Council of the Iroquois, spoke for the League at conferences
with Pennsylvania officials in 1742, 1744, and 1749. He is best remembered for quashing complaints of the Delaware Indians regarding
the fraudulent nature of the Walking Purchase of 1737 by asserting
that the tribe had nothing to say about it: "We conquered you; we
made women of you; you know you are women, and can no more sell
land than women." Then he ordered the Delawares to depart from
the Forks of the Delaware and to settle at Wyoming or Shamokin.
He died in 1750.

(Paul A. W. Wallace, Indians in Pennsylvania.)

CANAWESE INDIANS see CONOY INDIANS

CANONCHET, NARRAGANSET CHIEF. Canonchet was a formidable
young Narraganset chief and a determined foe of the English during

King Philip's War. Born about 1630 in Rhode Island, he was friendly
to white settlers until 1676 when the English attacked his people for
sheltering some of Philip's warriors. In a bloody battle at Patuxet
on March 26, 1676, most of the invading soldiers were killed. Afterward, he was compelled to flee from his homeland. Returning the
following month to obtain corn to feed his people, he was captured
by a Pequot warrior and turned over to the English for trial. At
Stonington, Connecticut, the colonists, who admired his bravery,
offered him freedom if he would order his warriors to lay down their
arms. But Canonchet refused to consider the proposal. Infuriated
by his courageous stand, Pequot and Mohawk warriors killed and beheaded him.

"With the death of Canonchet, Philip's ablest ally was gone and
the war was ebbing."--Albert Britt.

(Albert Britt, Great Indian Chiefs; Frederick J. Dockstader,
Great North American Indians; Douglas Edward Leach, Flintlock and
Tomahawk.)

CANONICUS, NARRAGANSET CHIEF. Canonicus was chief of the
Narragansets when the Pilgrims landed in Massachusetts in 1620.
His first reaction to the newcomers was hostile, sending them a
bundle of arrows wrapped in a snakeskin as an invitation to do battle, but his warlike ardor abated, and in time he befriended the
struggling colonists. In 1635 he gave land near the present Providence, Rhode Island, to Roger Williams, and three years later he
signed a treaty of amity with the Connecticut settlers. Not long
afterward he became deeply offended, however, when the English
seized his nephew Miantonomo and turned him over to the Mohegan
Indians, enemies of the Narragansets, for execution.

Canonicus died on June 4, 1647, at the approximate age of
88.

(Frederick J. Dockstader, Great North American Indians;
Herbert Milton Sylvester, Indian Wars of New England, I.)

CANOY INDIANS see CONOY INDIANS

CAPE NEDDOCK, MAINE, MASSACRE. Cape Neddock, a fishing village five miles from Wells, Maine, was twice laid waste by Abnaki
Indians. In September 1676 the hostiles destroyed the entire village, killing or capturing forty settlers. Only a half dozen people
escaped. In 1691 the Abnakis attacked Wells, failed to take it, and
vented their wrath on Cape Neddock, killing nine men and burning
the village once more.

(Edward L. Bourne, History of Wells and Kennebunk; Samuel
Adams Drake, The Border Wars of New England.)

CAPTAIN BULL, DELAWARE CHIEF, RAID. Captain Bull, son of
the important Delaware chief, Tedyuscung, blamed white settlers of
the Wyoming Valley of Pennsylvania for his father's death by fire
in the spring of 1763. In retaliation, on October 15, 1763, he struck
the valley with his Delaware warriors, wiping out the scattered

settlements except for a handful of people who managed to escape. About twenty settlers were captured, several of whom suffered a fiery death at the stake.

(Paul A. W. Wallace, Indians in Pennsylvania; Anthony F. C. Wallace, King of the Delawares: Teedyuscung.)

CAPTAIN JACOBS, DELAWARE CHIEF. Captain Jacobs, a fiery Delaware war chief, was a major scourge of the Pennsylvania frontier during the French and Indian War. He and his followers helped the French defeat Gen. Edward Braddock's British army near Fort Duquesne in 1755. Then joining forces with another redoubtable Delaware, Shingas, he ravaged the settlements of the Pennsylvania mountains from his village of Kittanning.

In October 1755 Jacobs and Shingas descended upon the settlers of the Great Cove, near the Maryland border, annihilating 47 families and burning 27 plantations. Early in 1756, following raids in Cumberland County, Pennsylvania, officials placed a $700 price on the heads of hostile Delaware chiefs, but the rewards did not deter Jacobs and Shingas. On February 29 they attacked David Davis's Fort in the Little Cove and McDowell's Mill on the Conococheague. On March 30 they struck Patterson's Fort, and the following day they overran McCord's Fort and ambushed pursuers at Sideling Hill. Shingas suffered a serious wound in a battle near Fort Cumberland, but Jacobs continued his assaults on Pennsylvania settlements and forts. On June 11 the Delawares seized Bigham's Fort.

On July 30 Jacobs and his warriors, assisted by a few Frenchmen led by Louis Coulon de Villiers, carried out his greatest coup of the war. They besieged Fort Granville and compelled it to surrender, to the shock and dismay of settlers throughout the Juniata region, as this was the first instance of a strongly defended fort capitulating to a Delaware war party.

But the victory was destined to lead to the death of Captain Jacobs. The commanding officer at Granville, Lt. Edward Armstrong, was killed in the attack. His brother, Col. John Armstrong, was the foremost Indian fighter in Pennsylvania, and he organized a retaliatory expedition against Kittanning. The Pennsylvanians struck the Delaware stronghold by surprise on September 8, 1756, destroying most of the village. They set fire to Jacobs's home and ordered him to surrender and save the lives of his family, but the fearsome chief, shouting that he could eat fire, continued to fight. It is asserted that he killed fourteen soldiers before he and his wife and child perished in the flames.

(William A. Hunter, Forts on the Pennsylvania Frontier; Paul A. W. Wallace, Indians in Pennsylvania.)

CAPTAIN LEWIS, SHAWNEE CHIEF. Captain Lewis (John Lewis, Quitewepes), an important Shawnee chief during the period following the War of 1812, fell into disrepute with his people because he signed the Treaty of Fort Meigs (September 29, 1817), ceding most Shawnee land in Ohio. Afterward he removed west of the Mississippi and attempted to persuade other Indians to do the same. There he assisted

the Cherokee chief Takatoka in his attempt to create an Indian confederacy in the West. He visited William Clark, Indian superintendent
at St. Louis, who felt that the plan would assist the government in
removing remaining Indians from Ohio, and he went on to Washington
where he received the support of President Madison. However, at
a council at Wapakoneta, Ohio, in May 1825, he found the Indians
as adamant as ever against agreement to depart from their ancient
homelands.

(Grant Foreman, The Last Trek of the Indians.)

CAPTAIN PIPE, DELAWARE CHIEF. Captain Pipe (Hopocan) was
one of the most influential war chiefs of the Delaware Indians during
the second half of the eighteenth century. Born in Pennsylvania
about 1725, he played an important role in tribal affairs during the
French and Indian War (on the side of the French), Pontiac's War,
and the American Revolution.

In 1763 Captain Pipe was captured by British forces while attempting to seize Fort Pitt. After Pontiac withdrew, the Delaware
settled in Ohio on the Muskingum River, where Pipe gained renown
as a negotiator and orator as well as a war chief.

At the outbreak of the American Revolution, Captain Pipe led
the pro-British party of his tribe. He took little part in the hostilities, however, until his brother was slain and his mother wounded
in February 1778 in a senseless attack on a defenseless Delaware village by American militiamen on the Shenango River. (See SQUAW
CAMPAIGN.) Afterward he fanned war fever among the Delawares
and had his revenge by burning Col. William Crawford at the stake
following the American defeat at the Battle of Upper Sandusky in
1782.

Hopocan participated in several peace treaties after the war,
particularly those of Fort McIntosh in 1785 and Fort Harmar in 1787.
He advised the Indians to remain at peace with the whites. His
death occurred in 1794.

(Frederick J. Dockstader, Great North American Indians; Paul
A. W. Wallace, Indians in Pennsylvania.)

CARHEIL, ETIENNE DE. Etienne de Carheil, a prominent Jesuit
missionary, was born at Carentoir, France, in 1633, educated at
Paris, ordained in 1666, and sent to Canada to serve the Indians soon
afterward. He was stationed among the Cayugas from 1668 until he
became ill in 1673. Then, after a brief recovery period, he returned
to that tribe for eight additional years.

Father Carheil was a powerful orator, adept at mastering Indian languages, and extremely zealous. Nevertheless, the fierce
Cayugas resisted his mission to introduce Christianity among them.
T. J. Campbell, historian of the New York Jesuits, reported that
Carheil "wandered from wigwam to wigwam, only to be driven out
with insults and blows, or trudged weary and hungry after his wild
people on their hunting or predatory excursions, often seeing the
tomahawk or knife of some angry savage above his head."

During his second mission to the Cayugas, however, Carheil's labors began to bear fruit. He baptized more than three hundred Indians, chiefly captive Hurons. In 1686 he was assigned to the Huron mission at Mackinac. There his determined opposition to the sale of liquor to Indians and to French cohabitation with native girls aroused hostility among the traders and soldiers. After the Indians left the mission to move to Detroit, he returned to Quebec in 1703. He died after serving as a missionary priest for sixty years.

(T. J. Campbell, Pioneer Priests of North America; Edna Kenton, ed., Black Gown and Redskins.)

CARLISLE, PENNSYLVANIA. Carlisle, Pennsylvania, founded in 1751, became a center of Scotch-Irish settlement and headquarters of an extensive Indian trade. Fort Louther was constructed there in 1755, replaced not long afterward by Fort Carlisle. The community served as a staging point for expeditions against the Indians, notably those of Col. Henry Bouquet in 1763 and 1764, as well as the site of treaty negotiations with tribes from Ohio by Benjamin Franklin and others.

In 1879 a school for Indians was established at Carlisle by Gen. R. H. Pratt. Thousands of Indians from tribes throughout the United States have attended the Carlisle Indian School, many of them remaining in the East after graduation and working on farms and in industrial plants, while others returned home and attempted to teach trades learned at Carlisle. The school became especially renowned for its outstanding athletic teams, for its band, and for publications written and printed by its students. It closed in 1918.

(F. W. Hodge, ed., Handbook of American Indians, I; Elaine Goodale Eastman, Pratt, the Red Man's Moses.)

CARTLIDGE, JOHN AND EDMUND. John and Edmund Cartlidge, brothers, were among very few Pennsylvania Quakers who became active Indian traders. They were granted land near the Conestoga Indian village in 1716 and entered the fur trade soon afterward. Many conferences between colonial officials and tribal representatives were conducted at their homes while they served as justices of the peace.

In 1721 the Cartlidge brothers, while on a trading expedition to Maryland, were accosted by an intoxicated Seneca Indian who demanded rum. When they refused, the Indian attacked them. John grappled with his assailant and threw him down. The warrior's head struck a tree, causing him to lose consciousness. When he revived he went to his cabin to arm himself. Edmund seized the Indian's gun and broke it over his head. John kicked him in the head when he tried to arise. He died the next day as a result of his injuries. Both brothers were imprisoned by colonial authorities, but soon afterward the Six Nations Council obtained their release, convinced that they had acted in self-defense.

John Cartlidge died in 1726, but Edmund continued trading operations, becoming one of the first Englishmen to seek furs west of the Alleghenies. He was sent to the Shawnees in 1731 by Pennsylvania officials to urge the tribe to return from Ohio to their former homes. The following year he served as interpreter when the chiefs came to Philadelphia for a conference. In 1732, while visiting the Delawares, he detected French activity on the Allegheny and notified the governor of Pennsylvania.

(Charles A. Hanna, The Wilderness Trail.)

CARVER, JONATHAN. Jonathan Carver, a Massachusetts cartographer and a survivor of the Fort William Henry massacre of 1757, was employed by Maj. Robert Rogers to explore the territory around the Great Lakes and upper Mississippi in search of a passage to the Pacific. In 1766 he accompanied French traders to Green Bay and to the Winnebago village on Doty Island. Then, having persuaded a band of Winnebago warriors to assist them, they visited several Sauk and Fox villages before arriving at the Mississippi at present Prairie du Chien. There Carver left most of his companions, crossed the Mississippi, and entered hostile Indian territory. With two companions he stood off an attack by a band of Chippewas. Proceeding up the Mississippi, he wintered with the Sioux near St. Anthony's Falls.

In the spring of 1767, Carver learned that Rogers was unable to finance further explorations. He went to Mackinac, turned over his maps and journals to traders for delivery to Rogers, and helped arrange a council with the tribes. He returned to his home at Boston in 1768.

Carver wrote a book about his travels which was published in London in 1778. The work was read widely and used by researchers until its reliability was called into question early in the twentieth century. Scholarly debate over its merits has continued for many years, but, although he must have included incidents related by other travelers as his own, the value of his narrative to students of Indian life is acknowledged: "... the charge that his literary and historical fame is undeserved, must in the light of recent discoveries be withdrawn."--Louise Phelps Kellogg.

(Jonathan Carver, Travels Through the Interior Parts of North America; Louise Phelps Kellogg, The British Regime in Wisconsin and the Northwest.)

CASCO, MAINE, RAIDS. Casco, Maine, a small settlement near the present city of Portland, was destroyed by Indians on two occasions. In May 1690 the Sieur de Portneuf, leading 50 Frenchmen and about four hundred Abnaki Indians, surrounded the town. Fort Loyal, located on a bluff overlooking the harbor, was garrisoned by about a hundred men commanded by Capt. Sylvanus Davis.

The predawn attack began prematurely when Indians fired at a settler, Robert Greason, walking toward the village. Citizens awakened by the sound of gunfire rushed to four garrison houses outside the fort, foiling Portneuf's plan to seize them asleep in their beds. Davis dispatched 30 men to assist the settlers, but the Indians ambushed them, slaying almost the entire detachment. Four wounded soldiers managed to stagger back into the fort.

The French and Indians burned most of the homes in the

village, but the garrison houses withstood their attacks throughout the day, and after nightfall all of the defenders escaped into the fort. A siege followed for five days until, almost out of ammunition, Davis surrendered upon assurance that the English would be permitted to go to another settlement. But, almost immediately, the Indians seized them, murdered the wounded men, and conveyed the survivors to Canada. About a hundred people were killed during the raid.

Rebuilt about 1692, Casco was destroyed again in August 1703. Some five hundred Indians, led by a French officer, took a position outside the fort and persuaded Maj. John March to parley beyond the walls under a flag of truce. Without warning, Chiefs Moxus, Assacombuit, and Wanungonet attacked him with tomahawks while other Indians opened fire on the fort. Soldiers sallied forth and rescued the commander, but two of them were slain before the others escorted March into the stockade.

The enemy burned the village and began to dig a mine from the shore to the fort. Fortunately, however, a heavily armed ship from Boston arrived and attacked the invaders, compelling them to withdraw before they could complete the tunnel and blow up the fort.

(Samuel Adams Drake, Border Wars of New England; Francis Parkman, A Half-Century of Conflict; Herbert Milton Sylvester, Indian Wars of New England, II-III.)

CASCO, MAINE, TREATIES OF. The first treaty of Casco was negotiated in 1678 by Massachusetts colonial leaders with chiefs of the Abnaki and Pennacook nations. Peace was restored with Indians participating in King Philip's War, upon their promise to release all English captives.

In January 1698 the hostile tribes of the Maine region, having temporarily lost French assistance as a result of the Peace of Ryswick, determined to end hostilities with the English. A treaty was negotiated at Mare Point on Casco Bay, with the Abnaki chiefs acknowledging their past crimes and agreeing to release their captives in the spring. Many of the captives had become so assimilated, however, that they refused to return to their white relatives.

In June 1703 Massachusetts Gov. Joseph Dudley called a conference with the Abnakis in an attempt to keep them at peace during Queen Anne's War. Some of the most hostile Indians intended to murder Dudley and other Englishmen present, but they were prevented from carrying out their designs by the intermingling of their own chiefs with the colonists. Declaring, therefore, that they desired peaceful relations, the Abnakis received vast quantities of gifts, and Dudley promised to see to their future needs by establishing trading posts and sending gunsmiths to serve them. Within six months, however, Indian attacks on the settlements resumed.

(Samuel Adams Drake, Border Wars of New England; Francis Parkman, A Half-Century of Conflict; Herbert Milton Sylvester, Indian Wars of New England, III.)

CASS, LEWIS, INDIAN RELATIONS. Lewis Cass was born at Exeter,

New Hampshire, in 1782. He moved to frontier Ohio in 1799, where he became a lawyer, a military officer, and one of the most successful Indian diplomats in United States history. During the War of 1812 he attained the rank of brigadier-general and fought against the British and Indians at the Battle of the Thames.

Cass served as governor of Michigan Territory and superintendent of Indian affairs of the Northwest Territory from 1813 to 1831 and as secretary of war from 1831 to 1836. During those years he negotiated several important treaties with the tribes. In 1817 he and Duncan McArthur obtained a cession of more than four million acres in Ohio, Indiana, and Michigan from the Wyandot, Chippewa, Ottawa, and Potawatomi tribes. He negotiated treaties with the Miami Indians in 1814, 1818, and 1826. In 1825 he and William Clark negotiated a treaty at Prairie du Chien with 134 Sauk and Fox, Menominee, Potawatomi, Sioux, Iowa, Winnebago, and Chippewa chiefs, promoting peace and defining boundaries between the lands of the various nations.

In addition to his treaty-making activities, Cass played an important part in preventing racial incidents from spreading into full-scale Indian wars. In 1820 he led a delegation to the head of Lake Superior and to Madeline Island to assure the Indians that the United States desired to be friends of the tribes. Although he incurred the wrath of the Chippewas by tearing down a British flag, his mission proved to be tremendously beneficial. In 1827 he prevented a major Winnebago war, brewing as a result of the murder of a white settler, by rushing regular troops to the scene. At that time he narrowly escaped death when a warrior's gun aimed at his heart misfired.

A student of Indian culture, Cass believed that the tribes must remove to the West or perish. His report entitled "Inquiries Concerning the Indians" has been of enduring value to ethnohistorians.

"Lewis Cass was one of the master architects of American Indian policy."--Francis Paul Prucha.

(Bert Anson, The Miami Indians; Grant Foreman, The Last Trek of the Indians; Carolissa Levi, Chippewa Indians of Yesterday and Today; Frank B. Woodford, Lewis Cass, the Last Jeffersonian; Francis Paul Prucha, Lewis Cass and American Indian Policy.)

CASTOR HILL, TREATIES OF. In October 1832 at Castor Hill (home of William Clark) a series of treaties with several Indian tribes obtained land cessions and provided for their removal to the West. On October 24, the Kickapoos ceded their lands in southwestern Missouri in exchange for a large tract near Fort Leavenworth. On October 26, the Shawnees and Delawares at Cape Girardeau ceded their lands and agreed to remove to a reservation in Kansas. On the following day, the Peoria, Cahokia, Michigamea, Tamaroa and Kaskaskia tribes exchanged their lands in Illinois and Missouri for 250 sections in Kansas. On October 29, the Wea and Piankashaw Indians ceded their territory in Illinois and Missouri and agreed to remove to the Illinois Indian reservation in Kansas. The United States government agreed to pay the cost of removal and to subsist the Indians for a year in their new homes.

(Grant Foreman, The Last Trek of the Indians; Charles J. Kappler, ed., Indian Affairs; Laws and Treaties, II.)

CAT NATION see ERIE INDIANS

CATSKILL INDIANS. The Catskill Indians, a small Munsee division, lived along the west side of the Hudson River, on Catskill Creek. They took part in the Esopus wars and, afterward, some of them moved to Pennsylvania to join the Mahicans and Moravians. Their numbers dwindled rapidly, and survivors merged with remnants of other tribes.
    (F. W. Hodge, ed., Handbook of American Indians, I; Allen W. Trelease, Indian Affairs in Colonial New York.)

CAUGHNAWAGA INDIANS. The Caughnawaga Indians, Iroquois who were converted to Christianity by Jesuit missionaries during the seventeenth century, moved to Sault St. Louis, in Canada, and established a town called Caughnawaga in 1676.
    They became fierce French allies, raiding the New York Iroquois as well as the English settlements. The narratives of the border wars contain numerous accounts of their exploits, especially at Deerfield and Fort Duquesne. At the conclusion of the French and Indian War some of the Caughnawagas removed to the Ohio Valley and abandoned the Christian religion.
    (F. W. Hodge, ed., Handbook of American Indians, I.)

CAYUGA INDIANS. The Cayuga Indians, one of the smaller nations of the Iroquois confederacy, were located in the area around Cayuga Lake, New York. During colonial times the tribe's population was estimated at only 1,000 to 1,500, but the Cayugas compensated for lack of numbers by their skill and courage as warriors.
    The Cayugas clashed frequently with the French until 1653, when a major war with the Erie Indians caused them to make a temporary peace with their European enemies. In 1656 they permitted Jesuits to establish the Mission Sainte Marie among them, but the renewal of Iroquois-French warfare caused its abandonment two years later. In 1661, because of an Iroquois war with the Susquehanna Indians, the Cayugas sought a resumption of peaceful relations with the French. The Jesuits established the Mission St. Joseph in Cayuga territory in 1668, but it was abandoned because of tribal hostility in 1682.
    During the last decade of the seventeenth century, the Cayugas and other Iroquois nations raided French settlements with great frequency. In retaliation, many of their villages were destroyed by French expeditions. In 1701, however, they made peace with the French and attempted to remain neutral during French-English clashes as they sought to increase trade with both nations.
    At the onset of the American Revolution the Cayugas favored the British. Led by Chief Fish Carrier, they proved to be formidable raiders, greatly feared by American settlers. In 1779 Gen. John Sullivan destroyed their villages, and many Cayugas fled to Canada, while the remainder settled with other tribes of the Six Nations.

In 1789 the Cayugas sold most of their New York lands to the state, many of them removing to the Ohio and joining the Senecas. Subsequently these bands removed to the Indian Territory. Others joined the Oneidas in Wisconsin, while a small number remained in New York.
(F. W. Hodge, ed., Handbook of American Indians, I; William C. Sturtevant, ed., Handbook of North American Indians, XV.)

CEDAR POINT, WISCONSIN, TREATY OF. On September 3, 1836, Col. Henry Dodge negotiated the Treaty of Cedar Point with the Menominee Indians. In exchange for an annuity of $20,000, extending for twenty years, the Menominees ceded a large portion of their lands in the areas along the Menominee, Wisconsin, and Wolf rivers.
(Charles J. Kappler, ed., Indian Affairs, Laws and Treaties, II.)

CELERON, PIERRE JOSEPH DE, OHIO RIVER EXPEDITION. Angered by the expansion of English trade in the Ohio Valley, the French sent Pierre Joseph de Celeron in 1749 to expel traders and to reassert French claims to the region. With his force of 20 French soldiers, 180 Canadians, and 55 Indians, he descended the Ohio to the Miami, burying lead plates at the mouth of every tributary claiming all of of the land for France. The Indian tribes encountered were unfriendly, but he managed to avoid active hostility while he warned them that the English traders would seize their lands.
As Celeron had gifts to distribute, the tribes agreed to his demands to trade with the French, and English traders temporarily abandoned their posts. Celeron brought his followers home without losing a man, but the expedition proved to be a failure, for English traders returned to the area as soon as French forces withdrew.
(Solon J. Buck, The Planting of Civilization in Western Pennsylvania; Albert T. Volwiler, George Crogan and the Westward Movement.)

CHABANAKONGKOMUN. Chabanakongkomun, a settlement of Christian Indians, was founded near Worcester, Massachusetts, about 1672. Known first to the English as Pegan Indians, and later classed as Nipmucs, they numbered less than fifty after white settlers established a town nearby. In 1793 some tribesmen still lived on a reservation near the original settlement.
(F. W. Hodge, ed., Handbook of American Indians, I.)

CHABERT DE JONCAIRE, PHILIPPE-THOMAS see JONCAIRE, PHILIPPE-THOMAS

CHABERT DE JONCAIRE DE CLAUSONNE, DANIEL see JONCAIRE, DANIEL DE, SIEUR DE CHABERT ET DE CLAUSONNE

CHAMBLY, POTAWATOMI CHIEF see SHABONEE, POTAWATOMI CHIEF

CHAMPLAIN, SAMUEL DE, IROQUOIS BATTLES. Samuel de Champlain, French navigator and founder of Quebec, made an alliance with the Algonquian and Huron Indians near the St. Lawrence River in 1608. He hoped that the agreement would assist him to make discoveries in parts of the New World closed to the French by enemy Indians. The following year, however, it resulted in a disastrous development that he had failed to foresee.

In June 1609 his new allies called upon him to assist them in attacking their powerful adversaries, the Iroquois. He agreed, and with two other Frenchmen and some sixty Indians he invaded the Iroquois country near Lake Champlain. On July 9 they attacked a force of two hundred Mohawks near Ticonderoga, and the ensuing encounter was described by Champlain as follows:

> I looked at them and they looked at me. When I saw them getting ready to shoot their arrows at us, I levelled my arquebuse, which I had loaded with four balls, and aimed straight at one of the three chiefs. The shot brought down two, and wounded another. On this, our Indians set up such a yelling that one could not have heard a thunder-clap, and all the while the arrows flew thick on both sides. The Iroquois were greatly astonished and frightened to see two of their men killed so quickly, in spite of their arrow-proof armor. As I was reloading, one of my companions fired a shot from the woods, which so increased their astonishment that, seeing their chiefs dead, they abandoned the field and fled into the depths of the forest.

In 1610 Champlain joined the Algonquians in another attack on the Iroquois. Finding the enemy barricaded, he led his Frenchmen and Indians over the obstacle, killing eighty-five warriors and capturing fifteen. Afterward he was sickened by the sight of his allies burning the captives to death.

In September 1615 Champlain and a dozen Frenchmen joined a Huron war party crossing Lake Ontario in search of the Iroquois. On October 15 they attacked the strongly defended village of Onondaga. This time they met more than their match. Champlain was wounded, several Hurons were killed, and the invaders retreated headlong.

Champlain's attacks on the Iroquois "kindled a fire of hatred towards the French, on the part of the Iroquois tribes, which that nation was never able to overcome, and had abundant reason to rue." --Frank H. Severance.

(William J. Eccles, The Canadian Frontier; Francis Parkman, Pioneers of France in the New World, II; Frank H. Severance, An Old Frontier of France.)

CHAPTICON INDIANS. The Chapticon Indians, a small tribe or band, lived in Maryland, a few miles south of the present Washington, D.C. By 1652 their lands were occupied by white settlers, and they were relegated to a reservation at the head of the Wicomico River.

(F. W. Hodge, ed., Handbook of American Indians, I.)

CHARDON, JEAN BAPTISTE. Jean Baptiste Chardon, a Jesuit priest, began his mission among the Indians of Wisconsin and Michigan about 1716. He was the last missionary at St. Francis Xavier, near De Pere, Wisconsin, an assignment that led him to labor among the Mascouten, Miami, Kickapoo, Sauk, Fox, Potawatomi, Winnebago, and Illinois Indians. Although he possessed unusual ability to master Indian languages and he carried out his ministry with energy and dedication, he enjoyed little success in gaining converts to Christianity in Wisconsin.

After many years at De Pere, Father Chardon moved to the Potawatomi mission, St. Joseph, near the southern end of Lake Michigan. Afterward he was assigned to serve as chaplain and interpreter at the French fort at Green Bay, Wisconsin. In 1743, after twenty-seven years among the Indians, he returned to Quebec, where he died a few years later.

(Louise Phelps Kellogg, The French Regime in Wisconsin and the Northwest.)

CHARLEVOIX, PIERRE FRANCOIS XAVIER DE. Father Charlevoix, a Jesuit priest from Picardy, arrived in Canada from France in September 1720. He was assigned by the crown not only to inspect the missions and forts of the Great Lakes and the Mississippi Valley, but to seek information from the Indians about a passage to the Western Sea. During the spring of 1721 he visited Mackinac and La Baye. Prevented by the hostility of the Sioux from penetrating their country, he went to Kaskaskia, where he interviewed Indians and traders about their knowledge of western rivers. Then he journeyed to New Orleans and Biloxi, became ill, and returned to France in 1722.

The most important result of the priest's travels was his report on the location and disposition of Mississippi Valley Indian tribes, and the establishment, five years later, of a French post in the Sioux country. In 1744 he published a book, Histoire et Description Générale de la Nouvelle France, which was praised by Thomas W. Field in his Indian bibliography as follows: "The extraordinary man who was the author of these volumes left no subject relating to the history of the affairs of his wonderful order in America untouched, and as the missions of the Company of Jesus among the Indians were the principal purpose of the fathers in both of the Americas, the curiosity of Charlevoix permeated every accessible square mile of their surface to learn the habits, the customs, and the secrets of the life of the strange people his brethren sought to subdue to the influence of the cross."

(Pierre François Xavier de Charlevoix, Histoire et Description Générale de la Nouvelle France; Thomas W. Field, An Essay Toward an Indian Bibliography; Louise Phelps Kellogg, The French Régime in Wisconsin and the Northwest.)

CHARTIER, MARTIN. Martin Chartier, a French-Canadian trader, had an extraordinary but poorly documented career on both sides of the international boundary. He asserted that he had escaped from French authorities in Canada in 1684, having been imprisoned for trading beaver skins without permission. However, La Salle charged that he had deserted his post at Fort Crèvecoeur in January 1680, gone to Mackinac with other deserters, robbed the post of furs, plundered the magazine at Niagara, and escaped into the wilderness with the spoils.

It is believed that Chartier lived with the Shawnees near Fort St. Louis, married a Shawnee woman, and moved with the band about 1692 to Maryland to establish a village on the lower Elk River. Maryland authorities suspected that he was a spy for the French, but he convinced the governor that he had every reason to avoid contact with his countrymen. After trading in Maryland for several years, he and his Indian associates moved up the Susquehanna River to Lancaster County, Pennsylvania, where he established a trading post prior to 1707.

Chartier served as an interpreter for the Shawnees during councils at Conestoga in 1711 and 1717. In 1717 he received a land grant at the mouth of Conestoga Creek. There he established a home and trading post, where he died the following year.

(Charles A. Hanna, The Wilderness Trail.)

CHARTIER, PETER. Peter Chartier, son of the French renegade, Martin Chartier, and a Shawnee woman, was brought up among members of that tribe in Maryland and Pennsylvania. He married a Shawnee and succeeded his father as trader in Lancaster County, Pennsylvania, in 1718. He expanded his trading posts to Paxtang and Harrisburg and, about 1734, he and his Shawnee followers moved to the Allegheny River. There he established Chartier's Town and became chief of his band.

Chartier became a fierce French partisan about 1744, convinced that English expansionism threatened Indian survival. In 1745 he abandoned Chartier's Town and led his followers to the Shawnee settlements of the Scioto, robbing English traders along the way. Soon afterward they moved southward to the Catawba country, where he urged the Cherokees and Creeks to expel English traders from their towns. He was still inciting the Southern Indians to attack the English in 1756 and, as a result of their refusal, he may have rejoined the Shawnees north of the Ohio at that time.

(Charles A. Hanna, The Wilderness Trail; Paul A. W. Wallace, Indians in Pennsylvania.)

CHARTRES, FORT DE. Built in 1719-20 near Kaskaskia, Illinois, and rebuilt several times within a few years because of deterioration, Fort de Chartres provided the site of French governmental functions in the Illinois country until after the French and Indian War. The last fort by that name was built of stone and generally considered the largest and strongest bastion in North America.

When the French and Indian War ended, hostile tribes prevented the British from taking possession of Fort de Chartres. Finally in 1765, the prominent Pennsylvania trader and Indian agent, George Croghan, gained access for the British by persuading Chief Pontiac to permit them to pass, and the French departed on October

10. In 1766 Croghan delivered 17 boatloads of goods to Fort de Chartres and negotiated a treaty with the tribes of the area, the Indians agreeing to acknowledge English sovereignty and to permit the establishment of trading posts in their villages.

Because of deterioration and flood damage Fort de Chartres was abandoned in 1772.

(Clarence W. Alvord, The Illinois Country; Dale Van Every, Forth to the Wilderness; A. T. Volwiler, Croghan and the Westward Movement.)

CHAUMONOT, PIERRE JOSEPH MARIE. Pierre Joseph Marie Chaumonot, born on March 9, 1611, to an impoverished family in Burgundy, begged from door to door to avoid starvation until taken in and cared for by the Jesuits. He became a missionary and sailed to Canada in 1639. For fifteen years he labored with great success among the Hurons, speaking their language fluently, fleeing with them during Iroquois incursions, and begging the people of Quebec to save them from starvation. For a time he lived with the Indians known as the Neutral Nation, but in less than six months he was compelled to flee by the threats of warriors to eat him alive.

In 1655 Chaumonot, accompanied by Father Claude Dablon, established the Onondaga mission, and he preached among the Oneidas and Cayugas as well. He managed to convert a few Indians to Christianity, but after three years of labor he had to flee to Montreal because of Iroquois hostilities. Resuming his work with the Hurons, he remained an active missionary until 1692, when illness compelled him to retire. He died on February 21, 1693.

(T. J. Campbell, Pioneer Priests of North America; Edna Kenton, ed., Black Gown and Redskins.)

CHAUVIGNERIE, LOUIS MARAY, SIEUR DE, FAMILY OF. Louis Maray, Sieur de Chauvignerie, a French-Canadian military officer, was born in 1671. He and his son Michel, and his grandson, Michel, Jr., were among the most successful Indian diplomats, and, as all were known as Ensign Chauvignerie, it is impossible at times to determine which man was referred to in Canadian official correspondence.

In 1705 Louis was sent to improve relations with the Ottawa Indians at Mackinac. Soon afterward he became a favorite of the New York Iroquois and, in 1711, it was he who notified the Five Nations of the outbreak of war between France and England. He probably was the Ensign Chauvignerie who served as interpreter at Niagara in 1721.

The date of birth of Michel, Sr., is not recorded, but it probably occurred about 1704. He served among Indians most of his life, playing an especially important part in French-Iroquois relations. In 1728 he (or his father), while on a mission to the Onondagas, refused to salute the British flag or to permit his Indian companions to do so while passing the fort at Oswego. This act gained great respect among the Iroquois for him. He was called upon frequently to hold councils with the Indians, to bargain for the release of captives, and to condole for warriors killed fighting the English. In 1756, as lieutenant of marines, he completed construction of Fort Machault.

Michel, Jr., born about 1739, became a prominent leader of Indian war parties while still in his teens. From his father's post at Fort Machault he led some thirty warriors against the English settlements "to burn cabins, ruin crops, run off the stock, take prisoners when they could, and when they could not, to kill and scalp. Such," said Frank H. Severance, "was the schooling of a French-Canadian lad in the year of war 1757!" Young Michel became separated from his warriors during his last raid, almost starved, and finally surrendered to the English. Imprisoned at Germantown for a short time, he was exchanged in 1758.

(Frank H. Severance, An Old Frontier of France.)

CHEESHATEAUMUCK, CALEB. Caleb Cheeshateaumuck was "the only New England Indian in early days who completed his studies at Harvard College, taking his degree in 1666." He died of tuberculosis.

(F. W. Hodge, ed., Handbook of American Indians, I.)

CHEQUAMEGON BAY. A southern indentation of Lake Superior, Chequamegon Bay was the location of the first French post in the present state of Wisconsin. It is believed that the explorers and traders, Radisson and Groseilliers, built a post there in 1658. Less than a decade later Father Claude Allouez established a mission there, and Father Jacques Marquette labored among the Indians of the area from 1669 to 1671.

(Louise Phelps Kellogg, The French Régime in Wisconsin and the Northwest.)

CHERRY VALLEY MASSACRE. Cherry Valley, New York, was strategically located, if strongly enough defended, to block British plans to overrun the Mohawk region during the American Revolution. In the spring of 1778 General Lafayette sent Col. Ichabod Alden's regiment there to man the fort, built by Cherry Valley citizens, which he renamed Fort Alden. (See ALDEN, ICHABOD.)

In November 1778, Capt. Walter Butler of the Tory Rangers was ordered to seize Fort Alden. He led 150 rangers, 50 British Regulars, and 321 of Joseph Brant's Iroquois Indians to Cherry Valley on November 11, capturing Alden's scout patrol asleep during a snowstorm the previous night. He divided his force, sending a detachment to capture Alden and most of his officers at their quarters at the home of Robert Wells outside the fort, while storming the stockade with his main force. Indians killed Alden trying to flee to the fort, but Maj. Daniel Whiting evaded them and assisted in throwing back Butler's first assault. The British and Brant's Mohawks attacked the fort for almost four hours, but the other Indians, having no desire to exchange shots with 300 barricaded continental soldiers, slipped away from Butler's army and began murdering civilians. Their desertion left Butler with fewer troops than the defenders and destroyed any chance of capturing Fort Alden.

Butler, when he learned of the massacre of settlers, sent a detachment of rangers to protect the survivors, but in the meantime

the Indians had slain 31 people, most of them women and children.
Brant prevented the murder of others. The rangers captured many
of the survivors and guarded them against attack during the remainder of the battle. When Butler ordered a retreat, he held more
than 70 prisoners, but he released most of the women and children
the following day.

Cherry Valley was struck by Indian raiders once more in the
summer of 1779. And, in the spring of 1780, a third incursion resulted in the death of 8 settlers, while 14 were captured.

(T. Wood Clarke, The Bloody Mohawk; Barbara Graymont, The
Iroquois in the American Revolution; Francis Whiting Halsey, The Old
New York Frontier; Dale Van Every, A Company of Heroes.)

CHICAGO, ILLINOIS CHIEF. Chicago (Chikagou), a chief of the
Illinois Indians, accompanied the Jesuit father, Nicholas Beaubois,
to Paris, France, in 1725. There he made several talks on Indian
life to gain support for the missionaries. When he returned to America and described the marvelous sights he had seen, the Indians refused to believe him.

Chicago remained a firm friend of the French. When the
Chickasaw Indians tried to induce him to attack the French settlements, he retorted that he would make war on the Indian allies of
the English instead.

(Edna Kenton, ed., Black Gown and Redskins.)

CHICAGO, ILLINOIS, MASSACRE see DEARBORN, FORT, MAS-
SACRE

CHICAGO, ILLINOIS, TREATIES OF. Two important treaties with
the Chippewa, Ottawa, and Potawatomi Indian tribes were negotiated
at Chicago. On August 29, 1821, the tribes were induced by Lewis
Cass and Solomon Sibley to cede extensive land holdings in southwestern Michigan. And on September 26, 1833, George B. Porter
and others persuaded them to cede millions of acres in Illinois and
Wisconsin and to take their people across the Mississippi.

(Charles J. Kappler, ed., Indian Affairs: Laws and Treaties,
II.)

CHICKATAUBET, MASSACHUSET CHIEF. Chickataubet, a Massachuset chief residing on the Neponset River, became a friend of the
Puritans soon after their arrival in America. In 1621 he submitted
to English authority and began to wear white men's clothing when
visiting the settlements. Two years later, however, furious over
the desecration of Indian graves by the English, he participated in
an attack on the settlers of Weymouth, but colonial authorities did
not condemn him for it.

In 1631 Chickataubet visited Governor Winthrop at Boston,
bringing him a gift of corn. Afterward he dined with Winthrop on
several occasions. The following year he joined the colonists in their
war against the Pequot Indians. In 1633 he died of smallpox.

(F. W. Hodge, ed., Handbook of American Indians, I; B. B.
Thatcher, Indian Biography, II.)

CHILLICOTHE, SHAWNEE VILLAGE. There were several Shawnee villages named Chillicothe, each established and then abandoned as white settlers overran tribal lands and forced the Indians to withdraw to the westward. In 1750 the village was located near the present Portsmouth, Ohio. It was destroyed by a flood about 1753. After white settlement of Kentucky, war parties from Chillicothe attacked, captured Daniel Boone, and held him at Chillicothe on the Little Miami. This village was destroyed by George Rogers Clark in 1780. A Chillicothe at the present site of Piqua, Ohio, was destroyed by Clark in 1782. A Chillicothe in Ross County, Ohio, was destroyed by Kentucky frontiersmen in 1787.

(F. W. Hodge, ed., Handbook of American Indians, I; Charles A. Hanna, The Wilderness Trail.)

CHIPPEWA INDIANS. The Chippewa (Ojibwa, Saultier) Indians, one of the largest and most powerful tribes in the present United States, were located around Lakes Huron and Superior, in much of Minnesota, and in northeastern North Dakota during the period of early European contact. Closely related to other Algonquian tribes of the area, particularly the Ottawas and Potawatomis, they warred incessantly with other Indians, especially the Sioux. But because of their distance from European settlements they played a less important part in French-English conflicts than did some smaller tribes of the region.

French and Chippewa relations began in the seventeenth century. It is believed that Jean Nicolet visited the tribe in 1633. Father Isaac Jogues was among them by 1642, and Father Claude Allouez preached to them in 1665. In 1668 Father Jacques Marquette founded a mission at the present site of Sault Ste. Marie, the center of Chippewa population.

While the tribe was not inspired by the religious teachings of the Jesuit fathers, its members were enthusiastic embracers of other aspects of French civilization, especially the use of firearms. They acquired guns at an earlier time than most of their Indian enemies and used them with deadly effect to drive the Sioux to the westward. Their friendship with traders led to much intermarriage, induced them to engage in the fur trade, and influenced them to become allies of the French in wars with the Iroquois.

When the English wrested Chippewa territory from the French, the tribe responded with great hostility. Chippewas made up a major component of Pontiac's forces. After the defeat of that Indian conspiracy, however, the Chippewas generally supported the English, as that nation provided the only source of trade goods on which they had become dependent for survival. In 1778 Chippewa warriors attacked the guard of Gen. Arthur St. Clair's camp on the Muskingum, killing or capturing several soldiers. After the Revolution, British traders continued to serve the northwestern Indians, holding their allegiance throughout the Tecumseh uprising and until after the War of 1812.

Even after accepting American sovereignty, many of the Chippewas remained hostile, provoked to violence by settlers invading

their territory. These hostilities invariably led to confiscation of
Chippewa land. The tribe resisted removal from the Great Lakes re-
gion, however, and was allotted lands in Wisconsin, Michigan, and
Minnesota. Only a few agreed to remove to Kansas and the Indian
Territory.

(George Copway, The Traditional History and Characteristic
Sketches of the Ojibway Nation; Carolissa Levi, The Chippewa Indians
of Yesterday and Today; Louise Phelps Kellogg, The French Regime
in Wisconsin and the Northwest; William C. Sturtevant, ed., Handbook
of North American Indians, XV.)

CHIPPEWANAUNG, INDIANA, TREATIES OF. Three treaties were
negotiated with separate bands of Potawatomi Indians by Abel C.
Pepper on September 20-23, 1836. The Indians ceded lands reserved
for them four years earlier and consented to move to the West within
two years.

(Charles J. Kappler, ed., Indian Affairs: Laws and Treaties,
II.)

CHITOMACHEN, CONOY CHIEF. Chitomachen (Tayac), a Conoy chief
in early seventeenth-century Maryland, was converted to Christianity
by Father Andrew White. In 1640, crediting the missionary with restoring him to health after all of his tribal conjurers had failed, he
and his wife and son were baptized in the presence of the governor
and other officials of the colony. Afterward he and his wife were
remarried during a Christian ceremony. The chief sought to have his
people converted and, although he died less than a year later, the
Conoys became such staunch Christians that they protected the
colonists from enemy Indian attack.

(C. C. Hall, ed., Narratives of Early Maryland; James McSherry, History of Maryland.)

CHOPTANK INDIANS. The Choptank Indians, a Nanticoke subdivision,
lived along the Choptank River in Maryland during colonial times. In
1741 they were assigned a reservation in Dorchester County, and
they did not move with most other Nanticokes to Ohio and Indiana
during the early years of the republic. A few of their descendants,
much mixed with other races, remain in that region today.

(F. W. Hodge, ed., Handbook of American Indians, I; John R.
Swanton, The Indian Tribes of North America.)

CHRISTIAENSEN, HENDRICK. Hendrick Christiaensen (Carstiens,
Corstiaenssen), a Dutch sea captain and explorer, made ten voyages
to America during the early seventeenth century. In 1614, while
exploring the Hudson River, he and Adriaen Block persuaded two
young Indians, sons of a principal sachem, to accompany them on
their return voyage to Holland. There they attracted much attention
before being returned to their tribe.

One of the youths, called Orson by the Dutch, led an attack
on Christiaensen's ship, the Black Bear, when it returned to the Hudson in 1618. Christiaensen and most of the crew members were killed.
One of the five survivors shot Orson to death.

(C. A. Weslager, Dutch Explorers, Traders and Settlers in the Delaware Valley.)

CHRISTINA, FORT. Fort Christina, at the present site of Wilmington, Delaware, was established on lands purchased from the Indians in March 1638 by Swedish settlers led by Peter Minuit. Named for the Queen of Sweden, the strongly constructed fort controlled the best trade route to the Conestoga Indians. A town developed around it which served as the capital of New Sweden. The citizens were quick to engage in the fur trade with the Conestoga and Delaware Indians, competing successfully with the Dutch traders of Fort Nassau. In 1655 the Dutch seized Fort Christina. In 1664 they, in turn, were ousted by English forces.

(John E. Pomfret, The Province of West New Jersey; C. A. Weslager, Dutch Explorers, Traders, and Settlers in the Delaware Valley.)

CHUBB, PASCHO. Capt. Pascho Chubb commanded the fort at Pemaquid, Maine, with a garrison of ninety-five men in 1696. In February, in response to an invitation by Gov. William Stoughton to exchange prisoners, the Abnaki chiefs Abenquid, Egeremet, and Moxus approached the fort under a flag of truce. Chubb and several of his men went out to meet them, attacked them without warning, and killed two of the chiefs. Only Moxus escaped.

The Indians and French were quick to retaliate, sending a large force in July to seize the Pemaquid fort. Chubb asserted that "he would fight, even if the sea were covered with French ships and the land with Indians," but he surrendered in short order when the French opened fire with cannon. He and his men were taken to Boston and exchanged for Abnaki prisoners held in that city.

In 1697 Indians went to Chubb's home at Andover, Massachusetts, and slew him and his wife as an act of retaliation.

(Samuel Adams Drake, The Border Wars of New England; Francis Parkman, Count Frontenac and New France Under Louis XIV.)

CHURCH, BENJAMIN. Benjamin Church, the most effective New England Indian fighter for more than a quarter century, was born in 1639 at Duxbury, Massachusetts. In 1674 he settled at Seconet (Little Compton), near the Massachusetts-Rhode Island border, where he established friendly relations with the neighboring Saconnet (Seconet) Indians. As militia colonel of Bristol County, he played an important role in the Indian relations of both the Plymouth and Rhode Island colonies.

In June 1675 Church attended a Saconnet dance at the village of their squaw sachem, Awashonks. There he discovered that King Philip was attempting to forge a conspiracy among New England tribes to attack the settlements. After urging Awashonks to ignore Philip's messengers, he hurried to Plymouth to warn the colonists. As a result of his timely warning, Governor Winslow appointed him to command an army of Plymouth and Rhode Island fighting men to withstand the Indian onslaught.

On June 18, 1675, King Philip's followers began attacking settlers of Swansea, Massachusetts, and Church led a dozen Plymouth
soldiers to scout the area. They rode into an ambush, one man was
mortally wounded, and his companions fled, leaving Church alone on
the field. Finally, after failing to persuade his forces to come out
and fight the Indians, he rode into Swansea convinced that he commanded a company of cowards. Less than a month later, however,
they proved their courage when Church led twenty men to scout
along the Sakonnet River. Attacked by Indians, the scouts fought
their way to the shore, formed a tight circle behind rocks, and
stood off the warriors until a sloop arrived to evacuate them.

In December 1675, while serving as an aide to Gen. Josiah
Winslow, Church was wounded in a bloody campaign against the Narraganset Indians. (See GREAT SWAMP FIGHT.) Afterward he retired from the fray until June 1676, when he received permission to
recruit a company of colonists and friendly Indians. He persuaded
Awashonks to withdraw her support of King Philip and to provide
him with Saconnet Indian scouts, an innovation that enabled him to
render his most successful service during the war.

Discarding traditional European marching formations as un-
workable in the wilderness, Church employed Indian tactics that
assisted him to avoid ambushes. He advanced quickly and silently in
spread formation, led by his Indian scouts, and he used the element
of surprise to strike suddenly, seize captives, and retreat before
substantial enemy forces could gather to overwhelm him. Time after
time he captured members of an enemy band and persuaded them to
inform him of the whereabouts of other hostiles.

By August 1676 Church, guided by turncoat warriors, was hot
on the heels of King Philip himself. He captured the chief's wife
and son, but Philip escaped the trap on that occasion. On August
12, however, he located Philip's camp at Mount Hope, launched a
surprise attack, and one of his braves killed the chief as he attempted
to escape. This feat, followed by his capture of chief Annawan,
virtually ended the war.

For more than ten years after King Philip's War, Church enjoyed the life of a prosperous planter. Then, in 1689, he began the
second phase of his career as an Indian fighter. The Abnaki Indians
were depredating in Maine and New Hampshire, and Church was
chosen to punish them. He sailed with a large force of Plymouth
settlers and friendly Indians to Falmouth, arriving on September 20.
The entire Casco Bay area was swarming with Indians, but he defeated them during a battle at Brackett's farm. Eleven of his soldiers
were killed and ten wounded before he drove the Abnakis away from
the area. Church, not always the most modest of men, asserted
that "this was the first time the eastward Indians were ever thoroughly whipped and put to flight."

In September 1690 Church's forces returned to Casco Bay and
marched against the Abnakis of Androscoggin. The Indians fled before him, but he captured a few warriors and recovered three white
women and two children. A half dozen of the captured Indians were

tortured to death as, Church reported, "an example to the rest."
Afterward he attacked a band of Abnakis on the Saco River, slew
two of them, and recovered an English captive. He pursued the
hostiles to Cape Elizabeth, where they made a stand. Seven soldiers
were killed and twenty-four wounded before he charged the Abnakis
and put them to flight.

In 1692 Church served with Sir William Phipps in an expedition
to rebuild the destroyed fort at Pemaquid. Church led strikes into
the Indian country while Phipps repaired the fort.

Four years later, Church led another expedition against the
Abnakis. When his quarry escaped into the wilderness, he turned
on the French settlements in Acadia, burning Beaubassin but failing
to capture a fort on the St. John River.

In 1704 Church made his final expedition against the Abnaki
Indians and their French allies. So angered by the massacre at
Deerfield that he disregarded poor health and a weight problem, he
rode horseback all the way to Boston and volunteered to clean out
the Indians in Maine and the French in Acadia. He recruited 550
colonists and friendly Indians, sailed to Penobscot Bay, killed all of
the Indians that he could catch, and destroyed St. Castin's fort.
Proceeding to Grand Pré, he destroyed that important Acadian village. He returned to Massachusetts with the same number of French
and Indian prisoners that had been taken in Hertel's attack on Deerfield. "It was a miserable retaliation for a barbarous outrage; as
the guilty were out of reach, the invaders turned their ire on the
innocent."--Francis Parkman.

Benjamin Church died as a result of a fall from his horse in
1718.

(Thomas Church, The History of the Great Indian War of 1675
and 1676; Samuel Adams Drake, The Border Wars of New England;
Douglas Edward Leach, Flintlock and Tomahawk; Francis Parkman,
A Half-Century of Conflict; Herbert Milton Sylvester, Indian Wars of
New England, II-III.)

CINCINNATI, OHIO. Cincinnati, Ohio, was established during the
winter of 1788-89. Fort Washington was built there in 1789 to protect the settlers against marauding Indians, and it served as the
staging ground for the Harmar, St. Clair, and Wayne expeditions.

"The squalid little town of Cincinnati ... suffered from the
Indian warparties in the spring (of 1791), several townspeople being
killed by the savages, who grew so bold that they lurked through
the streets at nights, and lay in ambush in the garden where the
garrison of Fort Washington raised their vegetables."--Theodore Roosevelt.

(Theodore Roosevelt, The Winning of the West, V.)

CLAESON, JACOB. Jacob Claeson (Jacob Young), a Dutch trader on
Chesapeake and Delaware bays and one of the few Europeans who
could speak the language of the Susquehanna Indians, frequently
served as an interpreter at councils and during treaty negotiations.
In 1661 he and the wife of a Swedish preacher ran away to live with

the Susquehannas, and he became a tribal leader during their wars with the Iroquois.

After the English gained possession of the Delaware region, Claeson returned to Maryland and resumed his activities as interpreter and Indian diplomat. In 1682, however, the Iroquois accused him of persuading them to attack the Piscataway Indians in order to secure a portion of the spoils. Arrested for treason, he escaped punishment by describing his many exploits on behalf of the colony. Afterward he negotiated treaties with several tribes and operated a ferry at the mouth of the Susquehanna River.

(Charles A. Hanna, The Wilderness Trail.)

CLAESSEN, LAWRENCE. Lawrence Claessen (Clawson, Clausen), a Dutch settler, arrived on the New York frontier before 1700. He became a respected trader, so admired for his honesty by the Iroquois that they gave him several small islands in the Mohawk River. One of the few white men able to speak the dialects of all of the Six Nations, he served as interpreter at conferences on several occasions. In 1728 he helped negotiate the sale of Iroquois land around Oswego to the English. He served the English as an Indian diplomat during the contest with the French for Iroquois support until 1730.

(Frank H. Severance, An Old Frontier of France.)

CLAIBORNE, WILLIAM, INDIAN RELATIONS. William Claiborne was born in Westmoreland County, England, about 1587, and arrived in Virginia in 1621. He served as that colony's surveyor and as secretary of state on several occasions. In 1631 he established a trading post on Kent Island, in Chesapeake Bay, where he soon came into conflict with Lord Baltimore. Maryland governor Leonard Calvert charged him with inciting the Indians to attack the colonists and seized his new trading post on Palmer's Island in 1637. In retaliation he and the Puritan settlers of Maryland seized Catholic settlements in 1644, but they were evicted two years later.

Claiborne's trade with the Indians of the Susquehanna region was highly successful. In addition, he commanded colonial troops in two victories over enemy Indians. Captured by the Choptank Indians, he was rescued in time to lead an expedition against the hostile natives, thoroughly defeating the Chickahominies and Pamunkeys. He died about 1677.

(Nathaniel C. Hale, Virginia Venturer; Charles A. Hanna, The Wilderness Trail; Louis B. Wright, The Atlantic Frontier.)

CLARK, GEORGE ROGERS, ILLINOIS CAMPAIGNS. George Rogers Clark's Indian campaigns in the Illinois country during the American Revolution were crucial events in acquiring that vast territory for the United States. In 1777, to stop Indian attacks on Kentucky settlements, he determined to strike the hostiles in their own strongholds. Recruiting volunteers in Virginia, Kentucky, and the Holston settlements, he trained them on Corn Island, near Louisville, and led 175 men down the Ohio on June 24, 1778.

Ten miles below the mouth of the Tennessee, Clark beached his boats and marched through the wilderness toward the French settlements of Illinois. He seized Kaskaskia on July 4 without firing a shot and, soon afterward, he induced Vincennes and other French settlements to adopt the American cause. He lacked adequate manpower to carry out his principal objective, the capture of Detroit, however, and British governor Henry Hamilton led a large force of soldiers and Indians from that post to drive Clark from the Illinois.

Hamilton recaptured Vincennes on December 17 and resumed dispatching Indian raiders against the settlements. He went into winter quarters at Vincennes, confident that Clark would make no move against him until the return of warm weather. But Clark determined to attack Vincennes while most of the Indians were away. He marched his men from Kaskaskia through a flooded wilderness, arrived at Vincennes in the middle of winter, and captured the fort on February 24, 1779. Most of Hamilton's Indians fled the scene, but some war parties, returning from raids, fell into Clark's hands before they realized that the Americans were in command of the fort. Clark and his men tomahawked them in retaliation for the scalps they had taken.

Clark's victories on the Illinois and Wabash rivers had a tremendous influence on the northwestern Indians. Among those making peace with the Americans were the Miamis, Michigameas, Weas, Wyandots, Kaskaskias, Peorias, Potawatomis, Piankashaws, Osages, Iowas, Winnebagos, Chippewas, Sauks, and Foxes. "With each of these tribes," reported Randolph C. Downes, "solemn ceremonies were held in which the tribesmen expressed their repentance, threw down the English war hatchet, and pledged peace and friendship with the Big Knife, their new American protectors."

While Clark's conquest gained crucial Indian allegiance that held most of the northwestern territory for the Americans during the remainder of the Revolution, its effect upon the tribes gradually eroded as a result of failure to provide them with adequate trade goods. By 1782 Clark found it necessary, as a result of renewed raids on the settlements, to lead another expedition against the northwestern tribes. On November 4 he led 1,000 men from the mouth of the Licking and, six days later, he attacked the Miami towns. Most of the Indians escaped, but Clark took ten scalps and seven prisoners, redeemed two white captives, and destroyed villages and crops. The success of this campaign insured the Kentucky settlements of security against major Indian attacks.

In 1786 the northwestern Indians, inflamed by the invasion of their lands by American squatters, renewed their hostile activities. In September, Clark led 1,200 volunteers to Vincennes in an attempt to chastise the Indians on the Wabash. The expedition fell apart, however, because of a mutiny among Clark's followers, and the men returned to their homes without engaging the enemy. "Nevertheless," wrote Theodore Roosevelt, "the expedition ... overawed the Wabash and Illinois Indians, and effectively put a stop to any active expressions of disloyalty and disaffection on the part of the French."

(Thomas P. Abernethy, Western Lands and the American Revolution; Clarence Walworth Alvord, The Illinois Country; Randolph C.

Downes, <u>Council Fires on the Upper Ohio</u>; Theodore Roosevelt, <u>The Winning of the West</u>; Dale Van Every, <u>A Company of Heroes</u>.)

CLARK, WILLIAM, INDIAN RELATIONS. William Clark, younger brother of George Rogers Clark, was born in Virginia on August 1, 1770. He became a soldier in Kentucky during his youth, served in several Indian campaigns, and gained renown as a result of his leadership, with Meriwether Lewis, of the famous expedition to the Pacific in 1804-1806. In 1807 he was appointed Indian agent to the northwestern tribes. The following year he established Fort Osage on the Missouri River. He served as governor of Missouri Territory from 1813 to 1821, and as Superintendent of Indian Affairs at St. Louis from 1822 until his death on September 1, 1838.

Clark became one of the most effective Indian diplomats in American history. In 1810 he assisted William Henry Harrison to counter the intrigues of Tecumseh and his brother the Prophet. During the War of 1812 he persuaded several important chiefs to visit Washington in an attempt to prevent them from supporting the British. During the spring of 1814 he led two hundred soldiers and volunteers up the Mississippi, defeated the Sauk Indians at Rock Island and imposed peace upon them, captured Prairie du Chien, and established Fort Shelby. He played an important part in resolving hostilities with the Winnebagos in 1827 and with the Sauks in 1832. (See WINNEBAGO INDIANS; BLACK HAWK WAR.) He negotiated several treaties with northwestern tribes. (See PRAIRIE DU CHIEN; CASTOR HILL.) In addition, he engaged in the Indian trade as a partner of Manuel Lisa in the St. Louis Missouri Fur Company, managing the firm's headquarters and serving as president from 1812 to 1814.

Clark's attitude toward Indians is reflected in his official report of 1826:

> The events of the last two or three wars, from General Wayne's campaign, in 1794, to the end of the operations against the southern tribes, in 1818, have entirely changed our position with regard to the Indians. Before those events, the tribes nearest our settlements were a formidable and terrible enemy; since then, their power has been broken, their warlike spirit subdued, and themselves sunk into objects of pity and commiseration. While strong and hostile, it has been our obvious policy to weaken them; now that they are weak and harmless, and most of their lands fallen into our hands, justice and humanity require us to cherish and befriend them. To teach them to live in houses, to raise grain and stock, to plant orchards, to set up landmarks, to divide their possessions, to establish laws for their government, to get the rudiments of common learning, such as reading, writing, and ciphering, are the first steps toward improving their condition. But, to take these steps with effect, it is necessary that previous measures of great magnitude should be accomplished; that is, that the tribes now within the limits of the States and Territories should be removed to a country

beyond those limits, where they could rest in peace, and enjoy in reality the perpetuity of the lands on which their buildings and improvements would be made.

By the time of his death, asserts Jerome O. Steffen, Clark had been able to see some of his recommendations enacted into law, but "the acts of 1834 did too little too late to curb the abuses perpetrated on the Indians by the white settler whose appetite for new land was insatiable."

(Jerome O. Steffen, William Clark, Jeffersonian Man of the Frontier; Francis Paul Prucha, American Indian Policy in the Formative Years.)

CLAUS, DANIEL. Daniel Claus was born in Germany and emigrated to America as a young man. Arriving in Philadelphia in 1749, he met Conrad Weiser and accompanied him to the Iroquois council at Onondaga. As a result, Claus lived with Indians, learned their languages, and eventually received an appointment as deputy Indian agent. In 1752 Claus lived at the home of Sir William Johnson and served among the Mohawks of Canajoharie. He became a close friend of Chief Hendrick, accompanied him to Philadelphia for conferences, and served with him at the Battle of Lake George. Afterward he received a commission in the Royal Americans.

By 1760 Claus moved to Montreal to serve as Sir William Johnson's deputy among the Indians of Canada. In 1762 he married Johnson's daughter Nancy and by the time of Sir William's death he had become one of Great Britain's most effective Indian diplomats.

In 1775 Claus persuaded the Caughnawaga and St. Regis Indians to stand by the British in the event of an invasion by the Americans. In September he participated in the siege of St. Johns, and, soon afterward, he went to England with Guy Johnson and Joseph Brant. When he returned the following year he persuaded a large force of Indians to accompany Col. Barry St. Leger's expedition, and he and his warriors played a prominent part in the Battle of Oriskany.

As the Revolutionary War neared its end, many Iroquois families left New York to settle in Canada. Claus provided newcomers with supplies and established a school for them. When the war ended he berated British officials for failing to protect the rights of the Indians during treaty negotiations. Returning to Europe in poor health, he died at Cardiff in 1787.

(Barbara Graymont, The Iroquois in the American Revolution; Arthur Pound, Johnson of the Mohawks.)

CLINTON, JAMES, EXPEDITION. In June 1779 Gen. James Clinton led a large force of soldiers and militiamen from Canajoharie to link up with Gen. John Sullivan's invasion of the Iroquois country. On his way to the rendezvous he burned cabins and crops at three Indian villages. Joining forces with Sullivan on August 22, he participated in the destruction of towns throughout the Six Nations. (See SULLIVAN, JOHN.)

"When one considers the terrible condition of the roads through the ... wilderness, the tremendous weight of the loads transported, the steady climb ..., and the fact that Brant and his followers were constantly hanging on the flanks of the army to pounce upon any wagon momentarily unprotected, one must agree ... that Clinton's march was one of the most remarkable feats of American military history."--T. Wood Clarke.

(T. Wood Clarke, The Bloody Mohawk.)

COBLESKILL, NEW YORK, RAIDS. On May 30, 1778, Joseph Brant led some 300 to 400 Indians and Tories to attack the settlement of Cobleskill, New York, ten miles west of Schoharie. After burning several buildings the raiders laid an ambush for troops quartered at a garrison house and killed 22 of them when they emerged to do battle. The surviving soldiers and settlers fled to Schoharie for safety.

In 1779 a party of 300 Onondaga Indians attacked the 19 families who had returned to Cobleskill. The settlers fled, their retreat covered by 7 Continental soldiers, holed up in a burning house, who continued to fight until they perished in the flames.

In September 1781 Indians and Tories raided the area around Cobleskill, slaughtering a settler and taking 7 captives.

(T. Wood Clarke, The Bloody Mohawk; Barbara Graymont, The Iroquois in the American Revolution; Francis Whiting Halsey, The Old New York Frontier.)

COCHECO, NEW HAMPSHIRE, MASSACRE. On June 27, 1689, the village of Cocheco (Dover), New Hampshire, was attacked by Pennacook Indians led by Chiefs Kankamagus and Mesandowit. The raid was intended to retaliate for the murder of Indians there at the conclusion of King Philip's War. (See WALDRON, RICHARD.) Indian women had been permitted to sleep inside each of the five garrison houses, and, at a signal from warriors concealed outside the pickets, they opened the gates. Four of the houses were seized, 23 settlers were killed, and 29 captives were marched to Canada and were sold to the French.

(Jeremy Belknap, History of New Hampshire, I; Samuel Adams Drake, Border Wars of New England.)

COCKENOE, MONTAUK INTERPRETER. Cockenoe, a Montauk youth, was captured by English settlers in 1637 during the Pequot War. He was employed as an interpreter by Rev. John Eliot and played an important part in translating the Eliot Bible. He translated for colonial officials during conferences with Indians until the time of his death about 1700.

(Ola Elizabeth Winslow, John Eliot, Apostle to the Indians.)

COLEMAN, THOMAS. Thomas Coleman, a legendary Indian fighter of Pennsylvania's Juniata Valley, was so feared by his adversaries that war parties avoided his area. About 1763, raiders seized Coleman's brother boiling sugar and boiled him "to a jelly" in a large iron kettle. After discovering his brother's body, Thomas devoted his

life to the destruction of Indians. During the American Revolution
he led a company of scouts, and he went out alone when his followers
were too frightened to accompany him. He suffered numerous knife
and tomahawk wounds, but he survived to enjoy a full measure of
revenge.

(U. J. Jones, History of the Early Settlement of the Juniata
Valley.)

CONNER, RICHARD. Richard Conner, a Maryland youth, became a
trapper and "long hunter" immediately after the conclusion of the
French and Indian War. While trading with the Shawnees he met
Mary Myers, a young captive, purchased her for $200, and married
her. As one of the provisions of the purchase he agreed to remain
with the tribe and to have his first son raised as an Indian.

In 1774 the Conners left the Shawnees under a provision of
the Treaty of Camp Charlotte. Soon afterward, however, they began
a journey to attempt to reclaim their son, James, from the tribe.
When they arrived at the Moravian mission on the Tuscarawas, they
gained such respect for the work of the missionaries that they decided to make their home with the Christian Delawares. Conner became an active and invaluable member of the mission, but in 1781 he
and the missionaries were compelled by the British and Wyandot Indians to go to Detroit. After the Revolution he and his family became the first settlers of St. Clair County, Michigan.

(Dale Van Every, Ark of Empire.)

CONESTOGA INDIANS see SUSQUEHANNA INDIANS

CONNOLLY, JOHN. Dr. John Connolly was the nephew of George
Croghan and Gordon Howard, two of the most prominent Pennsylvania
traders. He spent his childhood on the frontier and became adept
at Indian diplomacy at an early age. He served as a surgeon's mate
in the French and Indian War and, as his reward, he received a grant
of 2,000 acres at the present site of Louisville, Kentucky, from Lord
Dunmore, governor of Virginia. Afterward, Connolly and Dunmore
engaged extensively in western land speculation, losing it later as a
result of Tory activities.

During the Pennsylvania-Virginia boundary dispute over the
Pittsburgh area, Connolly served as Dunmore's agent. In 1774, acting as Virginia's justice of the peace in the contested area, he called
upon the citizens to organize a militia to repel an anticipated Indian
invasion. He led the militia (Virginia partisans) to seize Fort Pitt,
and he renamed it Fort Dunmore. Furious Pennsylvania partisans
accused him of using his office to seize the Indian trade for himself.
Reuben Gold Thwaites has pointed out that Dunmore and Connolly,
to counteract the spreading revolutionary spirit among the colonies,
"favored a distraction in the shape of a popular Indian war."

On April 25, 1774, Dunmore instructed Connolly to prepare the
citizens of Pittsburgh to fight an Indian war. As no immediate threat
of war existed, Connolly provoked one by calling upon Michael Cresap,
Daniel Greathouse, and other Indian haters to foment hostilities. Attacks

upon Indians began immediately (see LOGAN, JOHN). The Mingo Indians retaliated, but the Shawnees tried to avoid the conflict by escorting their traders safely to Pittsburgh. Connolly repaid this bid for peace by sending frontiersmen in pursuit of the Shawnee envoys, attacking them at Beaver Creek, and wounding one warrior before they escaped. This incident made war with the Shawnees inevitable.

Connolly served as a major in Dunmore's War of 1774. After the defeat of the Shawnees he concluded a treaty with the Indians that supplemented the Treaty of Camp Charlotte. However, the Virginia House of Burgesses, distrusting Connolly's motives, disregarded his treaty and appointed its own commissioners to ratify the agreement. Later Connolly admitted that it had been his intention to use the treaty negotiations as a vehicle to gain Indian support for the British in the impending conflict with the colonies.

In June 1775 Connolly conferred with a delegation of Delaware Indians at Pittsburgh and persuaded them to side with the British. Then, rewarded with a colonel's commission, he schemed to raise a regiment of frontier Tories, lead them to Detroit, and augment his forces by recruiting Indians from the Great Lakes and Ohio River regions. While going eastward to discuss his proposal with British officers, however, he was captured by American authorities near Hagerstown, Maryland, imprisoned, and compelled to use his influence to restrain the Indians from attacking the settlers.

After the Revolution, Connolly served as a clerk to Sir John Johnson in the British Canadian Department of Indian Affairs. In 1788, Lord Dorchester sent him to Louisville to investigate the likelihood of Indian support in the event of another war with the Americans. There he became involved in the Wilkinson-Miro intrigue to draw the western settlers away from the American union. Wilkinson, however, was supporting Spain's bid while Connolly sought British ascendancy in the region. After gaining as much information as possible from Connolly, Wilkinson employed an Indian to threaten his life and Connolly fled from the territory.

(Thomas P. Abernethy, Western Lands and the American Revolution; Randolph C. Downes, Council Fires on the Upper Ohio; Dale Van Every, Ark of Empire; Alexander Scott Withers, Chronicles of Border Warfare.)

CONOY INDIANS. The Conoy (Canoy, Ganawese, Kanhawas, Canawese, Piscataway) Indians, a powerful Algonquian tribe closely related to the Delawares and Nanticokes, lived in Maryland between the Potomac River and Chesapeake Bay at the time of initial English contact. They joined the Powhatans in the massacre of Virginia colonists in 1622. They were friendly to Maryland settlers, however, and in 1634 the Jesuits established missions among them. In 1640, following the lead of Chief Chitomachen, most of them were converted to Christianity. Afterward they engaged in the fur trade and served as an effective buffer between the Maryland settlements and hostile tribes.

The Conoys suffered so many casualties during warfare with the Conestogas that they were compelled to begin a gradual and partial withdrawal up the Potomac, many of them settling at the present site of Washington, D.C. Epidemics reduced their population from 2,000 to a few hundred. In 1673 they were assigned to a reservation in Maryland, but soon afterward the Conestogas drove them into Pennsylvania. In 1743, upon the insistence of the Iroquois, they settled at Shamokin. By 1758 most members of the tribe were absorbed by the Nanticokes, and, soon afterward, moved to New York. A few remained in Maryland to work on plantations.

(William C. Sturtevant, ed., Handbook of American Indians, XV; Paul A. W. Wallace, Indians in Pennsylvania.)

CONSERT, CORNELIUS. Cornelius Consert, a Dutch pirate, received an English pardon in return for his offer to fight against the Indians in King Philip's War. His effectiveness as an Indian fighter was praised by his contemporary, Nathaniel Saltonstall, as follows:

> About three days after the General (Thomas Savage), finding Cornellis to be a Stout Man, and willing to venture his life in the cause of the English, sent him with twelve Men under his Command to Scout about, with Orders to return in three Hours on Pain of Death; in his Way he met sixty Indians, ... set on them, killing thirteen, and took eight alive, persues the Rest as far as he could go for the Swamps.... By this time Cornellis and his twelve Men (all being preserved) returned to the Camp, but they were eight Hours absent: Whereupon a Council of War was called, who past the Sentence of Death on him, for exceeding the Order given him. Immediately was also Pardoned, and received thanks for his good Service done in the Expedition; and was in a short Time sent out on the like Design, and brought Home with him twelve Indians alive, and two Indians Heads.

(Charles H. Lincoln, ed., Narratives of the Indian Wars.)

CONVERSE, JAMES. Capt. James Converse was one of the most courageous New England Indian fighters during the last decade of the seventeenth century. In June 1691, with less than forty men, he defended Storer's garrison at Wells, Maine, against an attack by two hundred Abnaki warriors led by Chief Moxus. Moxus, while abandoning the assault, promised to return and, true to his word, he reappeared at Wells one year later with Chiefs Madockawando and Egermet, a large Abnaki war party, and several French soldiers. Converse commanded 29 soldiers and most of the Wells settlers. The Indians were repulsed in several attempts to seize the stockade. After losing a large number of warriors to the unerring defenders, both male and female, the Abnakis burned a prisoner to death and withdrew from the field.

Throughout the remainder of 1692 and most of 1693, Converse and his troops patrolled the area between Pemaquid and Piscataqua and up the Kennebec to Teconnet. During that time he kept the hostiles too scattered to mount a massive invasion of the Maine settlements.

(Samuel Adams Drake, Border Wars of New England; Francis Parkman, Count Frontenac and New France Under Louis XIV.)

CORBITANT, MASSACHUSET CHIEF. Corbitant, a Massachuset chief, was hostile to the Plymouth settlers and angry at Massassoit for befriending them. He attempted to create a conspiracy in 1621 with the Narragansets and other tribes to drive the colonists into the sea. While Miles Standish and his corps of Plymouth fighting men were away from the village, he seized their Indian friends, Hobomok and Squanto, and attacked Massassoit. Hobomok escaped, however, located Standish, and led the Plymouth men to Nemasket to rescue Squanto. As a result of this prompt and effective action, Corbitant and other hostile chiefs made peace with the Pilgrims.

(Neal Salisbury, Manitou and Providence; Alvin G. Weeks, Massasoit.)

CORLAER see VAN CURLER, ARENT

CORNPLANTER, SENECA CHIEF. Cornplanter (Gyantwahia, John O'Bail), son of a white trader and a Seneca woman, was born at Ganawagus, an Iroquois village on the Genesee River, before 1750. Raised by his mother's people, he became a war chief of the formidable Seneca tribe, leading raids on the English settlements during his youth. Upon the onset of the American Revolution he became a British partisan, striking the settlers at Cherry Valley, Wyoming Valley, Fort Freeland, the Canajoharie area, and elsewhere.

After the Revolution, Cornplanter made his peace with the Americans, signing the treaties of Fort Stanwix in 1784 and Fort Harmar in 1789. In 1790, during a visit to the nation's capital at Philadelphia, he appealed to George Washington for assistance to his suffering people.

For his help in persuading the Iroquois to stay out of the hostile Indian confederacy in the Northwest Territory, Cornplanter received a grant of land on both sides of the Allegheny River. There, asserted Paul A. W. Wallace, "he brought in Quaker teachers, established schools, made roads, built good houses, developed agriculture, bred large herds of cattle, and, in a word, turned the Cornplanter Grant into a model community." He lost the respect of some of his people because of his role in agreeing to land cessions, but he retained sufficient influence to induce the Senecas to support the Americans in the War of 1812.

Shortly before his death in 1836, Cornplanter dreamed that his friendship for the whites had been a mistake. As a result he destroyed all of the gifts that government officials had presented to him.

(Frederick J. Dockstader, Great North American Indians; Barbara Graymont, The Iroquois in the American Revolution; Paul A. W. Wallace, Indians in Pennsylvania.)

COSHOCTON, DELAWARE VILLAGE. Coshocton, an important Delaware Indian town, was located at the present site of Coshocton, Ohio, during the American Revolution. The residents were friendly to the Americans, but Gen. Daniel Brodhead, convinced that they intended to ravage the settlements, determined to destroy them first. On April 7, 1781, he led some 300 soldiers against Coshocton, surprising the settlement and burning it to the ground. The militia murdered 15 Delawares after they had surrendered, thus making the survivors bitter enemies of the Americans.

(Randolph C. Downes, Council Fires on the Upper Ohio; Dale Van Every, A Company of Heroes.)

COULON DE VILLIERS, LOUIS. Louis Coulon de Villiers was born in Canada in 1710. His father, Nicolas-Antoine Coulon de Villiers, was commandant at Fort St. Joseph, and Louis served under him as a cadet during his youth. He was wounded and his father and brother were killed during a fight with the Fox Indians near Green Bay in 1733. (See BUTTE DES MORTS.)

Louis, promoted to lieutenant in 1734, continued his wilderness career, serving in Bienville's Chickasaw campaign of 1739, and commanding at Crown Point and Fort Miamis. In 1754 he led a large force of Canadians and Indians to Fort Duquesne, and, upon his arrival in June, he learned that his brother Joseph had been killed by George Washington's Virginians and Indians. Louis commanded the French army that defeated Washington at Great Meadows (see NECESSITY, FORT).

During the early years of the French and Indian War, Louis led attacks upon the New York and Pennsylvania settlements. In July 1756 he and his Indian followers sank several boats on the Oswego River and collected 24 English scalps. On August 7, 1757, he fought a battle near Lake George, losing 21 Canadian and Indian lives, but inflicting an equally heavy toll on the English. He died of smallpox on November 2, 1757.

(Louis Antoine de Bougainville, Adventures in the Wilderness; Solon J. Buck, The Planting of Civilization in Western Pennsylvania; Dale Van Every, Forth to the Wilderness.)

COULON DE VILLIERS DE JUMONVILLE, JOSEPH. Joseph Coulon de Villiers de Jumonville, a Canadian military officer, has a place in American history because his death at the hands of George Washington's English and Indian forces set in motion a series of clashes that led to the French and Indian War. Born in 1718, he entered military service at an early age, and most of his experience was limited to Indian warfare. He served with Bienville in the Chickasaw campaign of 1739. Six years later, during King George's War, he participated in several French and Indian raids on the New England settlements.

On May 23, 1754, he was stationed at Fort Duquesne when ordered to lead 30 men to determine whether George Washington's army had entered territory claimed by the French. Informed of Jumonville's movements by Indian scouts, Washington led 40 men to intercept him. They attacked the French camp on the night of May 28, slaying Jumonville and killing or capturing most of his men. French officials were furious, insisting that Jumonville's party was an emissary without hostile intentions when attacked during a time of peace.

(Dale Van Every, Forth to the Wilderness.)

COURTEMANCH, AUGUSTIN LE GARDEUR DE REPENTIGNY see LE GARDEUR DE COURTEMANCHE, AUGUSTIN

COUTURE, GUILLAUME. Guillaume Couture, a young French-Canadian, accompanied the Jesuits, Isaac Jogues and René Goupil, on a canoe voyage into Iroquois territory in 1642. On the Lake of St. Peter the Iroquois attacked them and captured Jogues and Goupil. Couture escaped but, seeing the seizure of his companions, he returned and attempted to rescue them. He killed an Iroquois warrior before his enemies overwhelmed him.

Taken to a Mohawk town, the captives were subjected to the kind of torture that the tribe was adept at administering. The Iroquois tore out Couture's nails, gnawed his fingers, and pierced his hand with a sword. He withstood their torments with such courage that an Iroquois family adopted him to replace a lost son. (See GOUPIL, RENE; JOGUES, ISAAC.)

In July 1645 Couture went with the Mohawks to Canada on a peace-making mission. During thee years with the tribe he had achieved a great deal of influence over their chiefs, and he was in large measure responsible for their peace overture. During the conference he was restored to his own people, but later that year he returned to the Mohawks to spend the winter in an attempt to show them the benefits of Christianity.

(Francis Parkman, The Jesuits in North America, II; Edna Kenton, ed., Black Gown and Redskins.)

CRANE, WYANDOT CHIEF see TARHE, WYANDOT CHIEF

CRAWFORD, FORT. Fort Crawford was built at Prairie du Chien, Wisconsin, in 1816. Until the close of the Black Hawk War of 1832 it played an important part in protecting traders and settlers in the upper Mississippi Valley. The fort provided accommodations for the negotiation of numerous treaties with Indian tribes.

(F. L. Paxon, History of the American Frontier.)

CRAWFORD, HUGH. Hugh Crawford was one of the most prominent Pennsylvania traders and Indian managers of the eighteenth century. He entered the Indian trade by 1739, working at times for George Croghan or Thomas Smallman, but frequently trading on his own account. While in the wilderness he rendered important service to Pennsylvania by arranging conferences with Indian chiefs. About 1753 he claimed land on the Juniata River near the present city of Huntingdon, Pennsylvania.

Crawford participated in several important campaigns during the French and Indian War and Pontiac's War, serving as a lieutenant in the Pennsylvania militia in 1756 and as an ensign in the Forbes Expedition of 1758. In 1760 he was a trader at Fort Pitt, but he returned to military activities upon the outbreak of Pontiac's War. During the spring of 1763 he was captured by Indians at the mouth of the Maumee River, held for a few weeks, and delivered with other captives to Detroit on July 12. In 1765 he guided an English officer to Fort de Chartres seeking French surrender of that post. (See ROSS, JOHN.)

After peace was established with Pontiac, Crawford was assigned in 1766 to conduct that chief to Oswego to confer with Sir William Johnson. Johnson's biographer, Arthur Pound, noted that "Crawford brought Pontiac and his party over the long route with every attention calculated to ease the broken spirit of a grieving primitive."

In 1767 Crawford served as interpreter for the Mason-Dixon Expedition to establish the southern boundary of Pennsylvania. For this service he received a grant of 500 acres a few miles from Fort Pitt. He died in 1770.

(Charles A. Hanna, The Wilderness Trail; Arthur Pound, Johnson of the Mohawks.)

CREDIT ISLAND, BATTLE OF. The Battle of Credit Island was fought on September 5-6, 1814, at the present site of Davenport, Iowa, by Maj. Zachary Taylor and 334 American soldiers against a force of more than 1,000 British troops and Indians. Taylor, who had intended to seize British posts on the upper Mississippi, was compelled to retreat to St. Louis when the British attacked with cannon fire.

(K. Jack Bauer, Zachary Taylor; Reginald Horsman, The War of 1812.)

CRESAP, MICHAEL. Michael Cresap, son of Col. Thomas Cresap, was born on June 29, 1742, in present Alleghany County, Maryland. He spent his boyhood on the frontier and killed his first Indian at the age of ten when he revenged the death of a settler near Oldtown, shooting the warrior in the act of scalping his victim.

In 1767, while trading at Redstone, he killed the Delaware chief called Captain Peter in a dispute over rum. Theodore Roosevelt has provided the following characterization: "He was of the regular pioneer type: a good woodsman, sturdy and brave, a fearless fighter, devoted to his friends and his country; but also, when his blood was heated and his savage instincts fairly roused, inclined to regard any red man, whether hostile or friendly, as a being who should be slain on sight."

Cresap began making plans as early as 1767 to establish a post on the Ohio River. It was his intention, if opposed by the Indians, to destroy their villages. No attempt at settlement was made until the spring of 1774, however, at which time he, George Rogers Clark, and other frontiersmen assembled at the mouth of the Great Kanawha to descend the Ohio and build a post in Kentucky. When some of them were fired on while hunting, they proposed to attack a Shawnee village known as Horseshoe Bottom, but Cresap persuaded them to go to Wheeling to await developments. At Wheeling, Cresap and Clark were requested by John Connolly to hold their men ready to precipitate an Indian war. The opportunity arose on April 25 when Cresap learned that a Shawnee and a Delaware were descending the river. Cresap and his men ambushed the canoe and shot them to death. On April 27 he and his men pursued a party of friendly Shawnees who were returning from a conference at Fort Pitt, cornered them near Captina Creek, and killed two of them. These events touched off the conflict called Cresap's War or Dunmore's War. A few days later, Chief Logan's family was massacred by white men at Yellow Creek. Cresap was accused by Logan of leading the affair, but he was at Redstone at the time.

Cresap served as a captain at the bloody battle of Point Pleasant on October 10, 1774. He died of an illness on October 18, 1775.

(Randolph C. Downes, Council Fires on the Upper Ohio; Theodore Roosevelt, The Winning of the West, I; James H. Perkins, Annals of the West.)

CRESAP, THOMAS. Thomas Cresap was born in Yorkshire, England, about 1702 and emigrated to Maryland at the age of 15. He became involved in the Indian trade at an early age, and by 1740 he had established a frontier post at Shawnee Oldtown, athwart the trail taken by Iroquois and Cherokee war parties. At this strategic location he was highly instrumental in preserving the peace as an intermediary between the Maryland government and those powerful tribes.

In 1747 Cresap served as an advisor to the Ohio Company, recipient of a grant of 200,000 acres near present Louisville, Kentucky. As a friend of George Washington and other influential Virginians, he was appointed in 1752 to blaze a trail over the mountains from Fort Cumberland to the Redstone. (See NEMACOLIN'S PATH.) This trail became the route of Washington's Road, Braddock's Road, and the National Road.

In 1766 Cresap established a trading post at Redstone in the Indian country, prohibited by the Proclamation of 1763, but permitted by the Iroquois. There he competed so successfully with Pennsylvania traders that General Gage, Sir William Johnson, and George Croghan attempted to have him removed by the Indians. But Cresap, as fearless a frontiersman as ever roamed the Allegheny Mountains, defied them until his death about 1790.

(Thomas P. Abernethy, Western Lands and the American Revolution; Dale Van Every, Forth to the Wilderness.)

CROGHAN, GEORGE. George Croghan, one of the most important Indian traders and diplomats of the eighteenth century, was born in Ireland. The place and time of his birth are unknown, but he was a young man when he arrived in Pennsylvania in 1741. A distant relative of Sir William Johnson, he followed his kinsman's example by embarking immediately in the Indian trade.

During his first decade in America, Croghan operated a trading post near Harris's Ferry in Lancaster County, a location well calculated to command the trails leading westward to the Indian country. As his business expanded, this post became the first link in a chain that extended all the way to the Falls of the Ohio. He had been in America less than five years when he began competing with the French for the Indian trade at Sandusky and along the shores of Lake Erie. He and the famous French-Canadian partisans, the Joncaires, struggled for many years to influence the Iroquois, Ottawas, Miamis and other western tribes, and Croghan generally prevailed. In 1746 he became a counselor to the Six Nations. In 1747 he played a leading part in inciting the Wyandot chief, Nicolas, to murder five French traders, and he brought one of their scalps to the Governor of Pennsylvania. In turn, the French offered a $1,000 reward for his scalp.

Beginning in 1748, Croghan spent much of his time at Logstown, distributing presents to the Indians and advising them to hold fast to the English interest. In 1749 he countered the move of the Céleron Expedition to gain control of the tribes along the Ohio. He suffered severe financial reverses between 1749 and 1753, largely as a result of robberies by Indian allies of the French. And, near the end of that period, he was compelled to move his home to Aughwick, west of the settlements, in order to escape debtor's prison.

By 1754, most of the Ohio Indians had taken the part of the French. After George Washington's defeat at Great Meadows in July 1754, Indians still opposed to the French congregated at Croghan's post at Aughwick. Fort Shirley was built there in 1755, and Croghan, recipient of a captain's commission, was ordered to build three additional forts to protect the settlers.

When General Braddock assembled his forces to attack Fort Duquesne, Croghan provided Indian scouts for the expedition. He and eight Iroquois chiefs and warriors marched with the army and provided regular reports about enemy movements, information which Braddock largely ignored.

After Braddock's defeat, Croghan visited Sir William Johnson, and they, probably the two most knowledgeable men in America about Indian affairs, combined their talents to hold as many tribes as possible in the English interest. As Johnson's Deputy Superintendent in the Northern District, he participated in numerous conferences with the Iroquois and the Ohio tribes. In addition he provided warriors to assist Col. Daniel Webb in guarding the Oneida portage. In March 1757 he sent scalping parties of Iroquois, Susquehannas, Nanticokes, and Delawares against the French and Indians on the Ohio. In the spring of 1758, from headquarters at Fort Herkimer, he led Iroquois scouting parties deep into enemy territory. In July he brought some 400 Indians to assist Gen. James Abercrombie in an unsuccessful attempt to take Ticonderoga.

In October 1758 Croghan played a leading role in negotiating the Treaty of Easton. The eastern Delawares agreed to live in peace with the Pennsylvania settlers and to give up their English captives. This diplomatic achievement assisted Gen. John Forbes to drive the French from Fort Duquesne.

After the defeat of France, Croghan moved his headquarters to

Fort Pitt, where he conferred with Indian chiefs on many occasions in an attempt to maintain peace and to promote trade. Between 1759 and 1761 he redeemed more than three hundred white men, women, and children from captivity. In 1760 he went with Maj. Robert Rogers to take possession of the French post at Detroit. During the march he conferred with chiefs and promoted friendly relations.

Unable to obtain sufficient trade goods to satisfy the tribes, a major cause of Pontiac's War, Croghan left Fort Pitt shortly before it was attacked in 1763. Soon afterward he assisted Col. Henry Bouquet to obtain provisions for his successful march to relieve that vital fortification. After Pontiac's defeat, Croghan went to London to advise the Board of Trade on matters of Indian management. Some of his suggestions were adopted, but he failed to obtain assistance for traders who had suffered great losses during the recent wars.

In 1765 Croghan rendered what his biographer, Albert T. Volwiler, believed to be his greatest service, his role in occupying the Illinois country. Appointed to make peace with the Indians of that vast region, he assembled a large pack train of presents, only to have them confiscated by Pennsylvania frontiersmen. (See BLACK BOYS.) In May 1765, however, he departed from Fort Pitt with boats loaded with presents, stopping frequently to negotiate with formerly hostile chiefs. On June 8 a Kickapoo war party attacked his camp, killing five of his men and capturing the survivors. Croghan received a tomahawk wound, but he recovered in time to persuade his captors to become allies of the English. Released on July 1, he negotiated peace with the tribes of the Great Lakes and the Wabash. Afterward he escorted Pontiac to Detroit, where peace was proclaimed.

In 1768, Croghan conferred with more than a thousand Indians at Fort Pitt, dealing with grievances regarding settlers invading their lands. His influence was instrumental in averting a major uprising. Purchase of the contested territory was finalized later that year at Fort Stanwix by a treaty which Croghan helped to negotiate.

In 1772 Croghan resigned from the Indian service and shifted his activity to land speculation. He acquired extensive holdings in Pennsylvania and New York, but he lost a fortune in the attempt to establish a new colony called Vandalia, an undertaking doomed by the outbreak of the American Revolution.

Croghan supported the Americans during the war, but he was suspected of Tory leanings and tried for treason in 1778. Although acquitted, he lived in poverty at Lancaster and Philadelphia until his death on August 31, 1782.

"George Croghan was the leading exponent of the expansion of the Anglo-Saxon race into the Ohio region.... He was preeminent as an Indian trader, an Indian agent, a land speculator, and a projector of inland colonies."--Albert T. Volwiler.

(Albert T. Volwiler, George Croghan and the Westward Movement; Arthur Pound, Johnson of the Mohawks; Dale Van Every, Forth to the Wilderness; Howard H. Peckham, Pontiac and the Indian Uprising.)

CROWN POINT, NEW YORK see BLOODY POND, BATTLE OF

CRUZAT, FRANCISCO, INDIAN RELATIONS. Francisco Cruzat, a
Spanish military officer, was appointed lieutenant-governor of Upper
Louisiana in 1775 and again in 1780. During his second administration
he bestowed large stores of gifts upon the Indians of the St. Louis
area to prevent them from supporting the British during the American
Revolution. He succeeded in gaining the allegiance of the Sioux and
other powerful tribes on the upper Mississippi. In February 1781
his soldiers captured Fort St. Joseph (present site of Niles, Michigan) without the loss of a man.
    (John Anthony Caruso, The Mississippi Valley Frontier.)

CUMBERLAND, FORT, MARYLAND. Fort Cumberland, at the juncture
of the Potomac River and Wills Creek (present site of Cumberland,
Maryland), had its beginnings in 1750 when the Ohio Company erected
a small structure there. Stronger stockades were constructed in
1754-55, the last serving as an assembly point for the Braddock Expedition. In June 1755 a force of 130 Frenchmen and Indians slew
20 people in the vicinity of the fort. It was abandoned in 1765.
    (William A. Hunter, Forts on the Pennsylvania Frontier.)

CURLY HEAD, CHIPPEWA CHIEF. Curly Head, born about 1750,
lived near the present site of Crow Wing, Minnesota. He fought many
battles with the neighboring Sioux, but he was friendly toward white
settlers. During the winter of 1805-06 he received a United States
flag and a medal from Lt. Zebulon M. Pike. In 1825, after signing
the Treaty of Prairie du Chien, he died while returning to his home.
    (F. W. Hodge, ed., Handbook of American Indians, I.)

CUSTALOGA, DELAWARE CHIEF. Custaloga, chief of the Unalachtigo
Delawares in Coshocton County, Ohio, was one of the instigators of
the attack on Col. Henry Bouquet's army at the Battle of Bushy Run.
Described by Dale Van Every as "a veteran of many encounters with
white men, both at the council table and in the field," he took the
lead after Bouquet's Expedition in seeking a peaceful settlement.
    (Dale Van Every, Forth to the Wilderness.)

CUTSHAMEKIN, MASSACHUSET CHIEF see KUTSHAMAKIN, MAS-
SACHUSET CHIEF

CUYLER, ABRAHAM, FLOTILLA. Lt. Abraham Cuyler of the Queen's
Rangers departed from Niagara on May 23, 1763, with 96 men and 10
boatloads of supplies for the garrison at Detroit. Unaware of the
outbreak of Pontiac's War, he landed at Point Pelee, east of the mouth
of the Detroit River, on May 28 to camp for the night. At midnight
a party of Wyandot Indians attacked the camp, compelling the startled
rangers to flee for the boats. Many soldiers were slain in the disorganized retreat, and most of the survivors surrendered. Cuyler
was wounded, but he managed to escape with 40 of his men in two
boats. They sailed to Fort Sandusky, found it destroyed by the Indians, and returned to Niagara.
    The captured rangers faced a terrible fate. Taken to the

Indian camp outside besieged Fort Detroit, they were compelled to run the gantlet. Then, drunk from rum ransacked from Cuyler's boats, the Indians burned them at the stake, threw their bodies into the river, and roared defiance as the corpses floated past the defenders of Fort Detroit.

(Howard H. Peckham, Pontiac and the Indian Uprising; Arthur Pound, Johnson of the Mohawks; Dale Van Every, Forth to the Wilderness.)

-D-

DABLON, CLAUDE. Claude Dablon, one of the most dedicated Jesuit missionaries of Canada and the northeastern part of the present United States, was born at Dieppe on January 21, 1619. After study at Paris and elsewhere he arrived in Canada in 1655. A versatile man of strong intellect and prodigious physical power, he had prepared himself to influence the Indians by use of his skills as a musician.

Soon after coming to Canada, Father Dablon assisted Father Joseph Chaumonot in establishing a mission among the fierce Iroquois of Onondaga. He described their arrival as follows: "Very late that evening, the Elders held a Council ... where one of them, after greeting us on behalf of the nation made us ... presents ... of beads, to wipe our eyes, wet with tears shed over the murders committed in our country that year...."

Dablon and Chaumonot constructed the first Catholic chapel in the present state of New York near Onondaga. While Chaumonot preached to the Indians in their native language, Dablon, unable to speak Iroquois, attracted them to the services by playing the flute. At first their labors met with marked success. They negotiated a peace treaty between the Iroquois and Algonquians, baptized an Indian infant, and redeemed a French child from captivity. When the leading sachem accepted Christianity, the future of the mission appeared to offer great promise. The priests soon discerned, however, that the Onondagas desired French protection rather than conversion to Christianity. Not even the introduction of French settlers to Onondaga assuaged Iroquois hostility, and finally they fled to Canada to escape being murdered. (See ONONDAGA INDIANS.)

In 1661 Dablon served among the Algonquians near Hudson's Bay. After gaining a few converts there he returned to Quebec and remained in the French settlements until he accompanied Father Jacques Marquette to Lake Superior in 1669. He wintered with the Hurons in 1670–71, and founded the St. Ignace Mission at Mackinac at that time.

In 1670 Dablon was appointed superior of the Canadian missions and rector of the College of Quebec. He edited the Jesuit Relations for many years before he died at Quebec in 1697.

(T. J. Campbell, Pioneer Priests of North America; Louise Phelps Kellogg, The French Régime in Wisconsin and the Northwest; Edna Kenton, ed., Black Gown and Redskins; John Gilmary Shea, Discovery and Exploration of the Mississippi Valley.)

DALYELL'S DEFEAT   see   BLOODY RUN, BATTLE OF

DAVERS, ROBERT.   Robert Davers, an English traveler and scientist,
was the first white man to die during Pontiac's War.   With a friend,
Charles Robertson, he was exploring the Great Lakes region in a
canoe in 1763 when a band of Pontiac's supporters swarmed out of
the woods near Detroit, murdered them and boiled and ate them.
Pontiac used the tragedy as a means to attempt to intimidate the defenders of Fort Detroit, but the only result was tremendous anger
in England and determination to crush the uprising.
    (Dale Van Every, Forth to the Wilderness.)

DEAN, JAMES.   James Dean, a native of Groton, Connecticut, spent
his childhood among the northeastern Indians.   It is uncertain
whether he was held in captivity or lived with them voluntarily, but
he had mastered many dialects before serving as an interpreter to
missionaries at Oquaga.   Afterward he received a good education at
Dartmouth.
    At the outbreak of the Revolutionary War, Dean was sent by
the Americans to Onondaga as envoy to the Six Nations.   He visited
the Caughnawagas in Canada and urged them, with some initial success, to remain neutral.   Then he acted as interpreter at the Albany
Conference of August 25, 1775, at which time most members of the
Six Nations determined upon a course of neutrality.
    Beginning in 1776, Dean assisted Philip Schuyler in inducing the
Oneidas to stand with the Americans when other Iroquois took up
the hatchet for the British.   "His influence among the Oneidas in the
years ahead would be of immense importance."--Barbara Graymont.
    (Barbara Graymont, The Iroquois in the American Revolution.)

DEARBORN, FORT, MASSACRE.   Fort Dearborn was established in
1803 at the mouth of the Chicago River (present site of Chicago)
under terms of the Treaty of Greenville.   At the onset of the War
of 1812, the strong stockade was garrisoned by some 75 soldiers under the command of Capt. Nathan Heald.   The fall of Mackinac on
July 17, 1812, caused a great movement of Indians toward the British
cause and led Gen. William Hull to order the evacuation of Fort Dearborn.
    On August 9, 1812, Heald received Hull's order and began
preparations to evacuate the fort and to march to Fort Wayne.   At
that time some 600 Indians, chiefly Potawatomis, were gathered near
the fort, arguing among themselves whether to attack the garrison.
Capt. William Wells and 30 Miami Indian scouts from Fort Wayne arrived about August 14 to serve as protectors during the march, and
Heald arranged with Potawatomis believed to be friendly to provide
an additional escort.   Black Partridge, a friendly Potawatomi chief,
warned Heald to expect an attack, for the hostile chiefs Blackbird
and Mad Sturgeon had worked the warriors into a frenzy with demands
to strike a blow against the hated Americans.
    On August 15, 97 soldiers and settlers marched from the stock-
ade.   Wells and most of his Miamis took the lead, followed by the

soldiers and their wives and larger children. Two baggage wagons containing the smaller children and the families' belongings were guarded by a few soldiers and members of the Chicago militia. The remainder of the Miamis brought up the rear.

As the column advanced along the beach, a band of Potawatomis moved parallel to the soldiers and quickly disappeared behind a row of sand dunes. Detecting an ambush, Wells raced to the center of the column to give warning. His Miami scouts disappeared as soon as the action began. Heald ordered a charge and drove the Potawatomis from the dunes, but many soldiers died during the onslaught.

At the rear of the column, Indians surrounded the baggage wagons, killing the soldiers and wives who tried to protect the children. One warrior leaped into the wagon transporting the children and tomahawked all except one of them. Wells raced his horse toward the wagons in a desperate effort to save the survivors, but he was shot to death in the attempt. (See WELLS, WILLIAM.)

Having lost more than half of his soldiers, Captain Heald surrendered upon assurance that the lives of his men would be spared. Upon returning to the fort, however, the Indians murdered the wounded soldiers and burned 5 men at the stake. Afterward the Indians put the fort to the torch and marched the captives away to their villages. Some of the prisoners died in captivity. Twenty-seven survivors eventually were redeemed.

(Milo M. Quaife, Checagou; Louise Phelps Kellogg, The British Regime in Wisconsin and the Northwest.)

DECORAH, SPOON see DEKAURY, CHOUKELEA, WINNEBAGO CHIEF

DEERFIELD INDIANS see POCOMTUC INDIANS

DEERFIELD, MASSACHUSETTS, RAIDS. Deerfield, Massachusetts, founded in 1670, was one of the settlements most exposed to Indian attacks. During King Philip's War it was raided on September 1, 1675, with the loss of one settler and the destruction of several homes. (See BLOODY BROOK, BATTLE OF.) Afterward the village was deserted until rebuilt in 1682.

The attack known as the Deerfield Massacre occurred on February 29, 1704. At that time the town contained 289 settlers. It was guarded by a garrison of 20 men. Led by the French officer François Hertel, some 50 Canadians and 200 Abnaki and Caughnawaga warriors leaped over the palisades at dawn while many residents still slept. Unseen, they surrounded the houses and, at the signal of the war whoop, began their assault. Most of the citizens surrendered without resistance, but spirited defenses occurred at the garrison houses of John Sheldon and Benoni Stebbins. One of the Sheldon sons escaped out a window and sped to Hatfield for assistance before the Indians battered down the door and killed or captured all of the defenders. At the Stebbins house, several men and women stood off the attackers throughout the battle. Finally the French and Indians withdrew, having massacred 38 settlers and taken 119 captives. (See WILLIAMS, JOHN, FAMILY OF.) Some one hundred citizens escaped.

In June 1710 Deerfield was attacked by 180 Indians, led by a Frenchman. The citizens, many of whom had recently been redeemed from captivity, resisted so bravely that the raiders withdrew after killing 1 man and wounding 3 or 4.

(S. A. Drake, Border Wars of New England; Francis Parkman, A Half-Century of Conflict; Herbert Milton Sylvester, Indian Wars of New England, III.)

DEFIANCE, FORT. Gen. Anthony Wayne, on his way to punish the northwestern tribes at the Battle of Fallen Timbers, stopped at the junction of the Auglaize and Maumee rivers and built Fort Defiance in the very heart of hostile Indian country. The work began on August 8, 1794, and a strong stockade was completed within eight days.

After defeating the Indians at Fallen Timbers, Wayne's army returned to Fort Defiance on August 27. Warriors watched the fort from the surrounding wilderness and killed several soldiers in work parties outside the walls, but they never made any attempt to assault the stockade which had been its name because Wayne had defied "the English, Indians, and all the devils in hell to take it."

(Thomas Boyd, Mad Anthony Wayne; Theodore Roosevelt, The Winning of the West, V.)

DEKANISORA, ONONDAGA CHIEF. Dekanisora, an outstanding Onondaga orator, served as Iroquois speaker during negotiations with both French and English officials during the seventeenth and eighteenth centuries. In 1688 he was captured by Chief Adario in an attempt to disrupt Iroquois-French negotiations, but was quickly released as a gesture of friendship. He died at Albany in 1730 while negotiating a treaty.

(F. W. Hodge, ed., Handbook of American Indians, I; Frederick J. Dockstader, Great North American Indians.)

DEKAURY, CHOUKELEA, WINNEBAGO CHIEF. Choukelea Dekaury (Spoon Decorah) was the son of a French trader, Joseph des Caris, and the important Winnebago female chief Glory-in-the-Morning. Born in 1730 and raised on Doty Island (near the present Menasha, Wisconsin), he was a great war chief during conflicts with the Chippewas, but he generally remained friendly to white people. He played an important part in negotiating the treaty of June 3, 1816, at St. Louis, and died a short time afterward.

"Spoon Decorah was the founder of the great Decorah family of Winnebago, who to this day are influential among the tribe."-- Louise Phelps Kellogg.

(F. W. Hodge, ed., Handbook of American Indians, I; Louise Phelps Kellogg, The British Régime in Wisconsin and the Northwest.)

DEKAURY, KONOKA, WINNEBAGO CHIEF. The son of Chief Choukelea Dekaury, Konoka was born in 1747 and succeeded his father as Winnebago chief in 1816. Unlike his father, he participated in white men's wars, fighting against the Americans in the attack on Fort

Stephenson and in the Battle of the Thames. After the War of 1812, however, he chose to live in peace, signing the Treaty of Prairie du Chien on August 19, 1825. He avoided participation in the Winnebago War of 1827, but, he was held for a time as a hostage by the whites. He died on April 20, 1836.

(F. W. Hodge, ed., Handbook of American Indians, I.)

DELAWARE INDIANS. The Delaware (Lenni Lenape), an important Algonquian tribe, occupied all of New Jersey and portions of New York, Pennsylvania and Delaware at the time of initial European contact about 1524. Respected as the ancestor (grandfather) tribe by all of the Algonquians, they had a population estimated at 6,000 in 1600.

The Dutch established trading posts in the Delaware country early in the seventeenth century, and the tribe quickly adopted many aspects of European culture. Although they exhibited a generally peaceful demeanor they engaged in several conflicts with the Dutch on the Hudson during the mid-seventeenth century, losing many of their people and having their villages destroyed. (See ESOPUS INDIANS.) For the most part they enjoyed peaceful relations with the Swedes and English during that period.

In 1682 the Delawares held their first council with William Penn, and, largely because of their instinctive hospitality, they permitted the establishment of his Quaker colony in their territory. They were conquered by the Iroquois about 1720, and white settlers began occupying their lands in such numbers that most of the Delawares began to move westward, arriving on the Allegheny by 1724, the Susquehanna by 1742, and the Ohio by 1751. (See PENN, WILLIAM; WALKING PURCHASE.) Bands remaining in the East gradually ceded most of their lands and became concentrated on reservations.

The militant Shawnees began merging with the Delawares west of the Allegheny Mountains about 1750, assisting them to free themselves of Iroquois domination, and encouraging them to favor the French in the colonial rivalry for the North American continent. By the outbreak of the French and Indian War, the Delawares had evolved into a powerful tribe with militaristic inclinations and a deep resentment of wrongs suffered at the hands of the English. The result was a series of devastating raids on Pennsylvania settlements. (See CAPTAIN JACOBS; SHINGAS; KITTANNING; GRANVILLE, FORT.) The eastern Delawares were drawn away from the French interest by concessions gained at the Treaty of Easton in 1758 (see TEDYUSCUNG), and the western bands by daring diplomacy (see POST, CHRISTIAN FREDERICK).

By the onset of the American Revolution, deep divisions had occurred among Delaware chiefs and bands over Indian-white relationships. Chief White Eyes kept the tribe neutral for three years, but eventually he espoused the American cause and sought to incorporate his people into the Union as a fourteenth state. (See WHITE EYES.) The Moravian missionaries had converted many Delawares to Christianity, and the massacre of these peaceful "praying Indians" by American militiamen in 1782, as well as the destruction of

Coshocton, resulted in attacks on frontier settlements by the militant Delawares led by Captain Pipe during the remainder of the war.

After the Revolution, the Delawares wandered westward in scattered bands. Those living in Indiana supported Tecumseh during the War of 1812. Some settled in Missouri and later moved southward into Arkansas and Texas. Others lived with the Iroquois in Canada. By 1835 many Delawares had concentrated on a reservation in Kansas, removing to Oklahoma after the Civil War. More than a thousand of their descendants live there today.

(Charles A. Hanna, The Wilderness Trail; John R. Swanton, Indian Tribes of North America; William C. Sturtevant, ed., Handbook of North American Indians, XV; Paul A. W. Wallace, Indians in Pennsylvania; C. A. Weslager, The Delaware Indians.)

DELAWARE PROPHET. The Delaware Prophet Neolin was born about 1725 and lived on the Tuscarawas River in Ohio when he came to prominence as a prophet in 1759-60. Believed to be a psychopath by the whites, he conveyed his message by weeping and shouting, and he gained a tremendous following, for Indians "ascribed a special clairvoyance to madness."--Dale Van Every.

The Prophet charged that contact with white people led the Indians to sin. To attain salvation they must cleanse themselves by discarding every object that had ever been touched by a white man. If they heeded his message, the Prophet asserted, the Indians would defeat their enemies in an impending war and reclaim all of their lost hunting grounds.

The Prophet's claims had a profound effect upon the Delawares and other Indians who deeply resented the intrusion of white settlers upon their lands. His followers threw away goods obtained from traders, returned to the use of the bow and arrow, clothed themselves in animal skins, and rid themselves of liquor contamination by the use of a purgative drink. Some of them became wandering disciples, spreading his message to distant tribes.

When Pontiac heard of the Prophet's teachings he realized that he could use them to promote his own plans to make war on the whites. He became an advocate of the Prophet's philosophy, but he altered it slightly in order to condemn the British while holding fast to Indian friendship with the French. When Pontiac attacked the British posts in 1763, many of the Prophet's followers were among his most aggressive warriors. After Pontiac's war failed to expel the whites from the Indian country, the Prophet lost credibility and faded into oblivion.

(Frederick J. Dockstader, Great North American Indians; Randolph C. Downes, Council Fires on the Upper Ohio; Howard H. Peckham, Pontiac and the Indian Uprising; Dale Van Every, Forth to the Wilderness.)

DENONVILLE, JACQUES RENE DE see BRISAY, JACQUES RENE DE, MARQUIS DE DENONVILLE

DERMER, THOMAS. Thomas Dermer, an English seafarer, was

associated with Capt. John Smith, Ferdinando Gorges, and others in exploring the New England coast and rivers. In 1619, accompanied by the Indian, Squanto, who had been kidnapped and taken to England, Dermer was sent by Gorges to establish friendly relations and trade with the coastal tribes. At first he succeeded, but after Squanto left him to seek his own people, the Indians of Martha's Vineyard attacked Dermer and his crew, killing most of the Englishmen. Badly wounded, Dermer fled to his boat and escaped from the pursuing warriors. Near Long Island a second Indian attack impelled Dermer to set sail for Virginia. There he died of his wounds.

(Neal Salisbury, Manitou and Providence; C. A. Weslager, The English on the Delaware.)

DETROIT, MICHIGAN, INDIAN AFFAIRS. By the latter part of the eighteenth century, the French in Canada recognized the strategic importance of the strait that connects Lake Erie with Lake Huron in blocking the English from the Northwest, in curbing invasions by the Iroquois, and in providing a vital link in the proposed line of communications from the St. Lawrence to the mouth of the Mississippi. As a result, in 1686, they built a temporary stockaded post near the present site of Detroit.

In 1701 Antoine La Mothe Cadillac, in order to strengthen French claims to the region and to advance the fur trade, led 100 men to the site, constructed Fort Pontchartrain du Détroit, and invited the tribes of the Great Lakes region to establish villages nearby. This concentration of Indians led to intertribal hostilities that threatened to engulf the French fort.

In 1712 the Fox Indians, perhaps incited by the English, determined to destroy Detroit. They burned buildings outside the palisade, but the commandant, the Sieur Dubuisson, and his 30 men held the fort for 18 days until a large force of friendly Indians (Illinois, Missouris, Osages, Ottawas, and Potawatomis) arrived and drove the besieging Foxes and Mascoutens a few miles above the fort. There the hostiles were surrounded and attacked for 23 days by the French and their Indian allies before the survivors surrendered, only to be brought to the fort as slaves.

For the next 35 years Detroit grew in importance as a French military post and center of the Indian trade. During King George's War, the English attempted to incite the Indians to seize the fort, and, in 1747, the Huron chief, Nicolas, determined to make the attempt. His plans were betrayed by an Indian woman, however, and Nicolas had to content himself with waylaying French trappers approaching the fort.

In 1760, during the French and Indian War, a British military force took command of Detroit. The Indians did not resist, for they needed trade goods, and they failed to realize that the victorious Englishmen assumed ownership of their lands. When they learned the true state of affairs they joined the firebrand, Pontiac, in attacking all of the British posts in the West.

During 1763, Pontiac, after failing to seize Fort Detroit by intrigue (see GLADWIN, HENRY), besieged it for 15 months and inflicted heavy casualties upon British forces who sallied forth to attack the Indian camps (see BLOODY RUN, BATTLE OF). Col. John Bradstreet arrived at Detroit during the summer of 1764 and Pontiac's forces withdrew.

Fort Detroit served as the bastion of British power in the West during the American Revolution. Frequently, Gov. Henry Hamilton dispatched Indian war parties to attack American frontier settlements, and he received a large number of captives at Detroit until he, himself, was taken prisoner by George Rogers Clark. Clark's conquest of the Illinois was intended to be a preliminary action leading to the seizure of Detroit, but he was unable to recruit a sufficient force to make the attempt.

The end of the Revolution did not result in timely acquisition of Detroit by the Americans. The British retained the post until 1796, using it as a rallying point for resistance to American expansion during the Indian wars of that period.

During the War of 1812, Gen. William Hull invaded Canada from his headquarters at Detroit, but, becoming alarmed over the security of his base, he retreated and surrendered Detroit to Gen. Isaac Brock and his British and Indian forces on August 16, 1812. As a result, Detroit remained under British control until 1813.

(A. M. Gibson, The Kickapoos; Louise Phelps Kellogg, The British Regime in Wisconsin and the Northwest; Francis Parkman, A Half-Century of Conflict; Howard H. Peckham, Pontiac and the Indian Uprising; Dale Van Every, Forth to the Wilderness.)

DETROIT, MICHIGAN, TREATIES OF. On November 17, 1807, Gov. William Hull negotiated a treaty at Detroit with the Wyandot, Potawatomi, Ottawa, and Chippewa Indians, securing a large cession of land in Michigan and Ohio. The Indians received cash and gifts valued at $10,000.

On January 14, 1837, Henry R. Schoolcraft persuaded Chippewa chiefs to cede more than 100,000 acres in Michigan. The Indians received the proceeds of the sale of their lands to settlers, and they agreed to remove from the state.

On July 31, 1855, George W. Manypenny and Henry C. Gilbert conferred with Ottawa and Chippewa chiefs at Detroit. The United States allotted 80 acres to Indian families and 40 acres to single persons. Tribal organization was eliminated.

(Charles J. Kappler, ed., Indian Affairs: Laws and Treaties, II.)

DEVIL'S HOLE MASSACRE. On September 14, 1763, one of the bloodiest battles of Pontiac's War occurred near Niagara Falls, New York, at a place called Devil's Hole. It began when a wagon train from Fort Schlosser, escorted by 30 troopers, rode into an ambush at Devil's Hole. The Seneca Indians burst from concealment in heavy woods and pinned the train against the edge of the abyss. Some of the mules stampeded and dragged men and wagons over the brink. Soldiers attempting to make a stand were cut down by heavy musket fire or overrun and tomahawked by hordes of warriors. Only 2 escaped.

The sound of battle was heard by 80 British soldiers at Lewis-town, New York. Rushing to the rescue, they fell into a new am-bush not far from Devil's Hole, and half of them died in the first fire. The survivors engaged the charging Senecas in hand-to-hand combat, most of them being overwhelmed by superior numbers. Seventy-two soldiers were slain, while a few fled to safety at Fort Niagara.

(Howard H. Peckham, Pontiac and the Indian Uprising.)

DE VRIES, DAVID P. David P. De Vries, a Dutch navigator, was among the earliest explorers of the Delaware River region. In 1631 he established the colony of Zwaanendael for the West India Company near present Lewes, Delaware. After he returned to Europe, the en-tire settlement was wiped out by Indians. (See ZWAANENDAEL COLONY MASSACRE.)

When De Vries returned to his colony and learned that the 30 settlers were dead he decided to seek peace with the Indians instead of revenge. The chief accepted his invitation to hold a council and, after concluding a peace treaty, departed greatly pleased that no ac-cusation had been made against him for the destruction of the colony.

In 1633 De Vries visited Fort Nassau. During the journey he narrowly escaped death at the hands of Delaware Indians. Disre-garding the incident, he concluded a permanent peace with the bands of that area.

While at Fort Amsterdam in 1643, De Vries volunteered to ac-company a Canarsee chief to his village on Long Island to condole for the massacre of 80 peaceful Indians at Pavonia by the Dutch. He persuaded the chiefs of the offended tribes to negotiate at New Am-sterdam, and a peace treaty was signed on March 25.

(E. B. O'Callaghan, History of New Netherland, I; John E. Pomfret, The Province of West New Jersey.)

DICKSON, ROBERT. Col. Robert Dickson, a British trader, gained great influence over the tribes of the Great Lakes and Upper Mis-sissippi as early as 1786. In 1787 he served as interpreter at a major conference at Mackinac, and he rapidly rose thereafter as one of the region's foremost Indian diplomats. In 1797 he married the sister of a Sioux chief, and he attempted with some success to mo-nopolize the trade of that tribe.

Convinced by 1811 that war with the Americans was inevitable, Dickson gave all of his trade goods to the Indians near Prairie du Chien in a successful bid for their support. In the summer of 1812 he led 140 warriors to join the British in capturing the U.S. post at Mackinac. In September, while recruiting a large Indian force to help the British attack Detroit, he discovered that American sur-vivors of the Fort Dearborn massacre were held in captivity, and, with the help of a French trader, he secured the release of more than twenty men, women, and children. Having been appointed British Indian agent, he recruited warriors for attacks on Forts Meigs and Stephenson, but he ordered the Indians to perpetrate no more mas-sacres such as those that had occurred at Fort Dearborn and at the Raisin River.

During the winter of 1813-14, large numbers of Indians assembled at Lake Winnebago to participate in a planned spring offensive. By late spring 1814, Dickson and Robert McKay sent war parties to strike the settlements in Illinois and to raid along the Missouri. In July 1814 Dickson's Indians attacked a large flotilla near the mouth of the Rock River, killing 100 Americans. They continued their raids after the close of the War of 1812. Dickson died in 1823.

Robert Dickson, despite his efforts to curb the cruelties of his followers, is depicted in folklore as a blood-thirsty monster. Clarence Walworth Alvord has characterized him as "adroit but shifty, the despair of every military man but beloved by the Indians."

(Clarence Walworth Alvord, The Illinois Country; A. M. Gibson, The Kickapoos; William T. Hagan, The Sac and Fox Indians; Louise Phelps Kellogg, The British Régime in Wisconsin and the Northwest; Milo M. Quaife, Checagou.)

DIETZ, WILLIAM, FAMILY OF. Capt. William Dietz commanded a militia company at Berne, New York, during the American Revolution. In 1781 he became such a thorn in the side of Tories and Indians that they determined to exact revenge upon him and his entire family. A raiding party slipped into Berne and captured Dietz in his own home. They tied him to a gatepost and murdered his father, mother, wife, and each of his children while he was compelled to watch the atrocities. Then they marched him to Niagara and executed him.

(William L. Stone, Border Wars of the Revolution, I; Francis Whiting Halsey, The Old New York Frontier.)

DODGE, HENRY, INDIAN RELATIONS. Henry Dodge was born at Vincennes, Indiana, on October 12, 1782. He grew up on the frontier in Kentucky, Illinois, and Missouri, engaged in lead mining, and attained the rank of major-general in the Missouri militia. Having lost five uncles in Indian wars, his advice in handling the tribes was "first give them presents--then give them lead."

After serving as sheriff at Ste. Genevieve for 16 years, Dodge turned his attention to hunting hostile Indians during the War of 1812. Afterward he moved to Michigan Territory (present state of Wisconsin) and led a company of mounted militia in the Winnebago War of 1827. His greatest claim to fame as an Indian fighter occurred during the Black Hawk War of 1832. With 150 mounted rangers he patrolled the area north of the Rock River to prevent Black Hawk from breaking through to the Mississippi. He won a bloody battle with a Kickapoo war party on June 16, 1832, at the Pecatonica River. (See PECATONICA, BATTLE OF.) In addition, he played an important part in the battle with Black Hawk's forces attempting to cross the Mississippi on August 3. (See BAD AXE, BATTLE OF.) This engagement ended the Black Hawk War.

Dodge's record in the Black Hawk War resulted in his commission as major in the U.S. Army and an assignment to guard the upper Mississippi Valley. In 1833 he was promoted to colonel of dragoons.

To establish friendly relations between Plains tribes and Indians from the East, he led his troopers to the Pawnee villages on Red River in 1834 and to the Colorado Rockies in 1835. Elected governor of Wisconsin Territory in 1836, he obtained several land cessions from the tribes of that region. He died in 1867.

(Cecil Eby, That Disgraceful Affair, the Black Hawk War; Grant Foreman, Advancing the Frontier.)

DONGAN, THOMAS, INDIAN RELATIONS. Col. Thomas Dongan, an Irish nobleman, served as Governor of New York from 1683 until 1688. He instituted a vigorous Indian policy designed to wrest the fur trade from the French Canadians and to protect New York's interests against encroachment by Pennsylvania and other colonies. It appears, also, that he attempted to promote his own interests by obtaining a personal grant of land on the Susquehanna from the Iroquois and persuading the Indians to prevent Pennsylvanians from entering his domain.

In October 1683 Dongan conferred with the Iroquois chiefs, claimed New York provincial control of their lands south of Lake Ontario as a protectorate, and asserted the authority of the English to establish forts near their villages. In addition, he and Virginia officials negotiated peace between the Iroquois and southern tribes. As a result, raids that had resulted in the deaths of white settlers as well as their Indian neighbors at the hands of the Iroquois ceased for several years.

In 1684 Dongan authorized English traders to penetrate the Great Lakes region. They went as far as Mackinac, where they offered better prices for furs than the Indians had received from the French. The Indians invited them to return, but the French intercepted them on their voyage homeward and confiscated their furs. (See ROSEBOOM, JOHANNES.)

In 1687, when the French attacked the Seneca Indians, Dongan dispatched other warriors to resist the invasion. Afterward the Iroquois besieged Montreal, and French officials charged Dongan with arming and inciting them. Dongan denied the accusation and used his influence to break the siege.

Dongan believed that French priests among the Iroquois were intriguing against his administration. He asked the tribes to expel them and to accept English missionaries in their stead. His effort was not entirely successful, but by 1687 some of the Jesuit missions were abandoned.

Sir Edmund Andros succeeded Dongan as governor in August 1688. Dongan lived on Long Island until 1690, when he fled from the colony during the Leisler Rebellion.

(Allan W. Trelease, Indian Affairs in Colonial New York; Francis Whiting Halsey, The Old New York Frontier; Frank H. Severance, An Old Frontier of France; Francis Parkman, Count Frontenac and New France Under Louis XIV.)

DOVER, NEW HAMPSHIRE, MASSACRE see COCHECO, NEW HAMPSHIRE, MASSACRE

DREUILLETTES, GABRIEL see DRUILLETTES, GABRIEL

DREW, THOMAS, FAMILY OF. The Abnaki Indians destroyed the
village of Oyster River, New Hampshire, on July 18, 1694. More
than a hundred men, women, and children were captured or killed.
Among those marched to Canada were the newlyweds Mr. and Mrs.
Thomas Drew. Compelled to separate from his wife when the raiders
assigned prisoners to various bands, Drew was redeemed after two
years in enemy hands. Mrs. Drew endured a longer and more difficult captivity. On the long journey, during a snow storm, she gave
birth to a child. The Indians murdered the baby when the mother
was unable to feed it. She was held four years at Norridgewock,
surviving unbelievable hardships before being permitted to return to
her husband.
    (Jeremy Belknap, History of New Hampshire, I.)

DRUILLETTES, GABRIEL. Gabriel Druillettes, a Jesuit priest, was
born in 1610 and arrived in Canada to serve as a missionary in 1643.
Living first among the Indians of the St. Lawrence, he moved on to
the Abnaki villages in Maine in 1646, where he remained almost twenty
years. He struggled successfully with Indian sorcerers, cured the
sick, converted many Abnakis to Christianity, and was adopted into
the tribe.
    Druillettes proved to be an effective diplomat. In 1651 he
persuaded the Abnakis and Mahicans to unite forces with the French
in fighting the Iroquois. He got along well with the Plymouth settlers, visiting Puritan towns from time to time as Abnaki agent, and
always receiving a warm welcome. He was unsuccessful, however,
in persuading the English colonists to join forces in opposing the
Iroquois.
    In 1671 Father Druillettes assumed the direction of the Jesuit
mission at Sault Ste. Marie. After achieving great success as a
missionary there he died at Quebec in 1681.
    (Emma H. Blair, The Indian Tribes of the Upper Mississippi
Valley and the Region of the Great Lakes; Francis Parkman, The
Jesuits in North America.)

DUBLET, TOM see NEPANET, TOM, NIPMUC CHIEF

DUCOIGNE, JEAN BAPTISTE, KASKASKIA CHIEF. Jean Baptiste
Ducoigne, a French-Kaskaskia half-blood chief, developed a prefer-
ence for white manners and customs. William Henry Harrison noted
that "Ducoigne's long and well-proved friendship for the United
States has gained him the hatred of all the other chiefs and ought
to be an inducement with us to provide as well for his happiness,
as for his safety."
    Ducoigne signed the treaties of August 7 and 13, 1803, at
Vincennes. As a result he received a house and 100 acres of land.
He died about 1832.
    (F. W. Hodge, Handbook of American Indians, I.)

DUDLEY MASSACRE. During the British and Indian siege of Fort
Meigs in April and May 1813, a force of Kentuckians attempted to
relieve the garrison by capturing the enemy cannon. Led by Lt.
Col. William Dudley, a detachment of 800 men attacked the enemy
camp and spiked the cannon. Afterward, Dudley decided to disregard orders to retreat to the fort. Most of his men were captured,
and 40 were murdered before Tecumseh could compel his braves to
stop molesting the hated "Long Knives."
    (R. David Edmunds, The Shawnee Prophet.)

DUMMER'S WAR. Dummer's War was instigated in 1724 by Canadian
officials in an attempt to employ the Abnaki Indians to disrupt English settlement of Maine and Vermont. The Abnakis launched large
scale attacks on the most easterly English outposts in 1724 and 1725,
but they were repulsed with heavy losses at a fort on the St.
George River. In retaliation, the English destroyed the Abnaki
settlements of Old Town and Norridgewock. (See NORRIDGEWOCK
INDIANS.)
    (Francis Parkman, A Half-Century of Conflict; Herbert Milton
Sylvester, Indian Wars of New England, III.)

DUNLAP'S STATION RAID. After Harmar's defeat, the jubilant Indians launched attacks on the Ohio settlements during the winter
of 1790-91. In January, near Cincinnati, they raided Dunlap's
Station. The settlers, supported by 18 soldiers from Fort Washington, stood off Simon Girty's 300 Miami warriors, but before the
raiders departed they burned Abner Hunt, a captive, to death just
outside rifle range of the stockade.
    (Dale Van Every, Ark of Empire.)

DUNSTABLE, MASSACHUSETTS, RAID. On July 3, 1706, a war
party of Abnaki Indians from St. Francis surprised the garrison of
20 men at Dunstable. The soldiers had just been out on a scout
and were celebrating the successful return by "taking off their
equipments, and laying aside their arms ... (and) indulging in a
carousal in true barrack-room fashion, to make amends for the fa-
tigues of the day." Late in the evening Mr. and Mrs. John Cummings went outside the stockade to milk and were greeted by gunfire. Mrs. Cummings was killed and her husband captured. Afterward, the Indians "rushed through the open gate into the house before the astonished soldiers could have time to seize their arms....
A furious hand-to-hand fight took place, in which such of the soldiers
as had not lost their heads laid about them with chairs, clubs, or
whatever else they could lay hands upon, with such effect as finally to clear the house of assailants."--Samuel Adams Drake.
    "The Indians who were as much surprised as the soldiers ...
yielded the house, defeated by one quarter their number of unarmed
men."--Herbert Milton Sylvester.
    (Samuel Adams Drake, The Border Wars of New England; Her-
bert Milton Sylvester, Indian Wars of New England, III.)

DUQUESNE, FORT. In 1754 the Ohio Company began construction of a fort at the present site of Pittsburgh, Pennsylvania. Before its completion, however, it was captured by French forces who constructed Fort Duquesne at the strategic spot where the Allegheny and Monongahela rivers unite to comprise the Ohio. The fort was square shaped, each side about 80 feet long, and strengthened by protruding bastions at the corners. The strongest fortress in the region, it served as French headquarters for the Ohio, but the size of the garrison fluctuated with the seasons. There usually was a large Indian encampment near the fort, making it possible for some of the soldiers to return to Canada during the fall and winter.

The Virginians made an attempt to capture Fort Duquesne in 1754, but George Washington's defeat at the Great Meadows on July 3 brought the expedition to an end. (See NECESSITY, FORT.) A much more powerful force of British Regulars marched against Fort Duquesne in 1755, but they were crushed on July 9 by French and Indian forces. (See BRADDOCK'S DEFEAT.) Finally, in 1758, Fort Duquesne was destroyed by the French on November 24, when they lacked sufficient forces to withstand an assault by the John Forbes Expedition. The English built Fort Pitt at the site. (See FORBES EXPEDITION; PITT, FORT.)

(William A. Hunter, Forts on the Pennsylvania Frontier; Howard H. Peckham, Pontiac and the Indian Uprising; Dale Van Every, Forth to the Wilderness.)

DURHAM, NEW HAMPSHIRE, RAIDS   see   OYSTER RIVER, NEW HAMPSHIRE, RAIDS

DUSTIN, HANNAH, CAPTIVITY OF   see   DUSTIN, THOMAS, FAMILY OF

DUSTIN, THOMAS, FAMILY OF. On March 15, 1697, Indians attacked the Thomas Dustin family near Haverhill, Massachusetts. Mrs. Dustin, having recently given birth to a child, was in bed under the care of a nurse, Mary Neff. Thomas Dustin, at work in the fields, saw the Indians coming and realized that he could not reach the house in time to defend his wife. Shouting to his seven children who were playing nearby to run toward the garrison, he mounted his horse and kept between them and the Indians, riding and dismounting in turn so as to provide defense and cover until he followed them to safety inside the pickets.

The Indians seized Hannah and Mary, murdered the infant, and withdrew into the wilderness. They camped on an island near Concord, then divided into several parties, and most of them departed. The two women were retained by an Indian family consisting of two warriors, three women, and seven children. Also left at the scene was a white boy, Samuel Leonardson, who had been held in captivity a long time.

Hannah Dustin was determined not to spend her life in captivity. During the night she devised a plan with the boy and the nurse to slaughter the Indians as they slept. They seized tomahawks

and struck at the Indians' heads, completing the deadly work before
their captors could awake and arise. Then they scalped the Indians,
took a canoe, paddled downstream to Haverhill, and claimed a bounty
for the scalps.

(Samuel Adams Drake, Border Wars of New England; Herbert
Milton Sylvester, Indian Wars of New England, II; Alden T. Vaughan
and Edward W. Clark, eds., Puritans Among the Indians.)

-E-

EASTON, PENNSYLVANIA, TREATIES OF. An important series of
conferences intended to draw the Delawares, Shawnees, and Senecas
away from their support of the French took place at Easton, Pennsylvania, between 1756 and 1758. Beginning in July 1756 Pennsylvania governor William Denny, George Croghan, Conrad Weiser, and
several influential Quakers persuaded Chief Tedyuscung, leader of
the eastern Delawares, to restore peaceful relations with the English.

Easton was the scene of renewed negotiations during the summer of 1757, resulting in a peace treaty with the eastern Delawares
and other tribes. Although factionalism among Pennsylvania leaders
threatened to disrupt the proceedings, Croghan managed the meetings
skillfully. The English agreed to establish trading posts among the
tribes, and the Indians consented to submit land disputes to Sir
William Johnson for disposition. The treaty failed to end the Indian
war, however, for the Ohio Delawares continued their raids.

In 1758, at the request of Gen. John Forbes, a crucial council
was held at Easton to settle Indian grievances over land purchases.
On October 8, some 500 Delaware, Shawnee, and Iroquois Indians began negotiations with Gov. Francis Bernard of New Jersey in addition
to Governor Denny and other Pennsylvania officials. Croghan, supported by the Mohawk chiefs, dominated the conference, and on
October 26, the Treaty of Easton was signed. The governments of
the two colonies paid the Indians to satisfy land claims. More im-
portantly, negotiators returned to the Indians much of the Delaware
and Shawnee hunting grounds sold by the Iroquois during the Albany
Congress of 1754. The Indians agreed to release all white captives,
to live at peace with the English, and to urge the tribes on the Ohio
to do the same.

The Treaty of Easton was of great importance in withdrawing
Indian assistance from the French, a development that facilitated
Forbes's successful march to Fort Duquesne. (See POST, CHRISTIAN
FREDERICK.)

(Samuel Smith, The History of the Colony of Nova-Caesaria,
or New Jersey; Albert W. Volwiler, George Croghan and the Westward Movement; Paul A. W. Wallace, Conrad Weiser.)

ECORSE RIVER COUNCIL. On April 27, 1763, Pontiac the fiery Indian patriot summoned chiefs of the Great Lakes region to a council
at the Ecorse River, eight miles south of Detroit. He urged them to
unite to "exterminate from our land this nation whose only object is

our death." The chiefs arose as one in shouting approval, and Pontiac's War was underway.

(Francis Parkman, Conspiracy of Pontiac; Dale Van Every, Forth to the Wilderness.)

EDWARD, FORT. Fort Edward was built in 1755 on the Hudson River, not far from the south end of Lake George, to guard the trail to Montreal and to protect Albany from invasion by the French and Indians from Crown Point. On July 23, 1757, a French officer, Paul Marin, led a force of Canadians and Indians to scout around Fort Edward. They encountered soldiers near the fort, slew 32 men, and took 1 captive.

During the American Revolution, Fort Edward was abandoned when threatened by the invasion of Gen. John Burgoyne.

(Arthur Pound, Johnson of the Mohawks; T. Wood Clarke, The Bloody Mohawk.)

EDWARD AUGUSTUS, FORT   see   GREEN BAY, WISCONSIN

EDWARDS, JONATHAN, INDIAN MINISTRY. Rev. Jonathan Edwards, eminent eighteenth-century Congregational clergyman and metaphysician, and one of America's most forceful and controversial preachers, possessed little "aptitude nor training for the teaching of savages," but he accepted a post among the Stockbridge Indians after his dismissal as pastor at Northampton, Massachusetts, in 1750. The mission, which he had helped to establish in 1734, served some 218 Stockbridge Indians and several white families.

Expecting to enjoy a better opportunity there to reflect and to write, Edwards soon discovered that he faced different, but no less formidable, problems at his new location beyond the frontier line. He could neither speak nor understand the Indian languages, and members of his flock could not communicate with him. Having little interest in native cultures, he intended to transform Indians into Englishmen as quickly as possible by sending children to live with white families. Although most of the Stockbridges had been baptized, other Indians who camped near the mission to obtain food and trade goods had no inclination to embrace Christianity. The Mohawks, in particular, were so hostile that in 1754 the mission was transformed into a fortress.

Miscast as a missionary, Edwards was relieved to resign the Stockbridge position in 1757 to become president of Princeton University.

(Ola Elizabeth Winslow, Jonathan Edwards.)

EDWARDS, NINIAN, INDIAN RELATIONS. Ninian Edwards, a young lawyer from Kentucky, was appointed Governor of Illinois Territory in 1809. Believing the territory to be seriously threatened by Indians at the outbreak of the War of 1812, he organized an expedition against the Kickapoos, Miamis, and Potawatomis in the autumn of 1812. Backed by Col. William Russell and three companies of regulars, he led the Illinois militia against the villages around Lake Peoria. His forces surprised a large Kickapoo village on October 18, killed 24 Indians, and drove the survivors into a swamp. Soon afterward he destroyed a deserted Miami village. On November 11, he captured a Kickapoo village on the Wabash. These victories enabled Edwards to recruit more than 1,500 mounted volunteers, a sufficiently strong force to cow most of the remaining Indians into keeping the peace.

The attitude of Ninian Edwards toward Indians is revealed in a letter he wrote early in 1813: "The truth is that all the different tribes of Indians view our increase of population and approximation to their villages and hunting grounds with a jealous eye, are predisposed to hostility and are restrained only by fear from committing aggressions. I make no calculation upon their friendship, nor upon anything else but the terror with which our measures may inspire them, and therefore I am now and long have been opposed to temporizing with them."

(Emma H. Blair, The Indian Tribes of the Upper Mississippi Valley and the Region of the Great Lakes; A. M. Gibson, The Kickapoos; Clarence Walworth Alvord, The Illinois Country.)

EDWARDSVILLE, ILLINOIS, TREATIES OF. On September 25, 1818, at Edwardsville, Illinois, Ninian Edwards and Auguste Chouteau negotiated a treaty with the Peoria, Kaskaskia, Michigamea, Cahokia, and Tamaroa tribes, trading them land near Ste. Genevieve, Missouri, for their homes in Illinois.

On July 30, 1819, at Edwardsville, Auguste Chouteau and Benjamin Stephenson negotiated a treaty with the Kickapoo Indians. The tribe ceded more than 13 million acres between the Illinois and Wabash rivers in exchange for a tract on the Osage River in Missouri, and an annuity of $2,000 for 15 years.

(Grant Foreman, The Last Trek of the Indians; A. M. Gibson, The Kickapoos.)

EEL RIVER INDIANS. The Eel River Indians, a group of Miami bands that had fled to the Wea country to avoid being engulfed by white settlers, organized a temporary subtribe at Thorntown, Indiana, where they received a small reservation. In 1828 they sold the reservation and reunited with the Miamis on the Wabash.

(Bert Anson, The Miami Indians; F. W. Hodge, ed., Handbook of American Indians, I.)

EGEREMET, KENNEBEC CHIEF. Egeremet, characterized by Francis Parkman as "one of the terrors of the English border," led an Abnaki attack on New Dartmouth (New Castle, Maine) in 1689 in retaliation for the seizure of 16 Indians at Saco. Egeremet captured Henry Smith, Edward Taylor, and their families and marched them away to Teconnet. In June 1692 Egeremet led an attack on Wells, but 400 warriors failed to overcome the determined defenders. (See WELLS, MAINE.)

Egeremet was killed outside Fort Pemaquid under a flag of truce in February 1696. (See CHUBB, PASCHO.)

(Samuel Adams Drake, Border Wars of New England; Francis Parkman, Count Frontenac and New France Under Louis XIV.)

ELEKENS, JACQUES. Jacques Elekens, a Dutch West India Company trader, made an inadvertent discovery in 1622 that initiated an important innovation in Indian-European relations. He kidnapped a Pequot chief and threatened to behead him if his followers failed to offer a large ransom. The Pequots redeemed him with wampum. Although the company removed Elekens from North America for this act, they used his discovery of the value of wampum to greatly expand their trade with inland tribes lacking access to the highly prized shell beads that served as Indian currency.

(Neal Salisbury, Manitou and Providence.)

ELIOT, JOHN. John Eliot, often called "the Apostle to the Indians," was born in Essex County, England, in 1604. He was educated at Cambridge, embraced Puritan theology, and emigrated to New England in 1631. Appointed pastor at Roxbury, a post that he held throughout his lifetime, he displayed a sincere interest in the welfare of neighboring Indian tribes.

About 1640, with the assistance of a Montauk Indian named Cockenoe, Eliot began a study of Indian languages with intent to Christianize all of the tribes of New England. Soon afterward he began visiting Indian villages, in some cases at the risk of his life. On one occasion a hostile chief threatened him with a knife, only to be admonished by the imperturbable preacher that "I am about the work of the great God, and he is with me, so that I fear not all the sachems of the country."

Eliot began preaching to the Algonquians in their own langauges in 1646. He made such a profound impression that many Indian parents agreed to send their children to Christian schools. He soon discovered, however, that Indians were reluctant to live in English communities, so he began establishing "Praying Indian" towns beyond the line of frontier settlement. The first of these was built at Natick in 1651, and it proved to be so successful that 13 others were established by 1674. While subject to Massachusetts law, these towns were governed to a great degree by the Indians themselves. By the outbreak of King Philip's War they contained more than a thousand converts.

With the assistance of Cockenoe, Eliot began preparing a translation of the Bible into Algonquian. The New Testament was published in 1661 and the Old Testament in 1663. This impressive scholarly achievement, and Eliot's other religious writings, are of great historical and ethnological value, for not only was the Eliot Bible the first published in America, but it provides about all the information available on the Massachuset Indian language.

The outbreak of King Philip's War disrupted Eliot's missionary activities. Although the "Praying Indians" were faithful Christians, the Puritans ignored Eliot's pleas and compelled them to live in concentration camps. Eliot did all that he could to assist them, and, finally, he came under suspicion himself when he supported Captain Tom, an Indian accused of raiding the settlements, and comforted him on his way to the gallows. In addition to attempting to protect the "Praying Indians," Eliot denounced the Puritan practice of exiling

New England natives into West Indian slavery, pointing out that de-
portation would deny them the opportunity to become Christians.

When the war ended, Eliot learned that the Christian Indians
had lost faith in Puritan good intentions. Four Praying Indian towns
survived, but the inhabitants gradually returned to the wilderness.
The saddened missionary died in 1690.

(Ola Elizabeth Winslow, John Eliot, "Apostle to the Indians";
Alden T. Vaughan, New England Frontier; Martin Moore, Memoirs of
the Life and Character of Rev. John Eliot.)

ELLIOTT, MATTHEW. Matthew Elliott, an Irishman who arrived in
Pennsylvania in 1761 to enter the Indian trade, married a Shawnee
woman and lived with that tribe for many years. He first came to
prominence as an Indian diplomat during Dunmore's War of 1774. As
a messenger from Chief Cornstalk, he arranged the peace treaty of
Camp Charlotte.

Upon the onset of the American Revolution, Elliott was captured
by Wyandot Indians and delivered to the British at Detroit. Convinc-
ing them that he supported the Crown, he was released to return to
Pittsburgh, where he induced Alexander McKee and Simon Girty to
flee to the British. These three veteran frontiersmen became leaders
of the British Indian Service, and, according to Reuben Gold Thwaites,
renegades largely responsible for attacks on the settlements of Pennsylvania, Virginia, and Kentucky. Especially noteworthy was their
role as Indian leaders in Bird's invasion of 1780.

In 1781 Elliott led an Indian force to the Moravian mission at
Gnadenhutten to admonish the Christian Indians and their teachers to
shun the American cause. When he departed, the missionaries warned
the citizens of Wheeling to prepare for an attack. After the expedition failed, Elliott returned to Gnadenhutten, destroyed the mission,
and compelled the missionaries to remove to Detroit.

In 1782 Elliott was active in assaults upon Kentucky settlements.
As a member of Capt. William Caldwell's Indian army, he participated
in the siege of Bryan's Station and in the bloody Battle of Blue
Licks.

After the Revolutionary War ended, Elliott resumed his life as
a trader. Because the British refused to surrender their northwestern posts, he continued to serve them as an Indian agent, and
his trading post at Malden was a popular gathering place for the
tribes. In 1810, he provided arms for Tecumseh and encouraged Indian attacks on American settlements.

With the outbreak of the War of 1812, Elliott, although he was
about 70 years old, resumed active partisan leadership as Superintendent of the Indian Department. In August 1812 he commanded 600
Indians who assisted the British in compelling the Americans to surrender Detroit. In January 1813 he led about 700 warriors in the
victory over General Winchester, and he was partially to blame for
failing to curb the Indians at the Raisin River Massacre. In April
1813 he and Tecumseh led a large force of Indians in an unsuccessful
attack on Fort Meigs. He commanded the Indians in August 1813 in
the attempt to capture Fort Stephenson. He and his Indians covered

Col. Henry Proctor's retreat from Detroit in September 1813 and they continued to fight the Americans at the Battle of the Thames after British troops fled. After that defeat, he brought 2,000 Indians to his property on Burlington Bay and provided for their needs to the best of his ability. In December 1813 he led the Indians in the British capture of Fort George, Lewiston, and Buffalo, on the Niagara frontier. These exertions in bitter cold weather made Elliott seriously ill, and he died on May 7, 1814.

(Reginald Horsman, Matthew Elliott, British Indian Agent.)

ENDICOTT, JOHN, EXPEDITION. In 1636 John Endicott led 90 Massachusetts men in boats to Block Island and to the Pequot Indian country to punish the natives for the murders of John Oldham and John Stone. He was instructed to "spare the women and children, but put all the men to the sword." Upon arrival at Block Island, a landing party was attacked by 50 warriors, but after shooting their arrows the Indians fled. Endicott burned their villages and crops, reembarked his men, and sailed on to the land of the powerful Pequot nation. After a council in which the Indians made it clear that they didn't want war, the Puritans attacked them and destroyed their homes, crops, and canoes. Kutshamokin, a chief who accompanied the expedition, killed and scalped a warrior, thus making the Pequot War inevitable. The other Pequots escaped into the woods. Afterward, Endicott returned to Boston without having lost a man.

(Richard Drinnon, Facing West; John W. DeForest, History of the Indians of Connecticut; Neal Salisbury, Manitou and Providence.)

EPANOW, MARTHA'S VINEYARD CHIEF. Epanow, a Martha's Vineyard sachem, was captured and transported to England in 1611 by Capt. Edward Harlow. Intended for use as a guide and translator by Sir Ferdinando Gorges in an attempt to colonize New England, Epanow deceived his masters by offering to pilot them to rich gold mines in his homeland.

In 1614 Gorges sent Epanow with Capt. Nicholas Hobson to Martha's Vineyard to obtain the gold. As they were about to land, Epanow shouted instructions to warriors on the shore, and while he leaped overboard and swam to safety they released a barrage of arrows at Hobson's crew. Hobson and several of his men were so severely wounded that they abandoned the expedition.

In 1620 Epanow and his followers attacked Capt. Thomas Dermer's crew attempting to land at Martha's Vineyard, killing most of the men and compelling the ship to depart for Virginia. The captain died soon afterward of 14 arrow wounds sustained in the affray.

In 1621 Epanow made his peace with the English by signing a treaty with Pilgrim leaders.

(Herbert Milton Sylvester, Indian Wars of New England, I; Neal Salisbury, Manitou and Providence.)

EPHRATAH, NEW YORK, RAIDS. Ephratah, a German settlement eight miles east of St. Johnsville, was attacked by an Iroquois war party on April 30, 1773, during a militia drill. A brief battle ensued, and several militiamen were killed before the Indians withdrew. A year later, raiders struck Ephratah again, killing or capturing several families and burning the village.

(T. Wood Clarke, The Bloody Mohawk.)

ERIE INDIANS. The Erie Indians, an Iroquoian tribe called the Cat Nation, lived south of Lake Erie at the time of initial European contact. They were numerous and powerful, but they had little contact with whites until after they were crushed and the survivors absorbed by the Five Nations in 1655-56.

(William C. Sturtevant, Handbook of North American Indians, XV; Paul A. W. Wallace, Indians in Pennsylvania.)

ESHKEBUGECOSHE, CHIPPEWA CHIEF see FLAT MOUTH, CHIPPEWA CHIEF

ESOPUS INDIANS. The Esopus Indians, a division of the Munsee Delawares, lived near the present site of Kingston, New York, during the period of Dutch colonization along the Hudson River. At first they enjoyed friendly relations, but the sale of intoxicants to the Indians led to hostilities in 1655. On September 15, while many of the Dutch were away trying to conquer New Sweden, a war party so large that it arrived at New Amsterdam in 64 canoes attacked the settlement in retaliation for the murder of an Indian woman slain by a Dutchman for stealing a few peaches. The Dutch counterattacked, killed 3 warriors, and drove the others away. As a result, the settlers near the Esopus villages abandoned their farms.

By 1658 settlement of the Esopus Indian region resumed, and trouble arose again because of the sale of liquor. On May 1, some intoxicated Indians murdered a Dutchman and compelled the settlers to destroy their crops. Gov. Peter Stuyvesant informed the chiefs that if they continued to make trouble he would retaliate by killing or enslaving their women and children. As a result, the Indians agreed to keep the peace, and they sold Stuyvesant land on which to establish a new town in their territory.

In September 1659 a conflict known as the first Esopus War erupted when 8 drunken Indians alarmed the settlers. When the Indians fell asleep, the settlers fired among them, killing some and compelling the survivors to flee. The infuriated Indians declared war on the Dutch, besieged their fort, and destroyed farms and livestock. Numerous Dutch captives were taken, about 10 of them being tortured to death. Stuyvesant led 200 settlers and friendly Indians to the relief of the fort, and peace was restored in November as the result of the work of Mohawk and Mahican intermediaries.

Stuyvesant aroused the Indians to renew hostilities soon afterward, however, when he shipped some Esopus tribes people to the West Indies as slaves. During the spring of 1660 he recruited English settlers from Virginia and Swedes from the Delaware to help the Dutch wage war on the Esopus. On April 4, they ambushed a large Indian force, but most of the warriors escaped. On July 15, cowed by the size of Stuyvesant's forces, the Indians agreed to release their captives and withdraw from the region. This peace held for three years.

The second Esopus War began in 1663, when the Indians attacked Wiltwyck and New Town, killing a considerable number of Dutchmen, and capturing 45 men, women, and children. Stuyvesant recruited a strong force at Albany and New Amsterdam, and, commanded by Capt. Martin Krygier (Cregier), they invaded the Indian country in July and September, killing a chief, 14 warriors, and several women and children. After these battles, small detachments of soldiers pursued the Indians with such success that Esopus population decreased rapidly. The remnant of the tribe signed a peace treaty on May 16, 1664.

After the English seized New York from the Dutch in 1664 they obtained a large land cession from the Esopus. The tribe dwindled, thereafter, some scattering among other Munsees and some seeking refuge among the Iroquois. Eventually a considerable number of their descendants joined the Christian Indians at the Moravian missions.

(E. B. O'Callaghan, ed., Documentary History of the State of New York, II; Allan W. Trelease, Indian Affairs in Colonial New York.)

-F-

FAIRFIELD, NEW YORK, RAID. In March 1778 Indians and Tories raided the village of Fairfield, New York, not far from Herkimer. They killed one resident, captured a dozen others, and burned all of the houses.

(T. Wood Clarke, The Bloody Mohawk.)

FALLEN TIMBERS, BATTLE OF. Gen. Anthony Wayne devoted two years to training and drilling his army (Legion) before taking the field against the Indians that had defeated Generals Harmar and St. Clair. During the summer of 1794, determining that his 3,000 men, equally divided between regulars and mounted militia, were fully prepared for wilderness warfare, he led them to Au Glaize in the very heart of the Indian country. After establishing Fort Defiance at the present site of Defiance, Ohio, he marched down the Maumee, burning several Indian villages before camping within five miles of the British Fort Miami.

Chief Little Turtle, urged by his British advisors to attack Wayne before he reached Fort Miami, planned an ambush at a place called Fallen Timbers, where a tornado had created a two-mile-wide barrier to efficient movement of troops and an ideal setting for the type of wilderness warfare in which Indians excelled. He deployed his 1,300 warriors, supported by a few English and French volunteers, to form a barricade in the timbers. There they waited with mounting impatience for Wayne to march into the trap.

But Wayne was kept fully aware of enemy movements by his Chickasaw scouts, and he took every precaution against a surprise attack. Realizing that the Indians eventually would require rations from Fort Miami, he remained in camp for 48 hours. Finally, on August 20, 1794, many of the warriors left the field seeking food, and only 800 remained at the barricades when Wayne directed his army to advance, the mounted Kentucky militia in the lead and on the left, a squadron of dragoons on the right, and the Legion infantry in the center.

The Indians, confident that Wayne's army had entered a death trap, opened fire from the fallen timbers and then rushed forward as the militia fell back. But Wayne had prepared his Legion for this type of tactic. While the militia rode through their ranks and reformed in position to turn the enemy's right flank, the infantry advanced relentlessly toward the Indian center, driving the warriors back into the jumble of timbers. There Little Turtle attempted to make a stand, but Wayne's highly disciplined troops broke Indian resolve with bayonet charges. Driven from the timber, warriors encountered the cavalry completing its flanking maneuver. After 2 hours of battle the Indians retreated to Fort Miami, and, after the British refused them admission, they scattered into the wilderness.

American losses at Fallen Timbers amounted to 44 men slain and 87 wounded. Theodore Roosevelt asserted that the Indians "probably lost two or three times as many" and claimed that "it was the most complete and important victory ever gained over the northwestern Indians during the 40 years' warfare to which it put an end."

(Theodore Roosevelt, The Winning of the West, V; Fairfax Downey, Indian Wars of the U.S. Army; Dale Van Every, Ark of Empire.)

FALLS OF WOLF RIVER, TREATY OF. At the Falls of Wolf River, Wisconsin, on May 12, 1854, Francis Huebschmann negotiated a land cession treaty with the Menominee Indians. In exchange for land assigned to them six years earlier, they obtained a tract on Wolf River and payment amounting to $242,686.

(Charles J. Kappler, ed., Indian Affairs: Laws and Treaties, II.)

FALMOUTH, MAINE, RAIDS see CASCO, MAINE, RAIDS

FARMER'S BROTHER, SENECA CHIEF. Farmer's Brother (Honanyawus) was born near Lake Erie at an undetermined date, probably between 1716 and 1732. Celebrated for his oratory, he became both a war chief and peace advocate during a lengthy career as a leader in the councils of the Six Nations. He supported the French during the French and Indian War, the British during the American Revolution, and the Americans during the War of 1812. He signed treaties with the United States at Genesee on September 15, 1797, and at Buffalo Creek on June 30, 1802. When he died in 1814 he was buried with military honors in recognition of his services at the battles of Lake George and Lundy's Lane.

(F. W. Hodge, ed., Handbook of American Indians, I.)

FAST, CHRISTIAN, CAPTIVITY OF. In June 1780 Christian Fast, an American soldier from Westmoreland County, Pennsylvania, was captured near the Falls of the Ohio by Delaware Indians. While running the gantlet he displayed such fortitude that an old warrior adopted him to replace a son who had died in battle. Well treated as a member of the Delaware tribe during a two-year captivity, he was trusted sufficiently to accompany the Indians when they besieged Wheeling. During the third night of the siege he slipped away from the Delawares and ran to Fort Ross to warn the settlers of an impending attack. When the raiders arrived there, he helped repulse them. When he returned home he so nearly resembled an Indian that his parents failed to recognize him.

(W. W. Beach, The Indian Miscellany.)

FINLEY, JOHN. John Finley (Findlay), a Scotch-Irishman, emigrated to Carlisle, Pennsylvania, at an early age to enter the Indian trade. By 1752 he traded among the Shawnees at the Lower Pict Town (present Winchester, Kentucky), but the following year he was compelled to flee for his life during an attack on a dozen traders by Canadian Indians. In 1755 he and Daniel Boone became close friends while serving in Braddock's Expedition.

After the French and Indian War, Finley became a peddler, selling goods in frontier settlements from Pennsylvania to North Carolina. In 1769 he visited Boone at his home on the Yadkin River, and the two old friends determined to make a "long hunt" into Kentucky. The expedition ended disastrously when Boone was captured by Indians, one of their companions was killed, and all of their furs were confiscated.

Following the Kentucky debacle, Finley returned to Pennsylvania and resumed his trading activities. In 1771 a Seneca warparty robbed him of all of his trade goods, and afterward he is believed to have wandered through the wilderness until his death.

(Robert L. Kincaid, The Wilderness Road; Charles A. Hanna, The Wilderness Trail, II; Alexander Scott Withers, Chronicles of Border Warfare.)

FINNEY, FORT, TREATY OF. On January 31, 1786, American officials at Fort Finney, near the mouth of the Great Miami River, compelled the Shawnee Indians to cede their lands east of that stream. The tribe repudiated the treaty soon afterward, however, and the government found the Indians so hostile that it could not be enforced.

(Dale Van Every, Ark of Empire.)

FISH CARRIER, CAYUGA CHIEF. Fish Carrier (Hojiagede, Ojagegt) was one of the most active Iroquois chiefs in support of the British during the American Revolution. He participated in the Wyoming Valley Massacre of 1778, the Battle of Newtown in 1779, and the invasion of the Canajoharie area in 1780. In 1790 he signed a peace treaty, and as a result he received a land grant from the government and a medal from George Washington.

(Barbara Graymont, The Iroquois in the American Revolution; F. W. Hodge, ed., Handbook of American Indians, II.)

FISHER, JAMES, FAMILY OF. James Fisher, a retired British Army sergeant, lived with his wife and four children on Isle au Cochon, near Fort Detroit, at the beginning of Pontiac's War. Ottawa Indians invaded the island, killed Fisher, his wife, and one of his children, and carried the others into captivity. His infant daughter Marie died among the Indians a few weeks later. Another daughter was taken to an Indian village at Saginaw, and her subsequent fate is unknown. Betty Fisher, aged 7, was taken to an Ottawa camp. In 1764 she became ill with dysentery, soiled some of Pontiac's clothing, and he threw her in the Maumee River, where she drowned.

(Howard H. Peckham, Pontiac and the Indian Uprising.)

FITCH, JAMES. James Fitch, a Puritan clergyman at Norwich, Connecticut, became a missionary to the Mohegan Indians in 1671. Chief Uncas opposed Christianity and ordered his people to ignore him. By 1674, however, he had persuaded 30 Mohegans to attend Christian services. Because they were persecuted by other Mohegans, Fitch obtained a small reservation for them. The congregation grew slowly until King Philip's War brought an end to the mission.

(John W. DeForest, History of the Indians of Connecticut.)

FLAT MOUTH, CHIPPEWA CHIEF. Flat Mouth (Eshkebugecoshe), a chief of the Pillager Chippewas, was born in 1774, and lived at Leech Lake, Minnesota. He travelled widely during his youth and became known and respected by Plains and Woodland tribes alike. He fought bravely against the Sioux enemies of his people, but he counselled keeping the peace with the whites and spurned an offer to support the British during the War of 1812. His friendship with leaders of the new nation was in part responsible for his people retaining their lands when most other Indians were removed west of the Mississippi. He died in 1860.

(Frederick J. Dockstader, Great North American Indians; F. W. Hodge, ed., Handbook of American Indians, I.)

FLEMISH BASTARD, MOHAWK CHIEF. The son of a Dutch trader and a Mohawk woman, the chief generally referred to as the Flemish Bastard, was characterized by the Jesuit priest, Paul Ragueneau, as "an abomination of sin, and a monster produced between a heretic Dutch father and a pagan mother." As Canadian and church records abundantly illustrate, he was indeed a threat to the lives of French settlers and missionaries during the mid-seventeenth century.

Chosen a Mohawk chief, the Flemish Bastard led an Iroquois war party to prowl around Three Rivers during the summer of 1650. Sixty Frenchmen attempted to drive them away from the settlement, but the 25 marauders concealed themselves in weeds bordering a river and held their enemies at bay while they slew several French officers. Finally the Mohawks retreated in canoes, the French pursued, and more soldiers were killed.

In 1654 the ferocious chief attacked Father Simon Le Moyne and a band of Christian Onondagas travelling to Montreal. Most of the Onondagas were killed and Le Moyne was held as a captive for a brief period. Two years later, the chief and his followers murdered Father Leonard Garreau on the Lake of Two Mountains while the Jesuit was on his way to establish a mission among the Hurons.

During the winter of 1666-67, the Flemish Bastard attempted to divert a French army from attacking the Mohawk towns by releasing several French captives. As a result he was taken to Quebec and invited to eat at the governor's table, but dinner was disrupted when another Mohawk chief boasted of killing a Frenchman. The Flemish Bastard was forced to witness the execution of his fellow Mohawk, an experience that must have had a sobering effect upon him, for little is heard of his activities afterward.

(T. J. Campbell, Pioneer Priests of North America; Emma H. Blair, The Indian Tribes of the Upper Mississippi Valley and the Region of the Great Lakes; Francis Parkman, The Jesuits in North America, II; Herbert Milton Sylvester, Indian Wars of New England.)

FLINT RIVER, TREATY OF. Henry R. Schoolcraft represented the United States Government in negotiating a treaty with the Chippewa Indians at Flint River, Michigan, on December 20, 1837. The Saginaw band agreed to remove from their Michigan homes to lands near the head of the Osage River.

(Charles J. Kappler, ed., Indian Affairs: Laws and Treaties, II.)

FOND DU LAC, TREATY OF. On August 5, 1826, at Lake Superior's Fond du Lac, the Chippewa Indians negotiated a treaty with two United States officials, Lewis Cass and Thomas L. McKenney. The Chippewas agreed to maintain peace with the Sioux and to permit mining in their territory. They were compensated by a $2,000 annuity.

(Charles J. Kappler, ed., Indian Affairs: Laws and Treaties, II.)

FORBES EXPEDITION. British brigadier general John Forbes received orders in 1758 to lead an expedition against the French stronghold, Fort Duquesne. Realizing the importance of the role of Indians in the campaign, Forbes advocated neutralizing the tribes by rectifying their grievances over loss of hunting grounds, and he delayed his march until the Delawares and Shawnees had obtained satisfaction. (See EASTON, TREATY OF; POST, CHRISTIAN FREDERICK.) In addition, he recruited 600 Cherokee and Catawba warriors to scout in advance of his army and to deter western Indians from raiding frontier settlements.

Col. Henry Bouquet built a road across the western Pennsylvania mountains to facilitate the march of the main army of 6,000 men. The French commandant at Fort Duquesne, François Marchand de Ligneris, assumed that Forbes's army would follow the Braddock Road, and he dispatched war parties from the Great Lakes regions to guard it. When Forbes did not appear in due time, many of these Indians deserted the French and returned to their villages. A sufficient number of warriors remained, however, to defeat a premature attempt to seize Fort Duquesne by James Grant in September.

Forbes decided to build forts and supply bases along the new road, "thus taking possession of the country instead of merely marching through it."--Solon J. Buck. At one of these posts, Loyalhanna, his forces withstood a fierce French and Indian attack on October 12. On November 12, Forbes was informed by a former captive that Fort Duquesne was weakly defended. Abandoning plans to go into winter quarters, he directed his forces to push forward. On November 24, when within ten miles of their objective, they discovered that the French had burned the fort and retreated into the wilderness. The English occupied the ruins the following morning.

"In taking unopposed possession of the smoking embers of the French fort they were taking possession of the key to the west for their country and for the new country soon to be."--Dale Van Every.

(Solon J. Buck, The Planting of Civilization in Western Pennsylvania; Dale Van Every, Forth to the Wilderness.)

FOX INDIANS. The Fox (Mesquakie) Indians, a powerful Algonquian tribe, lived along the Fox River, Wolf River, Green Bay, Lake Superior, and Lake Winnebago during the period of French exploration. Bitter enemies of the Chippewas, they turned against the French for selling guns to that tribe, and they became the only Algonquian nation upon which the French waged war for extended periods. From the beginning of French contacts the Foxes became involved in the fur trade, but they refused to consider Christianization by the Jesuit missionaries.

In 1670 the Foxes accompanied Nicolas Perrot to Montreal to establish friendly relations. Soon afterward, however, they prevented French traders from using the Fox-Wisconsin waterway to the western tribes, and they began charging tribute for the use of other streams in their territory. In order to facilitate the fur trade, so essential in the development of Canada, the French determined to break through this Fox barrier.

Cadillac, instructed to regain control of the rebellious Fox Nation, persuaded them in 1710 to move to his post at Detroit. But, unlike other tribes who camped near the fort, the haughty Foxes displayed their hostility from the first day of arrival. Finally, in 1712, the French commandant incited other tribes to attack the Foxes, and the ensuing siege and massacre touched off a series of Fox wars that Louise Phelps Kellogg avers "brought New France to the verge of ruin, and without doubt contributed to its final overthrow." (See DETROIT, MICHIGAN, INDIAN AFFAIRS; LA PORTE DE LOUVIGNY, LOUIS DE; LE MARCHAND DE LIGNERY, CONSTANT DE; MARIN DE LA MALGUE, PAUL.) The vengeful Foxes retaliated against Indian tribes friendly to the French, particularly the Hurons, Illinois, Chippewas, Ottawas, and Potawatomis, and finally they found themselves under attack from all sides. During the 1730's they were almost exterminated, and the remnant obtained sanctuary with their kinsmen, the Sauks, both tribes fleeing to Iowa. (See SAUK INDIANS.) In 1737 the French granted a pardon to the united Sauks and Foxes. Afterward the Foxes remained at peace for four decades, rebuilding their population, but in 1780 they attacked the Chippewas at St. Croix Falls and were defeated with heavy losses.

The Foxes took little part in the French and Indian War, but they supported Pontiac in 1763 and sided with the British during the American Revolution. They established friendly relations with the Americans before the War of 1812, but most of them switched sides by 1814. In 1832 some of their warriors supported Black Hawk and his Sauks against the settlers. After the Black Hawk War, they ceded much of their land and moved to Iowa, and, a few years later, removed to a reservation in Kansas. About 1858 some Foxes returned to Iowa and settled near Tama, where their descendants still live.

(Emma H. Blair, The Indian Tribes of the Upper Mississippi Valley and the Region of the Great Lakes; William T. Hagan, The Sac and Fox Indians; Louise Phelps Kellogg, The French Régime in Wisconsin and the Northwest; Francis Parkman, A Half-Century of Conflict; John R. Swanton, Indian Tribes of North America.)

FOX ISLANDS MASSACRE. In 1724 the Abnaki Indians embarked along the Maine coast in 50 war canoes to prey upon New England fishermen. In the Fox Islands they attacked a fleet of fishing boats, killed 20 men, and seized 20 others to serve them as navigators. Afterward, while sweeping the shores clean of fishermen, they captured 14 additional fishing-smacks.

(Herbert Milton Sylvester, Indian Wars of New England, III.)

FRANKLIN, BENJAMIN, INDIAN AFFAIRS. While Benjamin Franklin's achievements in diplomatic, philosophical, scientific, and literary matters are widely acclaimed, his interests in Indian affairs and westward expansion have received comparatively little notice. Yet Franklin arrived at Philadelphia while it was a center of the Indian trade, he advocated fairness in relations with the tribes, and he was a keen student of comparative cultures.

Franklin was a dominant figure at the Albany Congress of 1754. (See ALBANY, NEW YORK, INDIAN TRADE AND DIPLOMACY.) He helped the Braddock Expedition of 1755 to obtain wagons to transport troops to fight the French and their Indian allies, and after Braddock's defeat he organized the settlements for defense against war parties that poured into western Pennsylvania. He led 500 men to the defense of the Lehigh Valley, built several forts, and prevented raids until after his forces were withdrawn.

In 1764 Franklin prevented the massacre of peaceful Indians at Philadelphia (see PAXTON BOYS MASSACRE). While he opposed unauthorized seizure of Indian lands by frontiersmen, he advocated acquisition of western territory by purchase from the tribes, including the 1768 Fort Stanwix Treaty.

(Sydney G. Fisher, The Quaker Colonies; Dale Van Every, A Company of Heroes.)

FRASER, JOHN. John Fraser was one of the first Pennsylvania Indian traders to move west of the mountains, establishing a post and gunsmith shop at Venango, near the junction of the Allegheny River and French Creek, in the 1740's. In 1749, during the Céleron expedition, the Delaware Indians declined to drive out their English traders because of their dependence upon Fraser's goods and services. Soon afterward, however, the French built Fort Machault at Venango, and Fraser was compelled to move his trading post to the mouth of Turtle Creek.

In 1754, Fraser served as lieutenant in Capt. William Trent's company that undertook the construction of Fort Prince George. He was at Turtle Creek attempting to save his trade goods when the French captured the fort.

(Solon J. Buck, The Planting of Civilization in Western Pennsylvania.)

FREELAND, FORT, RAID. Fort Freeland, located on the west bank of the Susquehanna River near Sunbury, Pennsylvania, was attacked on July 28, 1779, by Chief Cornplanter and 120 Indians and Capt. John McDonnell and 50 British Regulars and Tory Rangers. The garrison of 30 men, protecting 50 women and children, was taken by surprise and surrendered upon promise of good treatment.

Learning of the attack, Capt. Hawkins Boone led 80 Sunbury men to the relief of Fort Freeland. Boone's forces blundered into an ambush, and he and 15 of his men lost their lives. Afterward, the women and children were released and the adult male prisoners marched to Niagara.

(Barbara Graymont, The Iroquois in the American Revolution; Dale Van Every, A Company of Heroes.)

FREMIN, JACQUES. Father Jacques Frémin, a Jesuit missionary, was born at Rheims in 1628 and went to Canada in 1655 to offer Christianity to the Indians. In 1656 he helped Father Claude Dablon to establish a mission among the Onondaga Indians, remaining there until Iroquois hostilities compelled them to flee for their lives in 1658.

For several years Frémin served among Canadian Indians, but in 1666 he established a mission among the Mohawks. There he gained few Mohawk converts, but he comforted many Huron Christians held in Iroquois captivity. In 1668 he moved to a Seneca village, where he baptized Christian Indian captives about to be burned at the stake. Some time later he was sent to the Caughnawaga Indians (Christian Iroquois) at La Prairie. He died at Quebec in 1691 after spending 35 years with the Indians and baptizing 10,000 of them, principally sick children.

(T. J. Campbell, Pioneer Priests of North America.)

FRENCH MARGARET see MONTOUR, LOUIS, FAMILY OF

FRONTENAC, LOUIS DE BUADE, COMPTE DE, ONONDAGA CAMPAIGN. Governor Frontenac, in retaliation for Iroquois raids on Canadian settlements, determined in 1696 to destroy Onondaga. On July 4, he set out from Montreal with 2,000 Frenchmen and friendly Indians. Crossing Lake Ontario in canoes, they constructed a fort on Onondaga Lake, where they left a detachment to guard supplies. On August 4, they marched toward the main Onondaga castle,

Frontenac carried in an armchair as he was 78 years old and infirm. The Onondagas, well aware of the coming of their powerful enemies, burned their village and fled into the wilderness. Only one Indian too old to escape was captured, and the invaders tormented him to death. After destroying the Indians' crops, Frontenac withdrew, harassed all the way to his base camp by the infuriated Iroquois.

(T. Wood Clarke, The Bloody Mohawk; Cadwallader Colden, History of the Five Indian Nations.)

FROST, CHARLES. Maj. Charles Frost, one of the most successful guardians of the Maine-New Hampshire frontier, was born in Tiverton, England, in 1632 and came to America when he was about five years old. While still a youth he commanded the Yorkshire militia in fights with the Abnaki Indians. In 1676, at the conclusion of King Philip's War, he participated in the seizure of a large number of Indians under the pretense of holding a sham battle (see WALDRON, RICHARD). Some of the prisoners were hung for supporting Philip, and others were shipped to the West Indies as slaves.

For his part in this deception, the Indians determined that Frost must die. They tried on several occasions to capture him, but he managed to elude their war parties until July 4, 1697. That day was a Sunday, and Frost attended church services with family and friends. On his way homeward he was shot to death by Indians concealed in a thicket beside the road. So much did the Abnakis detest him that the night after his burial they dug up his body and impaled it upon a stake at the top of a hill.

(Samuel Adams Drake, Border Wars of New England; Herbert Milton Sylvester, Indian Wars of New England, II.)

FRYE, JONATHAN. Jonathan Frye, a 21-year-old preacher and graduate of Harvard, volunteered to serve as chaplain of a scalp-hunting expedition led by John Lovewell in May 1725. In a fight with the Abnaki Indians, most of Lovewell's men were killed or seriously wounded. (See PEQUAWKET INDIANS; LOVEWELL, JOHN.) Indian losses were heavy, also, and Frye scalped one of the dead warriors.

After several hours of battle, Frye sustained a mortal wound and "lay in his blood, praying from time to time for his comrades in a faint but audible voice." When the Indians withdrew at dusk, he tried to struggle homeward with the other survivors, but he collapsed after a few miles and told his companions to leave him. He was never seen again, but his "memory is still cherished, in spite of his uncanonical turn for scalping."--Francis Parkman.

(Francis Parkman, A Half-Century of Conflict.)

-G-

GALLOP, JOHN. During the summer of 1636 a trader, John Gallop, was sailing with a friend and 2 boys near the eastern end of Long Island when he saw that 16 Indians had seized a pinnace belonging to a neighbor named John Oldham. Ascertaining that they had

murdered the crew, Gallop, an unerring marksman, opened fire
on the Indians and brought down a warrior with every shot, while
his friend steered the boat in close pursuit.

When the Indians realized that Gallop was ready to ram them,
6 of the murderers leaped overboard and drowned while swimming for
shore. Two of the surviving Indians disappeared below as Gallop
boarded the pinnace, and the remaining pair surrendered. Gallop
bound their hands, but, suspecting that they would untie each other,
he threw one of them into the sea. Unable to capture the warriors
in the hold, he returned to his own boat and attempted to tow the
pinnace to port, but bad weather compelled him to loose her lines
and she drifted to shore.

Oldham's murder and Gallop's retaliation were direct causes of
the Pequot War of 1636-37.

(John W. DeForest, History of the Indians of Connecticut;
Alden T. Vaughan, New England Frontier; John Tebbel and Keith
Jennison, The American Indian Wars.)

GANAWESE INDIANS see CONOY INDIANS

GANOWAROHARE, ONEIDA TOWN. Ganowarohare, an Oneida village
located near the present Vernon, New York, was the site selected
by Jesuit missionaries for the establishment of the mission St. Francis
Xavier in 1667. (See BRUYAS, JAMES.) In 1777 the Oneidas supported the Americans, and Indian allies of the British burned Ganowarohare.

(F. W. Hodge, ed., Handbook of American Indians, I.)

GANSEVOORT, PETER, INDIAN RELATIONS. Col. Peter Gansevoort,
a young but experienced Albany, New York, military officer, was one
of the most effective Indian fighters during the American Revolution.
In May 1777 he repaired Fort Stanwix and successfully defended it
against Barry St. Leger's British and Indian army. After the siege
was lifted he was sent to Fort Edward to protect Albany from attack
by Brant's Mohawks and Tories.

In 1779 Gansevoort accompanied Gen. John Sullivan's invasion
of the Iroquois homeland. On September 29 he seized the lower Mohawk Castle at Fort Hunter, but quickly released his prisoners because of their neutrality. During the Battle of Newtown his 3rd
New York Regiment rescued Col. George Reid's New Hampshire troops
from an Iroquois assault and forced Brant to retreat.

After the war Gansevoort was promoted to brigadier-general
and served as commissioner of Indian affairs.

(T. Wood Clarke, The Bloody Mohawk; Barbara Graymont,
The Iroquois in the American Revolution.)

GARAKONTHIE, DANIEL, ONONDAGA CHIEF. Garakonthie was born
at Onondaga about 1600. He spent part of his youth at Montreal,
became friendly with the citizens, and helped redeem Frenchmen
from captivity. After returning to Onondaga, he assisted the Jesuit
missionaries to avoid an Iroquois massacre in 1658. By 1661 he had

become the principal chief and ablest diplomat among the Five Nations. At that time he went to Montreal to restore peace with the French and to request the missionaries to return to Onondaga. A few months later he restored 9 French captives to Quebec, and within the year he was responsible for the redemption of 18 additional prisoners.

In 1669, while visiting Quebec, Garakonthie was baptized by the bishop in his cathedral: "A guard of honor of troops was drawn up; cannon were fired; the governor of New France and the daughter of the intendant acted as godparents."--T. Wood Clarke. At that time he accepted "Daniel" as his Christian name.

During his remaining years Garakonthie made several journeys to the English as well as the French, promoting peaceful relations and attempting to save the lives of white people from the more warlike members of the Iroquois confederacy. In 1673, he persuaded the Iroquois to agree to the construction of Fort Frontenac, to bring furs there for sale to the French, and to permit other tribes to trade there. He died at Onondaga in 1676.

(T. Wood Clarke, The Bloody Mohawk; Frederick J. Dockstader, Great North American Indians.)

GARDINER, LION, INDIAN AFFAIRS. Capt. Lion Gardiner, an English expert on building fortifications, was sent to Saybrook, Connecticut, in 1635 to construct defenses against Indian attacks. At the onset of the Pequot War he attempted to dissuade John Endicott's Massachusetts forces from attacking the Indians, realizing that the Pequots would retaliate against Saybrook. Failing in this attempt, he sent 20 of his men with Endicott's expedition and strengthened his fort for the anticipated counterattack.

Just as Gardiner had expected, the Pequots harassed the Saybrook settlers, torturing some of them to death within sight of the post, and instituted a desultory siege. On March 4, 1637, while working outside the stockade, Gardiner received an arrow wound in the leg, but he managed to regain the safety of the fort. Afterward, when the Pequots requested a parley, Gardiner refused and dared them to assault his fortifications. He helped plan the campaign that exterminated most of the Pequots in May 1637. (See MYSTIC, BATTLE OF.)

In 1639 Gardiner purchased an island from the Indians at the eastern end of Long Island which still is known as Gardiner's Island. There, as a result of his influence over the Indians, he informed colonial authorities in 1642 of Narraganset plans to build a hostile confederacy.

(John W. DeForest, History of the Indians of Connecticut; Alden T. Vaughan, New England Frontier.)

GARDNER, JAMES B. Col. James B. Gardner of Ohio was appointed by the United States Government in March 1831 to persuade the Indians remaining in Ohio to remove west of the Mississippi. By the end of August he had convinced some 1,600 Shawnees, Senecas, Ottawas, and Wyandots that their only chance of survival lay in removal,

and they exchanged 370,000 acres for lands in the West. In 1832 he supervised their removal as far as the Mississippi, where he turned them over to army officers to complete their journey.
(Grant Foreman, The Last Trek of the Indians.)

GARNIER, JULIEN. Father Julien Garnier (known as the Apostle to the Senecas), was born in France on January 6, 1643, became a Jesuit in 1660, and sailed soon afterward to Canada to serve as a missionary. In 1671, after a short stay with the Onondagas, he joined Father Jacques Frémin at a mission among the Senecas. He remained there, ignoring frequent threats to his life, until a French war with the Iroquois impelled him to leave in 1684. When peace was restored in 1701, he returned to the Senecas, remaining eight years until the tribe bowed to English demands to expel him. Afterward he served the Indians of the St. Lawrence until his death in 1730.
(T. J. Campbell, Pioneer Priests of North America.)

GAUSTARAX, SENECA CHIEF. Gaustarax (Ostotax, Mud Eater) was an important eighteenth-century Seneca chief who strongly opposed the movement of English settlers onto Iroquois lands. It is believed that he was among the leading chiefs opposing Bouquet's army at Bushy Run in 1763.
(Paul A. W. Wallace, Indians in Pennsylvania.)

GAUTIER DE VERVILLE, CHARLES. Charles Gautier de Verville, nephew of the famous French-Canadian partisan, Charles Langlade, was a highly successful Indian diplomat in his own right during the American Revolution. While serving as interpreter for the British commandant at Green Bay, he proved to be so adept at managing Indians that he was appointed to help his uncle and other British supporters to recruit war parties to raid the American settlements.

In 1776 Gautier worked among the Sauk and Fox Indians to recruit warriors to defend Canada against an American invasion. In 1777 he provided Sauk and Fox scouts for Gen. John Burgoyne's invasion of New York. During the spring of 1778 he led 190 Sauk, Fox, Menominee, Sioux, and Winnebago warriors to Montreal. Later that year he was assigned to recruit Indians to defend Mackinac. In July 1779 he led 208 Indians to join Gov. Henry Hamilton's forces at Fort Vincennes, but when Hamilton was captured by George Rogers Clark, many warriors turned against the British, and Gautier barely escaped with his life.
(J. A. Jones, Winnebago Ethnology; Louise Phelps Kellogg, The British Régime in Wisconsin and the Northwest; Dale Van Every, A Company of Heroes.)

GAYAGAANHE, CAYUGA VILLAGE. Gayagaanhe, located on the eastern shore of Cayuga Lake, was the principal village of the Cayuga nation. The Jesuit mission of St. Joseph was established there in 1668. The village was destroyed by Col. William Butler during Sullivan's invasion of the Iroquois country in 1779.
(F. W. Hodge, ed., Handbook of American Indians, I.)

GELEMEND, DELAWARE CHIEF. Gelemend (Killbuck), an important
Delaware chief, was born in Pennsylvania about 1722. He succeeded
White Eyes as chief of the nation in 1778. A Christian and a friend
of the whites, he followed the example of his predecessor in striving
to lead his people toward acceptance of the beneficial aspects of
European civilization. In this regard he was overruled, however, by
the fiery war chief Captain Pipe, and he led his peace faction to an
island in the Allegheny River where he had been promised protection
by American authorities. In 1782 a band of militia, returning from
the massacre of the Moravian Indians, invaded the island and killed
several of Gelemend's followers. The chief himself barely escaped
by swimming the river. Afterward he gave up his authority and
lived with the surviving Moravians. His Christian name was William
Henry. He died in 1811.

(Frederick J. Dockstader, Great North American Indians; Paul
A. W. Wallace, Indians in Pennsylvania.)

GENESEO, SENECA VILLAGE. Geneseo was one of the largest and
most important Seneca villages. Located near the present site of
Geneseo, New York, it figured prominently in border warfare until
its destruction by Gen. John Sullivan in 1779.

(F. W. Hodge, ed., Handbook of American Indians, I.)

GERMAN FLATS, NEW YORK. German Flats, near the present site
of Herkimer, New York, was the scene of some of the most devastating Indian raids during the French and Indian War and the American
Revolution. Settled by Palatines early in the eighteenth century,
the highly productive agricultural area along the Mohawk River was
protected by Fort Herkimer.

In 1757 the Oneida Indians warned the residents of German
Flats of an impending attack by the French and Indians. The citizens failed to take heed and, on November 12, 300 warriors and
soldiers attacked the village north of the Mohawk. Some of the residents fled across the river to Fort Herkimer, while others sought
safety in five blockhouses. The soldiers at Fort Herkimer made no
sortie to assist the settlers, and after a brief battle the blockhouses
surrendered, one after another. Forty settlers were killed and 160
captured. Every house was burned to the ground.

During the spring of 1758 the French and Indians attacked the
section of German Flats south of the river, but they received a very
different reception. Capt. Nicholas Herkimer and a company of
rangers sortied from the fort and drove the attackers away from the
settlement.

During the American Revolution, the fertile fields of German
Flats produced the food so desperately needed by George Washington's
army. Seeking to deprive the Americans of that resource, Chief
Joseph Brant raided the area at frequent intervals. On September
17, 1778, a scout named John Adam Helmer raced into German Flats
to warn the settlers that a large force of Tories and Indians was
close behind him. The settlers rushed to take refuge at Forts Herkimer and Dayton and watched helplessly as Brant put the torch to

their homes, barns, mills, and crops, and confiscated their livestock.
Three men were killed.

In July 1782 Tories and Indians revisited German Flats and
devastated the settlement on the south side of the Mohawk. Only
the fort remained standing when they had completed their destruction.

(T. Wood Clarke, The Bloody Mohawk; Arthur Pound, Johnson
of the Mohawks; Francis Whiting Halsey, The Old New York Frontier;
Dale Van Every, A Company of Heroes.)

GERRISH, SARAH, CAPTIVITY OF. Sarah Gerrish, a seven-year-
old Cocheco, New Hampshire, child, was captured by Abnaki Indians
at her grandfather's home on June 28, 1689. (See WALDRON,
RICHARD.) Her captor threatened to burn her to death on several
occasions, but he finally marched her to Canada to sell to the French.
Within a week of her arrival at Quebec she was redeemed by the wife
of the intendant, who placed her in a convent. There she remained
for more than a year until she was exchanged as a result of William
Phips's expedition against Quebec.

(Samuel Adams Drake, Border Wars of New England.)

GIBSON, JOHN. Col. John Gibson was born at Lancaster, Pennsylvania, on May 23, 1740. He grew up near the frontier and acquired
an excellent knowledge of Indian languages and customs at an early
age. He participated in the Forbes Expedition of 1758, and after
the defeat of the French he entered the Indian trade at Fort Pitt.

Gibson was captured by Indians during Pontiac's War. While
other prisoners suffered a fiery death at the stake, he was saved
by an Indian woman and remained in captivity until Col. Henry Bouquet obtained his release in 1764. After Pontiac's defeat, the Delaware Indians, knowing that Gibson was a sincere friend to the tribes,
requested that he be appointed to serve as a trader among them.

In 1772 Gibson operated a trading post at Logstown. About
that time he married by Indian custom the sister of Logan the famous Mingo chief, and they had a son. When Logan's relatives were
massacred by white frontiersmen on April 30, 1774, Gibson's son was
found uninjured strapped to the back of his mortally wounded mother.
She lived long enough to persuade her murderers to send the baby
to Gibson. At the conclusion of Dunmore's War of 1774, Gibson was
sent by Governor Dunmore to seek peace with Logan, and at that
time the chief related to him the speech that became the most noted
of all samples of Indian oratory. (See LOGAN, MINGO CHIEF.)

In the autumn of 1775 Gibson participated in negotiating the
Treaty of Pittsburgh, guaranteeing the Indians that the Ohio River
boundary would be respected, and providing for Indian neutrality
during the conflict with Great Britain. Afterward he visited the
tribes, bearing the six-foot-long "Congress Belt" intended to insure
that Indians would resist pressure by British agents.

During the Revolution, Gibson was an effective officer in the
Continental Army. While commandant at Fort Laurens in 1779, he and
his starving troops withstood a siege by his archenemy, Simon Girty,

and a large force of Mingo and Wyandot Indians. (See LAURENS, FORT.) In the latter stages of the war, Gibson protected the Moravian missionaries and their Delaware Christian followers until infuriated American frontiersmen destroyed their missions in 1782. (See MORAVIAN INDIANS.) When survivors were brought as prisoners to Fort Pitt, Gibson released them to return to their villages.

After the Revolution, Gibson was appointed judge and major general of militia of the Pittsburgh area. From 1800 to 1816 he served as secretary of the Indiana Territory. During the War of 1812 he was acting governor, and his knowledge of Indian affairs enabled him to provide valuable assistance to William Henry Harrison while negotiating with Tecumseh at the council of Vincennes.

After his retirement to Pennsylvania, Gibson died in 1822.

(Randolph C. Downes, Council Fires on the Upper Ohio; Theodore Roosevelt, The Winning of the West, III.)

GILL, SAMUEL, CAPTIVITY OF. On June 10, 1697, Abnaki Indians raided Salisbury, Massachusetts, and captured a 10-year-old boy named Samuel Gill. Taken to St. Francis in Canada, he became assimilated quickly and never desired to return to his relatives. About 1715 he married a Kennebunk captive, Rosalie James, and their sons who married Indians became important Abnaki chiefs. By 1866, their descendants in Canada numbered more than 950.

(Emma Lewis Coleman, New England Captives Carried to Canada, II; Francis Parkman, A Half-Century of Conflict.)

GIRTY, GEORGE. Born in 1745 in Pennsylvania, George Girty was the youngest of three brothers who joined the British and Indians in terrorizing forts and settlements for many years. His father, Simon Girty, Sr., a trader, was killed by Indians in 1751 "during a drunken frolic," and his mother married John Turner. In 1756 the entire family was captured by Indians at the fall of Fort Granville (see GRANVILLE, FORT), and marched to Kittanning, where Turner was tortured to death. The surviving family members were divided among several tribes, George becoming an adopted Delaware.

After being released from captivity in 1759 as the result of a treaty, George and his mother and brothers made their home at Pittsburgh. There George worked for traders as an interpreter for a time, and then entered the Indian trade on his own account. Motivated by an opportunity to plunder, he joined the James Willing Expedition of 1778-79 that seized British property along the Mississippi River, but in May 1779 he deserted the Patriot cause and went to Detroit to join his brothers in the British Indian service. Gov. Henry Hamilton sent him to the Shawnees at Wapatomica to incite war parties to invade the Kentucky settlements.

George Girty was never as notorious as his brother, Simon, but he joined the Indians in some of the most sanguinary attacks of American history, including the David Rogers flotilla ambush, the siege of Bryan's Station, the Battle of Blue Licks, William Crawford's

defeat, and the attack on Wheeling (the last battle of the war) in
1782.

After the Revolution, George Girty lived with the Delawares,
married a woman of that tribe, and fathered several children. He
became increasingly assimilated, and he continued to oppose American
intrusion into the Indian country. In January 1791 he assisted Simon
in leading an attack on Dunlap's Station, near Cincinnati. He died
as a result of alcoholism shortly before the War of 1812.

(Consul W. Butterfield, History of the Girtys.)

GIRTY, JAMES. James Girty, born in 1743, was adopted into the
Shawnee tribe after the capture of his family at Fort Granville in
1756. Like his mother and brothers, he was redeemed from captivity in 1759 and grew up in Pittsburgh. He became an interpreter
and trader and, in 1778, he joined his brother Simon in supporting
the British and in inciting Indians to attack the Americans. Living
among the Shawnees and speaking their language fluently, he played
an important part in holding that powerful tribe in the English interest.

James participated in several Shawnee raids into Kentucky, the
most notable being the captures of Ruddle's and Martin's Stations in
the spring of 1780. At that time he earned a reputation for ferocity
to rival that of his brothers.

In August 1780 James and George Girty led the defense of the
Indian village of Piqua against an attack by George Rogers Clark.
Two years later, James served with Capt. Andrew Bradt and the
Tory Rangers and Indians in the final attack on Wheeling. After
the war he and his Shawnee wife established a successful trading
post at the head of the St. Mary's River. There he continued to
support Indians hostile to the Americans, and he had to flee during
the Harmar and Wayne campaigns.

After the Treaty of Greenville in 1795, James Girty returned
from his haven in Canada to resume trading activities, but he left
his wife and two children in Gosfield, Essex County, Canada. At
the beginning of the War of 1812 he rejoined them and died there in
1817.

(Consul W. Butterfield, History of the Girtys.)

GIRTY, SIMON. Simon Girty, born in Pennsylvania in 1741, was
captured at the fall of Fort Granville in 1756 and adopted by the
Seneca Indians. Released in 1759 as a result of a treaty, his fluent
command of several Indian languages enabled him to find employment
as an interpreter for traders and British officials.

Girty joined Lord Dunmore in waging war on the Shawnees in
1774. He served as a scout, delivering messages to Col. Andrew
Lewis before the Battle of Point Pleasant and shooting a warrior
during Dunmore's advance to the Shawnee villages. Afterward he
served as interpreter at Fort Pitt for the Indian agent, George Morgan. In May 1776 Morgan sent him with a peace belt to the Six Nations, and they agreed to his request for neutrality.

During the early stages of the American Revolution, Girty was active in organizing the Pittsburgh area to fight against the British, serving for a time as a lieutenant in the Patriot army. In February 1778 he accompanied Gen. Edward Hand on an expedition against the Delaware Indians. (See SQUAW CAMPAIGN.)

Shortly after returning from the Squaw Campaign, Girty was persuaded by Alexander McKee to desert to the British. They went to Detroit in the spring of 1778, causing great consternation among Pennsylvania settlers because of their influence over the Indians. British Governor Henry Hamilton employed Girty as an Iroquois interpreter and an instigator of attacks on Kentucky settlements. Soon after his arrival, Girty participated in a raid that returned from Kentucky with seven scalps and captured Mrs. Mary Kennedy and her seven children. While Hamilton became hated throughout the frontier and labeled "the hair-buyer," Girty gained his fearsome reputation as "the white savage." In January 1779, intent upon killing his enemy, John Gibson, he led an Indian force to Fort Laurens and ambushed detachments traveling between that post and Fort McIntosh. He returned the following month with 120 Mingo warriors to assist Capt. Henry Bird to besiege the fort for almost a month.

In the autumn of 1779 Girty led the Indians in a highly successful ambush of an American armament flotilla led by David Rogers on the Ohio River, killing 42 soldiers. In the spring of 1780 he served as interpreter for Colonel Bird during the capture and bloody aftermath of Ruddle's and Martin's stations. Early in 1781 he went to Upper Sandusky to arouse the Wyandot Indians, and he accompanied them on a Kentucky raid in March. His activities were curtailed soon afterward by a sword wound to his head inflicted during a quarrel with the Mohawk chief Brant, but by March 1782 he had recovered sufficiently to seize the Moravian missionaries and escort them to Detroit.

In May 1782 Girty's reputation for savagery increased when he refused a request by the captive Col. William Crawford to shoot him and end his torment while being burned at the stake by the Delaware Indians. There is ample testimony from other captives, including Simon Kenton, however, that he interceded for them and preserved their lives.

Girty played a leading part in the siege of Bryan's Station and in the Battle of Blue Licks that decimated the Kentucky militia in August 1782. In May 1783 he led a war party to within a few miles of Pittsburgh, killed several settlers, and captured a youth who informed him that the Revolutionary War had ended.

After the war, Girty rejoined his wife, a captive named Catherine Malott whom he had redeemed from the Shawnees, and they lived at peace for a short time in the Canadian town of Amherstburg. But the British were determined to keep control of the fur trade, and they employed Girty and others to incite the Indians to attack American traders and settlers. In 1791 he led the attack on Dunlap's Station, Ohio. The defenders repulsed the Indians and, with Girty's approval, the Indians burned a captive, Abner Hunt, to death within sight of the fort before withdrawing into the wilderness.

Girty was a leader in the defeat of Gen. Arthur St. Clair's

army in November 1791, leading the Wyandots so courageously that
his reputation as an Indian manager was greatly enhanced. In June
1792 it is probable that he led the Indian attack on Fort Jefferson,
killing or capturing 16 soldiers. A few months later he attended the
Au Glaize council and used his influence to keep the Indians hostile.

In 1794 Girty recruited a large force of warriors to help Chief
Little Turtle resist the invasion of the Indian country by Anthony
Wayne's army. He participated in the Indian attack on Fort Recovery, but he played little part in the decisive Battle of Fallen Timbers. Afterward he returned to his home at Amherstburg. He was
too infirm to take part in the War of 1812, but he was compelled to
flee with the Mohawks to Grand River when the Americans captured
the area. After the war he returned to his home, where he died on
February 18, 1818.

(Consul W. Butterfield, History of the Girtys; Charles Mc-
Knight, Our Western Border; Alexander Scott Withers, Chronicles of
Border Warfare.)

GLADWIN, HENRY. Maj. Henry Gladwin, a competent and courageous
British officer, gained firsthand knowledge of Indian fighting when,
as a young lieutenant, he fought under Braddock in the campaign
against Fort Duquesne in 1755. Three years later he was transferred to a new regiment especially trained to fight in the wilderness.

In August 1762 Gladwin went to Detroit to reinforce British
troops who had taken over the fort from the French. He was in
charge of Fort Detroit on May 7, 1763, when Pontiac appeared at the
gates with 300 warriors, intent upon seizing the stronghold. Pretending that they had come to pay their respects, they concealed
weapons under their coats. Pontiac planned to gain entry with a
few conspirators, to signal them to shoot Gladwin and his officers,
and to throw open the gates to a throng of Indians waiting outside.
But Gladwin had been warned of the plot, perhaps by an Indian woman,
perhaps by French citizens of Detroit, and when Pontiac entered the
gate he realized that the garrison was alert for any act of treachery.
Thwarted, he withdrew from the fort and instituted a prolonged but
unsuccessful siege. (See DETROIT, MICHIGAN, INDIAN AFFAIRS;
BLOODY RUN; PONTIAC; CAMPBELL, DONALD.) Promoted to
lieutenant-colonel during the siege, Gladwin retired from the army
after Pontiac's War and returned to England.

"Given a post to hold, Gladwin would hold it till the last man
was killed...."--Howard H. Peckham.

(Howard H. Peckham, Pontiac and the Indian Uprising; Dale
Van Every, Forth to the Wilderness.)

GLIKHIKAN, DELAWARE CHIEF. Glikhikan (Gun Sight) was an important Munsee Delaware chief who attempted to turn the Moravian
Indians away from Christianity and to restore their beliefs in native
religion. In 1769 he debated the Moravian missionaries, and, to the
consternation of his followers, the preaching of David Zeisberger converted him to Christianity. On December 24, 1770, he was baptized,
assumed the name Isaac, and accepted the appointment of Native Elder.

Glikhikan at once became a devout and resolute Christian. He arranged for the establishment of Moravian missions on the Beaver and Tuscarawas rivers, and he protected the Christian Indians from the hostility of pagan warriors. In addition, he prevented several raids on white settlements. His good works did not save him, however, from the wrath of the frontier militia during the American Revolution, for on March 8, 1782, he was murdered during the Moravian massacre. (See GNADENHUTTEN; MORAVIAN INDIANS.)

(F. W. Hodge, ed., Handbook of American Indians, I; Paul A. W. Wallace, Indians in Pennsylvania.)

GNADENHUTTEN, MORAVIAN VILLAGE. Gnadenhutten was the name given to several Christian Indian villages by the Moravian missionaries. The first was established in 1746 for Mahican Christians in Carbon County, Pennsylvania. The last and best known, located on the Muskingum River in Ohio, was founded in 1772.

The Moravian villages, usually occupied by Christian Delaware Indians, were the targets of hostilities by Indians, Frenchmen, British soldiers, and American frontiersmen at various times. On November 21, 1755, after Braddock's defeat, hostile Indians massacred the missionaries and residents of Gnadenhutten on the Lehigh River. Ten persons were killed. A second attack occurred three days later, and a third on January 1, 1756. The town was destroyed and 20 soldiers were killed.

During the American Revolution both the British and Patriots suspected the Moravian Indians at Gnadenhutten of assisting the enemy. In 1781 Wyandot Indians and British agents compelled the Moravians to move to Sandusky. When some of the Christian Delawares returned to Gnadenhutten in March 1782 Washington County militiamen, led by Col. David Williamson, massacred 100 unresisting men, women, and children. (See MORAVIAN INDIANS.)

(Solon J. Buck, The Planting of Civilization in Western Pennsylvania; William A. Hunter, Forts on the Pennsylvania Frontier; Theodore Roosevelt, The Winning of the West, III; Anthony F. C. Wallace, King of the Delawares: Teedyuscung; Edmund De Schweinitz, Life and Times of David Zeisberger.)

GODFROY, FRANCIS, MIAMI CHIEF. Francis Godfroy, a mixed-blood Miami chief, was a formidable warrior who became a successful businessman. Born about 1790, he developed into a gigantic warrior whose appearance made Indian enemies quail. He was little known by American frontiersmen, however, until the War of 1812. Then, as an ally of Tecumseh, he led 300 warriors in a dawn attack on Col. John B. Campbell's 600 soldiers on the Mississinewa River on December 18, 1812. The Miamis killed 10 soldiers and wounded 48. Campbell, convinced that he had been attacked by Tecumseh's entire confederacy, beat a hasty retreat.

After the war Godfroy took charge of his father's trading post and participated in several land cession treaties. He died in 1840.

(Bert Anson, The Miami Indians; Frederick J. Dockstader, Great North American Indians.)

GOMEZ, ESTEBAN. Esteban Gómez (Gomes), a Portuguese sea captain and explorer in the service of Spain, visited the New England coast in 1525. Near the mouth of the Penobscot River he captured 58 Abnaki Indians and conveyed them to Spain to sell as slaves, but King Charles V ordered their release.

(Neal Salisbury, Manitou and Providence; W. P. Cumming, R. A. Skelton, and D. B. Quinn, The Discovery of North America.)

GOOKIN, DANIEL. Daniel Gookin, one of New England's foremost friends of the Indians, was born in England in 1612. He came to America in 1634 and lived in Virginia and Maryland before moving to Massachusetts in 1644. He was a Puritan merchant who traveled along the Atlantic coast, met many Indians, and studied their history, culture, and trade practices.

In 1656 Gookin was appointed Superintendent of the Indians of Massachusetts, an office which he held most of his life, and which enabled him to protect the rights of Indians when conflicts arose between them and the settlers. Among his duties was the appointment of teachers, and he joined the Rev. John Eliot in supervising the spiritual activities in the so-called "Praying Indian" communities.

During King Philip's War, the New England colonists blamed the Christian Indians along with the hostiles for raids on the settlements. In vain did Gookin protest their innocence, and his friendship with Indians caused the citizens of Massachusetts to threaten his life. On February 9, 1676, a Praying Indian informed him that a war party planned to attack Lancaster, and Gookin arranged for troops to rush to the defense of the town. This prompt action saved a part of the community, but it failed to prevent Gookin from losing his office.

When Christian Indians were placed in a concentration camp on Deer Island, Gookin brought food and medicine that enabled them to survive. In spite of their mistreatment, many of these Indians, encouraged by Gookin and Eliot, held to their faith and rebuilt Christian communities after the war.

In later life Gookin served as major-general of Massachusetts military forces and published his studies of Indian life. His writings remain a valuable resource on that subject.

(Daniel Gookin, Historical Collections of the Indians of New England; Historical Account of the Doings and Sufferings of the Christian Indians in New England; Douglas Edward Leach, Flintlock and Tomahawk; Alden T. Vaughan, Puritans and Indians.)

GOSNOLD, BARTHOLOMEW, EXPEDITION. Bartholomew Gosnold, a seafarer who had been with the colonists of Roanoke Island, attempted to establish a settlement on the New England coast in 1602. On the shore of southern Maine his crew traded knives, hatchets, and beads to friendly Indians for animal skins. Then they sailed to the vicinity of Buzzard's Bay, built a breastwork on Cuttyhunk Island, and established trade with the natives.

Unfortunately, while Gosnold was exploring the bay in his ship, Concord, a dispute arose over objects of trade between the Indians

and the men left at the post. On June 11, Indians attacked two
Englishmen who were searching for food, wounding one with an arrow. This altercation caused Gosnold to abandon plans to establish
a colony in that region. He returned to England in July with a
valuable cargo of furs and stories of the wonders of the New World.
  (Alden T. Vaughan, New England Frontier; Neal Salisbury,
Manitou and Providence.)

GOUPIL, RENE. René Goupil, a young surgeon from France, accompanied Father Isaac Jogues in August 1642, to establish a mission
among the Hurons. On their way they were captured and tortured
by the Iroquois, an experience welcomed by Goupil, as he ardently
desired to die for his faith. After six weeks of captivity he was
tomahawked by a Mohawk warrior, receiving the martyrdom he sought
on September 29, 1642. (See JOGUES, ISAAC.)
  (Edna Kenton, ed., Black Gown and Redskins.)

GRANGULA, ONONDAGA CHIEF. Grangula (Otreouati, Big Mouth)
was a famous Onondaga orator and an influential Iroquois diplomat.
Wise enough to play the English against the French for the benefit
of the Five Nations, he refused in 1684 to agree to Governor Le
Febvre de la Barre's demand to break off trade with the English,
asserting that the Iroquois had no fear of the French and would trade
wherever they wished.
  In 1688 Grangula led 1,200 warriors to Montreal to establish a
truce and to arrange for chiefs from all the Five Nations to negotiate
a permanent peace. A preliminary treaty was signed, but the plan
for a general peace was disrupted by the duplicity of a Huron chief.
(See ADARIO.)
  "He shared with most of his countrymen the conviction that
the earth had nothing so great as the league of the Iroquois; but if
he could be proud and patriotic, so too he could be selfish and mean.
He valued gifts, attentions, and a good meal, and would pay for
them abundantly in promises, which he kept or not, as his own interests or those of his people might require."--Francis Parkman.
  (Cadwallader Colden, History of the Five Indian Nations; Francis Parkman, Count Frontenac and New France Under Louis XIV.)

GRANVILLE, FORT, PENNSYLVANIA. Fort Granville was built by
George Croghan late in 1755 on the Juniata River, near the present
site of Lewistown, Pennsylvania, and garrisoned by provincials under
the command of Capt. Edward Ward. It was so short of provisions
that on July 30, 1756, disregarding the threat of Indians who had
appeared outside the stockade a week earlier to challenge the soldiers
to come out and fight, Ward took all of his men except 24 to guard
a party of harvesters. During their absence the fort was attacked
by a large force of French soldiers under Louis Coulon de Villiers
and Indians led by Captain Jacobs, a formidable Delaware chief.
  The defenders, commanded by courageous Lt. Edward Armstrong,
stood off the enemy for a day and a night. Early the following morning the attackers burned a hole in the barricade and killed Armstrong

as he attempted to repair the damage. Then the French officer offered good terms, and John Turner surrendered the fort. Twenty-two soldiers, three women, and several children were captured. (See GIRTY, GEORGE; ARMSTRONG, JOHN; CAPTAIN JACOBS.) The fort was destroyed.

(William A. Hunter, Forts on the Pennsylvania Frontier.)

GRAY LOCK, WARANOKE CHIEF. The Waranoke Indians, an Algonquian band that lived near Westfield, Massachusetts, were led by the hostile chief Gray Lock during Queen Anne's War and Dummer's War. In July 1712 he attacked Springfield, Massachusetts, capturing several citizens. In August 1723 he raided Northfield and Rutland, murdering the Rev. Joseph Willard, two sons of Joseph Stevens, and several others, and taking captives. In 1725, after Dummer's War ended, he ceased his raids on the Massachusetts towns in the Connecticut Valley, but he declined to go to Montreal to sign a peace treaty.

(Herbert Milton Sylvester, Indian Wars of New England; William C. Sturtevant, ed., Handbook of North American Indians, XV.)

GREAT COVE MASSACRE. On October 31, 1755, the Delaware chiefs Shingas and Captain Jacobs led 100 warriors into the Great Cove, an area near the Maryland border at the present McConnellsburg, Pennsylvania. They massacred 47 families and destroyed 27 plantations.

(William A. Hunter, Forts on the Pennsylvania Frontier.)

GREAT MEADOWS see NECESSITY, FORT

GREAT SWAMP FIGHT. During King Philip's War the powerful Narraganset tribe built a strong stockaded town in the center of a swamp near the present site of West Kingston, Rhode Island. More than a thousand Indians took refuge there in December 1675, confident of safety throughout the winter as the English would be unable to find a path through the swamp. They did not suspect that one of their own people, Indian Peter, would turn traitor and guide their enemies to the stronghold.

On December 19, Indian Peter led Gen. Josiah Winslow's 300 colonists and 150 Mohegan Indians to the vicinity of the walled Narraganset town. Finding a gap in the enclosure, they raced through a withering fire to attack the Indians defending the wigwams inside.

Over the angry objections of Benjamin Church, a decision was made to set fire to the wigwams. Quickly the entire town was engulfed in flames. The colonial frontier historian, Douglas Edward Leach, noted that "how many old men, women, and little children perished inside the wigwams will ... never be known." In addition to the death of hundreds of people during the fight, the tribe lost its food supply, resulting in the threat of starvation. Seventy colonists were killed during the battle or died soon afterward of their wounds.

(Thomas Church, The History of the Great Indian War of 1675 and 1676; Douglas Edward Leach, Flintlock and Tomahawk.)

GREEN BAY, WISCONSIN. Green Bay, known during early frontier times as La Baye, was first seen by Europeans in 1634 when Jean Nicolet visited the area. Within a few years it became a rendezvous for French traders and missionaries. Fort St. Francis Xavier, established there in 1684, was abandoned 11 years later. Afterward French troops were stationed there periodically, particularly during the Fox Indian wars, until 1760.

In 1761 the British took possession of the former French post and named it Fort Edward Augustus. The commandant, Lt. James Gorrell, established friendly relations with the Fox, Sauk, Winnebago, and Menominee Indians, and those tribes protected the fort during Pontiac's War. Afterward British and French traders developed Green Bay into a center of the fur trade. Some of them instigated Indian hostility toward Americans until after the War of 1812. In 1816 Fort Howard was built at Green Bay and American settlement expanded.

(Louise Phelps Kellogg, The French Régime in Wisconsin and the Northwest; The British Régime in Wisconsin and the Northwest.)

GREENVILLE, TREATY OF. The Treaty of Greenville, one of the most important ever negotiated with Indians by the United States, was signed at Greenville, Ohio, on August 3, 1795. Gen. Anthony Wayne having defeated the Indians decisively at Fallen Timbers one year earlier, negotiated from a position of strength, and, in exchange for peace, chiefs of a dozen northwestern tribes agreed to open large areas of their lands to American settlement. The Indians ceded most of Ohio and Indiana as well as the sites of such strategic posts as Detroit, Mackinac, and Chicago. Provision was made for the release of prisoners, the opening of trade, establishment of boundaries, and payment of annuities. The Indians retained the right to remain on their land until it was purchased by the U.S. Government.

(Theodore Roosevelt, The Winning of the West, V; Dale Van Every, Ark of Empire; Charles J. Kappler, ed., Indian Affairs: Laws and Treaties, II.)

GROSEILLIERS, MEDART CHOUART DE. Medart Chouart de Groseilliers, one of Canada's earliest explorers and traders, was born in France about 1625. He went to Canada about 1640 and spent several years at a Huron mission studying Indian languages. Deciding to enter the Indian trade, he moved to Three Rivers, where he married a sister of Pierre-Esprit Radisson.

The trail of these famous explorers is murky, but Louise Phelps Kellogg believes that Groseilliers explored much of the Great Lakes region in 1654, returned to Three Rivers in 1656, and persuaded Radisson to accompany him to the Iroquois country in 1657. They made an unauthorized fur trading expedition in 1658, built the first European dwelling in Wisconsin, and returned to Montreal in 1660. There the governor seized their fortune in furs, causing them to desert to the English. They explored Hudson Bay for King Charles II in 1666, and Groseilliers obtained so many furs that "his success led to the establishment of the Hudson's Bay Company, which played a leading role in the economic development of Canada as well as that of the Mississippi Valley."--John Anthony Caruso.

Groseilliers, whose allegiance shifted between the English and French during later life, died in Canada after 1684. (See RADIS-SON, PIERRE-ESPRIT.)

(John Anthony Caruso, The Mississippi Valley Frontier; Louise Phelps Kellogg, The French Régime in Wisconsin and the Northwest.)

GROTON, MASSACHUSETTS, RAIDS. In March 1676 a Nipmuc war party led by Monoco (One-Eyed John) attacked the settlers of Groton. Most of the colonists defended themselves in garrison houses, but a few were killed or captured. The church and many houses were destroyed.

On July 27, 1694, Abnaki Indians led by Chief Moxus raided Groton. Twenty-two settlers were killed and 13 were captured. The Longley family alone lost the parents and 5 children slain and 3 children carried to Canada.

(Samuel Adams Drake, Border Wars of New England; Douglas Edward Leach, Flintlock and Tomahawk.)

GROUSELAND, TREATY OF. On August 21, 1805, William Henry Harrison negotiated a treaty at Grouseland, near Vincennes, with the Delaware, Miami, Wea, and Potawatomi Indians. The tribes made large land cessions in exchange for annuities.

(Charles J. Kappler, ed., Indian Affairs: Laws and Treaties, II.)

GUYANDOTTE INDIANS see WYANDOT INDIANS

GUYASUTA, SENECA CHIEF see KIASUTHA, SENECA CHIEF

GYANTWAHIA, SENECA CHIEF see CORNPLANTER, SENECA CHIEF

GYLES, JOHN. John Gyles, aged 9, was captured at Pemaquid, Maine, by Maliseet Indians on August 2, 1689. The raiders captured his parents, one brother, and two sisters. They murdered his father, but his mother and sisters were redeemed a few years afterward. His brother James escaped, but fell into Indian hands a second time, being tortured to death in 1692. John made the march to Canada, living with his captor for six years before being sold to the French.

John's life at the Indian village was threatened by visiting Micmac Indians who tortured him on several occasions. After six years, a dispute arose between his original captor and the widow of a second master to whom he had been sold. Some of the Indians suggested settling the dispute by killing the captive, but a priest arranged for his redemption by a French trader.

In 1698 the French permitted Gyles to return to New England. He secured government employment as an interpreter, serving skillfully for many years, and being trusted by his former captors in all matters of trade, prisoner exchange, and peace negotiation.

Gyles wrote an account of his experiences that remains one of the most interesting of narratives of captivity, as illustrated by the following incident: When a Jesuit priest offered to redeem him, his mother urged him to remain with the Indians. "'Oh, my dear child,' she lamented, 'if it were God's will, I had rather follow you to your grave, or nevermore see you in this world, than that you should be sold to a Jesuit; for a Jesuit will ruin you body and soul....' It pleased God to grant her request for she never saw me more."
(John Gyles, The Ordeal of John Gyles.)

-H-

HACKENSACK INDIANS. The Hackensack Indians, a subtribe of the Unami Delawares, lived in the area presently containing the cities of Newark, Jersey City, Passaic, Bayonne, and a part of Staten Island. Led by a chief known as Oritany (Oratamy), they numbered an estimated 1,000 people at the time the Dutch established settlements near them.

Trouble began between Dutchmen and Hackensacks in 1642 when farmers' livestock destroyed Indian crops. Settlers sold liquor to the Indians, then robbed a warrior of his furs when he became drunk. In retaliation, he murdered two settlers, and Gov. Willem Kieft threatened to declare war on the tribe. Oritany and other chiefs attempted to make amends by offering to compensate the widows, but Kieft demanded that they surrender the murderer. Oritany responded that he had fled from their territory, and he pointed out that the Dutch were at fault for selling liquor to Indians. But Kieft insisted upon war, and many peaceful Indians were slain. (See PAVONIA MASSACRES.)

On September 17, 1643, the Hackensacks attacked the bowery at Newark Bay, putting its defenders to flight. Afterward they burned the small settlement. A general Indian war ensued (see KIEFT, WILLEM; NEW AMSTERDAM), which ended in 1645, largely as a result of the desire of Oritany and his people to live in peace.
(F. W. Hodge, ed., Handbook of American Indians, I; E. B. O'Callaghan, ed., History of New Netherland, I; Allen W. Trelease, Indian Affairs in Colonial New York.)

HALF KING, ONEIDA CHIEF. The title "Half King" was used by the English in the eighteenth century to recognize an Iroquois chief assigned by the Six Nations to supervise tribes that they had conquered. Among the most prominent of these was Tanacharison, an Oneida chief, who served as vicegerent to the Delawares from 1747 until his death in 1754.

Half King established his headquarters at Logstown near the Forks of the Ohio. He hated the French for killing his father, and he was determined to prevent them from occupying the Ohio Valley. In 1752 he signed a treaty with Virginia authorities, and he served as advisor to George Washington, Christopher Gist, George Croghan, and other colonial leaders. He accompanied Washington in 1753 to demand French withdrawal from Forts Presque Isle and Le Boeuf. After failure of that mission he urged Virginia to fortify the forks, and he was present on April 17, 1754, when the French seized the unfinished fort.

When Washington led a force to evict the French, the Half King met him on May 28 and warned that a party of 34 French and Indians, led by Ensign Joseph Coulon de Villiers de Jumonville, was camped nearby. He assisted the Virginians in attacking the camp and asserted that he himself had killed Jumonville. Every member of the French party was killed or captured except 1, and the incident touched off the French and Indian War. French forces were quick to retaliate, and Washington, disregarding the Half King's advice, built Fort Necessity to oppose them. When Washington surrendered to superior French forces on July 3, the Half King moved his headquarters to George Croghan's post at Aughwick. He died there of pneumonia on October 4, 1754.

(Solon J. Buck, The Planting of Civilization in Western Pennsylvania; F. W. Hodge, ed., Handbook of American Indians, I; William A. Hunter, Forts on the Pennsylvania Frontier; Paul A. W. Wallace, Indians in Pennsylvania.)

HALF KING, WYANDOT CHIEF. Half King, a Wyandot chief, lived near Sandusky, Ohio, during the American Revolution. An ardent opponent of American frontier expansion, he was regarded, nevertheless, as a humane adversary who prevented atrocities by keeping liquor out of the hands of his warriors. He was honored by the Indians of the Great Lakes region as such an able warrior that he gained a following among the Ottawas, Chippewas, Shawnees and other tribes as well as his own Wyandots.

Half King has been credited with protecting the Moravian (Christian Delaware) Indians during and after the American Revolution. In 1777 he saved the Moravians of Lichtenau, Ohio, from massacre by hostile Indians. In 1781 he insisted upon the removal of the Moravians from the Muskingum to Sandusky, more as a protective measure than a hostile act, for they were threatened by enemies from all sides. In May 1782 Half King led the Indians in the victory over Col. William Crawford's army that had invaded his territory to wipe out the Moravians.

After the war he signed the Treaties of Fort McIntosh in 1785 and Miami Rapids in 1817.

(Dictionary of Indians of North America, I.)

HALL GIRLS, CAPTIVITY OF. Sylvia Hall, a 17-year-old Indian Creek, Illinois, girl, and her 15-year-old sister Rachel were captured by Potawatomi and Sauk Indians on May 20, 1832. (See INDIAN CREEK MASSACRE.) Carried to the Indian camp, they expected to be tortured to death when they witnessed the warriors dancing around the scalps of their parents and other victims.

On May 28, Henry Gratiot, the U.S. Indian agent to the Winnebagos, learned of the captivity of the Hall sisters. He sent two Winnebago chiefs, White Crow and Little Priest, to attempt to redeem them. The Sauks agreed to trade the captives for 11 horses, and the Winnebagos delivered them safely to Gratiot on June 2.

The Hall captivity, while by no means extraordinary, has become famous because the story was used so effectively to recruit soldiers to fight in the Black Hawk War.

(Cecil Eby, That Disgraceful Affair, the Black Hawk War; James Levernier and Hennig Cohen, eds., The Indians and Their Captives.)

HAMILTON, HENRY. Capt. Henry Hamilton, descendant of a noble Scottish family, entered the British army at an early age. He was sent to America in 1758 to fight in the French and Indian War. He participated in the Battles of Louisburg and the Plains of Abraham, and he was captured and held for a short time by the French in 1760. While a prisoner, he witnessed the effects of the employment of Indians in warfare against American settlers.

At the close of the French and Indian War, Hamilton was retired from the military service and in search of a government appointment. In April 1775 he was appointed lieutenant-governor of the British post at Detroit. Evading American forces surrounding Montreal, he arrived at Detroit on November 9. He was instructed to preserve Indian neutrality during the early stages of the American Revolution, but he stockpiled munitions for the day he expected orders to employ the tribes against the frontier settlements.

In March 1777 Hamilton received orders from Lord George Germain to instigate Indian warfare. On June 16, he summoned chiefs from Ohio and the Great Lakes region to Detroit, armed and entertained them, and urged them to wage war against their American enemies. He instructed them to spare women and children, but historians have asserted that he knew enough about Indian warfare to realize the futility of the admonition. By July he had dispatched 15 war parties to Kentucky, Virginia, and Pennsylvania, and they returned with 73 prisoners and 129 scalps. John Leeth, a trader imprisoned at Detroit, described the arrival of one of the war parties:

> ... the Indians produced a large quantity of scalps, the cannon fired, the Indians raised a shout, and the soldiers waved their hats.... This ceremony being ended, the Indians brought forward a parcel of American prisoners, as a trophy of their victories; among whom were eighteen women and children, poor creatures, dreadfully mangled and emaciated; with their clothes tattered and torn to pieces, in such a manner as not to hide their nakedness; their legs bare and streaming with blood; the effects of being torn with thorns.... To see these poor creatures dragged, like sheep to the slaughter, along the British lines caused ... my hair to rise with rage; and if ever I committed murder in my heart, it was then, for if I had had an opportunity ... I should certainly have killed the Governor, who seemed ... (to) delight in the exhibition.

In 1778 Simon Girty, Matthew Elliott, Alexander McKee and other experienced Indian managers joined Hamilton at Detroit, enabling him to increase the number of war parties and to seek the support of the southern Indians in driving all of the settlers east of the Alleghenies. His plans were foiled, however, when Americans captured him at Vincennes on February 24, 1779. (See CLARK, GEORGE ROGERS, ILLINOIS CAMPAIGNS.) Sent to Virginia as a prisoner of war, he was in constant danger from frontiersmen along the way who cursed him as a "hair buyer." At Williamsburg, the Governor and Council imprisoned him for inciting "the Indians to perpetrate their accustomed cruelties on the citizens of the states without distinction of age, sex, or condition." Hamilton, greatly indignant, defended his actions: "No party was sent out without one or more white persons, who had orders and instructions in writing to attend to the behavior of the Indians, protect defenceless persons and prevent any insult or barbarity being exercised on the Prisoners."

Hamilton signed a parole on October 10, 1780, and was exchanged on March 4, 1781. On April 7, 1782, he was appointed lieutenant-governor of Canada.

(John D. Barnhart, Henry Hamilton and George Rogers Clark in the American Revolution; Consul W. Butterfield, History of the Girtys; Louise Phelps Kellogg, The British Régime in Wisconsin and the Northwest; John Leeth, Leeth's Narrative; Theodore Roosevelt, The Winning of the West, II; Dale Van Every, A Company of Heroes.)

HAND, EDWARD. Gen. Edward Hand, a physician as well as a soldier, was born in Ireland in 1744. He came to America as an army surgeon in 1767, but he resigned his commission in order to practice medicine at Lancaster, Pennsylvania, in 1774. At the onset of the Revolutionary War, he sided with the Americans, participated in the siege of Boston, and fought in several major battles.

In 1777, Hand was promoted to brigadier-general and sent to western Pennsylvania to protect the frontier against British governor Henry Hamilton's Indian raiders. He attempted to recruit 2,000 frontiersmen to intimidate the Indians, but his appeals met with a minimum of success. In January 1778 he led 500 Pennsylvania militiamen to capture a British munitions depot at the mouth of the Cuyahoga River. Failing to find it, they vented their frustration by attacking undefended Delaware Indian villages. (See SQUAW CAMPAIGN.) In 1779, after participating in Gen. John Sullivan's invasion of the Iroquois country, he was assigned to a brigade fighting the British in the eastern sector. In 1783 he was promoted to major-general by brevet. He died in 1802.

(Randolph C. Downes, Council Fires on the Upper Ohio; Reuben Gold Thwaites and Louise Phelps Kellogg, The Revolution on the Upper Ohio.)

HANDSOME LAKE, SENECA CHIEF see SKANIADARIIO, SENECA CHIEF

HANNASTOWN, PENNSYLVANIA, RAID. Hannastown, a village of some thirty log cabins, served as county seat of Westmoreland County, Pennsylvania. On July 13, 1782, a large Seneca Indian war party, led by Kiasutha and Farmer's Brother, attacked the community. Fortunately, the citizens had received sufficient warning to enable them to take shelter in their small fort. The Senecas burned all of the structures outside the stockade, drove off the settlers' livestock, and ravaged the countryside.

(Solon J. Buck, The Planting of Civilization in Western Pennsylvania; Reuben Gold Thwaites and Louise Phelps Kellogg, Frontier Defense on the Upper Ohio.)

HANSON, JOHN, FAMILY OF. John Hanson, a Dover, New Hampshire, Quaker, took his eldest daughter to church on June 27, 1724, leaving his wife and younger children at home. Mohawk Indians from Canada invaded the house, killed and scalped two children, and captured Mrs. Elizabeth Hanson, her two-week-old infant, three other children, and their nurse.

After a difficult march crossing rivers and mountains for hundreds of wilderness miles, the warriors and their captives reached the Indian village. There the three older children were taken from their mother and sent to distant villages, while she and the baby remained with the war party leader. After six months of captivity, frequently forced to sleep in the snow to avoid mistreatment by her master, Mrs. Hanson was purchased by a Frenchman at Port Royal. Not long afterward, her husband redeemed her, three of the children, and the maid. He could not locate one of his daughters, however, and she eventually married a Frenchman and remained in Canada.

(Samuel G. Drake, Tragedies of the Wilderness; Herbert Milton Sylvester, Indian Wars of New England, III.)

HARDING, STEPHEN, FAMILY OF. Stephen Harding, a blacksmith and inn-keeper, settled at Wells, Maine, about 1700. He was friendly with the Abnaki Indians and accompanied them on hunting trips to the White Mountains. His knowledge of the country alarmed French traders, and they instigated the Indians to kill or capture him. But Harding thwarted their attempt, leading his wife and carrying their child out the back door just as the war party arrived at the front of the house. They fled through the wilderness to safety at Storer's garrison, almost ten miles away.

(Edward L. Bourne, History of Wells and Kennebunk; Herbert Milton Sylvester, Indian Wars of New England, III.)

HARLOW, EDWARD, EXPEDITION. Capt. Edward Harlow sailed from England in 1611 to seize some North American Indians to assist Sir Ferdinando Gorges as guides and interpreters during a projected colonization of New England. He landed at Monhegan Island, just off Penobscot Bay, and kidnapped three Indians. But one of them, a warrior named Pechmo, escaped, aroused the Abnakis, and attacked the Englishmen, wounding three sailors and compelling Harlow to sail

elsewhere in search of captives. At Martha's Vineyard he seized
Chief Epanow and two warriors. He transported his captives to
England, but Gorges was unable to employ them according to his
designs. (See EPANOW.)

(Neal Salisbury, Manitou and Providence.)

HARMAR EXPEDITION. In 1790 George Washington determined to
send an army to destroy the villages of the hostile Miami Indians,
located near the present site of Fort Wayne, Indiana. Chosen to
lead the expedition was Gen. Josiah Harmar, a brave officer who
lacked experience in fighting Indians. The Miamis were led by Little
Turtle, one of the best wilderness fighters in American history.
Harmar had only 300 Federal troops at his command, so 1,133 men
of the Kentucky and Pennsylvania militias were added to his force.
Unfortunately they were undisciplined, poorly trained, and badly
equipped.

Harmar marched from Fort Washington in October 1790, meeting
no resistance as the greatly outnumbered Indians burned their villages and retreated. But Little Turtle was watching for the right
opportunity for a surprise attack while drawing Harmar ever deeper
into the wilderness.

Eager to fight, Col. John Hardin received Harmar's approval
to make a reconnaissance with 210 men while the main army destroyed
the crops surrounding the deserted villages. Hardin's detachment
had advanced only a few miles, however, when Little Turtle attacked
with about a hundred warriors. At once the militia turned and fled.
Seventy panic-stricken men were overtaken and slain by the Miamis.
Hardin's 30 regulars fought bravely, but 22 of them lost their lives
before the survivors retreated.

Shocked by Hardin's defeat, Harmar decided that the destruction of the Miami villages and crops had accomplished the expedition's
objective, and he gave orders to begin a withdrawal. But Hardin
persuaded the general to permit him to make one more attempt to defeat the Miamis. Leading 400 men, most of them militia, he marched
on October 22 to retaliate for his recent defeat. Little Turtle
launched another attack with similar results. The militia fled. The
regulars stood and fought until most of them had been killed. Harmar, having lost 183 men in Hardin's two battles, resumed his retreat. "... he got his men out only because Little Turtle let them
go--and then had the gall to claim a victory."--Wilcomb E. Washburn.

(Dale Van Every, Ark of Empire; Robert M. Utley and Wilcomb E. Washburn, The American Heritage History of the Indian
Wars.)

HARMAR, FORT, TREATIES OF. Fort Harmar was built in 1786 at
the mouth of the Muskingum River, present site of Marietta, Ohio,
to protect surveyors and settlers. Two important treaties with Indians were negotiated there before its abandonment in 1795.

In December 1788 Arthur St. Clair met representatives of the
Seneca, Sauk, Wyandot, Potawatomi, Ottawa, and Chippewa nations
at Fort Harmar to demand enormous land cessions. The most hostile

nations, the Shawnees and Miamis, refused to attend. The Indians protested that the Americans wanted too much territory, but the Seneca chief Cornplanter countered that the Iroquois had ceded the disputed lands in 1784 (see STANWIX, FORT), and that other tribes had no choice in the matter. St. Clair insisted that the Indians had forfeited any claims to the lands because they had fought for the British and lost.

Finally, on January 9, 1789, St. Clair signed a treaty with the Iroquois, establishing their western limits and reaffirming the Treaty of Fort Stanwix. Afterward, a treaty was negotiated with other tribes in attendance, reaffirming the Treaty of Fort McIntosh and opening eastern Ohio to settlement. The treaties aroused such Shawnee and Miami hostility that four years of Indian warfare ensued. (See HARMAR EXPEDITION; ST. CLAIR'S DEFEAT; FALLEN TIMBERS; GREENVILLE, TREATY OF.)

(Dale Van Every, Ark of Empire; Charles J. Kappler, ed., Indian Affairs: Laws and Treaties, II; Randolph C. Downes, Council Fires on the Upper Ohio.)

HARPER, JOHN. Col. John Harper, founder of Harpersfield, New York, in 1771, was on excellent terms with the Iroquois Indians until the advent of the American Revolution. In February 1777, learning that Joseph Brant had assembled a large force of Indians at Oquaga, he went there painted as an Indian, joined in their dances, barbecued an ox for their feast, and inquired in their own language about their intentions. Brant responded that they would remain neutral during the Revolution unless the Americans attempted to seize Iroquois lands.

War erupted in the region soon afterward, however, and after the death of Gen. Nicholas Herkimer, Harper was placed in command of Mohawk Valley defenses. Discovering that a force of Tories and Indians had invaded the upper Schoharie, he rode to Albany for help, returned with a small cavalry detachment, charged the enemy, and drove them from the region. The victory crushed Tory sentiment in the Schoharie Valley.

As a ranger colonel, Harper rendered remarkable service against Tories and Indians throughout the remainder of the war. He participated in the Sullivan invasion of the Iroquois strongholds in 1779. In 1780, while he was away from home on a scout, Brant destroyed Harpersfield and captured his brother Alexander.

After the war, John Harper rebuilt Harpersfield. He and the Iroquois resumed friendly relations that lasted until his death in 1811.

(T. Wood Clarke, The Bloody Mohawk; Francis Whiting Halsey, The Old New York Frontier; Dale Van Every, A Company of Heroes.)

HARRIS, JOHN, FAMILY OF. John Harris, Jr., founder of Harrisburg, Pennsylvania, was the son of a Yorkshire, England, trader who migrated to Pennsylvania before 1718 and established a post and ferry on the Susquehanna shortly thereafter. Upon his father's death in 1748, John, Jr., operated the business, providing an important service to pioneers on their way to western Pennsylvania and Virginia. During most of his life he had the help of his mother, a fearless frontier woman who could fight Indians as well as any man, and his sister Elizabeth, wife of the famous trader John Finley.

The younger John Harris gained the friendship of the Indians by treating them fairly. When an Indian war erupted in 1755, he was in a position to inform Pennsylvania officials of the movements of hostiles. When war parties threatened his post, he built a stockade and hired veteran Indian fighters to help defend it. When circumstances permitted, he hosted Indian conferences, including a council with the Iroquois in 1757. He was a prominent frontiersman and trader until his death in 1791.

(Charles A. Hanna, The Wilderness Trail.)

HARRIS, MARY, CAPTIVITY OF. Mary Harris, a small child, was captured during an Indian raid on Deerfield, Massachusetts, in 1703, and carried to the western Pennsylvania wilderness. Her fate was unknown until 1750, when George Croghan and Christopher Gist met her near the Muskingum River on a small stream known as White Woman's Creek. Married to an Indian, she was the mother of several mixed-blood children. In 1761 Robert Eastman, a prisoner of the French, met Mary at Montreal. One of her sons was a prominent partisan during the French and Indian War.

(Frank H. Severance, An Old Frontier of France.)

HARRISON, FORT. Fort Harrison was established in 1811 by William Henry Harrison at the present site of Terre Haute, Indiana. Commanded by Zachary Taylor, it was intended to deter depredations by Tecumseh and his brother, the Prophet. Tecumseh had planned attacks on all of the western military posts, and he assigned the destruction of Fort Harrison to the Kickapoo Indians.

Chief Pakoisheecan led a large war party to Fort Harrison on September 3, 1812. In an attempt to convince Taylor that their intentions were peaceful, the warriors brought their wives and children with them. The stratagem failed, however, when young warriors could not resist killing two white men encountered outside the stockade. When Pakoisheecan requested permission to bring his "starving" women and children inside the post, Taylor wisely refused.

Realizing that Taylor could not be deceived, Pakoisheecan waited until night, then crawled to a corner of the stockade, heaped dry grass against the wall, and set it on fire. Simultaneously, the Kickapoos attacked the opposite side of the fort, diverting attention from the fire long enough for it to weaken the corner blockhouse. Perceiving the perilous situation in time, Taylor erected a barricade that barred the gap in the pickets.

Reluctant to risk the lives of many warriors by rushing the fort, Pakoisheecan resorted to siege tactics. As most of the defenders' food had been destroyed in the fire, they were reduced to eating livestock fodder during eight days under siege before a relief force arrived.

After the War of 1812, Fort Harrison was the site of negotiations of two important Indian treaties. On June 14, 1816, Benjamin Parke negotiated peace with the Kickapoos and Weas, and on August 30, 1819, he persuaded the Kickapoos of the Wabash to exchange their Indiana homeland for an extensive tract in Missouri. The Indians received an annuity of $2,000 for 10 years.

(R. David Edmunds, The Shawnee Prophet; A. M. Gibson, The Kickapoos; Charles J. Kappler, ed., Indian Affairs: Laws and Treaties, II.)

HARRISON, WILLIAM HENRY, INDIAN RELATIONS. William Henry Harrison, ninth President of the United States, was born in Virginia on February 9, 1773. Son of a signer of the Declaration of Independence, and a member of a wealthy and politically powerful family, he studied medicine at Hampden Sidney College, but abruptly changed his plans at the age of 18, and obtained an ensign's commission in the United States Army. In September 1791 he went to Fort Washington, arriving just in time to meet the survivors of the St. Clair Expedition, soundly defeated by the same Indians that he was destined to confront for the next quarter century.

Harrison's encounters with Indians established his place in American history as a military man and a highly successful treaty negotiator who opened millions of acres to settlement by United States citizens--exploits that led to high government office and contributed greatly to his campaign for the presidency. His achievements in Indian relations are well documented, but his attitude toward and methods of dealing with native Americans have remained matters of dispute among historians. His own correspondence indicates that when appointed Governor of Indiana Territory in 1800, he sympathized with the plight of the tribes: "The Indian chiefs," he acknowledged, "all profess and I believe that most of them feel a friendship for the United States ... but they made heavy complaints of ill-treatment on the part of our Citizens. They say that their people have been killed--lands settled on--their game wantonly destroyed--& their young men made drunk & cheated of the peltries which formerly procured the necessary articles of Clothing, arms and ammunition to hunt with. Of the truth of these charges I am well convinced."

To explain the transition from protector of Indian rights to perpetrator of deception in acquiring tribal lands in less than five years, Harrison's biographer, Freeman Cleaves, pointed out that President Jefferson pressured him to acquire all the land possible before Napoleon's acquisition of Louisiana led to French influence over the Indians, precluding future cessions. In 1802 he received official authority to make treaties.

Harrison set about his task with determination and skill. At Fort Wayne in June 1803 he negotiated boundary settlements with the Delaware, Shawnee, Potawatomi, Miami, Wea, Piankashaw, Kickapoo, and Kaskaskia Indians. Two months later he obtained more than eight million acres from the Illinois Indians. In August 1804 he acquired a large tract of land bounded by the Ohio and Wabash rivers from the Delawares. On November 3, 1804, he extracted 14 million acres from five Sauk chiefs who had come to St. Louis authorized only to surrender a warrior accused of murdering settlers. This cession, obtained, said William T. Hagan, as the result of "land hunger of the Americans ... and the stupidity or venality of the Indian negotiators set the stage for years of mutual hate and distrust." In 1809, Harrison, characterized by Dale Van Every as "a firm believer in the frontier principle of expulsion and/or extermination," concluded the treaty of Fort Wayne, obtaining 2 million acres in the Wabash River region, and so angering Tecumseh that that formidable Shawnee chief refused to permit occupation of the territory. These acquisitions demonstrated that "he seldom troubled himself about either the justice of the claims of the contracting party or the representative character of the chiefs, if signatures to a treaty could be obtained."--Clarence W. Alvord. (See WAYNE, FORT, TREATIES OF; GROUSELAND, TREATY OF; VINCENNES, INDIANA; ST. LOUIS, MISSOURI, INDIAN AFFAIRS.)

Harrison's treaties proved to be a major factor in generating Indian hostilities for years to come. Tecumseh, the Prophet, and other chiefs formed a conspiracy to retain Indian lands, and the movement led to Harrison's ascendancy as a military leader. Previously he had gained a reputation for bravery and prowess as aide-de-camp to Gen. Anthony Wayne at the Battle of Fallen Timbers, but his qualities of generalship were untested until he led American armies to three major victories over Tecumseh and the British. (See TECUMSEH; TENSKWATAWA; TIPPECANOE, BATTLE OF; MEIGS, FORT, SIEGES OF; THAMES, BATTLE OF THE.)

After the conclusion of the War of 1812, Harrison conducted negotiations with the Indians at Greenville, Ohio, in July 1814 and at Spring Wells, Michigan, on September 8, 1815. The resulting treaties established friendly relations with the tribes, extended United States protection over them, and arranged for a military alliance if needed. Afterward, he entered politics, serving as U.S. senator, minister to Colombia, and president. He died April 4, 1846.

(Freeman Cleaves, Old Tippecanoe; Clarence W. Alvord, The Illinois Country; Bert Anson, The Miami Indians; Grant Foreman, The Last Trek of the Indians; A. M. Gibson, The Kickapoos; Louise Phelps Kellogg, The British Régime in Wisconsin and the Northwest; Dale Van Every, The Final Challenge.)

HARTLEY, THOMAS, EXPEDITION. Col. Thomas Hartley, commanding a continental troop regiment protecting the Pennsylvania settlements during the American Revolution, determined to retaliate against the Iroquois for the Wyoming Massacre. In September 1778 he led 200 soldiers up the Susquehanna River and destroyed several villages, including Tioga, Queen Esther's Town, and Sheshequin. On the return march, Hartley's troop was attacked by the Indians, losing 4 men. After the loss of 10 warriors, the Iroquois abandoned the attack. The expedition's chief result was incitement of the Iroquois to increase depredations.

(Barbara Graymont, The Iroquois in the American Revolution; Dale Van Every, A Company of Heroes.)

HAVERHILL, MASSACHUSETTS, MASSACRES. Haverhill, Massachusetts, was the scene of two of the most destructive Indian raids in
New England history. Located on the Merrimac River, and containing
only about thirty houses, the town was a tempting target for Abnaki
and Canadian Indians who could approach it easily by water.

On March 15, 1697, a large war party invaded Haverhill and
assaulted every cabin. Within a matter of minutes, 27 settlers were
killed, 13 were captured, and every house was put to the torch.
(See DUSTIN, THOMAS, FAMILY OF.)

On August 29, 1708, a force of 400 Frenchmen and Indians attacked Haverhill before dawn. Led by François Hertel, the invaders
expected to take the town by surprise, but the citizens and a garrison of 30 soldiers had been warned by Peter Schuyler to prepare
for hostilities. Hertel and his followers attacked the fort and the
houses simultaneously and met sturdy resistance at every point. The
town minister, his wife, and child were among the 48 settlers slain,
but survivors managed to save most of the houses. Eight or 9 Indians were killed.

(Samuel Adams Drake, Border Wars of New England; Francis
Parkman, A Half-Century of Conflict; Herbert Milton Sylvester, Indian Wars of New England, II-III.)

HAVERSTRAW INDIANS. The Haverstraw Indians, a small subtribe
of the Unami Delawares, lived on the lower Hudson River, near the
present Haverstraw, New York, during early colonial times. They
joined neighboring tribes in attacking Dutch settlements in 1655,
but signed a peace treaty in 1660.

(Allen W. Trelease, Indian Affairs in Colonial New York.)

HAWKINS, ELIZABETH, CAPTIVITY OF. Elizabeth Hawkins, a small
Washington County, Pennsylvania, child, was captured by Shawnee
Indians in September 1781 and taken to their village north of the
Ohio. There she became completely assimilated, married an Indian,
and resisted return to her white relatives. Released by the Indians
after the Treaty of Greenville in 1795, she remained with her white
family for only a few weeks before insisting upon rejoining her Indian husband.

(C. Hale Sipe, Indian Wars of Pennsylvania.)

HAWLEY, GIDEON. Rev. Gideon Hawley, superintendent of the Indian school at Stockbridge, was sent to the Susquehanna Valley as
a missionary to the Indians of Oquaga in 1753. Forced to flee by
Indian hostiles during the French and Indian War, he served Sir
William Johnson as chaplain during the Crown Point expedition. After
the war, he served as a missionary to the Indians of Connecticut
and Massachusetts for almost half a century before his death in 1807.

(Francis Whiting Halsey, The Old New York Frontier.)

HEARD, JOHN, FAMILY OF. John Heard, a Cocheco, New Hampshire,
pioneer, married Elizabeth Hull, daughter of a Puritan minister. They
had five sons and five daughters, several of whom were casualties of

the New England Indian wars. They lived in one of five garrison houses designed to protect settlers in the small community, so greatly exposed to Abnaki incursions.

In 1676, when some of Cocheco's most prominent citizens entrapped 400 Indians and sold many of them into slavery (see WALDRON, RICHARD; FROST, CHARLES), an Abnaki youth fled to the Heard home, where Elizabeth concealed him. This act of kindness saved her life 13 years later when she was at the mercy of Indians retaliating for that deception.

In June 1689, a large war party attacked Cocheco at dawn. Elizabeth Heard and her children had gone to visit relatives at Portsmouth, and John was saved by the frantic barking of his dogs as the raiders attempted to enter his house. With the aid of William Wentworth, who braced himself against the gate until other men in the house were aroused, John was able to repel the invaders while the four other garrison houses were taken.

Elizabeth and her children returned in time to witness the surrender of one of the garrisons. Believing Waldron's to be secure, they sought entrance, only to discover that it was held by the Indians. The mother, believing that she lacked the strength to escape, ordered her children to flee and concealed herself in some bushes. Indians rushed to her hiding place, but the young warrior she had hidden years earlier recognized and protected her. It is probable that one of John Heard's daughters was captured during the raid, for the following year Benjamin Church recovered an Ann Heard of Cocheco when he attacked the Androscoggin Indian village.

John Heard, Jr., became a famous Indian fighter. On July 4, 1697, he and his wife, Phoebe, were on their way home after religious services, accompanied by Maj. Charles Frost. Indians stalking Frost because of his part in seizing their people in 1676 ambushed them in the woods, killing Frost and Phoebe Heard. John Heard, Jr., escaped with severe wounds.

Tristram Heard, another son of John and Elizabeth, was waylaid and slain by Indians while walking in the wilderness in 1723.

(Jeremy Belknap, History of New Hampshire, I; Samuel Adams Drake, Border Wars of New England; Herbert Milton Sylvester, Indian Wars of New England, II.)

HECKEWELDER, JOHN. Rev. John Heckewelder, one of the most important Moravian missionaries, was born at Bedford, England, in 1743. In 1754 he sailed with his parents to Pennsylvania and settled at Bethlehem. During his youth he felt called to the ministry, and he was especially eager to evangelize the Delaware Indians.

In 1762 he accompanied Rev. Christian Frederick Post to establish a mission on the Tuscarawas River, but they were compelled by hostile Indians to abandon it less than a year later. Afterward, he worked as a cooper at Bethlehem until he determined to resume missionary service. In 1772 he assisted Rev. David Zeisberger at the mission settlement of Friedensstadt. The following year he helped establish four missions in the Muskingum River region of Ohio.

The Ohio Moravian missions were highly successful until the

onset of the American Revolution. Then, suspected by each side of helping the other, the flourishing Christian Indian settlements were destroyed. Heckewelder was seized by Indian allies of the British in 1781 and taken to Detroit. After he convinced British officials of his innocence, he labored at missions in Michigan and northern Ohio until 1786, when he returned to his home at Bethlehem.

Heckewelder, fluent in Indian languages and familiar with tribal history and customs, was called upon by the U.S. Government to assist with treaty negotiations. On September 27, 1792, he and Rufus Putnam arranged a peace treaty with northwestern tribes at Vincennes, Indiana. A few months later, he assisted Timothy Pickering and others to negotiate a treaty with the Miamis.

In 1801, Heckewelder was appointed to superintend a reservation for Christian Indians at Gnadenhutten, Ohio. Nine years later he returned to Bethlehem, became active in the American Philosophical Society, and contributed substantially through his writings to knowledge of Indian history and customs. He died in 1823.

(John Heckewelder, History, Manners, and Customs of the Indian Nations; Reuben Gold Thwaites and Louise Phelps Kellogg, The Revolution on the Upper Ohio; Dale Van Every, A Company of Heroes; Edmund De Schweinitz, The Life and Times of David Zeisberger.)

HELMER, JOHN ADAM. John Adam Helmer was one of the Patriots' most effective scouts during the American Revolution. On September 17, 1778, he and three companions were watching the Unadilla trail in northern New York when Brant's Indians attacked them, killing his companions. Helmer escaped by diving into the Unadilla River.

Recognized as the best runner in the Mohawk Valley, Helmer rushed to warn the settlers of German Flats, 26 miles away. In an exploit celebrated in New York history as "Adam Helmer's Run," he raced through the wilderness with a pack of warriors in pursuit. He arrived at German Flats with "his clothing torn to tatters, his eyes bloodshot, his hands, face and limbs lacerated, and bleeding from the effects of brambles and bushes through which he had forced his headlong flight." Forewarned, the settlers fled to safety in Forts Dayton and Herkimer. Soon afterward, Brant and a large force of Indians and Tories destroyed the town, but they were unable to capture the forts. (See GERMAN FLATS.)

(T. Wood Clarke, The Bloody Mohawk; Francis Whiting Halsey, The Old New York Frontier.)

HENDRICK, MOHAWK CHIEF. Hendrick, a prominent Iroquois chief, was the son of a Mohegan father and a Mohawk mother. Known to New York frontiersmen as King Hendrick, and to the French as White Head, he was a faithful friend to Sir William Johnson and an important ally of the British. He was born about 1680 and grew up among the Mohawks of Canajoharie. Converted to Christianity during his youth, he became a chief as a young man, attended a conference with the governor of New York at Albany in 1700, and went to England to visit the queen in 1710.

Hendrick played an important role in the French and Indian War, raiding the Montreal region and joining Johnson in guarding the New York frontier. In 1754 he attended the Albany Congress to urge the colonies to create a united front against the French: "Look about your Country & see, you have no Fortifications about you, no, not even to this City.... Look at the French, they are Men, they are fortifying everywhere--but, we are ashamed to say it, you are like women bare and open without any fortifications." His address aroused the delegates to cooperate in the provision of mutual defense measures.

The following year, Hendrick, ignoring infirmities of age, led the Mohawks on Johnson's expedition against Crown Point. While on a scout, he was shot from his horse by the French and bayoneted to death on September 8, 1755.

(Frederick J. Dockstader, Great North American Indians; Arthur Pound, Johnson of the Mohawks; John Tebbel and Keith Jennison, The American Indian Wars.)

HENDRICKSEN, CORNELIS. Cornelis Hendricksen was one of the earliest explorers of the Delaware River region. In 1616, in the employ of Dutch merchants, he traded with the Conestoga Indians. Discovering that they held three Dutch traders in captivity, he redeemed them by paying a large ransom and assisted them to return to their post on the Hudson River.

(C. A. Weslager, Dutch Explorers, Traders, and Settlers in the Delaware Valley.)

HENRY, ALEXANDER. Alexander Henry, a native of New Jersey, became a fur trader while still in his teens. At the age of 21 he provided supplies for the British army that captured Montreal, and the following year he became the first English trader to establish a post at Mackinac. There he developed a brisk business, but the French traders hated him and the Ottawa and Chippewa Indians would have murdered him had it not been for the arrival of British troops.

With the onset of Pontiac's War in 1763, British troops and traders came under attack throughout the northwestern wilderness. Almost miraculously, Henry survived to write an account of amazing adventures. He was in his room writing letters when a crowd of warriors rushed inside the fort, pretending to retrieve a ball that had been thrown over the palisades during a game between the Chippewa and Sauk Indians. Once inside, they slaughtered every Englishman in sight. As the French traders were not molested, Henry sought sanctuary at the home of his neighbor Charles Langlade, but that famous French partisan refused to assist him:

> This was a moment of despair. But the next, a Pani Indian woman, a slave of M. Langlade's, beckoned me to follow her. She brought me to a door, ... telling me that it led to the garret, where I must go and conceal myself. I joyfully obeyed her directions....

> This shelter obtained, ... I was anxious to know what might still be passing without. Through an opening which afforded a view of the area of the fort, I beheld the ferocious triumphs of the barbarian conquerors. The dead were scalped and mangled, the dying were writhing and shrieking under the knife and tomahawk. From the bodies of some, ripped open, their butchers were drinking the blood, scooped up in the hollow of joined hands, and quaffed amid shouts of rage and victory.
>
> I was shaken, not only with horror but with fear. The sufferings which I witnessed I seemed on the point of experiencing.
>
> No long time elapsed before, everyone being destroyed who could be found, there was a general cry of "All is finished!!"

On the following day, Langlade betrayed Henry and conducted the Indians to his hiding place. A Chippewa prepared to stab Henry, but changed his mind abruptly and announced that the trader would be adopted into the tribe. Watawam, a Chippewa chief, adopted him and served as his protector until an opportunity arose to send him back to the English.

After Pontiac's War, Henry returned to Mackinac and reopened his fur trade. He and his partners visited many tribes and opened new areas of trade. He became wealthy, then lost his fortune and moved to Montreal. There he became a successful merchant.

(Alexander Henry, Travels and Adventures in Canada and the Indian Territories Between the Years 1760 and 1776; Frederick Drimmer, ed., Scalps and Tomahawks; Louise Phelps Kellogg, The British Régime in Wisconsin and the Northwest; Dale Van Every, Forth to the Wilderness.)

HERKIMER, NICHOLAS. Nicholas Herkimer was born in 1728 near the present city of Herkimer, New York. The son of a German fur trader, he grew up on the frontier, learned to speak the Iroquois language, and became an expert woodsman. Serving as a militia officer during the French and Indian War, he demonstrated his valor during the invasion of German Flats in 1758 by leading a sortie from the fort and driving the French and Indians away.

With the onset of the American Revolution, Herkimer, then a brigadier-general of militia, espoused the Patriot cause. In June 1777 he conferred with the Mohawk chief Brant in an unsuccessful attempt to promote Indian neutrality.

In August 1777 Gen. Barry St. Leger's army of British, Tories, and Indians invaded northern New York and besieged Fort Stanwix. Herkimer called upon every able-bodied man from 16 to 60 to march to the assistance of Fort Stanwix. Planning to coordinate his attack with a sortie from the fort, he went into camp to await a signal that his scouts had informed the defenders of his plans. The delay caused his subordinates to accuse him of disloyalty and cowardice. Angrily, on August 6, Herkimer gave orders to advance, and his forces marched into an ambush. Herkimer sustained a severe leg wound, but he seated himself with his back against a tree and calmly continued to command his troops for the duration of one of the bloodiest battles of the entire war. (See ORISKANY, BATTLE OF.)

Unable to break through British lines to relieve Fort Stanwix, Herkimer ordered the survivors of his 800-man army to retreat, and he was carried on a litter 35 miles to his home. He died a few days later as a result of leg amputation.

(T. Wood Clarke, The Bloody Mohawk; Fairfax Downey, Indian Wars of the U.S. Army; Barbara Graymont, The Iroquois in the American Revolution; Dale Van Every, A Company of Heroes.)

HERTEL, FRANÇOIS. François Hertel was born in 1642 at Three Rivers, Quebec, a settlement that bore the brunt of Iroquois hostility. He became an Indian fighter by the time he was 15. In 1661 he was captured by a Mohawk war party, taken to a village in New York, and put through such tortures as having his thumb cut off. He withstood the torments so bravely that an old woman adopted him. During his captivity he learned a great deal about the Indian way of life, particularly methods of waging wilderness warfare.

After two years of captivity, Hertel escaped, returned to Three Rivers, and resumed his role as guardian of the frontier. Skills acquired during his life with the Indians enabled him to become a leading partisan and a hero to the French-Canadian people. During wars with the English he was given command of Indian allies, and he led some of the most sanguinary invasions of New England villages. (See SALMON FALLS, NEW HAMPSHIRE; DEERFIELD, MASSACHUSETTS.) He and his sons participated in so many raids that they terrified settlers throughout New England. Ennobled for his services, he commanded Fort Frontenac from 1709 until 1712. At the age of 80 he died in 1722.

(Francis Parkman, Count Frontenac and New France Under Louis XIV; The Old Régime in Canada.)

HESSE, EMANUEL, EXPEDITION. Capt. Emanuel Hesse, a former soldier in Col. Henry Bouquet's Indian campaigns, became a fur trader at Prairie du Chien, and Indian manager for the British during the American Revolution. In an attempt to seize control of the Mississippi Valley, Gen. Frederick Haldimand appointed him to lead a large force of Indians to seize the Spanish and American posts along the river all the way to New Orleans.

Hesse recruited some 750 Sioux, Sauk, Fox, Chippewa, Ottawa, Menominee, and Winnebago warriors for an attack on St. Louis and Cahokia in the spring of 1780. With him as well were several prominent French and English traders and partisans. They came down the Mississippi from Prairie du Chien, expecting to take Cahokia by surprise, but the residents had been forewarned, and they sent for George Rogers Clark. His timely arrival discouraged the Indians from making more than a feint at Cahokia.

On May 26, however, Hesse led an attack on St. Louis, killing 22 citizens and capturing 70 near the north entrance to the city before the local militia rushed to that point and made a spirited resistance. The Indians had been promised easy victory and rich plunder, but the threat of George Rogers Clark had so intimidated them that they refused to sustain their initial assault. At the end of the day they retreated, pursued by a joint force of Spanish and American militia as far as Rock River, where Col. John Montgomery burned several Indian villages.

(John Anthony Caruso, The Mississippi Valley Frontier; Dale Van Every, A Company of Heroes.)

HIACOOMES, MARTHA'S VINEYARD MINISTER. Hiacoomes, a Martha's Vineyard Indian, was Thomas Mayhew's first convert, accepting Christianity in 1643. Less than a year later, this "man of a sad & a sober spirit" gained a strong following when a chief who led opposition to him was killed by lightning. In 1645 his standing was greatly enhanced when most of the Indians on the island fell sick while he and his family remained in good health.

Hiacoomes began preaching in 1646. He became an ordained minister in 1670, and he converted many of his people to Christianity at his church at Edgartown. He died in 1690.

(Dictionary of Indians of North America, I; Alden T. Vaughan, New England Frontier; William Kellaway, The New England Company, 1649-1776.)

HIGH HORN, SHAWNEE CHIEF see SPEMICALAWBA, SHAWNEE CHIEF

HILL, DAVID, MOHAWK CHIEF. David Hill, a Mohawk war chief, was an ardent British ally during the American Revolution. In 1778 he compelled some three hundred Oneida Indians, allies of the Americans, to change sides and fight for the British. He led some of the most destructive raids on the New York frontier settlements.

(Barbara Graymont, The Iroquois in the American Revolution.)

HILL, SAMUEL. Samuel Hill, a sea captain who lived at Wells, Maine, was captured along with his wife and children during a raid by Canadian Indians on August 10, 1703. After burning Hill's home, the Indians murdered the smaller children, marched the surviving members of the family to Canada, and turned them over to French officials.

While a prisoner in Canada, Hill managed to send a letter to New England, providing information about the location and condition of many captives. In May 1705 he was allowed to go to Boston to arrange a prisoner exchange. He reported that the French held 117 New England captives, while 70 more were in the hands of the Indians. As a result of his efforts, many of these captives regained their freedom.

(Edward L. Bourne, History of Wells and Kennebunk; Emma Lewis Coleman, New England Captives Carried to Canada Between 1677 and 1760 During the French and Indian Wars, I-II.)

HILTON, WINTHROP. Col. Winthrop Hilton, a prominent Exeter,
New Hampshire, shipper, served as a militia major in several invasions
of Abnaki Indian strongholds. In 1704 he joined Col. Benjamin
Church's attack on the Penobscots. The following year he led 270
Indian fighters on snowshoes to Norridgewock to retaliate against
the Kennebec Indians for raids on the Massachusetts and New Hampshire settlements. Finding the village deserted, he burned Indian
houses and the church of a Jesuit missionary. In 1708 he destroyed
the Indian village of Pigwacket (Pequawket).

Hilton's incursions resulted in Indian resolve to eliminate such
a dangerous enemy. Warriors watched his home and timberland for
the right opportunity, but Hilton evaded them until July 22, 1709.
Then, while directing the work of a crew of wood cutters, he was
shot and killed by an Abnaki war party.

(Samuel Adams Drake, Border Wars of New England; Herbert
Milton Sylvester, Indian Wars of New England, III.)

HIOKATOO, SENECA CHIEF. Hiokatoo, a Seneca war chief noted
for his ferocity during the French and Indian War and Pontiac's War,
was the leader of the Indians who murdered settlers during the
Cherry Valley Massacre of November 11, 1778. His wife, Mary
Jemison, a white girl who had been captured by Indians at the age
of 13, described his exploits:

> Hiokatoo was an old man when I first saw him....
> During the term of nearly fifty years that I lived with him,
> I received, according to Indian customs, all the kindness and
> attention that was my due as his wife. -- Although war was
> his trade from his youth till old age and decrepitude stopt
> his career, he uniformly treated me with tenderness, and
> never offered an insult....
>
> He was a man of tender feelings to his friends ...
> yet, as a warrior, his cruelties to his enemies perhaps were
> unparalleled.... In early life, Hiokatoo showed signs of
> thirst for blood, by attending only to the art of war, in the
> use of the tomahawk and scalping knife; and in practicing
> cruelties upon every thing that chanced to fall into his hands,
> which was susceptible to pain. In that way he learned to
> use his implements of war effectually, and at the same time
> blunted all ... tender sympathies.... He could inflict the
> most excruciating tortures upon his enemies, and prided him-
> self upon his fortitude, in having performed the most barbar-
> ous ceremonies and tortures, without the least degree of pity
> or remorse....
>
> At Braddock's defeat he took two white prisoners, and
> burnt them alive. In 1777, he was in the battle at Fort
> Freeland.... The fort contained a great number of women
> and children, and was defended only by a small garrison....
> After a short but bloody engagement the fort was sur-
> rendered.... Hiokatoo with the help of a few Indians toma-
> hawked every wounded American while earnestly begging with
> uplifted hands for quarters.

> In an expedition that went out against Cherry Valley
> ... they plundered and burnt every thing that came in their
> way, and killed a number of persons, among whom were sev-
> eral infants, whom Hiokatoo butchered or dashed upon the
> stones with his own hands.

Hiokatoo died of consumption in November 1811. He had been
a warrior for 76 years and was believed to have been 103 years old
at the time of his death.

(See JEMISON, MARY; CHERRY VALLEY MASSACRE.)

(Mary Jemison, A Narrative of the Life of Mrs. Mary Jemison;
Dale Van Every, A Company of Heroes.)

HOBOMOK, WAMPANOAG CHIEF. Hobomok, a Wampanoag chief and
medicine man, was a faithful friend of the Plymouth settlers from the
time he met them in 1621 until his death about 1642. One of Massasoit's favorite subordinates, he was highly instrumental in keeping
that powerful chief attached to the English interest. In 1621, during
a conspiracy by Chief Corbitant to depose Massasoit, Hobomok guided
Miles Standish and his men to attack Corbitant's village.

Hobomok rendered a vital service to the Pilgrims by keeping
them informed of hostile Indian movements, warning them whenever
Massachuset or Narraganset war parties threatened the safety of
the settlement. In 1622 he joined Standish in attacking the Massa-
chusets at Wessagusset. The hostiles were so terrified by his reputation as a fighter and magic worker that they fled from the field.

Hobomok became a Christian and spent his last years as a
citizen of Plymouth.

(Neal Salisbury, Manitou and Providence; Herbert Milton Sylvester, Indian Wars of New England, I; Alvin G. Weeks, Massasoit
of the Wampanoags; William Bradford, Of Plimoth Plantation.)

HOJIAGEDE, CAYUGA CHIEF see FISH CARRIER, CAYUGA CHIEF

HOLE-IN-THE-DAY, CHIPPEWA CHIEF. Hole-in-the-Day, a famous
warrior who befriended Americans and fought on their side during
the War of 1812, became war chief of the Chippewas in 1825. He
dedicated his life to the expulsion of the Sioux from the Lake Superior region, and with guns obtained from the Americans, he and
his followers took a heavy toll on their hereditary enemies and drove
them west of the Mississippi.

In 1838 Hole-in-the-Day attacked camps of Christian Sioux at
missions near the Chippewa River, killing several men, women, and
children. As a consequence, officers at Fort Snelling permitted the
Sioux to waylay him on his way home from visiting the fort, but he
escaped by exchanging his clothing and ornaments. He died in 1846.

(Frederick J. Dockstader, Great North American Indians; Doane
Robinson, A History of the Dakota or Sioux Indians.)

HONNIASONT INDIANS. The Honniasont (Honniasontkeronon) Indians,
a small and obscure Iroquian tribe, resided on the upper Ohio River

and streams in western Pennsylvania, Ohio, and West Virginia. They traded with the Dutch on occasion, but they were decimated by the Susquehannas during the early colonial period. The survivors seem to have been absorbed by the Senecas.

(John R. Swanton, Indian Tribes of North America.)

HOPEHOOD, ABNAKI CHIEF. Hopehood (Wahoa, Wohawa), a Kennebec Abnaki chief of Norridgewock, was one of the most formidable enemies of the New England colonists. His career as a raider began during King Philip's War when he attacked the settlement of Newichawanoc, Maine. Taken prisoner at an undetermined time by the settlers, he was sold into slavery at Boston, but he escaped after a season and returned to his people more determined than ever to drive the settlers into the sea.

In 1685 Hopehood signed a peace treaty because the Maine tribes were hard pressed by the Mohawks, and the English agreed to protect them. The peace held only until the outbreak of King William's War, however, and Hopehood led the Indians who joined François Hertel in the Salmon Falls massacre on March 18, 1690. He attacked Fox Point, New Hampshire, and Saco, Maine, in May, killing or capturing about twenty settlers. Soon afterward he went to Canada, where he was slain by Indians who mistook him for an enemy.

(Samuel Adams Drake, The Border Wars of New England; Herbert Milton Sylvester, Indian Wars of New England, II; Alden T. Vaughan and Edward W. Clark, Puritans Among the Indians.)

HOPKINS, SAMUEL, INDIAN CAMPAIGNS. Gen. Samuel Hopkins set out in October 1812 to destroy the Indian villages clustered around Prophetstown in support of Tecumseh and his brother, the Prophet. He led 4,000 Kentucky mounted militia up the Wabash Valley, but the expedition became lost on the prairie and returned to Fort Harrison without reaching its goal.

Less than a month later, Hopkins made a second invasion of the Indian country. He had only half of his original army, but he expected to join forces with troops led by Illinois Governor Ninian Edwards. This time he located Prophetstown, but found it deserted. After burning the town and several surrounding Kickapoo and Winnebago villages, he began his withdrawal, but he had not gone far before 150 mounted Indians overtook him and began harassing his troops. Kickapoo warriors shot Kentuckians from the saddle during the day and stole their horses under the cover of darkness. Finally, they set fire to the prairie, almost surrounding the bewildered militiamen in a ring of flames. Eighteen whites were killed and most of their baggage was burned before Hopkins could extricate his men and lead the survivors to safety in Kentucky.

(R. David Edmunds, The Shawnee Prophet; A. M. Gibson, The Kickapoos.)

HOPOCAN, DELAWARE CHIEF see CAPTAIN PIPE, DELAWARE CHIEF

HOWARD, BENJAMIN, EXPEDITION. During the War of 1812, Gen. Benjamin Howard, former governor of Missouri Territory, determined to strike the hostile Indians assembling near Lake Peoria before they had an opportunity to organize attacks on the western frontier settlements. In August 1813 he sent Maj. Nathan Boone with a scouting party into Illinois. They were compelled to retreat by a force of Sauk and Fox warriors.

A month later, however, Howard marched up the Illinois with 1,400 men. The hostiles retreated, and Howard burned their deserted villages near Lake Peoria. He retired to St. Louis in September, having alarmed the Indians so seriously that many of them made peace with the Americans.

(Louise Phelps Kellogg, The British Régime in Wisconsin and the Northwest.)

HOWE, JEMIMA, CAPTIVITY OF. In 1745 Indians attacked the Vermont home of Jemima Sawtelle Phipps, killing her husband, William, after he had slain two warriors. Jemima and her two small children escaped. The following year she married Caleb Howe, and within a few years she became the mother of five more children.

When Indians raided the Hinsdale Township area in July 1755, the Howe family took refuge at Bridgman's Fort. Soon afterward, Howe and his sons William and Moses, went with a work party into the fields near the fort. Suddenly, 12 Indians attacked, killing Howe and capturing the boys. The other men fled, and the Indians seized the fort when they discovered that only women and children remained to defend it.

The Indians marched the captives to Canada and sent Mrs. Howe and most of her children to St. Francis. There she became an old woman's servant. Her 10-year-old daughter Submit was sold to Gov. Pierre de Vaudreuil, and placed in a convent at Quebec. Mary, her 13-year-old daughter, was told to marry an Indian, but when Vaudreuil learned of it he had her sent to the same convent. Meanwhile, Jemima's youngest child, little more than an infant, died in captivity.

In 1759, Col. John Schuyler redeemed Mrs. Howe and her surviving sons. The following year, Jemima was able to obtain Submit's release from the convent despite the child's desire to remain. Mary married a Frenchman and refused to rejoin her family. After returning to New England, Jemima married Col. Amos Tute. She died in 1805.

(Howard H. Peckham, Captured by Indians.)

HUCKIN'S GARRISON HOUSE see OYSTER RIVER, NEW HAMPSHIRE, RAIDS

HUDDE, ANDRIES. Andries Hudde, a commissary official and Indian manager for the Dutch West India Company, came to Manhattan about 1634. In 1645 he was transferred to Fort Nassau on the Delaware, where he worked diligently to improve Indian relations and to compete with the Swedes in the fur trade. In 1646 he bought land from the Indians near the present site of Philadelphia, Pennsylvania, for a Dutch trading post. Two years later, he built Fort Beversreede on the east bank of the Delaware. This post and Fort Nassau were abandoned because of Swedish hostility and replaced by Fort Casimir, below the Swedish forts, in 1651. There Hudde acted as commissary until it was seized by the Swedes in 1654.

(C. A. Weslager, Dutch Explorers, Traders, and Settlers in the Delaware Valley.)

HUDSON, HENRY, INDIAN RELATIONS. Henry Hudson, a veteran English sea captain, made unsuccessful attempts to find a northwest passage in 1607 and 1608 for an association of Englishmen. After their company disbanded, he obtained backers in Holland and sailed in the Half-Moon to Maine in 1609. In July, he traded with the Indians of Penobscot Bay and Cape Cod. Late in August, he arrived at Delaware Bay and explored the Delaware River until he became convinced that it did not provide access to the Orient.

Early in September, Hudson explored Manhattan Island and anchored near the mouth of the river that bears his name. He traded extensively with Indians who boarded his ship, exchanging knives and beads for tobacco. Trouble began, however, when Hudson sent a boat to explore neighboring streams. The sailors seized Indian goods, and 26 warriors (probably Canarsees) retaliated with an attack on the boat. John Colman was killed and 2 of his mates were wounded.

Afterward, Hudson set sail up the Hudson River. On September 18, he anchored near the present Castleton, New York, invited the Mahican Indians to come aboard to trade, gave them liquor, and obtained a valuable cargo of furs. "Such," said E. B. O'Callaghan, "was the introduction among the Indians, by the first European to come among them, of that poison that ... caused within a few centuries, the almost entire extinction of the Red race."

After ascending the river as far as Albany, Hudson began his return to the coast. Near the present Peekskill an altercation arose when an Indian was shot to death while attempting a theft. Soon a swarm of angry warriors arrived in canoes and attacked the ship, but after 6 of them were killed, the survivors abandoned the attempt.

By early November, Hudson was back in Europe, having completed a voyage that made a major impact upon the Indians. "A number of red men," noted Allen W. Trelease, "had taken three steps toward civilization. They had seen the effect of firearms, they had got drunk and they had learned to want European goods."

Hudson made a second voyage to North America in 1610. After entering Hudson Bay, he was set adrift to perish by his mutinous crew.

(E. B. O'Callaghan, History of New Netherland, I; Allen W. Trelease, Indian Affairs in Colonial New York; C. A. Weslager, Dutch Explorers, Traders, and Settlers in the Delaware Valley.)

HULL, WILLIAM, INDIAN RELATIONS. Gen. William Hull, an officer decorated for bravery during the American Revolution, was appointed Governor of Michigan Territory in 1805. In that office he was called upon to conduct difficult negotiations with the northwestern Indian tribes, and his successful land cession treaties aroused the enmity of Tecumseh and his brother, the Prophet.

In 1807, the Prophet and his envoy, Blue Jacket, convinced Hull that the Shawnees were sincere friends of the United States. Two years later, when Ottawa and Chippewa Indians planned to attack the Prophet's followers, Hull persuaded them to leave the dangerous Indian confederation at Prophetstown unmolested. By 1810, however, Hull realized that he had been hoodwinked. He invited chiefs of the northwestern tribes to a conference near Brownstown, gave them presents and food, and urged them to prevent their warriors from going to Prophetstown.

At the onset of the War of 1812, Hull reluctantly accepted command of the Army of the Northwest, headquartered at Detroit. On July 11, 1812, he invaded Canada with an army of 2,000, including a regiment of regulars. Hesitating, however, to attack Fort Malden, as he feared that the fall of Mackinac would encourage the Indians to assist the British, he retreated to Detroit when informed that Tecumseh threatened his supply lines. On August 15, the British called upon Hull to surrender, informing him that they would be unable to restrain the Indians from massacring his men if they were taken in battle. Hull refused the demand, but when the British and Indians attacked Detroit the following day, he capitulated, apprehensive, he said, that warriors would slaughter the women and children who had taken refuge there. As a result, Hull was court-martialed for cowardice and sentenced to death, but President James Madison reprieved him because of his Revolutionary War record.

(R. David Edmunds, The Shawnee Prophet; Reginald Horsman, The War of 1812.)

HUNNIWELL, RICHARD. Richard Hunniwell, a Scarborough, Maine, settler, suffered the loss of his wife and child in an Abnaki attack during Queen Ann's War. From that time until his death, he became one of New England's most ferocious Indian fighters. His exploits have been recounted by Herbert Milton Sylvester:

> Regardless of all treaties, to Hunniwell an Indian was a savage butcher, who was to be killed at sight. Once he entered a clam house and found two friendly Indians visiting with the fishermen. He picked up one of their guns, pretended to examine it, then shot both of them with it. He is reported to have killed, upon another occasion, five Indians with a single shot.... Once, when mowing beside the Nonsuch, he discovered Indians across the stream. He kept at his work; but the savages, discovering the mower to be the famous Hunniwell, and that he had left his gun beside a haystack some little way off, determined to capture him. One of them forded the river (and) ... got the gun. Still creeping upon the ... mower the savage rose.... Instantly

Hunniwell whirled the scythe in the air. The savage fired; but ... the ball flew high, and the recoil threw the savage on his back. Before he could get to his feet Hunniwell had decapitated his enemy, and, fixing his head on a pole, placed it in full sight of the Indians across the river, challenging them to come over and he would serve them the same.

The Indians finally caught up with Hunniwell in 1713 when they ambushed 20 men rounding up cattle at Massacre Pond. They killed him instantly and mutilated his body.
(Herbert Milton Sylvester, Indian Wars of New England, III.)

HUNT, THOMAS. In 1614 an English sea captain, Thomas Hunt, a subordinate of Capt. John Smith, kidnapped 20 Patuxet and 7 Nauset Indians near the site of the future Plymouth colony and carried them to Spain. There he attempted to sell them as slaves, but priests intervened, and he left Spain without obtaining the expected profit. This crime convinced the New England Indians that white men were dangerous enemies.
(Neal Salisbury, Manitou and Providence.)

HURON INDIANS see WYANDOT INDIANS

HURONTOWN CONFERENCE. In 1786 Joseph Brant assembled a large number of chiefs of northwestern tribes at Hurontown on the Detroit River. He persuaded many of them to support the British and to renounce the recent treaties of Forts Finney, Stanwix, and McIntosh on grounds that no land cession was valid unless it had been approved by all of the tribes. Brant wrote a memorandum to Congress, signed by chiefs of 11 Indian nations, expressing a desire for peace, but insisting that the tribes would unite if necessary to expel interlopers from Indian lands. Congress ignored the message, and the Indians increased their raids on the settlements.
(Dale Van Every, Ark of Empire.)

HUTCHINSON, ANNE, MURDER OF. Anne (Mrs. William) Hutchinson, one of New England's most brilliant and controversial religious leaders, was banished from Massachusetts Bay for heresy in 1638. She removed with her family to the present site of Portsmouth, Rhode Island, where she purchased land from the Indians. In 1642, after her husband's death, she moved to New York and settled near Eastchester. In 1643 the Long Island Indians, joined by warriors from the Hudson, began a war with the Dutch. Among many Dutch and English settlers massacred in August and September were Anne Hutchinson and most of the members of her family. Her daughter Susanna was captured. Her supporters blamed her death on Puritan leaders who had driven her from Massachusetts. Her opponents responded by pronouncing her death "a judgement of God."
(E. B. O'Callaghan, History of New Netherland, I; Herbert Milton Sylvester, Indian Wars of New England, I; Emery Battis, Saints and Secretaries.)

HUTCHINSON, EDWARD. Capt. Edward Hutchinson, son of Anne
Hutchinson, was a farmer near Brookfield, Massachusetts, when
King Philip's War impended. He was sent on a mission to the Narraganset Indians to persuade them not to join Philip, and, with the
help of Roger Williams, he obtained their assurance of peaceful intentions. A few months later he undertook a similar mission to the
Nipmuc Indians. Accompanied by a small force of troopers, he rode
headlong into an Indian ambush. Hutchinson was wounded, and
several of his men were killed. The survivors fled to Brookfield.
They were not safe there, however, for the Indians besieged the village until help arrived. (See BROOKFIELD.) Hutchinson died of
his wounds three weeks afterward.

(Douglas Edward Leach, Flintlock and Tomahawk; Charles H.
Lincoln, ed., Narratives of the Indian Wars.)

-I-

ILLINOIS INDIANS. The Illinois Indians, a large Algonquian-speaking
confederacy comprising the Kaskaskia, Cahokia, Peoria, Tamaroa,
Michigamea, and Moingwena nations, were located in Illinois, Wisconsin, Iowa, and Missouri when first encountered by Europeans. Although they were scattered over a huge territory, they could assem-
ble large war parties from the various tribes when the need arose
as a result of their numerous conflicts with other Indians.

Seventeenth-century traders and missionaries characterized the
Illinois as friendly, tractable, and ideally suited for Christianization.
Fathers Claude Allouez and Jacques Marquette visited them between
1667 and 1673 and established missions soon afterward. La Salle and
Tonti gained their allegiance to France and built a fort at Starved
Rock for mutual protection. As allies, however, the Illinois tribes
suffered tremendous losses at the hands of Indian enemies of the
French, particularly the Fox, Iroquois, Potawatomi, and Sauk na-
tions.

Finally, terrified by Indian enemies, the Illinois tribes began
abandoning their hunting grounds and clustering around the French
settlements for protection. There they became increasingly weakened
by easy access to liquor and by susceptibility to European diseases.
Most of them became Christians, and intermarriages with the French
created a large mixed-blood population. After the French and Indian
War, they accompanied French settlers across the Mississippi to the
vicinity of St. Louis and Ste. Genevieve.

The Illinois Indians supported the Americans during the Revolutionary War and the War of 1812. As a result, they sustained repeated attacks by Indian allies of the British. Recognized by the
United States as the rightful owners of an immense territory, they
began selling land to the new nation before the beginning of the
nineteenth century, and by 1832 they completed the process and
moved to a reservation in Kansas. The remnants of the various
tribes merged into the Peoria and Kaskaskia nation on the Osage
River agency and became successful farmers. In 1867 they moved

to the Indian Territory and consolidated with the Wea and Piankashaw survivors in the northeastern portion of present Oklahoma.

(Clarence Walworth Alvord, The Illinois Country; Grant Foreman, The Last Trek of the Indians; Louise Phelps Kellogg, The French Régime in Wisconsin and the Northwest.)

INDIAN CREEK MASSACRE. One of the most atrocious attacks of the Black Hawk War occurred on May 20, 1832, when a Potawatomi war party wiped out most of the settlers of Indian Creek, near Ottawa, Illinois. The raid was in retaliation for abuse of Indians by one of the settlers, William Davis, a few days earlier. Sixteen settlers, including several women and children, were killed, and two girls were captured. (See HALL GIRLS, CAPTIVITY OF.)

"A ghastly sight met the eyes of the troops ... who went to bury the ... friends and relatives of the Hall girls.... The Indians had butchered their bodies. They had strung the women up by their feet and had practically chopped the children to pieces."--William T. Hagan.

(James A. Clifton, The Prairie People; Cecil Eby, That Disgraceful Affair, The Black Hawk War; William T. Hagan, The Sac and Fox Indians.)

INDUSTRY, FORT, TREATY OF. The Treaty of Fort Industry was negotiated at the present site of Toledo, Ohio, on July 4, 1805. Charles Jouett persuaded chiefs of the Chippewa, Ottawa, Potawatomi, Wyandot, Delaware, and Shawnee nations to cede almost three million acres west of the Cuyahoga River and south to the boundary established by the Treaty of Greenville. The tribes received a $1,000 annuity and retained the right to hunt and fish in the ceded territory.

(Charles J. Kappler, ed., Indian Affairs: Laws and Treaties, II.)

IROQUOIS INDIANS. The Iroquois Indians, known to colonial officials as the Five Nations (or Six Nations after 1722), were encountered in 1534 at the Bay of Gaspé by Jacques Cartier. They received the Frenchmen in a friendly manner and showed an eagerness to trade. Cartier kidnapped the sons of a chief, took them to France, and used them as guides when he sailed up the St. Lawrence as far as the present site of Montreal the following year.

Prior to 1570 the Iroquois nations--Mohawks, Oneidas, Onondagas, Cayugas, and Senecas--were at war with each other. Then two legendary leaders, Hiawatha and Dekanawida, induced them to establish the League of the Iroquois, a loose political and military union that established peace among them and enabled them to act as a powerful unit during conflicts with neighboring tribes. They attained strength disproportionate to their population (less than 15,000) because of their strategic location and their early acquisition of firearms. While the league assured members of mutual protection, it did not prevent any nation from waging war or making peace with outsiders, a situation which led to its dissolution two centuries later.

The Iroquois became hostile to the French in 1609 when Champlain and two of his men helped Algonquian Indians to defeat 200 Mohawks in battle. (See CHAMPLAIN, SAMUEL DE.) At that time the Iroquois discovered the importance of firearms, and they obtained them from Dutch traders after the founding of Albany in 1624. Soon the Iroquois were well enough armed to attack Montreal and Quebec and to carry out a war of extermination against the Algonquians, Hurons, and other Canadian allies of the French. By the early 1650's they were destroying Indian villages and enlarging their hunting grounds in the Great Lakes region and along the Ohio as well.

The fur trade with the Dutch (and later with the English) in New York enabled the Iroquois to conquer neighboring tribes, but it led to their dependency upon European trade goods. When the fur supply of northern and central New York became exhausted, the Iroquois attempted to obtain pelts from tribes farther west. A series of "beaver wars" began in the 1630's, and the Iroquois destroyed or decimated the neighboring Algonquian, Huron, Petun, Erie, and Susquehanna nations, replacing their own losses by adopting enemy survivors.

The French desired to make peace with the Five Nations, and, on occasion, league members stopped their attacks for brief periods in order to concentrate on wars with enemy Indians. In 1656 they permitted establishment of a French settlement and Jesuit mission at Onondaga, but it was abandoned two years later because of renewed Iroquois hostility. After the English supplanted the Dutch in New York in 1664, they relied upon superior trade goods to retain the Iroquois as allies. In general the strategy succeeded, but, beginning soon afterward, a minority of the Mohawks and Onondagas, influenced by the Jesuits, was induced to move to Canada and to fight against their own countrymen. (See CAUGHNAWAGA INDIANS.)

In 1667 the French destroyed several Iroquois villages, impelling the Five Nations to make peace while they sought to improve their position in the fur trade and to regather their strength. Beginning in 1679, members of the league made military alliances with the English, not realizing that the agreements endangered their independence by subjecting them to the crown. War with the French resumed in 1680 when the Iroquois attacked their allies, the Illinois Indians.

During King William's War (1689-97), the French and their Indian allies made numerous raids on New England towns and Iroquois villages. After the treaty of Ryswick in September 1697, the Iroquois, deprived of English support, made peace with the French and adopted a policy of neutrality, exercising a balance of power between the colonies of the two European nations that lasted until the French and Indian War. While maintaining neutrality, the league regained power and wealth, obtaining gifts from both camps and capitalizing on control of the fur trade. By 1757, however, realizing that the English probably would prevail, warriors joined them in the Crown Point and Niagara campaigns. (See JOHNSON, WILLIAM.)

French defeat terminated Iroquois tactics of playing one nation against another. Failing to fully comprehend English ability to encircle them, and under the powerful influence of Sir William Johnson, most of the Iroquois promised to remain faithful allies of the crown.

At the onset of the American Revolution, both sides initially urged the Iroquois to stay neutral. By 1777, however, both sought active Indian support. The Oneidas and Tuscaroras favored the Americans, while warriors from the other Iroquois nations joined the British expedition against Fort Stanwix. At the Battle of Oriskany, Six Nations warriors fought against each other, and the League of the Iroquois burst asunder. Under the leadership of Joseph Brant, the Mohawks, Onondagas, Senecas, and Cayugas raided the New York and Pennsylvania settlements, inflicting heavy casualties and great destruction. In 1779 the Americans retaliated by a destructive strike of their own (see SULLIVAN, JOHN), and compelled the hostiles to abandon their villages and to take refuge at Niagara. There they regrouped and resumed their raids until the end of the war.

After the Revolution, the Iroquois found that the British had relinquished tribal lands to the Americans. Many of them moved to Canada, where remnants reestablished the league. The Oneidas and Tuscaroras were rewarded for their support of the Americans by confirmation of their land possession at the Treaty of Fort Stanwix in 1784. Over time, however, the New York Iroquois sold most of their land and moved to reservations. (See MOHAWK, ONEIDA, ONONDAGA, SENECA, CAYUGA INDIANS.)

(Barbara Graymont, The Iroquois in the American Revolution; Allen W. Trelease, Indian Affairs in Colonial New York; Francis Parkman, A Half-Century of Conflict; T. Wood Clarke, The Bloody Mohawk; William J. Eccles, The Canadian Frontier; George T. Hunt, The Wars of the Iroquois; Cadwallader Colden, The History of the Five Indian Nations; Francis Jennings, ed., The History and Culture of Iroquois Diplomacy.)

IRWIN, LUKE. In 1751, Luke Irwin, a 28-year-old native of Ireland who came to Pennsylvania to engage in the Indian trade, visited tribes on the Allegheny and Ohio rivers. With three companions he obtained an enormous number of pelts, while defying French threats of eviction. Finally arrested near Sandusky, they were imprisoned at Montreal until released a year later as a result of persistent demands by the British ambassador to France.

To their seizure, said Frank H. Severance, "as much as any single act, may be ascribed the ultimate conflict between France and Great Britain in America."

(Frank H. Severance, An Old Frontier of France.)

-J-

JAMES, THOMAS. Thomas James, a New England clergyman, became the minister of the church at East Hampton, Long Island, about 1660. Interested in converting the Montauk Indians to Christianity, he mastered their language sufficiently to compose an Indian catechism.

In addition to his missionary activities, he served as an intermediary between the Indians and the colonists until his death in 1696.

(Allen W. Trelease, Indian Affairs in Colonial New York.)

JAMES, THE PRINTER, NIPMUC WARRIOR. James the Printer (Wowanus) was born about 1643. A member of the Reverend John Eliot's "praying Indian" communities, he was educated at the Cambridge, Massachusetts, Charity School. In 1659 he became the printer who helped Eliot publish an Indian Bible. In 1675, however, he joined King Philip's forces fighting the New England colonists.

One of Philip's few educated followers, he is believed to have served as secretary during the chief's negotiations that resulted in the release of Mrs. Mary Rowlandson from captivity. In addition, he posted a message written in English defending the Indian cause during the attack on Medfield.

After Philip's defeat, James surrendered at Cambridge on July 2, 1676. He received amnesty under a special declaration of mercy and became a teacher of Indians at Grafton. He died about 1728.

(Albert Britt, Great Indian Chiefs; Douglas Edward Leach, Flintlock and Tomahawk; Dictionary of Indians of North America, II.)

JEMISON, MARY, CAPTIVITY OF. Mary Jemison was born on shipboard in 1742 or 1743 while her parents were emigrating to America to settle on the Pennsylvania frontier. Soon after the outbreak of the French and Indian War, Shawnee Indians attacked the Jemison family, killed her father, mother, sister, and two brothers, and carried Mary into captivity. She was adopted as a sister by two Seneca women who treated her kindly, and within a short time she became substantially assimilated. After a pleasant interval with the Seneca family, she was informed that she must marry a Delaware warrior named Sheninjee. In later life she described the marriage thus:

> Sheninjee was a noble man; large in stature, elegant in appearance; generous in his conduct; courageous in war; a friend of peace, and a great lover of justice. He ... merited and received the confidence and friendship of all the tribes.... Yet, Sheninjee was an Indian. The idea of spending my days with him at first seemed perfectly irreconcilable to my feelings; but his good nature, generosity, tenderness, and friendship towards me soon gained my affection; and, strange as it may seem, I loved him! ... he was an agreeable husband, and a comfortable companion.

After Sheninjee's death, Mary and her three-year-old child hid in the woods to avoid redemption when the Indians were compelled to surrender their white captives. Not long afterward, she married a Seneca war chief named Hiokatoo, whose disposition differed substantially from that of her first husband. He treated her kindly, and she bore him six children, but he was one of the cruelest warriors in frontier history. (See HIOKATOO, SENECA CHIEF.)

During John Sullivan's destruction of the Iroquois homeland in 1779, she fled to Gardow Flats. There, to avoid starvation, she took a job as a farmhand for runaway slaves who had established a plantation. In 1797, the Indians gave her a large area of land at Gardow Flats, and she continued to live there after Hiokatoo died in 1811. In time the area became settled by white people, some of whom regarded her as a witch. Known in later life as "the white woman of the Genesee," she related her experiences to James E. Seaver in 1823, and her narrative remains one of the most informative and fascinating of all accounts of Indian captivity. She died in 1833.

(James E. Seaver, A Narrative of the Life of Mrs. Mary Jemison; Barbara Graymont, The Iroquois in the American Revolution; Howard H. Peckham, Captured by Indians; James Levernier and Hennig Cohen, eds., The Indians and Their Captives; Bernard W. Sheehan, Seeds of Extinction.)

JOGUES, ISAAC. Father Isaac Jogues, one of the most courageous Jesuit missionaries in the history of North America, was born at Orleans, France, on January 10, 1607. As a youth he entered a Jesuit college, and he was ordained in 1636. A few weeks afterward he sailed to Canada, determined to dedicate his life to the salvation of Indian souls.

In 1641 Father Jogues and Father Charles Raymbault served among the Chippewas of Sault Ste. Marie. The following year, while descending the St. Lawrence to obtain supplies for a mission, they were attacked near Three Rivers by the Iroquois. Father Jogues, two French companions, and several Huron Christians were captured. (See COUTURE, GUILLAUME; GOUPIL, RENE.) Taken to the Mohawk villages, they suffered the most severe tortures that Indians could inflict, one of the Frenchmen and most of the Hurons losing their lives. Jogues had a thumb cut off and all of his fingernails ripped out while tied to a scaffold, and when taken down and confined in a hut he had hot coals dumped upon him by the Indian children.

Father Jogues remained in captivity for two years. He had several opportunities to escape, but he chose to remain with his captors, as he never abandoned hope of converting them to Christianity. Finally, Dutch officials at Albany persuaded him to hide on a ship and assisted him to return to France.

Father Jogues rested in France for only a few months, for he remained as determined as ever to labor among the Indians. In July 1644, a Mohawk delegation concluded a peace treaty with the French at Three Rivers, and, in May 1646, Jogues visited them to ratify the agreement. The mission succeeded and the priest returned to Quebec convinced that the Iroquois would be receptive to his attempts to convert them. In September 1646, while he was enroute to their villages, a party of Mohawks seized him. Most of the warriors wanted to send him back to Canada, but when he entered a house to share their meal, a member of the fanatical Bear clan tomahawked him to death.

"Nature had given him no especial force of intellect or consti-
tutional energy, yet the man was indomitable and irrepressible."--
Francis Parkman.

(T. J. Campbell, Pioneer Priests of North America; T. Wood
Clarke, The Bloody Mohawk; George T. Hunt, The Wars of the Iroquois; Edna Kenton, ed., Black Gown and Redskins; Francis Parkman, The Jesuits in North America, I-II; Richard Van Der Beets,
Held Captive by Indians; E. B. O'Callaghan, History of New Netherland, I-II; Allan W. Trelease, Indian Affairs in Colonial New York.)

JOHNSON, GUY. Guy Johnson, nephew and son-in-law of Sir William Johnson, was born in Warrenton, Ireland, in 1740. He came
to America by 1756 and became Sir William's secretary soon afterward.
He served as lieutenant during the French and Indian War, commanding
a ranger company in the Amherst campaign of 1759-60.

In 1763, Guy Johnson married Sir William Johnson's daughter
Polly, and his mentor assisted him to rise rapidly in the British Indian Service. He was sincerely interested in Indian welfare, proved
to be an effective diplomat, and was recommended by the tribes to
succeed Sir William as superintendent of Indian affairs for the northern
department when the latter died in 1774.

At the onset of the American Revolution, Guy Johnson served
as colonel of the New York militia as well as Indian superintendent.
Intensely loyal to the crown, and helped by his secretary (the Mohawk chief Joseph Brant), he succeeded in holding most of the Iroquois in the British interest. In July, 1775, he conducted an important Indian conference at Oswego, and, afterward, he led a large
number of warriors and Tories to assist the British forces in Canada.
They helped defend St. Johns during the American invasion of September 1775. His proposal to send a large Indian force against the
New York settlements was turned down by Gov. Guy Carleton.

In November 1775, Guy Johnson and Joseph Brant sailed to
England in a successful attempt to strengthen their authority in the
Indian service. They returned to New York in July 1776. During
Sullivan's invasion of the Iroquois villages, Guy fought at the Battle
of Newtown, then retreated to Niagara, where he provided for the
needs of Indians who had been driven from their homes. Until March
1782, he remained at that post, inciting the Iroquois to frequent attacks upon the New York and Pennsylvania settlements. Then, replaced as Indian superintendent by Sir John Johnson, he sailed for
England and died in London in 1788.

(T. Wood Clarke, The Bloody Mohawk; Barbara Graymont, The
Iroquois in the American Revolution; Arthur Pound, Johnson of the
Mohawks.)

JOHNSON, JOHN. Sir John Johnson, son of Sir William Johnson,
was born on the New York frontier on November 5, 1742. While
still in his teens he served as a militia captain, fought at the Battle
of Lake George, and participated in Pontiac's War. He attended many
Indian conferences with his father, the British superintendent of Indian affairs, and he gained a considerable measure of influence over
the Iroquois.

Upon his father's death in 1774, John Johnson became one of the richest men in America and a leader of the New York Tories. With the outbreak of hostilities between the colonies and the mother country, he notified the British that he could recruit hundreds of Indians to fight for the crown. In May 1776, when New York Patriots attempted to arrest him, a large force of Mohawks protected him until he had time to escape to Canada, taking many Tories and Indians with him.

From a base in Canada, John Johnson organized a military unit known as the Royal Yorkers, or Johnson's Greens, to fight the Americans. They participated in some of the bloodiest battles and raids along the New York border, and Johnson became one of the most feared and hated partisan leaders. In 1777 he was a leader in the ambush of Nicholas Herkimer's army (see ORISKANY, BATTLE OF). In May 1780, he led a raid on the settlers near Johnstown, New York, killing 9 people, capturing 39, and destroying homes and crops. In October 1780, he led 265 warriors and a force of Tories into the Mohawk and Schoharie settlements, destroying the village of Stone Arabia and farms over a wide area. Although these were the only raids he led in person, he instigated many others from his headquarters at Niagara.

After the war, Sir John Johnson remained in Canada, serving as British superintendent of Indian affairs. He rendered excellent service in providing for the needs of the impoverished Indians. In September 1783, he attended an Indian conference at Sandusky, intended to maintain Britain's hold on the northwestern tribes and to prevent American acquisition of lands near the Great Lakes. He advised the tribes to stop raiding the settlements but to defend their lands against American encroachment.

Johnson obtained a large tract of land in Canada, became governor of Upper Canada, and maintained his influence with the tribes of that region until his death in 1830.

(T. Wood Clarke, The Bloody Mohawk; Barbara Graymont, The Iroquois in the American Revolution; Arthur Pound, Johnson of the Mohawks; Dale Van Every, Ark of Empire.)

JOHNSON, JOSEPH. Joseph Johnson, a Mohegan Indian, attended Eleazar Wheelock's Indian school which developed into Dartmouth College. When only 15 years old he became a teacher among the Iroquois. After a short time, however, he abandoned his school and became a sailor, leading a dissolute life on whaling voyages. In 1771, diseased and discouraged, he turned to the Scriptures for guidance, became a Mohegan missionary, and spoke at many meetings of philanthropic organizations in New York to raise funds to assist destitute Indians. He lived with the Iroquois during the American Revolution and attempted to keep them out of the war.

(John W. De Forest, History of the Indians of Connecticut.)

JOHNSON, WILLIAM. William Johnson was born in Ireland in 1715. In 1738 he sailed to America to supervise the land holdings of his uncle Admiral Peter Warren in the Mohawk Valley. From the time of his arrival he was brought into close association with the Mohawk Indians, and he proved to be the most compatible white man that this powerful nation had ever known. Johnson liked Indians instinctively, and he exhibited none of the usual attitudes of racial superiority that antagonized proud and powerful tribal leaders. He learned their customs, joined in their ceremonials, and cohabited so frequently with their women that he is said to have fathered more than a hundred half-Indian children. Within a year they adopted him, and while still a relative newcomer they made him a chief.

While supervising the admiral's estates at Warrensbush, he opened trading posts there and at Oquaga and Oswego that proved so profitable that he soon became one of North America's most successful merchants. His transactions were conducted with complete fairness toward the tribes and, unlike most traders, he refused to sell intoxicants to Indians.

Johnson's association with Indian girls who were relatives of Mohawk chiefs resulted in increasing his influence over the Six Nations. During his early years at Warrensbush he married his indentured servant, Catherine Weisenberg, shortly before her death. Afterward, by Indian custom he married Catherine, daughter of Chief Abraham, and lived with her about six years. After her death or departure, he installed Molly Brant, granddaughter of Chief Hendrick, as his "housekeeper," and she bore him eight children. Through her family connections, his standing throughout the Six Nations was greatly enhanced (see BRANT, MOLLY), and her brother Joseph Brant became Johnson's principal assistant in Indian management.

Johnson's biographer Arthur Pound noted that "probably he is the only squaw man in American history who never lost caste by reason of his consorts." As a matter of fact, colonial leaders realized that he was strategically connected and located so as to be able to render great service in the contest with France for control of the continent. By 1746, with Iroquois warriors firmly under his control, he was appointed commissary of Indian affairs. He responded by instigating or leading several invasions of Canada.

At the end of King George's War, Johnson was a commanding frontier leader, prepared to expand his activities to include political offices. Appointed to the Provincial Council in 1750, he thwarted French plans to establish a mission at Onondaga the following year by purchasing the land around Onondaga Lake. His prompt action prevented the establishment of a French fort and brought the Onondaga nation back to the British interest.

In 1753 Johnson warned that the French were preparing to seize the Ohio River region and that the British were perceived by the Iroquois as unprepared to repel them. Colonial officials responded by requesting that he use his influence among the tribes to persuade them to attend a council at Albany to resolve issues that had given rise to Indian grievances against the colonies. During this famous conference, the Iroquois sold land occupied by other tribes to Pennsylvania authorities, thus alienating the powerful Shawnees and Delawares.

After the French defeated George Washington's forces at Fort

Necessity, Johnson was appointed British Indian superintendent. When General Braddock arrived in America, he appointed Johnson major general as well as superintendent of Indian affairs. Johnson fortified his home with cannon, and it became known as Fort Johnson. In addition he constructed Forts Canajoharie, Hendrick, and Herkimer to protect the Mohawk settlements. In 1755 he led British troops and Iroquois warriors in a victory over Baron Dieskau's French forces near Crown Point (see LAKE GEORGE, BATTLE OF). As a result, he was rewarded with a barony by the crown, and Parliament awarded him £5,000. The following February he received a royal commission to serve as sole agent and superintendent of Indian affairs in the Northern Parts of North America.

In 1759, Johnson recruited the largest force of Indians in American history to join Gen. John Prideaux's campaign against the powerful French fort at Niagara. After Prideaux was killed, Johnson assumed command, won a bloody victory, and compelled the fort to surrender. (See NIAGARA, FORTS.)

In 1760, Johnson persuaded several Indian tribes to remain neutral while General Amherst led British troops across their lands during an invasion of Canada. After the capture of Montreal, he negotiated peace treaties with nine Canadian Indian nations.

The defeat of France led to Indian discontent, culminating in Pontiac's War, and, in 1761, Johnson discovered the beginnings of an Indian conspiracy. In an attempt to improve relations, he assembled representatives of 13 tribes at Detroit, distributed gifts, and dissuaded the Senecas from instigating hostilities. To defuse the plot, however, he was forced to play one nation against another, and by favoring the Senecas he infuriated Pontiac and the Ottawas. Pound considers this to be his "one great blunder in Indian diplomacy," and it was an important factor leading to a major Indian war.

During Pontiac's War, Johnson was able to prevent most of the Iroquois from joining the hostiles. In April 1764, he persuaded the Senecas to make peace. With the Iroquois united against Pontiac, he met representatives of other hostile nations at Niagara in July, distributed presents, and persuaded them to cease hostilities. Soon afterward, Pontiac surrendered.

For the remainder of his life, Johnson devoted most of his time to the welfare of Indians, particularly the protection of tribal lands from white encroachment. His reports to the Board of Trade were partially responsible for establishing a boundary line at the crest of the Appalachian Mountains beyond which white settlement was forbidden. Frontiersmen ignored the proclamation, however, and British officials in London decided to open lands beyond the line to settlement. In 1768, Johnson negotiated the Treaty of Fort Stanwix, persuading the Iroquois to cede land occupied by other tribes. This cession exceeded Johnson's instructions, and it was disapproved for a time by the Board of Trade. In analyzing Johnson's motivation, Barbara Graymont concluded that he "placed the king's interest above that of the Indians and ... did not neglect to enlarge his own land holdings at their expense," but he did serve "as a buffer between the red men and the colonists, did concern himself with their welfare, and did bother to learn and honor their customs."

Johnson's dedication to the crown made his role in Indian affairs increasingly difficult as events leading to the American Revolution divided the allegiance of tribesmen as well as settlers in the Mohawk region. Determined to prevent his Iroquois followers from breaking their "ancient covenant chain" with the British, he summoned them to a council at Johnson Hall on July 11, 1774. In poor health, and suffering from an old war wound, he harangued them for two hours, employing the vigorous oratorical style that had enabled him to dominate so many similar conferences. Suddenly he collapsed, was carried to bed, and died two hours later. (See BRANT, JOSEPH; JOHNSON, GUY.)

(Arthur Pound, Johnson of the Mohawks; T. Wood Clarke, The Bloody Mohawk; Barbara Graymont, The Iroquois in the American Revolution; Francis Whiting Halsey, The Old New York Frontier; Albert T. Volwiler, George Croghan and the Westward Movement.)

JOLLIET, LOUIS. Louis Jolliet (Joliet) was born at Quebec in 1645. He received a Jesuit education, intending to become a priest, but changed his mind about 1667 and embarked on a career as an explorer and fur trader. In 1669 he accompanied Jean Père to Lake Superior in search of a source of copper. While in the wilderness, he rescued an Iroquois warrior from Chippewa captivity and returned him to his people by way of Detroit and Lake Erie. Within two years he became familiar with much of the Great Lakes region, and, on June 14, 1671, he was at Saulte Ste. Marie when the Sieur de Saint Lusson took possession for France. "Thus," wrote Milo M. Quaife, "while still hardly more than a youth, Jolliet had ... disclosed to the French the direct route by way of the lakes from Quebec and Montreal to the Sault. The choice of Jolliet as leader of the expedition in search of the Mississippi was, therefore, entirely logical."

With Father Jacques Marquette as co-leader, Jolliet undertook, in 1673, an expedition to explore the great river which the Indians called the Mississippi. They began their voyage on May 17, went down the Mississippi as far as the Arkansas, and returned to Green Bay five months later. (See MARQUETTE, JACQUES.)

After his famous voyage, Jolliet was granted title to Anticosti Island, near the mouth of the St. Lawrence. He never returned to the West, but he explored Hudson Bay in 1679 and Labrador in 1694. He died in 1700.

(Edna Kenton, ed., Black Gown and Redskins; Louise Phelps Kellogg, The French Régime in Wisconsin and the Northwest; Milo M. Quaife, Checagou; John Gilmary Shea, Discovery and Exploration of the Mississippi Valley.)

JONCAIRE, DANIEL DE, SIEUR DE CHABERT ET DE CLAUSONNE. Daniel de Joncaire, seventh child of Louis-Thomas de Joncaire, was a member of one of the most successful families of Indian managers in North American history. (See JONCAIRE, LOUIS-THOMAS CHABERT DE; JONCAIRE, PHILIPPE-THOMAS.) Their names appear in several forms in the annals of Canadian history, and as Frank H. Severance has noted, it is impossible to determine in some instances which member of the family should be credited with a particular exploit or diplomatic coup.

Born at Montreal in 1716, Daniel spent most of his life among Indians. He was an adopted Seneca, and before he was twenty he had lived among the Iroquois, the Chippewas, the Ottawas, and the Shawnees. His knowledge of Indian languages and his adoption of many Indian customs enabled him, like his father and brother, to maintain a powerful influence over the tribes.

In 1736, Daniel negotiated peace between the Missisaugas and Iroquois, both nations French allies at that time. In 1739, he served in the French and Indian campaign against the Chickasaws. Between 1741 and 1743, while working out of Niagara, he visited tribes throughout the Great Lakes region, urging them to resist English attempts to gain their allegiance. When he learned that some Chippewas had attacked Niagara, he led a force that captured them and compelled them to fight for the French. His activities so alarmed English officials that they put a price on his head.

In 1748, Daniel was designated French commander of the Iroquois nations and sent to live among the Senecas. The superiority of English trade goods had lured many warriors to their interest, however, and 4 of them attacked him during a council, inflicting a knife wound. He killed 1 of his assailants with his tomahawk, however, and friendly warriors drove the 3 survivors from the council house. In 1749 he accompanied the Céleron Expedition down the Ohio River. In 1750, while attempting to thwart Sir William Johnson's attempt to seize the Indian trade of the Ohio region, he was bested by George Croghan in a confrontation at Logstown. The Indians signed a treaty with Croghan, insulted Joncaire, and drove him from the village.

Commissioned infantry lieutenant, Daniel was instructed in 1751 to establish Little Fort Niagara on the portage above the falls. The following year he dispatched warriors to attack Englishmen who spied upon the Niagara posts. In 1753 he assumed command of Fort Little Niagara as well as the portage, and, about that same time, he received instructions to establish forts on the Ohio. In 1754 he constructed Fort Machault at Venango.

During the French and Indian War, Daniel played a leading part in events along the Niagara-Great Lakes-Ohio frontier. In the summer of 1754 he led 500 warriors during Montcalm's capture of the British post at Oswego. Afterward, he returned to Niagara with orders to gain the allegiance of the Six Nations by improving trade relations. Inadequately supplied with government goods, he found it necessary to exhaust his own stores before the tribes would agree to attack English settlements.

In July 1758, Daniel equipped 216 Indians and Frenchmen at his own expense and hastened to Fort Duquesne to help defend it against the Forbes Expedition. He participated in Grant's defeat and escorted the English prisoners to Niagara. In 1759, when hordes of Indians congregated at Niagara, he exhausted his personal resources in an attempt to support them, and the French government failed to reimburse him.

When the British attacked Niagara in July 1759, Daniel led his small force through enemy lines into Fort Niagara. After the surrender of that strategic post to Sir William Johnson, he was freed in a prisoner exchange. Blamed along with many of his fellow officers for the loss of Canada, he was tried in France on charges of fraud and corruption. He received a reprimand for failing to keep adequate provisions at forts under his command, but the court acquitted him of more serious charges.

In 1764, Daniel went to London and attempted without success to persuade the king that he was the rightful owner of land around Niagara, his father having received it as a gift from the Iroquois. After taking the oath of allegiance to Great Britain, he was permitted to return to Montreal and engage in the Indian trade. He died at Detroit on July 5, 1771.

(Frank H. Severance, An Old Frontier of France.)

JONCAIRE, LOUIS-THOMAS CHABERT DE. Louis-Thomas Chabert de Joncaire, called Sonochiez by the Iroquois, was born in France about 1670. Entering military service at an early age, he came to Canada as a cavalry sergeant, probably between 1687 and 1689. About three years later, he and several other soldiers were captured by the Senecas. His companions were burned to death, and he was condemned to the same fate, but he exhibited such bravery under torture that the Indians spared his life and adopted him into the tribe. After a year of captivity, during which time he learned their language and became attached to their customs, the Indians permitted him to return to his own people.

"On that captivity, and Joncaire's subsequent adoption," declared Frank H. Severance, "depended the course of history in western New York for half a century. Joncaire passed much of his subsequent life among the Senecas, and though he won distinction for his service to his king and the cause of Canada, he seems never to have forfeited the confidence of his red brethren."

Joncaire married a Seneca woman during the 1690's and a French-Canadian, Marie Madelaine Le Gay de Beaulieu, at Montreal in 1706. He was the father of numerous children, two of whom, Philippe and Daniel, followed in his footsteps as Indian managers.

In July 1700, Joncaire interpreted at a meeting at Montreal intended to obtain the release of French captives held by the Iroquois. When agreement was reached, the chiefs requested that he take charge of arrangements. He brought 13 former captives to Montreal in September, the first of many that he redeemed during the next three decades. In 1701, he helped to negotiate an end to the war with the Iroquois, and the following year he played a leading role in preventing the Five Nations from becoming involved in Queen Anne's War. In 1704, while living with the Senecas, he debated Peter Schuyler in a Five Nations council at Onondaga over the merits of French or English trade. Afterward, he helped to outfit war parties to invade New England villages.

Commissioned lieutenant of the marine in 1706, Joncaire was sent on missions of friendship as far as the Illinois country, and he spent most of his time at Onondaga in an attempt to counter the influence of English agents. In 1709 he murdered a Frenchman named Montour who was serving the English. (See MONTOUR, LOUIS, FAMILY OF.) In 1710, learning that some Iroquois warriors intended to join the English in an invasion of Canada, he threatened French "vengeance if they shared in the hostile movement." Later that year he led an Iroquois force that participated in a French campaign against the English settlements.

In August 1711, Joncaire interpreted at a banquet for 800 Indians at Montreal. Announcing news that the English intended to attack Quebec, he brandished his tomahawk and began singing the Iroquois song of battle. Instantly, the Indians took up the chant, and all of them agreed to fight for the French.

During the next decade, Joncaire commanded Fort Frontenac and attempted to obtain Iroquois permission to establish a fort at Niagara. He spent the winter of 1719-20 with the Senecas, and by a generous distribution of liquor and gifts, he persuaded them to permit construction of the fort and to guard it against attack by the English. Afterward, he built a palisaded trading post at the present site of Lewiston, N.Y. He was appointed commandant of the post and master of the portage, and from that strategic location he managed an immense Indian trade.

In 1731 Joncaire received orders to use his influence to separate the Shawnees and Delawares from the English interest. He delivered a large store of goods to them and devoted the remainder of his life to countering the advances of English traders. He died at Fort Niagara on June 29, 1739.

"Up to the 1740's the French had far surpassed the rival nation in the possession of men ready and able to deal with the Indians and mould them to their will. Eminent among such was Joncaire, French emissary among the Senecas in western New York, who, with admirable skill, held back that powerful member of the Iroquois league from siding with the English."--Francis Parkman.

(Francis Parkman, A Half-Century of Conflict, I-II; Frank H. Severance, An Old Frontier of France.)

JONCAIRE, PHILIPPE-THOMAS. Philippe-Thomas Joncaire, eldest son of Louis-Thomas de Joncaire, was a highly successful Indian diplomat, much in the mold of his father and his brother Daniel. Born in 1707, he is said by several historians to have had an Iroquois Indian mother, but others assert that he was the son of his father's French-Canadian wife, Marie Madelaine Le Gay de Beaulieu.

At the age of 10, Philippe-Thomas was sent by his father to live with the Senecas "and desired their protection and favor for him, that after his death ... his son might be received amongst them in the same friendly manner as he himself had ever been...." He remained with the Indians long enough to learn their language and customs and to become so highly regarded by the nation that he succeeded his father as their agent in 1739. Like his father, he had both a French and an Indian wife.

Philippe-Thomas began his military career in 1726, served as a lieutenant of colonial troops for many years, and was promoted to captain in 1751. His entire career was spent on the frontier, most of it as an Indian manager, interpreter, and trader. Not only was he successful in countering English attempts to detach the Senecas from the French interest, but he strove with some success to prevent the French from retaliating against the tribe for hostile acts of their young warriors.

Closely associated with the Abbe Picquet, founder of the mission of La Presentation at the present site of Ogdensburg, N.Y., Philippe-Thomas was able to hold the Senecas and Shawnees in the French interest until William Johnson arrived in the Mohawk Valley in 1738. Afterward he and Johnson competed so fiercely for control of the tribes that each of them put a price on the head of the other.

In 1747 Philippe-Thomas became seriously ill and relinquished his role as Seneca agent to his brother Daniel. In 1749, however, he recovered sufficiently to serve with Daniel as advance agents of the Céleron Expedition, risking their lives to pave the way for forces that expelled English traders from the Ohio and claimed the region for France. In 1750, he established a trading post at Logstown.

In 1753, Philippe-Thomas drove the English trader John Fraser from Venango and established his own headquarters there. When George Washington encountered him there, Joncaire treated him hospitably, but informed him firmly that the French would never surrender the Ohio.

After the outbreak of the French and Indian War, most of the Iroquois supported the English, and by 1759 even the Senecas had deserted the French. Shortly before the fall of New France, Indians attacked Joncaire and his son-in-law. The two Frenchmen defended themselves until dark and then escaped into the night. Philippe-Thomas went to Niagara and was captured when the French surrendered the fort. After his parole, he went to France and died about 1766.

(Frank H. Severance, An Old Frontier of France.)

JUCHEREAU, CHARLES. Charles Juchereau, a French officer and entrepreneur, established the first business enterprise in the Mississippi Valley. In 1702 he led a company of Frenchmen to the mouth of the Ohio, employed Mascouten Indians as buffalo hunters, and opened a tannery to ship hides to market. Within weeks he had acquired a mountain of hides, but, before he could ship them to the east, an epidemic spread among his employees. He and most of his men succumbed, and the enterprise died with them.

(Louise Phelps Kellogg, The French Régime in Wisconsin and the Northwest.)

JUMONVILLE, JOSEPH COULON DE VILLIERS see COULON DE VILLIERS DE JUMONVILLE, JOSEPH

-K-

KANAGARO, SENECA TOWN. Kanagaro, an important Seneca Indian

town, was located a few miles south of the present site of Rochester, New York. It contained some 150 houses in 1677, and served as capitol of the Seneca nation for many years. In 1687 the residents destroyed their own town and moved to Kanadasega when the marquis de Denonville led 1,600 French troops and Indians against them.

(F. W. Hodge, ed., Handbook of American Indians, I.)

KANAGHSAWS, IROQUOIS VILLAGE. Kanaghsaws, a small Iroquois village in northern New York, was commanded by a black man known as Captain Sunfish. Its 17 houses were destroyed during Sullivan's expedition of 1779.

(F. W. Hodge, ed., Handbook of American Indians, I.)

KANAKUK, KICKAPOO PROPHET see KENEKUK, KICKAPOO PROPHET

KANAPIMA, OTTAWA CHIEF. Kanapima, an Ottawa chief, was born near Mackinac on July 12, 1813. His parents were Catholic converts, and his Christian name was Augustin Mammelin, Jr. It was intended that he should become a priest as well as a chief, and he spent several years at seminaries in Cincinnati, Ohio, and Rome, Italy. About 1835, however, he abandoned his studies, returned to America, and accepted the chieftainship of his band. On March 28, 1836, he signed a treaty ceding much Ottawa land to the United States.

(Dictionary of Indians of North America, II.)

KANHAWAS INDIANS see CONOY INDIANS

KASKASKIA INDIANS. The Kaskaskia Indians, most prominent tribe of the Illinois confederacy, were visited by French explorers about 1670. Their largest village, located in northern Illinois, contained 74 houses when Father Jacques Marquette established the mission Immaculate Conception near present Rockford in 1674. They became friends and allies of the French, and many of them accepted Christianity. In 1680 a large concentration of Kaskaskias near Starved Rock was decimated by an Iroquois attack. When La Salle established Fort St. Louis two years later, the survivors settled there seeking protection.

In 1703, Father Gabriel Marest removed the mission to a site near the mouth of the Kaskaskia River, and most members of the tribe moved with him. A few years later, a French post and settlement were founded nearby. Friction over land developed between whites and Indians, and, in 1719, Pierre Dugue de Boisbriant, commandant of Fort Kaskaskia, moved the Indians a few miles up the river.

The Kaskaskia nation dwindled steadily as a result of white men's diseases and vices. In addition, raids by Fox, Potawatomi, and Shawnee Indians took a heavy toll on the tribe. Despite adversity and ill treatment, the Kaskaskias remained firm in their alliance, supporting the French throughout their wars with the English and siding with the French and Americans during the Revolutionary War.

In 1803 the Kaskaskias, having absorbed remnants of other

Illinois tribes, began selling their lands to the United States. (See
VINCENNES; WAYNE, FORT, TREATIES OF.) In return, they were
promised protection from enemy tribes. In 1832, under terms of the
Treaty of Castor Hill, they ceded most of their remaining lands in
Illinois and Missouri and agreed to remove to a large tract in Kansas.
In 1867 the remnant of the Kaskaskia nation agreed to move once
more, uniting with the Peoria, Miami, Wea, and Piankashaw Indians
to occupy a reservation in northeastern Oklahoma. Afterward, they
were known as Peoria Indians. (See ILLINOIS INDIANS.)

    (F. W. Hodge, ed., Handbook of American Indians, I; William
C. Sturtevant, ed., Handbook of North American Indians, XV; Grant
Foreman, Last Trek of the Indians.)

KASKE, SHAWNEE CHIEF. Kaske, son of a Pennsylvania German and
a Shawnee woman, became one of the most fearsome chiefs of the
Shawnee nation and a staunch supporter of Pontiac. He married an
English girl, captured as an infant and thoroughly assimilated into
the Indian lifestyle. In 1764, when the Shawnees surrendered to
Col. Henry Bouquet's army, Kaske became so enraged that he withdrew from the nation to live among the Kickapoos. Less than a year
later, when the Kickapoos captured the English trader and diplomat
George Croghan, Kaske urged them to burn him at the stake. He
remained hostile to the English and Americans throughout his lifetime.

    (Dale Van Every, Forth to the Wilderness.)

KELLOGG, JOSEPH. Joseph Kellogg was captured by Indians at the
age of 12 during an attack on Deerfield, Massachusetts, in 1704.
Carried to Canada, he remained in Indian captivity for a year before
a French family paid for his freedom. He grew up in Montreal and
entered the fur trade in 1710. Probably the first English colonist
to see the western portion of the Great Lakes, he visited Mackinac,
explored Lake Michigan, and paddled down the Illinois River to trade
in the French villages. Afterward, he returned to Canada, where
he remained several years before going home to New England as the
result of a prisoner exchange. Subsequently, he served as an interpreter during negotiations with the French and Indians.

    (Louise Phelps Kellogg, The French Régime in Wisconsin and
the Northwest.)

KELLOGG'S GROVE, BATTLES OF. Kellogg's Grove, Illinois, near
the Wisconsin border, was the site of two Indian fights within a week
during the Black Hawk War. On June 16, 1832, a Sauk war party
encountered a company of soldiers led by Capt. Adam Snyder near
the settlement, withdrawing after their chief was wounded and four
warriors were killed. On June 25, Black Hawk attacked Maj. John
Dement's ranger battalion at Kellogg's Grove. Five of Dement's men
were killed and 26 horses stolen before the Sauks withdrew.

    Black Hawk, in his autobiography, paid tribute to Dement's
bravery: "I ordered my braves to rush upon them, and had the
mortification of seeing two of my chiefs killed, before the enemy

retreated. This young chief deserves great praise for his courage and bravery; but, fortunately for us, his army was not all composed of such brave men!"

(Black Hawk, Black Hawk, an Autobiography; Cecil Eby, That Disgraceful Affair, the Black Hawk War.)

KENEKUK, KICKAPOO PROPHET. Kenekuk (Kanakuk), known as the Kickapoo Prophet, was born about 1785. During the War of 1812 he emerged from obscurity as a pacifist among the warlike Kickapoos, inducing about 250 people to accept his prohibition of warfare, polygamy, and alcohol. Asserting that he had learned "the secrets of life during a visit to the Great Spirit," he persuaded his followers to establish a separate Kickapoo community on the Vermillion River in Illinois and to support themselves by farming instead of hunting. A majority of Kickapoos rejected his teachings, however, and held him in contempt as "a cowardly squaw." Most of them moved to Missouri, where they continued to live in the tribe's traditional ways.

Kenekuk developed a curious relationship with whites who settled near the Vermillion. Many of his teachings paralleled Christian beliefs, and at one time he served as an assistant to Jerome C. Berryman, a Methodist missionary. With Kenekuk's assistance, Berryman was able to convert many Indians to Christianity. Afterward, however, Berryman charged that Kenekuk "began to assert that he was the 'Son of God' sent to the red people, just as Jesus had been sent to the white people," and that he would rise from the grave three days after his death.

In 1819, traditionalist Kickapoo chiefs ceded all tribal lands in Illinois and led their followers to Missouri, but Kenekuk instructed his people to stay on their prosperous farms while he skillfully employed delaying tactics for more than ten years. His pacifistic and progressive doctrines enabled him to gain the support of many of his white neighbors, and officials permitted them to remain in disregard of the removal treaty. In time, however, new settlers coveted the choice lands of the Kickapoos, and, in 1832, superintendent of Indian affairs William Clark threatened forcible removal. Recognizing that it would be impossible to resist, the Illinois Kickapoos agreed under terms of the Treaty of Castor Hill to exchange their lands for a reserve in Brown County, Kansas. In 1833, Kenekuk led his 250 followers there and established homes near the Missouri River.

Within two years, Kenekuk and his people (including Potawatomis as well as Kickapoos) had reestablished their successful agricultural practices, profiting from the sale of crops to Fort Leavenworth. By 1845, Indian Agent Richard Cummins reported that they had "progressed faster in civilization" than any tribe familiar to him.

Kenekuk died of smallpox in 1852. The descendants of his people still live on their prosperous farms.

(Frederick J. Dockstader, Great North American Indians; A. M. Gibson, The Kickapoos; George A. Schultz, An Indian Canaan.)

KENNEBEC SETTLEMENTS. In 1558, David Ingram (a shipwrecked sailor) walked the entire shoreline from the Gulf Coast to the Penobscot

River. Rescued there by an English ship, he spread such stories of riches that Queen Elizabeth sent several ships to the coast of Maine (see GOSNOLD, BARTHOLOMEW; PRING, MARTIN; WAY-MOUTH, GEORGE; POPHAM, GEORGE). These expeditions led to the establishment of a short-lived settlement on the Kennebec River in 1607.

Seafarers traded with Indians on the Kennebec with such success that the Pilgrims, led by William Bradford, established a post there in 1622. Beginning in 1625, the Abnaki Indians began selling parcels of land to settlers, but 50 years later the tribe began a series of wars that destroyed or desolated most of the settlements.

(Charles M. Andrews, The Colonial Period of American History, I; William Bradford, Of Plimoth Plantation; Neal Salisbury, Manitou and Providence; Alden T. Vaughan, New England Frontier.)

KEOKUK, SAUK CHIEF. Keokuk, a famous Sauk chief and friend of the whites, was born near Rock Island, Illinois, about 1783. He was partially of French descent. During his youth he gained renown as a warrior during battles with the Sioux. While not a hereditary chief, his skill as an orator enabled him to lead a peace faction that opposed Black Hawk's militant British supporters during the War of 1812. In 1813, his prestige increased dramatically when he persuaded the Sauks to defend their capitol, Saukenuk, instead of fleeing west of the Mississippi when an American attack was anticipated. Although the attack never came, Keokuk became such a popular hero that he was able to challenge Black Hawk for tribal leadership.

William Clark, superintendent of Indian affairs, recognized Keokuk as a possible ally in his attempt to weaken the British supporters among the Sauks and Foxes. William T. Hagan, historian of these associated tribes, asserted that "the Americans had learned to appeal to his weak points, his cupidity and love of display." In 1821, when Keokuk surrendered two Sauks who had murdered a white man, Clark showered him and his followers with gifts. Afterward, Keokuk became increasingly inclined to accede to government requests for cooperation. Conveyed to Washington on several occasions, he became convinced of the futility of opposing so powerful a nation.

When Black Hawk refused to abandon tribal lands around Saukenuk without a fight, Keokuk kept his own followers from assisting his rival. After the Sauks were defeated, Americans imprisoned the hostile old man and designated Keokuk civil chief of the nation. In 1834, Black Hawk was released in Keokuk's custody upon the condition that he accept his rival's standing as principal chief of the nation.

Given control of tribal annuities, Keokuk was in a position to punish Sauks who opposed his policy of accommodating the government. He became increasingly unpopular with many of his own people. In 1845 he agreed to exchange tribal land in Iowa for a Kansas reservation. He died on that reservation three years later, and some of the Sauks have asserted that a follower of Black Hawk poisoned him.

"By the time of his death, Keokuk was alienated from Indian

and White alike. The Sauk distrusted him because of his willing-
ness to agree to every White wish; the latter no longer found him
useful because of his loss of influence among his own people."--
Frederick J. Dockstader.
(Frederick J. Dockstader, Great North American Indians;
William T. Hagan, The Sac and Fox Indians.)

KIALA, FOX CHIEF. Kiala, an early eighteenth-century chief, was
the leader of the anti-French faction of the powerful Fox Indian nation. "Little is known," wrote Clarence Walworth Alvord, "of the
Fox chief, Kiala, a veritable forerunner of Pontiac and Tecumseh,
who succeeded in building up a strong and far-reaching confederacy
of the discontented ... tribes." (See FOX INDIANS, SAUK IN-
DIANS.)
During the Second Fox War (1727-38), Kiala persuaded tribes
located as far apart as the Abnakis and the Sioux to cooperate in an
attempt to drive the French from Canada and the Mississippi. It
proved to be impossible, however, to hold so many diverse tribes
united in a common cause, and French traders managed to bring
about the defection of the Sioux from the confederacy. Moreover,
with the arrival of Gov. Charles de Beauharnois in Canada, the
French determined to wage a war of extermination against their Indian enemies. The Foxes suffered severe defeats near Lake Michigan
and in Wisconsin at the hands of the French and their Indian allies,
and, afterward, Kiala lost the support of most of the tribes.
By 1733 even the Foxes admitted that they must make peace
in order to avoid annihiliation. Kiala and his chief supporters surrendered to the French and were shipped as slaves to the West Indies.
(Clarence Walworth Alvord, The Illinois Country; William T.
Hagan, The Sac and Fox Indians; Louise Phelps Kellogg, The French
Régime in Wisconsin and the Northwest.)

KIASUTHA, SENECA CHIEF. Kiasutha (Guyasuta) was born in a
Seneca village on the Genesee River about 1720. More prominent as
an orator than a warrior, his first important role in history was as
a guide to George Washington in 1753 when the young officer warned
the French away from the Ohio. Afterward, he served as Six Nations regent or "half-king" among the tribes of the Ohio for many
years.
Kiasutha's role in Indian-white relations is a matter of disagreement among historians, although he is generally considered to
have made several sincere attempts to prevent warfare between the
races, attending peace conferences at Montreal, Fort Pitt, Fort Stanwix and elsewhere. His part in Pontiac's War is obscure. Paul A. W.
Wallace asserted that he attempted to prevent it, while Randolph C.
Downes described him as one of its instigators. Dale Van Every said
that he was one of the leaders in the attack on Bouquet's army at
Bushy Run, an assertion Wallace denied. There is agreement, however, that he was one of the leaders in negotiating peace with Bouquet.

Kiasutha attempted to prevent the Shawnees from fighting the English and Americans in Dunmore's War of 1774. He strove to keep the Six Nations neutral during the American Revolution, but when the Senecas decided to support the British, he reluctantly joined them. His one military exploit during the conflict was the raid on Hannastown, Pennsylvania, on July 13, 1782.

Kiasutha died of smallpox in 1794.

"All his life, although he was not a hereditary chief, he exerted vast influence among his own people and ... tried to adjust peacefully the differences that arose between Indians and white men." --Paul A. W. Wallace.

(Paul A. W. Wallace, Indians in Pennsylvania; Randolph C. Downes, Council Fires on the Upper Ohio; Dale Van Every, Forth to the Wilderness.)

KICKAPOO INDIANS. The Kickapoo Indians, a powerful and warlike Algonquian people closely related to the Sauks and Foxes, were located in southwestern Michigan and northwestern Ohio when first encountered by French explorers and missionaries in the 1660's. "Skilled in warrior craft and inventive strategy," asserts the ethnohistorian A. M. Gibson, "they were much in demand as frontier shock troops, and successively served as mercenaries for the French, Spanish, British, and Mexicans."

As a result of the influence of Nicolas Perrot, who opened a trading post in a Kickapoo village in 1685, the tribe became an ally of the French during their early wars with the Iroquois. A strongly conservative people, however, they clung to their own culture and resisted missionary attempts to convert them to Christianity. When the French attempted coercion, the Kickapoos turned against them, and joining the Foxes and Mascoutens, began waylaying travellers on the western waters.

In 1712, as a consequence of the siege of Detroit (see DETROIT, MICHIGAN, INDIAN AFFAIRS; FOX INDIANS), the Kickapoos and their allies opened a war without quarter against the French. Characterized by Gibson as "a people without pity," they launched so many attacks on traders that French commerce in Canada was virtually paralyzed. They were compelled to make peace in 1716, however, when Louis de Louvigny gained a victory for France over their allies, the Fox Indians. Afterward, the Kickapoos waged war against the Illinois Indians for assisting Louvigny's campaign. They crossed the Mississippi in 1727 and united forces with the Foxes in Iowa.

In 1728, the Kickapoos captured Father Michel Guignas and a party of Frenchmen on the Mississippi River (see BOUCHER, PIERRE EXPEDITION). The Fox Indians demanded that the Frenchmen be put to death, but the Kickapoos refused, intending to exchange them for Indians imprisoned by the French. So serious a dispute arose that the Kickapoos renounced their friendship with the Foxes in 1730 and became allies of the French. They helped defeat the Foxes in 1730 and supported the French during conflicts with the English and their Chickasaw allies.

During the French and Indian War, the Kickapoos defended

French interests along the Mississippi. After France's defeat, they strongly supported Pontiac, compelling the English to abandon several forts. They seized an envoy sent by Sir William Johnson to try to make peace with the tribes (see CROGHAN, GEORGE), and many of them became Spanish mercenaries after that nation acquired Louisiana.

At the onset of the American Revolution, the various Kickapoo bands divided their allegiances. Those living in Illinois scouted for George Rogers Clark, while the Wabash towns sided with the British initially, but joined the Americans after Clark's victories in the West. Because of American frontier expansion, however, they welcomed a British rapprochement in 1780. During the next decade, they raided American settlements frequently, killing some 1,500 people. They participated in Indian victories over Harmar and St. Clair, and they continued their raids even after the tribe officially made peace at Greenville in 1795.

Most Kickapoos were among Tecumseh's ardent supporters. They defeated a force of Kentuckians (see HOPKINS, SAMUEL, INDIAN CAMPAIGNS), but they failed to capture Fort Harrison because of Zachary Taylor's spirited defense (see HARRISON, FORT). Ninian Edwards destroyed their villages, but they continued their raids on the settlements. Some Kickapoo warriors accompanied Tecumseh to Canada, and, after his death, they continued to support his brother the Prophet. When the war ended, they remained as hostile as ever to the Americans, but the British finally persuaded them to make peace.

In 1819, the Kickapoos ceded their lands in Indiana and Illinois and moved to the Osage River in Missouri. Some of their bands went to Oklahoma, Texas, and Mexico, where they became renowned raiders and horse thieves. By 1839, so many had migrated to Mexico that they constituted a formidable force that raided the Texans and fought Apaches and Comanches. Their descendants live on the Texas-Mexico border today. The bands in Missouri eventually moved to the vicinity of Fort Leavenworth, where they abandoned the warpath and became successful farmers. (See KENEKUK.)

(A. M. Gibson, The Kickapoos; Grant Foreman, The Last Trek of the Indians.)

KIEFT, WILLEM. Willem Kieft was born in Amsterdam in 1597. Governor of New Netherland from 1638 until 1645, he was noted for his harsh Indian policy. In 1639 he attempted to recoup company expenses by taxing the Indians who lived near New Amsterdam, compelling them to pay in furs, corn, or wampum. This innovation so antagonized the tribes that in 1640 Kieft ordered preparations for an Indian war.

The first tribe to feel the wrath of Kieft's policy was the Raritan division of the Delawares. In 1640 the Raritans drove off a Dutch trading ship. Soon afterward, some Indians, perhaps Raritans, stole four hogs from a farmer, and Kieft sent 80 soldiers and sailors to demand restitution. This force attacked the village forthwith, shooting several Indians and torturing the chief's brother to death. The Raritans exacted revenge in June 1641, slaying four farmers on Staten Island.

In February 1643, Kieft sent powerful forces to attack two villages of Wecquaesgeek Indians, massacring more than a hundred men, women, and children in their sleep. (See ADRIAENSEN, MARYN; PAVONIA MASSACRES.) These events precipitated a war with 11 tribes and resulted in the deaths of many Dutch settlers before John Underhill's campaigns forced the Indians to make peace in 1645. The settlers blamed Kieft for the loss of lives and property, and Dutch officials determined to recall him. On his way home in 1647, he was lost at sea.

(E. B. O'Callaghan, History of New Netherland, I; Allan W. Trelease, Indian Affairs in Colonial New York.)

KILLBUCK, DELAWARE CHIEF   see   GELEMEND, DELAWARE CHIEF

KING BEAVER, DELAWARE CHIEF   see   TAMAQUE, DELAWARE CHIEF

KING HENDRICK, MOHAWK CHIEF   see   HENDRICK, MOHAWK CHIEF

KING NEWCOMER, DELAWARE CHIEF   see   NETAWATEES, DELAWARE CHIEF

KING PHILIP, WAMPANOAG CHIEF   see   METACOM; KING PHILIP'S WAR

KING PHILIP'S WAR. King Philip's War, a desperate conflict between the New England colonists and many of their Indian neighbors, was fought in 1675 and 1676. Characterized by the colonial historian Douglas Edward Leach as the "first major test for the budding civilization ..., a crisis of staggering proportions," it resulted in Indian attacks upon more than twenty towns and the deaths of 600 settlers. Calamitous as these losses were for the English, the fate of the Indians was far worse. They lost 3,000 men, women, and children, as well as their entire way of life.

The causes of King Philip's War have been a matter of disagreement among historians. Most scholars, including Leach, place the greatest emphasis on an insatiable demand for Indian land. On the other hand, Alden T. Vaughan has asserted that "there is no substantial evidence that resentment over land transactions spurred any tribe, even the Narragansett whose grievances were the most persistent, into violent reprisal." The chief for whom the war is named, Metacom (or King Philip) of the Wampanoags, began hostilities, Vaughan believes, because he realized that his power was eroding as a result of increasing English influence over the Indians of Massachusetts and Rhode Island.

Friendship between the English and the Indians, so important during the days of Chief Massassoit, began to wane as the colonists became increasingly self-sufficient. When Metacom succeeded his father, Massassoit, and his brother Wamsutta, in 1662, Plymouth officials demanded that he sell no land without their permission, yet they continued to make grants of their own near his villages. In 1667, the town of Swansea was established on land that Philip claimed for his own people, and when the chief reacted angrily, Plymouth officials fined him and demanded that his followers surrender their weapons. It appears probable that from that time forward he began to organize tribal alliances to attempt to drive the English into the sea. (See SASSAMON, JOHN.)

War began before Metacom had completed his plans when Swansea settlers fired upon Indians looting an abandoned house. He could not restrain his young braves, and they began ambushing settlers along forest trails. Armed forces from all of the New England colonies rushed to destroy the Wampanoags and to attack the Narragansets for refusing to surrender hostiles hiding among them. (See GREAT SWAMP FIGHT.) Other Indians that supported Philip were the Nipmucs, Abnakis, and the Connecticut River villages. Fortunately for the English, however, the Mohawks and Mohegans chose to oppose Philip's forces. Inexperienced in Indian warfare, colonial officers learned that without the guidance of friendly tribesmen they could not catch up with their enemies.

During the spring of 1676, Philip's supporters overran much of New England, inflicting heavy casualties, and driving the survivors to safety in larger settlements near the coast. (See DEERFIELD; GROTON; BROOKFIELD; LANCASTER; MARLBOROUGH; SUDBURY.) But by the beginning of summer, the advantage shifted toward the English because of their superior firepower, tribal deprivation and disease, and fear of the Mohawks. Gradually Philip's supporters began turning against them, some of them surrendering to the English and offering to serve as guides in locating the hiding places of the hostiles. One of these guides led the English to Philip's camp in a swamp in August 1676, and shot him to death when he tried to escape. Soon afterward, peace was restored in southern New England.

(Douglas Edward Leach, Flintlock and Tomahawk; Alden T. Vaughan, New England Frontier.)

KINZIE, JOHN, FAMILY OF. John Kinzie (Mackenzie) was born at Quebec on December 27, 1763, son of a British Army surgeon. During his childhood his father died, and his mother married William Forsyth, a trader, who took the family to live at Detroit. John grew up on the frontier, mastered several Indian languages, and became a trader himself at the age of 18, establishing a post at Miamitown (present Fort Wayne).

Like many traders, Kinzie was an employee of both the Canadian and United States Indian services during the years prior to the War of 1812. Apparently his loyalties lay with the British at first, for he fled from Gen. Josiah Harmar's army in 1790. After Harmar burned his post at Miamitown, he opened a trade with the Ohio Indians at the mouth of the Auglaize River. This post was destroyed by Anthony Wayne in 1794.

Kinzie married Margaret McKenzie, a captive who had been kidnapped by Indians at the age of 10 in Virginia. They had three children before her father, Moredock McKenzie, located her in 1795 and took her and her children to his home in Virginia. Afterward, Kinzie moved his trading activities to the St. Joseph River in southwestern Michigan.

In 1798, Kinzie married Eleanor Little McKillip, widow of Daniel McKillip, a former member of Butler's Rangers who had been killed during the Battle of Fallen Timbers. Eleanor, too, had been an Indian captive, taken near Pittsburgh in 1779 and held until 1784. She had several small children by her first husband, one of whom eventually married Lt. Linai Helm, an officer at Fort Dearborn.

In 1804, Kinzie moved his headquarters to the mouth of the Chicago River, near the newly established Fort Dearborn. At that time he is believed to have become an American citizen, for he served as justice of the peace of Indiana Territory. His business prospered, and he became the most prominent citizen of the small community that became the great city of Chicago.

At the onset of the War of 1812, Kinzie relied upon his friendship with the Potawatomi Indians to protect his family in the event of an attack on Fort Dearborn. He urged the commanding officer Capt. Nathan Heald not to evacuate the fort, warning that the troops and their families would be attacked by Indians during the retreat to Fort Wayne, but his advice was disregarded. On August 12, he accompanied Heald to a council with Indians congregated outside Fort Dearborn, and warned him afterward that they intended to massacre the garrison. When Heald insisted upon obeying Gen. William Hull's order to abandon the post, Kinzie made arrangements with friendly Indians to take his family by boat to safety on the St. Joseph River. They were still at their home, however, when the evacuation and attack occurred (see DEARBORN, FORT, MASSACRE). Kinzie saved the life of Mrs. Heald, who was badly wounded.

A few days after the massacre, Kinzie and his family fled to Detroit. There he was imprisoned by British officers who suspected him of communicating with the Americans. After the war, he returned to Chicago. He assisted with the negotiation of a treaty with the Indians in 1821, and he died at Chicago in 1828.

(Mrs. John H. Kinzie, Wau-Bun; Milo M. Quaife, Checagou.)

KIRK, WILLIAM. William Kirk, a Quaker, was authorized by federal officials to establish a mission among the Shawnee followers of Chief Black Hoof (Catahecassa) at Wapakoneta, Ohio, in 1807. With wisdom and dedication, he assisted the Shawnees to become successful farmers, clearing the heavily timbered land along the Auglaize River and splitting rails to enclose and protect their apple orchards and flourishing fields of corn and vegetables. He instructed the Indians, also, in improving their livestock, and he obtained a sawmill and gristmill, as well as the services of a blacksmith, to help them along the white man's road.

Unfortunately, Kirk was too involved with his "hands-on" instruction to devote the time required to keep adequate records. As a result, officials in Washington, suspecting him of mismanagement of government funds, dismissed him from his post on December 22, 1808.

After the loss of their advisor, the Indians of the Auglaize were unable to sustain their transformation to an agricultural way of life.
(R. David Edmunds, The Shawnee Prophet.)

KIRKLAND, SAMUEL. Samuel Kirkland was born in Norwich, Connecticut, on November 20, 1741. He decided early in life that he
would serve as a missionary among the Iroquois Indians, and, with
that goal in mind, he attended Eleazar Wheelock's school for Indians
at Lebanon. There he met Joseph Brant and other prominent Mohawk youths, became their close friend, and studied their language.
   Kirkland attended the College of New Jersey, where he espoused the teachings of Jonathan Edwards and the principles of the
"New Light" movement. When he became a Presbyterian missionary,
his insistence upon rejection of unregenerate persons kept his church
membership small, but it failed to limit his influence.
   In 1764, encouraged by Wheelock and Sir William Johnson, Kirkland established a mission among the Seneca Indians, the most warlike of the Six Nations. He began his labors in such destitution that
he was entirely dependent on the Indians for survival. At times,
reduced to eating acorns, he became convinced that Satan had determined to starve him to death. Scorned at first by the Seneca warriors, he made such a favorable impression on one of the sachems
that he became an adopted member of the family. This turn of
events enabled him to gain a small following, but when the sachem
died suddenly, some of the Senecas charged him with practicing
sorcery responsible for the death. His adopted relatives hid him in
the wilderness until the tribal council decided that the chief had
died of natural causes.
   As many of the Senecas remained hostile, Kirkland returned
to Connecticut in May 1766. He was ordained in June and commissioned by the Connecticut Board of Correspondents of the Society
of Scotland to establish a new mission among the Six Nations. With
the advice and encouragement of Sir William Johnson, he chose
Oneida as his headquarters, and he labored there among the Oneida
and Tuscarora Indians for the next 40 years.
   Kirkland gained tremendous influence over the Oneida Indians.
He instructed them in agriculture and industrial arts, reduced their
addiction to alcohol, and served as intermediary in settling tribal
disputes. His principal support came from young warriors who sought
to weaken the authority of the traditional sachems. By 1771, Sir
William Johnson began to see Kirkland's influence over the Indians
as a threat to his own domination and a possible source of trouble in
keeping the Six Nations faithful to the crown during the rising tide
of unrest in the colonies. As the possibility of insurrection increased, and Kirkland displayed Patriot inclinations, Johnson attempted to have him removed, only to encounter determined resistance by the Oneidas.
   With the onset of the American Revolution, Kirkland became
increasingly involved in Indian diplomacy, acting as an unofficial
agent of the Continental Congress. He was instrumental in persuading the League of the Iroquois to allow each member nation to act

independently in deciding whether to support the British or the Americans. While most of the Iroquois opted to fight for the British, he was able to enlist the Oneidas in the cause of the colonies and to persuade the Tuscaroras to maintain a neutral position. Guy Johnson, who succeeded Sir William as British commissioner of Indian affairs, threatened to kill Kirkland for his revolutionary activities.

During the war, Kirkland closed down his mission and organized the Oneidas as American scouts. He served as chaplain at Fort Stanwix during the siege of 1777, and he accompanied Sullivan's invasion of the Iroquois country in 1779. When Sullivan approached Kanadasega, site of Kirkland's former Seneca mission, he called upon the chaplain for advice in avoiding dangerous terrain.

After the war, Kirkland resumed his missionary and diplomatic activities. He assisted the Six Nations in establishing peace with the new government, and he was present during the negotiation of the Treaty of Fort Stanwix in 1784. In 1790 he escorted Cornplanter and other Iroquois chiefs to meet federal officials at Philadelphia. He assisted the government to obtain land cessions, and he settled his family on a tract given to him by the Oneidas in 1791. The following year, he was instrumental in preventing the Iroquois from assisting other tribes in fighting Gen. Anthony Wayne's army. He died in 1808.

"Love of his adopted people was the strength that was to carry him through many years of trial and discouragement."--Barbara Graymont.

(T. Wood Clarke, The Bloody Mohawk; Barbara Graymont; The Iroquois in the American Revolution; Francis Whiting Halsey, The Old New York Frontier.)

KISWAS, PEQUOT WARRIOR. Kiswas, a warrior who pretended to be a friend of the Connecticut colonists, served the Indians as a spy during the Pequot War of 1636-37. He spent much of his time at Fort Saybrook and, as he could speak English, he obtained information of use to the hostile Pequots. As soon as the war was well underway, he served as a guide for the Indians and participated in the murders of several settlers.

The Mohegan chief Uncas, an ally of the English, captured Kiswas near Fort Saybrook and requested permission to execute him according to Indian custom. Colonial leaders agreed, and the Mohegans burned him at the stake and danced around the fire while eating pieces of his flesh.

(Herbert Milton Sylvester, Indian Wars of New England, I.)

KITHTUWHELAND, DELAWARE CHIEF see ANDERSON, WILLIAM, DELAWARE CHIEF

KITTANNING EXPEDITION. Kittanning (Attigue) was the largest settlement established by the Delaware Indians after they moved from the Susquehanna River in 1724. Located on the Allegheny River in Armstrong County, Pennsylvania, it developed into a cluster of Delaware and Shawnee villages, known on the frontier as Alleghenia.

During the French and Indian War, it served as the staging area
for numerous raids on the Pennsylvania settlements, most of them
led by the fearsome Delaware chiefs, Shingas and Captain Jacobs.

After the Indians captured Fort Granville in July 1756, the
Scotch-Irish settlers of Cumberland County, Pennsylvania, determined to destroy Kittanning and to recover their friends and relatives believed to be held in captivity there. Led by Col. John Armstrong, some 300 militiamen and volunteers marched from Fort Shirley
on August 29, crossed the mountains without being seen, and attacked Kittanning at dawn on September 8. Residents of Shingas's
town, on the west side of the river, escaped when Armstrong's
forces failed to surround it, but the larger settlement, the home of
Captain Jacobs, was destroyed.

Armstrong described the action in his official report:

> Captain Jacobs immediately then gave the war-whoop,
> and with sundry other Indians, as the English prisoners after-
> ward told, cried the white men were at last come, they would
> then have scalps enough; but, at the same time, ordered
> their squaws and children to flee to the woods. Our men,
> with great eagerness, passed through and fired in the corn-
> field, where they had several returns from the enemy, as
> they also had from the opposite side of the river. Presently
> after, a brisk fire began among the houses, which from the
> house of Captain Jacobs was returned with a great deal of
> resolution, to which I immediately repaired, and found that
> from the advantage of the house and portholes sundry of
> our people were wounded and some killed; and, finding that
> returning the fire upon the house was ineffectual, I ordered
> the contiguous houses to be set on fire, which was performed
> by sundry of the officers and soldiers with a great deal of
> activity, the Indians always firing whenever an object pre-
> sented itself, and seldom missing of wounding or killing some
> of our people--from which house, on moving about to give
> the necessary orders and directions, I received a wound with
> a large musket-ball in the shoulders.

The battle raged until noon. Captain Jacobs and some 40 of
his followers were killed. The Pennsylvanians had 17 men killed
and a large number wounded. Eleven captives were recovered, but
the majority were taken to Venango and other villages deep in the
wilderness by Shingas and the warriors who escaped the attack.
Armstrong withdrew his forces from Kittanning when Indians from
neighboring towns began to organize a counterattack. (See ARM-
STRONG, JOHN; CAPTAIN JACOBS.) Soon afterward, some of the
Indians returned to Kittanning, but it never regained its position as
a center of hostile Indian activity.

(Solon J. Buck, The Planting of Civilization in Western Pennsylvania; Charles A. Hanna, The Wilderness Trail; William A. Hunter,
Forts on the Pennsylvania Frontier; U. J. Jones, History of the
Early Settlement of the Juniata Valley; Paul A. W. Wallace, Indians
in Pennsylvania.)

KONDIARONK, HURON CHIEF see ADARIO, HURON CHIEF

KONKAPOT, JOHN, MAHICAN CHIEF. Konkapot, a Mahican sachem, was born about 1700. Converted to Christianity, he received the name John at the time he joined the church. He helped lead many Mahicans to accept the white man's religion, and they became known as the Stockbridge Indians.

In 1734, colonial authorities awarded Konkapot a captain's commission, and, 10 years later, they recognized him as principal chief of the Mahican nation. He kept his people firmly in the English camp during the French and Indian War. He died shortly before the outbreak of the American Revolution.

"His leadership was respected by both groups in the New England region, and he protected his people to the best of his ability, often standing between them and the avaricious settlers...."--Frederick J. Dockstader.

(Frederick J. Dockstader, Great North American Indians; Dictionary of Indians of North America, II.)

KRYN, MOHAWK CHIEF. Kryn, known as "the Great Mohawk," led his warriors to a victory over invading Mahicans in 1669. During and after the battle, Father Jean Pierron followed the Mohawks and baptized the dying. His dedication in the face of danger so impressed the Mohawks that many of them became Christians and moved to Canada to establish the town of Caughnawaga. Kryn refused conversion at the time. But, influenced by his Christian wife, he visited Caughnawaga, decided to become a Catholic, returned to his village in New York, and led 40 followers to join their kinsmen in Canada.

Appointed chief of the Caughnawaga Indians by Father Jacques Frémin, he travelled to several tribes to preach about the virtues of Christianity. In addition, he served as the leader of the Christian Indians in attacks on English settlements. In 1690 he accompanied the French expedition that destroyed Schenectady, exhorting his Indians, says Parkman, "to wash out their wrongs in blood." He was killed a short time later when two Indian bands mistook each other for enemies and opened fire.

(T. J. Campbell, Pioneer Priests of North America; T. Wood Clarke, The Bloody Mohawk; Francis Parkman, Count Frontenac and New France Under Louis XIV.)

KUTSHAMAKIN, MASSACHUSET CHIEF. Kutshamakin (Cutshamekin), chief of the Massachuset Indians who lived around Dorchester, played an important part in instigating the Pequot War of 1636-37. While serving as a guide to English colonists during John Endicott's expedition to the Pequot country in 1636, he killed and scalped a warrior, so infuriating the tribe that they opted for war. Afterward, he served as English emissary to the Narraganset Indians, helping to convince them to fight against the Pequots.

Kutshamakin was converted to Christianity by the Reverend John Eliot. In 1642 he was arrested on charges of inciting the

Narragansets to make war on the English. Jailed for a brief period, he became so intimidated that he sold tribal land to the English and helped Massachusetts officials to obtain cessions from neighboring Indian nations. He became the leader of the Christian Indian town of Natick in 1651 and died soon afterward.

(Dictionary of Indians of North America, II; Neal Salisbury, Manitou and Providence; Alden T. Vaughan, New England Frontier.)

-L-

LA BALME, AUGUSTIN MOTTIN DE, EXPEDITION. Augustin Mottin de La Balme, a military officer believed to have come to America with Lafayette in 1779, recruited a force of French settlers at Vincennes and Kaskaskia to attack British posts in the West. In October 1780, he led some 140 Frenchmen and friendly Indians in an attempt to seize Detroit.

On his way northward, La Balme destroyed the trading post and the Miami village of Kekionga, putting the Indians and traders to flight. Soon afterward, he and his followers resumed their march, unaware that the Miami chief Little Turtle and his warriors were in close pursuit. When they camped for the night not far from the present site of Fort Wayne, the Indians attacked, killing La Balme and most of his men. (See ABOITE RIVER MASSACRE; LITTLE TURTLE, MIAMI CHIEF.)

(Clarence Walworth Alvord, The Illinois Country; Bert Anson, The Miami Indians; Louise Phelps Kellogg, The British Régime in Wisconsin and the Northwest.)

LA BARRE, JOSEPH-ANTOINE LE FEBVRE DE, EXPEDITION. Joseph-Antoine Le Febvre de La Barre, successor to Count Frontenac as governor of Canada, sailed to Quebec in 1682. Upon arrival he found the colony at war with the Iroquois. He determined to carry the war to the enemy villages, and in 1684, he led a poorly trained and ill-provisioned army of 1,100 Frenchmen and Indian allies to the mouth of the Salmon River. Before he could invade the Iroquois territory, however, an influenza epidemic incapacitated most of his men. There, at the mercy of Iroquois warriors who had advanced to intercept him, he agreed to a peace proposal that permitted him and his army to retreat to Montreal, but left the Illinois Indians without French protection. King Louis XIV, feeling that French honor had been sacrificed, summoned La Barre home in disgrace.

(William J. Eccles, The Canadian Frontier; Frank H. Severance, An Old Frontier of France.)

LA BAYE, FORT, CAPTURE OF. Fort La Baye, an English post at the present site of Green Bay, Wisconsin, was surrounded by hostile Indians in June, 1763, at the onset of Pontiac's War. The commanding officer Lt. James Gorrell realized that his garrison of 17 men could be overwhelmed at any time by the Winnebago, Menominee, Sauk, and Fox Indians. He agreed, therefore, to attend a council outside the

stockade. Fortunately, just as the hostiles were about to declare their intention to put the soldiers to death, a party of Sioux warriors arrived and demanded that the English be permitted to withdraw safely from the fort. One of the few garrisons to escape with their lives in the western country, Gorrell and his men evaded the hostile Chippewas at Mackinac and paddled to safety at Montreal.
(Dale Van Every, Forth to the Wilderness.)

LA BELLE FAMILLE, BATTLE OF. The Battle of La Belle Famille, an important British victory during the French and Indian War, was fought at the present site of Youngstown, N.Y., on July 24, 1759. Discovering that 1,200 French troops and Indians, led by Capt. Charles Aubry, were marching to the defense of Fort Niagara, Sir William Johnson and his Iroquois followers set a trap on the portage road. While the English launched a frontal attack, the Iroquois charged from the wilderness on both sides of the trail. Francis Parkman has described the action:

> The fight was brisk for awhile; but at last Aubry's men broke away in a panic. The French officers seem to have made desperate efforts to retrieve the day, for nearly all of them were killed or captured; while their followers, after heavy loss, fled to their canoes and boats above the cataract, hastened back to Lake Erie, ... burned the forts at Presq'Isle, Le Boeuf, and Venango ... and retreated to Detroit.

Approximately a thousand Frenchmen and Indians were killed or captured. Fort Niagara surrendered soon afterward.
(Francis Parkman, Montcalm and Wolfe, III; Frank H. Severance, An Old Frontier of France.)

LA DEMOISELLE, MIAMI CHIEF see OLD BRITON, MIAMI CHIEF

LAFONTAINE, FRANCIS, MIAMI CHIEF. Francis Lafontaine (Topeah), a mixed-blood Miami chief, was born about 1810. During his youth he became convinced that Indians must cooperate with the U.S. government or perish, and he began signing land cession treaties as early as 1834, usually receiving a land grant of his own as a reward. He operated a trading post near the forks of the Wabash after his appointment as principal chief in 1841.
For five years Lafontaine skillfully delayed Miami removal to the West. When his people finally departed in 1846, he obtained an exemption for himself, and died in Indiana on April 13, 1847.
(Bert Anson, The Miami Indians.)

LA FOREST, FRANÇOIS DAUPHIN DE. François Dauphin de La Forest, a friend and faithful lieutenant of La Salle's, came to Canada in 1679. During the following year he was promoted to major at Fort Frontenac, and he served at the frontier post for several years. He acted as goodwill ambassador to the Indians for Governors

Frontenac and Denonville, frequently distributing gifts to the western tribes.

In 1680, La Forest accompanied La Salle's exploration of the Great Lakes region. In 1687, he fought against the Senecas during the invasion of their villages led by Jacques Rene de Brisay, marquis de Denonville. After the death of La Salle in 1687, La Forest petitioned the crown to obtain the concession at Fort St. Louis for Henri de Tonti and himself. The request was granted in 1690, and the two explorers built Fort Pimitoui at the present site of Peoria soon afterward. There they developed an extensive trade with the Indians, but when it failed to achieve substantial profits, La Forest rejoined his military unit in Canada.

(Clarence Walworth Alvord, The Illinois Country.)

LAKE GEORGE, BATTLE OF. The Battle of Lake George was fought on September 8, 1755, between William Johnson's 5,000 provincial troops and Mohawk warriors and Gen. Ludwig August Dieskau's 1,700 French troops and allied Indians. Johnson, whose objective was to capture Fort St. Fréderic, near Crown Point, New York, established a camp at the south end of Lake George. On September 8, he sent a detachment led by Col. Ephraim Williams and Chief Hendrick to reconnoiter, and they were ambushed with great loss of life. (See BLOODY POND, BATTLE OF.) The survivors fled to Johnson's camp, just ahead of Dieskau's army.

Dieskau ordered an attack on Johnson's barricades, but his Indians and Canadians refused to assault the camp when they discovered that the English had cannon. The French regulars, however, drove toward the center of the encampment. Repulsed by a withering fire, they regrouped and rushed upon Johnson's right flank. A desperate hand-to-hand battle ensued while Johnson's artillery shelled the Indians who were concealed in a swamp. Finally, the French withdrew in disarray, pursued by the English and Mohawks who exacted a heavy toll. Dieskau was captured and most of his regulars killed. The survivors fled to Crown Point. Johnson's forces, weakened by the loss of 350 men, abandoned their objective to seize the French fort.

(T. Wood Clarke, The Bloody Mohawk; Arthur Pound, Johnson of the Mohawks; Dale Van Every, Forth to the Wilderness.)

LAKE POW-AW-HAY-KON-NAY, TREATY OF. On October 18, 1848, the Menominee Indians, as a result of negotiations with William Medill at Lake Pow-Aw-Hay-Kon-Nay, Wisconsin, agreed to cede all of their lands in the state for $350,000. They were permitted to settle upon lands obtained from the Chippewas.

(Charles J. Kappler, ed., Indian Affairs: Laws and Treaties, II.)

LAMBERVILLE, JEAN DE. Father Jean de Lamberville, a Jesuit missionary, was a native of Rouen, France, born about 1633. He went to Canada at an early age to labor among the Indians, and, in 1667-68, he established a mission at Onondaga. The undertaking was hazardous, for the Iroquois had become greatly addicted to liquor, and during their drunken frolics they frequently threatened his life. "I gave them presents," he related, "exhorting them at the same time to maintain peace with the French, to become Christians, not to annoy me with their drunkenness, to let me baptize the dying and the captives to be burned." In addition, he incurred the wrath of the Onondaga shaman by curing sick Indians with medicine brought from Montreal.

Father Lamberville and his brother Father Jacques de Lamberville were the last priests to leave the Iroquois when the French declared war upon the Senecas in 1684. They warned the governor of Canada that an attack on the Senecas would result in retaliation by the entire League of the Iroquois, but their advice was disregarded and the French invasion ended in disgrace. (See LA BARRE, JOSEPH-ANTOINE LE FEBVRE DE, EXPEDITION.)

When Gov. Jacques René de Brisay de Denonville arrived in Canada with orders to destroy the Iroquois, he deceived Father Lamberville into the belief that he intended to restore peace. In 1686, the priest acted as French ambassador to the Iroquois, making several trips to their villages to promote peace and to counter the efforts of Gov. Thomas Dongan of New York to strengthen their ties with the English. Later, Denonville paid tribute to his successful diplomacy: "You will be told ... how necessary Father de Lamberville is, and with what skill he averted the storm that threatened us, and how clever he is in controlling the Indian.... If you cannot send all these Fathers back to their missions, you may expect great misfortunes for this colony."

While Lamberville remained ignorant of Denonville's plans to attack the Iroquois, Dongan discovered them and sent a warning to the missionary to flee at once before the Five Nations realized that they had been deceived. Refusing to believe Dongan's emissaries, Lamberville declined their offer to escort him to safety. Soon afterward, however, some Onondagas learned of French intentions and warned him to flee for his life. Realizing that "all of his work and hopes" had been ruined, he went to Fort Cataroqui to serve as chaplain.

While at Cataroqui, Lamberville had several narrow escapes when Iroquois war parties attacked the post. In October 1687, while sailing to Niagara to obtain rations for the famished garrison, he helped repel an attack on the barque by a swarm of Iroquois in canoes. The following February, he became so ill with scurvy that a French officer and several Christian Indians determined to take him by dogsled to a hospital in Montreal. Pursued by hostile Indians, he had a narrow escape when the conveyance broke through the ice. The dogs prevented him from drowning, but he reached his destination so ill that he failed to recover for more than two years.

After the French attack on the Senecas failed to destroy their capability to make war, Denonville sent Lamberville to Onondaga to assist in restoring peace. The missionary was permitted to resume his activities there, but he was driven away in 1700. Two years later he returned, but in 1709, because of English intrigue, he had

to abandon his mission for the last time. Appointed mission pro-
curator, Lamberville spent his few remaining years in France. He
died in 1714.

"No man in Canada had done so much as the elder Lamberville to counteract the influence of England and to serve the interests of France...."--Francis Parkman.

(Francis Parkman, Count Frontenac and New France Under
Louis XIV; T. J. Campbell, Pioneer Priests of North America; Allen
W. Trelease, Indian Affairs in Colonial New York.)

LANCASTER, MASSACHUSETTS, RAIDS. Lancaster, a Massachusetts frontier settlement, was attacked by King Philip's warriors on
February 10, 1676. Fortunately for the settlers, they had taken
refuge in six garrison houses, five of which were so bravely defended that they held out until a relief force arrived from Marlborough and drove the Indians away. The home of Rev. Joseph
Rowlandson was set on fire, however, and the defenders abandoned
it. A dozen of them were slain as they emerged, and 24 survivors
were taken to captivity in Canada. (See ROWLANDSON, JOSEPH,
FAMILY OF.) Most of the town's buildings were burned.

In September 1697, an Abnaki war party invaded Lancaster.
Surprisingly unprepared for residents of a settlement so exposed to
Indian attack, the citizens were taken by complete surprise. Twenty
men, women, and children lost their lives, while five were carried
into captivity.

On July 31, 1704, a force of Frenchmen and Indians raided
Lancaster. They encountered a company of soldiers commanded by
Capt. Jonathan Tyng and drove them into garrison houses. Four
defenders were killed and most of the houses destroyed.

(Douglas Edward Leach, Flintlock and Tomahawk; Samuel
Adams Drake, Border Wars of New England.)

LANCASTER, PENNSYLVANIA, TREATIES OF. Lancaster, Pennsylvania, was the site of several important treaty negotiations with
powerful Indian tribes. In 1744, the Six Nations relinquished their
claims to land in Maryland and Virginia and agreed to side with the
English in King George's War. In exchange, they received payment
of £400 and a large store of gifts. In 1748, a treaty was negotiated at Lancaster with the Delawares, Shawnees, Miamis and Wyandots. The English agreed to send traders to the tribes, and the
Indians promised to protect them. In 1762, George Croghan negotiated a treaty at Lancaster with the Iroquois, Delaware, Shawnee,
Miami, Kickapoo, and Wea nations. The Indians released 30 prisoners and agreed to remain at peace, but they were greatly dissatis-
fied with the scanty distribution of gifts, and the outbreak of war
was delayed for only a short time.

(Randolph C. Downes, Council Fires on the Upper Ohio;
Howard H. Peckham, Pontiac and the Indian Uprising; Albert T.
Volwiler, George Croghan and the Westward Movement, Paul A. W.
Wallace, Indians in Pennsylvania.)

LANGLADE, CHARLES MICHEL DE. Charles Michel de Langlade,
grandson of a French officer of the Carignan regiment, and son of
a Canadian fur trader and an Ottawa Indian chief's sister, was born
in 1729. In his youth he became an important French military officer and partisan leader. According to frontier tradition, he participated in a French and Indian expedition against the Chickasaws when
he was only 10 years old. At the age of 21, having demonstrated
his ability as a wilderness fighter, he became a cadet in the French
colonial army.

Langlade's first famous exploit occurred on June 21, 1752,
when he led 240 Frenchmen and Indians in a surprise attack on the
English and their Indian allies at Pickawillanee. They killed some
30 Miami Indians and one Englishman, captured and ate the Miami
chief (see OLD BRITON), and completely destroyed British trade in
the region. "This act of war in time of peace had a profound influence on the affairs of both colonies. From this time forward ...
the French controlled both the fur trade and the occupancy of the
Ohio valley."--Louise Phelps Kellogg.

Langlade, as a leader of Indians, played an important role in
the French and Indian War. He led warriors against Braddock's
army with such success that Gen. John Burgoyne called him "the
author of Braddock's defeat." Afterward, he led war parties from
Fort Duquesne to attack English forces and settlements. On January
21, 1757, he and his followers defeated Rogers' Rangers and wounded
Maj. Robert Rogers near Crown Point. In August 1757, he participated in the capture of Fort William Henry, and his Indians joined
in the massacre of prisoners that followed.

In September 1757, Langlade was assigned to duty as second
in command at Fort Mackinac. In 1759, he recruited more than a
thousand Indians to defend Quebec, returning to Mackinac after the
fall of the city. In 1760, he helped defend Montreal, but left before
the surrender. He surrendered Mackinac to the English in 1761.

After the fall of New France, Langlade became a partisan of his
former enemies, the British. He was at Fort Mackinac when Pontiac's
followers seized it in 1763 (see HENRY, ALEXANDER), and moved to
Green Bay in 1764 to become an officer in the British Indian Service.
At his new post he engaged in the fur trade so successfully that he
became the town's most prominent citizen, frequently called the
"father of Wisconsin."

At the onset of the American Revolution, Langlade led 200 Ottawa and Chippewa Indians to defend Montreal, but they failed to
arrive in time to prevent the city's surrender. In 1777, he and his
followers supported Burgoyne's forces on Lake Champlain. They left
the army in August after Burgoyne censured them for their cruelty.
In 1778, he attempted to recruit warriors to help Gov. Henry Hamilton to retake Vincennes, but, after George Rogers Clark captured
Hamilton, Langlade could no longer incite the Indians to fight the
Americans. After the Revolution, he attempted to keep peace between the tribes. He died in 1800.

(Louise Phelps Kellogg, The French Régime in Wisconsin and
the Northwest; The British Régime in Wisconsin and the Northwest;
Frank H. Severance, An Old Frontier of France.)

LA POINTE, WISCONSIN, TREATIES OF. On October 4, 1842, Robert
Stuart negotiated a treaty with the Chippewa Indians at La Pointe.
In exchange for goods and $12,500 in cash, the tribe ceded much of
their land in upper Michigan and Wisconsin to the United States
government. On September 30, 1854, the Chippewas, at the second
Treaty of La Pointe, ceded additional lands in return for an annuity.
American negotiators were Henry C. Gilbert and David B. Harriman.
(Charles J. Kappler, ed., Indian Affairs: Laws and Treaties,
II.)

LA PORTE, SIEUR DE LOUVIGNY, LOUIS DE, EXPEDITIONS. Louis
de La Porte de Louvigny, a French army officer, was sent to Canada
in 1683 to help defend the colony against Indian attacks. For almost
four decades he served as an Indian fighter, negotiator, and
commander-in-chief of wilderness posts. In 1689, while leading 150
men to Fort Mackinac, he defeated an Iroquois war party, thereby
discouraging tribes of the Great Lakes region from waging war
against the French. He commanded at Mackinac and engaged in the
fur trade until 1699, when he assumed command of Fort Frontenac.
In 1712 he reopened the post at Mackinac which the French had
abandoned.
Louvigny's most important Indian campaign was conducted in
1716. At the request of the governor, he led 800 Frenchmen and
friendly Indians to punish the Fox tribe for murdering traders.
They attacked a fortified Fox village, defended by 3,500 Indians, at
Little Butte des Morts, near Lake Winnebago. When his artillery
failed to demolish the oak palisades, he dug trenches with the intention of planting explosives under the wall. As the Foxes had no
defense against this tactic, they accepted Louvigny's surrender
terms, which included releasing their captives, paying a ransom in
furs, ceasing their attacks on the French and allied Indians, and
recognizing French sovereignty. The expedition ended the first Fox
war, and Louvigny returned to Canada as a hero, but his Indian
allies were angered because he had lost the opportunity to annihilate
their enemies.
In 1725, Louvigny was lost at sea while sailing from France
to Canada to assume the office of governor of Three Rivers.
(John Anthony Caruso, The Mississippi Valley Frontier; Louise
Phelps Kellogg, The French Régime in Wisconsin and the Northwest.)

LA PRESENTATION. The development of the present city of Ogdensburg, New York, began in 1749 when the Abbé François Picquet
established the mission La Présentation at the mouth of the Oswegatchie
River. With the help of French troops, he built a fort at the site and
persuaded a large number of Iroquois to move there. The post became a rallying point for Iroquois raids on English settlements and a
supply depot for French posts farther west. "For a decade," wrote
Arthur Pound, "it was one end of the French pincers intended to
pull the Iroquois away from the British connection." It was captured by the British in 1760. (See PICQUET, FRANÇOIS; OSWE-
GATCHIE.)

(Arthur Pound, Johnson of the Mohawks; Michael Kammen, Colonial New York--a History; Francis Parkman, Montcalm and Wolfe; Frank H. Severance, An Old Frontier of France.)

L'ARBRE CROCHET, TREATY OF. L'Arbre Crochet, Michigan, was the site of treaty negotiations on July 6, 1820, between Lewis Cass and chiefs of the Chippewa and Ottawa Indians. As a result, the tribes ceded the St. Martin Islands, near Mackinac, to the United States. They accepted a large store of trade goods as remuneration.
(Charles J. Kappler, ed., Indian Affairs: Laws and Treaties, II.)

LA SALLE, RENE-ROBERT CAVELIER, SIEUR DE, FUR TRADE. Rene-Robert Cavelier, Sieur de La Salle, a favorite of Governor Frontenac, obtained title to Fort Frontenac, on May 13, 1675. Using it as a base for establishing the fur trade in the Mississippi Valley and the Great Lakes region, by 1680 he established trading posts from Lake Michigan to Niagara to the confluence of the Mississippi and the Ohio. With Frontenac's blessing, he attempted to monopolize the fur trade in this vast area, but the plan failed, largely because of the antagonism of other French traders. In addition, the Iroquois viewed La Salle's vessel, Le Griffon, as a threat to their role as middlemen in the trade.

In August 1679, Le Griffon transported La Salle from Niagara to Green Bay, and began a return voyage heavily loaded with furs. It never reached its destination, and its fate remains a mystery to this day. The loss of the ship resulted in La Salle incurring huge debts, and his men on the western waters began to desert him. With the recall of Governor Frontenac, he could no longer hope to monopolize the trade, and the new governor, Joseph-Antoine Le Febvre de La Barre, distrusted him and promised the Iroquois that he would be punished for trading guns to their enemies, the Illinois Indians.

His plan to establish a northern empire disrupted, La Salle attempted to recoup by exploring and colonizing the lower Mississippi. This venture led to his murder in Texas in 1687 by his own men.
(William J. Eccles, The Canadian Frontier; John Gilmary Shea, Discovery and Exploration of the Mississippi Valley; Francis Parkman, Count Frontenac and New France Under Louis XIV.)

LAURENS, FORT. Fort Laurens was constructed near the present site of Canton, Ohio, in 1778, by Col. John Gibson. It was established as one of a chain of forts intended to intimidate the Indians and to facilitate a campaign to capture Detroit. In neither aspect did it fulfill its purpose, however, for it quickly became the object of Shawnee, Mingo, and Wyandot hostilities that did not cease until it was deserted and destroyed.

Indian attacks began at Fort Laurens during the autumn of 1778. In January 1779, a Mingo war party led by Simon Girty ambushed a wagon train near the fort, killing two soldiers, wounding four, and driving the escort into the palisade. Girty besieged the

fort, and the defenders almost starved and froze during the fierce
winter. On February 23, a party of 19 soldiers slipped out the gate
in an attempt to secure firewood, but they were ambushed with 17
killed and 2 captured. Finally, in March, Gen. Lachlan McIntosh arrived with 500 men, drove the Indians away, and brought desperately needed supplies. Unfortunately, much of the rations proved to
be spoiled.

During the summer of 1779, Fort Laurens was evacuated. The
Indians burned it soon afterward.

(Randolph C. Downes, Council Fires on the Upper Ohio; Alexander Scott Withers, Chronicles of Border Warfare.)

LEATHERLIPS, WYANDOT CHIEF. Leatherlips (Shateiaronhia), a
Wyandot chief of Sandusky, was born about 1732. A signer of the
Treaty of Greenville in 1795, his friendship with the whites resulted
in distrust by Indian leaders. In 1810, Tecumseh and his brother
the Prophet, believing him to be an obstacle to their plans for uni-
fication of Indians to oppose the whites, accused him of practicing
witchcraft and sentenced him to death. Calmly accepting his fate,
he knelt beside his grave, chanted his death song, and collapsed
when Chief Roundhead's tomahawk penetrated his brain. He "clung
to life for several hours, a phenomenon that only seemed to confirm
his murderers' suspicions."--R. David Edmunds.

(R. David Edmunds, The Shawnee Prophet; Frederick J. Dockstader, Great North American Indians; Benjamin Drake, Life of
Tecumseh.)

LEBOEUF, FORT. Fort LeBoeuf was built in 1753 on French Creek
(present Waterford, Pennsylvania), as one of a line of posts intended
to prevent English occupation of the Ohio. The site was chosen to
protect the portage from French Creek to Lake Erie. Indians warned
the French against occupying the area, and when they were ignored
they requested English assistance. As a result, George Washington
was sent to Fort LeBoeuf to demand their departure. Refusal to
comply led to the outbreak of the French and Indian War.

After the fall of New France, a small English post was established at Fort LeBoeuf. At the onset of Pontiac's War in 1763, it
was manned by only 13 men, led by Ensign George Price. On June
18, Pontiac's followers attacked it repeatedly setting the stockade on
fire with flaming arrows. After resisting for several hours, Price
realized that the roof was ready to collapse and that his men would
perish beneath it. Under the cover of darkness, they cut through a
wall and crawled past the Indians. Most of them arrived safely at
Fort Pitt.

(Solon J. Buck, The Planting of Civilization in Western Pennsylvania; Dale Van Every, Forth to the Wilderness.)

LEE, THOMAS, CAPTIVITY OF. Thomas Lee was captured by Indians in Union County, Pennsylvania, on August 13, 1782. The six-
year-old captive watched while warriors shot his father and mother to
death and bashed his baby brother against a tree. He lived with his

captors until 1788, becoming completely assimilated. Then, when redeemed by relatives, he fled at the first opportunity in an unsuccessful attempt to return to the Indians. For a long time he remained resentful and sullen, but gradually he became reaccustomed to white civilization.

(C. Hale Sipe, The Indian Wars of Pennsylvania.)

LEECH LAKE, BATTLE OF. The Battle of Leech Lake, occurring in October 1898 in Minnesota, was one of the last fights in frontier history between Indians and United States troops. The trouble began on Bear Island when a Chippewa Indian murdered another member of the tribe. Witnesses refused to leave their reservation to testify at his trial, and 80 soldiers from Fort Snelling were sent to assist federal marshals in rounding them up. Unable to find the wanted men, they stacked arms for the noon meal, and Indians fired upon them from the dense underbrush. A battle raged for several hours, resulting in the deaths of a major and five troopers. Nine men were wounded, including Col. Timothy J. Sheehan. Few if any Indians were killed. A relief force arrived two days later and rescued the troops.

After the battle, the U.S. commissioner of Indian affairs persuaded many of the hostile Chippewas to surrender. Some of them were imprisoned, but executive clemency shortened their sentences.

(Charles E. Flandrau, The History of Minnesota and Tales of the Frontier.)

LEECH LAKE, TREATY OF. The Treaty of Leech Lake, Minnesota, was negotiated with the Pillager band of Chippewas by Isaac A. Verplank and Henry M. Rice on August 21, 1847. In exchange for an annuity of goods, the Chippewas ceded a large land area along the Leaf and Crow rivers.

(Charles J. Kappler, ed., Indian Affairs: Laws and Treaties, II.)

LEETH, JOHN. John Leeth, a 17-year-old orphan, went to work for a trader near the present site of New Lancaster, Ohio, in 1774. Soon afterward, Dunmore's War erupted, and Leeth was seized by the Shawnee Indians. Their plans to burn him to death were thwarted by a Delaware chief, who adopted him with these words: "Your mother has risen from the dead to give you suck. Your father has also risen to take care of you."

After the war, the Delawares informed him that he could return to his own people, but the youth enjoyed the Indian way of life. Still considering himself a member of the tribe, he resumed his life as a trader. In 1779, he married a captive, Salley Lowery, and they lived most of their lives with the Delawares.

(John Leeth, A Short Biography of John Leeth.)

LE GARDEUR DE COURTEMANCHE, AUGUSTIN. The Sieur de Courtemanche, grandson of Jean Nicolet, was born in Canada in 1663 and became a French military officer and Indian diplomat at an early age.

In 1689-90 he participated in the Portneuf expedition that captured the fort at Casco Bay, Maine. In 1691 he made a dangerous journey through the Iroquois country to bring news of French victories over the English to the troops at Mackinac. This information enabled the French to persuade their Indian allies to continue their attacks on Iroquois villages. In 1693 he fought against the Mohawks, and, afterward, he commanded a post on the St. Joseph. In 1700, when peace was restored between the French and Iroquois, Courtemanche visited the Miamis and other Indian allies and arranged for them to send chiefs to Montreal to participate in the final negotiations. His later years were spent in Labrador trading with the Eskimos. He died in 1717.

(Louise Phelps Kellogg, The French Régime in Wisconsin and the Northwest.)

LEININGER, BARBARA, CAPTIVITY OF. Barbara Leininger, aged 12, was captured by Allegheny Indians at Penn's Creek, Pennsylvania, on October 16, 1755. Her sister Regina, and a young neighbor, Marie Le Roy, were taken at the same time, while her father and brother were killed in the raid. During the march to the Indian stronghold of Kittanning, she was condemned to death for attempting to escape, but a young warrior saved her by begging for her life.

Barbara was at Kittanning when several captives suffered the fate she had so narrowly escaped after Col. John Armstrong attacked the town in December 1755. She described the death of a woman who had tried to escape during the battle as follows: "First, they scalped her; next, they laid burning splinters of wood, here and there, upon her body; and then they cut off her ears and fingers, forcing them into her mouth so that she had to swallow them. Amidst such torments, this woman lived from nine o'clock in the morning until toward sunset when a French officer took compassion on her, and put her out of her misery."

Soon after this attack, Barbara and Marie were taken to Fort Duquesne and assigned to work for the French, their Indian masters receiving their wages. Then they went to an Indian town on Beaver Creek, where they were compelled to labor in the fields. Eighteen months later, they moved many miles to the westward to a village she called Moschkingo.

Terrified by the knowledge of their fate if recaptured, Barbara and Marie, nevertheless, determined to try to escape. On March 16, 1759, they slipped away from the village with two English youths, David Breckinridge and Owen Gibson. They found a boat on the bank of the Muskingum River and crossed ahead of pursuers. For four days they fled through the wilderness to the Ohio, crossed on a raft, and finally reached Pittsburgh on the last day of March.

(J. Norman Heard, White into Red.)

LEININGER, REGINA, CAPTIVITY OF. Regina Leininger, sister of Barbara, was captured with her during a raid on Penn's Creek, Pennsylvania, on October 16, 1755. Ten years old when taken, she was compelled to carry a two-year-old captive strapped to her back for more than a hundred miles. When she arrived at her captors' village, she and the little girl she carried were given to an old Indian woman who compelled them to gather roots and bark to prevent starvation during the winter.

Regina remained in captivity nine years, finally being surrendered when Col. Henry Bouquet defeated the Indians and compelled them to give up their captives. Conveyed to Carlisle with hundreds of redeemed captives, she had forgotten her native language and had changed so dramatically that her mother did not recognize her. But Regina remembered some hymns that her mother had sung before her captivity, and through this means they were reunited. No one claimed the little girl who had been Regina's constant companion in captivity, so Mrs. Leininger took both of them home. The date was December 31, 1764.

(J. Norman Heard, White into Red.)

LE MARCHAND DE LIGNERY, CONSTANT. Constant Le Marchand de Lignery was born in France about 1663. He became a military officer, serving as a lieutenant in 1688, and being promoted to captain in 1705. Most of his career was spent in Canada, where he served as an Indian fighter and diplomat.

Lignery's initial Indian campaigns, in which he played a subordinate role, were against the Iroquois. In 1712, he was appointed commanding officer at Mackinac and instructed to develop the post into a headquarters of the Indian trade. There he served effectively as an arbiter of disputes between tribes. In 1715, he was ordered to punish the Fox Indians for attacking French traders, but the expedition failed to take place because he lacked adequate supplies. Four years later, he was relieved at Mackinac, but in 1722 he returned and reassumed command.

In 1724, Lignery negotiated a treaty that ended Fox attacks on the Chippewas, northern trading partners of the French, but failed to prevent incursions against the Illinois Indians and the colony of Louisiana. This pact was censured so strongly that, in 1726, he negotiated another, requiring the Foxes and their allies to make peace with the Illinois. It had little lasting effect, however, and beginning in 1728 a bloody war erupted between the French and the Foxes.

In June 1728, Lignery assembled some 500 Frenchmen and a large Indian contingent and marched to the main Fox village. The hostiles, having been forewarned of his movements, abandoned the town, and he captured only three women and a man who was too old to flee. These prisoners were given to his Indian allies as slaves, and the warriors celebrated their "victory" by burning the old man at the stake. After destroying the village and crops, Lignery led his forces back to Mackinac. He was severely criticized for failing to pursue the enemy. He died in 1731.

(John Anthony Caruso, The Mississippi Valley Frontier; Louise Phelps Kellogg, The French Régime in Wisconsin and the Northwest.)

LE MOYNE, CHARLES, BARON DE LONGUEUIL, INDIAN AFFAIRS.

Charles Le Moyne, eldest brother of Iberville, Bienville, and other members of the famous Canadian frontier family, was born at Montreal in 1656. His father, Charles Le Moyne, Sr., a prosperous pioneer and trader, sent him to France to be educated, and he chose a military career. In 1683, he returned to Canada as a lieutenant of infantry.

Le Moyne's career as an Indian fighter and diplomat began in 1687 when he served in the Denonville expedition against the Senecas. In 1689, he was severely wounded in a fight with the Iroquois who had massacred the French at Lachine Rapids. Because of his father's friendship with the Indians, however, he and his brother Paul Le Moyne de Maricourt were adopted by the Onondagas in 1694. With tribal adoption, he gained enough influence to prevent the Onondagas from supporting the English.

Beginning in 1704, Le Moyne spent most of his time with the Iroquois, keeping a majority of them neutral during Queen Anne's War. In 1720, he persuaded the Senecas to permit him to establish a post at Niagara. Four years later, he became governor of Montreal, while continuing his role of Indian diplomat. With his brother Paul, he succeeded in obtaining the release of many Frenchmen held in Indian captivity. He died in 1729.

(Frank H. Severance, An Old Frontier of France.)

LE MOYNE, SIMON. Father Simon Le Moyne, a Jesuit missionary, was born in France about 1604. Educated at Rouen, he taught at the Jesuit college there for 10 years before being assigned to the Canadian missions in 1638. For several years he labored among the Hurons. After their dispersal by the Iroquois, he followed the survivors in their wilderness wanderings until his superiors called upon him to undertake a perilous journey to the land of the Iroquois in New York.

In 1654, Father Le Moyne visited the Onondagas to investigate the possibility of establishing a mission among them. The Indians received him hospitably and permitted him to preach to their Huron captives. He returned to Quebec with a favorable report, and his request to establish a mission was granted. While on his way to Montreal, however, his party was attacked by Mohawks, and he barely escaped with his life. Disregarding this misadventure, he visited the Mohawks in 1655. The chiefs welcomed him, but warriors threatened his life so frequently that he returned to Canada, convinced that he would succeed better among the upper Iroquois.

In 1661, Father Le Moyne accompanied a party of Onondagas to their principal village. There he was received with shouts of joy, but within a short time several attempts were made on his life. Once he was bound to a stake and his legs were badly burned. Ignoring illness as well as his wounds, in August 1662, he conveyed 18 French captives to safety at Montreal. Refused permission by his superiors to return to Onondaga, he remained in Canada until his death on November 24, 1665.

(T. J. Campbell, Pioneer Priests of North America; T. Wood Clarke, The Bloody Mohawk; Edna Kenton, ed., Black Gown and Redskins.)

LENEUF DE LA VALLIERE DE BEAUBASSIN, ALEXANDRE, RAID.
In 1703 Gov. Philippe de Rigaud de Vaudreuil of New France determined to drive the English settlers out of Maine. To accomplish this
objective, French partisans aroused the Abnaki Indians, and, on
August 10, 500 Indians and Canadians, led by Captain Leneuf de La
Vallière de Beaubassin (son of the governor of Acadia), raided all
the English villages from Wells to Falmouth. More than 160 English
settlers were killed or captured before the raiders were turned back
at Falmouth by the arrival of an armed provincial galley. The raid
was in retaliation for the English destruction of Beaubassin in 1696.
     "Maine had nearly received her death blow. Throughout her
entire border nothing was left standing except a few isolated garrisons, and it was a question if even these could hold out much longer.
The deception had been so complete, the onset so sudden, that organized resistance was out of the question. The English, heedless
of the signs of the gathering storm, had been lulled into a state of
false security, and the awakening was terrible indeed."--Samuel
Adams Drake.
     (Samuel Adams Drake, The Border Wars of New England; Wil-
liam J. Eccles, The Canadian Frontier.)

LENNI LENAPE INDIANS see DELAWARE INDIANS

LE TORT, JACQUES, FAMILY OF. Jacques Le Tort, a Huguenot,
sailed to Pennsylvania in 1686 as a representative of English in-
vestors who had purchased 30,000 acres on the Schuylkill River from
William Penn. He and a few fellow Huguenots established a settlement in Chester County. In 1692 his wife, Anna, and his son,
James, joined him at his home, located on an important Indian trail
that followed the Schuylkill. By 1695 he was a well-established
trader.
     After the death of her husband, Anna Le Tort continued his
trading activities, establishing headquarters at Conestoga in 1704.
In 1707, James was an unlicensed trader among the Shawnees. He
was jailed at least two times by Pennsylvania authorities, suspected
of "evil designs against the government." In 1713, however, he
was licensed to trade. He established a profitable post at the forks
of the Susquehanna by 1726, trading with Shawnees, Delawares, and
Mingos. One of the first to follow the Delawares when they moved
westward to the Allegheny Mountains, he traded along the Ohio as
early as 1728, and he may have settled there. It is believed that he
had died by 1742.
     (Charles A. Hanna, The Wilderness Trail.)

LEWIS, JOHN, SHAWNEE CHIEF see CAPTAIN LEWIS, SHAWNEE
CHIEF

LEWISTOWN, OHIO, TREATY OF. On July 20, 1831, at Lewistown,
Ohio, some Shawnee and Seneca Indians negotiated a treaty with
United States Commissioners James B. Gardiner and John McElvain.
In exchange for presents, they ceded lands near Lewistown and

agreed to remove west of the Mississippi.

(Charles J. Kappler, ed., Indian Affairs: Laws and Treaties, II.)

LIENARD DE BEAUJEU, DANIEL-HYACINTHE-MARIE. Capt. Daniel-Hyacinthe-Marie Liénard de Beaujeu, son of a mayor of Quebec, was born at Montreal on August 19, 1711. At an early age he entered military service, and he quickly developed into a successful Indian diplomat. After participating in the capture of Grand Pré in 1747 he was sent to Niagara, where he managed the Iroquois with great skill.

In 1755 he was sent to Fort Duquesne to defend it against Braddock's advancing army of 3,000 men. On July 9 he led 244 Frenchmen and 637 Indians forth to ambush the English. He was killed early in the battle, but Lt. Jean-Daniel Dumas rallied the French and Indians and they gained a decisive victory (see BRAD-DOCK'S DEFEAT).

(Solon J. Buck, The Planting of Civilization in Western Pennsylvania; Frank H. Severance, An Old Frontier of France; Dale Van Every, Forth to the Wilderness.)

LIGNERIS, FRANÇOIS MARCHAND DE. François Marchand de Ligneris, one of the most prominent partisan leaders during the French and Indian War, was born in Canada in 1704. He became a noted Indian fighter in his youth, commanding the frontier town of Three Rivers in 1731, serving in the French army in Acadia, and participating in the Chickasaw campaign of 1747. In 1748-49, he was especially effective in negotiating prisoner exchanges with the English in New York.

Ligneris played an important part in the French and Indian victory over Braddock's army on July 9, 1755. From Fort Duquesne he led numerous attacks on frontier settlements, but he was compelled to destroy that key French bastion in October 1758, when he had only 200 men to defend it against the large army of Gen. John Forbes. Afterward, he led his men to Venango, where he continued to engage in wilderness warfare until called to defend Niagara against Sir William Johnson's army in 1759. (See NIAGARA, FORTS.) While attempting to relieve Fort Niagara, he was mortally wounded at the Battle of La Belle Famille on July 24.

(Frank H. Severance, An Old Frontier of France.)

LIGNERY, CONSTANT MARCHAND DE see LE MARCHAND DE LIG-NERY, CONSTANT

LIGONIER, FORT. Fort Ligonier was built at Loyalhanna (present Ligonier, Pennsylvania), by Capt. Harry Gordon during the Forbes Expedition of 1758. On October 12, while the fort was under construction, a large force of Frenchmen and Indians attacked it repeatedly, but Col. James Burd's 1,500 defenders repulsed them. The English lost 60 men in the battle, considerably more casualties than the attackers sustained.

During Pontiac's War, Ligonier was the only small post west of the Appalachians that held out against Indian attack. In June and July 1763, Capt. Archibald Blane's small garrison repulsed several attempts to seize the fort. Soon afterward, reinforcements arrived from Fort Bedford.

(Solon J. Buck, The Planting of Civilization in Western Pennsylvania.)

LILY OF THE MOHAWKS see TEKAKWITHA, KATERI, MOHAWK NUN

LINCOLN, ABRAHAM, IN THE BLACK HAWK WAR. Abraham Lincoln served as captain of the First Regiment of the Brigade of Mounted Volunteers during the Black Hawk War. After the company disbanded, he volunteered to serve as a scout. He was never involved in battle, but he saved the life of an aged Indian who blundered into camp and was set upon by soldiers who were ready to slaughter any red man who fell into their hands. Lincoln said later of his military career, "In the days of the Black Hawk War, I fought, bled (the blood being drawn by mosquitoes) and came away."

(Fairfax Downey, Indian Wars of the U.S. Army; John Tebbel and Keith Jennison, The American Indian Wars; Allan W. Eckert, Twilight of Empire.)

LITTLE ABRAHAM, MOHAWK CHIEF see ABRAHAM, MOHAWK CHIEF

LITTLE BEARD, SENECA CHIEF see SEQUIDONGQUEE, SENECA CHIEF

LITTLE SANDUSKY, TREATY OF. The Delaware Indians negotiated a treaty at Little Sandusky, Ohio, on August 3, 1829, with John McElvain. In exchange for $3,000, they ceded three square miles of their territory located adjacent to the Wyandot reservation.

(Charles J. Kappler, ed., Indian Affairs: Laws and Treaties, II.)

LITTLE TURTLE, MIAMI, CHIEF. Little Turtle (Michikinikwa) was born near the present Fort Wayne, Indiana, in 1752. His father was a Miami and his mother a Mahican. Not a hereditary chief, he was elevated to the status of war chief during his youth because of his ability as a warrior, his skill as an orator, and his familiarity with white people (perhaps having received a brief Jesuit education).

In 1789, Little Turtle led 15 warriors in raids on the settlements near Fort Washington. In 1790 he surprised and defeated Col. Augustin de la Balme's army that had destroyed the principal Miami town, Kekionga. (See ABOITE RIVER MASSACRE.) This victory elevated him to chief commander of the Miami confederacy. In that capacity, he led the Indians to tremendous victories over the American armies of Josiah Harmar in 1790 and Arthur St. Clair in 1791. (See HARMAR EXPEDITION, ST. CLAIR'S DEFEAT.) In 1794, however, he found Gen. Anthony Wayne too wise to entrap. After an unsuccessful attempt to take Fort Recovery, he advised the tribes to make peace with "the general who never sleeps." Other Indians refused, and Little Turtle relinquished command of the allied tribes to the Shawnee chief, Blue Jacket, but he participated in the Battle of Fallen Timbers as leader of Miami warriors.

After Wayne's decisive victory at Fallen Timbers, Little Turtle strove with such determination to maintain peace that many Indians disdained him as "a government chief." He signed the Treaty of Greenville and most of the subsequent treaties through 1809 that ceded Indian lands. In 1798, he went to Philadelphia to urge Pres. John Adams to prevent the sale of liquor to Indians. Four years later, he visited Pres. Thomas Jefferson, reiterated his request for an end to the liquor trade, and pleaded for federal supervision of annuity distribution. In addition, he visited Chicago, Detroit, Montreal, and Quebec, speaking to assemblies and becoming somewhat of a popular hero. A staunch opponent of Tecumseh's, he managed to prevent his people from joining that formidable chief's conspiracy. The Indian defeat at Tippecanoe in 1811 restored a measure of tribal respect for his leadership and wisdom, but by that time he had become severely afflicted by gout. Treated by the army surgeon at Fort Wayne, he died there on July 14, 1812, and was buried with respect by white citizens.

"Like so many other exceptional leaders, his frequent contacts with white civilization had left him halfway between the two cultures."--John Tebbel and Keith Jennison.

(Harvey Lewis Carter, The Life and Times of Little Turtle; Calvin M. Young, Little Turtle; Bert Anson, The Miami Indians; John Tebbel and Keith Jennison, The American Indian Wars; Frederick J. Dockstader, Great North American Indians; Dale Van Every, Ark of Empire.)

LITTLEFIELD FAMILY, WELLS, MAINE. Edmund Littlefield, a religious follower of John Wheelwright, settled in Wells, Maine, in 1641. He and his numerous descendants became the wealthiest citizens and, beginning with King Philip's War, the most celebrated Indian fighters of that frontier community. His grandson Isaac Littlefield, a youth of 16, was killed during an Abnaki attack on Wells in 1676.

By 1692, Jonathan Littlefield had established a sturdy garrison house. In June of that year, when a large force of Frenchmen and Indians attacked, he and his wife successfully defended it by displaying hats on sticks to confuse the enemy and firing an occasional shot.

In August 1703, Aaron and Tabitha Littlefield, children of Moses Littlefield, were captured by Indians and carried to Canada. Both of them refused all attempts to redeem them and lived with the French and Indians for the remainder of their lives. In 1707, the wife of one of the Littlefield men was ambushed and killed along with three other settlers while on her way through the woods from York to Wells.

In April 1708, Josiah Littlefield was captured by Indians, carried to Canada, and turned over to the French, where he was pressed into service as a skilled engineer. His captors attempted to obtain a large ransom for him, but New England officials refused "lest they make a market for their poor women and children." He was released in 1710 and returned home, but he died during an Indian attack on Wells on April 18, 1712.

(Edward L. Bourne, History of Wells and Kennebunk; Herbert Milton Sylvester, Indian Wars of New England, II-III.)

LIVINGSTON, ROBERT, INDIAN AFFAIRS. Robert Livingston was born in Scotland on December 13, 1654. He grew up in Holland and emigrated to Albany, New York, in 1674. Speaking both English and Dutch, he obtained the office of city clerk and acted as secretary to the Board of Commissioners of Indian Affairs. He married a sister of Peter Schuyler, and the two young men made a fortune in the fur trade. Within a few years, he was sufficiently wealthy to purchase extensive land holdings from Indians along the Hudson, and his speculations were so successful that he amassed one of the great fortunes of the time. A shrewd student of Indian affairs, his advice proved invaluable to colonial governors for many years. He died on October 1, 1728.

(Allen W. Trelease, Indian Affairs in Colonial New York.)

LOCHRY, ARCHIBALD, EXPEDITION. Col. Archibald Lochry, commanding officer of the Westmoreland, Pennsylvania, militia, responded in 1781 to a call by George Rogers Clark to provide men for a campaign against the British forces at Detroit. He led 100 frontiersmen to rendezvous with Clark's forces at Wheeling, but Clark, beset by desertions, departed down the Ohio before his arrival. Lochry tried desperately to overtake Clark's army. Unfortunately, a messenger he sent ahead to ask Clark to wait was captured by Joseph Brant's Mohawks, alerting the Indians that a small force of Americans was coming downriver.

On August 24, Brant forced the captured courier to decoy Lochry's boats to the shore near the mouth of the Great Miami. There his 90 warriors waited in ambush, and they opened a deadly fire on the unsuspecting Pennsylvanians. About a third of Lochry's men died in the battle, and the survivors were captured. Several of the captives, including Lochry, were tortured to death.

(C. Hale Sipe, Indian Wars of Pennsylvania; Randolph C. Downes, Council Fires on the Upper Ohio; Dale Van Every, A Company of Heroes.)

LOGAN, CAPTAIN, SHAWNEE CHIEF see SPEMICALAWBA, SHAWNEE CHIEF

LOGAN, JAMES, INDIAN AFFAIRS. James Logan was born in Ireland on October 20, 1674. Employed by William Penn as a secretary, he accompanied him to Pennsylvania in 1699. He administered Penn's affairs in America, made a fortune in land speculation, and lived in a mansion at Germantown.

Logan was a skillful administrator of Indian affairs. In order to safeguard Quaker colonists who opposed warfare, he took the lead in negotiating a treaty with the Iroquois in 1731 that recognized Six Nations domination of Pennsylvania tribes, thus placing the colony under League protection. He entertained leading chiefs at his home, and they regarded him as a true friend.

Logan added to his power and wealth by developing a prosperous fur trade. His traders competed with the French for furs on the Beaver, Ohio, Muskingum and other rivers of the western wilderness. He died on October 31, 1751.

"The formulation of Pennsylvania's Indian policy in 1731-32 was the work of three men: James Logan, Provincial Secretary and one of the ablest students of Indian affairs that the English ever produced; Conrad Weiser, ... and Shickellamy."--Paul A. W. Wallace.

(Paul A. W. Wallace, Indians in Pennsylvania.)

LOGAN, MINGO CHIEF. Logan (John Logan, Tachnechdorus, Tahgah-jute) was the son of a Cayuga mother and a Frenchman who had been captured and raised by the Iroquois. He was born at Shamokin, Pennsylvania, about 1725. A firm friend of the English settlers, he took the name Logan because of his admiration for James Logan, Pennsylvania provincial secretary. A skillful hunter, he supported his family for many years by selling dressed animal skins to the colonists. He supported the English during the French and Indian War and Pontiac's War.

About 1770, Logan and his followers moved to the Ohio. There the white frontiersmen did not hold him in the same high regard that he had enjoyed in the more settled regions of Pennsylvania. In April 1774, they murdered 13 of Logan's relatives in an unprovoked affray known as the Yellow Creek Massacre. This tragedy transformed the peaceful chief into a firebrand bent upon revenge. In June, he led 8 warriors into Virginia, killed 13 settlers (equal to the number of his slain relatives), and captured William Robinson and Thomas Hellen. Logan saved both of the captives when his warriors sought to burn them to death.

Logan's raids on the settlements were partially responsible for beginning Dunmore's War. When the Indians requested an end to the war, Logan refused to participate in treaty negotiations. Lord Dunmore sent an officer, John Gibson, to urge him to attend the proceedings, and Logan led him into the woods and related with tears in his eyes the story of the murders of his relatives. Gibson recorded the chief's words, and the oration has become famous as Logan's Lament.

After Dunmore's War, Logan became increasingly morose and addicted to liquor. Some observers considered him to be deranged. While returning from a trip to Detroit in 1780, he was murdered by his nephew.

(Randolph C. Downes, Council Fires on the Upper Ohio; Theodore Roosevelt, The Winning of the West, II; Dale Van Every, Forth to the Wilderness; Paul A. W. Wallace, Indians in Pennsylvania; Alexander Scott Withers, Chronicles of Border Warfare.)

LOGANSPORT, INDIANA, TREATY OF. The Treaty of Logansport

was negotiated by William Marshall with the Potawatomi Indians on
December 17, 1834. The Indians ceded four sections of land and
agreed to remove west of the Mississippi. Goods were presented to
the chiefs.

(Charles J. Kappler, ed., Indian Affairs: Laws and Treaties,
II.)

LOGSTOWN. Logstown, located on the Ohio River just below Pittsburgh, was an important center of the Indian trade during the mid-
eighteenth century. Established by Delaware and Shawnee Indians,
it expanded by 1749 to a settlement of 40 houses occupied by warriors of several Indian nations. Abandoned about 1750, it was reoccupied soon afterward by Mingos and other tribes allied with the
English.

In June 1752, George Croghan and representatives of the Ohio
Company negotiated a treaty with the Indians at Logstown, obtaining
permission to build forts in their territory. By 1754, however, some
of the residents were coming under French influence, and Croghan,
who had a trading post there, was compelled to provide many presents in order to avoid being expelled.

In 1754, after the French destroyed the fort at the mouth of
the Monongahela, the Indians at Logstown who supported the English
burned their town and fled to Redstone for protection. The following year, the French rebuilt the settlement for their allies, the
Shawnees. By 1756, the town was occupied by 100 Shawnees and
30 white captives. With the French loss of Fort Duquesne in 1758,
the Indians deserted Logstown.

(Charles A. Hanna, The Wilderness Trail; Albert T. Volwiler,
George Croghan and the Westward Movement; Randolph C. Downes,
Council Fires on the Upper Ohio.)

LONGLEY FAMILY, GROTON, MASSACHUSETTS. The Abnaki chief
Moxus raided Groton on July 27, 1694, killing 22 colonists and capturing 13. Among the slain were a man named Longley, his wife,
and 5 children. His children Lydia, John, and Betty were carried
to Canada. Betty died soon in captivity. Lydia became a nun and
remained in Canada the rest of her life. John, aged 12 when taken,
was redeemed four years later, but he had become so completely
assimilated that he had to be tied to prevent his running away to
rejoin the Indians.

(Emma Lewis Coleman, New England Captives Carried to Canada
Between 1677 and 1766; Samuel Adams Drake, Border Wars of New
England.)

LONGUEUIL, CHARLES LE MOYNE see LE MOYNE, CHARLES, BARON
DE LONGUEIL

LORIMIER, PIERRE LOUIS. Pierre Louis Lorimier (Laramie), a
French-Canadian trader, founded a post in western Ohio about 1769.
There he gained a strong influence over the Shawnee Indians.
During the American Revolution, he was an active British partisan,

providing the Indians with firearms and accompanying them when they raided American settlements. He was with the Shawnees in 1778 when they captured Daniel Boone and his fellow saltmakers at the Blue Licks, and he tried to persuade them to attack Boonesborough at that time. His post was destroyed by George Rogers Clark near the end of the war.

To avoid the Americans, Lorimier and about 400 Shawnees moved to the Mississippi. He established Cape Girardeau in 1793 on a Spanish land grant and prospered through the Indian trade and the sale of extensive land holdings. He lost his property when France sold Louisiana to the United States in 1804.

(John Bakeless, Daniel Boone.)

LOUVIGNY, LOUIS   see   LA PORTE, SIEUR DE LOUVIGNY, LOUIS DE

LOVEWELL, JOHN. Capt. John Lovewell was one of New England's most famous frontiersmen and scalp hunters. He led a band of Dunstable men into the Indian country with the expectation of claiming rewards for their kills.

In 1724, Lovewell and his men raided north of Winnipiseogee Lake, but found only one warrior and a boy. They killed the man for his scalp and brought the boy to Boston to claim their reward.

Disappointed at the meager return, Lovewell recruited 35 men for a raid on the Abnaki stronghold of Pigwacket (present Fryeburg, Maine), in the spring of 1725. Upon approaching Pigwacket at dawn on May 8, they saw an Indian hunting ducks and mortally wounded him, but he lived long enough to shoot Lovewell in the stomach. Not realizing that he had received a death wound, Lovewell placed his men in a defensive position when warriors attacked them from behind trees. After Lovewell died, Ensign Seth Wyman assumed command, and a bloody battle ensued for the entire day. Finally, Wyman killed the Indian medicine man and put an end to the fight. Only 18 of the English survived to return to Dunstable. (See FRYE, JONATHAN; PEQUAWKET INDIANS.)

(Jeremy Belknap, History of New Hampshire, I; Francis Parkman, A Half-Century of Conflict; Herbert Milton Sylvester, Indian Wars of New England, III.)

LOWERY, LAZARUS, FAMILY OF. Lazarus Lowery emigrated to Lancaster County, Pennsylvania, from northern Ireland about 1729. He opened a trading post in 1730 and made frequent trips with his goods as far west as the Ohio. His five sons, James, John, Daniel, Alexander, and Lazarus, accompanied him on his travels until his death in 1755.

John Lowery was blown to pieces in the Ohio country in 1749 when an Indian set fire to a keg of gunpowder near the spot where he was resting. James became a successful trader and assisted George Croghan in preventing many of the Indians from deserting the English interest. In January 1753, he was captured by the Caughnawaga Indians, but he managed to escape a few days later.

He lost all of his goods and was forced to sell his land. Alexander joined the trading firm of Edward Shippen, operated posts at Logstown, Carlisle, and Fort Pitt, and acquired a considerable fortune.

(Charles A. Hanna, The Wilderness Trail.)

LOYALHANNA, BATTLE OF THE see LIGONIER, FORT

LUTER EXPEDITION. During the winter of 1643-44, a group of Boston merchants organized an expedition to trade among the Indian tribes who lived along the Delaware River. Led by a man known as Captain Luter, a half dozen traders loaded a boat with firearms, powder, and trinkets and traded them for a valuable cargo of pelts. Then a new party of Indians arrived, and when the traders began examining their pelts, the warriors whipped out their tomahawks and murdered Luter and most of his men. They captured a man and a boy, looted the vessel, and began making off with the spoils. Another war party overtook them, killed the original robbers, and seized the goods for themselves. They sold the captives to the Swedish governor, Johan Printz, who returned them to Boston.

(C. A. Weslager, The English on the Delaware.)

LYDIUS, JOHN HENRY. John Henry Lydius, son of a Dutch clergyman, worked for Sir William Johnson at Albany, overseeing the shipment of trade goods and furs. In that capacity he gained a considerable influence over the Iroquois, and, about 1748, he helped a group of Connecticut settlers (representing the Susquehanna Company) to purchase the Wyoming Valley, a transaction that, according to Arthur Pound, resulted in "a sowing of devil's teeth which reached harvest in the frightful Wyoming massacre of 1778." Johnson, who no longer trusted Lydius, destroyed his trading post in 1755, and Fort Edward was built at the site. Lydius retained the support of Gov. William Shirley of Massachusetts, however, and represented him in negotiations with the Six Nations. In 1776, Lydius moved to England, where he died in 1791.

(Arthur Pound, Johnson of the Mohawks; Anthony F. C. Wallace, King of the Delawares: Teedyuscung.)

LYMAN, CALEB, EXPEDITION. Caleb Lyman, a Northampton, Massachusetts, settler, was told in 1704 that Indians allied with the French had established a village on the upper Connecticut River. He recruited five friendly Indians to help him ascertain the truth of the story, and, after traveling nine days through the wilderness, they located a large wigwam in a thicket. Convinced that their quarry had participated in a recent raid on Northampton, Lyman determined to attack. Under cover of a thunderstorm, the Massachusetts men fired into the wigwam, then charged with their tomahawks, killing seven warriors. Afterward, they collected a bounty of £31 for the Indians' scalps.

(Samuel Adams Drake, Border Wars of New England; Francis Parkman, A Half-Century of Conflict.)

-M-

M'ALLUM, DAN, CAPTIVITY OF. Dan M'Allum was captured in the
Wyoming Valley of Pennsylvania by Mohawk Indians soon after the
beginning of the American Revolution. Only two years old at the
time he was taken, he became completely assimilated. When the war
ended, the Indians released their captives, but Dan tried desperately
to rejoin his beloved Mohawk adopted mother. Returned to his real
mother, he never made a secret of the fact that he loved his Indian
mother the most. He told neighbors that "I wish to God I had never
left the Indians, for I was a good Indian, but I shall never make a
white man." He finally settled down, however, married, and became a successful farmer.
(George Peck, Wyoming.)

McCORD'S FORT, PENNSYLVANIA, RAID. McCord's fort, located
near Chambersburg, Pennsylvania, was attacked on April 1, 1756,
by the Delaware warriors of the fearsome chief, Shingas. Defenders
of the small, privately owned fortification were compelled to surrender, and 27 persons were killed or captured. Fifty militiamen pursued the raiders, overtook them at Sideling Hill, and engaged them
in a bloody battle. Capt. Alexander Culbertson and 19 of his men
were killed, and 12 others were wounded. Five captives were recovered, including two daughters of William McCord. A third daughter, Mary, was accidentally shot by the militia. The wife of John
McCord was carried to Kittanning and rescued during Col. John Armstrong's attack on that Delaware stronghold on September 8, 1756.
(William A. Hunter, Forts on the Pennsylvania Frontier.)

MCCOY, ISAAC. Isaac McCoy, a Baptist missionary, was born near
Uniontown, Pennsylvania, on June 13, 1784. With his parents he
moved to Kentucky when he was six years old, and there he received
a rudimentary education. In 1803 he married Virginia Polke, a religious girl who encouraged him to become a missionary. In 1804
they moved to Indiana, where he obtained a license to preach, and,
in 1817, he became a missionary to the Indians.

Within a few months, McCoy concluded that to Christianize the
Indians he would have to live among them, educate their children,
and put a stop to the activities of liquor traders. In 1822, he was
appointed by Lewis Cass, superintendent of Indian affairs of the
Northwest Territory, to supervise the educational progress of the
Potawatomi and Ottawa Indians. Soon he had 70 Potawatomi youths
enrolled in school.

McCoy, who had a genuine concern for the welfare of the Indians, became convinced that their only salvation lay in removing
them from the harmful influences of contact with white frontiersmen.
In 1828, he served on a commission intended to promote tribal removal
west of the Mississippi. This experience led him to envision a separate Indian territory, where tribes could work together to develop
their own nation. The idea appealed to Andrew Jackson and other
advocates of Indian removal, and he made frequent trips to Washington

to promote his plans. Appointed surveyor in 1830, he assisted tribes who ceded their lands to select reservation sites in the West. He chose a site near the Ottawa mission in Kansas as the future capital of an Indian state, but the plan failed because of too many diverse tribes and too much white encroachment on available lands.

In 1842, McCoy was appointed secretary and general agent of the Indian Mission Association. He died at Louisville, Kentucky while fulfilling those duties.

(George A. Schultz, An Indian Canaan.)

MCCREA, JANE, MURDER OF. Jane McCrea, a young woman with Loyalist leanings during the American Revolution, was engaged to be married to a Tory officer of Burgoyne's army named David Jones. During Burgoyne's invasion of New York, she went to Fort Edward, expecting its imminent occupation by the British. There, on July 27, 1777, she was shot to death and scalped by a Wyandot warrior named Panther, a scout for Burgoyne's forces. The circumstances of her death are a matter of historical dispute. Some authorities assert that Panther was employed by Jones to bring Miss McCrea to army headquarters and that she was shot accidentally by an American soldier. Others contend that two warriors captured her, disputed ownership, and settled the matter by murdering her. A third version holds that Panther shot her because her beautiful long hair would make such an impressive trophy.

Most authorities agree that Panther brought Jane's scalp to the British camp, that Jones recognized it, and that only Burgoyne's prompt action in placing the warrior under arrest prevented the grieving lieutenant from exacting vengeance on the spot. Burgoyne threatened to execute Panther, but released him when informed that all of his Indian allies would desert if he carried out the sentence.

The murder of Jane McCrea had important repercussions. Infuriated colonists rushed to join American armies. Tories were badly shaken over the death of one of their people at the hands of Indian allies. Even in England, politicians debated the wisdom of continuing to employ Indians against the Americans.

(Fairfax Downey, Indian Wars of the U.S. Army; Barbara Graymont, The Iroquois in the American Revolution; James Levernier and Hennig Cohen, eds., The Indians and Their Captives.)

M'CULLOUGH, JOHN, CAPTIVITY OF. John M'Culloch was 8 years old when captured by Delaware Indians near Fort Loudon, Pennsylvania, on July 26, 1756. Adopted by a warrior to replace a brother who had been killed, he became so thoroughly Indianized that he fled from his white father who had paid a ransom for his release. Many years later, after readjusting to white civilization, he wrote an interesting account of his successful attempt to rejoin the Indians:

> The next morning my father and two others came to
> our camp and told me ... I must go home with my father; to
> see my mother and the rest of my friends; I wept bitterly,
> all to no purpose; my father was ready to start. They laid

hold of me and set me on a horse, I threw myself off; they
set me on again, and tied my legs under the horse's belly,
and started away for Pittsburgh; we encamped about ten or
fifteen miles from Venenggo; before we lay down, my father
took his garters and tied my arms behind my back. ...
About midnight ... I ran off as fast as I could.

John remained with the Indians two more years. Finally, after
eight years as an adopted Indian, he was recovered by the Bouquet
Expedition.

(Archibald Loudon, ed., Selection of Some of the Most Interesting Narratives of Outrages Committed by the Indians, in Their
Wars With the White People.)

MCCUTCHEONVILLE, OHIO, TREATY OF. James B. Gardiner negotiated a treaty with the Wyandot Indians at McCutcheonville on January 19, 1832. The Wyandots ceded 16,000 acres and agreed to accept
as payment the proceeds of the sale of the land to settlers.

(Charles J. Kappler, ed., Indian Affairs: Laws and Treaties,
II.)

MCDOWELL'S MILL, PENNSYLVANIA, RAID. McDowell's Mill, a private fort belonging to John McDowell, was established in Franklin
County, Pennsylvania, in November 1755. On February 29, 1756,
the stockade was attacked by 80 Delaware warriors led by Chiefs
Captain Jacobs and Shingas. Fourteen soldiers and 12 Pennsylvania
frontiersmen defended the fort successfully until reinforcements arrived and drove the raiders away. Three of the defenders were
killed. So many settlers were slain near McDowell's Mill that a
stronger post (Fort Loudon) with a much larger garrison was constructed in December 1756.

(William A. Hunter, Forts on the Pennsylvania Frontier.)

MCINTOSH, FORT, TREATY OF. The Treaty of Fort McIntosh was
negotiated in January 1785 by Richard Butler, George Clark, and
Arthur Lee with representatives of the Delaware, Chippewa, Ottawa,
and Wyandot nations. The chiefs, who acted without full tribal
authorization, failed to understand the implications of the treaty
when they ceded a large portion of the state of Ohio in exchange for
goods to be distributed among the tribes. Three chiefs served as
hostages until all American captives were released. The Indians
repudiated the treaty soon afterward.

(Charles J. Kappler, ed., Indian Affairs: Laws and Treaties,
II; Solon J. Buck, The Planting of Civilization in Western Pennsylvania; Dale Van Every, Ark of Empire.)

MCINTOSH, LACHLAN, EXPEDITION. Gen. Lachlan McIntosh, a
Georgia veteran of the southern Indian wars, was appointed in July
1778, to establish a chain of forts in Ohio and to lead an expedition
against the British center of Indian control at Detroit. He succeeded
only in constructing Forts McIntosh and Laurens, and he was unable

to maintain the latter because of repeated Indian attacks. (See LAURENS, FORT.) In the opinion of the Ohio Valley historian Randolph C. Downes, he "assumed a bombastic air of superiority and marched into the Indian country as if he were Caesar occupying a conquered province," but he soon found it necessary to beg food from friendly tribes. The weakness of the expedition was so apparent that even the Delawares began to attack McIntosh's men. The march toward Detroit soon was abandoned.

(Randolph C. Downes, Council Fires on the Upper Ohio; Dale Van Every, A Company of Heroes.)

MCKEE, ALEXANDER. Alexander McKee, son of the prominent Pennsylvania trader, Thomas McKee, was for 40 years one of the most successful British Indian diplomats. He spent most of his life among Indians, his mother having been either a Shawnee or a white captive taken in infancy by that tribe. He married a Shawnee woman, and several of his sons became chiefs of that warlike nation.

McKee's youth was spent as an Indian trader in the Chillicothe area. At the age of 20, he became an associate of the important Indian diplomat George Croghan, and served as his principal assistant during Pontiac's War. He was in charge of Indian affairs at Fort Pitt during the siege of 1763, and he assisted Croghan at that post for the following decade. He gained such tremendous influence over the Indians that when Croghan retired from the British Indian Service in 1772, McKee succeeded him as Sir William Johnson's deputy Indian agent among the tribes of the Ohio.

At the onset of the American Revolution, McKee was suspected of Loyalist leanings. Richard Butler, appointed by the Continental Congress to the post of Indian Agent, forbade McKee to negotiate with the tribes or to leave Pittsburgh without his permission. Butler allowed him to attend an important Indian conference at Pittsburgh during the summer of 1775, however, and McKee publicly advocated Indian neutrality while secretly advising the tribes to prepare for an opportune time to attack the Americans.

In the spring of 1778, McKee fled from Fort Pitt and went to British headquarters at Detroit, where he was welcomed by Gov. Henry Hamilton and assigned to lead Indians against the American frontier settlements. "No other instance of Tory disaffection during the Revolution produced consequences so catastrophic," asserted Dale Van Every.

McKee led or dispatched Indian raids into Kentucky, Virginia, and Pennsylvania throughout the remainder of the Revolution. Afterward, as a trader and British agent, he provided arms for war parties and incited them to continue raiding frontier settlements. In September 1783, he assembled representatives of 35 tribes at Sandusky to urge them to defend their lands against American expansion, and he implied that they could expect British support. For the next 15 years, as a colonel and administrator of Britain's Indian affairs in the West, he continued to urge the tribes to drive the Americans back across the Ohio. In 1796, McKee moved to Malden, Ontario, where he died on January 14, 1799.

(Dale Van Every, A Company of Heroes; Ark of Empire;
Charles A. Hanna, The Wilderness Trail; Theodore Roosevelt, The
Winning of the West, II-III, V.)

MCKEE, THOMAS. Thomas McKee was a prominent Pennsylvania
trader who settled among the Delaware Indians of Shamokin at an
early age. In January 1743, the Indians planned to murder him, but
he was warned by a Shawnee woman (perhaps a white captive), and
fled to the settlements. Afterward, he married the woman and they
became the parents of Alexander McKee, a British Indian diplomat.
His trading enterprises expanded rapidly, and by 1748 he operated
posts on the Susquehanna and the Allegheny.

McKee served as a captain during the French and Indian War.
He participated in Indian conferences at Fort Pitt in 1759 and 1760.
He died in 1772.

(Charles A. Hanna, The Wilderness Trail.)

MCKENNEY, THOMAS L. Thomas L. McKenney was born in Hope-
well, Maryland, on March 21, 1785. His Quaker upbringing did not
prevent him from participating in the War of 1812, and afterward he
served as an officer in the Washington militia. Although he had little knowledge of Indian affairs when appointed superintendent of
Indian trade by President Madison in 1816, he became an ethnological
authority by collecting tribal artifacts and books, articles, and paint-
ings illustrative of Indian life. The collections formed the basis of
his important work, co-authored with Judge James Hall, entitled
Indian Tribes of North America.

While serving as superintendent of Indian trade, McKenney
supervised the operation of government factories. In 1819, he played
a leading role in insuring the enactment of the Indian Civilization
Act, important legislation that provided funds for the establishment
and operation of schools for Indians, mainly by missionaries. Three
years later, however, his office was abolished, largely because of
complaints by traders against the government factory system.

In 1824, Secretary of War John Calhoun created the Bureau
of Indian Affairs within the War Department and appointed McKenney
to direct it. During the next six years, McKenney became a leading proponent of Indian removal, abandoning his earlier efforts to
integrate Indians into white society. He negotiated the treaties of
Fond du Lac with the Chippewas in 1826, Butte des Morts with the
Menominees and Winnebagos in 1827, and others with the Creeks,
Choctaws, and Chickasaws shortly thereafter. In 1830 he was ousted
from office in a political move by Pres. Andrew Jackson.

Historians differ as to McKenney's motives and methods of administering Indian affairs. Richard Drinnon, who characterized him
as "more high-handed than high-minded," asserted he was motivated
in large measure by his determination to please his superiors and to
keep his job. Herman J. Viola, on the other hand, contended that
he was a "sincere humanitarian" who "did his best to maintain a
balance between national desires and national honor by just treatment
of the Indians."

(Herman J. Viola, Thomas L. McKenney, Architect of America's Early Indian Policy; Richard Drinnon, Facing West; J. P. Kinney, A Continent Lost--A Civilization Won.)

MACKINAC. Mackinac (Michilimackinac), at the juncture of Lakes Michigan and Huron, became a center of French missionary and fur trade activities during the latter part of the seventeenth century. Father Jacques Marquette established the St. Ignace Mission there to serve the Huron Indians in 1670. Antoine La Mothe Cadillac commanded a French fort there in 1694, and he persuaded most of the Indians of the area to accompany him when he established Detroit in 1701. By 1750, Mackinac had become the headquarters of French fur traders and coureurs de bois.

In 1761, the British seized Fort Mackinac, then located on the south shore of the Mackinac Straits, and several English traders moved there. (See HENRY, ALEXANDER.) Maj. George Etherington, the commanding officer, was warned by the traders that the Chippewa Indians were threatening to massacre his small garrison, but the troops were taken completely by surprise when warriors rushed through the gate on June 4, 1763, under the guise of retrieving a ball that had sailed over the stockade wall during a game of lacrosse. The Indians, Chippewas and Sauks, attacked English soldiers and traders, killing 20 and capturing more than a dozen. Several of the captives were tortured to death, while the others were turned over to Ottawa Indians and saved by a French priest.

Near the end of Pontiac's War, the English regained control of Fort Mackinac. During the American Revolution it served as a headquarters of British-Indian diplomatic realtions. In 1783, the United States obtained possession of Mackinac as a result of the Treaty of Paris, but the British and their Indian allies compelled the Americans to surrender the post during the War of 1812 and continued to hold it for 15 years. It served as a center of the British fur trade until 1830.

(Louise Phelps Kellogg, The British Regime in Wisconsin and the Northwest; Francis Parkman, A Half-Century of Conflict; Howard H. Peckham, Pontiac and the Indian Uprising; Dale Van Every, Forth to the Wilderness.)

MADISON, FORT. Fort Madison (Fort Bellevue) was built on the Mississippi River at the present site of Fort Madison, Iowa, during the winter of 1808-09. Its establishment was opposed by Chief Black Hawk and his Sauk and Winnebago supporters, and they made several determined attempts to drive the small garrison away. During the spring of 1809, Black Hawk used a dance outside the stockade as a ruse to rush inside the gate, only to be confronted by cannon. Realizing that the soldiers were ready to repulse the attack, Black Hawk and his followers withdrew.

At the onset of the War of 1812, the Indians renewed their attempts to destroy Fort Madison. Beginning early in 1812, a siege was instituted by Potawatomi Indians, but they withdrew when the garrison received reinforcements. Two attacks were made in July

1813, and several soldiers were slain. Finally, in November 1813, when the small garrison was again surrounded by hostile Indians and faced starvation, the commandant ordered an evacuation. The soldiers dug a trench to the river and escaped in boats, and the last man to leave set a fire that destroyed the fort.

(William T. Hagan, The Sac and Fox Indians; Louise Phelps Kellogg, The British Régime in Wisconsin and the Northwest.)

MADOKAWANDO, PENOBSCOT CHIEF. Born about 1630, Madokawando became one of the most prominent Abnaki sachems who at first favored peaceful relations with the early English settlers of Maine. Incited by the French, however, and angered by English occupation of Penobscot lands, he finally opted to join hostile chiefs in raiding the settlements. Although he became a formidable enemy, he earned a measure of respect by his humane treatment of captives, especially during the seizure of Pemaquid in 1689 when he was responsible for sparing the lives of Lt. James Weems and 6 other soldiers. In 1691, he led the attack on York, Maine, killing 77 citizens and destroying the town.

After the Baron de St. Castin married Madokawando's daughter he shared tribal leadership with the chief. By 1693, they realized that the English eventually would defeat the French and Indians during King William's War and that it would be wise to make peace in order to restore trade and redeem Abnaki prisoners. In August, Madokawando negotiated peace during a conference at Pemaquid, much to the displeasure of chiefs determined to continue their raids. He died in 1698.

(Francis Parkman, Count Frontenac and New France Under Louis XIV; Herbert Milton Sylvester, Indian Wars of New England.)

MAGNUS, NARRAGANSET CHIEF. Magnus was a female chief of the Narraganset Indians during King Philip's War. The sister of Chief Ninigret, she was married to a son of the powerful sachem, Canonicus. Her principal village was located near Exeter, Rhode Island.

Magnus and her followers were Philip's firm allies. Pursued by Maj. John Talcott and his Connecticut troops, she was encamped in a swamp near Warwick, Rhode Island, when the colonists launched a surprise attack on July 2, 1676. Carolyn Thomas Foreman described the action as follows:

> During King Philip's War much savagry was displayed by the whites as well as the red men, but on neither side was there an act of signal vengeance more shocking than that of Major Talcot, who, with a force of 300 mounted men-- English and Indians--overtook a body of nearly the same number of Narragansetts in a swamp in their country. Those who were not killed in the first assault were made prisoners, and 90 so taken were put to death. Among them was the Squaw Sachem Magnus....

(Carolyn Thomas Foreman, Indian Women Chiefs; Douglas

Leach, Flintlock and Tomahawk; F. W. Hodge, ed., Handbook of American Indians, I.)

MAGUAGA, BATTLE OF. The Battle of Maguaga (Monguagon) was fought on August 9, 1812, near Maguaga, Michigan, when Col. James Miller led 600 regulars and Michigan and Ohio volunteers in an attempt to reopen Gen. William Hull's supply route to Fort Detroit. Miller's forces were ambushed by 250 Indians led by Tecumseh and 150 British soldiers commanded by Capt. Adam Muir. In a fierce battle, approximately 100 British and Indians were killed. Miller suffered 80 casualties. Tecumseh was compelled to retreat, but Miller failed to reopen communications, and Hull surrendered Detroit soon afterward.

   (Reginald Horsman, The War of 1812.)

MAHICAN INDIANS. The Mahican Indians, a large and powerful Algonquian tribe, occupied both banks of the upper Hudson River when encountered by Henry Hudson, who traded with them in 1609. They were allies of the Delawares and bitter enemies of their neighbors, the Mohawks. The first North American Indians to sign a treaty with Europeans, they permitted the establishment of a Dutch trading post in their territory in 1614. Afterward, they sold large portions of their land to the Dutch and served the newcomers as middlemen in their extensive fur trade.

   After 1628, when the Mohawks seized their lands west of the Hudson, the Mahicans waged war on tribes located to the east of that river in order to obtain beaver skins to trade with the Dutch. Just before the English seized New Amsterdam in 1664, the Mahicans raided Dutch settlements. After the English negotiated peace between the Mahicans and Mohawks in 1673, the two tribes began raiding Virginia and the Carolinas to increase their fur supplies.

   By 1730 the Mahican villages, formerly 40 strong, had become widely scattered. Many had relocated in Pennsylvania's Wyoming Valley, while a few had moved as far west as Ohio and Indiana. In 1736 those Mahicans occupying the Housatonic Valley moved to a mission at Stockbridge. (See STOCKBRIDGE INDIANS; SERGEANT, JOHN.) Soon afterward, Moravian missionaries converted many Mahicans to Christianity.

   Some of the western Mahicans sided with the British during the American Revolution. After Gen. John Sullivan's American army invaded Indian lands in 1779, they fled to Niagara for British protection. Four years later, some of them moved to Canada. A few Mahicans remained on the Hudson after the Revolution, but that remnant gradually faded away.

   "Despite the fact that the Mahican were in existence and available for observation for at least three generations after colonization had begun, comparatively little is known of them today."--Allen W. Trelease.

   (Allen W. Trelease, Indian Affairs in Colonial New York; William A. Sturtevant, ed., Handbook of North American Indians, XV; John R. Swanton, Indian Tribes of North America.)

MAIN POC, POTAWATOMI CHIEF. Main Poc (Main Poche, Main Poque), a prominent Potawatomi shaman and orator, exerted tremendous influence over the Sauks, Winnebagos, and Chippewas during the early nineteenth century. He was such a successful leader of war parties that his followers believed his medicine protected him from arrows and bullets. While most of his hostilities were directed at enemy Indians, particularly the Osages, he played an important role as a British partisan during the War of 1812.

In 1807, Main Poc became an ally of Tecumseh and the Shawnee Prophet. The following year, he was persuaded by William Wells to visit President Jefferson at Washington. After receiving numerous gifts and an ample supply of liquor, he promised to remain at peace with the Americans. The Treaty of Fort Wayne infuriated him, however, and he rejoined the Shawnee Prophet in June 1810. In 1811 he attacked the southern Illinois settlements so furiously that most of the citizens abandoned their homes and fled to Kentucky.

During the spring of 1812, Main Poc used his enormous influence to persuade northwestern tribes to support the British in their war with the United States. He harried Gen. William Hull's forces near Detroit, inflicting heavy casualties. After a battle at Brownstown, he murdered an American officer. With the defeat of the British and the death of Tecumseh at the Battle of the Thames, he conferred with an American official, Thomas Forsyth, and agreed to call a halt to his raids on the settlements.

James A. Clifton has characterized Main Poc as a "man with an insatiable desire for killing" and "a strong infatuation for the whiskey jug."

(James A. Clifton, The Prairie People; Emma H. Blair, The Indian Tribes of the Upper Mississippi Valley and the Region of the Great Lakes; R. David Edmunds, The Shawnee Prophet.)

MAKATAIMESHEKIAKIAK, SAUK CHIEF see BLACK HAWK, SAUK CHIEF

MALOTT, PETER, FAMILY OF. Peter Malott of Maryland was moving his family down the Ohio River by flatboat when, on April 1, 1780, a party of Delaware Indians attacked the flotilla near the mouth of Captina Creek, killing three men and capturing 21 men, women, and children. Of the three boats in the company, two escaped to the Kentucky settlements. Malott manned one of the fortunate boats, but his family was traveling on the one that was taken. Mrs. Malott and her five children were marched to the Muskingum and scattered among Indian villages. The eldest daughter Catherine (aged 15) was held by the Shawnees of Mad River, while the fate of the other children is unknown.

Malott despaired of recovering his family and returned to Maryland, but his wife was redeemed from captivity by the British at Detroit, and she employed Simon Girty, the famous British partisan known as "the white savage," to help her locate her lost children. He found Catherine in 1783 and fell in love with the beautiful young woman, but the Indian family that had adopted her refused his efforts to redeem her. Finally, Girty persuaded them to permit him to take her to Detroit to visit her mother, promising a prompt return to the tribe. Once in Detroit, he married her and made a home for her in Canada.

(Consul W. Butterfield, History of the Girtys; Charles Mc-Knight, Our Western Border.)

MANHATTAN INDIANS. The Manhattan Indians, a member of the Wappinger confederacy, lived on Manhattan Island and along the east bank of the Hudson River when encountered by the Henry Hudson Expedition. They paddled out in canoes to attack Hudson's ship when he returned down the river in 1609. Afterward, they permitted the Dutch to settle on Manhattan Island, and Peter Minuit purchased it from them on May 6, 1626, for goods and trinkets valued at 66 guilders. Later, they sold their remaining lands to white settlers.

(F. W. Hodge, ed., Handbook of American Indians, I; E. B. O'Callaghan, History of New Netherland, I.)

MARIETTA, OHIO, RAID. New England farmers established the village of Marietta, Ohio, at the mouth of the Muskingum River in 1788. They befriended the natives and were spared the horrors of Indian warfare until after Harmar's defeat two years later. Then early in 1791, the exultant Indians infiltrated the settlements around Marietta and wreaked particular havoc on the hamlet called Big Bottom. Theodore Roosevelt has described the attack as follows:

> There were some twenty-five Indians in the attacking party; they were Wyandots and Delawares.... The assault was made in the twilight, on the 2d of January, the Indians crossing the frozen Muskingum and stealthily approaching a blockhouse and three cabins. The inmates were frying meat for supper, and did not suspect harm, offering food to the Indians; but the latter, once they were within doors ... shot and tomahawked all save a couple of men who escaped and the five who were made prisoners. The captives were all taken to the Miami, or Detroit....

More than a dozen settlers were killed in or around Marietta that day.

(Theodore Roosevelt, The Winning of the West, V; Dale Van Every, Ark of Empire.)

MARIN DE LA MALGUE, PAUL. Paul Marin de La Malgue, an officer in the Canadian Army, was born at Montreal in 1692. He was assigned to the western frontier by 1720 and spent most of his life as a soldier and trader among the Indians of the Great Lakes region. In 1722, he assumed command of the French post at Chequamegon Bay (present Ashland, Wisconsin), and attempted to insure that Indian tribes remained at peace with the French and each other.

In 1728, the second Fox war against the French erupted, and

Marin was assigned to subdue them. He established his headquarters among the Menominee Indians in 1729, and he defeated the Foxes at Butte des Morts in 1730. Afterward, he proved to be as effective a diplomat as a fighter, and Louise Phelps Kellogg has asserted that "it was his policy of conciliation that succeeded in ending the Fox wars, after the policy of terrorism had failed." In 1740, he escorted chiefs from all the western tribes to Montreal to assure the French of their friendly intentions.

After the defeat of the Foxes, Marin was transferred to Green Bay, where he amassed a fortune in the fur trade. In 1750, he established a fort near Lake Pepin and traded profitably with the Sioux. His connivance with Gov. Pierre-Jacques de Taffanel, Marquis de La Jonquière, in controlling the Indian trade resulted in practices which eventually hastened the fall of New France, but at the time he rendered valuable service by maintaining peace between all of the western tribes.

In 1753, Marin was ordered to block English expansion along the Ohio by building a chain of French forts and a road to the head of the Allegheny River. Old and infirm at the time, he constructed forts at Presque Isle and Le Boeuf, but died at the latter on October 29, 1753, of food poisoning, before completing his task.

(Louise Phelps Kellogg, The French Régime in Wisconsin and the Northwest.)

MARLBOROUGH, MASSACHUSETTS, RAID. On March 26, 1676, Indians attacked Marlborough while the citizens were attending church services. The town was partially destroyed. Pursued by Ephraim Curtis and 40 settlers, the invaders were overtaken not far from the town, and several warriors were slain before the war party fled into the wilderness. Afterward, most of the citizens of Marlborough abandoned the town and sought safety at the larger communities on the Atlantic coast.

(Douglas Edward Leach, Flintlock and Tomahawk.)

MARQUETTE, JACQUES. Jacques Marquette was born at Laon, France, on June 10, 1637. In early childhood he aspired to be a missionary, and he entered the Jesuit order in 1654. In 1666, he was sent to Canada to labor among the Indians. Apt at learning Indian languages, he mastered the speech of the Algonquians at Three Rivers, and was assigned to the Ottawa mission at Sault Ste. Marie in 1668. The following year, he succeeded Father Claude Allouez as missionary to the Hurons at Chequamegon Bay, and he accompanied them in 1671 when they fled from the Sioux to Mackinac. There he established the mission of St. Ignace.

While working with the tribes in the Great Lakes region, Father Marquette interviewed Indians who had seen the Mississippi, and he developed a deep interest in exploring that river, rumored to provide a passage to the Orient. More important to the missionary was the prospect of Christianizing the Illinois Indians, a nation he believed to be less hostile than those of the Lakes. While awaiting that opportunity, he studied the Illinois language.

While serving the Hurons, Marquette met a French-Canadian explorer, Louis Jolliet, who aspired to visit the Mississippi. The opportunity arose when, in 1672, Jolliet was commissioned to explore the great river and chose Marquette to accompany him. With a few companions, they began their journey in canoes as soon as the ice melted in the spring of 1673. On June 17, they entered the Mississippi and began their journey through the shores which Indians warned were infested by dangerous monsters.

On June 25, the explorers visited a village of the Illinois Indians. There they were received with great hospitality. Marquette spoke to the assembled Indians about their need to accept Christianity. In response, the chief said "I thank thee, Black Gown ... for having taken so much trouble to come visit us.... I beg thee to have pity on me, and on all my Nation. It is thou who Knowest the great Spirit who has made us all.... Come and dwell with us, in order to make us know him." Marquette promised that after the expedition was completed he would establish a mission among them.

Proceeding down river, Marquette's party met the Michigamea Indians. The priest described the encounter as follows:

> They were armed with bows, arrows, hatchets, clubs, and shields. They prepared to attack us, on both land and water; part of them embarked in great wooden canoes ... in order to intercept us.... One of them then hurled his club which passed over without striking us. In vain I showed the Calumet, and made them signs that we were not coming to war against them. The alarm continued, and they were already preparing to pierce us with arrows from all sides, when God suddenly touched the hearts of the old men, who were standing at the water's edge.

After pacifying the Michigameas with presents, the party resumed its southward journey and arrived at an Arkansas (Quapaw) village. The chief was friendly, but he warned them not to continue their voyage, as the lower river banks were infested by hostile Indians and visited by Spaniards. His own warriors wanted to kill them, but he had refused to permit an attack on his guests.

Convinced that the Mississippi flowed into the Gulf of Mexico instead of the Pacific, and concerned that their maps and journals would fall into the hands of the Spaniards, Marquette and Jolliet decided that their objective had been achieved and began their return journey.

Upon arriving at De Pere, Marquette, ill and exhausted, remained there a year attempting to regain his strength. In October 1674, the missionary set out for the Illinois country to fulfill his promise to bring Christianity to the tribe. Near the mouth of the Chicago River he became seriously ill and remained there until spring. Late in March 1675, he arrived at Kaskaskia and established his Illinois mission, but his condition worsened, and he set out with a few companions to seek medical attention at St. Ignace. He died on May 18, 1675, before reaching his destination.

"Marquette seems to have been one of those gifted beings to whom the satisfaction of desires is granted, because in themselves the desires are so pure and altruistic."--Louise Phelps Kellogg.

(Louise Phelps Kellogg, ed., Early Narratives of the Northwest; The French Regime in Wisconsin and the Northwest; Edna Kenton, ed., Black Gown and Redskins; Agnes Repplier, Père Marquette; John Gilmary Shea, Discovery and Exploration of the Mississippi Valley; Joseph P. Donnelly, Jacques Marquette, S.J.)

MARSHALL, EDWARD, FAMILY OF. Edward Marshall, a Pennsylvania woodsman, was the only man who completed the Walking Purchase land acquisition journey in 1737. As a result, he was hated by the Delaware Indians. During the French and Indian War, hostile Indians killed his wife and son and wounded his daughter. Soon afterward he died, "old and unhappy, complaining that Thomas Penn had not paid him for his services in the famous Indian Walk." (See WALKING PURCHASE.)

(Anthony F. C. Wallace, King of the Delawares: Teedyuscung.)

MARTHA'S VINEYARD INDIANS. The Indians of Martha's Vineyard, Algonquian-speaking subjects of the Wampanoags, were numerous when first encountered by Europeans. In 1602, Bartholomew Gosnold, an English seafarer, traded with the tribe. In 1611, Capt. Edward Harlow kidnapped three of their people and took them to England. Three years later, one of them returned with Capt. Nicholas Hobson, and he instigated an attack on the ship. (See EPANOW.) In 1620, the Martha's Vineyard Indians attacked and killed most of the crew of Capt. Thomas Dermer's ship.

In 1641, when the Thomas Mayhew family moved to the island, they succeeded in Christianizing most of the 3,000 inhabitants. The converts refused to participate in attacks on the English during King Philip's War. While warfare had little impact on the Indians of Martha's Vineyard, their population decreased rapidly as a result of debauchery by traders. By 1807, only a few mixed-bloods remained.

(F. W. Hodge, ed., Handbook of American Indians, I; Neal Salisbury, Manitou and Providence.)

MASCOUTEN INDIANS. The Mascouten Indians, a powerful Algonquian tribe, lived on the Fox River, in Wisconsin, when the French explorer Nicolas Perrot visited their village before 1669. They confiscated his trade goods and would have burned him to death but for the intervention of the Fox Indians. By 1670, the Jesuit missionary Claude Allouez visited them, and Father Jacques Marquette was among them in 1673.

In 1679, the Mascoutens attempted to block La Salle's approach to the Illinois country. Suffering severely as a result of Iroquois attacks, most of them settled among the Kickapoos in 1691. Soon afterward, infuriated by French trade with the Sioux, they began attacking coureurs de bois. In 1712, they camped near the new French post at Detroit, where they joined the Foxes in attempting to destroy the fort. Tribes friendly to the French attacked them, killing more than 800 warriors. Afterward, the Mascoutens, Foxes, and Kickapoos waged a relentless war against the Illinois Indians and other tribes allied with the French.

In 1728, the Mascoutens and Kickapoos captured 12 Frenchmen on the Mississippi and refused a demand by the Foxes to put them to death. The resulting quarrel led them to become French allies, and they joined in attacks upon their former friends. Most of them moved to the present site of Lafayette, Indiana, about 1740. In 1747, they assisted the French in attacking the Chickasaws.

After French departure from North America, the Mascoutens allied themselves with the English, but they avoided participation in the American Revolution. Soon afterward, they were absorbed by the Kickapoos and Sauks.

(Louise Phelps Kellogg, The French Régime in Wisconsin and the Northwest; William C. Sturtevant, ed., Handbook of North American Indians, XV.)

MASHPEE RESERVATION. In 1660 a reservation was established in Barnstable County, Massachusetts, for remnants of New England and Long Island Indian bands. They numbered about 400 by the end of the century. Afterward they intermarried with whites and blacks, and a culture of a mixed-blood population replaced that of the Indians.

(F. W. Hodge, ed., Handbook of American Indians, I.)

MASON, JOHN. John Mason was born in England about 1600. He became a professional soldier and fought in the Netherlands before coming to Massachusetts by 1633. In 1635, he was a leader in founding Windsor, Connecticut.

Mason played a major role in the war against the Pequot Indians in 1637. While commanding Connecticut forces raised to punish the Pequots, he defeated a war party that besieged Saybrook. Then, with a force of 500 colonists and Narraganset Indians, he attacked a large palisaded Pequot town, slaughtering hundreds of Indians. (See MYSTIC, BATTLE OF.)

After the defeat of the Pequots, Mason was appointed major general of Connecticut forces, a position that he held until his death. In addition, he served as deputy governor from 1660 until 1670. For many years he handled Indian affairs for the New England Confederation. He died in 1672.

(John Mason, A Brief History of the Pequot War; John W. De Forest, History of the Indians of Connecticut.)

MASSACHUSET INDIANS. The Massachuset Indians, an Algonquian confederacy, were located in the Massachusetts Bay area when first encountered by Europeans about 1500. Champlain visited them a century later. Captain John Smith counted 20 villages in 1614, but they were decimated by a plague three years later. The Puritans settled among the survivors in 1620, and, except for a brief clash in 1622 (see WESSAGUSSET), avoided hostilities. Many of them became Christians and were gathered by missionaries into "praying

Indian" communities. Soon they ceased to exist as a distinctive tribe.

(John R. Swanton, Indian Tribes of North America; Neal Salisbury, Manitou and Providence.)

MASSACHUSETTS, FORT. Fort Massachusetts was constructed at the present site of Adams, Massachusetts, in 1744. It was the most exposed of four forts intended to guard the Deerfield Valley against Indian attacks. In August 1746, the Marquis de Vaudreuil led 500 Frenchmen and 200 Abnaki Indians in an attack on the fort, garrisoned at the time by only 22 men, half of them disabled by dysentery.

On the day before the attack, Sgt. John Hawks, who had been left in charge when the commanding officer attended a meeting to plan an invasion of Canada, sent 15 men to Deerfield to replenish the fort's scanty powder supply. When the attackers appeared and began a heavy fire on the fort, Hawks was compelled to conserve ammunition, but the defenders managed to kill an Abnaki chief and to wound Vaudreuil and 16 of his men.

On the second day of the attack, the defenders, almost out of powder, agreed to surrender upon receiving a promise that they would not be turned over to the Indians. But, except for Hawks, the chaplain, three women, and five children who were marched to Canada, the defenders fell into Abnaki hands. The fort was destroyed. The detachment returning from Deerfield with powder was ambushed, 15 men being killed and the remainder captured.

The fort was being rebuilt in 1747 when a large force of Frenchmen and Indians surrounded it. The defenders anticipated them with a sortie, and the invaders withdrew.

(Francis Parkman, A Half-Century of Conflict; Herbert Milton Sylvester, Indian Wars of New England, III.)

MASSAPEQUA INDIANS. The Massapequa Indians, an Algonquian tribe, lived on Long Island when first encountered by Europeans. In 1643, they sold some of their lands to the Dutch. Their chief, Takapoucha, was hostile toward both the Dutch and English settlers, but he signed a treaty with Governor Stuyvesant in 1655 offering to support the Dutch in their Indian wars.

(F. W. Hodge, ed., Handbook of American Indians, I; Allen W. Trelease, Indian Affairs in Colonial New York.)

MASSASOIT, WAMPANOAG CHIEF. Massasoit (Osamequin), a famous warrior and friend of the Pilgrims, was born about 1580 and became chief of the Wampanoags about 1607. Most of his people had been wiped out in a plague shortly before the Pilgrims arrived, and he saw the settlers as possible protectors against his powerful Indian neighbors, particularly the Narragansets. On March 22, 1621, he signed a peace treaty with the settlers, gave them land, and helped them to survive in their strange new environment. He and 90 of his people provided food for, and participated in, America's first Thanksgiving celebration with the Pilgrims.

Massasoit exerted influence over small New England tribes who desired peaceful relations with the newcomers, but his peace treaty was ignored by more hostile Indians who branded him a traitor. In 1632, the Narragansets sought to assassinate him, and he fled to Plymouth for protection. He died in 1662, after remaining a dependable friend of the colonists for 40 years.

"When we consider the wonderful sagacity, the political wisdom of Massasoit's move in seeking to establish friendly relations with the invaders of his soil and to pave the way for the two races to live side by side in peace and harmony, ... we cannot fail to be impressed by his foresight.... That his judgment was in error, and his confidence misplaced was no fault of his, but the misfortune of his people. Had the colonists shown half the regard for the spirit of the treaty they made with him, and for the obligations they thereby assumed towards him and his, that he manifested for forty years of his life after its signing, what a different story would be the annals of New England today." --Alvin G. Weeks.

(Alvin G. Weeks, Massasoit; Frederick J. Dockstader, Great North American Indians; William Bradford, Of Plimoth Plantation; Alden T. Vaughan, New England Frontier, Neal Salisbury, Manitou and Providence.)

MASSIE, NATHANIEL. Nathaniel Massie founded Massie's Station near the present Manchester, Ohio, in 1791. The first settlement of Virginia veterans of the American Revolution north of the Ohio under the state's military reserve policy, the settlement contained 30 cabins enclosed by a strong stockade by 1794. Massie, while surveying lands in the Indian country for future settlers, was compelled to fight off several Indian attacks, once outrunning 150 warriors from the present site of Xenia, Ohio, to his own station. In 1795, while leading 60 prospective settlers to Paint Creek, he attacked an Indian camp, precipitating the last battle before the Treaty of Greenville ended the Indian wars in that region. One settler and several Indians were killed. He founded Chillicothe in 1796.

(James B. Finley, Life Among the Indians; John Anthony Caruso, The Great Lakes Frontier.)

MATINECOC INDIANS. The Matinecoc Indians, a small Algonquian tribe, inhabited portions of Queens and Suffolk counties, New York, during early contacts with Europeans. Decimated by Mohawk attacks and white men's vices, they were almost extinct by 1650.

(F. W. Hodge, ed., Handbook of American Indians, I.)

MATTABESEC INDIANS. The Mattabesec Indians, an Algonquian tribe believed to have belonged to the Wappinger confederacy, inhabited the Connecticut River Valley from Wethersfield to Middletown and lands to the westward. Once a powerful nation consisting of several subtribes, they became involved in wars with the Dutch in 1650. Afterward, they sold their lands and dwindled away. Survivors eventually were absorbed by the Delawares.

(F. W. Hodge, ed., Handbook of American Indians, I.)

MAUMEE COUNCIL. The Maumee River, scene of many Indian battles (see FALLEN TIMBERS), provided the setting, also, of important negotiations between the northern tribes and the United States. In August 1793, the Indians assembled there and determined to insist upon the Ohio River as the boundary between the tribes and the new government. They sent the following message to American commissioners waiting at Detroit for permission to proceed to the conference with proposals to negotiate peace: "Brothers: you have talked to us about concessions. It appears strange that you should expect any from us, who have only been defending our just rights against your invasions. We want peace. Restore to us our country, and we shall be enemies no longer."

When President Washington learned that the Indians, encouraged by the British to expect their support, had refused to consider American proposals, he ordered military operations against them. (See WAYNE, ANTHONY.)

(John Anthony Caruso, The Great Lakes Frontier; Dale Van Every, Ark of Empire; Randolph C. Downes, Council Fires on the Upper Ohio.)

MAUMEE, OHIO, TREATY OF. On February 18, 1833, a treaty was concluded by George B. Porter, representing the U.S. government, and the Ottawa Indians. The tribe ceded lands on the Miami River in exchange for funds needed to pay their debts.

(Charles J. Kappler, ed., Indian Affairs: Laws and Treaties, II.)

MAYHEW FAMILY, MARTHA'S VINEYARD, MASSACHUSETTS. Thomas Mayhew, Sr., a merchant of Wiltshire, England, was born in 1593 and emigrated to Massachusetts by 1632. In 1641, he purchased Martha's Vineyard. In 1642, he sent his son Thomas, Jr., to colonize the island, joining him there a few years later.

Thomas, Jr., who was born in England and came to America with his father, was determined to convert the Indians to Christianity. He became New England's first missionary to the Indians and gained his first convert in 1643. (See HIACOOMES.) Within a few years, he made Christians of most of the 3,000 inhabitants, training some of them to preach, and he founded a school for Indian children in 1652. Five years later, while on a voyage to England, he was lost at sea.

In 1657, Thomas Mayhew, Sr., succeeded his son as missionary. For the next quarter century he visited Indian villages to preach, and his popularity prevented the Martha's Vineyard Indians from supporting King Philip in 1675-76.

After the senior Mayhew died in 1682, his grandson John assumed the duties of missionary. He organized several Indian

congregations and placed them under native preachers. John died
in 1689, and his son Experience became the island's missionary in
1693. Experience had spent his entire youth with Indians, was
fluent in their language, and served them with great success for 65
years. Before his death in 1759, he published several influential
tracts on missionary work and translated sermons into Algonquian.
He was highly influential in interesting clergymen and lay leaders in
England as well as America in the importance of missionary work
with the Indians.

"By practicing as well as preaching the gospel and by understanding the value of native institutions, the Mayhews gave Martha's
Vineyard a felicitous pattern of Indian-White relations seldom dupli-
cated in the conquest of the North American continent."--Charles W.
Akers.

(Charles W. Akers, Called into Liberty.)

MECINA, KICKAPOO CHIEF. Mecina was the chief of a band of
Kickapoos that refused to abide by the removal treaty of Edwardsville, which, in 1813, ceded the tribe's lands between the Illinois and
Wabash rivers. When ordered by William Clark to move west of the
Mississippi, he responded by repeating Tecumseh's claim that no
tribe could dispose of Indian land without the approval of all the
tribes.

From their village near Lake Peoria, Mecina's band roamed from
the Illinois to the Wabash, stealing stock and terrorizing the settlers.
Raiders traded their loot to Potawatomi Indians and renegade whites
for guns and ammunition, defying the government to remove them for
more than a decade. Finally, some of Mecina's warriors joined Black
Hawk's raiders while he led his remaining followers to merge with
other Kickapoo bands.

(A. M. Gibson, The Kickapoos.)

MEDFIELD, MASSACHUSETTS, RAID. Medfield, a small settlement
some 20 miles southwest of Boston, was attacked by King Philip's
warriors on February 21, 1676. Two hundred soldiers stationed in
the town were sleeping when several hundred Indians infiltrated the
community before dawn and concealed themselves near the houses in
which troops were quartered. At first light the invaders opened fire
as soldiers and civilians stepped outside. They destroyed about 50
houses before being driven away by cannon fire from the town's
main fort.

(Douglas Edward Leach, Flintlock and Tomahawk.)

MEEKER, JOTHAM. Jotham Meeker, a Baptist missionary, was born
in Ohio on November 8, 1804. Trained as a printer, he began his
missionary activities in 1825, serving in Michigan among the Ottawas,
Potawatomis, and Chippewas, as an assistant to Rev. Isaac McCoy.
In 1831, he assisted Rev. Abel Bingham at a Chippewa mission at
Sault Ste. Marie. Two years later, he moved to Shawnee Mission,
Kansas, where he undertook the publication of religious books, jour-
nals, and newspapers in various Indian languages.

In 1837 Meeker established a mission of his own among the Ottawa Indians near the present site of Ottawa, Kansas. There he enjoyed tremendous success in converting the Indians to Christianity and in helping them adjust to white civilization. Before his death in 1855, he had helped them to develop model farms and to build comfortable homes.

(George A. Schultz, An Indian Canaan.)

MEIGS, FORT, SIEGES OF. Fort Meigs was built near the present site of Maumee, Ohio, in 1813 as a supply base for William Henry Harrison's operations against Detroit and other British forts in the Northwest and Canada. Harrison considered the fort, containing eight blockhouses, four battery elevations, and 15-foot pickets, to be the most secure in North America. The garrison of 1,200 men was less than adequate, however, to defend such an immense fortification, and the enlistments of many of the militiamen were due to expire.

Meanwhile, British Gen. Henry A. Proctor determined to seize Fort Meigs before it could fulfill its purpose. Chiefs Tecumseh, Roundhead, and Main Poc recruited warriors from south of the Great Lakes to assist him, and a formidable force of more than 2,000 Indians, British regulars, and Canadian militia surrounded the fort on April 28, 1813, primed to destroy it with artillery and to annihilate the defenders as they fled the scene.

Proctor's plans to shell the fort into submission were thwarted, however, by virtually impregnable bastions and pickets and by the spirited resistance of the well-entrenched Americans, determined to hold out until reinforcements arrived from Kentucky. A siege was instituted that lasted 10 days. British artillery boomed and Indians fired from the cover of stumps and ravines, but with negligible results. Finally a frustrated Tecumseh challenged Harrison to cease hiding "in the earth like a ground hog" and lead his men out to battle an equal number of Indians. On May 4, Proctor sent an officer under a flag of truce to request surrender in order to "spare the effusion of blood," but Harrison, daily expecting reinforcements, refused.

On May 5, Gen. Green Clay approached the fort with 1,200 Kentucky militiamen. Acting on Harrison's orders, they prepared to storm the enemy batteries while a sortie from the fort kept the Indians occupied. The plan was partially successful, but many of the Kentuckians were captured and killed by the Indians. (See DUDLEY MASSACRE.) Clay succeeded, however, in bringing 500 reinforcements into the fort.

After a detachment of regulars (led by Col. John Miller) captured the British cannon, the Indians lost heart and began drifting away. Proctor tried two other times to persuade the Americans to surrender, but Harrison refused to be bluffed. An exchange of prisoners was arranged, and, after two days of little activity, Proctor abandoned the siege on May 8. American casualties inside the fort were 77 killed and 196 wounded.

Proctor had not given up hope, however, of capturing Fort

Meigs. On July 21, he returned, reinforced by 2,000 warriors recruited by Tecumseh, Main Poc, and Robert Dickson. The defenders,
then commanded by General Clay, refused to be drawn outside the
walls by Tecumseh's ruse of a sham battle, and the siege was
abandoned after a week of ineffective small-arms fire.

(Freeman Cleaves, Old Tippecanoe; Louise Phelps Kellogg,
The British Régime in Wisconsin and the Northwest; R. David Edmunds,
The Shawnee Prophet.)

MEIGS, FORT, TREATY OF. The Treaty of Fort Meigs was negotiated on September 29, 1817, by Lewis Cass and Duncan McArthur
with the Wyandot, Potawatomi, Ottawa, Shawnee, Delaware, and
Seneca tribes. More than one hundred chiefs signed the treaty that
ceded a large area north of the territory acquired by the Treaty of
Greenville. The Wyandots alone ceded more than four million acres
in Ohio, Indiana, and Michigan.

(Grant Foreman, Last Trek of the Indians; John Anthony
Caruso, The Great Lakes Frontier.)

MENARD, PIERRE. Pierre Ménard was born at St. Antoine, Quebec,
on October 7, 1766. About the age of 21, he was employed as an
Indian trader at Vincennes, Indiana, by Col. Francis Vigo. He
moved to Kaskaskia in 1791, and, four years later, he became a
major of the militia there.

Ménard was a founder of the St. Louis Missouri Fur Company
in 1809. He made a trading expedition to the Three Forks of the
Missouri the following year, but the Blackfoot Indians compelled him
to leave their country. He returned to Kaskaskia, where during
subsequent years he held several government offices, including that
of lieutenant governor.

Ménard, a sincere friend of the Indians, served as subagent
to several tribes, including the Shawnees, Delawares, and Illinois.
He provided supplies for Indians emigrating to the West, and, in
1819, he conducted the Peoria and Piankashaw tribes to their homes
beyond the Mississippi. He helped to negotiate numerous treaties.
When the Ottawas removed to the West in 1834, they regarded him
so highly that they gave him the tract of land containing bones of
their ancestors, relying upon him to maintain the graves. He died
on June 13, 1844.

(Grant Foreman, Last Trek of the Indians.)

MENARD, RENE. René Ménard, a Jesuit missionary, was born in
Paris, France, on September 7, 1605. After study at Paris, Rouen,
and elsewhere, he sailed to Canada in 1640 to Christianize the Indians. He labored among the Hurons and Nipissings in Canada for
16 years before being assigned in 1656 to assist in the establishment
of a French settlement among the Iroquois. He ministered first to
the Cayugas, where even the children attacked him, then to the
Oneidas, and finally to the Onondagas. He baptized some women
and children, but his work was disrupted in 1658 when all of the
French settlers fled to Canada to escape massacre by the Onondagas.

In 1660, Menard accompanied an Ottawa Indian flotilla to their village on Keweenaw Bay. The following year, finding the Ottawas increasingly hostile, he set out through the Wisconsin wilderness to serve a band of Christian Hurons hiding from the Iroquois. Apparently he lost his way, for he never was seen again. "So died this holy man; alone in the wilderness, no one knows how or where," wrote T. J. Campbell, but "his breviary and cassock are said to have been used by the Sioux in their ... incantations."

(T. J. Campbell, Pioneer Priests of North America; Edna Kenton, ed., Black Gown and Redskins; Louise Phelps Kellogg, The French Régime in Wisconsin and the Northwest.)

MENOMINEE INDIANS. The Menominee Indians, an Algonquian tribe, lived in the area of the Menominee and Fox rivers and westward from Green Bay when encountered by the French explorer Jean Nicolet about 1634. Jesuit missionaries and Canadian traders were among them by 1671, and Menominee bands went far and wide to obtain the furs that enabled them to prosper.

The Menominees, faithful allies of the French, asserted that they had never killed a white man. This record was broken in 1758, however, when they joined an Indian uprising at Green Bay that resulted in the murders of 14 Frenchmen. The following year they attempted to make amends by executing 2 of the murderers.

After the British supplanted the French in Wisconsin, the tribe accepted them as friends and allies. Some Menominees became followers of the Shawnee Prophet in 1807 and supported the British until 1815. After the Americans gained possession of Wisconsin, the Menominees began selling their lands. Finally, in 1854, they ceded all that remained except for a reservation on Wolf River. There, notes Louise Phelps Kellogg, they "still live on portions of the land that was theirs when Nicolet first visited them--a remarkable record of an unbroken residence in the same region."

(Louise Phelps Kellogg, The French Régime in Wisconsin and the Northwest; William C. Sturtevant, ed., Handbook of North American Indians, XV.)

MENOMINEE, POTAWATOMI PROPHET. Menominee, chief of a band of Potawatomis that inhabited northern Indiana after the War of 1812, was revered as a prophet by Indians of that region and accorded a measure of respect by neighboring white people for his efforts to improve the lives of his followers. In his youth he must have received some Christian teaching, for he incorporated Catholic rituals into his religious ceremonies.

In 1821, Menominee met a Baptist missionary, Isaac McCoy, and persuaded him to remove his mission to a Potawatomi village. McCoy was favorably impressed by Menominee's efforts to eradicate drinking and gambling among the Indians, but taken aback when he discovered that the "Potawatomi Preacher" was a polygamist.

By 1835, Menominee had become a practicing Roman Catholic, and many of his people followed his example. He attempted to prevent tribal removal west of the Mississippi by assisting his followers

to establish successful farms and to adapt to many aspects of white
civilization, but his efforts failed because of the insatiable demands
of settlers for Indian lands. In 1838, the Indiana militia seized
Menominee's band while many of them were in church, handcuffed
the prophet, and marched them off to the West.
(James A. Clifton, The Prairie People; Grant Foreman, Last
Trek of the Indians; George A. Schultz, An Indian Canaan.)

MERCER, HUGH. Hugh Mercer was born in Aberdeenshire, Scotland,
about 1725 and educated as a physician at the University of Aber-
deen. About 1746, he emigrated to Pennsylvania, where he practiced
medicine at the frontier settlement of Mercersburg for 10 years.
During that period he served as a militia officer, and, at the onset
of the French and Indian War, he was thrust into a leading role in
protecting Pennsylvania settlements against Indian attacks.

Promoted to colonel, Mercer participated in Braddock's expedi-
tion of 1755 and was wounded in the disastrous defeat of July 9.
He was wounded once more in Armstrong's attack on Kittanning in
September 1756, became separated during the withdrawal from the
destroyed Delaware Indian town, and was lost in the wilderness for
two weeks before finding his way to Fort Lyttelton. He commanded
Pennsylvania troops in the Forbes expedition that occupied Fort
Duquesne in 1758.

In 1759, Mercer assumed command of Fort Pitt. In March of
that year, he led an expedition against the French forts on the
Ohio, but was turned back by a combination of floods and Indian attacks. While commanding at Fort Pitt, he played an important role
in pacifying some of the Delaware Indians and in persuading other
tribes to attend a peace conference.

After the French and Indian War, Mercer, upon the advice of
George Washington, established a medical practice at Fredericksburg,
Virginia. During the American Revolution he served as a general in
Washington's army, participated in several major battles, and was
killed by the enemy in January 1777.
(Solon J. Buck, The Planting of Civilization in Western Penn-
sylvania; Randolph C. Downes, Council Fires on the Upper Ohio;
William A. Hunter, Forts on the Pennsylvania Frontier.)

MESQUAKIE INDIANS see FOX INDIANS

METACOM, WAMPANOAG CHIEF. Metacom, usually known as King
Philip, was the son of Massasoit, the Wampanoag chief who had remained a firm friend of the English colonists until his death. Born
at Pokanoket about 1639, Metacom showed an early interest in Christianity, but he discarded the notion as it became increasingly apparent that land disputes eventually would lead to hostilities with the
colonists.

After the death of Massasoit and his elder son, Philip became
the head chief of the Wampanoags in 1662. Douglas Edward Leach,
historian of King Philip's War, has characterized him as "a man of
firm will, ambitious, proud-spirited, quick to resent an affront to

his dignity." Such an affront occurred in 1671, when he was fined by Plymouth officials for fomenting discord and compelled to acknowledge that the Wampanoags were subject to English law. At that time, Leach believes, "he was gradually brought face to face with the awful alternatives--total submission to the English and their way of life, or a bloody war to clear them from the country...."

Realizing that the Wampanoags were too weak to withstand the power of the English, Metacom spent several years developing alliances with most of the New England tribes. He planned an attack on Plymouth, hoping that war with the other colonies could be avoided, but his meetings with neighboring tribes aroused hostility toward all the English. Violence erupted at Swansea before his plans were completed, and afterward there was no turning back. (See KING PHILIP'S WAR.) He did not participate personally in many battles, but he visited Indian villages throughout southern New England inciting the chiefs to drive the enemy into the sea. He failed, however, to obtain the support of the Iroquois, and Mohawk hostility proved to be a major cause of his ultimate defeat.

English officials offered a reward for Metacom's head, and, by the summer of 1676, some of his followers deserted his cause and guided the colonists to his strongholds and hiding places. Colonial forces came close to catching him on August 1, and did capture his wife and son, sending them into West Indian slavery. Col. Benjamin Church learned, a few days later, that he was at Mount Hope, and a deserter led the English to his hideaway in a swamp. On August 12, 1676, they surrounded the Indian camp and shot Philip to death as he attempted to flee from the swamp. Church ordered his men to decapitate the fallen chief and displayed his head on a gibbet at Plymouth.

Students of the Indian wars differ as to the abilities of Metacom to command. Leach asserts that evidence is lacking that Philip acted as supreme commander: "Instead, he seems to have sunk into the position of a leader among leaders." Albert Britt considers him "a modern commander, more modern than any of his opponents." Wilcomb E. Washburn has written that "the events of the struggle show that Philip was hardly masterminding a campaign to drive the English into the sea; his actions were haphazard and inexplicable except as reactions to circumstances beyond his control."

(Douglas Edward Leach, Flintlock and Tomahawk; Albert Britt, Great North American Indians; Robert M. Utley and Wilcomb E. Washburn, The American Heritage History of the Indian Wars; Thomas Church, The History of the Great Indian War of 1675 and 1676.)

METEA, POTAWATOMI CHIEF. Metea, a powerful Potawatomi chief, played an important role in the War of 1812 and its aftermath. He was one of the leading participants in the Fort Dearborn massacre, he led hostiles who attacked William Henry Harrison's troops enroute to Fort Wayne in 1812, and he continued to fight the Americans until after the Battle of the Thames. He signed peace treaties for the Potawatomis in 1817 and 1818, and he negotiated the Treaty of the Wabash in 1826, ceding the tribe's lands in Indiana. He died during a drunken brawl at Fort Wayne in 1827.

    (F. W. Hodge, ed., Handbook of American Indians, I.)

MEURIN, SEBASTIEN LOUIS. Sebastien Louis Meurin, a Jesuit missionary, was born in France in 1707. Assigned to the Canadian missions in 1741, he labored among the Illinois Indians from 1742 until the French suppressed the Jesuits in 1763.

    As the Indians urged him to remain with them, he went to New Orleans and received permission from the Superior Council of Louisiana to return to the Illinois country, where he became pastor of the French parish at Ste. Genevieve. His health had deteriorated so greatly that he was unable, except on special occasions, to cross the river and preach to the Indians. He died at Prairie du Rocher in 1777.

    (Clarence Walworth Alvord, The Illinois Country; Edna Kenton, ed., Black Gown and Redskins.)

MIAMI BAY, OHIO, TREATY OF. The Treaty of Miami Bay was negotiated by James B. Gardiner with the Ottawa Indians on August 30, 1831. The tribe ceded a large area around the Auglaize and Miami rivers and agreed to remove across the Mississippi.

    (Charles J. Kappler, ed., Indian Affairs: Laws and Treaties, II.)

MIAMI, FORT, OHIO, CAPTURE OF. Fort Miami (Miamis) was built by the French about 1749 at the site of the present Fort Wayne, Indiana. After the French and Indian War, a small British garrison commanded by Ensign Robert Holmes was stationed there to protect the Maumee-Wabash portage. In May 1763, with the outbreak of Pontiac's War, a Miami Indian girl, Holmes's mistress, agreed to lure him to his death. On May 27, she persuaded him to accompany her to visit her sick mother. Once outside the stockade, he was shot to death by two concealed warriors. The post sergeant went out to investigate and was immediately killed. Then the Indians sent a French trader into the fort to demand surrender, and while the 11 remaining soldiers were considering the matter, they emphasized their demand by hurling Holmes's severed head over the wall. Leaderless and terrified, the enlisted men opened the gates. All of them were slain except 1 man who was adopted by an Indian family.

    (Howard H. Peckham, Pontiac and the Indian Uprising; Dale Van Every, Forth to the Wilderness.)

MIAMI INDIANS. The Miami Indians, a powerful Algonquian tribe, were located near Green Bay, the headwaters of the Fox River, and the southern shores of Lake Michigan when first visited by the French explorers, Radisson and Groseilliers, in 1654. Soon afterward, they established villages on the St. Joseph and Wabash rivers, but the pressure of other tribes forced many of them to move to the Miami River. They were influenced greatly by French traders and missionaries during the late seventeenth century, and a rift developed when a part of the tribe became Christians.

While the Iroquois remained a threat, the Miamis served as allies and trading partners of the French. Widely scattered in their attempts to improve their fur trade profits, their bands camped temporarily at Forts St. Louis, Pontchartrain, and Miamis. When British traders began contacting the Miamis, offering superior goods, the French attempted to persuade the tribe to move northwestward, but with little success.

A Miami chief, Old Briton, established the village of Picka-willanee on the Miami River in 1748 in order to gain easier access to British goods. This event so infuriated the French that they and their Indian allies destroyed the settlement in 1752. (See OLD BRITON; LANGLADE, CHARLES MICHEL DE.) From that time until the French withdrawal from North America, the Miamis remained their nominal, if lukewarm, allies. About 250 Miami warriors participated in the French and Indian victory over Gen. Edward Braddock on July 9, 1755.

The Miamis, greatly reduced in population by warfare and pestilence, were reluctant to participate in Pontiac's War, but victories by other tribes persuaded them to help seize two British forts. (See MIAMI, FORT; OUIATENON, FORT.) They did not take part in the siege of Detroit, and they sought peace with the British soon afterward.

At the onset of the American Revolution, the Miamis promised to remain neutral. By 1777, however, the British commandant at Detroit, Henry Hamilton, persuaded them to attack American settlements. This support vanished after Hamilton was captured by George Rogers Clark, but the destruction of their principal village, Kekionga, in 1780 by a French officer leading an expedition against Detroit, resulted in bloody retaliation. (See ABOITE RIVER MASSACRE; LA BALME, AUGUSTIN MOTTIN DE; LITTLE TURTLE.)

After the Revolution, British agents influenced the Miamis to resist American occupation of their lands. Indian insistence upon maintaining the Ohio River boundary resulted in the development of the Miami confederacy, with its headquarters on the Maumee River, to repel American settlement north of the Ohio. The confederacy included warriors of tribes from Canada and the Great Lakes region; as well as those located along the Ohio. With the Miami chief Little Turtle as their leader, they defeated two American armies in 1790 and 1791 (see HARMAR EXPEDITION; ST. CLAIR'S DEFEAT). They were themselves defeated in 1794, however, by Gen. Anthony Wayne (see FALLEN TIMBERS), and compelled to make peace.

The Miamis ceded some of their lands in 1795 at the Treaty of Greenville. Soon afterward, some Miamis began moving west of the Mississippi, but others clung to their homelands for another half century. Rejecting Tecumseh's attempts to involve them in his Indian conspiracy, they remained neutral during the War of 1812 until they were attacked by American troops (see MISSISSINEWA CAMPAIGN). In spite of protestations that their neutral village had been attacked, Miami retaliation for the Mississinewa affair provided the Americans with a reason to demand a land cession. The Treaty of St. Mary's in 1818, characterized as a "land grab" by the historian Bert Anson, deprived them of some 7 million acres and concentrated them on four reservations. Even these were lost in 1840 as a result of white encroachment, debt, and the belief that removal west of the Mississippi would permit the tribe to survive. Most of the Miamis were on the Osage River in Kansas by 1846, but two bands fled to the wilds of Michigan to escape removal. Afterward, the Kansas Miamis moved to northeastern Oklahoma and became citizens, with lands allotted to them in severalty.

(Bert Anson, The Miami Indians; W. Vernon Kinietz, The Indians of the Western Great Lakes; Grant Foreman, Last Trek of the Indians; Randolph C. Downes, Council Fires on the Upper Ohio.)

MIANTONOMO, NARRAGANSET CHIEF. Born about 1600, Miantonomo was the nephew of Chief Canonicus, and he assisted him as leader of the powerful Narraganset nation. In 1632, after he had become their principal chief, he visited the governor in Boston and went to church with the colonists. By 1636, however, Puritan leaders began suspecting him of provoking native hostility, and he returned to Boston on several occasions to assure them of his loyalty.

In March 1637, Miantonomo and four other chiefs sold land in the vicinity of Narragansett Bay to William Coddington and other Englishmen. While supporting the colonists during the Pequot War, he aroused the enmity of Uncas, a Mohegan chief and a staunch English ally. Uncas schemed to convince colonial authorities that Miantonomo was fomenting hostility against them. In 1642, Miantonomo was confined briefly at Boston under suspicion of treachery and warned sternly to mend his ways.

Despairing of maintaining friendship with the English, in 1643 Miantonomo sought to weld a confederacy of New England tribes to resist colonial expansion. Unwisely, he sought to bring Uncas into the alliance. The Mohegan chief seized him and turned him over to the English. Tried by officials of the United Colonies, Miantonomo was convicted of attempting to murder Uncas and sentenced to death. They instructed Uncas to take him to Mohegan territory and execute him. With his death (in September 1643) "went the last possibility of an effective native resistance to English Puritan hegemony."-- Neal Salisbury.

(Neal Salisbury, Manitou and Providence; Herbert Milton Sylvester, Indian Wars of New England, I; Frederick J. Dockstader, Great North American Indians; John W. DeForest, History of the Indians of Connecticut.)

MICHIGAMEA INDIANS. The Michigamea Indians, southernmost tribe of the Illinois confederacy, were located along the Mississippi River in southern Missouri and northern Arkansas when Jolliet and Marquette encountered them in 1673. About 1700, the Chickasaws and Quapaws drove them northward into Illinois, where they settled near the French Fort de Chartres. Because of their friendship with the French, they frequently were attacked by Indian allies of the English. As their numbers decreased, they were absorbed by the Kaskaskias.

(Clarence Walworth Alvord, The Illinois Country; F. W. Hodge, ed., Handbook of American Indians, I.)

MICHIKINIKWA, MIAMI CHIEF   see   LITTLE TURTLE, MIAMI CHIEF

MICHILIMACKINAC   see   MACKINAC

MILET, PIERRE. Father Pierre Milet, who led one of the most amazing and adventurous lives of the Jesuits who labored among the Iroquois, was born at Bourges, France, about 1615, and entered the order at the age of 20. In accordance with his desire to serve as a missionary, he was assigned to labor among the Indians of Canada.

In 1668, the famous Iroquois chief, Garakonthie, visited Montreal and induced Father Milet to serve among his people at Onondaga. Four years later, Milet moved to Oneida, the Iroquois nation immediately to the eastward of the Onondagas. There, according to the Jesuit historian T. J. Campbell, "at the very outset he exercised a marvellous influence ... [and] could have made them all nominal Christians if he wished; but the delinquencies, especially of the men, were too great, and only a limited number of braves were admitted to baptism."

In 1686, Gov. Jacques René de Brisay, marquis de Denonville, deceived Father Milet into persuading several Iroquois chiefs to confer with French officers at Cataroqui about improving relations. The French seized the chiefs and compelled them to serve as galley slaves. The priest realized that the Iroquois would accuse him of complicity in the plot, so he remained at Cataroqui to serve as chaplain to the garrison.

In June 1689, some Iroquois chiefs came to Cataroqui bearing a flag of truce, and urged Milet to accompany them to console some wounded Christian Indians who had requested the last rites of the Church. Once outside the palisade, the Indians seized him and threatened to burn him to death on the spot, but an Oneida chief demanded the right to return him to the nation where he had served for so many years. At Oneida, the captive attended a council called to determine his fate, and largely through the influence of Christian Iroquois women, he was held in captivity instead of being tortured to death.

While still regarded as a captive, the priest was adopted to replace a chief who had died. He attended tribal councils as a sachem, and in time, he gained such tremendous influence that English traders tried to persuade warriors to kill him. Most of the Iroquois sided with the English in their wars with the French, but Father Milet worked constantly to restore peace. In 1693, he induced Iroquois chiefs to confer with officials at Quebec, and the following year the Indians agreed to release all of their French captives as a price of peace. Among those released, although he could scarcely be considered still a captive, was Father Milet. Afterward, he remained at Montreal and served as spiritual advisor to Oneidas who had removed to that area. He died on December 31, 1708.

(T. J. Campbell, Pioneer Priests of North America; Cadwallader Colden, History of the Five Indian Nations; Francis Parkman, Count Frontenac and New France Under Louis XIV.)

MINGO BOTTOM. Mingo Bottom, named for the Indians who occupied
the area, was located near the present site of Steubenville, Ohio.
It was used frequently during the American Revolution as a staging
area by the militia for expeditions against Indian villages.
(Theodore Roosevelt, The Winning of the West, III.)

MINGO INDIANS. The Mingo Indians, detached bands of Iroquois
who had settled near the upper Ohio shortly before and during the
French and Indian War, became more closely associated with the
Shawnees and Wyandots than with the Six Nations. In 1761, English
settlers began invading their hunting grounds, so antagonizing them
that they were among the most hostile Indians during Pontiac's War.
The murder of Chief Logan's family by American frontiersmen in 1774
aroused the tribe to take the lead in Dunmore's War, and Logan led
several raids against the Virginia settlers.
Mingo warriors were among the most active raiders during the
American Revolution, with the new Kentucky stations bearing the
brunt. In 1777, joined by Shawnees, Delawares, and Wyandots,
they besieged Boonesborough and Wheeling and drove many frontier
settlers back across the mountains. They calmed down considerably
after George Rogers Clark defeated their allies in 1779, however, and
refused to take part in the siege of Fort Laurens.
After the Revolution, some Mingo bands joined the Cayuga nation, others became associated with the Shawnees, and the rest retained their identity at a village on the Sandusky River. In 1831,
most of them ceded their lands and removed to Kansas. In 1867,
they moved to Oklahoma, where their descendants still live.
(Randolph C. Downes, Council Fires on the Upper Ohio; Dale
Van Every, A Company of Heroes; Forth to the Wilderness.)

MINISINK INDIANS see MUNSEE INDIANS

MINISINK, NEW YORK, RAIDS. Minisink, near the present town of
Goshen, New York, was a favorite target of the Mohawk chief Joseph
Brant during the American Revolution. His first incursion, on a
relatively small scale, was made on the settlements near Minisink in
July 1778. There, only 35 miles from George Washington's headquarters, he drove off cattle and appropriated grain to feed his followers while diverting attention from the British and Indian invasion
of the Wyoming Valley.
In July 1779, in an attempt to delay Sullivan's campaign against
the Iroquois towns, Brant struck Minisink a more serious blow. He
led 87 warriors and Tories into the town and attacked the main fort,
but failed to capture it. The invaders burned houses, barns, and
mills, and killed 4 men, including the schoolmaster Jeremiah Van
Auken, who sacrificed his life to gain time for the children to escape.
Fugitives from Minisink fled to Goshen to give the alarm, and a militia company went in pursuit of the raiders. Brant lured the militia,
149 men, into an ambush near Laxawaxen ford and slaughtered most
of them. Indian losses, also, were heavy.
In 1780, Brant returned to Minisink, but details of the action

have received little attention because of his burning of Harpersfield during the same campaign.

(Barbara Graymont, The Iroquois in the American Revolution; William Stone, Border Wars of the American Revolution; Dale Van Every, A Company of Heroes.)

MINQUA INDIANS   see   SUSQUEHANNA INDIANS

MINUIT, PETER, INDIAN RELATIONS.   Peter Minuit, a native of Wesel, Germany, was the first director general of New Netherland (1626–31), and the founder of New Sweden in 1638.   In 1626, he purchased Manhattan Island from the Indians for trinkets valued at $24.   After his recall by the Dutch in 1631, he persuaded Queen Christina to permit him to establish a Swedish colony near New Netherland.   The following year, he returned to America, purchased land from the Delaware Indians near the present site of Trenton, and established Fort Christina as a Swedish trading post.   Leaving a small garrison at the fort, he sailed to St. Christopher to trade and was killed by a hurricane.

(Albert Cook Myers, ed., Narratives of Early Pennsylvania, West New Jersey, and Delaware; E. B. O'Callaghan, History of New Netherland, I; Allen W. Trelease, Indian Affairs in Colonial New York; C. A. Weslager, Dutch Explorers, Traders, and Settlers in the Delaware Valley.)

MISSIASSIK INDIANS.   The Missiassik Indians, an Algonquian tribe or band closely associated with the Abnakis, lived in a large village at the mouth of the Missisquoi River in northern Vermont.   They were decimated by a plague about 1730, and the survivors fled to St. Francis in Canada.

(F. W. Hodge, Handbook of American Indians, I.)

MISSISSINEWA CAMPAIGN.   The Mississinewa River served as a place of refuge for Indian bands that had rejected Tecumseh's movement and desired to remain neutral during the War of 1812.   A number of villages, including those of the Delaware chief Silver Heels and the Miami chief Metocina, were located along the river, protected, their leaders believed, by their longstanding friendship with the Americans.

But William Henry Harrison feared that the Indians on the Mississinewa were a danger to Fort Wayne and a potential threat to his rear troops during a campaign against Detroit.   Therefore, in December 1812, he ordered Col. John B. Campbell to lead 600 men against the Miami villages on the Mississinewa.   Campbell was instructed to spare Silver Heels's village, but he attacked it on December 17, killing 8 warriors and capturing 42 men, women, and children.   Afterward, he burned Metocina's village and moved on to another Miami town, where the warriors resisted stoutly before being driven away.

Returning upriver, Campbell camped near the ruins of Silver Heels's village on December 18.   There, before daylight, a force of infuriated Miamis attacked the camp. Led by Chiefs Little Thunder, Francis Godfroy, and Joseph Richardville, warriors killed 10 soldiers and wounded 48, compelling Campbell to abandon plans to attack other Indian towns.

The Miamis regarded the Mississinewa campaign as "an unprovoked destruction of neutral and defenseless villages filled with noncombatants--an early Sand Creek Massacre."--Bert Anson.

(Bert Anson, The Miami Indians.)

MOGG, ABNAKI CHIEF. Mogg, chief of Norridgewock, was converted to Christianity by a Jesuit missionary. He was a staunch friend of the French and a stalwart opponent of English expansion. His village was burned by the English and their Iroquois allies in 1705, 1722, and 1724. Refusing to retreat on the final occasion, Mogg defended his wigwam, killing a Mohawk before being tomahawked by the dead warrior's brother. Afterward, the colonists killed the chief's wife and children.

(Herbert Milton Sylvester, Indian Wars of New England, III; F. W. Hodge, ed., Handbook of American Indians, I.)

MOHAWK INDIANS. The Mohawk Indians, the most easterly of the Six Nations of Iroquois, were the first to encounter Europeans. In 1609, they were attacked near Lake Champlain by Samuel de Champlain, 2 other Frenchmen, and some Algonquian Indians. The Frenchmen killed 2 chiefs and wounded a third, and the Mohawks, who had never seen guns, fled in terror. In 1610, Champlain led the Algonquians in an attack on a stockaded Mohawk village, slaying 85 warriors. These encounters made the Mohawks deadly enemies of the French and convinced them that they must obtain firearms in order to survive.

In 1624, Fort Orange was established by the Dutch at the present site of Albany, New York, and soon afterward the settlers began trading guns to the Mohawks for beaver skins. The tribe, which had been small and weak, was transformed into the terror of the region. Mohawks defeated their Indian enemies who lacked firearms, seizing their furs, and refusing to permit them to come to Fort Orange to trade. Between 1640 and 1652, they conquered most of their Indian neighbors, increasing their power by incorporating captives into the tribe.

The Mohawks fought several bloody wars with the French, negotiating peace for brief periods in order to trade. They became increasingly dependent upon European goods, and when the English supplanted the Dutch in New York in 1664, they continued to come to Albany to obtain what they needed. The superiority of English trade goods was of major importance in making the Iroquois allies of the English during the ensuing wars between the two European nations.

In 1666, a French expedition destroyed the Mohawk villages and crops. The following year, the tribe found it expedient to make peace with the French and to permit missionaries to live among them. Some Mohawks embraced Christianity and moved near Montreal. They allied themselves with the French, and joined in attacks on the Iroquois of New York. (See CAUGHNAWAGA INDIANS.) In 1693, the French and Caughnawaga Indians destroyed the Mohawk villages of the Mohawk Valley. They compelled the Iroquois to make peace in 1701.

During Queen Anne's War (1702-13), the Mohawks of Canada became the scourge of the New England settlements. The New York Mohawks remained neutral during that struggle, playing one nation against the other to improve their position in the fur trade. With the establishment of Fort Hunter near the Mohawk villages in 1712, English settlers began buying land from the Indians and building homes in the area. In 1738, William Johnson became a trader among the Mohawks and gained tremendous influence over the tribe. He made firm British allies of them during the French and Indian War. (See HENDRICK, MOHAWK CHIEF; LAKE GEORGE, BATTLE OF.)

During the Revolutionary War, the Mohawks and most of the other Iroquois supported the British, but the Oneidas and Tuscaroras sided with the Americans. This division caused the League of the Iroquois to split asunder. Chief Brant led the Mohawks in numerous battles and raids against the New York settlements. (See BRANT, JOSEPH; CHERRY VALLEY MASSACRE; ORISKANY, BATTLE OF; COBLESKILL; ANDRUSTOWN; SPRINGFIELD; SCHOHARIE; MINISINK.) After the war, many of the Mohawks moved to Canada to settle on lands Brant had acquired. Others remained in New York, signed land cession treaties, and moved to reservations. Many of their descendants live at the St. Regis Reservation, astride the U.S.-- Canadian boundary, today.

(William C. Sturtevant, ed., Handbook of North American Indians, XV; Barbara Graymont, The Iroquois in the American Revolution; E. B. O'Callaghan, History of New Netherland, I-II; Allen W. Trelease, Indian Affairs in Colonial New York; Arthur Pound, Johnson of the Mohawks; T. Wood Clarke, The Bloody Mohawk.)

MOHEGAN INDIANS. The Mohegan Indians, a branch of the Pequot nation, split off and formed a separate tribe when Chief Uncas rebelled against the principal sachem, Sassacus. His people established their village near Norwich, Connecticut, and allied themselves with the colonists during the Pequot War of 1637. After the defeat of the Pequots, the Mohegans absorbed the survivors and, supported by the English, laid claim to a large territory in southern New England.

The Mohegans served the English as allies during King Philip's War. At the conclusion of that war, they were the most powerful tribe in southern New England, but their numbers decreased rapidly thereafter. They sold their lands to the English, and moved to a reservation on the Thames River in Connecticut where the survivors were absorbed by the Scaticook and Brotherton Indians, most of them becoming converts to Christianity. A few remained at their old town, Mohegan, where a remnant of mixed-bloods still resides.

(John W. DeForest, History of the Indians of Connecticut; F. W. Hodge, ed., Handbook of American Indians, I; John R. Swanton, Indian Tribes of North America.)

MOINGWENA INDIANS. The Moingwena Indians, a small tribe or band of the Illinois confederacy, were located on the west side of the Mississippi when seen by Father Marquette during his descent of that river in 1673. They faded from history soon afterward, and it is believed that they were absorbed by the Peoria tribe.
(F. W. Hodge, ed., Handbook of American Indians, I.)

MONTAUK INDIANS. The Montauk Indians, an Algonquian tribe, inhabited eastern and central Long Island. Tributaries of the Pequots until the destruction of that nation in 1637, they were attacked frequently by the Narragansets and lost most of their population as a result of wars and plagues. About 1759, most of the survivors joined the Brotherton Indians. Those who remained on the island have mixed-blood descendants living on the Shinnecock Reservation today.
(Allen W. Trelease, Indian Affairs in Colonial New York; John R. Swanton, Indian Tribes of North America.)

MONTGOMERY, JOHN, EXPEDITION. Col. John Montgomery, a division commander in George Rogers Clark's army during the Revolutionary War, was dispatched after the successful defense of St. Louis and Cahokia in 1780 to pursue the retreating Indians. He failed to overtake them, but he burned several Sauk and Fox villages on the Rock River. (See HESSE, EMANUEL, EXPEDITION.)
(F. A. Jones, Winnebago Ethnology; Dale Van Every, A Company of Heroes.)

MONTOUR, LOUIS, FAMILY OF. "Authorities regarding the Montours are not always consistent and are sometimes not reconcilable as to statements of material facts" acknowledged J. N. B. Hewitt in an article in the Handbook of American Indians that related experiences of members of this mixed-blood family that played such important roles in American frontier history. And, indeed, some of their deeds remain a matter of such historical dispute that it is difficult to determine which Montour was involved in a particular event, or even whether the event actually transpired.

A Canadian official, Benjamin Sulte, compiled a Montour genealogy that illuminates early family history: Pierre Couc, son of Nicholas Couc, a nobleman of Cognac, came to Canada and settled at Three Rivers. In 1647, he married an Algonquian Indian woman, Marie Metiwameghwahkwe, and they had eight children. The eldest son, Louis, born in 1659, took the name of Montour. About 1683, he married Madeleine, a Saco Indian girl, and they had a son and two daughters. In 1694, he was seriously wounded by Mohawk Indians in a battle near Lake Champlain. At or about that time, his children were captured by the Iroquois and taken to their villages. Afterward, Louis deserted the French colony and became an Indian diplomat for the English. In 1709, Governor Vaudreuil instructed his Indian agent Louis-Thomas Chabert de Joncaire to arrest Montour and bring him to Canada to be hung for inciting Indians to attack the French. Joncaire murdered Montour when he could not take him alive.

The children of Louis Montour (Jean, Margaret, and their sister who is known in frontier annals as Madame Montour) were captured by the Iroquois and raised by the Miamis. Jean's life was not well documented. Some historians assert that he, rather than his father, was murdered by Joncaire in 1709, but he was still alive in 1733. Margaret married a Miami chief and probably spent the remainder of her life with that tribe.

Madame Montour, whose name is believed to have been Madeleine, was captured at the age of 10. She became greatly assimilated, married a Seneca Indian named Roland before 1712, and they had six children: Andrew, Henry, Robert, Lewis, Margaret, and another daughter whose name history fails to record. After the death of her first husband, she married an Oneida chief, Big Tree, who adopted the name Robert Hunter. He was killed in a battle with Catawba Indians about 1729.

Madame Montour hated the French because of the murder of her father. She gained great influence over the Indians and used it so successfully in the English interest that French officials offered her a reward if she would return to Canada.

By 1711, Madame Montour had become an interpreter at conferences between the Iroquois and New York officials. In 1712, she helped dissuade the Five Nations from helping the Tuscaroras fight Carolina settlers. In 1727, she served as interpreter at Philadelphia during negotiations between the Six Nations and Pennsylvania officials. For her services, she regularly received a man's pay. Her old age was spent at the site of Montoursville, Pennsylvania, where she became blind before her death in 1753.

Three of Madame Montour's sons (Andrew, Henry, and Lewis) served Pennsylvania colonial officials as interpreters. Lewis is believed to have been killed during the French and Indian War. Another son, perhaps it was Robert, became a Seneca war captain who fought under Sir William Johnson at the Battles of Lake George and Niagara. Her eldest son, Andrew, became one of the most successful Indian diplomats in the history of Pennsylvania, so effective that the French put a price on his head.

Andrew (Sattelihu), was a close friend of the Moravian missionaries. In 1742, he guided Count Nikolaus Zinzendorf to the Wyoming Valley. The following year, he served as interpreter for the Delaware Indians at a conference at Shamokin with Pennsylvania officials. He accompanied Conrad Weiser to a Six Nations council at Onondaga in 1745. In 1748, he and Weiser went to Logstown on the Ohio to confer with several tribes who had been trading with the French. In 1752, Governor Hamilton of Pennsylvania granted him land northwest of Carlisle, and he lived there several years. He interpreted for Virginia officials during land cession treaties in 1752 and 1753.

At the outbreak of the French and Indian War, Andrew was appointed to lead Indian allies of the English. He and his scouts were with George Washington at Fort Necessity in 1754, and with Gen. Edward Braddock during the defeat of 1755. In 1756, he visited the Iroquois to urge them to prevent the Delawares from attacking Pennsylvania settlements. He accompanied Sir William Johnson to the relief of Fort Edward, serving as captain of scouts.

In 1758, Montour resumed his interpreting duties. On October 8-26, he translated at the important Council at Easton for the governors of Pennsylvania and New Jersey. On December 4, he interpreted for Colonel Bouquet at a conference with the Delawares at Fort Pitt. On February 8-9, 1759, he served as interpreter for Gen. John Forbes at Philadelphia, and later that year he translated at the Pittsburgh conference with the Iroquois, Delawares, Shawnees and Wyandots.

In 1760, Montour marched with Rogers' Rangers to take possession of the former French post at Detroit, returning the following year. On August 12-29, 1762, he interpreted for Pennsylvania officials at a council at Lancaster with the Iroquois, Shawnees, Delawares, and Miamis.

In 1763, during Pontiac's War, Montour scouted hostile Indian country to warn the settlers of impending attacks. In February 1764, he led Indian scouts to destroy the Delaware town of Kanestio, and they returned with 41 prisoners. The following year, he served with Col. John Bradstreet at Niagara, guarding the carrying place and redeeming captives. In 1766, he is believed to have accompanied George Croghan to Fort de Chartres and New Orleans.

In 1768, Montour interpreted at the Council of Fort Pitt in April and May, and at the Council of Fort Stanwix in October and November. These services marked the end of his active career, for he settled down on his land near Fort Pitt, one of several tracts awarded him for many years of government services. He died a very wealthy man a few years later. Andrew's son John, born in 1744 of a Delaware chief's daughter, was educated at Philadelphia. He fought for the English in Dunmore's War and for the Americans during the Revolutionary War. Afterward, he served as an interpreter. He lived on Montour's Island near Pittsburgh.

One of Madame Montour's daughters, name unrecorded, is known to have existed only because she was present at the negotiation of the Treaty of Lancaster in 1744. Her other daughter, known in frontier annals as French Margaret, was born between 1700 and 1705. She married a Mohawk chief, Peter Quebec (Katarionecha), and they had six children: Nicolas, John, Roland, Mary, Catherine, and Esther. They lived for a time in Ohio, but moved to the present site of Williamsport, Pennsylvania (then called French Margaret's Town), after 1745. She enjoyed great influence over the Iroquois and kept liquor traders away from her town.

On the onset of the French and Indian War, French Margaret and her family moved to a village near Tioga, where her son-in-law Eghohowin was chief. There she persuaded the chief to release three white captives. She died of smallpox soon afterward.

One of French Margaret's sons, probably Nicolas, was killed during a battle with Creek Indians in 1753. John and Roland became Iroquois war chiefs who attacked the settlements during the Revolutionary War and probably participated in the Wyoming Massacre in 1778.

Mary Montour, French Margaret's daughter, married the White Mingo (John Cook, Kanaghragait), a Seneca chief. She became a

Christian as a child while staying with her mother in Philadelphia, and after her husband's death, she moved with the Moravian Indians from Salem to Canada.

Mary's sister Catherine married Telemut (Thomas Hudson), a noted Seneca chief, and they had a son, Amochol, and two daughters. She and her husband participated in the Treaty of Easton in October 1758. The village where she lived, known as Catherine's Town, was destroyed by Gen. John Sullivan in 1779, and she lived the remainder of her life in Canada, near Niagara. Her son Amochol became a Moravian, and was living at New Salem in 1788.

The most legendary and controversial member of the Montour family was Esther, a third daughter of French Margaret. She was educated at Philadelphia and developed an admiration for white people and their way of life. She married a Munsee Delaware chief, Eghohowin, and gained great influence over the Iroquois. In 1772, after her husband's death, she established a new village nearby known as Queen Esther's Town.

Esther's presence at, and involvement in, the Wyoming Massacre are matters of historical dispute. The Handbook of American Indians asserts that she accompanied her son Gencho to the battlefield, and that after Gencho was killed she exacted such revenge on American prisoners that she became known as "the fiend of Wyoming." J. N. B. Hewitt described the alleged atrocity as follows:

> Without mercy and with the most fearful tortures, they were ruthlessly butchered ... after having surrendered themselves as prisoners of war. Placed around a huge rock and held by stout Indians, 16 men were killed one by one by the knife or tomahawk of "Queen Esther." In a similar circle 9 others were killed in the same brutal manner.... This slaughter ... gave Esther her bloody title.

Some historians have blamed the massacre on Catherine, Esther's sister. Others assert that the murder of captives never took place. "All this is fictional," wrote Barbara Graymont. "No women were along on the expedition, and no such sanguinary tortures took place." "The tradition is out of key with her character," asserted Paul A. W. Wallace. "She treated the Strope family, who had been her prisoners since May of that year, with great kindness.... On the other hand, we know that Queen Esther, whatever her normal character, may have been inflamed to avenge the death of her son...."

In the fall of 1778, Queen Esther's town was destroyed by American troops commanded by Col. Thomas Hartley. According to some accounts, Esther was killed by Sullivan's army at the Battle of Newtown. Wallace believes, however, that after the war she married a Tuscarora chief and lived at Cayuga Lake.

(Charles A. Hanna, The Wilderness Trail; Paul A. W. Wallace, Indians in Pennsylvania; Barbara Graymont, The Iroquois in the American Revolution; F. W. Hodge, ed., Handbook of American Indians, I.)

MORAVIAN INDIANS. The Moravian Indians, chiefly Delawares, Munsees, and Mahicans, were converted to Christianity by Moravian missionaries. Beginning among the Mahicans in New York in 1740, the missionaries moved their converts to Pennsylvania in 1746 and established the community of Friendenshutten on the Susquehanna River. A small Moravian Indian settlement was established near Bethlehem, but it was broken up by white settlers who threatened the Indians until the governor marched them to Philadelphia for their own protection. A mob of frontiersmen followed them there, but was prevented from attacking the defenseless natives by Benjamin Franklin and Quaker leaders.

The Moravian town of Gnadenhutten, on the Lehigh River near the present town of Leighton, Pennsylvania, was attacked by hostile Indians on November 24, 1755, slaying 14 Christians. Afterward, troops sent to protect the town were attacked by Chief Tedyuscung's Delaware band on January 1, 1756. Twenty soldiers were slain and the town was burned.

Alarmed by the hostility of both Indians and whites, the missionaries moved their settlements westward, stopping for a time on the Beaver River in western Pennsylvania, and then in 1773, establishing the towns of Schoenbrunn, Gnadenhutten, and Salem on the Muskingum River in Ohio. There the Indians established homes and farms and lived peacefully until the outbreak of the American Revolution. With their villages located halfway between Indian allies of the British on the Sandusky and the American settlements south of the Ohio, they found themselves suspected by each side of favoring the other. The Sandusky Indians, after failing to induce the Moravians to become British allies, attempted to implicate them by stopping at their towns when returning from raids. The British at Detroit believed that the Americans would use the Moravian towns as a staging area for attacks, while the Americans were convinced that Moravian Indians joined war parties that invaded Pennsylvania settlements. In vain did the missionaries protest that they and their converts were neutrals.

In the fall of 1781, the British Indian agent Matthew Elliott, the Wyandot chief Half-King, and the Delaware chief Captain Pipe led a large force of warriors into the Moravian towns, seized the missionaries and marched them to Detroit, and compelled the Indian inhabitants to accompany them to Sandusky.

In the spring of 1782, some 150 Moravian Indians on the point of starvation fled from Sandusky and returned to their towns to tend their crops. There, on March 7, they were surrounded by 100 Pennsylvania militiamen led by Col. David Williamson. The inhabitants of Schoenbrunn received enough forewarning to enable them to escape, but those of the other towns were rounded up and confined in two houses at Gnadenhutten. The ensuing tragedy has been described by Theodore Roosevelt:

> As soon as the unsuspecting Indians were gathered in
> the two houses, the men in one, the women and children in
> the other, the whites held a council as to what should be

done with them. The great majority was for putting them instantly to death. Eighteen men protested, and asked that the lives of the poor creatures be spared, and then withdrew, calling God to witness that they were innocent of the crime about to be committed.... One of them took off with him a small Indian boy, whose life was thus spared....

When the murderers told the doomed Moravians their fate, they merely requested a short delay in which to prepare themselves for death. They asked one another's pardon for whatever wrongs they might have done, knelt down and prayed, kissed one another farewell, "and began to sing hymns of hope and praise to the Most High." Then the white butchers entered the houses and put to death the ninety-six men, women, and children that were within their walls.

The surviving Moravian Indians, led by the Reverend David Zeisberger, removed to Canada in 1791, establishing the town of Fairfield on the Thames River. Fairfield was destroyed by American troops during the War of 1812, but it was rebuilt on the opposite side of the river.

(Theodore Roosevelt, The Winning of the West, III; Solon J. Buck, The Planting of Civilization in Western Pennsylvania; Dale Van Every, Forth to the Wilderness; F. W. Hodge, ed., Handbook of American Indians, I; William A. Hunter, Forts on the Pennsylvania Frontier.)

MORGAN, GEORGE. George Morgan was born in Philadelphia on February 14, 1743. Orphaned at age 6, he was apprenticed at 13 to Baynton, Wharton, and Company, the foremost American firm engaged in the Indian trade. Eight years later, he married the daughter of one of the proprietors and became a full partner in the company. His friendship with George Croghan opened the door to profitable trade with the western tribes, and in 1765, he assisted Croghan in sending a pack train of goods to the Indians in an attempt to restore peace with Pontiac's supporters. The train was ambushed and goods confiscated by Pennsylvania frontiersmen (see BLACK BOYS). The following year he accompanied Croghan down the Ohio to the Illinois country with 17 boatloads of goods for the Indians.

Morgan remained in the Illinois as his company's representative in the Indian trade, and he became a leader in the movement to establish civil government there. In 1768, he was appointed judge of the civil court, a fortunate development, for the trading firm had passed into receivership. During the same year, the Treaty of Fort Stanwix opened large areas of ceded Indian lands to settlement, and Morgan became an officer in the Indiana Company, organized to profit from land speculation.

At the onset of the Revolutionary War, Morgan sided with the Americans. In April 1776, Congress appointed him to succeed Richard Butler as Indian agent of the middle department (west of the Allegheny Mountains). His first assignment was to counter the efforts of British governor Henry Hamilton to control the western tribes, so in June he sent Simon Girty to invite the Iroquois and other nations to a peace conference at Pittsburgh. At the conference in October, he received pledges of neutrality and distributed a large shipment of presents. Hamilton's inducements were greater, however, and war parties ranged far into the Virginia and Kentucky settlements.

In 1777, Morgan attempted to organize another Indian conference at Pittsburgh, but frontiersmen murdered some of the chiefs, and Morgan hid others in his own home to protect them. Afterward, he was accused of being a Tory and placed under arrest briefly, but was cleared of the charges and reinstated. He continued to promote peace with the Indians until 1779, when he resigned in frustration and went east to serve as a colonel in the war against the British.

After the war, Morgan lived on a farm in New Jersey and resumed his land speculation ventures. Receiving little Congressional encouragement, in 1788 he approached Spanish officials about establishing a colony on the west bank of the Mississippi. As a result, he founded New Madrid, Missouri, in 1789, but Gov. Esteban Miro of Louisiana put an end to the undertaking, and he returned to his New Jersey home. He died on March 10, 1810.

"Perhaps no man was personally involved in more important events over the whole of the early frontier's most critical period, from before Pontiac's War to after the Louisiana Purchase, than was George Morgan."--Dale Van Every.

(Dale Van Every, Ark of Empire; Thomas P. Abernethy, Western Lands and the American Revolution; Solon J. Buck, The Planting of Civilization in Western Pennsylvania; Randolph C. Downes, Council Fires on the Upper Ohio; Clarence Walworth Alvord, The Illinois Country.)

MORRIS, THOMAS, EXPEDITION. During the summer of 1764, Col. John Bradstreet, confident that a treaty he had signed with some Indians had ended Pontiac's War, dispatched Capt. Thomas Morris to inform hostile tribes and the French at Fort de Chartres that peace had been restored and to warn them not to attack British troops. Neither of the officers realized that Pontiac was still inciting the tribes to resist and that several of them remained as hostile as ever.

Morris was accompanied by the Iroquois chief Thomas King and two Frenchmen. At the Ottawa village on the Maumee, Morris had a confrontation with Pontiac, but Thomas King threatened the chief with an Iroquois war, and Pontiac agreed to permit them to continue their journey.

When Morris arrived at the Miami Indian town of Kekionga on September 7, he found the Indians even more hostile. He described his encounter as follows: "The Shawnees & Delawares begged of the Miamis either to put us to death ... or to tie us & send us prisoners to their village...." He was stripped and tied to a post, but before the torture could begin, a young Miami chief, Pacanne, untied him, announcing, "I give this man his life." Thereupon Morris abandoned his mission and returned to Detroit to inform Bradstreet that Pontiac's followers were by no means ready to give up the fight.

(Bert Anson, The Miami Indians; Howard H. Peckham, Pontiac and the Indian Uprising; Dale Van Every, Forth to the Wilderness.)

MORSE, JEDEDIAH, EXPEDITION. The Reverend Jedediah Morse, an advocate of founding an Indian state, was commissioned by two missionary societies "to visit Indian tribes of the U.S. and ascertain their condition, and devise measures for their benefit and advancement." His expenses were paid by the federal government in exchange for helpful advice in handling Indian relations.

Morse departed from New Haven, Connecticut, on May 10, 1821, and visited tribes as distant as the Great Lakes. He interviewed Indians, missionaries, traders, and agents during a journey that lasted through August. In 1822 he published A Report to the Secretary of War of the United States, on Indian Affairs, which contained invaluable information on the size, condition, and attitude toward the government of the tribes he had seen.

(Emma H. Blair, The Indian Tribes of the Upper Mississippi Valley and the Region of the Great Lakes; J. P. Kinney, A Continent Lost--A Civilization Won.)

MORTON, THOMAS. Thomas Morton, an English adventurer, accompanied Andrew Weston to Massachusetts in 1622, remained a brief time at Wessagusset, and returned to England. By 1625 he was back near Plymouth, working at Woolaston's Plantation. He ousted the owner's overseer, renamed the plantation Merry Mount, and erected a maypole, around which he danced with Indian women. He traded guns to the Massachuset, Narraganset, and Wampanoag Indians for furs, violating Puritan laws as well as ethical values.

William Bradford and other Plymouth leaders concluded that Morton was a sinner, an outlaw, and a dangerous enemy. In 1628, Capt. Miles Standish arrested him and sent him to England for trial on charges of selling guns and liquor to Indians. He was acquitted, however, and returned to Merry Mount in 1629. Less than a year later, the Pilgrims deported him, charging that he had treated Indians unfairly, an invalid accusation as he enjoyed great popularity with the natives. Because of lack of evidence, he was freed by the courts, and he devoted several years as a legal assistant to Sir Ferdinando Gorges in attempting to revoke the Massachusetts Bay charter.

In 1643, Morton returned to Plymouth, intending to settle in Maine. Again arrested, he was imprisoned in Boston for a year, and he died soon after being released.

(William Bradford, Of Plimoth Plantation; Neal Salisbury, Manitou and Providence; Richard Drinnon, Facing West.)

MOSELEY, SAMUEL. Capt. Samuel Moseley, a privateer from Jamaica who became one of New England's foremost Indian fighters, captured a crew of pirates in 1675 and recruited them to fight in King Philip's War. In August 1675, they seized 15 Indians living at Marlborough, accused them of being hostiles, and marched them to Boston for trial. The prisoners were acquitted, but they narrowly escaped a lynch mob.

In September 1675, Moseley and his men invaded Pennacook Indian territory and burned the village of the friendly chief Wannalancet. Massachusetts officials, anxious to keep peace with the Pennacooks, disavowed the attack. In 1676 Moseley seized the peaceful Indians of John Hoar's workhouse at Concord, marched them to Boston, and had them interred on Deer Island.

Moseley and his men captured a considerable number of hostiles during the war, especially after he agreed to use friendly Indians as scouts. He became a popular hero to the hard-pressed settlers of southern New England.

(Douglas Edward Leach, Flintlock and Tomahawk.)

MOXUS, PENOBSCOT CHIEF. Moxus (Taxous, Agamus), a powerful Penobscot chief, led some of the most destructive raids in the history of New England. In 1689 he and the Baron de St. Castin captured Pemaquid, marching many colonists into captivity. (See GYLES, JOHN.) Two years later, he led an attack on Wells, Cape Neddock, and York, killing 9 citizens. In July 1694, his war party, accompanied by French officers, slew more than 100 settlers near the present city of Durham. (See OYSTER RIVER.) Soon afterward, he struck at Groton, Massachusetts, killing 22 colonists and taking 13 prisoners. In February 1696, he narrowly escaped death at Pemaquid when the commanding officer of the fort, Capt. Pascho Chubb, ignored a flag of truce and attacked him. In 1703 it was his turn to ignore a flag of truce when he lured Maj. John March outside the walls of the Casco fort. March was saved by a sally from the fort, and Moxus withdrew his warriors under the bombardment of a ship's cannon.

Moxus interspersed his raids with the negotiation of peace treaties. He signed treaties with New England officials in 1689, 1699, 1702, 1713, and 1717.

(Samuel Adams Drake, Border Wars of New England; Francis Parkman, Count Frontenac and New France Under Louis XIV.)

MRIKSAH, NARRAGANSET CHIEF. The eldest son of the important Chief Canonicus, Mriksah succeeded his father as leader of the Narragansets in 1647. He strengthened his power by marrying a sister of Chief Ninigret (see MAGNUS), and cooperated closely with Ninigret during King Philip's War.

(F. W. Hodge, ed., Handbook of American Indians, I.)

MUGG, AROSAGUNTACOOK CHIEF. Mugg, a reluctant participant in King Philip's War, was drawn into the conflict by English abuse. Early in 1676 he went to Boston to seek a peace treaty for his tribe and for the Penobscots. Promptly arrested and thrown into prison, he was released within a short time, but, indignant over his incarceration, he recruited 100 warriors and raided Black Point, Maine, on October 12, 1676. Most of the residents fled, and he destroyed the settlement. Less than a week later, he appeared at Wells and demanded the surrender of Wheelright's garrison, but he withdrew after killing 2 colonists when the defenders announced that they would fight to the last man.

Next, Mugg turned his attention to capturing boats off the coast of Maine. He seized a 30-ton ketch by cutting its cable and used it to capture fishing and trading boats. He planned to use his fleet to attack the villages along the coast and to blockade Boston, but he was killed at Black Point on May 16, 1677.

"Mugg was a brilliant naval strategist and ship handler, a sort of Indian Nelson who feared neither the English nor their cannon-armed ships."--Wilcomb E. Washburn.

(Robert M. Utley and Wilcomb E. Washburn, The American Heritage History of the Indian Wars; Jeremy Belknap, History of New Hampshire, I; Edward L. Bourne, History of Wells and Kennebunk; F. W. Hodge, ed., Handbook of American Indians, I.)

MUNSEE INDIANS. The Munsee Indians, a division of the Delawares who spoke an Algonquian dialect akin to that of the Mahicans, lived in northern New Jersey and New York west of the Hudson River when encountered by Henry Hudson in 1609. When whites began to encroach on their lands, many of them abandoned their villages to join other Delaware bands. Some removed to the Allegheny River in Pennsylvania as early as 1724. In 1737, Pennsylvania officials defrauded them of most of their lands (see WALKING PURCHASE), and they were settled on the Susquehanna by the Iroquois. In 1756 the Munsees remaining in New York were placed on a reservation and controlled by the Mohawks.

Many of the Munsees were converted to Christianity by the Moravian missionaries before the Revolutionary War, and they suffered greatly at the hands of other Indians, the Americans, and the British, during that conflict. (See MORAVIAN INDIANS.) Others merged with the Stockbridge Indians and were assigned to a reservation near Green Bay, Wisconsin, in 1833. In 1857, the Christian Munsees were granted lands in Kansas, and most of them removed to Oklahoma in 1866. Some Munsees migrated to Canada to join the Moravians there.

(F. W. Hodge, ed., Handbook of American Indians, I; John R. Swanton, Indian Tribes of North America; Allen W. Trelease, Indian Affairs in Colonial New York.)

MURPHY, TIMOTHY. Timothy Murphy, a legendary Indian fighter in New York and Pennsylvania, was born at Minisink, New York, in 1751. He moved to Pennsylvania as a child and grew up on the frontier. According to tradition, his wife and children were killed by Indians and he swore to spend the rest of his life exacting revenge on that race. Reputedly, he had killed 40 Indians by the close of the Revolutionary War.

On one occasion, Murphy led a small band of soldiers to attack a Tory and Indian camp near Unadilla. Most of the warriors were away, and Murphy's men clubbed and tomahawked the old men, women, and children. Then Murphy hid in a hollow log until the warriors returned, shot one of them, and escaped into a thicket.

While scouting the Seneca country for the Sullivan Expedition, he was one of the few who escaped the Iroquois ambush of Lt. Thomas

Boyd's detachment. (See BOYD, THOMAS.) Known as the "Savior of the Schoharie," he roamed the wilderness, "as savage and vindictive as his enemies" until his death in 1818.

(James Levernier and Hennig Cohen, eds., The Indians and Their Captives; Francis Whiting Halsey, The Old New York Frontier.)

MURRAY, WILLIAM, PURCHASES. In 1768, William Murray, a Scotch trader, represented a company that provisioned the British Army in America. Afterward, he went to work for the David Franks Company of Lancaster, Pennsylvania, traders in the Illinois country. In 1773 he arranged to purchase a large part of southern Illinois from the Cahokia, Kaskaskia, and Tamaroa Indians for the Illinois Land Company. The price of the enormous tract was 20 guns, 500 pounds of powder, 4,000 pounds of lead, 10,000 pounds of flour, some livestock, kettles and other goods. Two years later, Murray purchased for himself, Governor Dunmore of Virginia, and other speculators, a large tract extending to the Wabash River for similar considerations.

The British government refused to approve Murray's land transactions, and perhaps for that reason, he supported the Americans during the Revolutionary War. If so, it was all for naught, for Congress voided the sales because public policy prohibited the purchase of Indian lands by private individuals.

(Grant Foreman, Last Trek of the Indians; Clarence Walworth Alvord, The Illinois Country.)

MYSTIC, BATTLE OF. During the Pequot War of 1637, Capt. John Mason and the Mohegan chief Uncas led 100 Connecticut and Massachusetts soldiers and hundreds of friendly Indians to attack a Pequot stronghold near the present site of Mystic, Connecticut. On May 26 they stormed the palisaded town before dawn at a time when most of the warriors were away, setting the wigwams on fire while the Mohegans waited outside the walls to shoot down any Pequot attempting to flee through the flames.

Mason described the slaughter as follows:

> We called up our Forces with all expedition, gave Fire upon them through the Pallizado; the Indians being in a dead indeed their last Sleep: Then we wheeling off fell upon the main Entrance ... indeed such a dreadful Terror did the Almighty let fall upon their spirits, that they would fly from us and run into the very Flames, where many of them perished....
>
> And thus in little more than one Hour's space was their impregnable Fort with themselves utterly Destroyed, to the Number of six or seven Hundred.... There were only seven taken Captive & about seven escaped.

The bloodbath at Mystic broke the back of the Pequot resistance and brought the war to an early conclusion. (See PEQUOT INDIANS.)

(John Mason, A Brief History of the Pequot War; John W. De-
Forest, History of the Indians of Connecticut; Neal Salisbury, Manitou and Providence.)

-N-

NAHPOPE, SAUK CHIEF. Nahpope (Neapope) was one of Black
Hawk's leading lieutenants in that formidable Sauk chief's war of
1832. A determined opponent of white settlement on Indian lands,
he is said to have deceived Black Hawk into expecting British assistance if the Sauks defended their homeland. He led the Indians
during the Battle of Wisconsin Heights, near the present site of Sauk
City, Wisconsin, holding off a large militia force until the Indians
could cross the Wisconsin River to temporary safety.

Historians differ regarding Nahpope's role in the Black Hawk
War after the Battle of Wisconsin Heights. Most authorities believe
that he remained with Black Hawk throughout the war and was captured with him. Cecil Eby asserts, however, that he deserted Black
Hawk after the battle and fled to the Winnebagos. He was confined
briefly with Black Hawk at Jefferson Barracks at the conclusion of
the conflict. After release he rejoined the Sauks in Iowa.

(Black Hawk, Black Hawk, an Autobiography; Cecil Eby, That
Disgraceful Affair, the Black Hawk War; F. W. Hodge, ed., Handbook of American Indians, II.)

NANAGOUCY, MOHEGAN CHIEF. Nanagoucy, a Mohegan subchief,
was among the New England Indians who fled to the St. Joseph
River after their defeat by the colonists during King Philip's War.
There he became a hunter for French traders, and in 1681, an advisor to La Salle in his plan to establish an Algonquian settlement
on the Mississippi to serve as a buffer against the Iroquois. Nanagoucy recruited additional warriors from New England, and he assisted with the Indian settlement around Fort St. Louis in 1682.

(George T. Hunt, The Wars of the Iroquois; Francis Parkman,
La Salle and the Discovery of the Great West.)

NANTICOKE INDIANS. The Nanticoke (Wiwash) Indians, a large
Algonquian tribe, were located on the eastern shore of Maryland and
in southern Delaware at the time they came to the notice of Capt.
John Smith in 1608. They were feared by other Indians because of
their use of witchcraft and poison, and they were dangerous enemies
of the early settlers of Maryland. In 1642, Maryland officials organized the settlers to retaliate for Nanticoke raids, and the tribe
signed the first of several peace treaties to avoid the invasion of
their territory. The treaties failed to prevent white encroachment,
however, and hostilities flared up from time to time during the next
four decades.

About 1680, the Nanticokes sought Iroquois protection, becoming tributaries of the League. Most of them began a northward
movement after 1722, halting briefly at the juncture of the Juniata

and Susquehanna rivers, and finally settling in places assigned to them by the Iroquois, including Chenango and Oswego. During their migrations they transported the bones of their ancestors, finally interring them in the Wyoming Valley of Pennsylvania in 1748. About 1753, they were formally adopted into the Iroquois confederacy and given representation at Six Nations councils.

In 1784, most of the Nanticokes moved westward to Ohio and joined their kinsmen, the Delawares. A few, known to the whites as Wiwashes, remained in Maryland and Delaware, where their mixed-blood descendants still live.

(John R. Swanton, Indian Tribes of North America; William C. Sturtevant, Handbook of North American Indians, XV; Paul A. W. Wallace, Indians in Pennsylvania.)

NARRAGANSET INDIANS. The Narraganset Indians, one of New England's largest, wealthiest, and most culturally advanced Algonquian tribes, occupied the present state of Rhode Island at the time of Puritan settlement of the area around Massachusetts Bay. They were hostile at first toward the Plymouth settlers, but they cooperated with other Puritans in conducting trade with interior tribes, and by 1632 they had become friends of all of the English colonies.

In 1636, Roger Williams established the Providence colony in the Narraganset country and gained a considerable measure of influence over the tribe. At the onset of the Pequot War, the Narragansets declined to join the hostiles in attacking the English settlements. Their attempts to remain neutral were thwarted by colonial suspicion, however, and they were compelled to sign a treaty of alliance with the English. At the conclusion of the war, they received trade advantages formerly enjoyed by the vanquished Pequots.

In 1643, the creation of a confederation called the United Colonies--Massachusetts, Connecticut, New Haven, and Plymouth--posed a threat to the settlers of Providence and to their friends, the Narragansets. A conflict involving rival chiefs Uncas and Sequasson led to warfare between the Mohegans and Narragansets. When the English encouraged Uncas to murder Chief Miantonomo, the Narragansets appealed unsuccessfully to King Charles I to protect their people and lands from colonial threats and encroachments. The United Colonies responded by declaring war on the tribe. To avoid invasion the chiefs were compelled to sign a treaty in 1645, agreeing to pay an annual tribute, cede the lands formerly controlled by the Pequots, and provide hostages as proof of friendly intentions. Afterward, peace prevailed for 30 years, but the colonists remained alarmed over the perceived threat of 2,000 Narraganset warriors on their borders.

At the onset of the King Philip's War in 1675, the English demanded that the Narragansets help them capture fugitive Wampanoag warriors. When the Narragansets were reluctant to comply, the English became convinced of the tribe's hostile intentions. The Narragansets, already incensed by competition among the colonies to gain control over Indian lands, attempted to maintain an appearance of neutrality while providing shelter for the families of King Philip's warriors. Colonial authorities compelled the Narragansets to sign a peace treaty in July 1675, but the chiefs ignored their agreement to turn in Wampanoags seeking sanctuary.

In the fall of 1675, the English determined to attack the Narragansets to compel them to observe their treaty obligations. In an attempt to weaken the tribe before its leaders could prepare for war, an army led by Gov. Josiah Winslow invaded Narraganset territory, and on December 19, burned a stockaded village in a swamp, massacring hundreds of men, women, and children. (See GREAT SWAMP FIGHT; CHURCH, BENJAMIN.)

After the war, surviving Narragansets settled among the Niantics, and the united tribes were assigned to a reservation near Charlestown, Rhode Island. There, hemmed in by encroaching white settlements, the Indian population continued to decrease. In 1788, most of the survivors moved to New York to join the Brotherton Indians.

(John W. De Forest, History of the Indians of Connecticut; Douglas Edward Leach, Flintlock and Tomahawk; Neal Salisbury, Manitou and Providence; William C. Sturtevant, ed., Handbook of North American Indians, XV.)

NASHOBA, MASSACHUSETTS. Nashoba, a Christian Indian town, was established by the Reverend John Eliot at the present site of Littleton, Massachusetts, prior to the outbreak of King Philip's War. Attacked frequently by the Mohawks, the community managed to function under constant threat until 1675. Then its 50 residents were removed to Concord.

(Alden T. Vaughan, New England Frontier; F. W. Hodge, ed., Handbook of American Indians, II.)

NASSAU, FORT, NEW JERSEY. Fort Nassau was established as a Dutch trading post on the Delaware River, some 16 leagues from its mouth, in May 1623, by Cornelius Jacobsen Mey. The Indian trade fell short of expectations, and the fort was not garrisoned during certain seasons of the year. In 1635, the English occupied the empty post, but when the garrison returned the intruders were captured. Too weak to prevent Swedish trade with the Indians on the west bank of the Delaware, the post was abandoned in 1651.

(C. A. Weslager, Dutch Explorers, Traders, and Settlers in the Delaware Valley.)

NASSAU, FORT, NEW YORK. Fort Nassau was built on Castle Island in the Hudson River (present site of Albany) in 1614, by the Dutch West India Company. The small stockaded post was garrisoned by a dozen traders and protected by cannon. For three years the fort enjoyed a flourishing fur trade with neighboring tribes, but a flood forced its abandonment in 1617.

(Allen W. Trelease, Indian Affairs in Colonial New York.)

NATICK, MASSACHUSETTS. Natick, a Christian Indian village, was founded on the Charles River at the present site of Natick,

Massachusetts, by the Reverend John Eliot in 1651. Containing 150 inhabitants, mainly Massachuset Indians, it served as a model for other Christian native communities. By 1670 about 50 Indians had been accepted as communicants. At the onset of King Philip's War, the Christian chiefs of Natick warned the colonists of Philip's hostile intentions.

Soon after King Philip's War, white settlers occupied the area around Natick, and by 1734, they began gaining control of the town's affairs. Many of the Indians served the English in the French and Indian War, and the native population decreased as a result of war casualties and diseases. By 1764, the majority of Natick residents were white, and the community was incorporated as an English town in 1781. The last Natick Indian died in 1821.

(Alden T. Vaughan, New England Frontier; Douglas Edward Leach, Flintlock and Tomahawk; F. W. Hodge, ed., Handbook of American Indians, II.)

NATTAHATTAWANTS, NIPMUC CHIEF. Nattahattawants, chief of the Nipmucs of Musketaquid (present Concord, Massachusetts), was a friend of the Puritan settlers and sold large tracts of tribal lands to Gov. John Winthrop. In later life he became a Christian and encouraged his people to follow his example.

(F. W. Hodge, ed., Handbook of American Indians, II.)

NAUSET INDIANS. The Nauset Indians, an Algonquian tribe closely associated with the Wampanoags, occupied most of Cape Cod at the time of initial European contact. In 1606, they had a friendly visit with the French explorer Samuel de Champlain, but in 1614, their hostility was aroused against Europeans by the kidnapping of seven Nausets by Capt. Thomas Hunt. Upon the colonization of Plymouth in 1620, they attacked 20 Englishmen with bows and arrows, but were driven away with no loss of life on either side. Afterward, they befriended the Pilgrims, sending them food during the difficult days of 1622.

By 1665, most of the Nausets had become converts to Christianity and had subjected themselves to Massachusetts law. They supported the colonies during King Philip's War, and afterward, they absorbed remnants of defeated tribes. Their population fell drastically during the eighteenth century as a result of disease, but a small number of their descendants still live at the Mashpee Reservation on Cape Cod.

(John R. Swanton, Indian Tribes of North America; Neal Salisbury, Manitou and Providence; Alden T. Vaughan, New England Frontier.)

NAVASINK INDIANS. The Navasink Indians, an Algonquian tribe and a branch of the Delawares, were located near the present site of Navesink, New Jersey, when encountered by Henry Hudson in 1609. Friendly to European visitors, they boarded Hudson's ship to trade tobacco for goods and trinkets. In 1663 and 1664, they sold most of their land to the Dutch. When the English acquired New

Netherland, the Navasinks raided their settlements, but Col. Richard Nicholls used gifts and diplomacy to overcome their hostility. Afterward, their population dwindled rapidly as a result of proximity to white settlements.

(Allen W. Trelease, Indian Affairs of Colonial New York.)

NAWKAW, WINNEBAGO CHIEF. Nawkaw, an important Winnebago chief, was born about 1735 near Green Bay, Wisconsin. A supporter of the British during the War of 1812, he fought beside Tecumseh at the Battle of the Thames. After the war, he signed several treaties with the Americans and became an advocate of peace with the settlers. He kept his people out of the Black Hawk War and helped to restore peace during the hostilities aroused by Chief Red Bird's followers. He died in 1833.

(F. W. Hodge, ed., Handbook of American Indians, II.)

NEAPOPE, SAUK CHIEF see NAHPOPE, SAUK CHIEF

NECESSITY, FORT. Fort Necessity was built at the Great Meadows near the present site of Farmington, Pennsylvania, by George Washington in May and June 1754. Expecting French retaliation for his attack upon one of their detachments (see COULON DE VILLIERS DE JUMONVILLE, JOSEPH), Washington erected a small, stockaded fort to accommodate 160 men. Before its completion, reinforcements arrived, bringing his force to 360 effectives, some of whom camped outside the fort.

On July 3, an army of 500 Frenchmen and 400 Indians surrounded Fort Necessity. They began firing from the woods about mid-morning and kept it up until dark. At 8 p.m. they proposed that the defenders surrender and withdraw with the honors of war. As Washington had sustained 100 casualties and almost exhausted his food and ammunition, he accepted the terms. On July 4, he began the march to Virginia, and the French and Indians destroyed Fort Necessity.

(William A. Hunter, Forts on the Pennsylvania Frontier; Dale Van Every, Forth to the Wilderness.)

NEGWAGON, OTTAWA CHIEF. Negwagon, an Ottawa chief who lived near Mackinac, Michigan, supported the Americans during the War of 1812. He fought in several battles against Tecumseh and the British and lost a son in one of the engagements. After the war, he signed several treaties with U.S. government negotiators.

(F. W. Hodge, ed., Handbook of American Indians, II.)

NEHANTIC INDIANS see NIANTIC INDIANS

NEMACOLIN'S PATH. In 1752, a Delaware chief, Nemacolin, was employed by Christopher Gist and Thomas Cresap to blaze a direct trail over the mountains from the Potomac River to the Monongahela. This trail was used by George Washington in 1754 and Edward Braddock in 1755 in their unsuccessful efforts to oust the French from the Ohio. It eventually became a part of the National Road.

(Charles A. Hanna, The Wilderness Road; Dale Van Every, Forth to the Wilderness.)

NEOKAUTAH, WINNEBAGO CHIEF. Neokautah was born about 1780 and lived near Lake Winnebago. He became an ardent supporter of Tecumseh and fought beside him against the Americans at Fort Meigs and Fort Sandusky. On June 3, 1815, he signed a peace treaty at Mackinac with the Americans, and 10 years later, he signed the Treaty of Prairie du Chien.

(F. W. Hodge, ed., Handbook of American Indians, II.)

NEOLIN, DELAWARE PROPHET see DELAWARE PROPHET

NEPANET, TOM, NIPMUC CHIEF. Tom Nepanet, known to the colonists as Tom Dublet, was a Christian Indian and a firm friend of the English during King Philip's War. Imprisoned on Deer Island as a suspected supporter of King Philip, he proved his loyalty by rescuing English prisoners from Nipmuc captivity. Among those recovered with his assistance were members of the Joseph Rowlandson family. In May 1676, he helped Massachusetts troops ambush a Nipmuc war party near Lancaster.

(Douglas Edward Leach, Flintlock and Tomahawk; Dictionary of Indians of North America, II.)

NEPAUPUCK, PEQUOT CHIEF. Nepaupuck was a leader among the hostiles during the Pequot War of 1637. Among the colonists slain by him was Abraham Finch of Wethersfield, whose hands were cut off and delivered to Chief Sassacus. He survived the war, but wandered into New Haven sometime later and was recognized and imprisoned. Tried and condemned to death, he was decapitated and his head was displayed on a pole in the marketplace.

(Herbert Milton Sylvester, Indian Wars of New England, I.)

NESUTAN, JOB. Job Nesutan, a Christian Natick Indian, was of tremendous assistance to Reverend John Eliot in translating the Bible and other religious works into Algonquian. In July 1675, shortly after the outbreak of King Philip's War, he was killed while scouting for the colonial forces attempting to locate Philip in his Mount Hope hiding place.

(Alden T. Vaughan, New England Frontier.)

NETAWATEES, DELAWARE CHIEF. Netawatees (King Newcomer) was born in eastern Pennsylvania about 1678. During his youth he befriended William Penn. By 1718, he had become an important chief of the Unami Delawares, signing the Treaty of Conestoga in that capacity. Feeling the pressure of white encroachment on Indian lands, he migrated to the Ohio by 1737, settling first at Cuyahoga Falls, and establishing Newcomerstown on the Muskingum River around 1766. In 1770, he moved his headquarters to Gekelemukpechuenk, a town which he abandoned in 1773 or 1774 to remove to Coshocton.

After the death of Sassooan, Netawatees was elevated to principal chief of the Delaware nation. Inclined toward peace with the whites, he played an important part in persuading Tedyuscung to cease hostilities against the English in 1757. During Col. Henry Bouquet's invasion of the Indian country in 1764, however, Netawatees refused to discuss peace terms, and as a result, Bouquet deposed him. After the army's departure he resumed his role as principal chief.

In later life, Netawatees became a supporter of the Moravian missionaries, attended services regularly, and may have become a Christian. He died at Pittsburgh on October 31, 1776.

(Paul A. W. Wallace, Indians in Pennsylvania.)

NEUTRAL INDIANS. The Neutral Nation, an Iroquian confederacy, was located in southern Ontario, western New York, northeastern Ohio, and southeastern Michigan when first encountered by French explorers. In 1616, Samuel de Champlain reported them to be an agricultural people, powerful enough to put 4,000 warriors into the field. French missionaries labored among them as early as 1626. In 1640, tribes hostile to the French attempted to persuade the Neutrals to murder the missionaries, but the request was refused.

The Neutrals, who received that name because they declined to become involved in wars between the Iroquois and Hurons, may have signed their own death warrants by refusing to take the part of the latter. As soon as the Iroquois had defeated the Hurons, they turned on the Neutrals in 1650-51, utterly destroying them as a nation, and incorporating the survivors into the Seneca villages. A small remnant fled to the Carolinas and joined the Catawbas.

(George T. Hunt, The Wars of the Iroquois; F. W. Hodge, ed., Handbook of American Indians, II; John R. Swanton, Indian Tribes of North America.)

NEW AMSTERDAM. New Amsterdam was founded on Manhattan Island by the Dutch West India Company in July 1625. During the next decade, settlement expanded steadily, and most of the colonists engaged in trade with the Indians for furs and foodstuffs. (See MINUIT, PETER; MANHATTAN INDIANS.) In 1638, Director-General Willem Kieft instituted a harsh Indian policy, requiring the neighboring tribes to pay tribute, and reserving trading rights to the company. As a result, hostilities developed between Indians and settlers, and a sporadic state of warfare prevailed for the next six years, costing many lives and threatening the destruction of New Amsterdam. (See PAVONIA MASSACRES.) Hostilities ended in 1644-45 when chiefs of neighboring tribes assembled at New Amsterdam and pledged that their people would cease attacks on the settlers in exchange for a Dutch guarantee of Indian rights "to cultivate their fields in peace."

An uneasy peace prevailed at New Amsterdam until the outbreak of the Esopus War of 1655. Then on September 15, a large war party invaded New Amsterdam in 64 canoes, shot a settler to death in retaliation for his murder of an Indian woman for stealing peaches, and raced through the streets threatening to destroy the entire town. Dutch soldiers from Fort Amsterdam killed three of the hostiles and compelled the war party to retreat to their canoes. Afterward, the Indians paddled to Pavonia, killed numerous settlers, and captured most of the women and children. This conflict has become known as the Peach War.

With the fall of New Netherland to the English in 1664, New Amsterdam became New York City. Indian relations in the immediate area declined in importance, but a small illegal rum trade persisted throughout the remainder of the century.

(E. B. O'Callaghan, History of New Netherland, I-II; Allen W. Trelease, Indian Affairs in Colonial New York.)

NEW HAVEN COLONY. The New Haven colony was established in 1638 on the northern side of Long Island Sound by Puritans who had recently arrived in America. The region had been cleared of hostile Indians as a result of the Pequot War, and the newcomers recognized an opportunity to trade with the friendly tribes who remained. The first settlement was made on land purchased from the Quinnipiac Indians at the site of the present city of New Haven, Connecticut. Additional communities soon sprang up on both sides of the sound.

The principal founders, John Davenport and Theophilus Eaton, became disenchanted with prospects for the fur trade in the area by 1641 and began to acquire land along the Delaware River as a means of improving their prospects. Settlers from New Haven made trading expeditions to the Delaware that year, but they were driven away by their Dutch and Swedish competitors in 1642.

New Haven became a member of the United Colonies of New England in 1643. In 1664 it was absorbed by Connecticut.

(Neal Salisbury, Manitou and Providence; Alden T. Vaughan, New England Frontier; C. A. Weslager, The English on the Delaware.)

NEW YORK CITY see NEW AMSTERDAM

NEWTOWN, BATTLE OF. During Gen. John Sullivan's invasion of the Iroquois country in 1779, his march led him to Newtown, an Indian village near the present site of Elmira, New York. There Maj. John Butler awaited him in ambush on a ridge with 600 warriors and Tories. Butler and the Mohawk chief Joseph Brant realized that Sullivan's forces were too strong for them, but the Indians refused to consider a retreat.

As Sullivan approached on August 29, the Iroquois were concealed on a hilltop on his right. On his left, Brant and the Tory Rangers lay behind breastworks. The center was held by a few British soldiers and some Indians and Tories. Butler attempted to lure Sullivan into making a frontal assault, but the general held back his main force while he sent a brigade to make an enveloping movement. Meanwhile, he opened fire on the hill and the breastworks with cannon, compelling the Indians to abandon their strongest positions. Brant led an attack on the flanking brigade, but his poorly disciplined warriors gave way before bayonet charges by the American Regulars. Butler recognized the danger of envelopment and ordered a retreat. Warriors fled to their villages, and effective Iroquois resistance came to an end.

While the Battle of Newtown proved decisive, casualties were surprisingly limited. Sullivan had 5 men killed and 36 wounded, while Butler lost 5 rangers and 12 Indians.

(Barbara Graymont, The Iroquois in the American Revolution; Dale Van Every, A Company of Heroes.)

NIAGARA, FORTS. Niagara, on the border between New York and Ontario, was one of the most strategic sites during the struggle for control of the North American continent. The frontier historian Dale Van Every has written that "Fort Niagara, below the Falls, Little Fort Niagara, above the Falls, and the portage road that ran between the two forts comprised the indispensable link that connected the Atlantic ... and Oswego, with the immense trade empire of the Great Lakes region. That 14 miles of cart paths along the cliffs of the Niagara gorge was the geographical, military, and economic key to the northwest."

La Salle was the first European to recognize Niagara's importance to the fur trade. In 1679, he persuaded the Senecas to permit him to build a fortified post near the falls, but it was destroyed by fire less than a year later. In 1687, the marquis de Denonville erected a temporary post at the mouth of the Niagara River during his campaign against the western Iroquois. In 1720, Louis-Thomas de Joncaire, an adopted Seneca, persuaded that nation to permit the construction of a small fort at the lower end of the portage (present site of Lewiston, New York). Six years later, the French built Fort Niagara, a large stone structure at the juncture of the Niagara River with Lake Ontario (near the present Youngstown, New York).

Fort Niagara became increasingly important to the French as a center of Indian diplomacy and trade during the years immediately preceding the French and Indian War. Moreover, with the establishment of French fortifications on the Ohio, all troops, trade goods, and munitions shipped to the western country went by way of Niagara. From Niagara the French were able to maintain control of the western tribes and to influence even the Senecas for several years.

At the onset of the French and Indian War, the Seneca, Shawnee, and Delaware Indians congregated at Fort Niagara, where war parties were organized by the commandant and sent against the New York, Pennsylvania, and Virginia settlements. (See POUCHOT, FRANÇOIS.) The British determined in 1755 to eradicate this French and Indian stronghold, but the first attempt, by William Shirley, became sidetracked by supply and transportation problems. In the summer of 1759, however, an army of more than 3,000 British Regulars and colonial militiamen commanded by Gen. John Prideaux, and Iroquois warriors led by Sir William Johnson, besieged Fort Niagara. Prideaux was killed when one of his cannon burst, but Johnson took command, won a decisive victory over a relief force of French and Indians (see LA BELLE FAMILLE), and compelled Fort Niagara to surrender. The victory enabled the British to gain control of French posts farther west.

Fort Niagara played an important role in Pontiac's War, the American Revolution, and the War of 1812. In September 1763, Seneca Indian supporters of Pontiac ambushed a British army wagon train at the falls and massacred 72 soldiers. (See DEVIL'S HOLE MASSACRE.) After Pontiac's defeat, Sir William Johnson conducted a council at Fort Niagara in July 1764, with more than 2,000 Indians of a dozen tribes. Friendship was restored and land cessions negotiated.

During the American Revolution, Fort Niagara served the British as an Indian rallying point and an outfitting center for raids on the American settlements by John Butler, Guy Johnson, and Joseph Brant. After Gen. John Sullivan's invasion of the Iroquois country in 1779, the Indians took refuge at Niagara and organized war parties that preyed upon Pennsylvania and New York settlements. (See BRANT, JOSEPH.) After the war, Fort Niagara remained in British possession until turned over to the Americans in August 1796.

During the War of 1812, the British regained possession of Fort Niagara, capturing it on December 19, 1813, by charging through an unguarded gate. More than 60 Americans were killed and 350 captured. The Indian allies of the British seized Lewiston, got drunk on liquor stored there, and murdered several citizens.

Fort Niagara was restored to the United States by the Treaty of Ghent.

(Frank H. Severance, An Old Frontier of France; Arthur Pound, Johnson of the Mohawks; Dale Van Every, Forth to the Wilderness; Barbara Graymont, The Iroquois in the American Revolution; Howard H. Peckham, Pontiac and the Indian Uprising; Reginald Horsman, The War of 1812.)

NIANTIC INDIANS. The Niantic (Nehantic) Indians, a New England Algonquian tribe, were split into eastern and western branches when the powerful Pequot nation invaded their territory. The eastern branch lived in western Rhode Island and along the coast of Connecticut, while the western band occupied the coast from Niantic Bay to the Connecticut River. The two branches had little contact with each other when Europeans first entered the area.

The Pequot War had a devastating effect on the western Niantics. In 1634 they murdered a trader, Capt. John Stone, an act which led to English hostility toward their Pequot protectors. In the war that followed, the western Niantics were almost destroyed, and the survivors were assigned to the supervision of the Mohegan Indians. Some of their descendants joined the Brotherton Indians after the American Revolution, while others were absorbed by the Mohegans.

The eastern Niantics became close associates of the Narraganset Indians before King Philip's War of 1675-76. They took no part in the conflict, but they permitted Narraganset survivors to settle among them. Afterward, the tribes merged and the eastern Niantics became known as Narragansets.

(F. W. Hodge, ed., Handbook of American Indians, II; John R. Swanton, Indian Tribes of North America; William C. Sturtevant, ed., Handbook of North American Indians, XV; John W. De Forest, History of the Indians of Connecticut.)

NICELY, JACOB, CAPTIVITY OF. Jacob Nicely was captured at the age of five by Seneca Indians near his home in Westmoreland County, Pennsylvania. In 1828, after almost four decades of Jacob's captivity, his family learned that he was living on a Seneca reservation with an Indian wife. Almost completely assimilated, he refused at first to visit his aged mother, but relented and set out with his brother on the road to Pennsylvania. They had not gone far, however, when Jacob changed his mind and returned to the reservation. He agreed to make the trip the following summer, but failed to keep his promise and lived the rest of his days as an Indian.

(C. Hale Sipe, Indian Wars of Pennsylvania.)

NICOLAS, WYANDOT CHIEF. Nicolas (Orotony), a Wyandot (Huron) chief, became hostile to the French at Detroit and moved his village to Sandusky Bay in 1738. There he supported the English and permitted Pennsylvania traders to live in his village. In 1747, he seized five French traders, and, perhaps at the instigation of George Croghan, he condemned them to death. He attempted to unite the western tribes in a war against the French, and one of his supporters attacked Fort Miami. (See OLD BRITON.) The conspiracy failed however, and Nicolas burned his own village and fled to the White River. Little is known of his later life, but in 1779 he refused to participate in the British and Indian attack on Fort Laurens.

(R. David Edmunds, ed., American Indian Leaders; Howard H. Peckham, Pontiac and the Indian Uprising; Charles A. Hanna, The Wilderness Trail.)

NICOLET, JEAN. Jean Nicolet, one of North America's greatest explorers and Indian diplomats, was born at Cherbourg, France, about 1598. He sailed to Quebec in 1618 and was sent by Samuel de Champlain in 1620 to live with the Indians and learn their languages. After two years with the natives of Allumette Island, he accompanied 400 members of that tribe on a successful mission to make peace with the Iroquois. In 1624, he served as interpreter at a conference during which the Iroquois opted for peace with the French. His work was so highly regarded that Canadian officials appointed him interpreter for the Nipissing tribe. During nine years with that nation, Nicolet was elevated to chief, and he imposed extraordinary authority over the people.

While at home on Lake Nipissing, Nicolet received instructions from Champlain to explore the western country to the farthest reaches yet reported by Indians. His explorations were intended to expand the fur trade, and, if possible, to discover a passage to China. In 1634, accompanied by seven Huron warriors, he went by canoe to Georgian Bay, Mackinac, Lake Michigan, and Green Bay. Some historians believe that he explored the Fox River as far as the Mascouten Indian villages and completed his journey in Illinois. He returned to Canada by the same route, arriving at Quebec in 1635. Although his exploits have taken on the aura of folklore, a reliable Jesuit friend related that Nicolet negotiated peace between the Hurons and Winnebagos clad in such "a grand robe of China damask, all strewn with flowers and birds of many colors" and carrying "thunder in both hands--for thus they called the two pistols that he held." His appearance and demeanor drew more than 4,000 Indians to feast with him, and he brought peace negotiations to a successful conclusion.

"He was the first white man to set foot on what became, a century and a half later, the Northwest Territory, including the present states of Ohio, Indiana, Illinois, Michigan, Wisconsin, and that part of Minnesota lying east of the Mississippi River."--John Anthony Caruso.

After his journey, he served as interpreter at Three Rivers. In 1641, he negotiated peace with the Iroquois. The following year he was drowned at Sillery when his boat capsized in a storm while on a mission to redeem an Abnaki Indian from captivity.

(John Gilmary Shea, Discovery and Exploration of the Mississippi Valley; Edna Kenton, ed., Black Gown and Redskins; Louise Phelps Kellogg, ed., Early Narratives of the Northwest; The French Régime in Wisconsin and the Northwest; John Anthony Caruso, The Mississippi Valley Frontier.)

NIMHAM, DANIEL, WAPPINGER CHIEF. Daniel Nimham (Ninham) was born about 1710 and became chief of the Wappingers in 1740. In 1755, he and most of his warriors enlisted in Sir William Johnson's Indian forces to fight for the British during the French and Indian War. In 1762, he went to England to protest that Wappinger lands on the east side of the Hudson River had been seized by white settlers. His charges received a sympathetic hearing, and British officials promised restitution, but when he returned to New York he found colonial authorities reluctant to rectify the situation.

Hoping to gain favor with the Americans, Nimham led his warriors to battle the British during the Revolutionary War. They fought valiantly at Cortland's Ridge on August 30, 1778, and Nimham was killed the following day during the Battle of Kingsbridge.

(Frederick J. Dockstader, Great North American Indians; F. W. Hodge, ed., Handbook of American Indians, II.)

NINIGRET, NIANTIC CHIEF. Ninigret, an important Niantic chief, has remained a controversial figure in New England history for more than three centuries. Born about 1600, he became a chief at Wekapaug (present Westerly, Rhode Island) at an early age and demonstrated such diplomatic skills that he was able to retain his territory throughout his long life.

While striving to remain at peace with the English, Ninigret became a powerful leader in intertribal warfare. Neutral during the war between Pequots and Narragansets of 1632, he was charged by the Mohegan chief Uncas with harboring fugitive Pequots. A cousin and ally of the Narraganset chief Miantonomo, he went to war against the Mohegans after Uncas executed that powerful sachem in 1643. The English supporters of Uncas compelled Ninigret to sign a peace treaty in 1647.

Between 1647 and 1654, New England colonial leaders listened
to constant complaints by Indians and settlers that Ninigret was
conspiring to resurrect the hostile Pequot nation, to assassinate
Uncas, to arouse the Mohawks against them, and to provoke a war
between the Dutch and the English. He made frequent trips to Boston to plead his innocence, but little credence was placed in his pleas.
When he was late in paying tribute exacted upon his tribe, colonial
forces went to his village to collect it and to threaten him with death
if he failed to mend his ways. Finally, in 1654, Maj. Simon Willard
and more than 300 men seized Ninigret and threatened to have "his
head sett up upon an English pole." Willard forced the chief to sign
a new peace treaty, but only the presence of a New England coastal
patrol compelled him to keep the agreement.

Ninigret was an enemy of Metacom the Wampanoag chief, and refused to support him against the English during King Philip's War.
He sought the role of mediator, but never received the opportunity
to use his diplomatic skills to bring an end to the war.

After peace was restored in New England, several attempts
were made to convert Ninigret to Christianity, but he refused to consider it until "whites learned to behave in a Christ-like manner."
He died unconverted in 1678.

"In his dealings with the English he ... never kept his agreements ... unless he was actually forced to do so. He was proud,
self-seeking, and always went about with a chip on his shoulder."--
Herbert Milton Sylvester.

"... he seems to have preserved his pride, of which he possessed an inordinate amount, and his property as well, without being
obliged to fight for either."--Alexander F. Chamberlain.

"... he managed to establish irregularly peaceful relationships
with the Whites for most of his life. Owing to the times, and the in-
cessant hostilities between the colonists and ... the tribes ... this
balance was achieved only by dextrous diplomacy."--Frederick J.
Dockstader.

(Frederick J. Dockstader, Great North American Indians; F. W.
Hodge, ed., Handbook of American Indians, II; Herbert Milton Syl-
vester, Indian Wars of New England, I; Alden T. Vaughan, New
England Frontier; Douglas Edward Leach, Flintlock and Tomahawk.)

NINIVOIS, FOX CHIEF. Ninivois, who was born about 1740, was an
ardent supporter of Pontiac. In 1763, he played an important part
in Pontiac's siege of Detroit.

(Dictionary of Indians of North America, II; Howard H. Peckham, Pontiac and the Indian Uprising.)

NIPMUC INDIANS. The Nipmuc Indians, an Algonquian tribe, resided in scattered villages in Rhode Island, eastern Connecticut, and
central Massachusetts before King Philip's War. Many of them became converts to Christianity, living in so-called "praying villages."
Dominated by the more numerous Narragansets, they supported that
nation against the English during King Philip's War, and one of their
bands attacked Mendon, Massachusetts, on July 14, 1675, murdering

several settlers. After the war, they fled to Canada or took refuge with tribes on the Hudson River. Some of them settled eventually with remnants of other tribes at the Christian town of Scaticook, in New York.

(John W. De Forest, History of the Indians of Connecticut; Douglas Edward Leach, Flintlock and Tomahawk; John R. Swanton, Indian Tribes of North America; Alden T. Vaughan, New England Frontier.)

NISSOWAQUET, OTTAWA CHIEF. Nissowaquet (LaFourche), an Ottawa chief who lived at Mackinac, was a staunch enemy of the English during the French and Indian War. A brother-in-law of Charles Michel de Langlade, he is believed to have accompanied that French partisan in the attack on Braddock's army and in other battles and raids.

(F. W. Hodge, ed., Handbook of American Indians, II.)

NOQUET INDIANS. The Noquet Indians, an Algonquian tribe or band affiliated with the Chippewas, lived in northern Michigan when first encountered by early French explorers. In 1659, they were congregated at the mission of St. Michel in southern Wisconsin. Never prominent in frontier history they probably were absorbed soon afterward by the Chippewas or the Menominees.

(John R. Swanton, Indian Tribes of North America.)

NORMAN'S KILL, TREATY OF. The Treaty of Norman's Kill was negotiated by the Dutch with the Iroquois near the present site of Albany, New York, in January 1618. Providing for peace and alliance, it remained in effect until the English acquired New York.

(E. B. O'Callaghan, History of New Netherland, I.)

NORRIDGEWOCK INDIANS. The Norridgewock Indians, an Abnaki subdivision, occupied the Kennebec Valley at the time of initial European contact. Their principal village was located near the present site of Norridgewock, Maine. A powerful and warlike people, they proved to be among the most formidable foes of the New England colonists.

In 1607, George Popham established a colony at the mouth of the Kennebec and traded with the Indians, but he died the following year and the English abandoned the area. In 1688, the French established a mission at Norridgewock and the tribe supported them in their rivalry with the English. Father Sebastian Rasles, in particular, exerted tremendous influence over the tribe, and English officials were convinced that he incited the Indians to attack the Massachusetts settlements.

In 1705, Col. Winthrop Hilton led 270 New England frontiersmen in a retaliatory raid against Norridgewock, found the village deserted, and burned it. The Indians rebuilt it soon afterward and enclosed it in a tall and sturdy stockade. The mission was reconstructed outside the enclosure. The Norridgewocks, fearing another English invasion, halted hostilities until abuse by unscrupulous rum traders and land-hungry settlers aroused renewed attacks on the New England settlements. In 1721, they destroyed 26 isolated settlers' cabins. Soon afterward, Col. Thomas Westbrook led 300 men to Norridgewock and attempted to capture Father Rasles, but he escaped into the woods. This expedition infuriated the Indians, and they retaliated by burning the village of Brunswick, capturing 9 English families.

The final destruction of Norridgewock occurred on August 23, 1724, when Capt. Jeremiah Moulton surprised the town with 80 experienced Indian fighters. They killed and scalped Father Rasles and put the Indians to flight, many of whom drowned while attempting to swim the river to safety. (See RASLES, SEBASTIAN; MOGG.) The survivors fled to St. Francis in Canada.

A few Indians returned to Norridgewock, but they were attacked by the colonists in 1749. At the onset of the French and Indian War, the remnant resettled at St. Francis.

(Jeremy Belknap, History of New Hampshire, I; Francis Parkman, A Half-Century of Conflict; Herbert Milton Sylvester, Indian Wars of New England, III; F. W. Hodge, ed., Handbook of American Indians, II.)

NOYELLES, NICOLAS JOSEPH DE, EXPEDITION. In 1735, Capt. Nicolas Joseph de Noyelles led 80 Frenchmen and several hundred friendly Indians across the Mississippi to attack a band of hostile Sauk and Fox Indians. On April 19, they located the enemy village near the Des Moines River and besieged it for four days. Out of rations, the French and their Indian allies were at the point of starvation, and as the defenders gave no indication that they would surrender, Noyelles called off the attack upon their agreement to return in peace to their former homes at Green Bay. The promise was not kept, however, and "the battle proved nothing save the endurance and intrepidity of the French."--John Anthony Caruso.

(John Anthony Caruso, The Mississippi Valley Frontier.)

NUMBER FOUR, NEW HAMPSHIRE. Number Four, a fort located near the present site of Charlestown, New Hampshire, was settled in 1740 by colonists from Massachusetts. The northernmost outpost on the Connecticut River, it was far removed from the settlements below and exposed to attacks by the French and Indians. A small garrison of Massachusetts soldiers manned the 180-foot-square stockade, and about a dozen families lived nearby.

Fort Number Four was attacked by the French and Indians on April 19, 1746, and four other times during May and June. The able commander Capt. Phineas Stevens repelled the invaders with small loss of life, but most of the settlement's livestock was stolen. In April 1747, the French and Indians returned, 400 strong, besieged the fort for three days, and were prevented from burning it only by the courage of defenders who crawled outside the walls and extinguished the flames. After two demands to surrender were refused, the attackers abandoned the siege and retreated from the area.

(Jeremy Belknap, History of New Hampshire, I; Francis Parkman, A Half-Century of Conflict; Herbert Milton Sylvester, Indian Wars of New England, III.)

NUTIMUS, DELAWARE CHIEF. Nutimus, a prominent eighteenth-
century Delaware chief, was born in New Jersey but moved to the
Lehigh Valley of Pennsylvania at an early age. Friendly to the
Quaker settlers, he adopted many of their ways, learned the blacksmith trade, and used his knowledge of native medicine to cure Indians and settlers alike. Angered by the duplicity of Thomas Penn
(see WALKING PURCHASE), he abandoned his home and established
Nutimus Town on the North Branch of the Susquehanna River in
1737. There he lived in a large house with five sons and their families, attended by five black servants, until the French and Indian
War. He moved to Canisteo, New York, to avoid being embroiled in
the conflict, and afterward, to the West Branch of the Susquehanna
during Pontiac's War.
    (Paul A. W. Wallace, Indians in Pennsylvania.)

-O-

O'BAIL, JOHN see CORNPLANTER, SENECA CHIEF

O'BEAL, JOHN see ABEEL, JOHN

OCCOM, SAMSON, MOHEGAN CLERGYMAN. Samson Occom, a Mohegan Indian, was born in 1723 at New London, Connecticut. He was
educated by Rev. Eleazar Wheelock and lived with Wheelock's family
for three years. Converted to Christianity in 1741, he prepared
himself through the study of English, Latin, Greek, and Hebrew for
a career as a teacher and missionary to the Indian nations. After
teaching briefly at New London, he went to Long Island to serve as
religious instructor to the Montauk Indians. There he married Mary
Montauk (Fowler), and they had 10 children. For a decade he supported his family by hunting and fishing, repairing guns, binding
books, and making wooden spoons and churns. Meanwhile, he converted many Montauks to Christianity. On August 29, 1759, he was
ordained by the Suffolk Presbytery of Long Island.
    Occom's life took a dramatic turn in 1765 when he was selected
to sail to England to help raise money to support Wheelock's Indian
Charity School. The first Indian ever to preach in England, his
appearance aroused great interest and approbation. John W. De
Forest, historian of the Connecticut Indians, has noted that in 1766
and 1767 "he delivered between three and four hundred sermons.
Large contributions were taken up after his discourses; the king
himself ... gave 200 pounds; and, in the whole enterprise, seven
thousand pounds were collected in England, and two or three thousand in Scotland. The success of this attempt resulted in trans-
ferring Wheelock's school to New Hampshire.... It was there incorporated as Dartmouth College...."
    Returning to America, Occom traveled among New England
tribes, teaching the way to the white man's religion and civilization.
In 1773, he was instrumental in removing New England Indians to a
reservation in New York State. After the American Revolution, he

served as minister to the Brotherton Indians. He died at New Stockbridge, New York, on August 2, 1792.

(John W. De Forest, History of the Indians of Connecticut;
Frederick J. Dockstader, Great North American Indians.)

OGDEN LAND PURCHASES. David A. Ogden, who had obtained the
preemptive rights to western New York lands formerly held by the
government of Massachusetts, was an early nineteenth-century advocate of Iroquois removal to the West. In 1819, he attempted unsuccessfully to secure the removal of the Senecas. In 1826 and 1838,
however, the Ogden Company purchased from the Senecas and other
New York Iroquois most of their lands in the state. The Senecas
retained their Allegheny and Cattaraugas reservations.

(J. P. Kinney, A Continent Lost--A Civilization Won.)

OGDENSBURG, NEW YORK see LA PRESENTATION; OSWEGATCHIE

OGHWAGA see OQUAGA

OHIO COMPANY OF VIRGINIA. The Ohio Company of Virginia was
organized in 1747 to profit from Indian trade and land speculation.
The crown granted the company 500,000 acres in 1749. In 1750 and
1751, Christopher Gist explored the Ohio Valley and established
friendly relations with the Indians. In 1752, at the Treaty of Logstown, the tribes confirmed the deed to the territory granted by the
Iroquois at the Treaty of Lancaster, agreed to permit the company
to build a fort at the forks of the Ohio, and promised to protect it.
The fort was captured by the French in 1754, however, and the ensuing French and Indian War prevented the company from achieving
its goals. (See TRENT, WILLIAM.)

(Kenneth P. Bailey, The Ohio Company of Virginia; Clarence
Walworth Alvord, The Mississippi Valley and British Politics; Randolph
C. Downes, Council Fires on the Upper Ohio.)

OJAGEGHT, CAYUGA CHIEF see FISH CARRIER, CAYUGA CHIEF

OJIBWA INDIANS see CHIPPEWA INDIANS

OLD BRITON, MIAMI CHIEF. Old Briton (La Demoiselle), chief of
a Miami village located in northwestern Indiana, was a leader in the
Indian movement to abandon the French interest and to become English supporters in order to enhance trade opportunities. An ally of
the Wyandot chief Nicolas, he participated in a conspiracy to massacre
French troops and traders in 1747 by attacking Fort Miami and capturing eight soldiers. In 1748, he established a village, Pickawillanee,
on the Miami River (present site of Piqua, Ohio). By 1750, George
Croghan and other Pennsylvania traders had establishments at the
village, and their superior trade goods attracted increasing numbers
of Indians to the English interest.

The French and their Indian allies made several attempts to
capture Old Briton and to destroy Pickawillanee. As a result of one

such attack in 1751, Old Briton became so enraged that he condemned three of his French prisoners to death and cut off the ears
of a fourth to be sent as a warning to Canadian officials.

In 1752, the prominent French partisan Charles de Langlade
attacked Pickawillanee with 240 warriors. Old Briton and a few followers put up a stiff resistance, but badly outnumbered, he eventually agreed to a parley. Langlade demanded that he surrender in return for a guarantee of safety for members of his family. Reluctantly, Old Briton surrendered and was immediately killed. Langlade's
warriors boiled his body and ate it as a warning to his people to
return to the French interest.

(Bert Anson, The Miami Indians; R. David Edmunds, ed.,
American Indian Leaders.)

OLDHAM, JOHN. John Oldham, a sea captain and trader, was expelled from the Plymouth Colony in 1624 for "plotting and writing
against the Colony and attempting to excite a sedition." In 1625,
he returned to Plymouth to visit his wife and children and, as related by William Bradford, they "appointed a gard of musketers wch
he was to pass throw, and ever one was ordered to give him a
thump on ye brich, with ye but end of his musket, and then was
conveied to ye water side, wher a boat was ready to cary him away."

After living for brief periods at Nantasket and Watertown, Oldham joined Richard Vines in establishing a settlement in 1630 on the
Saco River in Maine. In 1633, he explored the Connecticut River,
traded with the Indians for beaver skins, and interested Plymouth
leaders in establishing a trading post in that region. Afterward,
he settled with his family at Dorchester and made regular voyages
along the coast to trade with the Indians.

In 1636, the Narraganset chief Canonicus gave Oldham an island in Narragansett Bay on condition that he establish a trading
post there. But before he could do so, he made a voyage to trade
with the Pequot tribe. This expedition angered Indian enemies of
the Pequots, and during his return journey, the natives of Block
Island boarded his boat, tomahawked him, and captured two boys who
constituted his entire crew. Canonicus redeemed the boys and returned them to their homes. Oldham's death was revenged by another trader who discovered his body in his drifting boat. (See
GALLOP, JOHN.) The murder was a contributing factor to the
Pequot War.

(Herbert Milton Sylvester, Indian Wars of New England, I;
John W. De Forest, History of the Indians of Connecticut; William
Bradford, Of Plimoth Plantation.)

ONANGIZES, POTAWATOMI CHIEF. Onangizes (Shimmering Light of
the Sun) was an important seventeenth-century Potawatomi chief.
He probably was Nicolas Perrot's guide during the Frenchman's explorations in 1668. He persuaded the Potawatomis to trade with the
French, made frequent trips to Montreal as the tribe's envoy, and
wore a medal presented by Governor Frontenac. He established a
center of trade at Rock Island, greeted La Salle there in 1679, and

assisted La Salle's followers who had fled from the Iroquois in 1680.
In 1694, he arranged for tribes of the Great Lakes region to make
an alliance with the French.

(James A. Clifton, The Prairie People.)

O'NEAL MASSACRE. In February 1812, the Kickapoo Indians massacred 10 members of the O'Neal family at their farm near Peoria,
Illinois. They desecrated the bodies and burned every building on
the property. The tragedy so terrified residents of the area that most
of them fled to the east. Gov. Ninian Edwards reported that the
chiefs openly boasted of the deed, but he lacked sufficient troops to
punish them.

(A. M. Gibson, The Kickapoos.)

ONEIDA INDIANS. The Oneida Indians, the least numerous tribe of
the League of the Iroquois, occupied a single village during historic
times. It was moved from the headwaters of Oneida and Oriskany
creeks to the vicinity of Oneida Lake. It is estimated that the Oneidas had fewer than a hundred warriors, but they raided and hunted
over a vast territory from the St. Lawrence to the Susquehanna.
Warfare continually reduced their population, and they replenished it
by adopting captured Algonquians and Hurons and by incorporating
remnants of tribes into the nation. When the Tuscaroras moved from
North Carolina to become the Sixth Nation, they settled on Oneida
lands, and according to Allen W. Trelease, "they were as much an
adjunct to the Oneida as they were an equal member of the confederacy."

The Oneidas joined their Mohawk neighbors in attacking the
French and Algonquians during the first half of the seventeenth
century. They usually enjoyed amicable relations with the Dutch
and the English, and quickly became dependent upon them for European trade goods. During the latter half of the century, they experienced periods of peace with the French, and in 1667, they permitted a Jesuit missionary to live among them (see BRUYAS, JAMES).
By 1687, however, they were firmly in the English camp, and Gov.
Thomas Dongan of New York granted them protection as subjects of
Great Britain. In 1696, Count Frontenac sent a detachment to
Oneida to destroy habitations, cattle, and crops, and the French
made prisoners of 35 members of the tribe.

The Oneidas attempted to maintain neutrality during the French
and Indian War. But strong pressure to take sides was applied by
both combatants, and at last, they reluctantly consented to become
British allies. This decision resulted in disaster for the tribe, for
in addition to the ravages of war they suffered greatly from famine.

In 1764, a Presbyterian missionary, Samuel Kirkland, began
living with the Oneidas, and he soon gained tremendous influence
over the tribe. With the Revolutionary War on the horizon, Kirkland,
a fiery American patriot, contested with Sir William Johnson for
Oneida allegiance. Johnson demanded Kirkland's expulsion, but the
Oneidas refused. As most of the Six Nations were firmly in the
British interest, the refusal of the Oneidas to join them led to dissolution of the League of the Iroquois.

The Oneidas proved to be valuable allies during the Revolution. They kept the Americans informed of hostile Iroquois movements, and they formed a contingent of General Herkimer's army that fought the British and Indians during Barry St. Leger's invasion of 1777. (See ORISKANY, BATTLE OF.) In 1780, the British and Tories destroyed the Oneida village. As a result, some of the starving Indians fled to Schenectady, while others joined Iroquois British supporters at Niagara.

At the end of the war, the Oneidas rebuilt their village, and as a reward for their services, Congress guaranteed them possession of their lands at the Treaty of Fort Stanwix of 1784. New York authorities sought to open their territory to white settlement, however, and negotiated a series of land cession treaties with the tribe. In 1816, many Christian Oneidas moved to Green Bay, Wisconsin, where they eventually received lands in severalty. In 1838, the Treaty of Buffalo required all Iroquois still living in New York to remove to Kansas, but the Oneidas refused. A few removed to Canada, while those remaining in New York were allotted lands in severalty in 1843.

(William C. Sturtevant, ed., Handbook of North American Indians, XV; Cadwallader Colden, The History of the Five Indian Nations; Barbara Graymont, The Iroquois in the American Revolution; Allen W. Trelease, Indian Affairs in Colonial New York; T. Wood Clarke, The Bloody Mohawk.)

ONEKA, MOHEGAN CHIEF. Oneka, son of the famous Mohegan chief Uncas, fought on the side of the New England colonists during King Philip's War. In 1675, at the urging of Uncas, he led 50 warriors to Boston to volunteer their services. They were at Rehoboth, Massachusetts, when Philip escaped from his Mount Hope hiding place, and they almost captured the Wampanoag chief. Oneka participated in the destruction of the Narraganset stronghold in the Great Swamp Fight on December 19, 1675.

(Douglas Edward Leach, Flintlock and Tomahawk; F. W. Hodge, ed., Handbook of American Indians, II.)

ONONDAGA INDIANS. The Onondaga Indians, a powerful and warlike Iroquois tribe, were located in the Onondaga Valley of northern New York during the seventeenth century. Their hunting grounds extended from the eastern shores of Lake Ontario to the Susquehanna River. At the time of first European contact, they could send 300 warriors against their enemies.

As the central nation of the League of the Iroquois and the keeper of its ceremonial fire, Onondaga occupied a strategic position during the Indian wars of the region as well as the rivalry among European nations for control of the continent. Onondaga chiefs were under pressure from all sides, and seldom was the nation united in its relations with the French or the English. This ambivalence kept them at risk of attacks by French, English, and American armies.

In 1615, Samuel de Champlain besieged Onondaga, arousing hostility against the French that prevailed for many years. In 1653, however, the Onondagas made peace with the French in order to wage war on neighboring tribes, and at that time they permitted the establishment of a mission in their principal town. Eager also for the establishment of a French settlement to protect them against their Erie Indian enemies, they allowed the Jesuit fathers Claude Dablon and Joseph Marie Chaumont, 2 lay brothers, 10 soldiers, and 40 settlers to build the St. Jean the Baptist mission and a settlement surrounded by a stockade. By 1658, however, the Eries had been defeated, and the Onondagas no longer valued the presence of a French settlement among them. Hostility became increasingly evident, and a Christian Indian warned the French to flee for their lives. In the loft of the mission, therefore, the Frenchmen built six boats, stocked them with provisions, and launched them into the lake one night while the Indians were enjoying a banquet. Several weeks later, they arrived safely at Quebec.

During their brief labors at Onondaga, the priests had gained a sufficient number of converts to create a pro-French tribal faction, and as a result, the Indians requested missionaries to return. In 1661, therefore, the Onondaga mission was reestablished. (See LE MOYNE, SIMON; GARAKONTHIE, DANIEL; LAMBERVILLE, JEAN DE.) It was abandoned in 1687 because of a war between the French and the Senecas.

In 1689, Governor Frontenac led a large expedition of Frenchmen and Indians to punish the Onondagas for their hostilities. The Onondagas abandoned their town, and the invaders burned the village and destroyed its food supply. When peace was restored in 1701, the Jesuit mission was opened once more, but it was abandoned eight years later.

During the late 1740's, about half of the Onondagas moved to the mission at La Présentation. They fought against the English in the French and Indian War, while members of the tribe remaining at Onondaga attempted to maintain neutrality.

During the American Revolution, the Onondagas split into three factions--neutrals, pro-Americans, and pro-British. In 1779, the Americans destroyed Onondaga (see VAN SCHAICK, GOOSE), and consequently, most of the survivors fled to Niagara to join the British. In retaliation, they wiped out the settlement of Cobleskill, New York.

After the Revolution, many Onondagas removed to Canada, while those remaining in New York were assigned reservations. In 1788, they ceded most of their land, but a significant number still live near Syracuse, New York.

(William C. Sturtevant, ed., Handbook of Indians of North America, XV; Barbara Graymont, The Iroquois in the American Revolution; Allen W. Trelease, Indian Affairs in Colonial New York; T. Wood Clarke, The Bloody Mohawk; Cadwallader Colden, The History of the Five Indian Nations.)

ONTARIO, FORT, TREATY OF. Fort Ontario, built by the British just east of Fort Oswego in 1755, was the scene of Pontiac's final agreement to make peace with British officials. In July 1766, after conferring with Sir William Johnson, he addressed a conference of Indian and white negotiators, promised to live in peace, and agreed to use his influence to persuade other hostile Indians to bury the hatchet. A peace treaty was signed, the chiefs received presents, and the Indians departed for their villages.

(Howard H. Peckham, Pontiac and the Indian War.)

OQUAGA, IROQUOIS VILLAGE. Oquaga (Ouquaga, Oghwaga), a large and prosperous Iroquois village, was located on the east branch of the Susquehanna River in Broome County, New York. It was the site of Sir William Johnson's highly successful trade headquarters for many years. Some 750 Indians, mainly Mohawks, lived there at the close of the French and Indian War.

At the onset of the American Revolution, Oquaga provided a rallying point for Tories and hostile Indians. (See HARPER, JOHN.) In 1777, Joseph Brant assembled 700 warriors there and led them against the Susquehanna and Unadilla settlements. In October 1778, while the warriors were away, Col. William Butler's American army destroyed Oquaga.

(T. Wood Clarke, The Bloody Mohawk; Arthur Pound, Johnson of the Mohawks; Dale Van Every, A Company of Heroes.)

ORANGE, FORT. Fort Orange was built at the present site of Albany, New York, in 1624 by representatives of the Dutch West India Company. A village named Beverwyck developed around the fort and quickly evolved into a major fur trading center. The Dutch traded firearms to the Iroquois that enabled them to terrorize the French and their Indian allies.

On August 30, 1645, Willem Kieft, director-general of New Netherland, negotiated an important peace treaty at Fort Orange with neighboring tribes, ending an Indian war that had lasted five years. In 1664, the English captured Fort Orange. (See ALBANY, NEW YORK.)

(E. B. O'Callaghan, History of New Netherland, I; Allen W. Trelease, Indian Affairs in Colonial New York.)

ORATAMIN, HACKENSACK CHIEF. Oratamin, an important Hackensack chief, played major roles in restoring peace between New York Indian tribes and Dutch settlers. In 1643, he represented several tribes during peace negotiations that concluded hostilities that had begun with the Pavonia Massacres. (See NEW AMSTERDAM.) War erupted again soon afterward, however, and Oratamin led negotiations that restored peace on August 13, 1645. In 1655, a major conflict erupted between the Dutch and the Esopus Indians. Oratamin served as an intermediary, and in 1663 the bloody war ended. (See ESOPUS INDIANS.) Oratamin died about 1667.

(F. W. Hodge, ed., Handbook of American Indians, I; Allen W. Trelease, Indian Affairs in Colonial New York.)

ORDWAY, JOANNA, CAPTIVITY OF. Joanna Ordway, aged 18, was captured by Abnaki Indians at Haverhill, Massachusetts, in 1704. For several years she roamed the wilderness with her captors. In the spring of 1707, a party of Deerfield scouts opened fire on the band and wounded Joanna. A scout rushed forward to scalp her and was startled to see that she was a white woman. She scrambled out of his grasp and fled into the woods. Soon afterward, she must have married an Indian, for she had a half-blood child named Marguerite Abenaki, who was baptized by a Catholic priest on June 22, 1710. She lived in Montreal in 1713.

(Emma Lewis Coleman, New England Captives Carried to Canada.)

OREHAOUE, CAYUGA CHIEF. Orehaoue, a seventeenth-century Cayuga war chief, violently opposed Christianity. To a considerable extent he prevented Father Etienne de Carheil from converting Cayugas during many years of missionary activity. In 1687, he was captured by the Denonville expedition and sent to France as a galley slave. Returning to America in 1689, while on shipboard he was befriended by Governor Frontenac. Afterward, he became a French ally and a Christian, and on his deathbed in 1698 he informed his confessor that "if he had been present when Christ was crucified he would have revenged him by lifting the scalps of the Jews."

(Francis Parkman, Count Frontenac and New France Under Louis XIV; F. W. Hodge, ed., Handbook of American Indians, II.)

ORISKANY, BATTLE OF. The Battle of Oriskany, one of the bloodiest of the American Revolution, was fought on August 6, 1777, near Fort Stanwix, New York. When British colonel Barry St. Leger, besieging the Americans at Stanwix, learned that Gen. Nicholas Herkimer was marching to the relief of the fort with 800 militiamen, he sent the Mohawk chief Joseph Brant and Sir John Johnson with 400 Indians and 80 Tories to intercept them.

Brant and Johnson prepared an ambush in a ravine two miles west of Oriskany Creek. They opened fire on the column as it entered the trap, killing most of Herkimer's officers at the beginning of the battle. Herkimer's rear guard fled from the scene, many of the terror-stricken militia pulled down by pursuing Mohawks. The 500 men of the main column, caught in the trap, fired from behind trees and engaged the enemy in hand-to-hand combat, sustaining heavy losses until a cloudburst interrupted the action.

During the interval, Herkimer ordered his men into formation on high ground. Severely wounded, he lighted his pipe and sat with his back to a tree while directing such a spirited defense that the Indians withdrew from the battle. The British soon followed suit, and the Patriots retained possession of the field. But their losses were so severe, almost 500 men having been killed, wounded, or captured, that they abandoned the attempt to relieve the fort. The Tories and Indians had 33 men killed and 29 wounded.

(T. Wood Clarke, The Bloody Mohawk; Barbara Graymont, The Iroquois in the American Revolution; Dale Van Every, A Company of Heroes.)

ORONO, PENOBSCOT CHIEF. Orono, a devout Roman Catholic of mixed French-Abnaki ancestry, lived a life of obscurity until his old age. During the French and Indian War, he attempted to keep his people at peace, but when the English declared war upon the Abnakis he participated in raids on the New England settlements. At the onset of the American Revolution, he adopted the cause of the colonists and assisted them in their fight for independence. After the war, he sold several land tracts to the whites. It is believed that he was 108 years old when he died on February 5, 1802.

(F. W. Hodge, ed., Handbook of American Indians, I.)

ORONTONY, WYANDOT CHIEF see NICOLAS, WYANDOT CHIEF

OSAMEQUIN, WAMPANOAG CHIEF see MASSASOIT, WAMPANOAG CHIEF

OSHKOSH, MENOMINEE CHIEF. Born near Green Bay in 1795, Oshkosh became a formidable warrior who fought for the British in the War of 1812 and for the Americans in the Black Hawk War. As a 17-year-old, he joined Col. Robert Dickson's British Indian forces that captured Mackinac in July 1812. Afterward, he fought American troops at Fort Sandusky and elsewhere.

Oshkosh was designated principal chief of the Menominees in 1827 by U.S. Indian agent Lewis Cass, as the tribe lacked a leader to negotiate the Treaty of Butte des Morts. After becoming reconciled to United States control of the Great Lakes region, he signed a treaty in 1848 that ceded the tribe's land in Wisconsin. (See LAKE POW-AW-HAY-KON-NAY, TREATY OF.)

Oshkosh was addicted to alcohol, and he died in a brawl that followed a drinking bout on August 30, 1858.

(Frederick J. Dockstader, Great North American Indians; F. W. Hodge, ed., Handbook of American Indians, II.)

OSWEGATCHIE, IROQUOIS TOWN. Located at the present site of Ogdensburg, New York, Oswegatchie was a Christian Iroquois village that became increasingly important in frontier history when the Abbé Picquet established the mission La Présentation there in 1748. During the French and Indian War, the town's 3,000 residents supported the French against their Iroquois kinsmen.

During the Revolutionary War, the people of Oswegatchie, greatly reduced in number by smallpox, fought on the side of the British. Eventually, the survivors were absorbed by the Onondagas at St. Regis. (See LA PRESENTATION.)

(Frank H. Severance, An Old Frontier of France, I; F. W. Hodge, ed., Handbook of American Indians, II.)

OSWEGO, NEW YORK. In 1722, English traders established Oswego on the south shore of Lake Ontario in an attempt to seize the fur trade that had been going to the French at Niagara. The enterprise proved to be highly successful, and within a short time 150 traders congregated there, many of them standing on the beach waving rum bottles to induce passing Indians to paddle to shore.

In 1724, the Iroquois, concerned that the French at Niagara

held too much power, agreed as a counterbalance to permit Gov. William Burnet of New York to build an English fort at Oswego. The French protested but failed to take action to prevent construction of Fort Oswego, a sturdy stone structure that Arthur Pound has characterized as "a hinge on which the fate of empire creaked through a half-century of crisis." Oswego not only provided an observation point for detecting French military transport, but it "gave directly on Nature's best fur farm, the ... triangle between the Mississippi and the St. Lawrence." In fact, Francis Parkman observed, "Oswego became the great centre of Indian trade while Niagara, in spite of its more favorable position, was comparatively slighted by the Western tribes."

During the French and Indian War, Gen. Joseph de Montcalm captured Oswego on October 14, 1756. After the American troops surrendered, Indian allies of the French attempted to massacre them, but Montcalm ordered his troops to fire upon his own warriors to save the lives of the prisoners. Afterward, he destroyed Oswego, informing the Iroquois that the English had intended the post as a means of their subjugation.

In 1759, the British regained possession of Oswego, and Sir William Johnson used the reconstructed fort as a staging ground for almost a thousand Indians in preparation for the Niagara campaign. After his departure to join the British Army, the small force left at Oswego under Gen. Frederick Haldimand withstood a French and Indian attack. In 1760, numerous Iroquois chiefs negotiated peace with the British at Oswego.

During the early years of the Revolutionary War, Oswego served as a major British stronghold. In 1777, Col. Barry St. Leger used the fort as a base during his invasion of the Mohawk Valley. In July 1778, however, American troops from Fort Stanwix found the post unguarded and destroyed it.

During the War of 1812, Oswego was captured once more by the British.

(Arthur Pound, Johnson of the Mohawks; Francis Parkman, A Half-Century of Conflict; T. Wood Clarke, The Bloody Mohawk; William C. Eccles, The Canadian Frontier; Louis Antoine de Bougainville, Adventures in the Wilderness.)

OTREOUATI, ONONDAGA CHIEF   see   GRANGULA, ONONDAGA CHIEF

OTSINOGHIYATA, ONONDAGA CHIEF. Otsinoghiyata (The Bunt) was a principal chief of the Onondaga nation. An ally of Sir William Johnson's, he assisted him at numerous conferences with the Iroquois and signed the Treaty of Fort Stanwix in 1768.

(Arthur Pound, Johnson of the Mohawks; F. W. Hodge, ed., Handbook of American Indians, II.)

OTSIQUETTE, PETER, ONEIDA CHIEF. Peter Otsiquette, a well-educated Oneida chief who signed the Treaty of 1788, visited France and called upon the Marquis de Lafayette. He died at Philadelphia in 1792 while attending a conference with United States officials, and he was buried there with military honors.

(F. W. Hodge, ed., Handbook of American Indians, II.)

OTTAWA INDIANS. The Ottawa Indians, an important Algonquian tribe, lived in Canada at the time of initial European contact. Samuel de Champlain, who met them in 1615, considered them to be "great warriors, hunters, and fishermen." Firm friends of the French from earliest times, they moved to the Great Lakes area and supplanted the Hurons as middlemen in the early fur trade. In 1665, Father Claude Allouez established the mission of St. Esprit for them at Chaquamegon Bay, where he converted one band to Christianity, but most members of the tribe rejected his teaching. Because of Sioux hostility, a large number of Ottawas moved to Manitoulin Island in Lake Huron to receive French protection. They removed to Mackinac by 1680, settling alongside the Hurons at the St. Ignace mission. With the establishment of Detroit in 1701, some Ottawas moved there, but most remained at Mackinac, and others were scattered in fur hunting camps from Georgian Bay to the St. Joseph River.

The Ottawas supported the French during the colonial wars. During King George's War in 1744-48, they raided the New York settlements. In the French and Indian War, they participated in Braddock's defeat and tortured British prisoners to death. They attacked settlements in Virginia and Pennsylvania, killed 160 English soldiers on Lake George, and massacred troops who had surrendered after the siege of Fort William Henry.

After the French surrendered Canada, many Ottawas became English allies. Not all of them followed the lead of their famous chief Pontiac during his war of 1763-64, and others deserted him after he failed to capture Detroit. Pontiac and those who remained loyal to him were persuaded to make peace with the English by the threat of an Iroquois war.

During the Revolutionary War, the Ottawas were British allies. War parties attacked the Kentucky settlements in 1777, but George Rogers Clark's capture of British governor Henry Hamilton cooled their ardor, and some began siding with the Americans. A similar dichotomy prevailed during the War of 1812, although many of them had been followers of the Shawnee Prophet.

The Ottawas, who had begun making land cessions as early as 1795, sold most of their territory during the 1830's and moved first to Iowa and then to a reservation in Kansas. (See MEEKER, JOTHAM.) Those who remained in Michigan were allotted lands in severalty in 1833.

In Kansas, tribal members sold their allotments and resettled on the Quapaw agency in Oklahoma. Some Ottawas remain in Oklahoma today, while others live in Michigan and Canada.

(Howard H. Peckham, Pontiac and the Indian Uprising; Grant Foreman, Last Trek of the Indians; William C. Sturtevant, ed., Handbook of North American Indians, XV; E. W. Voegelin, Anthropological Report on the Ottawa, Chippewa, and Potawatomi Indians; William C. Eccles, The Canadian Frontier.)

OUIATENON, FORT. Ouiatenon, a Wea village at the present site of Lafayette, Indiana, was the headquarters of French traders in the Wabash region. A French fort, established there in 1720, was turned over to the English when Canada was lost in 1760. At the onset of Pontiac's War, the Weas and Kickapoos captured Lt. Edward Jenkins and the 20-man English garrison, destroyed the fort, and took the prisoners to Fort de Chartres.

The Indian village of Ouiatenon was destroyed by Kentucky militia commanded by Gen. Charles Scott in 1791.

(Howard H. Peckham, Pontiac and the Indian Uprising; Dale Van Every, Forth to the Wilderness; F. W. Hodge, ed., Handbook of American Indians, II.)

OWEN, THOMAS. Col. Thomas Owen, U.S. Indian agent, played an important role during the Black Hawk War by persuading the Potawatomi Indians to remain neutral. He employed Potawatomi scouts to watch the hostiles and to report their movements to U.S. commanders.

(Cecil Eby, That Disgraceful Affair, the Black Hawk War.)

OWENS, DAVID. David Owens, a Pennsylvania trader and a deserter from the British army, married a Shawnee woman and fathered four half-blood children. In 1764, when Pennsylvania offered a bounty on Indian scalps, he murdered his wife and children and attempted to collect the bounty. Gov. John Penn refused to pay, and ordered Owens to join Col. Henry Bouquet's expedition against the Shawnees. When Bouquet sent him as a messenger to propose peace, the Indians threatened to burn him in retaliation for murdering his family. Owens responded that if they killed him, Bouquet would destroy their villages. After debating the matter for three days, the Indians released Owens and sent him to inform Bouquet that they were ready to make peace.

(Charles A. Hanna, The Wilderness Trail; Dale Van Every, Forth to the Wilderness; Francis Parkman, The Conspiracy of Pontiac; Archibald Loudon, A Selection of Some of the Most Interesting Narratives of Outrages Committed by the Indians in Their Wars With the White People, II.)

OYSTER RIVER, NEW HAMPSHIRE, RAIDS. Oyster River, a New Hampshire settlement at the present site of Durham, was spread out along both sides of the river that gave it its name. During the late seventeenth and early eighteenth centuries, it was the target of some of the most destructive Indian raids in northern New England history. In September 1689, Abnaki Indians cut off all of the men of the Huckins garrison house when they went to the fields. Eighteen settlers were killed while only 1 escaped. Immediately afterward, the war party attacked the house where the women and children had taken refuge. Two young boys put up a spirited defense, but they had to surrender when the Indians set fire to the roof. As they emerged from the burning building, 3 or 4 of the children were slaughtered, and the survivors were carried into captivity.

On July 18, 1694, 230 Penobscot warriors and a few French-men scattered throughout the settlement before dawn, intending to surround all 12 of the garrison houses. A premature gunshot killed John Dean, however, and alerted some of the settlers so that they had time to escape. Five of the garrisons were taken, with the loss of about 104 settlers. The other 7 garrisons were defended with such determination that the Indians finally gave up the attempt and with-drew, taking 27 prisoners with them.

On April 26, 1706, a war party attacked a house outside the garrison, killing 8 men. The women of the settlement disguised themselves as men and opened fire on the attackers with such deadly effect that the Abnakis fled from the scene.

(Jeremy Belknap, History of New Hampshire, I; Francis Park-man, Count Frontenac and New France Under Louis XIV; Herbert Milton Sylvester, Indian Wars of New England.)

OZINIES INDIANS. The Ozinies, a small tribe or band associated with the Nanticokes, lived on the south side of the Chester River in Maryland when encountered by Capt. John Smith in 1608. In 1642, they became hostile to the Maryland settlers, and as they could place 60 warriors in the field, the Kent Island residents were greatly alarmed.

(James McSherry, History of Maryland; F. W. Hodge, ed., Handbook of American Indians, II.)

--P--

PAPUNHANK, MUNSEE CHIEF. Papunhank (Papoonhank, Minsi John), a Munsee Delaware prophet, was born about 1705. During his youth he was a frequent visitor to Philadelphia, and not liking the way of life of white people, he began to urge the Indians to cling to their own culture. In 1752, with 20 families of followers, he established a village at Wyalusing in Bradford County, Pennsylvania. Within a few years, however, he came under the influence of the Quakers and Moravians and decided to become a Christian.

During Pontiac's War, Papunhank led 21 Moravian Indians to Philadelphia for their own protection. In 1765, he donated land at Wyalusing to the Moravians for the establishment of the Friedenshut-ten mission. Seven years later, he moved with the Moravians to the Tuscarawas River. He died in 1775.

(Paul A. W. Wallace, Indians in Pennsylvania.)

PARKER, ELY SAMUEL, SENECA CHIEF. Ely Samuel Parker, a mixed-blood grandson of the famous orator Red Jacket, was born at Indian Falls, New York, in 1828. He became a chief in 1852, studied at Rensselaer Polytechnic Institute, and was employed as an engineer by the United States government. A close friend of Lewis Henry Morgan, he helped that pioneer anthropologist with his research on the League of the Iroquois.

Parker fought on the side of the Union during the Civil War, serving with General Grant at Vicksburg and rising to the rank of brigadier general. After the war, he remained in military service until 1869, when he resigned to accept President Grant's appointment as commissioner of Indian affairs. In that office he encountered the opposition of politicians who had used their positions for personal gain. In 1871, he was exonerated of charges of defrauding the government, but he became so distressed by the racial bias of Washington bureaucrats that he resigned his office.

In 1876, the New York City Police Department appointed Parker building superintendent, a position he held until his death on August 31, 1905. He was buried at Buffalo.

(Frederick J. Dockstader, Great North American Indians; F. W. Hodge, ed., Handbook of American Indians, II; Robert Winston Mardock, The Reformers and the American Indian.)

PARKER, JOHN, FLOTILLA. Lt. Col. John Parker of the Jersey Blues commanded a flotilla of 22 barges on Lake George that was attacked by Ottawa Indians and a few Frenchmen on July 27, 1757. Parker's forces had 160 men killed and about the same number captured. Only 2 barges escaped.

(Arthur Pound, Johnson of the Mohawks.)

PARSONS, WILLIAM, FAMILY OF. During the summer of 1703, an Abnaki war party attacked the town of Wells, Maine, killing or capturing a considerable number of its citizens. Samuel and William Parsons, small children of William and Hannah Parsons, were killed, and a daughter was captured and sold to the Mohawks. William, Sr., Hannah, and two children who survived the attack found refuge at York, Maine, with the Arthur Bragdon family. Less than two months later, however, York was attacked, the Bragdon family was massacred, and the Parsons family carried into captivity. William, Sr., died among the Indians soon after they captured him.

(Edward L. Bourne, History of Wells and Kennebunk; Samuel Adams Drake, The Border Wars of New England.)

PASCOMMUCK, MASSACHUSETTS, MASSACRE. Pascommuck, Massachusetts, now known as Easthampton, was attacked by 72 Frenchmen and Indians on May 13, 1704. The garrison was taken by surprise, having failed to post a watch, and several settlers were slain in their beds. When the Indians set fire to the garrison house, the defenders surrendered. Twenty citizens died during the attack, and the survivors were marched away as captives. One wounded man was released to warn pursuers to turn back or take responsibility for the massacre of the captives. Unfortunately, he was slain by Indian stragglers before he could convey the message to a relief party. Seeing themselves pursued, the Indians killed 19 of the captives and conveyed 3 to Canada. The relief party rescued 8 of the prisoners.

(Samuel Adams Drake, The Border Wars of New England; Herbert Milton Sylvester, Indian Wars of New England, III.)

PASHIPAHO, SAUK CHIEF. Pashipaho, principal chief of the Sauk nation, was born about 1760. He was one of the chiefs responsible for ceding all Sauk lands east of the Mississippi between the Illinois and Wisconsin rivers (15 million acres) under terms of the Treaty of St. Louis on November 4, 1804. Condemned by the historian Cecil Eby as "one of the most notable swindles in American history," the treaty created such hostility that it eventually brought on the Black Hawk War.

In 1809, Pashipaho led an attack on Fort Madison. He refused to participate in the Black Hawk War of 1832, however, and supported Keokuk's peace policy. Afterward, he signed the Treaty of Fort Armstrong, ceding 6 million acres as reparation for depredations committed during the war. He moved with his tribe to Kansas, and it is believed that he died there about 1842.

(F. W. Hodge, ed., Handbook of American Indians, II.)

PASSACONAWAY, PENNACOOK CHIEF. Passaconaway, a powerful Pennacook chief, was born about 1565 and lived near the present site of Concord, New Hampshire. At the time English settlers arrived in the area, his domain included a large portion of New England. In 1642, Massachusetts soldiers kidnapped his wife and son, but released them with an apology when colonial officials realized that the Pennacooks were ready to wage war.

In 1664, Passaconaway signed a peace treaty, placing his people under English authority. Reputedly a visionary and sorcerer, he foresaw the destruction of all Indians who resisted rule by the white race, and on his deathbed in 1665 he warned the Pennacooks to maintain peace with the colonies.

"He excelled," said Jeremy Belknap, "in sagacity, duplicity, and moderation, but his principal qualification was his skill in some of the secret operations of nature, which gave him the reputation of a sorcerer, and extended his fame and influence among all the neighboring tribes. They believed that it was in his power to make water burn, and trees dance, and to metamorphose himself into flame." He told his followers that "he had been a bitter enemy of the English, and by the arts of sorcery had tried his utmost to hinder their settlement and increase, but could by no means succeed."

(Jeremy Belknap, History of New Hampshire, I; Frederick J. Dockstader, Great North American Indians.)

PASSAMAQUODDY INDIANS. The Passamaquoddy Indians, an Algonquian people, lived in Maine and Canada at Passamaquoddy Bay and along the St. Croix River. A small tribe affiliated with the Abnakis, they were the easternmost Indians in the present United States. Their first European contacts were with French and Portuguese fishermen. Samuel de Champlain befriended them in 1603, resulting in the establishment of amicable relations with the French.

In general, the Passamaquoddy people maintained peace with the English colonists. After the Revolutionary War, most of them settled on the United States side of the boundary. In 1794, they were assigned 23,000 acres in Washington County, Maine, and their descendants live there today.

(William C. Sturtevant, ed., Handbook of North American Indians, XV; John R. Swanton, Indian Tribes of North America.)

PASSAYONK INDIANS. The Passayonk Indians, a Delaware band, occupied the west bank of the Delaware River when first encountered by Europeans. In 1633, they sold part of their land to the Dutch West India Company, and Arent Corssen constructed a trading post there. In 1648, Andries Hudde obtained tribal land on the Schuylkill and established Fort Beversreede among them. Swedish colonists objected, but the Passayonks defended the Dutch right to remain on that river.

(C. A. Weslager, Dutch Explorers, Traders, and Settlers in the Delaware Valley.)

PATTERSON, JAMES AND WILLIAM. Capt. James Patterson, a Pennsylvania trader, was born in 1715 and began selling goods to the Indians while still in his teens. In 1751, he founded the first settlement in Juniata County. He was feared by the Indians because of his skill with a rifle, and hated because he had claimed a large tract of their land. It is believed that he commanded a company of rangers during Braddock's campaign, and he refused to abandon his home during the Indian raids that followed Braddock's defeat. In 1755, war parties attacked Patterson's fort repeatedly, but James and his family and neighbors repulsed every raid.

In 1756, James Patterson assisted Col. James Burd's troops build forts and military roads. The following year he commanded Fort Hunter, keeping scouts in the field to warn settlers of impending Indian attacks. In 1758, he served in the Forbes expedition, and in 1763, he fought in Pontiac's War. He died at his home, leaving many descendants in the Juniata Valley.

Capt. William Patterson, son of James, was born in Lancaster County, Pennsylvania, in 1737, and accompanied his father to the Juniata Valley. He married a daughter of the pathfinder John Finley. Reputed to be the best shot in the wilderness, he helped his father defend their home against Indian attack. As an officer in Colonel Burd's company, he fought in the Battle of Loyalhannon in 1758. In 1767, he arrested Frederick Stump for murdering 10 Indians and delivered him to Philadelphia for trial. He died in 1801.

(Charles A. Hanna, The Wilderness Trail; U. J. Jones, History of the Early Settlement of the Juniata Valley.)

PATUXENT INDIANS. The Patuxent Indians, an Algonquian tribe closely associated with the Conoys, lived in Calvert County, Maryland, when Capt. John Smith visited the area in 1608. With the beginning of English settlement at St. Mary's in 1634, the "King of Patuxent" declared his friendship at a banquet while seated between the governors of Maryland and Virginia. Soon afterward, missionaries made many converts among the Patuxents. In 1651, the tribe was placed on a reservation at the head of the Wicomico River.

(James McSherry, History of Maryland; C. C. Hall, ed., Narratives of Early Maryland.)

PATUXET INDIANS. The Patuxet Indians, a band or village of the Massachuset tribe, had a population of 2,000 at the time of initial European contact. In 1614, Capt. Thomas Hunt kidnapped 20 Patuxets, including the famous Squanto, and sailed to England. In 1617, smallpox spread by seafarers depopulated Patuxet, and when Squanto returned in 1619 he discovered that few of his people had survived.

After Plymouth was founded on land formerly possessed by the Patuxets, Squanto attempted to rebuild the band by assembling scattered remnants. He hoped to challenge the Wampanoags and to lessen his dependence upon the English, but his plans failed to materialize.

(Neal Salisbury, Manitou and Providence.)

PAUGUSSET INDIANS. The Paugusset Indians, a small Algonquian tribe believed to have belonged to the Wappinger confederacy, resided along the Housatonic River in Connecticut. In 1660, they sold most of their land to the colonists. In 1762, a small remnant moved to Scaticook.

(F. W. Hodge, ed., Handbook of American Indians, II.)

PAVONIA MASSACRES. Pavonia, a pioneer New Jersey settlement, was founded as a patroonship across the Hudson from Manhattan by Michael Pauw in 1630. The patroonship, which included Staten Island as well as the Jersey City-Bayonne area, was located along the path used by inland tribes to transport furs to New Amsterdam. Pauw failed to provide an adequate number of settlers and surrendered his lands to the Dutch West India Company in 1635.

Director-General Kieft imposed a tax on the tribes, an act that so infuriated Indians passing through Pavonia that, in 1641, they murdered a settler named Garret Jansen Van Hoorst. Kieft demanded the surrender of the murderers, but the Indians ignored him. In 1642, Mohawk Indians massacred several Pavonia settlers, and the survivors fled to Manhattan.

On February 26, 1643, Kieft dispatched a military expedition to attack peaceful Indians who had encamped at Pavonia to escape from the Mohawks. Asserting that New Amsterdam was in danger of Indian attack, he instructed the troops to kill warriors, but to spare women and children. But E. B. O'Callaghan, historian of New Netherland, has written that the soldiers spared no one: "Eighty Indians were slaughtered ... while in repose. Sucklings were torn from their mothers' breasts, butchered before their parents' eyes, and their mangled limbs thrown ... into the river or the flames. ... others were thrown alive into the river; and when their parents ... rushed in to save them ... both parents and offspring sank into one watery grave."

In retaliation for this bloodbath, according to Sydney G. Fisher, "the Indians revenged themselves by massacring the Dutch again and again, every time they attempted to reestablish Pavonia."

On September 15, 1655, a large party of Indians attacked the settlers of Manhattan (see NEW AMSTERDAM), and after being driven back to their canoes, they crossed the Hudson and destroyed Staten Island and Pavonia. Fifty settlers were killed and a hundred carried into captivity.

(E. B. O'Callaghan, History of New Netherland, I; Sydney G. Fisher, The Quaker Colonies; John E. Pomfret, The Province of East New Jersey; Allen W. Trelease, Indian Affairs in Colonial New York; William Christie McLeod, The American Indian Frontier.)

PAWATOMO, KICKAPOO CHIEF. Pawatomo, a Kickapoo chief who participated in the Pigeon Roost massacre, narrowly escaped death when Gov. Ninian Edwards destroyed his village during the autumn of 1812. Losing 24 of his followers and all of his horses, he established a village for the survivors on Rock River, outside the militia's field of operations. In 1814, he assisted Robert Dickson, a British agent, in the destruction of Illinois and Missouri settlements.

After the war, Pawatomo moved his village to Lake Peoria, where he attempted unsuccessfully to incite the Potawatomis and Miamis to join the Kickapoos in raiding the settlements. In 1819, he removed his followers to Missouri.

(A. M. Gibson, The Kickapoos.)

PAWTUCKET INDIANS see WAMESIT INDIANS

PAXINOS, MINISINK AND SHAWNEE CHIEF. Paxinos, a Minisink chief, joined the Mohawks in organizing an attack on the French in 1680. Afterward, he lived among the Delawares and befriended the Moravian missionaries. Before 1754 he removed to the Ohio, became known as "the old chief of the Shawnees," and fought against the English during the French and Indian War. He died soon afterward.

(F. W. Hodge, ed., Handbook of American Indians, II.)

PAXTON BOYS MASSACRE. On December 14, 1763, a band of 57 Pennsylvania backwoodsmen known as the Paxton Boys attacked a peaceful Indian settlement at Conestoga. Led by Lazarus Stewart, they murdered 8 Susquehanna Indians. After the governor issued an order for their arrest, they showed their disdain for colonial authority by returning on December 27 and slaying the 14 survivors of the previous attack, most of them women and children. Learning that other Indians had fled to Philadelphia for protection, the Paxton Boys marched to the city. But finding Philadelphians prepared to repel them, they dispersed without carrying out their plan to lynch the terrified refugees.

The Paxton Boys became heroes throughout the frontier regions of Pennsylvania, ravaged recently by Delaware war parties during Pontiac's War, but they were regarded as outlaws by the Quakers and residents of areas safe from Indian raids. Benjamin Franklin ridiculed them as "the valorous, heroic Paxtons, prating of God and Bible, fifty-seven of whom armed with rifles, knives, and hatchets, had actually succeeded in killing three old men, two women and a boy."

(Sydney G. Fisher, The Quaker Colonies; Paul A. W. Wallace, Indians in Pennsylvania; Howard H. Peckham, Pontiac and the Indian Uprising; Dale Van Every, North to the Wilderness.)

PAYNE, ADAM AND AARON. Adam Payne, an Illinois minister of
the New Lights Church, felt called to serve as a missionary to the
Indians during the Black Hawk War. While riding his horse near the
Fox River in 1832, he was attacked by Potawatomi Indians. Being
unarmed, he attempted to beat them off with his Bible. A few days
later, soldiers found his head affixed to a pole and sent it to his
brother, Aaron, also a preacher, for burial. Bent upon exacting an
eye for an eye and a tooth for a tooth, Aaron joined the army
pursuing Black Hawk and was killed at the Battle of Bad Axe.
    (Cecil Eby, That Disgraceful Affair, the Black Hawk War.)

PECATONICA, BATTLE OF. On June 16, 1832, during the Black
Hawk War, 5 settlers were murdered at Fort Hamilton, Wisconsin, by
Kickapoo Indians. Gen. Henry Dodge and 29 volunteers pursued the
Kickapoos to the Pecatonica River and charged the embankment where
they had taken refuge. During the battle, 11 Indians and 3 soldiers
were killed before the Kickapoos fled from the scene.
    (Cecil Eby, That Disgraceful Affair, the Black Hawk War.)

PEMAQUID, MAINE. Pemaquid, the site of an Abnaki village, was
frequented by European fishermen before 1600 and settled by the
English about 1625. A palisaded post, built there in 1631, was
destroyed by Indians in 1676. Afterward, a stone fortress mounting
7 or 8 cannon, was built that became the easternmost bastion of
colonial defense during King Philip's War.
    In 1689, the troops at Pemaquid mutinied, and only Lt. James
Weems and 30 soldiers were there on August 2, when 100 Abnaki
allies of the French destroyed the settlement and compelled the fort
to surrender. The Indians murdered several soldiers, burned the
fort, and marched the survivors to captivity in Canada.
    In 1692, Sir William Phips built Fort William Henry at Pemaquid.
A tall stone structure with walls 8 feet thick, it appeared to be in-
destructible to the Indians who signed a peace treaty at Pemaquid in
1693. In August 1696, however, a large force of French and Indians
invested the fort, the English surrendered, and "the victorious enemy ... threw down the walls, constructed with so much labor; yet
defended with so little spirit."--Samuel Adams Drake.
    (Samuel Adams Drake, The Border Wars of New England; Her-
bert Milton Sylvester, Indian Wars of New England, I-II.)

PENN, WILLIAM, INDIAN RELATIONS. William Penn, founder of
Pennsylvania, was born in London, England, on October 14, 1644.
Son of an English admiral, he became a member of the Society of
Friends and an advocate or religious toleration. He was imprisoned
on more than one occasion for preaching unorthodox sermons, but
his father's services to the crown assisted him and others to establish a Quaker colony in West Jersey. In 1677, he created the charter
for the colony, providing for fair treatment of Indians, including
equal participation on juries during trials when Indians were involved.
    Penn's efforts in behalf of civil rights in New Jersey provided
a prelude for his more famous experiences, when in 1681, he received

a grant from the king of an immense territory now known as Pennsylvania. Even before his departure for North America he sent a message of brotherhood to the Indians:

My Friends

There is one great God and power that has made the world and all things therein, to whom you and I and all people owe their being and well-being, and to whom you and I must one day give an account for all that we do in this world. This great God has written his law in our hearts, by which we are taught and commanded to love and help and do good to one another, and not to do harm and mischief one unto another. Now this great God has been pleased to make me concerned in your parts of the world, and the king of the country where I live has given unto me a great province therein, but I desire to enjoy it with your love and consent, that we may always live together as neighbors and friends, else what would the great God say to us, who has made us not to devour and destroy one another, but live soberly and kindly together in the world.

Now I would have you well observe, that I am very sensible of the unkindness and injustice that has been too much exercised towards you by the people of these parts of the world, who have sought themselves, and to make great advantages by you, rather than by examples of justice and goodness unto you; which I hear has been matter of trouble to you and caused great grudgings and animosities, sometimes to the shedding of blood, which has made the great God angry. But I am not such a man, as is well known in my own country. I have great love and regard toward you, and I desire to win and gain your love and friendship by a kind, just and peaceful life; and the people I send are of the same mind, and shall in all things behave themselves accordingly.

Penn remained true to the convictions expressed in his letter, and although he resided in America only three years, he made at least seven land purchases from the Indians based solely upon spoken assurances that the Friends and Indians would treat each other justly. He traveled unarmed through the Indian country as far as the Susquehanna, studied Indian customs, and mastered their languages. "Penn's fair treatment of the Indians kept Pennsylvania at peace with them for about 70 years," Sydney G. Fisher observed; "in fact, from 1682 until the outbreak of the French and Indian Wars, in 1755...." Until his descendants departed from his principles of fairness (see WALKING PURCHASE), Pennsylvania developed without the Indian wars that ravaged other colonies.

William Penn died on July 30, 1718. "... to this day the Indians revere his memory."--Paul A. W. Wallace.

(Sydney G. Fisher, The Quaker Colonies; Charles A. Hanna, The Wilderness Trail; John R. Soderland, ed., William Penn and the

Founding of Pennsylvania; Paul A. W. Wallace, Indians in Pennsylvania.)

PENNACOOK INDIANS. The Pennacook Indians, a confederation of Algonquian tribes, lived in northeastern Massachusetts, southern Maine, and south-central New Hampshire during colonial times. They were influenced by the neighboring Abnakis to become allies of the French, and in spite of heavy depletion resulting from smallpox, their population was estimated at 1,250 in 1674.

In 1644, the Pennacooks, impressed by English power exhibited during the Pequot War, permitted Massachusetts to exercise sovereignty over their lands. (See PASSACONAWAY; WANNALANCET.) Most of them attempted to remain at peace during King Philip's War, but the treacherous seizure of 200 of their people in 1676 infuriated the tribe. (See WALDRON, RICHARD.)

After the war, most of the Pennacooks abandoned their homes and moved to St. Francis in Canada or settled among the Mahicans in New York. Those in Canada remained hostile to the English and participated in French and Indian raids until after their new home became British territory. Pennacooks in New York became converts to Christianity and finally settled at Scaticook.

(Alden T. Vaughan, New England Frontier; Samuel Adams Drake, The Border Wars of New England; John R. Swanton, Indian Tribes of North America; F. W. Hodge, ed., Handbook of American Indians, II.)

PENN'S CREEK MASSACRE. On October 16, 1755, a Delaware Indian war party attacked the small settlement on Penn's Creek, in Snyder County, Pennsylvania. Nineteen settlers were killed and more than ten were carried into captivity. (See LEININGER, BARBARA.) Homes were burned and livestock slaughtered in this first outburst of Delaware hostility since William Penn had established a "league of peace and amity" with them in 1682. On October 25, a party that went to Penn's Creek to bury the dead was attacked, several men being killed.

(Randolph C. Downes, Council Fires on the Upper Ohio; William A. Hunter, Forts on the Pennsylvania Frontier.)

PENOBSCOT INDIANS. The Penobscot Indians, a powerful Algonquian tribe and a member of the Abnaki confederacy, lived along the Penobscot River and Bay when first encountered by European explorers and fishermen before 1600. Samuel de Champlain visited them in 1604, and they became allies of the French during the colonial wars. They were greatly influenced by the Baron de St. Castin, a French officer and trader.

In 1688, French priests established a mission among the Penobscots. Later that year, Gov. Edmund Andros plundered St. Castin's trading post at Penobscot. "The baseness of the act," admitted the New England antiquarian Samuel Adams Drake, "so like to that of some roving buccaneer, aroused the indignation of St. Castin's tribesmen, the Penobscots, ... and they were now ready to dig up the hatchet whenever he should give the signal."

From that time until they signed a peace treaty in 1749, the Penobscots dispatched numerous war parties against the New England settlements. In addition, during Dummer's War of 1724-25, they captured English fishing boats on the high seas. During the French and Indian War, they attempted at first to remain neutral, but English attacks compelled them to take the war path. During the Revolutionary War, the tribe supported the Americans, and some of them participated in Benedict Arnold's attack on Quebec in 1775. As a result, they retained part of their homeland, where their descendants still live.

(Samuel Adams Drake, Border Wars of New England; Francis Parkman, A Half-Century of Conflict; William C. Sturtevant, ed., Handbook of North American Indians, XV.)

PENTRY, MRS. EDWARD. Mrs. Edward Pentry, a French-Canadian frontier woman, married an Englishman in Maine. In 1672, they established a trading post near the Upper Kennebec River. While her husband was away, she was paddling a canoe on Moosehead Lake when two Indians attempted to pull the boat to the shore. She shot one of them through the heart and struck the other over the head with her gun. When he began trying to swim to shore, she shot him to death.

Several hours later, she heard firing, rushed to the scene, and saw two Indians attacking her husband. She shot one of them as he was charging the wounded Pentry with a tomahawk, then stabbed his companion to death. Afterward, she carried her husband to their cabin and nursed him back to health.

Mrs. Pentry lived in the northern wilderness most of her life. She died at the age of 96, leaving numerous descendants to carry on the Indian trade.

(William W. Fowler, Woman on the American Frontier.)

PEORIA INDIANS. The Peoria Indians, an Algonquian tribe of the Illinois confederacy, contained 300 lodges when visited by Jolliet and Marquette near the mouth of the Des Moines River in 1673. Before the explorers' return voyage, however, they had moved across the Mississippi and established their principal village near the present site of Peoria, Illinois. The explorers made such a favorable impression on the Peorias that the tribe supported the French, even at the cost of sustaining severe losses at the hands of the Iroquois and other Indians allied with the English. The Sauk and Fox Indians massacred many of them, and some of the survivors resettled on the Missouri.

The main body of Peorias remained on the Illinois River until they sold their lands east of the Mississippi to the United States in 1818. Then, with remnants of other Illinois tribes, they moved to a reservation on the Osage River. In 1868, after uniting with the Wea and Piankashaw tribes, they removed to the Indian Territory.

(William C. Sturtevant, ed., Handbook of North American Indians, XV; Grant Foreman, The Last Trek of the Indians.)

PEQUAWKET INDIANS. The Pequawket (Pigwacket) Indians, a tribe of the Abnaki confederacy, lived on the headwaters of the Saco River near the Maine-New Hampshire boundary during the colonial wars. A warlike people, they attacked the New England settlements and took many captives until a band of English scalp hunters fought a bloody battle with them in 1725. (See LOVEWELL, JOHN.) Afterward, they removed to the source of the Connecticut River.

(F. W. Hodge, ed., Handbook of American Indians, II; Francis Parkman, A Half-Century of Conflict.)

PEQUOT INDIANS. The Pequot Indians, a powerful Algonquian tribe, were encountered by Dutch explorers along the Connecticut coast in 1614. They traded with the Dutch and sold land to them in 1633. The following year, however, a disagreement led the Dutch to murder a Pequot chief. A brief war resulted, and the Pequots permitted the English to settle in Connecticut.

In 1634, the Niantic Indians, allies of the Pequots, killed a sea captain, John Stone, and Massachusetts officials demanded retribution of the Pequots. War was averted, however, when the tribe signed a peace treaty on November 1. Two years later another captain, John Oldham, was murdered by the Indians of Block Island, and John Endicott led a force of Massachusetts and Connecticut troops to avenge him. After attacking the Block Islanders, Endicott advanced into Pequot territory, accomplishing little except to arouse the tribe's hostility to a fever pitch. Raids against Connecticut settlements followed, and the English declared war on the Pequots on May 1, 1637.

A force of Connecticut and Massachusetts soldiers, bolstered by hundreds of Indian allies, marched into Pequot territory, torched the tribe's principal village, and burned hundreds of Indians to death. (See MASON, JOHN; MYSTIC BATTLE OF.) This massacre so decimated the tribe that the survivors attempted to flee to the Mohawks. Most of them were intercepted and captured or killed. Captives were turned over to the Mohegans, Narragansets, and Niantics until 1655, when the English resettled them near the Mystic River. Their descendants still live in that area.

(John W. DeForest, History of the Indians of Connecticut; Richard Drinnon, Facing West; Neal Salisbury, Manitou and Providence; William C. Sturtevant, Handbook of North American Indians, XV.)

PERROT, NICOLAS. Born in France in 1644, Nicolas Perrot went to Canada at an early age to assist the Jesuit missionaries. In 1665, he became a fur trader and began a life in the wilderness that lasted 35 years. In 1668, he was among the Potawatomis of Green Bay, and two years later, he escorted the Sieur de St. Lusson to assert formal possession of the Northwest for France. As a prominent coureur de bois, he learned the Indian customs and languages so thoroughly that he gained tremendous influence over them. He understood the importance of uniting the western tribes to oppose the Iroquois, and he succeeded in halting wars between tribes and in uniting them in the French interest.

In 1683, Perrot became France's official representative among the tribes of Wisconsin. The following year, he participated in

Governor La Barre's unsuccessful Iroquois expedition. Afterward, as commandant at Green Bay, he established a profitable trade with the Sioux, gained an alliance with the Iowas, built several French forts on the Mississippi, and claimed the upper Mississippi for France. As the tribes of Green Bay resented his selling guns to the Sioux, they invested his post at Fort St. Antoine. He invited six chiefs to parley inside the stockade, seized them, and compelled them to call off the siege. In 1689, he ameliorated Fox Indian hostility, thereby preventing a massacre of French traders.

In 1693, Perrot played a vital role in preserving the fur trade of the Great Lakes for the French. The Iroquois were intercepting the fur fleets until he and Henri de Tonti organized a flotilla large enough to fight its way through. Afterward, he dispatched war parties to attack Iroquois villages. In 1695, he was seized by Miami Indians who threatened to burn him at the stake, but a band of friendly Fox warriors arrived just in time to save him from death. The following year, all traders' licenses were revoked, and Perrot, whose fur warehouses had been destroyed by hostile Indians, returned to Montreal and a life of poverty in 1698. Although he never returned to the West, he served his country in 1701 as interpreter during a peace conference at Montreal between the western Indian nations and the Iroquois. Afterward, he wrote his Mémoire sur les Moeurs, Costumes et Relligion des Sauvages de l'Amérique Septentrionale. He died at Montreal in 1718.

"The Algonquians loved and esteemed him; and the various tribes of the bay honored him as their father."--Emma H. Blair.

"Perrot formed a series of alliances with the tribes ... which laid the foundation for the French sovereignty in the Northwest."-- Louise Phelps Kellogg.

(Emma H. Blair, The Indian Tribes of the Upper Mississippi Valley and the Region of the Great Lakes; Louise Phelps Kellogg, ed., Early Narratives of the Northwest; The French Régime in Wisconsin and the Northwest; James A. Clifton, The Prairie People.)

PESHEWAH, MIAMI CHIEF. Peshewah (John B. Richardville) was born near Fort Wayne, Indiana, about 1761. He was the grandson of a French nobleman and the son of Joseph Drouet de Richardville, a French-Canadian trader, and Tecumwah, sister of the Miami principal chief Pacanne. A warrior in his youth, he became much more noteworthy in later life as a diplomat and businessman.

Peshewah inherited a small fortune from his parents, traders and operators of a lucrative portage business. He became a successful trader and farmer himself, and added to his income by cooperating with U.S. government negotiators in obtaining Indian land cessions.

When Pacanne died in 1814, Peshewah succeeded him as principal chief of the Miami nation. Speaking French and English fluently, he was well prepared to manage tribal affairs during an era in which his people's welfare depended more upon diplomacy than ability to wage war. He skillfully maneuvered to prevent Miami removal to the West for many years. At the same time, he arranged land cession treaties, however, and was well rewarded by the government for his assistance.

Finally, in 1840, Peshewah signed a treaty at the Forks of the Wabash that compelled about half of the tribe to remove beyond the Mississippi. Many Miamis reacted furiously, especially because Peshewah was allowed to remain in Indiana. But Bert Anson, historian of the tribe, believes that "the Miamis would have been completely destroyed had they been led by a less astute man." He died in 1841, reputedly the wealthiest Indian in North America.

(Bert Anson, The Miami Indians.)

PESSACUS, NARRAGANSET CHIEF. Pessacus, an important Narraganset chief, was born in 1623. A brother of Miantonomo, he became increasingly hostile to the New England colonists after the execution of that famous chief in 1643. In 1645, an English force was sent to punish Pessacus, but the Narragansets avoided an attack by agreeing to terms imposed by the commissioners of the United Colonies.

In 1669, Pessacus was accused of assisting chief Ninigret to develop a conspiracy to attack the colonies. Evidence indicated that no conspiracy existed, however, and Pessacus was cleared of the charges. With the outbreak of King Philip's War, Pessacus once more provided assurance of Narraganset peaceful intentions. The tribe hoped to delay involvement until they could determine which side would be victorious, but Pessacus could not control young warriors who supported the hostiles. In October 1675, he signed a treaty pledging to surrender Wampanoag warriors to the English, but he failed to deliver them. Soon afterward, the English determined to wage war against the Narragansets.

During the war, Pessacus served as a leader of King Philip's forces. By April 1676, however, he advocated an end to hostilities. He survived the war, but he was killed in 1677 in a fight with the Mohawks.

(F. W. Hodge, ed., Handbook of American Indians, II; Alden T. Vaughan, New England Frontier; Douglas Edward Leach, Flintlock and Tomahawk.)

PHELPS-GORHAM PURCHASE. In 1788, Oliver Phelps and Nathaniel Gorham purchased preemption rights from the Massachusetts government to acquire Seneca Indian lands in New York. They persuaded the Indians to sell territory east of the Genesee and other large tracts for $5,000 and a $500 annuity.

(William C. Sturtevant, ed., Handbook of North American Indians, XV.)

PHILLIPS, WILLIAM. In July 1780, Capt. William Phillips led 10 frontiersmen to scout the Woodcock Valley and the Great Cove in Pennsylvania for signs of hostile Indians. They spent a night in an abandoned cabin, and in the morning they found themselves surrounded by 60 warriors. They repulsed repeated attacks until mid-morning, but when the roof burst into flame, Phillips "cried for quarters, and told the savages that he would surrender, on condition that his men should be treated as prisoners and not injured." The Indians agreed, and they carried Phillips and his son into captivity, but they tied 7 of his men to trees and shot them to death. The survivors were held in various Indian villages until their release after the end of the Revolutionary War.

(U. J. Jones, History of the Early Settlement of the Juniata Valley.)

PIANKASHAW INDIANS. The Piankashaw Indians, a division of the Miamis in ancient times, were recognized as a distinct tribe in 1682, the year they arrived at La Salle's Fort St. Louis on the Illinois River. By 1717, they resided on the Wabash River, and the French established the Vincennes post among them in 1731.

The Piankashaws abandoned the French interest by February 1751, requesting the English to send traders to their villages. Later that year, they murdered several Frenchmen near Kaskaskia and attempted to influence neighboring tribes to become English allies. At the onset of the Revolutionary War, they supported the British, but they changed sides after the Americans captured Vincennes.

By 1800, some of the Piankashaws migrated west of the Mississippi, and all of them left Illinois by 1828. In 1832, they combined with the Weas and settled in Kansas. About 20 years later, they united with remnants of Illinois tribes under the name Peorias and Kaskaskias, and in 1867, all of them removed to Oklahoma, where they became known as Peoria Indians.

(Clarence Walworth Alvord, The Illinois Country; Albert T. Volwiler, George Croghan and the Westward Movement; Grant Foreman, Last Trek of the Indians; William C. Sturtevant, ed., Handbook of North American Indians, XV.)

PICKAWILLANEE, MIAMI TOWN. Pickawillanee was established on the Miami River near the present site of Piqua, Ohio, in 1748. It was the principal Miami Indian town by 1751, when Christopher Gist reported that it "consists of about 400 Families, and ... is accounted one of the strongest Indian Towns upon this Part of the Continent." George Croghan and 50 other English traders established posts there, and French traders and troops made several attempts to expel them. Finally, in 1752, they and their Ottawa Indian allies burned Pickawillanee (see OLD BRITON; LANGLADE, CHARLES DE), captured most of the English traders, and ate the Miami chief. The fall of Pickawillanee put an end to the English fur trade in that region until after the French and Indian War.

(Bert Anson, The Miami Indians; Albert T. Volwiler, George Croghan and the Westward Movement; Dale Van Every, Forth to the Wilderness; John Tebbel and Keith Jennison, The American Indian Wars.)

PICQUET, FRANÇOIS. François Picquet, a Sulpitian abbé who was born at Bourg, France, in 1708, founded the mission La Présentation at the present site of Ogdensburg, New York, in 1749. He gained influence over the Iroquois and converted many to Christianity. In addition, he persuaded tribes of the Great Lakes to adopt the French interest, and he accompanied them on their raids against English settlements. (See LA PRESENTATION.) During the late stages of the French and Indian War, Picquet, who knew that he would be treated roughly if he fell into English hands, led 25 soldiers and a large group of Indians down the Mississippi to New Orleans, arriving safely in

July 1761. He died 10 years later.

(Louis Antoine de Bougainville, Adventures in the Wilderness; Francis Parkman, Montcalm and Wolfe; Frank H. Severance, An Old Frontier of France.)

PIERCE, MICHAEL. During King Philip's War, Capt. Michael Pierce led a force of 85 Plymouth troops and friendly Indians in pursuit of hostile Narragansets. Near the Pawtucket River, they were ambushed and surrounded by a powerful Narraganset war party. Pierce and his men formed a tight circle and fought desperately, but they were too badly outnumbered to prevail. Forty-two men were slain, and the others broke through the enemy line and escaped.

(Douglas Edward Leach, Flintlock and Tomahawk.)

PIGEON ROOST MASSACRE. During the War of 1812, Kickapoo Indians who were frustrated by failure to seize Fort Harrison, raided the settlements along the White River. Their most lethal attack was launched in September 1812, against the small settlement of Pigeon Roost, not far north of Louisville, Kentucky. There they massacred 21 settlers, including children brained against trees. In retaliation, Ninian Edwards recruited an army that destroyed several Kickapoo villages.

(R. David Edmunds, The Shawnee Prophet; A. M. Gibson, The Kickapoos.)

PIGWACKET INDIANS see PEQUAWKET INDIANS

PINE, CHARLES. Charles Pine and his fellow scout, Richard Hunniwell, were among the most famous frontiersmen in southern Maine during Queen Anne's War. Pine was noted for stalking Indians with two guns, firing both from concealment at warriors seated around a campfire, and vanishing into the wilderness before the startled survivors could take up his trail.

(Herbert Milton Sylvester, Indian Wars of New England, III.)

PISCATAWAY INDIANS see CONOY INDIANS

PITT, FORT. On November 24, 1758, the French burned Fort Duquesne, at the present site of Pittsburgh, Pennsylvania, and retreated from that strategic location. The English forces of Gen. John Forbes occupied the position immediately afterward and quickly began construction of Fort Pitt, named for the prime minister William Pitt. Instructed by Pitt to build a fortress of such strength that neither French nor Indians could control the Ohio or threaten the colonies, the British built a structure that enclosed eight acres and accommodated 1,000 men. Soon afterward, a village of some two hundred civilians sprang up outside the stockade.

The strength of Fort Pitt was put to the test in 1763, when Pontiac's War caused the destruction of most western posts. On July 24, a Delaware chief warned the commanding officer Capt. Simeon Ecuyer that a large Indian army was approaching Fort Pitt and offered to escort the 338 men of the garrison to safety. Suspecting treachery, Ecuyer responded that he could hold the fort against any attack and warned the Delawares to keep out of the war. As a parting gift, he presented the chief with blankets infected with smallpox.

On July 27, those Indians not suffering from smallpox attacked the fort but the defenders used their muskets and cannon with such deadly results that the assault was abandoned on August 1. Col. Henry Bouquet, after defeating the Indians at the Battle of Bushy Run, reinforced Fort Pitt on August 10.

British troops garrisoned Fort Pitt until 1772. With the onset of the Revolutionary War, it came under American control and served as a base for operations against the British and Indians in the West. After 1782, the fort became badly dilapidated.

(Solon J. Buck, The Planting of Civilization in Western Pennsylvania; Howard H. Peckham, Pontiac and the Indian Uprising.)

PITTSBURGH, PENNSYLVANIA, TREATIES OF. Three important treaties were negotiated with Indians at Pittsburgh during the Revolutionary War. On October 7, 1775, commissioners of the Continental Congress promised the tribes that the Americans would adhere to the Ohio River boundary. The Indians agreed to release captives taken during Dunmore's War and to remain neutral in the conflict between the colonies and Great Britain. As a result of this treaty, an Indian war was averted.

In September 1776, a second treaty was negotiated at Pittsburgh, intended to counter the efforts of Henry Hamilton at Detroit to enlist the Indians as allies of the British. Col. George Morgan, Indian agent for the Middle Department, met with chiefs of the Delaware, Shawnee, Seneca, Ottawa, and Wyandot nations, distributed presents, and secured renewed assurances of neutrality.

On September 17, 1778, a treaty was signed at Pittsburgh by chiefs White Eyes and Killbuck permitting the Americans to build a fort among the Delaware Indians and agreeing to provide warriors to fight the British. Andrew and Thomas Lewis assured the tribe that their territorial rights would be respected.

(Solon J. Buck, The Planting of Civilization in Western Pennsylvania; Charles J. Kappler, ed., Indian Affairs: Laws and Treaties, II.)

PIZHIKI, CHIPPEWA CHIEF. Pizhiki (Buffalo) was born about 1759 and lived to be almost one hundred years old. Converted to Catholicism, he signed many treaties with American officials. For signing the Treaty of La Pointe in 1854, he was awarded a section of land near La Pointe, Wisconsin.

(F. W. Hodge, ed., Handbook of American Indians, II.)

PLAISTED-WHEELRIGHT WEDDING. In 1712, Elisha Plaisted married Hannah Wheelright at her father's home, the John Wheelright garrison house at Wells, Maine. After the ceremony, guests preparing to depart encountered the Abnaki chief, Abomazine, and 200 warriors surrounding the house. During a sortie, the bridegroom was captured and his companions driven back inside. Afterward, under a flag of truce, they bargained for his release, but the Indians refused. Fighting was resumed, and three settlers were killed before the Abnakis departed, taking Plaisted with them. A few days later, however, a large reward gained his release, and he was restored to his bride.

(Edward L. Bourne, History of Wells and Kennebunk; Francis Parkman, A Half-Century of Conflict.)

POCOMTUC INDIANS. The Pocomtuc (Deerfield) Indians, an Algonquian tribe, inhabited northwestern Massachusetts and nearby sections of Connecticut and Vermont during colonial times. In 1651, they joined neighboring tribes in assisting the French to wage war on the Iroquois. Their principal village was destroyed by the Mohawks in 1666, and Deerfield, Massachusetts, was established near that site in 1669.

The Pocomtucs supported the hostile tribes during King Philip's War. Afterward, they fled to Scaticook, and eventually they removed to St. Francis in Canada.

(John R. Swanton, Indian Tribes of North America.)

PODUNK INDIANS. The Podunk Indians, a small tribe closely associated with the Poquonnocks, resided along the Podunk River in Hartford County, Connecticut, during early colonial history. They ceded much of their territory to Hartford settlers, but in 1657, they rejected an attempt by Rev. John Eliot to preach a sermon, asserting that "the English ... had already taken away their land, and now they were only attempting to make the Podunks their servants."
Most of them accompanied other hostile tribes away from New England after King Philip's War, but a few remained near Hartford until about 1750.

(John W. De Forest, History of the Indians of Connecticut.)

POKANOKET INDIANS. see WAMPANOAG INDIANS

POMHAM, NARRAGANSET CHIEF see PUMHAM, NARRAGANSET CHIEF

PONCET, JOSEPH ANTOINE DE LA RIVIERE, CAPTIVITY OF. Father Joseph Antoine de La Rivière Poncet, a Jesuit missionary from Paris, was captured by Mohawk Indians during an attack on Quebec in 1653. Conveyed to a Mohawk castle, he was tied to a scaffold, and an Indian chewed off one of his fingers. During three days of torture, he kept up his courage by singing religious songs. Spared from death by an old woman who adopted him, he was released soon afterward to serve as an envoy of the Mohawks when they desired to negotiate peace with the French.

(T. J. Campbell, Pioneer Priests of North America; Edna Kenton, ed., Black Gown and Redskins; E. B. O'Callaghan, History of New Netherland, II.)

PONTIAC, OTTAWA CHIEF. Little is known of Pontiac's life that preceded his sudden emergence in 1763 as the chief conspirator in a powerful Indian confederation intended to drive the English east of the Appalachians. Historians differ as to the time and place of his birth, but the Indian scholar, Frederick J. Dockstader, believes that it occurred about 1720 on the Maumee River in Ohio.

During King George's War (1744-48), Pontiac probably fought for the French. It is probable that he participated in Braddock's defeat in 1755. After the fall of Quebec in 1760, it is said that he guided Robert Rogers and his rangers to occupy the former French posts in the western wilderness. Soon afterward, he became incensed by British trade policies, and early in 1763, he urged tribes of the Great Lakes region to join an abortive plot hatched by the Senecas to expel English traders. Afterward, he took the lead in uniting the tribes in making a determined effort to drive the British and their American colonists from their western forts and settlements.

An accomplished orator, Pontiac persuaded the Ottawas, Chippewas, Potawatomis, Hurons, and other western tribes to attack the British posts nearest their villages, while he reserved the leadership of the campaign against Detroit for himself. (See GLADWIN, HENRY; CAMPBELL, DONALD.) Fort Detroit held out against his numerous warriors, as did Fort Pitt against the Delawares, but the smaller forts had all fallen by July 1. (See ST. JOSEPH, FORT; SANDUSKY, FORT; MIAMI, FORT; OUIATON, FORT; MACKINAC; LA BAYE, FORT; PRESQU'ISLE, FORT; LE BOEUF, FORT.) By the end of July, some of his allies who had been besieging Detroit began to lose heart, but his victory over Capt. James Dalyell during a sortie on the last day of the month (see BLOODY RUN), restored their enthusiasm.

News that France and England had signed a peace treaty in October 1763, sapped Pontiac's support once more, however, and the chief's murder of a white child held in captivity turned other followers against him. Afterward, he abandoned the siege and withdrew to Illinois, hoping to resume the war in the spring of 1764. His designs were thwarted, however, when the French at Fort de Chartres refused his request for military supplies and advised the Illinois Indians to ignore him.

During the winter of 1764-65, Pontiac, back at the Ottawa village on the Maumee, tried once more to arouse the Indians of that area to hostility, and he hoped for support from the Creeks and Choctaws. He finally abandoned hope in the spring of 1765, and in July, George Croghan persuaded him to make peace. In July 1766, he conferred with Sir William Johnson at Fort Ontario and agreed to use his influence to curtail hostilities by the Great Lakes Indians. On April 20, 1769, he was murdered at Kaskaskia by a Peoria warrior, perhaps at the instigation of British traders.

"His meteoric career blazed against the western sky, casting a lurid glow over the whole vast wilderness, inflaming the tumult of more than 20 sieges and battles, and scorching the white frontier from end to end."--Dale Van Every.

"The 'Conspiracy of Pontiac' was less a conspiracy than a war, and a far greater war than Pontiac could have managed."--Arthur Pound.

"It was the impatience and waywardness of his Indians that beat him in the end, but he held them to it for six months, the only siege in Indian history long enough to be dignified with that title."-- Albert Britt.

(Howard Peckham, Pontiac and the Indian Uprising; Francis Parkman, History of the Conspiracy of Pontiac; Dale Van Every,

Forth to the Wilderness; Albert Britt, Great Indian Chiefs; Frederick
J. Dockstader, Great North American Indians; Arthur Pound, Johnson of the Mohawks.)

POOSEPATUCK INDIANS. The Poosepatuck Indians, a Long Island
tribe closely associated with the Montauks, inhabited a 30-mile stretch
of the south shore east of Patchogue. In 1666, they moved to a
reservation near Mystic, and a few of their descendants still live
there.
       (F. W. Hodge, ed., Handbook of American Indians, II.)

POPHAM PLANTATION see SAGADAHOC COLONY

POQUIM, MOHEGAN CHIEF see UNCAS, MOHEGAN CHIEF

POQUONNOCK INDIANS. The Poquonnock Indians, a small Algonquian
tribe closely associated with the Podunks, lived near the mouth of
the Farmington River in Hartford County, Connecticut. They disposed of their lands to white settlers about the middle of the seventeenth century and disappeared as a tribal entity.
       (John W. De Forest, History of the Indians of Connecticut.)

PORTAGE DES SIOUX, MISSOURI, TREATIES OF. Three treaties
were negotiated with Indian tribes at Portage des Sioux by William
Clark, Auguste Chouteau, and Ninian Edwards during the summer of
1815. On July 18, they negotiated peace with the Piankashaw and
Potawatomi Indians and obtained assurances of the release of captives
taken during the War of 1812. On September 2, they negotiated a
similar peace treaty with the Kickapoos. On September 13, they persuaded the Sauk Indians of the Missouri to remain separate from
those of the Rock River and to lend them no assistance during hostilities against the United States.
       (Charles J. Kappler, ed., Indian Affairs: Laws and Treaties,
II.)

PORTSMOUTH, NEW HAMPSHIRE, TREATY OF. On October 29, 1712,
the settlers of Portsmouth informed the hostile Indians that the Peace
of Utrecht had concluded Queen Anne's War. This event led to a
peace treaty that was signed on July 11, 1713. The Abnakis "acknowledged their perfidy, promised fidelity, renewed their allegiance,
submitted to the laws, and begged the queen's pardon for their
former miscarriages. The frequent repetition of such engagements
and as frequent violations of them, had by this time much abated the
sense of obligation on the one part, and of confidence on the other.
But it being for the interest of both parties to be at peace, the
event was particularly welcome."--Jeremy Belknap.
       (Jeremy Belknap, History of New Hampshire, I.)

POST, CHRISTIAN FREDERICK. Christian Frederick Post, a lay missionary of the Moravian Church, was born about 1710 in Conitz,
East Prussia. He emigrated to North America in 1742 and labored

among the Christian Indians of Connecticut and New York. In 1743, he married a Wampanoag Indian woman. She died three years later, and in 1749 he married a Delaware convert, and they lived among the tribes of the Wyoming Valley of Pennsylvania. When his second wife died, he accompanied a mission to Laborador, and barely survived an attack by the natives.

Post returned to the Wyoming Valley in 1754 and began his service as an Indian diplomat that resulted in amazing achievements. After Braddock's defeat, the Delawares became hostile, and Post rushed eastward to warn the Pennsylvania settlements to prepare for attacks by Chief Tedyuscung. In June 1758, he went to the village of the then repentant Tedyuscung, conferred with several chiefs, and persuaded the eastern Delawares to withdraw from the war.

In July 1758, Gov. William Denny of Pennsylvania sent Post to the Delawares and other tribes of the Ohio to persuade them to follow the lead of the eastern Delawares in defecting from the French interest. "Heroically and calmly," wrote Albert T. Volwiler, "he went into the heart of the enemy's country and placed himself in the hands of a treacherous and crafty foe." While addressing an Indian council across the river from Fort Duquesne, he would have been arrested by French officers if the Indians had not protected him. He informed the tribe that if they failed to make peace, an army led by Gen. John Forbes would annihilate them.

As a result of Post's mission to the Ohio, chiefs went to Philadelphia to confer with Governor Denny. The Council of Easton convened on October 8, and representatives of the tribes visited by Post became convinced of the government's good intentions when officials repudiated the Treaty of Albany and agreed to restore lands west of the Alleghenies to the Indians.

After the signing of the Treaty of Easton, Post and a small military escort set out to inform the western Indians that the British desired peace with the tribes, that Forbes was advancing toward Fort Duquesne, and that they must not defend the French. After leaving the military escort at the Allegheny and proceeding toward the Ohio, Post learned that the soldiers had been attacked by hostile Delawares, five of them killed, and five taken captive. Realizing that his own life was in great danger, Post relied upon friendly chiefs to protect him.

The Indians, unsure of which way to turn, finally permitted Post to deliver his messages to the assembled tribesmen. "On Nov. 20, 1758, the great decision was made that sealed the doom of Fort Duquesne. On the afternoon of that day, Post, at Kuskuski, read the news of the treaty of Easton.... In the evening a French captain from Fort Duquesne arrived ... and offered a string of wampum to one of the leaders who declined to take it."--Randolph C. Downes.

After the surrender of Fort Duquesne, Post worked at Indian missions on the Ohio and in Nicaragua. He died in 1795.

(Solon J. Buck, The Planting of Civilization in Western Pennsylvania; Randolph C. Downes, Council Fires on the Upper Ohio; Albert T. Volwiler, George Croghan and the Westward Movement.)

POTAWATOMI INDIANS. The Potawatomi Indians, a powerful Algonquian tribe closely associated with the Chippewas and Ottawas, lived
near Green Bay, Wisconsin, when first encountered by French explorers and missionaries during the 1640's. They became French
allies in wars with the Iroquois, and they developed a flourishing fur
trade with Montreal, but most of them resisted attempts to convert
them to Christianity until those on the St. Joseph River became
Catholics in the early eighteenth century.

"From 1690 to 1760 the Potawatomi loyally served the French
as their most reliable allies against--first--those tribes who threatened
the preeminence of New France by making accommodations with the
English and--eventually--the English themselves."--James A. Clifton.

In 1703, after the Iroquois made peace, some of the Potawatomis
established a village at Detroit. During the Fox and Mascouten siege
of Detroit in 1712, they rescued the French and almost exterminated
their Indian enemies. In 1746, incited by the French, they began
raiding English settlements, and during the French and Indian War
they attacked villages and farms in New York, Pennsylvania, Maryland, and Virginia. They participated in the victory over Braddock
and in the capture of Fort William Henry. After the English captured
Quebec in 1759, the Potawatomis made peace in order to obtain trade
goods, but in 1763 they joined Pontiac's movement to seize English
forts and settlements.

During the American Revolution, the Potawatomis sided with
the British and began raiding Kentucky and New York settlements in
1776. By that time the tribe was widely scattered, and the western
villages, retaining their dislike of the British, turned to the Spanish
for trade goods.

The Potawatomis came under the influence of Tecumseh and his
brother the Prophet by 1807. In 1812, before the beginning of the
war, Tecumseh attempted to restrain them from attacking Americans,
but their medicine man Main Poc led raids against settlements from
Indiana to the Mississippi even before war was declared. Potawatomis
slaughtered the soldiers and civilians evacuating Fort Dearborn (see
DEARBORN, FORT, MASSACRE), attacked Fort Meigs, and participated in the massacre of prisoners on the Raisin River. The Americans countered by burning their villages.

After Tecumseh's death at the Battle of the Thames, most
Potawatomis withdrew from the conflict. They signed peace treaties
in 1814 and 1815, and began selling off their lands. In 1837, the
last of 34 land cession treaties was signed, finalizing "the demise of
the Potawatomi tribe as a viable political, social, and cultural unit."--
James A. Clifton. Most of them moved west of the Mississippi by
1841, but those living in Indiana refused to leave their homelands
until troops rounded them up, destroyed their homes, and marched
them away. The Catholic Potawatomis at L'Arbre Croche, Michigan,
likewise were marched west under guard.

Located on reservations in Iowa and Kansas, they were crowded
out by white farmers, and they removed to the Indian Territory by
1870. Members of the tribe still live in Oklahoma, Kansas, Michigan,
and Wisconsin.

(James A. Clifton, The Prairie People; Grant Foreman, Last Trek of the Indians; Milo M. Quaife, Checagou; R. David Edmunds, The Shawnee Prophet; William C. Sturtevant, ed., Handbook of North American Indians, XV; Francis Paul Prucha, The Great Father, I.)

POTAWATTIMIE MILLS, INDIANA, TREATY OF. On December 16, 1834, the Potawatomi Indians negotiated a treaty at Potawattimie Mills with William Marshall. They ceded two sections of land in exchange for $700 and payment of their debts.

(Charles J. Kappler, ed., Indian Affairs: Laws and Treaties, II.)

POUCHOT, FRANÇOIS. Capt. François Pouchot, a French military officer, was born at Grenoble in 1712. His regiment arrived in Canada in 1755. A talented engineer, he built a strong fort at the mouth of the Niagara River and used it as a base for sending Indian war parties to raid the English settlements. Many captives and scalps were delivered to him during the next four years.

In 1759, Sir William Johnson captured the fort (see NIAGARA, FORTS; LA BELLE FAMILLE). Pouchot was exchanged, returned to Montreal, and sent in 1760 to build Fort Lévis near Ogdensburg, New York. There he was compelled to surrender once more when the English captured the fort. He returned to France in 1761, and was killed in Corsica fighting for the French in 1769.

"... he was a dogged, sturdy fighter; and although he surrendered twice to the British, never did he show the white feather."-- Frank H. Severance.

"Sieur Pouchot ... seems to have won the affection of the Indians who have given him the name of Galegayogen, that is to say the 'Center of Good Fortune.'"--Louis Antoine de Bougainville.

(Louis Antoine de Bougainville, Adventures in the Wilderness; Frank H. Severance, An Old Frontier of France.)

POWESHIEK, FOX CHIEF. Born in Iowa about 1813, Poweshiek was an important Fox chief during the Black Hawk War. He fought beside Black Hawk in several battles, and after their defeat at Bad Axe, he was compelled to cede tribal lands. In 1833, he went to Washington to plead for better treatment of his people. He died about 1845.

(Frederick J. Dockstader, Great North American Indians.)

PRAIRIE DU CHIEN, WISCONSIN. Located on the Mississippi River in southwestern Wisconsin, Prairie du Chien began as an Indian village that was visited by Louis Jolliet and Father Jacques Marquette in 1673. About a dozen years later, Nicolas Perrot established Fort St. Nicolas at the site, and it developed rapidly into a center of the French fur trade. When Great Britain acquired the region in 1763, English traders joined the French, and Prairie du Chien became increasingly important as a fur trade capital.

During the Revolutionary War, the British built a fort at Prairie

du Chien that served as a base for an attack on the Spanish and
Americans at St. Louis and Cahokia. When their invasion failed, the
British and Indians (see HESSE, EMANUEL) retreated to Prairie du
Chien and destroyed the fort to prevent its capture by the Americans.
Prairie du Chien was an important post during the War of 1812.
The Americans were driven out and the British used the area as a
staging point for Indian raids. (See DICKSON, ROBERT.) In June
1814, William Clark seized the settlement for the Americans and built
Fort Shelby there. Soon afterward, the British and Indians re-
captured it and named it Fort McKay. After the war, the British
burned the fort and withdrew. It was replaced by the Americans as
Fort Crawford in 1816.

Prairie du Chien was the scene of several important treaty
negotiations with the Indians. On August 19, 1825, William Clark
and Lewis Cass negotiated peace between the tribes of the area and
established their boundaries. On July 29, 1829, Caleb Atwater,
Pierre Ménard, and John McNeil obtained land cessions from the
Chippewa, Ottawa, and Potawatomi tribes near Lake Michigan at the
cost of a $16,000 annuity and a large load of presents. On August
29, 1829, the Winnebagos ceded large tracts near the Wisconsin and
Rock rivers for goods and an $18,000 annuity. On July 15, 1830,
William Clark and Willoughby Morgan negotiated land cession treaties
with the Sauk and Fox Indians and Plains tribes. Much of Iowa and
adjoining lands in Missouri and Minnesota were obtained in exchange
for annuities.

The Black Hawk War, resulting to a considerable degree from
Sauk dissatisfaction with the Treaty of 1830, involved troops stationed at Prairie du Chien. When Black Hawk surrendered he was
confined there by Zachary Taylor.

(William T. Hagan, The Sac and Fox Indians; Louise Phelps
Kellogg, The British Régime in Wisconsin and the Northwest; Charles
J. Kappler, ed., Indian Affairs: Laws and Treaties, II.)

PRESQU'ISLE, FORT. Fort Presqu'Isle was built by the French in
1753 at the present site of Erie, Pennsylvania. It served as a center of troop movements until it came under British control in 1759.
At the outbreak of Pontiac's War, the fort was garrisoned by Ensign
John Christie and 26 soldiers. On June 15, 1763, a force of Seneca,
Ottawa, Chippewa, and Huron Indians surrounded the fort and began
a well-organized siege. They broke through the barricade, occupied
several buildings, and rained fire arrows on the blockhouse. Finally,
cut off from the well and threatened by a trench dug below the walls
of the blockhouse, Christie surrendered the fort upon Indian assurances that his men would be permitted to march to Fort Pitt. But
as soon as the soldiers marched out, they were seized and sent to
several Indian towns. Christie was released to the English at Fort
Detroit, but two of his men were tortured to death by the Hurons.

(Howard H. Peckham, Pontiac and the Indian Uprising; William
A. Hunter, Forts on the Pennsylvania Frontier; Dale Van Every,
Forth to the Wilderness.)

PRING, MARTIN, EXPEDITION. Martin Pring, an English sea captain, was sent to explore the New England coast in 1603 by a company of Bristol merchants. At the harbor of Provincetown, Massachusetts, he built a barricade to protect the sailors from Indian attacks. The Nauset Indians proved to be friendly, however, and visited the English so often that they wore out their welcome. Finally, Pring set the Englishmen's dogs upon them, and "they were obviously disturbed by this less than reciprocal conduct."--Neal Salisbury. Warriors attacked the barricade, but were driven away by gunshots and dogs. Soon afterward, Pring departed, oblivious to Indian invitations to remain.

(Neal Salisbury, Manitou and Providence.)

PRINTZ, JOHAN. Johan Printz, a Swedish cavalry officer, was appointed governor of New Sweden in 1642. Upon his arrival in America the following year he constructed Fort Elfsborough to guard the entrance to the Delaware River and three fur trade posts on the Schuylkill. Instructed to treat the Indians fairly and to convert them to Christianity if possible, he endeavored to divert their trade away from the Dutch by offering better prices for furs. In addition, he warned that the Dutch intended to massacre every Indian on the Delaware. In 1646, he bought additional land from the Indians to prevent Dutch settlement. Until his replacement several years later, he dominated the fur trade, denying both Dutch and English the opportunity to prosper.

(E. B. O'Callaghan, History of New Netherland, I; C. A. Weslager, Dutch Explorers, Traders, and Settlers in the Delaware Valley.)

PROVIDENCE, RHODE ISLAND, RAID. On March 29, 1676, during King Philip's War, Providence was attacked by Narraganset Indians. A majority of the inhabitants took refuge in the garrison house, and only one colonist was killed, refusing to run from the Indians as he believed that his Bible would protect him. Most of the town was burned to the ground.

(Douglas Edward Leach, Flintlock and Tomahawk; Charles H. Lincoln, ed., Narratives of the Indian Wars.)

PUMHAM, NARRAGANSET CHIEF. Pumham (Pomham), born about 1730 in Rhode Island, was a strong supporter of King Philip during the war of 1675-76. The English burned his village near the present site of Warwick in 1675. In July 1676, he and his followers were on the verge of starvation when a force of colonists and Christian Indians attacked them near Dedham, Massachusetts. Pumham and most of his people were killed.

(Douglas Edward Leach, Flintlock and Tomahawk.)

PURPOODUCK, MAINE, RAID. Purpooduck, Maine, now known as Cape Elizabeth, was attacked by Abnaki Indians in August 1703. Twenty-five citizens were killed, and eight survivors were carried into captivity. Most of the male residents were away from home fishing and thus escaped the attack.

(Herbert Milton Sylvester, Indian Wars of New England.)

-Q-

QUABAUG see BROOKFIELD, MASSACHUSETTS

QUEEN ALLIQUIPPA see ALLIQUIPPA, QUEEN

QUEEN ESTHER see MONTOUR, LOUIS, FAMILY OF

QUINNAPIN, NARRAGANSET CHIEF. Quinnapin, a Narraganset
sachem born about 1630, was related by birth or marriage to some
of the most important chiefs in New England colonial history. A
nephew of Miantonomo and a brother-in-law of Metacom, he was married to the famous female Wampanoag chief, Wetamoo. Like most of
his relatives, he played a leading role in King Philip's War, particularly in the raid on Lancaster, Massachusetts, of February 10, 1676.
Near the end of the war, he was captured by the colonists, tried
by court-martial at Newport, Rhode Island, and executed.
    (F. W. Hodge, ed., Handbook of American Indians, II; Douglas
Edward Leach, Flintlock and Tomahawk.)

QUINNEY, JOHN W., STOCKBRIDGE CHIEF. John W. Quinney (The
Dish) was born in 1797 at New Stockbridge, New York, of a distinguished line of Mohegan chiefs. He was educated at Westchester,
New York, and returned to live with his people, then known as the
Stockbridge Indians. In 1822, he and chiefs of neighboring tribes
purchased land from the Menominee Indians near Green Bay, Wisconsin, as a home for Indians from New York, but the U.S. government claimed the property after the Menominees disavowed the sale.
Quinney went to Washington to protest, but he had to settle for a
payment of $25,000 for the loss of the Indians' improvements. Soon
afterward, the Stockbridges and other New York Indians were
granted land on Lake Winnebago largely as a result of his efforts.
    Quinney created a constitution for his people in 1837 that sub-
stituted election of chiefs for traditional hereditary elevation. In
1846, as a result of allotment of lands in severalty, the Stockbridges
began selling their holdings to whites until Quinney managed to have
the procedure repealed. After his election as principal chief in 1852,
he persuaded the government to cede 460 acres of their former New
York land back to his people, and they returned to Stockbridge. He
died there on July 21, 1855.
    (Frederick J. Dockstader, Great North American Indians; Wil-
liam C. Sturtevant, ed., Handbook of North American Indians, XV.)

QUINNIPIAC INDIANS. The Quinnipiac Indians, a small Algonquian
tribe, lived along the Quinnipiac River in New Haven County, Connecticut, during early colonial times. In 1638, they sold most of
their land to the English for a large quantity of goods, retaining
hunting rights and a small tract for their principal town. In 1768,
some of them settled among the Tunxi Indians. The tribe had
dwindled to a handful of people by 1774.
    (John W. De Forest, History of the Indians of Connecticut;
F. W. Hodge, ed., Handbook of American Indians, II.)

-R-

RADISSON, PIERRE-ESPRIT. Pierre-Esprit Radisson was born in France in 1636 and moved with his parents to Canada about the age of 15. In 1652, while hunting with friends near Three Rivers, he was captured by the Mohawk Indians and marched to their village. The Mohawks murdered his companions, but they spared his life because he demonstrated great bravery under torture. He was adopted by a chief, treated kindly, and became partially assimilated.

Radisson was torn between a desire to return to his parents and an enjoyment of the wild, free life of the Indians. Somewhat reluctantly, he agreed to a proposal by an Algonquian Indian prisoner that they escape while on a canoe trip. During their escape they murdered three Mohawks. Quickly recaptured and returned to the village, Radisson endured severe tortures, and he was about to be burned at the stake when he was rescued by the chief who had adopted him. After visiting Iroquois villages throughout New York, he fled from his captors and reached safety among the Dutch at Fort Orange in October 1653.

Radisson's exploring experiences after his arrival at Three Rivers in 1654 were recounted in manuscripts that he wrote many years afterward. Their veracity has been disputed by historians ever since their discovery in 1880. John Anthony Caruso has conceded that Radisson's chronology was "hopeless," that he narrated other explorers' adventures as if they had been his own, and that he lied about visiting places that he had never seen. Nevertheless, Caruso asserted, "Radisson proved that a man may fabricate and still be valuable, even to historians."

Louise Phelps Kellogg, after careful study of the manuscripts and contemporary Canadian documents, concluded that Radisson did not accompany his brother-in-law in 1654 as claimed to establish trade with the western tribes. (See GROSEILLIERS, MEDART CHOUART DE.) But he probably was a member of the French colony at Onondaga in 1657-58 (see ONONDAGA INDIANS), and he did accompany Groseilliers to Green Bay and the Illinois country in 1658. They returned to Montreal in 1660 with a fortune in furs, but the governor confiscated them because the expedition had been made without his authorization.

After this disappointment, Radisson and Groseilliers deserted the French and helped the English to establish the fur trade on Hudson Bay. Radisson died in England about 1710.

"After Nicolet he was the first Frenchman whose account of voyages to the Northwest has been preserved. According to the various interpretations of his journals he may have been the first white man in Iowa, in Minnesota, and in the Dakotas, or in Manitoba, and possibly he was the first white man to visit the Mississippi River."--Louise Phelps Kellogg.

(Pierre-Esprit Radisson, Voyages; Louise Phelps Kellogg, The French Régime in Wisconsin and the Northwest; John Anthony Caruso, The Mississippi Valley Frontier.)

RAGUENEAU, PAUL. Father Paul Ragueneau, a Jesuit missionary, was born in Paris on March 18, 1608. After study at Clermont and Bourges, he sailed to Canada in 1636 and labored among the Huron Indians until the missions were destroyed by the Iroquois in 1649. Afterward, he served as superior of all Canadian missions from 1650 to 1653.

Ragueneau's work among the Indians of the present United States began in 1657 when he set out from Quebec to Onondaga with 45 Iroquois warriors and 50 Christian Hurons. During the journey, the Iroquois massacred the Hurons. "Some of them were stabbed or tomahawked in my arms and on my breast as I tried to shield them," Ragueneau wrote in one of his many reports published in the Jesuit Relations and Allied Documents.

While serving as superior at the French settlement at Onondaga, Ragueneau was warned that the Iroquois intended to murder the French. He planned and directed their escape to Quebec in April 1658. (See ONONDAGA INDIANS.) He returned to France in 1662 and died there in 1680.

(T. J. Campbell, Pioneer Priests of North America; Edna Kenton, ed., Black Gown and Redskins.)

RAISIN RIVER MASSACRE. In January 1813, Gen. James Winchester, commanding Gen. William Henry Harrison's left wing during the Detroit campaign, responded to appeals by citizens of Frenchtown on the Raisin River to rescue them from the British. He sent 700 Kentuckians, commanded by Cols. John Allen and William Lewis, who defeated a force of British and Indians on January 17 and occupied the settlement. Winchester arrived with 300 reinforcements soon afterward, but he failed to heed warnings of an impending attack by Col. Henry Proctor and a large army of British and Indians from Amherstburg, just across the Canadian border from Detroit. When Proctor attacked at dawn on January 22, Winchester was asleep at a private home away from his troops. When he finally arrived at the scene and ordered a retreat, his men were under such heavy attack by the Indians that it was impossible to effect an orderly withdrawal. Many of the Kentuckians were killed. Winchester was captured, and under threat of an Indian massacre, he ordered his 500 survivors to surrender.

Fearing that Harrison was on his way to the scene, Proctor retreated to Fort Malden, taking with him all of the American prisoners able to walk. Left in two houses at Frenchtown were 64 wounded Americans under the supervision and care of a British officer and two doctors. During their march, the British traded whiskey for the Americans claimed as Indian captives. Afterward, aroused by the liquor, the Indians returned to Frenchtown and set fire to the building housing the wounded Americans. Elias Darnall, who escaped in spite of his wounds, described the ensuing massacre:

> I saw my fellow soldiers, naked and wounded, crawling out of the houses to avoid being consumed in the flames. Some that had not been able to turn themselves on their bed

for four days, through fear of being burned to death, arose
and walked out.... A number, unable to get out, perished
in the flames.... The savages rushed on the wounded ...
shot and tomahawked and scalped them, and cruelly mangled
their naked bodies while they lay agonizing and weltering in
their blood. A number were taken towards Malden, but,
being unable to march with speed, were massacred. ... the
road was strewn for miles with mangled bodies left for the
birds and beasts tɔ tear to pieces and devour.

The Indians took the heads of their victims to Detroit and
mounted them on poles. The atrocity so aroused the Americans that
"Remember the River Raisin" became a rallying cry during the duration of the War of 1812.
(Elias Darnall, A Journal Containing an Interesting and Accurate Account of the Hardships, Sufferings, Battles, Defeat, and
Captivity of Those Heroic Kentucky Volunteers and Regulars, Commanded by General Winchester, in the Year 1812-1813; John Anthony
Caruso, The Great Lakes Frontier; Frederick Drimmer, ed., Scalps
and Tomahawks; Fairfax Downey, Indian Wars of the U.S. Army.)

RALE, SEBASTIEN see RASLES, SEBASTIAN

RAMSAY, DAVID. David Ramsay was born in England, came to
America as a British soldier, and fought in the French and Indian
War. Afterward, he became an Indian trader on Lake Erie among the
Missisaugas and Chippewas. Notorious for selling liquor to Indians
and murdering them when they became intoxicated, he brought the
scalps of three men, a woman, and an infant to Niagara in 1772. But
the commanding officer confined him and refused to pay the bounty.
When the Indians learned of his presence at Niagara, they demanded
that he be turned over to them for punishment. Upon being refused, they threatened to burn down the fort. To avoid an attack,
the commandant sent him to Montreal for trial, where after more than
a year in confinement, he was released for lack of evidence.
(Charles A. Hanna, The Wilderness Trail.)

RAPIDS OF THE MIAMI, TREATY OF THE. Lewis Cass and Duncan
McArthur negotiated the Treaty of the Rapids of the Miami on Sep-
tember 29, 1817. Land cessions were obtained from the Chippewa,
Potawatomi, and Wyandot Indians in exchange for annuities.
(Charles J. Kappler, ed., Indian Affairs: Laws and Treaties,
II.)

RARITAN INDIANS. The Raritan Indians, a branch of the Delaware
nation, lived along the Raritan and Delaware rivers during early
colonial times. Their principal village was located near the present
site of Trenton, New Jersey. Hostilities arose with the Dutch in
1633 when warriors attacked traders, but peace was negotiated the
following year. In 1640, the Dutch accused them of attacking a
yacht, and in retaliation, 70 soldiers murdered the chief's brother

and destroyed the tribe's corn. In 1641, the Raritans killed four Dutch soldiers on Staten Island, and New Amsterdam officials offered rewards for their scalps. When a settler brought in the head of a Raritan chief, the tribe decided to make peace and pay the hated tax that Dutch officials had imposed.

The Raritans gradually sold their lands to Dutch and English settlers. After merging with remnants of other New Jersey tribes, they lived on the Brotherton Reservation until 1802, when they joined the Brotherton Indians in New York. In 1833, the few remaining Raritans moved with the Stockbridge Indians to Lake Winnebago in Wisconsin.

(F. W. Hodge, ed., Handbook of American Indians, II; E. B. O'Callaghan, History of New Netherland, I; Allen W. Trelease, Indian Affairs in Colonial New York.)

RASLES, SEBASTIAN. Sebastian Rasles (Sébastien Râle), a Jesuit missionary, was born in France between 1654 and 1657. He studied at Lyons and sailed to Canada in 1689. He was assigned first to missions near Quebec, where he quickly mastered the Algonquian languages. In 1691, he was sent to the Illinois Indians, and three years later, he was transferred to the Abnaki mission at Norridgewock, on the Kennebec River, in the present state of Maine.

Rasles was greatly beloved by the Norridgewock Abnakis, who built a chapel and attended his services regularly. Not long after his arrival, Malecite Indians visited Norridgewock, and the missionary converted the entire tribe to Christianity. When Protestant missionaries from Massachusetts attempted to influence his converts, he threatened to leave Norridgewock if they listened to the English.

While peace prevailed between France and England, Father Rasles attempted to prevent his Indians from attacking the settlements. But at the onset of Queen Anne's War in 1702, he was recruited by French officials to serve as an instrument of their colonial policy. The New England historian Jeremy Belknap has asserted that

> knowing the power of superstition over the savage mind, he took advantage of this, and of their prejudice against the English, to promote the cause, and strengthen the interest of the French among them. He even made the offices of devotion serve as incentives to their ferocity, and kept a flag, in which was depicted a cross, surrounded by bows and arrows, which he used to hoist on a pole, at the door of his church, when he gave them absolution, previously to their engaging in any warlike enterprise.

In 1705, the governor of Massachusetts called upon the Norridgewocks to drive out their priest, and when they refused, he organized a military expedition that burned the church and compelled Rasles to hide in the woods. In 1721, a second English expedition, 300 men led by Col. Thomas Westbrook, burned the church which had been rebuilt and put the priest to flight. In 1724, during Dummer's War, Col. Jeremy Moulton led a force of New England frontiersmen through the forest and took Norridgewock by surprise. Almost every Indian was killed or captured. Father Rasles was shot to death as he stood loading a gun in his doorway. The colonists mangled his body and took his scalp to Boston, where the people viewed it with much joy and relief.

(Jeremy Belknap, History of New Hampshire, I; Francis Parkman, A Half-Century of Conflict; Herbert Milton Sylvester, Indian Wars of New England, III; James Axtell, The Invasion Within.)

THE RAT, HURON CHIEF see ADARIO, HURON CHIEF

RAWLINS, AARON, FAMILY OF. In 1723, 18 Indians from Canada surrounded the home of Aaron Rawlins on the Piscasick River, near Lamprey Landing, on the Maine-New Hampshire frontier. Unaware of the presence of the war party, Mrs. Rawlins and 2 small children came outside the house and were immediately seized by the Indians. Rawlins and his elder daughter stood off the attackers, firing at every Indian who attempted to enter until he was killed by a random shot. Then the Indians rushed through the door and tomahawked his daughter. They carried Mrs. Rawlins and her son and small daughter to Canada. The boy was adopted, became thoroughly assimilated, and lived the remainder of his life with the Indians. The girl grew up in Canada and married a Frenchman.

(Jeremy Belknap, History of New Hampshire, I; Herbert Milton Sylvester, Indian Wars of New England, III.)

RECOVERY, FORT. Fort Recovery was established in 1793 at the site of St. Clair's defeat near the Ohio-Indiana boundary. Garrisoned only by 150 men under the command of Maj. William McMahon, the fort was surrounded by 2,000 warriors from Ohio and the Great Lakes region on June 30, 1794. Unaware of the war party's presence, McMahon and 90 of his men emerged from the fort with 300 pack horses, preparing to depart for Greenville. When the Indians opened fire, McMahon was killed and the pack train captured. A cavalry force that sortied to the rescue was compelled to flee back inside the stockade.

Chief Little Turtle and several British and French rangers urged caution in attempting to carry the fort, but the jubilant warriors launched a headlong attack. The defenders held them at bay with cannon and rifle fire during two days of fierce combat. Finally, having sustained greater losses than they had suffered during their defeat of St. Clair, the Indians gathered their fallen warriors and abandoned the attack. Those from the lakes left Little Turtle and returned to their villages.

(Dale Van Every, Ark of Empire; Theodore Roosevelt, The Winning of the West, V; Randolph C. Downes, Council Fires on the Upper Ohio.)

RED BIRD, WINNEBAGO CHIEF. Red Bird (Wanig-suchka) was born about 1788 near Prairie du Chien, Wisconsin. He was friendly to white settlers and tried to protect them from hostile Indians until, in

1827, a misunderstanding caused him to become involved in events that culminated in the so-called Red Bird War. Two Winnebagos were arrested for the murder of a white family, and an erroneous rumor reached the tribe that they had been turned over to Chippewa Indian enemies and bludgeoned to death. Without waiting to learn the truth, the Winnebago council instructed Red Bird to retaliate.

At first, Red Bird intended only to destroy livestock, but when Winnebago warriors called him a coward, he determined that some settlers must die. On June 26, 1827, he and two companions knocked on the door of the Registre Gagnier family and were invited inside to partake of a meal. While they were eating, Gagnier became alarmed by their hostile demeanor and reached for his rifle. Instantly, Red Bird shot him to death. While the Indians were occupied in killing a neighbor named Solomon Lipcap, Mrs. Gagnier and her son escaped, leaving behind an infant whom the Indians had stabbed, incorrectly assuming that it was mortally wounded.

Afterward, Red Bird returned to his village to plan another attack. Three days later, he and his followers fired upon several keelboats on the Mississippi, killing two crewmen and wounding four. He hoped that this action would incite other Indians to attack the settlers, but he failed to obtain their support.

Notified that troops would be sent to annihilate the Winnebagos, Red Bird surrendered on September 27 to give up his life for his people. He was convicted of murder, but he died in prison at Prairie du Chien before sentence was pronounced.

(R. David Edmunds, ed., American Indian Leaders; Frederick J. Dockstader, Great North American Indians.)

RED JACKET, SENECA CHIEF. Red Jacket (Sagoyewatha) was born about 1756 at Canoga, New York. More renowned for his oratory than his prowess as a warrior, he fled from the field during the Battle of Oriskany in 1777, avoided combat during the Wyoming Valley invasion of 1778, and was first to take to his heels at the Battle of Newtown in 1779. Afterward, when the Americans advanced to Kanadesaga, he killed a cow and smeared his tomahawk with blood to back up his boast that he had slain a soldier. These incidents caused Joseph Brant and Cornplanter to call him the cowardly cowkiller.

In 1779, during Sullivan's invasion of the Iroquois villages, Red Jacket advocated signing a peace treaty with the Americans. He became a determined opponent, however, of tribal acceptance of white culture traits, and he resisted, particularly, the work of missionaries among the Senecas. In 1792, he went with a delegation of chiefs to Philadelphia and received a medal from President Washington. Perhaps this recognition played a role in his decision to support the United States during the War of 1812, but at least one American officer accused him of treasonable conduct during that conflict.

After the war, Red Jacket led Iroquois attempts to preserve ownership of Indian lands, and in 1821, he persuaded the New York legislature to guarantee Indian title to their reservations. Soon afterward, however, he became greatly addicted to alcohol, and his followers deserted him. He was deposed as chief in 1827, but the Office of Indian Affairs reinstated his authority soon afterward. He died on January 20, 1830.

"Although he argued hotly against land sales, he also ratified many agreements disposing of Iroquois land."--Frederick J. Dockstader.

"In later years, at least, some of his tribesmen were able to overlook his shortcomings as a warrior and hold him in high esteem because of his ability as a civil leader."--Barbara Graymont.

(Frederick J. Dockstader, Great North American Indians; Barbara Graymont, The Iroquois in the American Revolution; F. W. Hodge, ed., Handbook of American Indians, II.)

REHOBOTH, MASSACHUSETTS, RAID. Rehoboth, Massachusetts, was located not far from King Philip's village. When that formidable chief began the war that bears his name, Rehoboth was among the first settlements to feel his wrath during the spring offensive of 1676. On March 26, a Narraganset war party killed several Rehoboth men during an attack on a military force commanded by Capt. Michael Pierce. Two days later, they attacked the village itself. Most of the citizens survived by defending themselves in garrison houses, but the remainder of the town was burned to the ground.

(Douglas Edward Leach, Flintlock and Tomahawk.)

RICE, SILAS AND TIMOTHY, CAPTIVITY OF. Silas Rice, 9, and his brother Timothy, 7, were captured by Iroquois Indians in 1704. Taken to an Indian village on the St. Lawrence, they were adopted into the families of chiefs as replacements for sons killed in battle. They became completely assimilated, married Indian girls, and in time, exhibited such qualities of leadership that they became prominent chiefs of the Caughnawagas.

In 1749, a relative found Timothy and persuaded him to visit his original home, but the white chief returned at the first opportunity to his Indian family. Timothy lived until 1777 and Silas until 1779. They left almost 700 descendants, many of whom became Iroquois leaders.

(J. Norman Heard, White into Red.)

RICHARDVILLE, JOHN B. see PESHEWAH, MIAMI CHIEF

RIVER RAISIN MASSACRE see RAISIN RIVER MASSACRE

ROBERTSON, CHARLES, EXPEDITION. British lieutenant Charles Robertson was stationed at Fort Detroit in 1763. Unaware of the impending Pontiac's War, he left Detroit on May 6 with a scientist named Sir Robert Davers, seven soldiers, 2 sailors, and a Pawnee Indian guide to obtain soundings at Lake Ste. Claire. At the mouth of the Ste. Claire River, a Chippewa war party opened fire on them without warning. Robertson, Davers, and the two sailors died instantly, the first casualties of Pontiac's War, and their companions were captured. The Chippewas consumed Robertson's body except for an arm that a warrior transformed into a tobacco pouch.

(Howard H. Peckham, Pontiac and the Indian Uprising; Dale Van Every, Forth to the Wilderness.)

ROBINSON, ALEXANDER, POTAWATOMI CHIEF. Alexander Robinson (Cheecheebingway), son of a Scottish father and an Indian mother, was born at Mackinac, Michigan, in 1789. A friend of the whites, he tried to prevent the Fort Dearborn massacre in 1812 and succeeded in saving the life of the commandant Capt. Nathan Heald. In 1827, he prevented the Potawatomis from making an assault on Fort Dearborn.

Robinson was a signer of several land cession treaties as well as the Treaty of Prairie du Chien which established boundaries between the northwestern tribes. He fought on the side of the settlers during the Black Hawk War.

(James A. Clifton, The Prairie People.)

ROCHESTER, NEW HAMPSHIRE, RAIDS. Between 1746 and 1748, Rochester, New Hampshire, sustained four Indian raids. In June 1746, warriors killed four men and captured a man and a boy at work in the fields. On August 6, they returned to Rochester, but the only settler to die was shot by mistake by a soldier. In June 1747, a war party attacked the men in the fields, but it was repulsed, largely because of the courage of teenagers John Place and Paul Jemens, who held them at bay. On May 1, 1748, Indians were discovered by Mrs. Jonathan Hodgedon when she went to milk her cows. She gave the alarm and lost her own life, but the citizens had time to take refuge in garrison houses, and the marauders withdrew.

(Jeremy Belknap, History of New Hampshire, I; Herbert Milton Sylvester, Indian Wars of New England, III.)

ROGERS, ROBERT. Maj. Robert Rogers, the most famous ranger and Indian fighter of the French and Indian War, was born at Methuen, Massachusetts, in 1731, and grew up on the New Hampshire frontier. Much of his youth was spent in exploring the wilderness and in trading with the Indians. These experiences, combined with his intense hatred of the French and their Indian allies, prepared him to lead amazing wilderness raids and scouting expeditions from Canada to the Carolinas.

In 1755, Rogers recruited a band of New Hampshire frontiersmen to repel Indian raids on New England settlements. His tactics succeeded so well that a dozen such small forces were raised, and Rogers, appointed captain by William Shirley, was placed in command of them all. Between 1756 and 1758 he scouted the area around Crown Point and Ticonderoga, fighting several battles with the French and Indians, inflicting and suffering many casualties, and narrowly escaping to safety at Fort Edward.

In 1759, Rogers performed the most daring exploit of his career--the destruction of the Abnaki town of St. Francis, Quebec, source of some of the most devastating raids against the New England settlements. Promoted to the rank of major, he was instructed by Gen.

Jeffrey Amherst to "take your revenge, but don't forget that, though those dastardly villains have promiscuously murdered women and children of all ages, it is my order that no women or children be killed or hurt."

After enduring incredible hardships that compelled 40 of his 220 men to turn back, Rogers arrived on October 6 at St. Francis, located on the St. Francis River near its juncture with the St. Lawrence. He described the action as follows:

> At half an hour before sunrise I surprised the town when they were all fast asleep, on the right, left, and center, which was done with so much alacrity by both the officers and men, that the enemy had not time to recover themselves, or take arms for their own defence, till they were chiefly destroyed, except some few of them who took to the water. About forty of my people pursued them, who destroyed such as attempted to make their escape that way, and sunk both them and their boats. A little after sunrise I set fire to all their houses, except three, in which there was corn.... The fire consumed many of the Indians who had concealed themselves in the cellars and lofts of their houses. About seven o'clock in the morning the affair was completely over, in which time we had killid at least two hundred Indians....

Rogers lost only 1 man, a Stockbridge Indian scout. He redeemed 5 captives. Six hundred English scalps were found displayed on poles throughout St. Francis.

Rogers participated in the Montreal campaign in 1760. Afterward, he was sent to the western posts to accept the surrender of the French garrisons. At the mouth of Grand River he met Pontiac, overcame his hostility with presents and praise, and according to his own assertion, persuaded him to escort the rangers to Detroit.

In 1761, Rogers led a company of rangers to South Carolina to fight the Cherokees. In 1763, he accompanied a relief force to Detroit, besieged by Pontiac, and on July 31, he played a major role in extricating the survivors of a disastrous sortie led by Capt. James Dalyell. (See BLOODY RUN.)

After Pontiac's War, Rogers indulged in illicit trade with the Indians, earned the disfavor of Sir William Johnson, and sailed to England to seek fame and fortune. Greatly lionized in London, he published his journals and received the appointment of commandant at Mackinac. There he concocted a plan to establish a western colony, with himself as governor, to explore the continent as far as the Pacific in search of the Northwest Passage (see CARVER, JONATHAN), and to rid the region of French traders. In 1767, he averted a war between the Chippewas and the Sioux by distributing an immense load of presents. He went heavily into debt and tried to recoup by trading rum to the Indians. Arrested on charges of violating his orders, he stood trial by court martial, and although he was acquitted for lack of evidence, he lost his command. He made a second trip to London seeking to improve his financial position, but there he was confined in debtor's prison until relatives secured his release.

In 1775, Rogers returned to America and attempted to gain favor of both sides at the onset of the Revolutionary War. American officers distrusted him, however, and imprisoned him as a spy. Escaping to the British he fought on their side throughout the war. Afterward, he lived in London until he died in poverty in 1795.

"He was ambitious and violent, yet able in more ways than one, ... and so skilled in woodcraft, so energetic and resolute, that his services were invaluable."--Francis Parkman.

(Robert Rogers, Journals of Major Robert Rogers; Francis Parkman, Montcalm and Wolfe; Howard H. Peckham, Pontiac and the Indian Uprising; Arthur Pound, Johnson of the Mohawks; Louise Phelps Kellogg, The British Régime in Wisconsin and the Northwest.)

ROSEBOOM, JOHANNES, EXPEDITIONS. Johannes Roseboom (Rooseboom) was a member of an influential Albany, New York, Dutch family at the time the English gained control of the colony. In 1685, a French deserter visited Albany and offered to guide English traders to a rich fur country controlled by the Ottawa Indians. Appointed by Gov. Thomas Dongan to lead the expedition, Roseboom was the first non-Frenchman known to have visited the Great Lakes. Welcomed by the Ottawas and Hurons, he traded goods, trinkets, and rum, and he returned safely with 11 canoes deeply laden with furs.

In 1687, Roseboom commanded an expedition of 20 canoes that undertook a second fur trading expedition. They encountered a French military force on Lake Erie, had their goods confiscated, and were imprisoned at Niagara and elsewhere until protests by English officials secured their release.

(Louise Phelps Kellogg, The French Régime in Wisconsin and the Northwest; Frank H. Severance, An Old Frontier of France.)

ROWLANDSON, MARY, CAPTIVITY OF. Mary Rowlandson, wife of the Reverend Joseph Rowlandson, was born in England in 1635 and emigrated with her parents to Salem, Massachusetts, by 1638. In 1653, they moved to Lancaster, Massachusetts, and three years later, Mary married the town's minister. They had four children: Mary (born 1657, died 1660); Joseph (born 1661); Mary (born 1665); Sarah (born 1675).

With the onset of King Philip's War in 1675, the residents of Lancaster slept in six stockaded garrison houses, and the Rowlandson home sheltered some 40 citizens. Warned by scouts that a war party intended to attack Lancaster, Rev. Rowlandson rushed to Boston in February 1676 to plead for troop reinforcements. Before he returned, the Narraganset Indians struck the settlement on February 10. Mary, whose story became one of the most famous and historically important of all narratives of captivity, described the assault:

>   Their first coming was about sun-rising. Hearing the
> noise of some guns, we looked out: several houses were

burning.... At length they came and beset our own house, and quickly it was the dolefulest day that ever mine eyes saw ... the bullets seemed to fly like hail; and quickly they wounded one man among us, then another, then a third. About two hours ... they had been about the house before they prevailed to fire it (which they did with flax and hemp which they brought out of the barn ...). They fired it once, and one ventured out and quenched it, but they quickly fired it again, and that took. Now is the dreadful hour come.... Some in our house were fighting for their lives, others wallowing in their blood, the house on fire over our heads, and the bloody heathen ready to knock us on the head if we stirred out.... Then I took my children ... to go forth and leave the house: but as soon as we came to the door and appeared, the Indians shot so thick ... one went through my side (as would seem) through the bowels and hand of my dear child in my arms ... the Indians laid hold of us, pulling me one way, and the children, another, and said, "Come, go along with us."

Mary, carrying her mortally wounded infant daughter, Sarah, was marched to the Narraganset village. There she was sold to Quinnapin, a Narraganset war chief, and his wife, Wetamoo, sister-in-law of King Philip. On February 18, Sarah died of her wound. Her other children, Joseph and Mary, were held nearby, but she was forbidden to speak with them. Soon afterward, her captors joined King Philip, and the hostiles moved quickly through southern Vermont and New Hampshire. She sewed for Philip and other Indians in order to obtain food.

Finally, in May 1676, Massachusetts authorities ransomed Mary, and she joined her husband. Her son was redeemed in June, and her daughter escaped to the settlements soon afterward. When the surviving members of the family were reunited, they lived in Boston until the war ended. In 1677, Rev. Rowlandson became pastor of the church at Wethersfield, Connecticut. He died in 1678, and Mary lived on a widow's pension. The date of her death is unknown.

(Mary Rowlandson, The Narrative of the Captivity and Restoration of Mrs. Mary Rowlandson; Howard H. Peckham, Captured by Indians.)

RYE BEACH, NEW HAMPSHIRE, RAID. Rye Beach, near Portsmouth, New Hampshire, was attacked by Indians who came in canoes on an autumn day in 1690. They ranged through the settlement throughout the day, killing or capturing 21 citizens.

(Herbert Milton Sylvester, Indian Wars of New England, II.)

-S-

SAC INDIANS see SAUK INDIANS

SACO, MAINE, RAIDS. Several settlements were established along
the Saco River in southwestern Maine in the early 1630's. While
most of the settlers were farmers and fishermen, many participated
in the Indian trade as well. Abnaki hostility during King Philip's
War compelled them to abandon the Saco Bay and River settlements
in 1675.

Reoccupied after the war, the Saco settlements were subjected
to Abnaki attacks for almost a century. On January 23, 1689, a
large war party killed 8 or 9 settlers. The Abnakis returned the
following year, slaughtered 9 citizens, and destroyed their homes.
In 1703, Frenchmen and Indians attacked the cabins at Saco Falls,
killing 11 people and capturing 24. In 1746 and 1747, the Abnakis
raided the Saco settlements repeatedly, murdering men in the fields
and marching captives to Canada.

(Samuel Adams Drake, The Border Wars of New England; Herbert Milton Sylvester, Indian Wars of New England, II-III.)

SADEKANAKTIE, ONONDAGA CHIEF. Sadekanaktie (Adaquarande),
a famous Onondaga orator, was born about 1640. He spoke at the
Onondaga council of 1690 with such eloquence that the Indians carried him, ill and lame, on a litter to Albany in 1693 to act as their
principal speaker. He died in 1701.

(Cadwallader Colden, The History of the Five Indian Nations;
Frederick J. Dockstader, Great North American Indians.)

SAGADAHOC COLONY, MAINE. Sagadahoc, the Kennebec River region, was settled in 1607 by George Popham with the assistance of
Tahanedo, an Indian chief who had been kidnapped and taken to
England by Capt. George Waymouth two years earlier. The colony
was abandoned within a few months as the result of Indian hostility,
bitter winter weather, and the deaths of Popham and other leaders.

(Charles M. Andrews, The Colonial Period of American History,
I; Neal Salisbury, Manitou and Providence.)

SAGAUNASH, POTAWATOMI CHIEF. Sagaunash (Billy Caldwell), son
of a British Army officer and an Indian mother, was born in Canada
about 1780. His father had him educated in a Catholic school near
Amherstburg, and as he spoke English and French fluently, he served
as an interpreter during his youth. About 1799, he became a fur
trader, first as an independent, and later in the service of John
Kinzie. During the War of 1812, Sagaunash served as secretary to
Tecumseh and as British liaison to Indian allies. He was assigned
the responsibility of preventing Indian atrocities during and after
battles.

After the war, Sagaunash switched his allegiance to the Americans. He lived at Chicago after 1820, served as justice of the peace,
and helped to quell the Winnebago uprising known as the Red Eird
War in 1827. During the Black Hawk War, he was a leader of the
Potawatomi scouts that served United States forces. In 1833, he
signed a series of treaties that ceded Potawatomi land in Illinois and
Wisconsin. Afterward, he joined the Potawatomis living west of Lake

Michigan and moved with them to Iowa. He died at Council Bluffs on September 28, 1841.

(James A. Clifton, The Prairie People; Frederick J. Dockstader, Great North American Indians.)

SAGINAW, MICHIGAN, TREATIES OF. On September 24, 1819, Lewis Cass obtained a large land cession from the Chippewa Indians by means of a treaty negotiated at Saginaw. The United States agreed to pay an annuity of $1,000 and to provide agricultural tools, livestock, and the services of a blacksmith.

On January 23, 1838, Henry R. Schoolcraft negotiated a treaty at Saginaw with the Chippewas. It resolved problems regarding land sales arranged under previous treaties.

(Charles J. Kappler, ed., Indian Affairs: Laws and Treaties, II.)

SAGOYEWATHA, SENECA CHIEF see RED JACKET, SENECA CHIEF

SAINT-CASTIN, JEAN VINCENT D'ABBADIE, BARON DE. Jean Vincent d'Abbadie, Baron de Saint-Castin, was born in France, became an army officer, and sailed to Canada with the Carignan Regiment in 1665 to fight the Iroquois. After the Treaty of Breda in 1667, he commanded the post at Pentagoet (present site of Castin, Maine), in territory disputed by the French and English. After his regiment disbanded, he operated Pentagoet as a trading post, married the daughter of the Abnaki chief Madockawando, and gained tremendous influence over the Indians.

Saint-Castin traded with the English colonies until 1688. Then, in the spring, an English force led by Gov. Edmund Andros raided his post during his absence, confiscated his goods, and destroyed his home and fort. Infuriated, the Frenchman incited the Indians to retaliate in a series of raids that contributed to the onset of King William's War. He participated in the capture of Pemaquid in 1689, (perhaps) in the siege of Fort Loyal in 1690, the raid on Wells in 1692, and the destruction of Fort William Henry in 1696. (See CASCO, PEMAQUID.) In 1701, he returned to France, leaving his trading interests to his half-Indian son.

(Francis Parkman, Count Frontenac and New France Under Louis XIV; Jeremy Belknap, History of New Hampshire, I; Herbert Milton Sylvester, Indian Wars of New England, II-III.)

ST. CLAIR'S DEFEAT. After Gen. Josiah Harmar failed to subdue the hostile Indians of the Old Northwest, President Washington appointed Arthur St. Clair, governor of the Northwest Territory, to undertake the task. St. Clair had served with distinction as one of Washington's officers during the revolutionary war, but by 1791 he had become "a sick, weak, elderly man, high minded and zealous to duty, but totally unfit for the terrible responsibilities of such an expedition against such foes."--Theodore Roosevelt. To make matters far worse, his officers were inexperienced and his troops (2,300 regulars and 300 militia) were poorly trained, ill equipped, and

underfed. Almost half of them had withdrawn from his army through
expired enlistments or desertion before they ever encountered an
enemy.

Chief Little Turtle had recruited a force of 1,500 Miami, Shawnee,
Delaware, and Potawatomi warriors, and they confidently awaited the
right opportunity to destroy St. Clair's army in the same manner as
Harmar's. Little Turtle, a talented military tactician in his own right,
was advised and assisted by such experienced British partisans as
Alexander McKee, Matthew Elliott, and Simon Girty. They recognized their opportunity to launch a surprise attack when St. Clair
went into camp on November 3 in a snow-covered clearing near the
Wabash River (present site of Fort Recovery). Because of swampy
terrain, the militia had camped across a creek from the regulars, and
it was upon this untrained contingent that Little Turtle launched his
initial attack shortly before dawn on November 4, 1791.

The militia, taken completely by surprise, fled across the
stream and disrupted attempts by the regulars to maintain defensive
positions. The Indians selected officers and cannon crews as targets, downing many of them during the first onslaught. St. Clair
survived, although six bullets pierced his uniform, and he attempted
to rally his men. But discipline had disintegrated, and the soldiers
milled helplessly while sustaining heavy losses.

The slaughter continued for three hours. Then St. Clair
ordered a bayonet charge that drove a gap through the Indian lines,
permitting the survivors to escape from the trap and flee to Fort
Jefferson. The army had sustained more than 900 casualties, the
largest loss ever suffered in a single Indian attack.

"Allowed to resign without censure by President Washington,
... St. Clair and his career were finished. So was most of the
American army."--Fairfax Downey.

(Dale Van Every, Ark of Empire; Theodore Roosevelt, The
Winning of the West, V; Fairfax Downey, Indian Wars of the U.S.
Army; John Anthony Caruso, The Great Lakes Frontier.)

ST. JOSEPH, FORT. Fort St. Joseph, at the present site of Niles,
Michigan, was established to guard the portage between Lake Michigan and the Illinois River. Originally the site of a Jesuit mission,
it developed into a fur trading post and a small French settlement.
After the French and Indian War, the British built a small fort
there, commanded by Ensign Francis Schlosser and garrisoned by 15
men at the beginning of Pontiac's War.

On May 25, 1673, the Potawatomi Indians seized Schlosser and
three of his soldiers, slaughtered the others, and plundered the fort.
Schlosser, who had been unaware that a war had begun, and the
other survivors were taken to Detroit and exchanged for Potawatomi
prisoners held by the British.

During the American Revolution, Fort St. Joseph was garrisoned
by 17 British soldiers. On February 12, 1781, a Spanish militia
force from St. Louis, led by Lt. Eugenio Pourée, purchased Potawatomi neutrality by offering gifts and a portion of the booty, and
seized the fort. Pourée had to provide additional presents to prevent
the Potawatomis from slaughtering the prisoners.

(Howard H. Peckham, Pontiac and the Indian Uprising; Dale Van Every, Forth to the Wilderness; John Anthony Caruso, The Mississippi Valley Frontier.)

ST. JOSEPH, MICHIGAN, TREATIES OF. The first Treaty of St. Joseph was negotiated with the Potawatomi Indians by Lewis Cass on September 19, 1827. Tribal lands were ceded, and provision was made for the consolidation of scattered Potawatomi bands.

The second Treaty of St. Joseph was negotiated with the same tribe by Lewis Cass and Pierre Menard on September 20, 1828. In exchange for an increased annuity, the tribe ceded land near Lake Michigan.

(Charles J. Kappler, ed., Indian Affairs: Laws and Treaties, II.)

ST. LOUIS, FORT, ILLINOIS. Fort St. Louis was established by La Salle on Starved Rock in 1683 as a bastion to protect his projected Illinois colony. Built on top of a rock that rises 125 feet above the Illinois River, it led to the concentration of Illinois Indian tribes, some 20,000 people, who sought its protection against Iroquois invaders.

When La Salle left Fort St. Louis to seek a concession from the crown, his chief lieutenant, Henri de Tonti, managed the Indians with great skill and developed a profitable fur trade with the Illinois and Miami tribes. In 1684, the fort withstood an Iroquois assault.

After La Salle's death, Tonti and François La Forest were awarded the concession of Fort St. Louis. They abandoned the Starved Rock site and moved their headquarters to Lake Peoria (Fort Pimitoui) in 1692.

(Clarence Walworth Alvord, The Illinois Country.)

ST. LOUIS, MISSOURI, INDIAN AFFAIRS. St. Louis was established as a Louisiana Fur Company post in 1764 by Auguste Chouteau and Pierre Laclede Liguest. It developed into a major center of the fur trade, and a French village grew up around it, especially after Illinois settlers moved across the Mississippi to avoid becoming British subjects. In 1766, Spanish troops were sent to St. Louis, but the community retained its affinity for France.

During the Revolutionary War, both France and Spain became allies of the Americans. The British determined to seize St. Louis as an avenue to the conquest of the Mississippi Valley. On May 24-26, 1780, they led a large force of Indians against Spanish soldiers guarding the city and Americans across the Mississippi at Cahokia, but they were defeated by Gov. Fernando de Leyba and George Rogers Clark. (See HESSE, EMANUEL, EXPEDITION.)

After the United States acquired St. Louis in 1803, many Americans moved there to engage in the fur trade. William Clark, the Indian agent, managed the western tribes successfully, conferring with chiefs at his St. Louis headquarters and arranging negotiations for purchasing Indian lands.

Several important treaties were signed at St. Louis. On

November 4, 1804, William Henry Harrison and Pierre Chouteau obtained a cession of 15 million acres from several inebriated Sauk chiefs who lacked the proper authority to negotiate for the tribe. In a transaction condemned by the historian Cecil Eby as "a treaty that must certainly rank as one of the most notable swindles in American history," the Sauks ceded their land east of the Mississippi between the Illinois and Wisconsin rivers for a $1,000 annuity. Dissatisfaction over the treaty was a major cause of the Black Hawk War.

On May 13, 1816, William Clark, Ninian Edwards, and Auguste Chouteau negotiated a treaty with the Sauks at St. Louis, confirming the Treaty of 1804 and compelling the Indians to return property stolen from settlers. Failure to comply would have deprived them of their annuities.

On June 3, 1816, Clark, Edwards, and Chouteau negotiated a treaty at St. Louis with the Winnebago Indians of the Wisconsin River. The Winnebagos agreed to remain at peace with the United States and to release American captives.

On August 24, 1816, the same negotiators obtained a land cession from the Chippewa, Ottawa, and Potawatomi Indians in exchange for annuities. The tribes were permitted to continue to hunt on the ceded lands.

Finally, on March 30, 1817, Clark, Edwards, and Chouteau negotiated a treaty with the Menominee Indians. The tribe confirmed land cessions and agreed to release their captives.

(John Anthony Caruso, The Mississippi Valley Frontier; Charles J. Kappler, ed., Indian Affairs: Laws and Treaties, II; Cecil Eby, That Disgraceful Affair, the Black Hawk War.)

ST. MARY'S, TREATIES OF. The St. Mary's River, near the Ohio-Indiana boundary, was the site of many treaty negotiations during the early nineteenth century. On September 17, 1818, Lewis Cass and Duncan McArthur held a council there with chiefs of the Seneca, Shawnee, Ottawa, and Wyandot tribes, establishing reservations and increasing annuities. On September 20, 1818, Cass negotiated a treaty with the Wyandots, exchanging lands in Michigan with the tribe. On October 2, 1818, Cass, Jonathan Jennings, and Benjamin Parke obtained a cession from the Potawatomi Indians of a large tract in Indiana for an annuity of $2,500. On the same day, they obtained from the Wea Indians a cession of all their lands (except for a small reservation) in Indiana, Ohio, and Illinois for an annuity of $1,850. On the following day, the Delawares ceded their Indiana lands for territory west of the Mississippi, payment for their improvements, and an increase in their annuities. On October 6, 1818, the same negotiators obtained a large land cession from the Miami Indians.

After these rapid-fire transactions, treaty negotiation ceased at St. Mary's for a time, but Cass returned on June 16, 1820, to obtain a cession from the Chippewas of land on which to construct a fort at Sault Ste. Marie.

On September 24, 1829, George Vashon negotiated a treaty at St. Mary's with the Delaware Indians. The tribe's annuities were increased as recompense for their agreement to remove from the White

River to the fork of the Missouri and Kansas rivers.

(Charles J. Kappler, ed., Indian Affairs: Laws and Treaties, II.)

ST. PETER'S, WISCONSIN, TREATY OF. On July 29, 1837, Henry Dodge secured a large land cession from the Chippewa Indians as a result of negotiations at St. Peter's. The government agreed to provide $19,000 worth of trade goods and $9,500 in cash and to pay the debts of the tribe.

(Charles J. Kappler, ed., Indian Affairs: Laws and Treaties, II.)

ST. REGIS SETTLEMENT. St. Regis was established on the St. Lawrence River about 1755 by Catholic Iroquois Indians. A Jesuit mission, St. Francis Regis, was built there, and a large Indian population congregated around it. When the boundary between the U.S. and Canada was surveyed, it ran through the community, and as a result, a part of the St. Regis Reservation is administered by each nation. About 2,500 of the St. Regis citizens (Mohawks) reside on the New York side of the boundary.

(F. W. Hodge, ed., Handbook of American Indians, II; Bernard Klein and Daniel Icolari, eds., Reference Encyclopedia of the American Indian; Barbara Leitch, A Concise Dictionary of Indian Tribes of North America.)

SAKARISSA, TUSCARORA CHIEF. Sakarissa, a Tuscarora sachem friendly to the English, was born about 1730 at Niagara Landing, New York. He negotiated a number of treaties, including that at Ft. Stanwix in 1768. In 1802, he went to North Carolina to resolve the tribe's land ownership problems in that state. He became a Christian, invited missionaries to his village, and founded the Tuscarora Congregational Church in 1805.

(Frederick J. Dockstader, Great North American Indians.)

SAKAWESTON, CAPTIVITY OF. Sakaweston, an Indian who lived on one of the New England coastal islands, was captured by Capt. Edward Harlow in 1611 and taken to England. He remained there many years, became an English soldier, and fought in Bohemia.

(F. W. Hodge, ed., Handbook of American Indians, II.)

SALMON FALLS, NEW HAMPSHIRE, RAID. In January 1690, a war party of 27 Frenchmen commanded by François Hertel and 25 Abnaki Indians led by Chief Hopehood, attacked the town of Salmon Falls, on the New Hampshire-Maine border. The settlers defended themselves with great bravery, but they were overwhelmed by the raiders. Thirty settlers were killed and 54, mainly women and children, were marched to Canada as captives. The town was completely destroyed.

(Jeremy Belknap, History of New Hampshire, I; Herbert Milton Sylvester, Indian Wars of New England, II.)

SAMOSET, PEMAQUID CHIEF. Samoset, a prominent Pemaquid chief of Monhegan Island, Maine, met many English sea captains during his youth. On March 21, 1621, soon after the Pilgrims arrived at Plymouth, they were amazed when Samoset walked among them and called out, "Welcome, Englishman!" He proved to be of great service to them, informing them of the geography of New England and of the disposition of Indian tribes. He and Squanto played leading roles in the negotiation of a treaty between Plymouth and the Wampanoag Indians in 1621.

In July 1625, Samoset sold 12,000 acres of Pemaquid land to John Brown, a Maine settler. He continued to befriend the English and to sell land to settlers until his death about 1653.

"In nobility of character, Samoset was the equal of Massasoit; and in natural intelligence, greatly his superior."--Herbert Milton Sylvester.

(Frederick J. Dockstader, Great North American Indians; Neal Salisbury, Manitou and Providence; Herbert Milton Sylvester, Indian Wars of New England, I.)

SANDUSKY CONFERENCE. In September 1783, a conference of chiefs of 35 tribes was held at the Wyandot town of Sandusky. Initiated by the Iroquois to formulate plans for mutual defense, it resulted from Britain's failure to provide assistance for her Indian allies at the conclusion of the American Revolution. Alexander McKee, British Indian agent, urged them to oppose American expansion in the Northwest. He advised them to cease attacking the settlements, but to expect British support if the Americans invaded their lands. The tribes determined to defend the Ohio River boundary.

(Dale Van Every, Ark of Empire; Randolph C. Downes, Council Fires on the Upper Ohio.)

SANDUSKY, FORT. Fort Sandusky was built by the British at Sandusky, Ohio, in 1761 and garrisoned by Ensign Christopher Paulli and 15 enlisted men. It was the first fort to fall to the Indians during Pontiac's War. On May 16, 1763, 7 neighboring Wyandot Indians, incited by Ottawas from Detroit, requested a conference with the commanding officer. Unaware of Pontiac's conspiracy, Paulli complied and the Indians seized him. Bursting through the gate, the Wyandots slaughtered all of the soldiers except Paulli, whom they took to Pontiac's camp at Detroit. There he was tortured, but saved from death by an Indian woman who adopted him. On July 3, he escaped and fled to safety inside the fort.

(Howard H. Peckham, Pontiac and the Indian Uprising; Dale Van Every, Forth to the Wilderness.)

SARATOGA, NEW YORK, MASSACRE. Saratoga (present Schuylerville), New York, was the northernmost English village during King George's War. A small community of Dutch farmers, it developed around a fort intended to protect Albany against invasion from Canada. The fort was in such disrepair, however, that the garrison withdrew at the onset of winter, and it was vacant on November 28, 1745, when 400 Frenchmen and 220 Indians attacked the town. Taken by surprise, the settlers offered little resistance. The invaders killed 30 citizens, captured 100, and burned the fort and town.

(Francis Parkman, A Half-Century of Conflict; T. Wood Clarke, The Bloody Mohawk.)

SASSACUS, PEQUOT CHIEF. Sassacus was born near Groton, Massachusetts, about 1560. During his youth, he became a noted warrior, so successful in raids that the Pequots believed he possessed magical powers. He became principal chief in 1632, ruling a territory that extended from Narragansett Bay to the Hudson River.

In 1634, Sassacus sought to improve relations with the colonists, a move which alienated many of his followers. His son-in-law Uncas and other discontented Pequots withdrew from the tribe and established the Mohegan nation.

When the Pequot War began in 1637, Sassacus led his people into a swamp where they took refuge in a strong stockade. John Mason attacked it on May 26 and killed about 700 Indians. (See MYSTIC, BATTLE OF.) Sassacus escaped with about 20 of his warriors, only to be slain by the Mohawks in 1638. His scalp was presented to the governor of Massachusetts.

(John W. De Forest, History of the Indians of Connecticut; Frederick J. Dockstader, Great North American Indians; Herbert Milton Sylvester, Indian Wars of New England, I; Alden T. Vaughan, New England Frontier.)

SASSAMON, JOHN. John Sassamon, a Christian Indian, was educated at Harvard. Afterward, he served as secretary to King Philip and then rejoined the Christian Indians at Natick. He became such a model Puritan that he served as a preacher to the Indians at Nemasket.

Shortly before the outbreak of King Philip's War, Sassamon informed English authorities that the tribes were conspiring to attack the settlements. Word of this warning reached the Wampanoags, and three warriors were appointed to murder the informer. On January 29, 1675, his body was found beneath the ice of a frozen lake. A jury of Englishmen and Indians condemned the murderers to be hanged, and the sentence was carried out on June 8.

(Douglas Edward Leach, Flintlock and Tomahawk.)

SASSOONAN, DELAWARE CHIEF. Sassoonan (Allumapees, Olumapies), a Unami Delaware chief, moved from the Schuylkill River to the present site of Harrisburg, Pennsylvania, by 1709. In 1718 he sold an enormous tract between the Delaware and the Susquehanna to the Penn family. Afterward, he moved to Shamokin, where he died in 1747.

(Paul A. W. Wallace, Indians in Pennsylvania; Charles A. Hanna, The Wilderness Trail.)

SAUK AND FOX AGENCY, TREATY OF. John Chambers negotiated a treaty with the Sauk and Fox Indians at their agency headquarters in Iowa on October 11, 1842. In exchange for $800,000 and payment

of their debts, the tribe ceded their lands west of the Mississippi and agreed to move to the Missouri River or one of its tributaries.
(Charles J. Kappler, ed., Indian Affairs: Laws and Treaties, II.)

SAUK INDIANS. The Sauk (Sac) Indians, a large Algonquian tribe, were located around Green Bay and along the Fox River when first encountered by seventeenth-century French explorers. Missionaries were among them as early as 1666, and Father Claude Allouez characterized them as a large, wandering tribe, more savage than any other Indians he had met.

The Sauks served as allies of the French until 1733. Then, when they provided sanctuary for some Fox Indian fugitives, the governor of Canada ordered troops to attack them. As a result, the Sauks and Foxes became affiliated, and after a bloody battle near the present Appleton, Wisconsin, they removed across the Mississippi to Iowa. (See BUTTE DES MORTS.) Ten years later, the French persuaded some of them to return to the Fox River. By 1762, a large village had developed on the Wisconsin River, and Sauk bands lived along the Mississippi from the Rock to the Des Moines rivers.

During the French and Indian War the Sauks favored first one side and then the other, and they were of two minds once more at the onset of the American Revolution. Some warriors participated in the attack on St. Louis (see HESSE, EMANUEL, EXPEDITION), and in retaliation, the Americans burned their Rock River villages. Afterward, the Sauks united as British supporters and refused to sign a peace treaty at the conclusion of the war.

In 1804, an event occurred that profoundly affected the future of the Sauk nation. A few warriors murdered settlers, and 5 chiefs went to St. Louis for a conference intended to prevent retaliation against peaceful members of the tribe. William Henry Harrison seized the opportunity to obtain a land cession. After receiving presents and consuming much liquor, the chiefs, without tribal authorization, ceded all Sauk lands east of the Mississippi and some to the west of that river. (See ST. LOUIS, MISSOURI, INDIAN AFFAIRS.) An article of the treaty specified that the Sauks could continue to live and hunt upon the ceded lands as long as the government owned them, and misunderstandings over that provision led to hostilities that culminated in the Black Hawk War.

The Sauks became followers of Tecumseh and his brother the Prophet, early in the nineteenth century, and the establishment of Fort Madison in 1808 made them increasingly hostile. In 1813, they used a dance as a ruse to invade the fort, but abandoned the scheme when confronted by cannon. Most of the Sauks supported the British during the War of 1812, but others accepted the protection of the United States and chose to remain neutral. The war faction attacked American boats near Rock Island, killing 100 soldiers. After the war, tribal factionalism increased. Black Hawk's militants, known as the British band, traded in Canada, while others, increasingly influenced by Keokuk, opted for peace and accommodation.

In 1815, Sauk chiefs who had removed their followers to the

Missouri River ratified the Treaty of St. Louis and proclaimed permanent separation from the Black Hawk faction. In 1816, Black Hawk agreed to make peace with the United States, and he and his followers established villages in Iowa.

In 1830, the Sauks ceded a portion of their Iowa lands and agreed to vacate the territory east of the Mississippi that they had sold in 1804. Black Hawk disregarded the agreement, however, and early in 1832, he and his followers returned to Illinois and reoccupied their former homes on Rock River. When ordered to leave, the Sauks refused, and troops were sent to evict them. (See BLACK HAWK WAR.)

As a result of Black Hawk's defeat, the Sauks and Foxes were compelled to cede the remainder of their Iowa lands and to remove to the Missouri River. They settled on the Osage River in Kansas in 1845, but ceded their reservation in 1867 and removed to the Indian Territory. In 1899, they were allotted lands in severalty there. Some Sauks returned to Iowa, and their descendants live at Tama today.

(Black Hawk, Black Hawk: An Autobiography; Cecil Eby, That Disgraceful Affair, the Black Hawk War; William T. Hagan, The Sac and Fox Indians; Grant Foreman, The Last Trek of the Indians; William C. Sturtevant, ed., Handbook of North American Indians, XV.)

SAULT STE. MARIE, MICHIGAN, TREATY OF. On June 16, 1820, Lewis Cass and Chippewa Indian chiefs negotiated a land cession treaty at Sault Ste. Marie. In exchange for goods and the right to fish in the area, the Indians ceded a large tract along the St. Mary's River.

(Charles J. Kappler, ed., Indian Affairs: Laws and Treaties, II.)

SAULTIER INDIANS see CHIPPEWA INDIANS

SAWCUNK, DELAWARE VILLAGE. Sawcunk was an important Delaware village located at the present site of Beaver, Pennsylvania. The home of the notorious warchief Shingas, it was a major center of the French fur trade until the fall of Fort Duquesne in 1758 forced its abandonment.

(F. W. Hodge, ed., Handbook of American Indians, II.)

SAWYER, THOMAS AND ELIAS, CAPTIVITY OF. Thomas Sawyer and his 15-year-old son, Elias, were captured by Abnaki Indians at Lancaster, Massachusetts, on October 15, 1705. Taken to Montreal, Thomas bargained for his freedom with an offer to build a sawmill for the French, but the Indians who captured him prepared to burn him at the stake. Suddenly a priest appeared, declaring that he held the key to purgatory and that he would send all of the Indians there if they refused to release the prisoner. The captors consented, Thomas built the mill, and he returned to New England late in 1706.

Elias helped his father construct the sawmill, but the Indians refused to release him. After his father's departure, he fell in love with an Abnaki Indian girl, and at first he declined to go home when the French purchased his freedom. After much persuasion he agreed to go, and eventually he married a Massachusetts woman, but he regretted the loss of his Abnaki sweetheart until the day of his death.

(Emma Lewis Coleman, New England Captives Carried to Canada; James Axtell, The Invasion Within.)

SAYBROOK, FORT. Fort Saybrook was established at the mouth of the Connecticut River (present site of Old Saybrook, Connecticut), by Lion Gardiner in 1635, on land donated by the Niantick Indians. In July 1636, Gov. John Winthrop, Jr., summoned the Pequot chiefs to Fort Saybrook to demand tribute and the surrender of warriors who had murdered a trader, John Stone. The chiefs refused, and the English began making alliances with neighboring tribes to compel Pequot submission.

With the onset of the Pequot War, Fort Saybrook was subjected to Indian raids and sieges. During the fall of 1636, seven men were captured while working in the fields, and most of them were tortured to death. In February 1637, Gardiner was wounded and two of his men killed while working a short distance outside the stockade. "Elated with those successes," wrote John W. De Forest, "the Pequots, some dressed in English clothes, some armed with English weapons, would occasionally come round the fort, and calling to the soldiers, address them with jeers and defiance ... (and) call on them, if they were men, to come out and revenge their slaughtered friends."

Fort Saybrook suffered through a desultory siege for nine months. Finally, troops from Massachusetts and Connecticut attacked the enemy stronghold (see MYSTIC) in May 1637, destroying Pequot power and restoring tranquility to Fort Saybrook.

(John W. De Forest, History of the Indians of Connecticut; Neal Salisbury, Manitou and Providence; Robert M. Utley and Wilcomb E. Washburn, The American Heritage History of the Indian Wars; Alden T. Vaughan, New England Frontier.)

SAYENQUERAGHTA, SENECA CHIEF. Sayenqueraghta, a prominent eighteenth-century Seneca war chief and orator, resided near the present site of Buffalo, New York. Between 1758 and 1775 he spoke for the Six Nations during several conferences with English officials, and he signed the Treaty of Easton in 1758 and the Treaty of Johnson Hall in 1764. During the American Revolution at age 70 he led the Senecas at the Battle of Oriskany, the assault on the Wyoming Valley, and the Battle of Newtown. He died in 1788.

"Sayenqueraghta was not only an excellent orator but the most distinguished warrior in the Confederacy, well over six feet tall and of commanding presence. In both battle and in council he was outstanding, possessing at the same time great bravery and a superior intellect."--Barbara Graymont.

(Barbara Graymont, The Iroquois in the American Revolution; F. W. Hodge, ed., Handbook of American Indians, II.)

SCAROUADY, ONEIDA CHIEF. Scarouady (Scaroyady, Monacatootha), a prominent Oneida orator and warrior, was appointed by the Six Nations in 1747 to supervise the Shawnees on the Ohio, assuming the title of Half King less than a decade later. A firm English ally, he conferred with George Washington at Logstown in 1753 and scouted for him during the campaign against the French in 1754. After Washington's defeat at Great Meadows, he moved his headquarters to Aughwick to escape French retaliation.

Scarouady led warriors who served in the Braddock Expedition of 1755. On July 6, British soldiers fired upon their Iroquois scouts by mistake, killing Scarouady's son, but the chief continued to serve them until Braddock's defeat three days later. Afterward, he gave a scathing characterization of Braddock: "He is now dead; but he was a bad man when he was alive; he looked upon us as dogs; would never hear anything that was said to him. We often endeavored to advise him, and to tell him of the danger he was in with his soldiers; but he never appeared pleased with us, and that was the reason a great many of our warriors ... would not be under his command."

Soon after Braddock's defeat, Scarouady discovered that the Delaware Indians had defected to the French. He went to Philadelphia to warn Pennsylvania officials to protect frontier settlements, but the Quakers ignored his advice. Afterward, with Six Nations support, he attempted to control the hostile Delawares until the assembly finally accepted his recommendation and declared war on the tribe.

Scarouady died at Lancaster, Pennsylvania, in 1757.

(Charles A. Hanna, The Wilderness Trail; Albert T. Volwiler, George Croghan and the Westward Movement; Paul A. W. Wallace, Indians in Pennsylvania.)

SCATICOOK, CONNECTICUT. Scaticook, an Indian village near the present site of Kent, Connecticut, became the residence of remnants of several New England tribes about 1732. A Moravian mission was established there, and many of the Indians were converted to Christianity. Their numbers dwindled rapidly as a result of disease, and by 1752 only 18 families remained.

(F. W. Hodge, ed., Handbook of American Indians, II; John W. De Forest, History of the Indians of Connecticut.)

SCATICOOK, NEW YORK. Scaticook was a Mahican Indian village located on the Hudson River in Rensselaer County, New York. After King Philip's War, remnants of the Wampanoag, Narraganset, Nipmuc, and Pennacook nations settled there at the invitation of New York officials. By 1702, the population exceeded 1,000, but French-Canadians induced so many of them to move to Caughnawaga or St. Francis that only 200 remained in 1721. Some Scaticooks joined the French in raiding the New England settlements in 1754, and afterward, most of them removed to Canada.

(F. W. Hodge, ed., Handbook of American Indians, II.)

SCHENECTADY, NEW YORK, MASSACRE. Schenectady, New York, was founded near the Mohawk villages in 1661 by Arent van Curler and 14 Dutch families. By 1690, it contained approximately 400 people and 80 substantial buildings. Early that year, Governor Frontenac dispatched 3 large war parties to attack the New York and New England settlements. One of them, led by François Hertel, turned aside from the targeted city of Albany when the Indians decided that it was too strong to attack, and surrounded Schenectady during the night of February 8-9. The inhabitants were totally unprepared, for a blinding snowstorm was raging, and even the sentinels were sound asleep in their barracks when the invaders, 300 Indians and coureurs de bois, entered the stockade gate and surrounded every house in the settlement. Then, reported Cadwallader Colden, "they raised their War Shout, entered the Houses, murdered every Person they met, Men, Women, and Children, naked and in cold Blood; and at the same Time set Fire to the Houses. A very few escaped, by running into the Woods in this terrible Weather: And several hid themselves, till the first Fury of the Attack was over, but these were soon driven from their lurking Places by the Fire, and were all made Prisoners."

Sixty citizens died during the attack, and 27 were captured and marched off toward Canada. As soon as the Mohawks learned of the massacre they joined the Albany militia in pursuing the raiders, cutting off stragglers all the way to Montreal.

(Cadwallader Colden, History of the Five Indian Nations; T. Wood Clarke, The Bloody Mohawk; Herbert Milton Sylvester, Indian Wars of New England, II.)

SCHOENBRUNN, MORAVIAN INDIAN MISSION. Schoenbrunn was established in 1772 by Moravian missionaries near the present site of New Philadelphia, Ohio, as a haven for Christian Delaware Indians. It was the site of the first schoolhouse in Ohio and the birthplace of the first white child in the state. At the onset of the American Revolution, Schoenbrunn and other Ohio Moravian towns were suspected by both sides of assisting the other. In September 1781, the British commandant at Detroit sent a force of French-Canadians and Indians to forcibly remove the inhabitants to Sandusky. In March 1782, American militiamen destroyed the town. (See GNADENHUTTEN.)

(Reginald Horsman, Matthew Elliot, British Indian Agent; Edmund De Schweinitz, The Life and Times of David Zeisberger.)

SCHOHARIE VALLEY, NEW YORK, RAIDS. Settled by German Palatines in 1714, the Schoharie Valley was the scene of several Indian invasions during the American Revolution. In 1778, a party of 300 Tories and Indians destroyed settlements and took prisoners in the valley until Col. John Harper drove them out at the head of a cavalry squadron from Albany. By 1780, so many residents had been attacked that blockhouses had been built to protect women and children while the men formed companies to harvest their crops. In October 1780, Sir John Johnson led a large force of Tories and Indians into

Schoharie, attacked two of the three forts, and after failing to capture them, destroyed homes and crops owned by Patriots throughout
the valley. Most of the settlers were safe in the forts, but those
who tried to defend their homes lost their lives in the futile attempt.

(T. Wood Clarke, The Bloody Mohawk; Francis Whiting Halsey,
The Old New York Frontier.)

SCHUYLER, HAN JOST. During Gen. Barry St. Leger's siege of
Fort Stanwix in 1777, a major role in thwarting his plans was played
by Han Jost Schuyler, a mentally retarded youth who was revered by
the Indians. Schuyler lived at Little Falls, New York, with his
mother and brother, staunch Tories in spite of the fact that Mrs.
Schuyler was a sister of the Patriot general Nicholas Herkimer.

On August 12, 1777, Han Jost and his mother and brother
were captured while attending a Tory rally at Shoemaker's Tavern.
The two brothers were condemned to death, but the mother pleaded
so earnestly for their lives, that Gen. Benedict Arnold agreed to
spare them if they would help break the siege of Fort Stanwix.
After shooting holes in Han's coat to make it appear that he had
narrowly escaped, Arnold sent the youth to the camp of the Indians
who were supporting St. Leger. Meanwhile, he held Han's brother
as a hostage, threatening to hang him if the mission failed.

Han wandered among the Indians, many of whom believed that
he had the gift of vision, and warned them that Arnold was advancing with troops as numerous as leaves on the trees. As a result,
the Indians deserted in such numbers that St. Leger abandoned the
siege of Fort Stanwix.

(T. Wood Clarke, The Bloody Mohawk; Barbara Graymont, The
Iroquois in the American Revolution.)

SCHUYLER, PETER. Maj. Peter Schuyler, called Quider by the Iroquois, was born at Albany, New York, on September 17, 1657. The
son of a pioneer settler who had become wealthy in the fur trade, he
grew up near the Iroquois villages and became beloved and respected
by their chiefs. As a result, he was highly influential in holding
the Six Nations in the Dutch, and later in the English, interest.

In 1686, Schuyler was appointed mayor of Albany and head of
the Board of Indian Commissioners. He negotiated treaties with tribes,
and he and his brother-in-law Robert Livingston made fortunes in
the fur trade. As colonel of the Albany militia, he commanded Iroquois warriors as well as his own troops during fights with the French.
In 1691, he led 120 settlers and 146 Mohawks and Mahicans to attack
the French fort at La Prairie, across the river from Montreal. Greatly outnumbered, he was compelled to withdraw, only to find his retreat cut off by troops from Fort Chambly. A bloody battle ensued
before Schuyler drove them back to their stockade. According to
Cadwallader Colden, the French lost 300 men in the campaign. In
February 1693, he led the militia and Iroquois in pursuit of 600
French and Indians who had destroyed Mohawk villages. A fierce
fight occurred near Saratoga, and the enemy was driven back into
Canada.

In 1710, Schuyler conveyed several Mohawk chiefs to England. There, after observing the strength and wealth of the English, they went home dissuaded from seeking an alliance with France. The visit played an important role in determining the outcome of Queen Anne's War. The French continued to court the Iroquois, however, and in 1720, Schuyler visited the Senecas to counteract the influence of their agent, Joncaire. He died in 1724.

(Cadwallader Colden, History of the Five Indian Nations; T. Wood Clarke, The Bloody Mohawk; Francis Parkman, A Half-Century of Conflict; Allen W. Trelease, Indian Affairs in Colonial New York.)

SCHUYLER, PHILIP. Philip Schuyler was born at Albany, New York, on November 22, 1733. He became a military leader and Indian diplomat during his youth and, as a major of New York troops, he fought with distinction during the French and Indian War. In 1755, he commanded a company during Sir William Johnson's Crown Point campaign. The following year, he accompanied Col. John Bradstreet's expedition to Oswego, and in 1758, he assisted Bradstreet in the campaign against Fort Frontenac.

In 1775, Schuyler served as a delegate in the Second Continental Congress. At the onset of the American Revolution, he was appointed major general in command of the Northern Department, and sent to the Six Nations to seek their neutrality. In January 1776, he attempted to seize Sir John Johnson on suspicion of inciting the Iroquois to attack the Americans, but the Mohawks protected the prominent Tory. Later that year, he conferred with Iroquois chiefs at Albany and at German Flats, accused some of them of fighting against the Americans, and received their apologies. The following year, aware that many Indians were supporting the British, he abandoned his plan for neutrality and called upon the Iroquois to defend the Americans. When only the Oneidas and Tuscaroras agreed, he urged George Washington to send an army to invade the Iroquois home land.

In 1777, Schuyler, short of troops and equipment, was compelled to retreat before the Burgoyne invasion. In spite of the fact that his strategy saved Fort Stanwix, he was relieved of command before the Battle of Saratoga, and he retired from the army in 1779. During the winter of 1780-81, he saved the Oneidas and Tuscaroras from starvation after Joseph Brant had destroyed their towns. After serving in Congress for many years, he died at Albany in 1804.

(T. Wood Clarke, The Bloody Mohawk; Barbara Graymont, The Iroquois in the American Revolution.)

SCOTT, CHARLES, EXPEDITION. Gen. Charles Scott, a veteran Indian fighter, was assigned in 1791 to lead the Kentucky militia against hostile villages on the Wabash. In May, he led 700 men to the upper Wabash, learned that the Kickapoo and Wea warriors had gone to defend the Miami villages on the Maumee, and then attacked the old men, women, and children. Thirty-two Indians were killed and 58 captured, 5 villages were burned, crops were destroyed, and bales of furs were confiscated.

Scott was "a rough Indian fighter and veteran of the Revolutionary

War, who afterwards became governor of the State. Scott had moved
to Kentucky not long after the close of the war with England; he had
lost a son at the hands of the savages, and he delighted in war
against them."--Theodore Roosevelt.

(Theodore Roosevelt, The Winning of the West, V; A. M. Gibson, The Kickapoos; Dale Van Every, Ark of Empire; Randolph C.
Downes, Council Fires on the Upper Ohio.)

SECOWOCOMOCO INDIANS. The Secowocomoco Indians, a small Algonquian tribe closely associated with the Conoys, resided along the
Wicomico River in Maryland, near its juncture with the Potomac, at
the time of initial European contact. An agricultural people, they
were among the first Indians encountered by Maryland colonists in
1634. In 1651, they abandoned their lands to the English and removed to a reservation at the head of the Wicomico.

(F. W. Hodge, ed., Handbook of American Indians, II.)

SENECA INDIANS. The Seneca Indians, the largest and one of the
most warlike members of the Six Nations of Iroquois, occupied an extensive area of western New York and a portion of northern Pennsylvania during the period of early European contact. They were estimated at that time to be able to put more than a thousand warriors
into the field, and although they sustained many losses in battle,
they replenished their population by destroying neighboring tribes
and incorporating survivors into their ranks.

Seneca involvement in warfare with Europeans began in 1627
when they joined other Iroquois in attacking the French and their
Indian allies on the St. Lawrence. Soon afterward, they became involved in the fur trade with the Dutch at Fort Orange, acquired
firearms, and almost annihilated the Hurons, Eries, and the Neutral
Nation. In 1654, they made peace with the French, and shortly
thereafter, they invited Jesuit missionaries to visit their villages.

The Senecas were defeated in battle by the Susquehanna In-
dians, assisted by English settlers from Maryland, in 1663. Their
losses led them to seek French support, and therefore, they permitted
Father Jacques Frémin to establish a mission among them in 1668.
By 1675, however, the Senecas had crushed the Susquehannas and
no longer felt that they needed to maintain peace with the French.
In 1680, they attacked the Illinois Indians, bringing on war with the
French and their Indian allies. (See BRISAY, JACQUES RENE DE,
MARQUIS DE DENONVILLE, EXPEDITION.) Although Denonville destroyed Seneca villages and crops, he failed to put an end to their
attacks, and the tribe remained at war with the French until the end
of the century.

By 1700, the Senecas had split into eastern and western divisions when some of them migrated toward the Ohio country. The
tribe made peace with the French in 1701, and the western villages
became increasingly friendly with them, largely as the result of the
able diplomacy of such agents as the Joncaire family. During the
French and Indian War, they favored the French, while the eastern
division, influenced by Sir William Johnson, supported the English.

During Pontiac's War, the western Senecas captured the British posts at Venango, Le Boeuf, and Presqu'Isle. In addition, they inflicted heavy losses on British forces near Niagara (see DEVIL'S HOLE MASSACRE). After Pontiac's defeat, the Senecas signed a peace treaty at Niagara, and Sir William Johnson compelled them to cede four miles on each side of that river to the English.

The Senecas served as fierce British partisans during the American Revolution. They participated in the siege of Fort Stanwix, the Battle of Oriskany, and the attacks on Cherry Valley and the Wyoming settlements. In 1779, their villages were destroyed by American armies (see BRODHEAD, DANIEL; SULLIVAN, JOHN), but the Indians merely moved to Niagara and stepped up their raids on the settlements.

After the war, some of the Senecas removed to Canada, while those remaining in New York and Pennsylvania were compelled to cede most of their lands under terms of the Treaties of Fort Stanwix, Fort Harmar, and Canandaigua. In 1788, they sold much of their territory to a private company (see PHELPS-GORHAM PURCHASE), and beginning in 1826, they parted with most of the remainder (see OGDEN LAND PURCHASE). Some Senecas moved to Kansas, and later to Oklahoma, but many remain on the Allegheny, Cattaraugas, Oil Spring, and Tonawanda Reservations in New York.

(Barbara Graymont, The Iroquois in the American Revolution; Howard H. Peckham, Pontiac and the Indian Uprising; Allen W. Trelease, Indian Affairs in Colonial New York; William C. Sturtevant, ed., Handbook of North American Indians, XV.)

SEQUIDONGQUEE, SENECA CHIEF. Sequidongquee (Little Beard), lived at Little Beard's Town (present site of Cuylerville, New York) at the onset of the American Revolution. A fierce enemy of the Americans, he and his warriors were responsible for many of the murders during the Cherry Valley Massacre of November 11, 1778. In 1779, his town was destroyed by the Sullivan expedition.

(T. Wood Clarke, The Bloody Mohawk; Francis Whiting Halsey, The Old New York Frontier.)

SERGEANT, JOHN. Rev. John Sergeant, a pioneer New England clergyman, founded a mission at Stockbridge in 1736 and visited tribes in New York and Pennsylvania in the service of the Society in Scotland for Propagating the Gospel. He died in 1749.

(Francis Whiting Halsey, The Old New York Frontier.)

SHABONEE, POTAWATOMI CHIEF. Shabonee (Chambly), a prominent Potawatomi chief, was born about 1775 and lived near the present site of Shabbona, Illinois. Born an Ottawa, this grandnephew of Pontiac became a Potawatomi peace chief when he married into that tribe. A friend and follower of Tecumseh, he was a leader in the Battle of Tippecanoe, and he was present when Tecumseh died at the Battle of the Thames. He saved the lives of several whites during the Fort Dearborn Massacre, however, and after the War of 1812, he became an ally of the United States. He prevented most of the

Potawatomis from joining the Winnebago War of 1827 and the Black Hawk War of 1832, and he warned settlers of impending Indian attacks. (See INDIAN CREEK MASSACRE.) His friendship for white people turned many Indians against him, and he narrowly escaped death when his son and nephew were slain during a Sauk and Fox ambush.

The government rewarded Shabonee for his services with two sections of land, but when he assisted Potawatomis to remove west of the Mississippi in 1836, officials claimed that he had abandoned his land and sold it to speculators. Afterward, citizens of Ottawa, Illinois, bought him a small farm near Seneca, and he lived there on a government pension until his death in 1859.

(Cecil Eby, That Disgraceful Affair, the Black Hawk War; James A. Clifton, The Prairie People; Frederick J. Dockstader, Great North American Indians.)

SHACKAMOXON, TREATY OF. Shackamoxon, a Delaware Indian village near Philadelphia, was the site of a treaty signed by William Penn with the tribe in 1683. Penn did not seek a land cession, but merely attempted to assure the Indians of his goodwill and to provide methods of peacefully settling problems arising between the races.

(Jennings C. Wise, The Red Man in the New World Drama.)

SHAMOKIN. Shamokin, located on the Susquehanna River near the present site of Sunbury, Pennsylvania, was an important Indian community during the early eighteenth century. Some 300 Delaware, Shawnee, and Iroquois Indians lived there under the supervision of an Iroquois half-king, and cabins extended along major trails leading to the Ohio, the Potomac, and the Wyoming Valley.

At the outbreak of the French and Indian War, Delawares friendly to the English were driven from Shamokin by the hostiles. In order to protect them and the Pennsylvania settlements, Fort Augusta was established at Shamokin in 1756. The fort withstood several attacks the following year. (See AUGUSTA, FORT.)

(F. W. Hodge, ed., Handbook of American Indians, II; William A. Hunter, Forts on the Pennsylvania Frontier.)

SHAVEHEAD, POTAWATOMI CHIEF. Shavehead, a fearsome Potawatomi chief who resided near Lake Michigan southwest of the present site of Kalamazoo, was a terror to both whites and enemy Indians during the early nineteenth century. A follower of Tecumseh and an ally of the British, he was a leader in the Fort Dearborn Massacre, and he participated in raids and battles during the War of 1812. He was accustomed to displaying enemy scalps as personal ornaments, and he reputedly collected a string of 99 tongues of his victims.

After the War of 1812, Shavehead stationed himself at a ferry crossing of the St. Joseph River and demanded that passengers pay tribute to the Potawatomis for the right to cross their lands. There are many legends about his death. According to one account, he was shot to death by a survivor of the Fort Dearborn Massacre when he boasted of his role in the atrocity.

(F. W. Hodge, ed., Handbook of American Indians, II.)

SHAWNEE PROPHET see TENSKWATAWA

SHELDON, JOHN, FAMILY OF. John Sheldon, a resident of Deerfield, Massachusetts, was away from home when Abnaki and Caughnawaga warriors attacked the town on February 29, 1704. His wife and
small daughter were killed, and 4 of his children were captured. His
eldest son, John, Jr., escaped and ran to Hatfield for help.
        Sheldon made several trips to Montreal to try to recover his
children. In 1705, he obtained the release of two of his children
and his daughter-in-law. In 1706, he redeemed 44 captives. On a
third trip, in 1707, he secured freedom for 7 additional Deerfield
citizens.
        (Samuel Adams Drake, The Border Wars of New England; Fran-
cis Parkman, A Half-Century of Conflict; Alden T. Vaughan and
Edward W. Clark, eds., Puritans Among the Indians.)

SHENANDOAH, ONEIDA CHIEF see SKENANDOA, ONEIDA CHIEF

SHENANGO. Shenango, an important Indian town, was located on
the Ohio River a few miles northwest of Pittsburgh. The residence
of Iroquois, Ottawas, and Indians of several other tribes, it was a
focal point of the fur trade before the establishment of Fort Pitt.
        (Solon J. Buck, The Planting of Civilization in Western Penn-
sylvania; F. W. Hodge, ed., Handbook of American Indians, II.)

SHICKSHACK, WINNEBAGO CHIEF. Shickshack, a Winnebago chief
who lived in Illinois near the Sangamon River during the early nineteenth century, was friendly to white settlers. He supported them
during the Black Hawk War, and he probably was among the Winnebagos who captured Black Hawk. It is probable that his death occurred in Kansas after removing there with his followers.
        (F. W. Hodge, ed., Handbook of American Indians, II.)

SHIKELLAMY, ONEIDA CHIEF. Shikellamy (Swataney), an important
Iroquois chief during the first half of the eighteenth century, was of
mysterious origins. He told William Bartram that he was born of
French parents at Montreal, captured by the Cayugas, and adopted
by the Oneidas. Frederick J. Dockstader, who believes that Shikellamy's father was French and his mother was an Indian, asserts that
"it seems certain that he was captured at the age of two by Oneida
warriors and was raised by that tribe."
        Shikellamy's youth was spent on the Schuylkill River in Penn-
sylvania. The Iroquois recognized his diplomatic abilities by appoint-
ing him about 1727 to administer their affairs with other tribes and
white settlers at Shamokin. As resident representative of the Iroquois (half-king), he played a major role in settling disputes between
the English and Indians, and he is credited with saving the lives of
several white people. He protected Indians from self-destruction by
persuading colonial officials to curtail the liquor trade. Frequently,
he attended conferences with Pennsylvania officials at Philadelphia.
He was of great assistance to Conrad Weiser in obtaining cessions of

Indian lands, occurrences that led to war with the Delawares but preserved peace with the Iroquois.

In later life, Shikellamy came under the influence of the Moravian missionaries. He died as a Christian at Shamokin on December 6, 1748.

(Frederick J. Dockstader, Great North American Indians; F. W. Hodge, ed. , Handbook of American Indians, II; Paul A. W. Wallace, Indians in Pennsylvania.)

SHINGABAWASSIN, CHIPPEWA CHIEF. Singabawassin, a Chippewa chief who played an important role in Indian-white relations during the early nineteenth century, was born in Michigan in 1763. While residing at the mouth of the St. Mary's River, he was a leader in warfare against the Sioux, but he became a friend of white settlers. He was the principal Chippewa speaker during the negotiation of the Treaties Sault Ste. Marie in 1820, Prairie du Chien in 1825, Fond du Lac in 1826, and Butte des Morts in 1827. He died between 1828 and 1837.

(F. W. Hodge, ed. , Handbook of American Indians, II.)

SHINGAS, DELAWARE CHIEF. Shingas, one of the most formidable Delaware chiefs during the French and Indian War, grew up on the upper Schuylkill River, but he moved to the Ohio country after the sale of his home territory to the English in 1732. In 1752, he was appointed "king of the Delawares" by the Iroquois half-king Tanacharison, at the suggestion of English officials. Until the outbreak of the French and Indian War, he transacted all affairs between the western Delawares and the colonists.

With Washington's defeat, the Delawares began a shift toward the French interest. Shingas, who appeared to favor neutrality, asserted that he met Braddock's army on the way to attack Fort Duquesne and urged the British general to leave the Delawares unmolested on their own lands, but when Braddock responded that "no savage should inherit the land," Shingas determined to support the French.

At Kittanning in the autumn of 1755, Shingas and Captain Jacobs organized war parties that carried devastation to the Pennsylvania frontier settlements. They raided the Great and Little Coves in November 1755, the Juniata and Sherman's Creek settlements in January 1756, and the Conococheague region the following month with such fury that Pennsylvania officials placed a price on the head of "Shingas the Terrible." During the late winter and spring of 1756, they attacked David Davis's Fort, McDowell's Mill, Patterson's Fort, and McCord's Fort, and defeated a force of pursuers at Sideling Hill. On April 18, Shingas was wounded near Fort Cumberland and retired to Kittanning to recuperate. There, a few months later, he narrowly escaped during an attack by Col. John Armstrong (see KITTANNING).

After the destruction of Kittanning, Shingas ceased his attacks on the settlements and moved, first to the Scioto, and then to Beaver River. In 1758, he was deposed by the Delawares and replaced by his brother King Beaver (Tamaque). He died during the winter of 1763-64.

(Randolph C. Downes, Council Fires on the Upper Ohio; Charles A. Hanna, The Wilderness Trail; William A. Hunter, Forts on the Pennsylvania Frontier; Paul A. W. Wallace, Indians in Pennsylvania.)

SHINNECOCK INDIANS. The Shinnecock Indians, an Algonquian tribe of the Montauk confederacy, lived on Long Island from Shinnecock Bay to Montauk Point. By 1671, they were under English domination. Many of them left their homes to join the Brotherton Indians about 1788. The most dramatic event in their more recent history occurred in December 1876, when 28 men died in an attempt to save a ship that was stranded off the Long Island shore. A few Shinnecocks still live on a reservation near Southampton, Long Island.

(F. W. Hodge, ed., Handbook of American Indians, II; John R. Swanton, Indian Tribes of North America.)

SHORT, MERCY, CAPTIVITY OF. Mercy Short, aged 15, was captured by Abnaki Indians in 1690 during an attack on Salmon Falls, New Hampshire. She witnessed the murders of her parents and brothers and sisters. Carried to Canada, she endured a year of Indian captivity. After her redemption, she was sent to live with a Massachusetts family.

In 1692, Mercy began experiencing hallucinations of captivity among demons. Cotton Mather attempted for weeks to free her from demonic possession. After a time, her imaginary tormenters began to assume the form of Indians, and she gave such vivid descriptions of war dances that onlookers slashed the air around her bed with swords in an attempt to destroy the invisible Abnakis.

During the Massachusetts witchcraft hysteria of 1692, Mercy joined other girls in condemning innocent citizens to death at Salem. Richard Slotkin has asserted that she, like many other redeemed captives, wished to condemn New England society for its smug ignorance of the nightmare of captivity.

(Richard Slotkin, Regeneration Through Violence.)

SIMMONS, JOHN, FAMILY OF. John Simmons, a soldier, was stationed with his family at Fort Dearborn at the onset of the War of 1812. When the fort was evacuated and the column attacked by Potawatomi Indians, Simmons was slain while attempting to protect the civilians. (See DEARBORN, FORT, MASSACRE.) His two-year-old son, David, was one of a dozen children tomahawked by a warrior who climbed into the wagon in which they were riding.

Mrs. Simmons, carrying an infant daughter in her arms, survived the massacre, but she was captured by Indians from Green Bay. She carried the baby to their village, 200 miles through the wilderness. Beaten with switches and clubs, she held the infant to her breast while running the gantlet. After her ordeal, she and the child were protected and cared for by an old Indian woman.

Mrs. Simmons and her daughter were redeemed after several months of captivity. They lived in Iowa, where the mother died in

1857. Her daughter, who lived until 1900, was the last survivor of the Fort Dearborn massacre.

(Milo M. Quaife, Checagou.)

SINKHOLE, BATTLE OF THE. On May 24, 1815, Black Hawk and a Sauk war party ambushed a small American detachment near Green Bay, killing 4 soldiers. Troops pursued the Indians till they took refuge in a sinkhole. There the warriors held the whites at bay, killing 11 and wounding 3, until they were able to escape during the night. Five of Black Hawk's warriors were killed in the sinkhole.

(William T. Hagan, The Sac and Fox Indians.)

SIWANOY INDIANS. The Siwanoy Indians, one of the more important tribes of the Wappinger confederacy, lived along the northern shore of Long Island Sound and inland to the vicinity of the present White Plains, New York. Their principal village, Poningo, was located near the present Rye, New York. After wars with the Dutch, they gradually sold their lands to the whites, dwindled in numbers, and were absorbed by other Algonquian tribes.

(F. W. Hodge, ed., Handbook of American Indians, II; John R. Swanton, Indian Tribes of North America.)

SKANIADARIIO, SENECA CHIEF. Skaniadariio (Handsome Lake) was born at Ganawagus in the Genesee Valley, New York, about 1735. He was a half-brother of the prominent chief Cornplanter. As a young warrior, he fought in the French and Indian War and the American Revolution. Afterward, according to Paul A. W. Wallace, he "suffered the moral and mental collapse that came to many Iroquois at the turn of the 19th century as they watched the breakup of their national home and saw the end of the Six Nations' heroic role in North American affairs." He became a drunkard, his health deteriorated, and he was near death when he experienced a vision that restored him to health and instructed him to lead the Iroquois to a style of life based upon self-control and a return to traditional Iroquois religion and customs.

Handsome Lake's teachings gained a large following among the Senecas and, in 1801, he was elevated to chief. In 1802, he visited Pres. Thomas Jefferson, explained the basis of his beliefs, and urged the government to guarantee Iroquois land ownership and to eliminate the sale of liquor on their reservations. He made a favorable impression on the president, but his teachings alienated several important Iroquois chiefs, and he was exiled from his village for a short time.

Skaniadariio persuaded most of his followers to remain at peace during the War of 1812. He went from village to village preaching that Iroquois survival depended upon substitution of farming for hunting and conquering the craving for alcohol. He gained great popularity among the Senecas, and his message was well received at Onondaga, but he died there suddenly on August 10, 1815.

After his death, Handsome Lake's teachings were codified, and they retain their importance as guides to right conduct among the Iroquois of the United States and Canada.

(Frederick J. Dockstader, Great North American Indians; William C. Sturtevant, ed., Handbook of North American Indians, XV; Paul A. W. Wallace, Indians in Pennsylvania.)

SKENANDOA, ONEIDA CHIEF. Skenandoa (Shenandoah) was born of Susquehanna Indian parents about 1706 and adopted by the Oneidas at an early age. As a youth he was addicted to alcohol, but he broke the habit after Albany citizens robbed him while he lay in a stupor on a city street. Afterward, he became a noted warrior and a favorite of other braves who were attempting to wrest power from the hereditary chiefs. He fought on the side of the British during the French and Indian War.

By 1767, Skenandoa had become greatly influenced by the teachings of Rev. Samuel Kirkland, a Presbyterian missionary. At the onset of the American Revolution, he assisted Kirkland in keeping the Oneidas and Tuscaroras from joining other Iroquois as British allies. He resisted attempts by his son-in-law, Joseph Brant, to persuade him to join the British at Niagara, but in 1780, when he went there to arrange a prisoner exchange, he was confined until he agreed to change his allegiance. Afterward, he accompanied Brant on at least one raid. When the war ended, he apologized to the Americans and was restored to their good graces. Afterward, the Oneidas split into factions, and he led those who favored Christianity and the white man's way. In later life, he signed several land cession treaties.

Skenandoa was a farmer until he became blind. He died a devout Christian in 1816 and was buried beside Kirkland at his own request.

(Frederick J. Dockstader, Great North American Indians; Barbara Graymont, The Iroquois in the American Revolution; William C. Sturtevant, ed., Handbook of North American Indians, XV.)

SLOCUM, FRANCES, CAPTIVITY OF. Frances Slocum, a five-year-old Quaker girl, was captured in 1778 by a Delaware war party during a raid on the Wyoming Valley settlements. She remained with the Indians the rest of her life. Her mother and brothers made several journeys into the wilderness, offering large rewards for her return, but they gave up the search after failing to locate her.

Frances became the adopted daughter of a Delaware chief. Treated tenderly, she enjoyed life as an Indian. She married a warrior at an early age, but divorced him when he insisted upon moving west of the Mississippi. Afterward, she married Shapoconah, a Miami warrior who succeeded Little Turtle as war chief. They moved to the Mississinewa River after the War of 1812, and she was left a widow with four children about 1833.

In 1837, Frances revealed her identity to a white visitor, and he informed her brothers that she lived near the Wabash River. They visited her at once and urged her to return to her old home in Pennsylvania, but she refused, stating that she was "an old tree who could no longer move about." Then they petitioned the government to grant the land to her on which her cabin was built in order to exempt her from removal with the Indians to the West. She died there on March 9, 1847.

(Bert Anson, The Miami Indians; George Peck, Wyoming.)

SLOVER, JOHN, CAPTIVITY OF. John Slover was captured by Miami Indians at the age of eight near the Kanawha River. His father was killed in the raid. He and his mother survived the march to Ohio, but his two younger sisters died of fatigue. His mother was ransomed within a short time, but John remained with the Miamis and Delawares until he was 20. Then, in 1773, while visiting Fort Pitt with the Shawnees, he was recognized by relatives and urged to return to the family home. He yielded reluctantly, having become strongly attached to the Indians and their way of life.

During the American Revolution, Slover served as a guide for Col. William Crawford's army that invaded the Indian country. Crawford was defeated by the Delawares and Shawnees, and Slover found himself a prisoner once more. Condemning him for turning against them, the Indians determined to burn him to death. They fastened him to a stake and set fire to the faggots, but a sudden downpour of rain extinguished the fire, causing postponement of his ordeal to the next day. During the night his guards fell asleep, however, and he loosened his bonds and escaped to Wheeling.

(Frederick Drimmer, Scalps and Tomahawks; John A. M'Clung, Sketches of Western Adventure; Theodore Roosevelt, The Winning of the West, III.)

SMITH, JAMES. James Smith was born about 1737 near the Tuscarora Mountain in Franklin County, Pennsylvania. Raised on the frontier, he became one of Pennsylvania's foremost pathfinders and Indian fighters. At the age of 18, he was captured by Delaware Indians while serving as a road builder for Braddock's ill-fated army in 1755. Taken to Fort Duquesne, he withstood torture so courageously that the Indians spared his life while burning other captives from Braddock's army at the stake.

Taken to the Muskingum River, he was adopted by a Caughnawaga Indian family. During the winter of 1757-58, famine stalked the Indian camps, and Smith escaped without pursuit. He had not gone far, however, before he killed a buffalo and decided to bring meat to his hungry Indian relatives. He remained with the Caughnawagas an additional 18 months before he escaped while on a visit with them to Montreal.

Returning to Pennsylvania, Smith became a prosperous farmer and justice of the peace. In 1763, during Pontiac's War, he organized a company of rangers, taught them to fight Indian style, and protected the southwestern Pennsylvania settlements. After the war, he persuaded a large band of frontiersmen to prevent pack trains from delivering ammunition, liquor, and other trade goods to the Indians. (See BLACK BOYS.) In 1764, he served in Bouquet's expedition against the Ohio Indians. Two years later, he explored much of Tennessee and Kentucky. As a militia officer, he fought Indians in western Pennsylvania from 1776 until he moved to Kentucky in 1778.

Much of his later life was spent as a Presbyterian missionary to the Indians whom he had fought with such determination during his youth. He died about 1814.

Smith's account of his adoption ceremony is of much value to students of Indian customs:

> ... a number of Indians collected about me, and one of them began to pull the hair out of my head ... as if he had been plucking a turkey, until he had all the hair clean out of my head, except a small spot about three or four inches square on my crown. They cut this off with a pair of scissors, except three locks, which they dressed up in their own mode. Two of these they wrapped round with a narrow-beaded garter ..., and the third they plaited at full length and then stuck full of silver brooches. After this they bored my nose and ears, and fixed me up with earrings and nose jewels. They ordered me to strip off my clothes and put on a breechclout, which I did. Then they painted my head, face and body in various colors. They put a large belt of wampum on my neck, and silver bands on my hands and right arm. Next, an old chief led me out ... and ... holding me by the hand, made a long speech very loud, and handed me to three young squaws. They led me ... into the river ... and washed and rubbed me severely.

After this ceremony, the chief informed Smith that "you are now flesh of our flesh and bone of our bone. By the ceremony which was performed today, every drop of white blood was washed out of your veins. You are taken into the Caughnawaga nation and initiated into a warlike tribe. You are to consider yourself as one of our people."

(James Smith, An Account of the Remarkable Occurrences in the Life and Travels of Col. James Smith; Francis Parkman, Montcalm and Wolfe, I; Frederick Drimmer, ed., Scalps and Tomahawks; Dale Van Every, A Company of Heroes.)

SMITH, JOHN, NEW ENGLAND EXPLORATIONS. While Capt. John Smith is more renowned for his Virginia adventures, he played an important part in the exploration of the coast of New England as well. In 1614, he commanded two ships that sailed from north of Penobscot to Cape Cod, hunting whales and seeking precious metals. When these ventures failed, he established trade with the Indians, securing more than a thousand beaver skins and studying the languages and customs of the inhabitants. In addition, he made an accurate map of the New England coast. He had a few minor fights with Indians, but before returning to England three months later he established friendly relations with the coastal tribes.

During the winter of 1614-15, Smith published glowing accounts of the fertility of New England soil, and he urged the establishment of plantations using native labor in the manner employed by Spain in her New World possessions. He persuaded Sir Ferdinando Gorges to project a colony in New England, but financial reverses prevented fruition, and Smith never returned to America.

(Neal Salisbury, Manitou and Providence; Alden T. Vaughan, New England Frontier.)

SMITH, RICHARD. Richard Smith, a Rhode Island trader, established a post on the western shore of Narragansett Bay during the 1630's. He gained tremendous influence during 40 years of commerce with the Indians, selling them goods that they needed and liquor that they craved.

At the onset of King Philip's War, Smith attempted to persuade the Narragansets to remain at peace with the English. His diplomacy succeeded until the colonists determined to attack the Narragansets and used Smith's post at Wickford as a base. After the army withdrew from Wickford, the Indians destroyed the post.

(Douglas Edward Leach, Flintlock and Tomahawk; Alden T. Vaughan, New England Frontier.)

SOULIGNY, MENOMINEE CHIEF. Souligny, the grandson of a French trader and an Indian woman, was born in 1785. He became a Menominee war chief and fought on the side of the British during the War of 1812. He participated in the capture of Mackinac and the attack on Fort Meigs. After the death of his friend Tecumseh, he made peace with the Americans and supported them in the Black Hawk War. He died in 1864.

(F. W. Hodge, ed., Handbook of American Indians, II.)

SPEMICALAWBA, SHAWNEE CHIEF. Spemicalawba (High Horn, Captain Logan), a nephew of Tecumseh, was born at Wapakoneta, Ohio, about 1776. As a small boy he was captured by Gen. James Logan and educated as a member of Logan's family in Kentucky. After returning to the Indians during an exchange of prisoners, he attempted to dissuade Tecumseh from waging war on the settlers.

During the War of 1812, High Horn served as a scout for the Americans. He evacuated woman and children from Fort Wayne and guided them to safety before Indians invested the place. Afterward, he killed Winamac, a hostile Potawatomi chief who had played a leading role in the Fort Dearborn Massacre. He himself was killed on November 24, 1812, on a scouting expedition for General Winchester. He was buried with military honors, and the town of Logansport, Indiana, was named for him.

(Frederick J. Dockstader, Great North American Indians; Benjamin Drake, Life of Tecumseh.)

SPENCER, OLIVER M., CAPTIVITY OF. Oliver M. Spencer, a 10-year-old boy, was captured by Shawnee Indians near Cincinnati, Ohio, in 1792, while on his way home from a Fourth of July celebration. On the march to the Shawnee village, he attempted to escape, and the Indians were about to kill him when a Mohawk warrior interceded in order to hold him for ransom. Severely beaten and forced to walk barefooted through 100 miles of brambles, he was so near death on arrival that the Mohawk turned him over to an aged medicine woman and her granddaughter to nurse. They treated him kindly, and he began to enjoy Indian life. He had become considerably assimilated by the time he was ransomed in February 1793, by a British trader.

(O. M. Spencer, The Indian Captivity of O. M. Spencer.)

SPENCER, THOMAS, ONEIDA CHIEF. Thomas Spencer (Ahnyero), an Oneida chief who served Mohawk Valley settlers as a blacksmith, played an important part in preserving their lives during the American Revolution. He spied upon the activities of the British and Tories and warned Patriot settlers when war parties were preparing a raid.

In July 1777, Spencer learned of St. Leger's plan to attack Fort Stanwix. He suggested to the defenders that they block Wood Creek with fallen trees, a plan that delayed St. Leger's arrival until August 2. Meanwhile, he warned Mohawk Valley settlers that the Oneidas would go over to the British if the fort surrendered. Gen. Nicholas Herkimer called out the militia to march to Fort Stanwix, and Spencer was killed during the Tory and Indian ambush at Oriskany.

(T. Wood Clarke, The Bloody Mohawk; Barbara Graymont, The Iroquois in the American Revolution.)

SPOTTED ARM, WINNEBAGO CHIEF. Spotted Arm (Broken Arm, Manahketshumpkaw), an important Winnebago chief, was born about 1772. A British supporter, he was wounded at the siege of Fort Meigs in 1813. He signed the Treaty of Green Bay in 1828. In 1832, he was held hostage to insure that the Winnebagos did not join the hostiles during the Black Hawk War. Afterward, he moved with his people across the Mississippi, where he died a few years later.

(F. W. Hodge, ed., Handbook of American Indians, II.)

SPRING WELLS, MICHIGAN, TREATY OF. On September 8, 1815, the Delaware, Wyandot, Shawnee, Seneca, and Miami tribes ended a state of warfare with the United States at Spring Wells, near Detroit. Negotiating the treaty for the government were William Henry Harrison, Duncan McArthur, and John Graham.

(Charles J. Kappler, ed., Indian Affairs: Laws and Treaties, II.)

SPRINGFIELD, MASSACHUSETTS, RAID. Springfield, a Massachusetts frontier settlement, was attacked by Indians on October 5, 1675, during King Philip's War. Lt. Thomas Cooper was mortally wounded while scouting near the Indian camp, but he lived long enough to ride into Springfield and give the alarm. The settlers took refuge in garrison houses, and only one man was killed, but the Indians burned 30 buildings before withdrawing when a relief force arrived.

(Douglas Edward Leach, Flintlock and Tomahawk.)

SPRINGFIELD, NEW YORK, RAID. Springfield, a village located on Lake Otsego, New York, was attacked on July 18, 1778, by Joseph Brant and 500 Iroquois raiders. Eight men were slain and 14 captured. Brant assembled the women and children in one house and burned every other building in town.

(Barbara Graymont, The Iroquois in the American Revolution; Francis Whiting Halsey, The Old New York Frontier.)

SQUANDO, ABNAKI CHIEF. Squando, a Sokoki Abnaki sachem known to the New England colonists as the Sagamore of Saco, played an important part in King Philip's War of 1675-76. The reason for his hostility toward the English colonists is made evident in the following passage:

> But the war at the eastward is said to have grown out of the foolish conduct of some of the inhabitants. An insult was offered to the wife of Squando, a chief Sachem on the river Saco. Some irregular sailors, having heard that young Indians could swim naturally, like those of the brute creation, met the wife of Squando with an infant child in a canoe, and to ascertain the fact, overset it. The child sunk to the bottom, but the mother diving down, immediately brought it up without apparent injury. However, it fell out, that the child died shortly after, and its death was imputed to the treatment it had received from the sailors. This so enraged the chief, that he only waited a fit time to commence hostilities.--Thomas Church.

Squando participated in the destruction of the Saco settlements. After the war, he signed a peace treaty at Cocheco.

(Thomas Church, The History of the Great Indian War of 1675 and 1676; William C. Sturtevant, ed., Handbook of North American Indians, XV.)

SQUANTO, PATUXET CHIEF. Squanto (Tisquantum), a famous Patuxet chief, was born about 1580 and taken to Europe early in the seventeenth century. Historians agree that he was kidnapped, but the time and circumstances are uncertain. Based upon a record provided by Sir Ferdinando Gorges, doubted by most historians, he was seized by Capt. George Waymouth in 1605. Neal Salisbury asserted that he was captured by Capt. Thomas Hunt and sold into slavery in Spain in 1614. Henry F. Howe, in the article on Massachusetts in the Dictionary of American History, wrote that he was taken to Europe by Captain John Smith's expedition of 1614. Herbert Milton Sylvester believed that he was kidnapped by Waymouth in 1605 and possibly returned to America in time to have been stolen by Hunt in 1614.

How Squanto arrived in England is unclear, but he was living in London in the home of John Slany, an officer of the Newfoundland Company, in 1617. In 1618, he is said to have met Capt. Thomas Dermer in Newfoundland and returned to England with him. It is known that he sailed to New England with Dermer in 1619, helped him to establish friendly relations with the Wampanoags, and left him to return to the Patuxets.

When Squanto arrived at his former home, he discovered that a plague had wiped out his people. Thereafter, he lived with the Wampanoags as an interpreter for Massasoit (according to Frederick J. Dockstader) or as a captive (according to Neal Salisbury). He was there when the Pilgrims arrived, and he helped arrange a treaty between the tribe and the colonists in 1621. Afterward, he lived with the Pilgrims, instructed them in the cultivation of corn, advised them about the geography of New England, and helped them with Indian relations.

While Squanto was of great assistance in enabling the settlers to survive, he created difficulty for them by plotting the murder of Massasoit. The Wampanoags wanted to execute him for the threat to their chief, but the Pilgrims protected him because they needed his services. He died of natural causes at Cape Cod in December 1622, while assisting the colonists to buy food from the Indians.

(William Bradford, Of Plimoth Plantation; Frederick J. Dockstader, Great North American Indians; Neal Salisbury, Manitou and Providence; Herbert Milton Sylvester, Indian Wars of New England, I, Alden T. Vaughan, New England Frontier.)

SQUAW CAMPAIGN. The so-called Squaw Campaign took place in February 1778, when Gen. Edward Hand led 500 Pennsylvania militia to capture British supplies at the mouth of the Cuyahoga River. The undisciplined troops disregarded orders and fired at the first Indians they met, not waiting to ascertain whether they were friends or foes. After heavy rain prevented them from reaching their objective, they attacked two friendly Delaware Indian villages on the Shenango River and Mahoning Creek, slaying several women and children, wounding the mother of Captain Pipe, and killing that formidable chief's brother, the only grown man present to defend the inhabitants. As a result of this unfortunate expedition, Captain Pipe declared war on the Americans, and many Delawares became British allies.

(Dale Van Every, A Company of Heroes; Paul A. W. Wallace, Indians in Pennsylvania; Randolph C. Downes, Council Fires on the Upper Ohio.)

SQUAW SACHEM OF POCASSET see WEETAMOO, WAMPANOAG SACHEM

STANDISH, MILES. Miles Standish was born in England about 1584. He embarked on a military career and served in the Low Countries before accepting an appointment as a military leader with the Pilgrims bound for America in 1620. He sailed on the Mayflower, and upon landing at Plymouth Rock, he became the first commissioned military officer in New England.

Historians differ in regard to Standish's success as an Indian manager. While most assert that his skillful handling of the tribes enabled the colony to survive, some contend that peaceful relations established by Squanto and Samoset were strained by Standish's aggressive policy of threats and extortions. Herbert Milton Sylvester has characterized him as "something of a savage. No one who has ever written of him has credited him with either a predominating intellect or a superabundance of moral principle. He was, undoubtedly, the man for the time and the place--the bully by proxy for the community."

Standish regarded Indians as natural enemies. His proclivity for robbing food caches and burial grounds interfered with Pilgrim intentions to establish peaceful trade relations. On the other hand, when war erupted he was an effective commander. He organized a militia company and constructed a barricade to protect the settlement. When the Narraganset Indians sent the Pilgrims arrows wrapped in a snakeskin, he defied the threat by returning the skin filled with gunpower and lead.

When the village of Wessagusset was threatened by Indians in 1622, Standish led eight militiamen to its relief. They enticed four Indian leaders into a cabin, stabbed three of them to death, and hanged the fourth as an example. The other Indians fled from the scene. After this decisive action, the colony escaped Indian attacks for 50 years.

Standish founded the town of Duxbury in 1632 and died there in 1656.

(William Bradford, Of Plimoth Plantation; Neal Salisbury, Manitou and Providence; Herbert Milton Sylvester, Indian Wars of New England, I; Alden T. Vaughan, New England Frontier.)

STANWIX, FORT. Fort Stanwix was built by Gen. John Stanwix in 1758 at the great Oneida carrying place between the Mohawk River and Wood Creek, a strategic location for the protection of settlements along the Mohawk and Hudson valleys. Constructed near the present site of Rome, New York, it was one of the strongest bastions on the continent, usually garrisoned by more than 400 men. It was destined to be the site of three of the most important events in American frontier history.

In the autumn of 1768, Sir William Johnson and George Croghan invited the Six Nations, the Delawares, Shawnees, and other tribes to attend a conference and receive presents at Fort Stanwix. More than 3,000 Indians accepted. Most of them believed that the conference would be useful to the tribes in establishing a united front to prevent white settlers from occupying their lands. They were dismayed to discover that the Iroquois had already agreed to sell lands south of the Ohio River as far west as the Tennessee, claimed by right of conquest, but occupied by other tribes. The cession included large portions of the present states of New York, Pennsylvania, West Virginia, and Kentucky. Thus the Iroquois protected their homeland by diverting settlement southward and westward onto the hunting grounds of the Shawnees, Delawares, and Mingos. The treaty, signed on November 5, aroused such anger among displaced tribes that it led to Dunmore's War.

The second crucial event that transpired at Fort Stanwix was the British and Indian siege of 1777. British general John Burgoyne, attempting to capture Albany and overrun the lower Hudson Valley, sent a large force led by Col. Barry St. Leger to seize the Mohawk settlements. Fort Stanwix was the only position strong enough to impede his campaign, and he surrounded it with 1,400 regulars, Tories, and Indians on August 2. Commanding the 550 defenders, Col. Peter Gansevoort refused to surrender, and the British and Indians began a siege, firing steadily at the fort for two days.

On August 5, learning that Gen. Nicholas Herkimer was leading a large army to the relief of Fort Stanwix, St. Leger sent a force of Indians and Tories to ambush the column. (See ORISKANY, BATTLE OF.) While they were away, Col. Martinus Willett sallied forth with 250 men and destroyed their camps, greatly discouraging St. Leger's Indian allies. Afterward, Gen. Benedict Arnold alarmed the Indians so greatly by spreading rumors that he would attack them with troops as numerous as leaves on the trees (see SCHUYLER, HAN JOST) that warriors deserted St. Leger in droves. Thus deprived of a substantial portion of his forces, St. Leger abandoned the siege on August 22 and retreated to Oswego.

The final major event in frontier history that occurred at Fort Stanwix was the Treaty of October 22, 1784. In order to restore peace with the victorious Americans, the Iroquois ceded land in New York and Pennsylvania north and west of the boundary established by the Treaty of 1768. In addition, they abandoned claims to lands west of the Ohio occupied by other tribes. Only a few chiefs signed the agreement with American negotiators Richard Butler, Arthur Lee, and Oliver Walcott, and other Indians strongly objected. Afterward, settlers flocked to the region.

(T. Wood Clarke, The Bloody Mohawk; Francis Whiting Halsey, The Old New York Frontier; Barbara Graymont, The Iroquois in The American Revolution; Albert T. Volwiler, George Croghan and the Westward Movement; Dale Van Every, Forth to the Wilderness.)

STARK, JOHN, CAPTIVITY OF. John Stark, a future Indian fighter and Revolutionary War general, was captured by Abnaki Indians in May 1752 while hunting on Baker's River. He was taken up the Connecticut River to an Indian village and compelled to run the gantlet. Afterward, he was adopted by an Indian family and treated kindly until his redemption. His experiences with the tribe prepared him to be a partisan leader and a member of Rogers' Rangers in the French and Indian War.

(Jeremy Belknap, History of New Hampshire, I.)

STATEN ISLAND, NEW YORK. Staten Island was purchased from the Indians by Dutch officials in 1630. Peace between the races prevailed for several years, but in 1640 hostilities began when settlers accused the Raritan Indians of slaughtering livestock. The Indians ignored a summons from New Amsterdam to make reparations, and Cornelis van Tienhoven led 80 soldiers and sailors to punish them. They captured several Indians and tortured them to death. In retaliation, the Raritans murdered 4 Staten Island farmers the following year.

In September 1655, Indians attacked New Amsterdam, then crossed to Staten Island and destroyed the village. Twenty-three settlers were slain.

(E. B. O'Callaghan, History of New Netherland; Allen W. Trelease, Indian Affairs of Colonial New York.)

STEPHENSON, FORT. Fort Stephenson, located on the Sandusky River at the present site of Fremont, Ohio, was commanded by Maj. George Croghan during the War of 1812. He had only 120 men and one cannon when 1,200 British soldiers and Indians, commanded by Gen. Henry A. Proctor, attacked the fort on August 1-2, 1813. A heavy assault was made on the stockade, but the defenders held their fire until the enemy reached pointblank range, then sent them reeling with accurate rifle and cannon fire. Deserted by many of his Indians, Proctor abandoned the attack and withdrew from the area on August 3. The British and Indians sustained more than a hundred casualties, while only 1 American was killed.

(Louise Phelps Kellogg, The British Régime in Wisconsin and the Northwest; John Tebbel and Keith Jennison, The American Indian Wars; Reginald Horsman, The War of 1812; R. David Edmunds, The Shawnee Prophet.)

STEVENS, PHINEAS. In August 1723, Deacon Joseph Stevens and his 4 sons were attending religious services at the Rutland meeting house in Massachusetts when Chief Gray Lock and a Waranoke war party attacked. The deacon escaped, but 2 of his sons were killed and the other 2 captured. Phineas, one of those taken prisoner, learned the tactics of wilderness warfare so thoroughly during his captivity that after redemption he became one of New England's leading Indian fighters.

On May 24, 1746, Stevens, then a military officer, rushed to the relief of 21 soldiers besieged by Indians at Fort Number Four, the most northerly post in the Connecticut Valley (present Charlestown, New Hampshire). A fierce fight ensued with 5 men on each side being slain. Afterward, the fort was abandoned, but Stevens reoccupied it with 30 men in March 1747.

Early in April 1747, a French officer, Jean Baptiste Boucher de Niverville, attacked Number Four with 400 soldiers and Indians. The Indians attempted to set fire to the fort, but the defenders dug trenches extending outside the stockade and doused the flames. For two days, the attackers fired at the fort, riddling the walls, but managing to wound only 2 defenders. Then Niverville demanded surrender, Stevens refused, and the attack was resumed. On the third day, the French and Indians abandoned the siege and withdrew.

In 1749, Stevens was appointed by the governor of Massachusetts to attempt to redeem New England captives in Canada. This was the first of many such missions. Among captives he redeemed was John Stark, a future general of the Revolutionary War, for whom he traded a pony.

"Stevens, a native of Sudbury, Massachusetts, one of the earliest settlers of Number Four, and one of its chief proprietors, was a bold, intelligent, and determined man."--Francis Parkman.

(Francis Parkman, A Half-Century of Conflict; Jeremy Belknap, History of New Hampshire, I; Herbert Milton Sylvester, Indian Wars of New England, III.)

STILLMAN'S RUN. In May 1832, during the Black Hawk War, Maj. Isaiah Stillman patrolled the Kyte River region with 275 men. On May 15, a discouraged Black Hawk sent 7 warriors to Stillman's camp with a proposal to surrender his entire band. The soldiers suspected trickery and opened fire on the Sauk emissaries, killing 3 and sending the others on a frantic ride back to Black Hawk's camp.

Black Hawk, hearing the sound of soldiers in pursuit, stationed his 40 warriors behind trees to await them. As the vanguard of troops spurred into camp, the Sauk chief sprung his trap. The startled riders turned tail at the first fire. As they fled, they met other troopers advancing and threw them into panic with shouts that a thousand Indians were in pursuit. Soon Stillman's entire force, with the exception of a few men who were slain attempting to make a stand, joined the frantic retreat all the way to Fort Dixon. First arrivals reported that a massacre had occurred, spreading terror throughout the nearest settlements. Actually, only 11 soldiers were killed in the fiasco that is recorded in history as "Stillman's Run."

(William T. Hagan, The Sac and Fox Indians.)

STOCKBRIDGE INDIANS. The Stockbridge Indians, a member of the Mahican confederacy originally called Housatonics, lived along the Housatonic River in southwestern Massachusetts. They were renamed when they became Christians and the town of Stockbridge was founded among them in 1738 by the Reverend John Sergeant. A school was established at Stockbridge, where the Indians studied agriculture and manual arts and acquired many traits of white civilization.

The Stockbridges fought for the colonists during three major wars. In the French and Indian War, their villages suffered from so many raids that only 200 Stockbridges survived. Their warriors fought against Pontiac, sustaining additional losses. Then as American allies, they lost almost half of their men fighting the British.

After the Revolution, white settlers moved into Stockbridge and made life so unbearable that the Indians removed to Oneida Creek, in New York. There they adopted many of the ways of their white neighbors, and by 1800, they had created a stable agricultural settlement. Another removal was required in 1828-29 because of pressure by whites, and the Stockbridges joined remnants of other tribes in Wisconsin. In 1833, they settled with the Munsees on a reservation near Green Bay. Ten years later, they were granted citizenship. Their descendants live in Wisconsin today.

(F. W. Hodge, ed., Handbook of American Indians, II; John R. Swanton, Indian Tribes of North America; William C. Sturtevant, ed., Handbook of North American Indians, XV.)

STONE, JOHN.   John Stone, a mariner, a trader, and by most accounts a rogue, sailed to Massachusetts from Virginia in 1633 with
a cargo of cattle.   In Boston he was convicted of disorderly conduct
and expelled from the colony.   At Plymouth he made an attempt on
the life of the governor.   Finding himself unwelcome elsewhere, he
and an eight-man crew set sail for the Connecticut River.

   At the mouth of the river, Stone opened trade with the Niantic
Indians, welcoming sachems and warriors to visit his ship.   One day
in 1634 he sent three men ashore to hunt, and the others to work
in the galley, while he took a nap in his cabin.   Silently, a party of
Indians boarded the ship and tomahawked the sleeping captain.   About
the same time, warriors slew the hunters ashore.   The remaining crewmen attempted to defend themselves, but some of them died in a powder explosion and the others were overwhelmed.   The Niantics plundered the ship and gave some of the goods to Pequot chiefs.

   New England authorities made little objection at the time, but
later they demanded that the Pequots, neighbors and protectors of
the Niantics, surrender the murderers for trial.   Three years after
Stone's death, they used the incident as one of their reasons for
waging war on the Pequots.

   (John Mason, A Brief History of the Pequot War; Herbert Milton Sylvester, Indian Wars of New England, I; Alden T. Vaughan,
New England Frontier.)

STORER, JOSEPH, FAMILY OF.   Joseph Storer was born in 1648.
He established a lumber business at Wells, Maine, in 1661, and as
the village was a frequent target of Abnaki Indian attacks, he built
one of the strongest garrison houses in New England.   During King
Philip's War, his brother Benjamin was killed by the Indians on
April 13, 1677, and afterward, Joseph enclosed his home with a
strong palisade and invited neighbors to take refuge there at the
first sign of danger.   With the onset of King William's War in 1689,
he inspired the settlers to stand firm in the face of French and Indian invasions.

   In June 1691, Capt. James Converse and some 35 men withstood an attack on Storer's garrison house by the Abnaki chief Moxus
and 200 warriors.   One year later, Converse and 29 soldiers joined
the settlers at Storer's in repulsing an attack by Chiefs Madockawando, Moxus, and Egeremet and the French officers St. Castin and
Portneuf.   The 500 attackers failed to capture the fort and had to
settle for torturing a prisoner outside the stockade.

   On August 10, 1703, a war party of Canadian Indians led by
French officers, attacked Wells and captured Joseph Storer's 18-
year-old daughter, Rachel.   Taken to Canada, she joined the Catholic Church and rejected attempts by Rev. John Williams to redeem
her.   Shortly before Storer died in 1730, he provided a large sum in
his will for Rachel if she would leave her husband, a Canadian military officer, and return to New England.   But the legacy was rejected and she lived at Montreal until her death in 1747.

   (Edward L. Bourne, History of Wells and Kennebunk; Samuel
Adams Drake, The Border Wars of New England; Herbert Milton

Sylvester, Indian Wars of New England, II-III; Alden T. Vaughan
and Edward W. Clark, eds., Puritans Among the Indians.)

STOUGHTON, ISRAEL. Capt. Israel Stoughton, an English officer
who had fought under Cromwell, led Massachusetts soldiers during
the late stages of the Pequot War. In 1637, with the help of the
Narraganset Indians, they captured 100 Pequots, executed more than
20 warriors, and divided the women and children among the colonists and their Indian allies to serve as slaves. Stoughton requested
Governor Winthrop to permit him to keep "the fairest and largest"
of the women for himself. Those sent to Boston tried so desperately
to escape that the Puritans branded several of them on the shoulder.
     (Herbert Milton Sylvester, Indian Wars of New England, I;
Alden T. Vaughan, New England Frontier.)

STUDEBAKER, ELIZABETH, CAPTIVITY OF. Elizabeth Studebaker,
a small child, was captured by Delaware Indians in Cumberland County,
Pennsylvania, in 1755. While living with the Indians, she developed
into a beautiful maiden and a great favorite of the tribe. After nine
years of captivity, she was among the 206 prisoners delivered up to
Col. Henry Bouquet near the Muskingum River as a result of his
successful campaign against the Delawares and Shawnees. The redeemed captives were taken to Fort Pitt, and along the trail it was
necessary to watch many of them to prevent their running away to
rejoin the Indians. One of the most determined to escape was Elizabeth Studebaker. Ten days after the march began, she slipped
away into the wilderness to rejoin her adopted people.
     (C. Hale Sipe, Indian Wars of Pennsylvania.)

STUMP, FREDERICK, MASSACRE. In January 1768, Frederick Stump,
a Pennsylvania frontiersman, and his hired man, John Ironcutter, invited a band of 10 Indians to his home on the west side of the Susquehanna River. They plied them with liquor, and while the guests
were too inebriated to defend themselves, they murdered and scalped
them. Among the victims were the Seneca chief John Cook (called
the White Mingo), and some Shawnee and Delaware women. Thus,
wrote Dale Van Every, "at one stroke Stump had managed to incense
not only the already infuriated Ohio Indians but England's chief Indian allies, the Iroquois, upon whose pacifying influence so much
depended."
     The Iroquois demanded that Sir William Johnson punish the
murderers, and as a result, George Croghan went before the Pennsylvania Assembly to warn of an Indian war unless the tribes obtained satisfaction. Officials ordered Stump's arrest, and Capt. William Patterson seized him and his cohort and took them to jail at
Carlisle. One day afterward, however, a band of frontiersmen broke
into the jail and released Stump and Ironcutter. Neither of them
ever went to trial.
     (Charles A. Hanna, The Wilderness Trail; U. J. Jones, His-
tory of the Early Settlement of the Juniata Valley; Dale Van Every,
Forth to the Wilderness.)

STUYVESANT, PETER, INDIAN RELATIONS. Peter Stuyvesant, a
veteran Dutch military officer and colonial official, arrived at New
Amsterdam to serve as director-general of New Netherland on May
11, 1647. Soon afterward, he attempted to curtail Dutch trade of
arms and ammunition to the Indians, but in 1648, he was accused of
indulging in that trade himself, and he made no further attempt to
prohibit the practice. He negotiated a treaty with the Susquehanna
Indians in 1649. In an attempt to wrest the Indian trade from the
Swedes, he built Fort Casimer on the Delaware River in 1651.

In 1652, Stuyvesant nullified purchase of lands from Indians
by individuals and decreed that he personally would supervise such
transactions in the future. He denied charges by New England officials that he incited war parties to attack their settlements, and he
proposed cooperation among the Dutch and English in handling Indian affairs, but the Puritans refused.

Hostilities with the Esopus Indians began in 1658, when a
warrior murdered a settler and Stuyvesant demanded his surrender.
The Indians responded that young warriors who bought liquor from
the Dutch were beyond their control. A few months later, Dutch
settlers murdered several drunken Indians, and the Esopus tribes
threatened war. Stuyvesant led 150 soldiers and friendly Indians
up the Hudson and forced the hostiles to disperse.

During the spring of 1660, provoked by Esopus depredations,
Stuyvesant determined to conquer the confederation and seize tribal
lands. His soldiers destroyed a village, captured 12 warriors, and
sent them into slavery at Curaçao. Afterward, the Esopus made
peace and ceded much of their territory. In June 1663, the Esopus
attacked several Dutch villages, killing or capturing numerous settlers. In retaliation, Stuyvesant dispatched a Dutch army that drove
the Indians out of the area and destroyed their houses and crops.
(See ESOPUS INDIANS.)

After the English captured New Netherland in 1664, Stuyvesant
retired to his Manhattan bowery. He died in 1672.

(E. B. O'Callaghan, History of New Netherland, II; Allen W.
Trelease, Indian Affairs in Colonial New York.)

SUDBURY, MASSACHUSETTS, RAID. One of the bloodiest battles
of King Philip's War was fought at Sudbury, Massachusetts, on April
12, 1676. About 500 Indians invested the town, and finding the citizens concentrated in garrison houses, they burned the vacated buildings. Meanwhile, relief forces began to reach Sudbury from neighboring communities. The first to arrive, a dozen settlers from Concord, were annihilated almost immediately. Soon afterward, a larger
force from Watertown entered the fray and cleared the eastern part
of Sudbury of Indians.

While the raiders still occupied the western side of the Sudbury
River, 50 or 60 Marlborough citizens hastening to Sudbury's relief
found themselves surrounded by hundreds of warriors. A fierce
battle began, with the Marlborough men defending themselves on a
hilltop. Finally, the Indians set fire to the grass, and the whites
attempted to flee through the smoke. More than 30 men, including

Capt. Samuel Wadsworth, their commander, were killed. Afterward, the Indians withdrew from the town, leaving most of it a smoking ruin.

(Douglas Edward Leach, Flintlock and Tomahawk.)

SULLIVAN, JOHN, EXPEDITION. In 1779, George Washington determined to destroy Iroquois strongholds in retaliation for Indian and Tory raids on New York frontier settlements. He appointed Gen. John Sullivan, a New Hampshire lawyer who had served ably in the Continental Congress and had fought under his command during the first three years of the Revolutionary War, to lead the expedition. T. Wood Clarke has characterized Sullivan as a "brave, competent, and thorough soldier, a commander who stood high in the esteem and confidence of General Washington."

Sullivan planned a campaign that would destroy the Six Nations' villages from end to end. While he led three brigades from Easton, Pennsylvania, up the Susquehanna against the Seneca strongholds, Gen. James Clinton would march along the Mohawk and wipe out the warriors and Tories of the Oquaga-Unadilla area. The third force, led by Col. Daniel Brodhead, would march northward from Pittsburgh and strike the Senecas in northern Pennsylvania and western New York. (See CLINTON, JAMES; BRODHEAD, DANIEL.)

Sullivan's army drove the Indians from Chemung in August, sustaining 20 casualties in a brief encounter with some Delaware warriors. After destroying the town, he marched to Tioga, where he was joined by Clinton's brigade, their combined forces numbering almost 4,500 men. They resumed the march on August 26 and fought the decisive battle of the campaign three days later, compelling the Indians led by Joseph Brant and John Butler to retreat. (See NEWTOWN, BATTLE OF.)

Meeting little resistance, Sullivan resumed his invasion, destroying Catherine's Town on September 2, Kendaia (Appletown) on September 5, and Canadasaga and neighboring villages on September 8. While burning Kanaghsaws a few days later, he sent a detachment to scout the area toward Geneseo castle. It was ambushed and almost annihilated (see BOYD, THOMAS, EXPEDITION).

After destroying Gathtsegwarohare, an important town on the Genesee River, on September 14, Sullivan sent detachments to devastate the Cayuga villages and the lower Mohawk castle. (See GANSEVOORT, PETER.) Then he led his main army back to Tioga, abandoning his major objective of capturing Niagara because of the lateness of the season. By the end of the campaign he had burned 40 villages while losing less than 40 soldiers. He had failed to destroy the fighting power of the western Iroquois, however, and he antagonized the neutral Onondagas. As a result, the Iroquois congregated at Niagara and increased their attacks on the New York and Pennsylvania settlements.

(Barbara Graymont, The Iroquois in the American Revolution; T. Wood Clarke, The Bloody Mohawk; Dale Van Every, A Company of Heroes; Francis Whiting Halsey, The Old New York Frontier.)

SUSQUEHANNA INDIANS. The Susquehanna (Conestoga, Minqua)

Indians, a large and powerful Iroquoian tribe, lived during early historic times on the Susquehanna River and its tributaries. By 1608, when encountered by Capt. John Smith, they had conquered the tribes of the Chesapeake region and controlled the lands as far north as Seneca territory.

During the first half of the seventeenth century, the Susquehannas sustained heavy assaults by the Iroquois and a series of smallpox epidemics, reducing their population from 3,000 to less than 600. The survivors usually were allies and trading partners of the English, Dutch, and Swedish settlers until 1674, when hostilities with southern tribes led to war with Maryland and Virginia settlers. Then, beset by enemies on all sides, they were compelled to move to New York under Iroquois supervision. Later they returned to their homeland, but tribal population dwindled steadily, and the last survivors were massacred by Pennsylvania frontiersmen in 1763. (See PAXTON BOYS.)

(Charles A. Hanna, The Wilderness Trail; Paul A. W. Wallace, Indians in Pennsylvania; Allen W. Trelease, Indian Affairs in Colonial New York; William C. Sturtevant, ed., Handbook of North American Indians, XV; F. W. Hodge, ed., Handbook of American Indians.)

SWAANENDAEL COLONY MASSACRE see ZWAANENDAEL COLONY MASSACRE

SWAMP FIGHT see GREAT SWAMP FIGHT

SWANSEA, MASSACHUSETTS. At the onset of King Philip's War, Swansea was the nearest settlement to the hostile stronghold at Mount Hope. The small community, containing a few scattered families, was poorly prepared for defense, when in June 1675, Wampanoag warriors began looting and burning abandoned buildings.

On June 21, settlers from neighboring communities were dispatched by Gov. Josiah Winslow to assist Swansea citizens. Benjamin Church led a small military force from Taunton and stationed soldiers in garrison houses. Soon afterward, hostilities escalated with the shooting of an Indian looter. On June 24, the Wampanoags attacked six settlers gathering corn, and before the end of the day, nine men had been slain.

On June 28, reinforcements arrived. A few soldiers crossed a bridge leading to lands controlled by the Indians, were fired upon from the woods, and retreated with the loss of one man. (See CHURCH, BENJAMIN.) On the following day, the Indians abandoned the area.

(Edward Douglas Leach, Flintlock and Tomahawk; John Tebbel and Keith Jennison, The American Indian Wars.)

SWARTON, HANNAH, FAMILY OF. On May 16, 1690, during King William's War, Abnaki raiders led by French officers attacked the Maine settlements. Hannah Swarton described her experience succinctly: "I was taken by the Indians when Casco Fort was taken. My Husband being slain, and four Children taken with me. The

Eldest of my Sons they kill'd, about two Months after I was taken, and the rest scatter'd from me."

Mrs. Swarton almost starved while on the trail to Canada. She was turned over to the French at Quebec, and in 1695, redeemed and permitted to sail to Boston. Her youngest child was recovered, but she never saw the others again. Her daughter Mary became a Catholic and married a Canadian.

(James Levernier and Hennig Cohen, eds., The Indians and Their Captives; Alden T. Vaughan and Edward W. Clark, eds., Puritans Among the Indians.)

SWETT, BENJAMIN, EXPEDITION. In 1677, Capt. Benjamin Swett, a Hampton, New Hampshire, Indian fighter, led 40 settlers and 200 Natick Indian allies to attack a concentration of Abnakis at the falls of Taconick on the Kennebeck River. The hostiles retreated two miles, then turned suddenly upon their pursuers. Most of Swett's men were put to flight. Swett was killed while trying with a few experienced fighters to protect the retreat. Sixty of his followers were killed or wounded.

(Jeremy Belknap, History of New Hampshire, I.)

-T-

TACHNECHDORUS see LOGAN, JOHN

TACKAPOUSHA, MASSAPEQUA CHIEF. Tackapousha, chief of an Algonquian tribe on western Long Island, was an ally of the Dutch during the Esopus Wars. Afterward, he became involved in a series of land disputes with the Dutch and English colonists, compelling them to pay tribute on numerous occasions. During King Philip's War, he was suspected of hostile intentions, and the settlers seized the tribe's firearms, returning them when he kept his braves out of the war. He died about 1694.

(Allen W. Trelease, Indian Affairs in Colonial New York.)

TAIMAH, FOX CHIEF. Born about 1790, Taimah became an important Fox chief and medicine man, especially famous for his ability to cure the sick. A friend of the settlers, he saved the life of the Indian agent at Prairie du Chien when a warrior attempted to murder him. After the tribe moved to Iowa, he continued to lead them with the respect of both races until his death about 1830.

(Frederick J. Dockstader, Great North American Indians.)

TALCOTT, JOHN. Maj. John Talcott of Hartford, Connecticut, was one of the most effective Indian fighters during King Philip's War. In June 1676, he led 440 English and Indian allies to victory over the hostiles, killing or capturing 52 people. Soon afterward, he repulsed a raid on Hadley. On July 2, he and his soldiers slew 171 Indians during an attack on a Narraganset village. On the following day, they assaulted Potuck's Narraganset band that was attempting to surrender, killing or capturing 67 people. Douglas Edward Leach, historian of King Philip's War, commented that "apparently men who themselves had loving wives and children waiting for them at home could stain their swords with the blood of Indian women and children without a qualm."

(Douglas Edward Leach, Flintlock and Tomahawk; Samuel G. Drake, ed., The Old Indian Chronicle.)

TAMANEND, DELAWARE CHIEF see TAMENEND, DELAWARE CHIEF

TAMAQUE, DELAWARE CHIEF. Tamaque (Beaver, King Beaver) was an important chief of the Turkey division of the Delaware Nation. He lived on the Schuylkill River until the lands of that area were sold to the settlers in 1732. Then he moved to the Ohio, residing at various times on Beaver River, Kuskuski, and Tuscarawas.

A brother of the fierce war chief Shingas, he joined the hostiles after Braddock's defeat in 1755. By 1758, however, he desired to make peace, and when Shingas was deposed as principal chief that year, Tamaque succeeded him. In 1762, he warned the whites of an impending Indian war.

At the onset of Pontiac's War, Tamaque reverted to hostility. He became a fierce raider on the Pennsylvania frontier until Col. Henry Bouquet compelled him to stop fighting and to release his white captives.

In later life, Tamaque was converted to Christianity by the Moravian missionaries. He died at the Moravian town of Gnadenhutten, Ohio, in 1769.

(Paul A. W. Wallace, Indians in Pennsylvania; F. W. Hodge, ed., Handbook of American Indians, II.)

TAMAROA INDIANS. The Tamaroa Indians, a member of the Illinois confederacy, lived near the mouth of the Illinois River when visited by early French explorers, and they remained friendly to the French thereafter. In 1680 the Iroquois drove the other Illinois tribes west of the Mississippi, but the Tamaroas refused to abandon their homes. As a result, they were almost annihilated during the next Iroquois invasion. A mission was established among the survivors in 1699, but they were absorbed soon afterward by other Illinois tribes.

(Clarence Walworth Alvord, The Illinois Country; F. W. Hodge, ed., Handbook of American Indians, II.)

TAMENEND, DELAWARE CHIEF. Tamenend (Tamanend, Tammany), chief of the Unami Delawares, is believed to have lived in the present Bucks County, Pennsylvania, when William Penn established his colony nearby. A legendary figure, the dates of his birth and death are unknown, but it is certain that on June 23, 1683, he signed a treaty with Penn at Shackamoxon. In 1694, at a meeting of the Pennsylvania Provincial Council, he promised eternal friendship, and he seems to have honored the pledge.

John Heckewelder wrote of him that "the name of Tamanend is held in the highest veneration among the Indians. Of all the chiefs and great men which Lenape nation ever had, he stands foremost.... The fame of this great man extended even among the whites.... In the Revolutionary War his enthusiastic admirers dubbed him a saint, and he was established under the name of St. Tammany, the Patron Saint of America." The Tammany Societies were named for him.

(Frederick J. Dockstader, Great North American Indians; John Heckewelder, History, Manners, and Customs of the Indian Nations; Paul A. W. Wallace, Indians in Pennsylvania; F. W. Hodge, ed., Handbook of American Indians, II.)

TAMMANY, DELAWARE CHIEF see TAMENEND, DELAWARE CHIEF

TANACHARISON, ONEIDA CHIEF see HALF KING, ONEIDA CHIEF

TANKITEKE INDIANS. The Tankiteke Indians, an Algonquian tribe of the Wappinger confederacy, lived astride the New York-Connecticut line during the time of Dutch settlement. Their chief, Pachamis, pretended friendship with the colonists, but he incited other tribes to attack them. In 1644, John Underhill burned a large Indian village in Westchester County, New York, which is believed to have been Tankiteke. More than 500 people perished in the flames.

(E. B. O'Callaghan, History of New Netherland, I; Allen W. Trelease, Indian Affairs of Colonial New York.)

TANNER, JOHN. John Tanner was nine years old when Indians captured him in Kentucky in 1789. After two years of harsh treatment he was adopted by an old Ottawa woman and grew up as a complete Indian, living most of the time with the Chippewas in the Great Lakes region. He married two Indian women and fathered several children.

In 1817, Tanner determined to visit his white relatives. Lewis Cass, governor of Michigan Territory, helped him to locate them, and he spent some time with his brothers and sisters in Kentucky. Afterward, he returned to his Indian family and worked for the American Fur Company. He trapped for several years and then served as interpreter for Henry Rowe Schoolcraft, U.S. Indian agent at Sault Ste. Marie. He related the story of his life with the Indians to Dr. Edwin James in 1830, and it was published.

Tanner tried desperately to resume the life of a white man. He had his Indian children educated, married a white woman, and fathered a child by her, but he was distrusted and abused by settlers who considered him a "white savage" and refused to accept him into their society. When his wife divorced him, he became subject to fits of violence and spent time in jail.

In 1846, James L. Schoolcraft, brother of the Indian agent, was murdered, and Tanner was never seen thereafter. Henry Schoolcraft accused Tanner of committing the crime. Policemen and soldiers searched for him, but no trace was found. Years later, it was reported that another man had killed Schoolcraft and then murdered Tanner to cover up the crime.

(Edward James, A Narrative of the Captivity and Adventures of John Tanner; Frederick Drimmer, Scalps and Tomahawks.)

TARBELL, JOHN AND ZECHARIAH, CAPTIVITY OF. John Tarbell (12), his brother, Zechariah (7), and their older sister, Sarah, were captured by Indians at Groton, Massachusetts, about 1707. Sarah was redeemed by the French, but the boys remained the rest of their lives with the Caughnawaga Indians in Canada. In 1739 they visited their relatives at Groton, but they spurned offers of money and land and returned to their Indian families.

In time, both John and Zechariah became chiefs of the Caughnawagas. They founded the mission at St. Regis about 1760.

(Emma Lewis Coleman, New England Captives Carried to Canada; Francis Parkman, A Half-Century of Conflict.)

TARHE, WYANDOT CHIEF. Tarhe (the Crain) was born near Detroit in 1742. As a youth he became a distinguished warrior. He fought the English at the Battle of Point Pleasant, and he was wounded at Fallen Timbers. Afterward, however, he realized that the Indians could not turn back the tide of American settlement, so he signed the Treaty of Greenville in 1795.

Tarhe rejected Tecumseh's plea to help hold the line against American expansion. During the war of 1812, although 70 years old, he served in General Harrison's army and fought the British and Indians at the Battle of the Thames. After the war, he befriended the settlers of Ohio, and upon his death in November 1818, both whites and Indians came great distances to attend his funeral.

"As a warrior, he was among the bravest of the brave; but, Indian as he was, no stain of cruelty, barbarity, or injustice, rests upon his character."--James B. Finley.

(Frederick J. Dockstader, Great North American Indians; R. David Edmunds, The Shawnee Prophet; James B. Finley, Life Among the Indians.)

TARRATEEN INDIANS see ABNAKI INDIANS

TATEMY, MOSES FONDA, DELAWARE CHIEF. Tatemy was born near the present Cranbury, New Jersey, during the latter part of the seventeenth century. He became a firm friend of the English during his youth, and as a reward for his services as an interpreter, he was awarded a 300-acre tract in Northampton County, Pennsylvania, in 1737. He was converted to Christianity by David Brainerd in 1745, and he served Brainerd as an interpreter until the latter's death in 1747.

Tatemy, who had been given the name Moses Fonda when baptized, served as interpreter at several important Indian conferences at Philadelphia and Easton, and he was instrumental in inducing the Delawares to cease hostilities during the French and Indian War. He died in 1761, "beloved," said John Heckewelder, "by all who knew him."

(John Heckewelder, History, Manners, and Customs of the Indian Nations; F. W. Hodge, ed., Handbook of American Indians, II.)

TAXOUS, ABNAKI CHIEF see MOXUS, ABNAKI CHIEF

TAYAC, CONOY CHIEF   see   CHITOMACHEN, CONOY CHIEF

TECUMSEH, SHAWNEE CHIEF. Tecumseh, considered by many historians to have been the greatest North American Indian who ever
lived, was born in 1768 at Piqua, a Shawnee village in Ohio. His
father, Puckeshinwa, was a Shawnee chief, and his mother, Methoataske, was of Creek and Cherokee descent. One of eight children,
he was raised by his brother Cheesekau, and his sister Tecumapease,
after his father was murdered by white hunters and his mother deserted the family.
      Tecumseh, about the age of 13, fled during a fight with Ken-
tucky frontiersmen, but he became a full-fledged warrior in time to
accompany Cheesekau on a raid of the Cumberland settlements about
1788. Cheesekau was slain, and Tecumseh and his followers avenged
him by killing three white settlers. He raided the frontier settlements repeatedly, participated in the victories over Harmar and St.
Clair, fought with great courage at Fallen Timbers, and refused to
attend peace negotiations in 1795.
      After the Treaty of Greenville, Tecumseh went to Indiana to
prepare himself for leadership in the movement to stem the tide of
white encroachment. About 1800 he fell in love with a white woman,
Rebecca Galloway, who taught him history and literature, but she
declined his proposal of marriage when he insisted upon retaining his
Indian lifestyle.
      Tecumseh came into his own as a leader early in the nineteenth
century when he proclaimed that no tribe could sell land to the whites
without permission of all of the tribes. He and his brother Tenskwatawa (the Shawnee Prophet) combined their philosophies and oratorical
skills to attract Indians from throughout the Ohio Valley and Great
Lakes regions to gather at the village of Prophetstown on the Wabash
River in 1808. Afterward, he visited tribes in the West and South,
urging them to join an Indian confederation intended to maintain the
Ohio River as a permanent boundary between whites and Indians.
      Gov. William Henry Harrison was alarmed by Tecumseh's activ-
ities, and at a conference at Vincennes in August 1810, war almost
erupted when the fiery young chief called the governor a liar. Incensed by the cession of a vast territory at the Treaty of Fort
Wayne, Tecumseh declared that any attempt by whites to settle on
lands thus fraudulently obtained would be met by armed resistance.
      Early in November 1811, while Tecumseh was recruiting war-
riors in the South, Harrison led a large army toward Prophetstown.
Disregarding Tecumseh's orders to avoid battle, Tenskwatawa attacked the soldiers while they were camped for the night, resulting
in an Indian defeat and the destruction of Prophetstown. (See TIP-
PECANOE, BATTLE OF.)
      When Tecumseh returned to find his plans disastrously dis-
rupted, he realized that his best hope to prevent American expansion
lay in an alliance with the British. With the onset of the War of
1812, he recruited large parties of warriors from many tribes to support the British offensive against Detroit and other American forts.
Commissioned brigadier general, he played a major role in compelling

General Hull to surrender Detroit on August 16, 1812. Afterward, recruits flocked to his camp, swelling his Indian force for a time to 15,000. With the death of Gen. Isaac Brock on October 13, 1812, however, Tecumseh had to cooperate with a less effective British commander, Col. Henry Proctor, whom the chief believed to be a coward. Their joint forces failed to capture other American strongholds (see MEIGS, FORT; STEPHENSON, FORT), and finally retreated to Canada. During these battles, Tecumseh gained the admiration and respect of American leaders by his intercession to save prisoners from torture and death.

After Perry's victory on Lake Erie, Tecumseh and his Indians covered Proctor's withdrawal deeper into Canada until, in exasperation, he demanded that the British make a stand near the Thames River. There, the Indians took position in a swamp, while the British occupied wooded terrain near the river. General Harrison's forces crushed the British, compelling Proctor to flee, but Tecumseh and his Indians resisted fiercely until the chief was slain. Fairfax Downey asserted that Tecumseh's "great voice, shouting orders, soared over the rackets of conflict. Indian bullets emptied the saddles of 15 of [Col.] Richard Mentor Johnson's vanguard troops. The colonel ... pistoled an Indian chief attacking him. He may have shot Tecumseh, who had already been many times wounded.... Slowly the Indians ... faded back through the swamp. They must have carried the body of Tecumseh with them, for it was never found...."

Tecumseh, only 44 years old at the time of his death, has received greater recognition for character and achievements than any other Indian. His biographer Glenn Tucker believes that "no other Indian had asserted such power.... He led ... poorly armed people against a great nation and won victories. He and Isaac Brock achieved the preservation of Canada for the British empire...."

Wilcomb E. Washburn acclaimed him as "the first native leader with vision enough to see that if white encroachments were to be stopped, the stopping could not be done by a single tribe, or even a confederation, but only by a great union of all tribes to fight for their common homeland."

Frederick J. Dockstader characterized him as "a brave, skilled fighter, but ... a leader who would not stand for barbarism or arbitrary, unnecessary killing--a code which made him respected throughout his life."

Even his adversary William Henry Harrison conceded that he was "one of those uncommon geniuses, which spring up occasionally to produce revolutions and overturn the established order of things."

(Glenn Tucker, Tecumseh, Vision of Glory; Frederick J. Dockstader, Great North American Indians; R. David Edmunds, The Shawnee Prophet; Sam Dale, Life and Times of Sam Dale; Fairfax Downey, Indian Wars of the U.S. Army; Robert M. Utley and Wilcomb E. Washburn, The American Heritage History of the Indian Wars; Benjamin Drake, Tecumseh.)

TEDYUSCUNG, DELAWARE CHIEF. Tedyuscung (Teedyuscung), one of the most important and controversial Delaware chiefs, was born

about 1705 at the present site of Trenton, New Jersey. During his
youth, he made a poor living as a broom manufacturer, wandering
throughout the settlements along the Delaware River. At that time
he acquired an admiration of European civilization, and in later life,
he attempted to influence his people to adapt the lifestyle of their
white neighbors.

About 1730, Tedyuscung moved to Pennsylvania and settled at
the forks of the Delaware. In 1737, this land was acquired by Pennsylvania authorities as a result of the controversial Walking Purchase,
a transaction that Tedyuscung condemned as a fraud. Afterward, he
came under the influence of Moravian missionaries, settled at their
town of Gnadenhutten, Pennsylvania, and was baptized as "Gideon"
in 1750. In 1753, he and the Christian Mahican chief Abraham established a village in the Wyoming Valley under Iroquois supervision.
His move, a defection from Moravian discipline, expedited his plan to
gain a position of leadership among his own people, and he was rewarded by designation as war chief of the Wyoming Valley Delaware
band.

After Braddock's defeat in July 1755, the Delawares of the
Ohio urged Tedyuscung's followers to join in their raids on English
settlements. Tedyuscung sought assurances of English protection,
but failing to receive them, and fearful of an attack by the French,
he and his warriors joined the hostiles in December 1755. He led his
warriors on a raid of the Weeser Plantation on December 31, killing
two farmers and capturing Leonard and William Weeser. On the following morning, they attacked two other plantations, taking four scalps
and four prisoners. On their way home they murdered elderly Peter
Hess when he was unable to keep up with their pace.

Abandoning Wyoming as too exposed to English retaliation,
Tedyuscung and his followers moved to Tioga. He did not personally
take the warpath again, but he sent packs of warriors to harry the
settlements.

In the spring of 1758, the Iroquois compelled the eastern Delawares to stop fighting the English. Tedyuscung, having discovered
that the French could not supply the goods his people needed to
survive, attended three peace conferences at Easton between 1756
and 1758, calling himself the "King of the Delawares" and claiming
that he could speak for 10 to 18 Indian nations. Royally entertained
by Pennsylvania officials, he gained the support of Isaac Pemberton
and other influential Quakers when he demanded restitution of lands
lost by the Delawares as a result of the Walking Purchase. In spite
of Iroquois attempts to brand him a pretender, he played an important
role in restoring peace between the Delawares and the English.

In 1762, Tedyuscung accepted a large sum of money from Pennsylvania officials to withdraw his charge of fraud regarding the Walking Purchase. At the end of the war, they built him a home in the
Wyoming Valley, and he agreed to return there with his followers
to prevent occupation of the area by Connecticut settlers. When the
Connecticut vanguard arrived, he compelled them to leave, but they
returned the following year. On April 19, 1763, Tedyuscung's home
caught fire and he perished in the flames. The circumstances remain

a matter of conjecture, some historians believing that settlers set the fire, others accusing the Iroquois of responsibility, while a third theory asserts that the chief himself caused the conflagration while in a drunken stupor.

"The murder of Teedyuscung, and the consequent massacre of those who arranged for and profited from his death, provide a fitting climax to a story which is the epitome of the tragic relation of white men and red in America..... Teedyuscung ... was somehow the only person able to sense the heart of the problem: to grasp the principle that while the 'civilizing' of the Indian was inevitable, it had to be a process undergone peacefully, in security, on Indian land, in Indian communities, at the Indian's pace."--Anthony F. C. Wallace.

(Anthony F. C. Wallace, King of the Delawares: Teedyuscung; Frederick J. Dockstader, Great North American Indians; F. W. Hodge, ed., Handbook of American Indians, II; Paul A. W. Wallace, Indians in Pennsylvania; Charles A. Hanna, The Wilderness Trail.)

TEFFT, JOSHUA. Joshua Tefft, a Pettaquamscut, Rhode Island, settler either voluntarily joined or was captured by the Narraganset Indians prior to King Philip's War. At the outbreak of war in 1675, the colonists regarded him as a renegade and an advisor to Indian enemies. On January 14, 1676, he was captured near Providence while leading hostiles who were stealing cattle. Tried by military court, he was convicted of treason and hanged and quartered.

(Douglas Edward Leach, Flintlock and Tomahawk.)

TEGAKWITHA, KATERI see TEKAKWITHA, KATERI

TEHORAGWANEGEN, CAUGHNAWAGA CHIEF. Tehoragwanegen (Thomas Williams), a mixed-blood grandson of the famous New England captive Eunice Williams, was born in Canada about 1758. During the American Revolution he accompanied Caughnawaga raids on the New England settlements, but upon his grandmother's request, he made every effort to prevent the massacre of women and children and to help captives survive the march to the Indian villages. During Burgoyne's campaign, Williams complained so bitterly about Indian cruelty that the general rebuked his warriors, causing many of them to desert the British army. He attempted, also, to curb the cruelties of the warriors who accompanied John Johnson's raids in the Mohawk region.

After the war, Tehoragwanegen visited his white relatives in New England, and in 1780, he took two of his sons there to be educated (see WILLIAMS, ELEAZER). He supported the Americans during the War of 1812. He died at Quebec on August 16, 1849.

(F. W. Hodge, ed., Handbook of American Indians, II.)

TEKAKWITHA, KATERI, MOHAWK NUN. Tekakwitha (Tegakwitha, Lily of the Mohawks) was born in 1656 at Caughnawaga, near the present site of Auriesville, New York. Her father was a Mohawk Indian and her mother, an Algonquian Indian captive, was a Christian. Her parents died of smallpox when she was a small child, and she was raised by an uncle, a Mohawk chief.

About the age of 10 she served meals to some Jesuit missionaries who visited her uncle, and over his strong objections, she decided to become a Christian. In 1675 she was baptized by Father Jacques de Lamberville, taking the name Kateri (Catherine). For the next two years she was abused by her uncle and shunned by the villagers, but in 1677, a Christian Iroquois chief named Louis Garonhiague took her to a Catholic Indian community near Montreal. There she became the first Indian nun to serve her people.

Always in poor health, Kateri died on April 17, 1680, at the Ville Marie of St. Francis Xavier, at the age of 24. Her brief life as a nun had been so remarkable for her devotion to Christ and her self-denial that both Indians and French-Canadians came to her grave to pray. So many of them asserted that they were cured of their illnesses or that they received visions of heaven that, in 1844, church authorities recommended her canonization. She was beatified in 1980.

(T. J. Campbell, Pioneer Priests of North America; Frederick J. Dockstader, Great North American Indians; F. W. Hodge, ed., Handbook of American Indians, II.)

TENSKWATAWA, SHAWNEE PROPHET. Tenskwãtawa (the Shawnee Prophet), a brother of Tecumseh, was born in 1775, shortly after his father, Puckeshinwa, was murdered by white hunters. His mother, Methoataske, deserted the family, and he was raised by his sister Tecumapease. At an early age he lost the sight of one eye in an accident while playing with a bow and arrow. As a youth he became addicted to alcohol, and he never developed into a successful hunter or warrior. He took no part in the victories over Generals Harmar or St. Clair, and although he was present during the Battle of Fallen Timbers, history is silent in regard to his participation.

Until 1805, Tenskwãtawa led a quiet life, lounging around the fire and frequently indulging his addiction to the point of unconsciousness. When one winter day he collapsed and almost fell into the fire, the Shawnees believed that he had died. But Tenskwãtawa was having a vision, and when he emerged from the trance he related a tale of visiting the spirit world and seeing both the past and the future. He vowed to abandon his dissolute lifestyle, and as the successor of the tribe's recently deceased medicine man, to lead his people to a glorious future.

When the Prophet demanded that tribes abandon the customs of white people and return to those of their ancestors, he struck a responsive chord among chiefs who realized that their lives were increasingly dominated by traders and settlers. Many Shawnees flocked to his standard, and when he accurately predicted a solar eclipse in 1806, leaders of other tribes accepted his teachings.

Tenskwãtawa provided a spiritual basis for Tecumseh's movement to unite all Indians in an attempt to prevent white encroachment on tribal lands. Assured by the Prophet that he could preserve them from death during battles, warriors from throughout the Ohio Valley and Great Lakes region joined him at Prophetstown, the headquarters that he established on the Wabash River near the mouth of Tippecanoe Creek in 1808.

At first Gen. William Henry Harrison believed that the Prophet's movement was beneficial, but by 1809 he realized that Tecumseh was developing an anti-American attitude at Prophetstown. The Treaty of Fort Wayne embittered the Indians and transformed the religious movement into preparations for war. Tecumseh, who had gradually supplanted his brother as leader, departed to recruit tribes in the South, admonishing the Prophet to avoid armed clashes with the whites until his return. But Harrison determined to seize the opportunity to crush the movement, and he led a large force of soldiers toward Prophetstown.

Tenskwatawa, forgetting or disregarding Tecumseh's instructions, persuaded his people to attack Harrison's camp during the night, promising to protect them from enemy bullets. His medicine failed, and Harrison defeated the Indians (see TIPPECANOE, BATTLE OF), and destroyed Prophetstown.

Afterward, the Indians turned against Tenskwatawa. Chiefs threatened his life, and even Tecumseh, upon his return, denounced him as a false prophet. Thoroughly discredited, he followed Tecumseh to Canada during the War of 1812. He fled at the beginning of the Battle of the Thames, and he remained in Canada after the British defeat. In 1824, American officials employed him to persuade the Shawnees to remove to the West, and he accompanied them to Kansas in 1828. In 1838, he died at Kansas City.

(R. David Edmunds, The Shawnee Prophet; Frederick J. Dockstader, Great North American Indians; Glenn Tucker, Tecumseh: Vision of Glory; Freeman Cleaves, Old Tippecanoe.)

THAMES, BATTLE OF THE. The Battle of the Thames, occurring on October 5, 1813, on the Thames River in Canada, was fought by Gen. William Henry Harrison's American army against the British and Indians led by Henry A. Proctor and Tecumseh. Proctor, who had been retreating steadily to avoid battle with Harrison's larger army, finally acceded to Tecumseh's demands to halt and make a stand. The decision was destined to lead to the chief's death and to Proctor's disgrace.

Hoping to ambush the Americans, Tecumseh chose the battleground, deploying most of the Indians in a swamp on the British right flank. Proctor's 700 regulars occupied high ground between two swamps, wooded terrain that offered protection for troops fighting in open order. Harrison recognized the ambush and discovered that the British had taken an open order alignment. Accordingly, he ordered a cavalry charge, the British gave way, and Proctor fled from the scene.

Meanwhile, a part of Harrison's cavalry, Kentuckians led by Col. Richard Mentor Johnson, charged Tecumseh's warriors in the swamp. The chief, imploring his followers to "be brave, stand firm, shoot straight," was wounded in the chest, but he continued to fire, and his warriors responded with spirit. When their ammunition gave out, they fought with their tomahawks until Tecumseh died. Then they retreated into the swamp and the battle came to an end. Six hundred British soldiers were captured and 18 killed, but while 33 of Tecumseh's warriors died and many were wounded, not one of them surrendered. American casualties were 18 killed and 25 wounded.

(Glenn Tucker, Tecumseh: Vision of Glory; Freeman Cleaves, Old Tippecanoe; Reginald Horsman, The War of 1812.)

THAYENDANEGEA, MOHAWK CHIEF see BRANT, JOSEPH, MOHAWK CHIEF

THORPE, HANNAH, CAPTIVITY OF. Hannah Thorpe (Tharp) was captured by Indians near Connersville, Indiana, during the War of 1812. A young girl when taken, she married a Mississinewa warrior called Captain Dixon (Metahkekequah), and became the mother of two children. Unlike many young white captives, she never became substantially assimilated. Detesting her life in an Indian village, she drowned herself about 1850.

(Bert Anson, The Miami Indians.)

THURY, PIERRE. Father Pierre Thury, a priest of the Quebec Seminary, established a mission among the Penobscot Indians of Maine in 1688. He encouraged his flock to wage war on the English settlements, and sometimes he accompanied their raiding parties. He was present at the capture of Pemaquid in 1689, at the sacking of Oyster River in 1694, and the recapture of Pemaquid in 1696.

Characterizing Thury as "among the most prominent apostles of carnage," Francis Parkman charged that when Chief Madockawando desired to make peace with the English, "Thury, wise as the serpent," persuaded other chiefs to keep up their attacks. "Whether acting from fanaticism, policy, or an odious compound of both," Parkman asserted, he was praised by the governor of Canada "in the same breath for his care of the souls of the Indians and his zeal in exciting them to war."

(Francis Parkman, Count Frontenac and New France Under Louis XIV.)

TICONDEROGA. Ticonderoga, originally called Fort Carillon, was built by the French in 1755 to guard the passage between Lake Champlain and Lake George. On July 8, 1758, British general James Abercrombie assaulted the fort with 16,000 soldiers and Indians. The fight lasted five hours, but the attackers never could dislodge General Montcalm's 3,600 defenders. After losing almost 2,000 men, Abercrombie ordered a retreat. French losses numbered 377.

During the summer of 1759, Gen. Jeffrey Amherst led 11,000 troops and Indians against Ticonderoga. The French, badly outnumbered once more, destroyed the fort and withdrew.

Fort Ticonderoga, rebuilt by the English, was captured by the Americans in 1775. In 1777, Gen. John Burgoyne's British and Indian forces menaced the fort and the Americans abandoned it on July 6.

(Michael Kammen, Colonial New York; Arthur Pound, Johnson of the Mohawks; T. Wood Clarke, The Bloody Mohawk.)

TIKUMIGIZHIK, CHIPPEWA CHIEF. Tikumigizhik was born at Gull

Lake, Minnesota, about 1830. A friend of white settlers, he became
a Christian after moving to White Earth about 1868. He refused to
attack American soldiers during the Minnesota uprising of 1862. In
later life he became a successful farmer.

(F. W. Hodge, ed., Handbook of American Indians, II.)

TILLEY, JOHN. John Tilley, a Boston merchant, undertook a voyage
up the Connecticut River to trade at Hartford during the Pequot War
of 1637. Disregarding Lion Gardiner's warning to stay away from
shore, he beached his boat a few miles above Fort Saybrook. The
Pequots captured him and killed all of the men in his crew. For
three days they tortured Tilley, flaying his skin for hatbands and
cutting off his hands and feet. They greatly admired his courage,
for he died without emitting so much as a moan.

(Herbert Milton Sylvester, Indian Wars of New England, I;
Alden T. Vaughan, New England Frontier.)

TIOGA, INDIAN VILLAGE. Tioga, located on the Susquehanna River
near the present site of Athens, Pennsylvania, was a point of settlement for fragments of Algonquian tribes under Iroquois supervision.
The southern gateway to the Six Nations, it straddled several important war trails. It served as a staging area for Gen. John Sullivan's expedition against the Iroquois, and it was burned by American soldiers on September 27, 1778.

(F. W. Hodge, ed., Handbook of American Indians, II; Dale
Van Every, A Company of Heroes.)

TIONONTATI INDIANS see WYANDOT INDIANS

TIPPECANOE, BATTLE OF. The Battle of Tippecanoe was fought
at Prophetstown, near the juncture of the Wabash River and Tippecanoe Creek, on November 7, 1811, between Gen. William Henry Harrison's army and Indian followers of Tecumseh and his brother the
Shawnee Prophet. Harrison, eager to fight the Indians assembled
at Prophetstown while Tecumseh was away, marched his 1,000-man
army to within a mile of his destination on November 6. The Prophet
sent a delegation of chiefs under a flag of truce, and they persuaded
Harrison to camp for the night, offering to parley the following
morning.

During the night, pressed by the Winnebagos for an immediate
attack on the camp, the Prophet proposed to send warriors before
dawn to assassinate the general and his officers. He assured the
Indians that with Harrison removed the soldiers would offer little
resistance. Moreover, he would use his magical powers to make enemy powder "as harmless as sand" and "bullets as soft as rain."

At 4:00 a.m. the appointed assassins began creeping into the
camp while the entire Indian force surrounded the sleeping soldiers.
Alert sentries fired at the shadowy figures and raised an alarm that
brought the troops scrambling into positions previously assigned. A
few officers were slain in their tents, but Harrison's life was saved
when he mounted a black horse instead of the gray that he usually
rode.

The Indians launched three frenzied attacks, compelling soldiers to fall back at times, but Harrison hurried to each threatened position, bringing reinforcements as needed, and "giving orders," recalled one of the regulars, in a "calm, cool, and collected manner" that inspired confidence in his men.

At daybreak, the Indians, furious because enemy powder and bullets were as effective as ever, began to condemn the "false prophet" and to slacken their attack. Harrison ordered a bayonet charge that cleared both flanks, and drove the hostiles into a swamp. Harrison did not pursue them, but on the following day he destroyed Prophetstown.

Harrison heralded the Battle of Tippecanoe as a great victory, and indeed, it propelled him into the White House three decades afterward, but historians have questioned the general's assessment: "... a closer examination of the battle and its outcome indicates that Harrison's claims were exaggerated. Both white and Indian losses were much the same. The American forces numbered close to 1,000 officers and men. They suffered 188 casualties, of which 62 were fatal. The number of Indians engaged in the contest is much more difficult to ascertain, but there probably were between 600 and 700 warriors ... probably at least 50 were killed and 70 wounded."--R. David Edmunds.

"Criticism ... made it possible for him to turn a defense into an imposing offensive of self-glorification. They kept Tippecanoe-- a minor engagement that settled little or nothing--so much in the public eye that in time it loomed up as one of the decisive battles of American history."--Glenn Tucker.

(Freeman Cleaves, Old Tippecanoe; Glenn Tucker, Tecumseh: Vision of Glory; R. David Edmunds, The Shawnee Prophet.)

TIPPECANOE, TREATIES OF. Tippecanoe served as the site of several treaties with the Potawatomi Indians during the 1830's. On October 20, 1832, John W. Davis, Jonathan Jennings, and Marks Crume obtained a large land cession near Lake Michigan in exchange for presents, payment of tribal debts, and a $15,000 annuity. Six days later the same commissioners obtained another large cession for a $20,000 annuity and $30,000 in goods. On December 10, 1834, William Marshall negotiated a cession of six sections of land for a $1,000 annuity and goods valued at $400. In April 1836, Abel C. Pepper negotiated treaties with several Potawatomi bands, in each instance obtaining land in exchange for annuities.

(Charles J. Kappler, ed., Indian Affairs: Laws and Treaties, II.)

TISQUANTUM, PATUXET CHIEF see SQUANTO, PATUXET CHIEF

TOMAH, MENOMINEE CHIEF. Tomah, a prominent Menominee chief, was born near Green Bay, Wisconsin, about 1752. An accomplished diplomat and orator, he served as a scout for Zebulon M. Pike in 1805. Pike considered him to be "a fine fellow ... much attached to the Americans," but the chief's attitude changed when Tecumseh

persuaded him to help hold Indian lands free of American settlers.
During the War of 1812, Tomah belatedly led 100 warriors to take
part in the capture of Forts Mackinac and Sandusky. A British medal
chief, he strongly supported the partisan leader Robert Dickson in
1814. He died in 1817.

(Frederick J. Dockstader, Great North American Indians;
Louise Phelps Kellogg, The British Régime in Wisconsin and the
Northwest.)

TOPEAH, MIAMI CHIEF see LAFONTAINE, FRANCIS

TOPENEBEE, POTAWATOMI CHIEF. Topenebee, an important Potawatomi chief of the St. Joseph River band, first came to note as a
signer of the Treaty of Greenville in 1795. The treaty was one of
many he signed during the next four decades, usually ceding Potawatomi lands to the U.S. Government. He became a follower of the
Shawnee Prophet and Tecumseh by 1807 and fought for the British
during the War of 1812. He attempted, however, to warn the Fort
Dearborn garrison that they would be attacked, and he saved several
soldiers and civilians during the massacre. He refused to join the
hostiles during the Black Hawk War. He signed the treaty requiring
Potawatomi removal to the West in 1833, but managed to have himself
and his relatives exempted. He died in Michigan in 1840.

(F. W. Hodge, ed., Handbook of American Indians, II; Mrs.
John H. Kinzie, Wau-Bun.)

TOTIAKTON, SENECA TOWN. Totiakton, a large, palisaded Seneca
town, was located in present Monroe County, New York, during the
seventeenth-century wars between the French and the Five Nations.
In early July 1687, an army of 3,000 Frenchmen and Indian allies led
by Jacques René de Brisay, Marquis de Denonville, invaded the Seneca country, fought off an attack by 450 warriors, and forced the
residents of Totiakton to flee to the Cayuga country. Denonville
burned the town and surrounding Seneca villages on July 4, and
destroyed the Indians' corn fields. "Two old men only were found
in the Castle, who were cut into Pieces and boyled to make Soop for
the French Allies."--Cadwallader Colden.

(Cadwallader Colden, The History of the Five Indian Nations;
Allen W. Trelease, Indian Affairs in Colonial New York.)

TRACY, ALEXANDRE DE PROUVILLE, MARQUIS DE, EXPEDITION.
Alexandre de Prouville, Marquis de Tracy, arrived in Canada in 1665
with a large force of French troops intended to punish the Iroquois.
In October 1666, he led 1,300 regulars, militia, and friendly Indians
in an invasion of the Mohawk country. Cadwallader Colden described
the campaign succinctly:

> This certainly was a bold Attempt, to march about 250 Leagues
> from Quebeck, through unknown Forrests; but all they were
> able to do, was to burn some of their Villages, and to
> Murder some Old Men, that (like the Old Roman Senators)

would rather dye than desert their Houses. This Expedition, however, gave the Five Nations Apprehensions they had
not before; for they never before that saw so great a Number of Europeans, whose Fire-Arms were extremely Terrible,
and they therefore thought proper to send and beg a Peace,
which was concluded in 1667.

As a result of this chastisement of the Iroquois, a great in-
crease in French immigration to Canada began.
(Cadwallader Colden, The History of the Five Indian Nations;
Francis Parkman, The Old Régime in Canada.)

TRENT, WILLIAM. William Trent was born in 1715, probably at
Philadelphia. During his youth he served in the Pennsylvania militia, was promoted to captain in 1746, and served on the New York
frontier. Afterward, he moved to Winchester, Virginia, and engaged
in the Indian trade with tribes along the Ohio.
In 1752, as an employee of the Ohio Company, Trent attended
a conference with the Indians at Logstown. Discovering that many
of the tribes were intriguing with the French, he went to Pickawillanee to distribute presents to placate the Miamis. In 1753, he appealed to the Iroquois to form an alliance with the Cherokees, Catawbas, and Wyandots to resist French intrusion along the Ohio. The
Six Nations agreed to the proposal when Trent promised that Virginians would build a fort and trading post at the forks of the Ohio.
In 1754, Trent was assigned to build the fort. After constructing a storehouse at Redstone, he reached the forks on February
15. Governor Dinwiddie had given him a captain's commission and
authorized him to enlist 100 men to prevent French occupation of the
Ohio. The fort was under construction in April when a French force
seized it during his absence. (See DUQUESNE, FORT.)
In 1758, Trent accompanied the Forbes expedition that recaptured the forks from the French and established Fort Pitt at the site.
Afterward, he joined the firm of Simon, Trent, Levy, and Franks,
and traded at Fort Pitt with the Indians. He was one of the fort's
defenders during Pontiac's War, and he and his partners sustained
heavy business losses during that conflict. They tried to recoup at
the Treaty of Fort Stanwix in 1768, but the grant of land they received along the Ohio from the Six Nations was never confirmed by
the British government. Trent spent several fruitless years in
England representing the "Suffering Traders" and land speculators
of the Indiana and Vandalia projects.
He returned to America in 1775, unsuccessfully seeking confirmation of his claims from the Continental Congress. Afterward,
he lived at Trenton, New Jersey, until moving to Philadelphia shortly
before his death about 1787.
(Randolph C. Downes, Council Fires on the Upper Ohio; Solon
J. Buck, The Planting of Civilization in Western Pennsylvania.)

TUNXIS INDIANS. The Tunxis Indians, a large and warlike Algonquian-speaking tribe, lived near the present site of Farmington,

Connecticut, during colonial times. In 1633 they had a population
of more than 3,000 but wars with the Mohegans and other neighboring
tribes greatly reduced their strength. In 1640 they began selling
land to English settlers. Early in the eighteenth century, most of
them moved to a reservation at Farmington, where they were joined
by remnants of other New England tribes. In 1738, they accused
whites of illegally occupying their lands, but their claims were ignored.

By 1761, only a few families remained at Farmington, others
having moved to Stockbridge, Massachusetts. In 1804, this remnant
held property under the care of an overseer. By 1850, reported
John W. De Forest, "they have all disappeared from their ancient
home. One miserable creature, a man named Mossock, still lives at
Litchfield, perhaps the sole remnant of the tribe."

(John W. De Forest, History of the Indian Tribes of Connecticut.)

TURNER, JOHN. John Turner, a Pennsylvania trader and militia
corporal, was the stepfather of the famous "white savage," Simon
Girty. During the summer of 1756, at the siege of Fort Granville,
he surrendered the garrison to the Delaware Indians after his commanding officer had been killed. The Indians recognized him as the
murderer of one of their people, marched him to Kittanning, and
executed him while his wife and children were compelled to watch.

(William A. Hunter, Forts on the Pennsylvania Frontier; Consul
W. Butterfield, History of the Girtys.)

TURNER, WILLIAM, EXPEDITION. During King Philip's War, Capt.
William Turner learned that a large number of hostiles were fishing
near the Connecticut River falls. He recruited 160 men and boys
from Hatfield, Northampton, and Hadley, Massachusetts, and on the
night of May 18, 1676, he led them into a camp of sleeping Indians.
Scattering throughout the camp, they opened fire on the wigwams
with deadly results. Survivors fled to the river, pursued by the
settlers who fired from the bank. Those who escaped being shot
were swept over the falls. More than a hundred men, women, and
children were slain.

Warriors from other fishing camps up and down the Connecticut were awakened by the sound of battle and rushed to the scene.
Turner ordered a retreat to Deerfield. The Indians pursued the
whites to Green River, where Turner was slain. Samuel Holyoke,
after the loss of 40 men, led the survivors to Deerfield. Indian
losses were substantially greater.

(Edward Douglas Leach, Flintlock and Tomahawk.)

TUSCARAWAS. Tuscarawas, a Delaware and Wyandot village, was
located on the Tuscarawas River in Ohio, near the mouth of the Big
Sandy. After the fall of Fort Duquesne, it became the headquarters
of the hostile Delaware chief Tamaque, and was called King Beaver's
Town by the whites. It was deserted in 1764 when the inhabitants
fled from Col. Henry Bouquet's army. While Bouquet camped there,

several chiefs came to Tuscarawas to request a peace conference.
(F. W. Hodge, ed., Handbook of American Indians, II.)

TWIGHTWEE INDIANS see MIAMI INDIANS

-U-

UNCAS, MOHEGAN CHIEF. Uncas (Poquim), son of the Mohegan
chief Owenoco, was born about 1606. In 1626, he married the daughter of the Pequot principal chief Sassacus, who ruled Mohegans and
Pequots as one tribe at the time English settlers arrived in Connecticut. Uncas was jealous of the influence of Sassacus, and he led the
Mohegan element of the tribe into rebellion against his chief on several occasions. At times he lived with the Narragansets, and in 1636,
he and his followers offered their services to the English at the onset of the Pequot War.

After the destruction of the Pequot nation and the death of
Sassacus in 1638, Uncas assumed leadership of the surviving Pequots
and other New England tribes that had been under Pequot domination.
In a favored position because of his support of the English during
the war, he undermined rival chiefs by warning colonial officials of
imaginary Indian conspiracies. In 1640, he strengthened his standing
with Connecticut leaders by ceding lands of tributary tribes to the
colony. "He was faithful to them [the English]," John W. De Forest
commented, "just as the jackal is faithful to the lion; not because he
loves the lion, but because it gains something by remaining in his
company."

In 1642, Uncas convinced colonial authorities that the Narraganset chief Miantonomo was conspiring against them. Although Miantonomo pleaded his innocence, he spent some time in a Boston jail.
Afterward, he attacked the village of Uncas, was captured by the
Mohegans, tried by United Colony officials, and sentenced to death.
Uncas carried out the execution in September 1643. (See MIAN-
TONOMO.) The death of their chief enraged the powerful Narraganset nation against the colonies as well as the Mohegans. Uncas
waged war against them, the Mohawks, and other tribes, for many
years.

By 1646, Uncas had become so high-handed that English officials reprimanded him for "obnoxious conduct" and unwarranted attacks upon his Indian neighbors. He regained their support, however, by spying for them on the activities of Indian leaders, and in
1653, he asserted that the Narragansets, incited by the Dutch, were
planning to overrun New England.

During King Philip's War of 1675-76, Uncas sent several hundred Mohegans to assist the colonies. Afterward, he was suspected
of murdering chiefs who had supported King Philip. He became increasingly addicted to alcohol, and he quarreled with whites and Indians alike, objecting strenuously to attempts by missionaries to convert his followers to Christianity. He died about 1683.

"He was a past-master in stratagem, and cared more for plunder

than glory. He was careful of his own men, and, therefore, popular. An apt politician, he was selfish, jealous, and inclined to play
the tyrant. Possessed of many bad traits, he had no great ones.
He served the English as the means to an end, which was the con-
summation of his own personal animosities."--Herbert Milton Sylvester.
    (John W. De Forest, History of the Indians of Connecticut;
Frederick J. Dockstader, Great North American Indians; Neal Salisbury, Manitou and Providence; Herbert Milton Sylvester, Indian
Wars of New England, I; Alden T. Vaughan, New England Frontier.)

UNDERHILL, JOHN. Capt. John Underhill, son of an English soldier
of fortune serving the Dutch, was born in the Netherlands about
1597 and trained for a military career. In 1630 he arrived in Mass-
chusetts to train the militia, receiving a captain's commission and a
land grant for his services. In 1636 he helped punish the Indians
of Block Island for the murder of John Oldham. During the Pequot
War, he joined John Mason's expedition at Saybrook and participated
in the massacre of hundreds of Indians at Mystic. Afterward, he
rescued some Narraganset Indians who were cut off by the Pequots,
asserting that he and his 30 soldiers killed or wounded at least a
hundred enemy warriors.
    Underhill became embroiled in a religious controversy and was
expelled from Massachusetts in 1637. He went to England and published an account of his experiences in the Pequot War. Afterward,
he returned to America and settled at Dover, New Hampshire, serving
temporarily as governor of that colony. In 1643, he moved to Stam-
ford, Connecticut, where he was recruited by the Dutch to fight their
Indian enemies. In February 1644, he led 130 soldiers to attack an
Indian town in which 500 people lived in three rows of houses. "Re-
calling Mason at Mystic," Herbert Milton Sylvester imputed, he "wanted
the village fired. It was a night surprise, and those savages who
escaped the flame of their blazing wigwams were compelled to return
to them by the guns and sabers of the Dutch. It was afterward asserted that in this foray five hundred savages--men, women, and
children were killed--and that only eight escaped." This slaughter
brought the war to an end. (See TANKITEKE INDIANS.)
    Afterward, Underhill settled on Long Island. In May 1653, at
the request of English officials he sought information from Indians
about Dutch attempts to incite raids on New England settlements.
He was arrested for sedition, but released without going to trial.
Upon returning to Long Island, he was employed by Rhode Island
officials to lead raids on Dutch settlements during the war of 1653.
    In 1658, Underhill settled at Oyster Bay on land he received
as a gift from an Indian tribe. He served as sheriff of Queen's
County and died there in 1672.
    (Jeremy Belknap, History of New Hampshire, I; E. B. O'Calla-
ghan, History of New Netherland, II; Allen W. Trelease, Indian Affairs in Colonial New York; Herbert Milton Sylvester, Indian Wars
of New England.)

UPPER SANDUSKY, OHIO, TREATY OF. On March 7, 1842, John

Johnston negotiated a treaty at Upper Sandusky with the Wyandot tribe. In exchange for an annuity of $17,500, reimbursement for their improvements, and payment of their debts, the Indians ceded all of their territory in Ohio and Michigan.

(Charles J. Kappler, ed., Indian Affairs: Laws and Treaties, II.)

-V-

VAN CAMPEN, MOSES. Moses Van Campen was born in New Jersey in 1757 and grew up on the Pennsylvania frontier. He fought against the British and Indians in the American Revolution, serving as a scout in Sullivan's expedition. After the Battle of Newtown, he returned to his home in the Wyoming Valley to recover from illness. There he was captured by a Mohawk war party, but on the march to their village he and 2 fellow captives cut their bonds during the night and attacked the sleeping Indians with their own guns and tomahawks. Only 1 of their 10 captors escaped. They scalped the warriors to collect a bounty, and Van Campen recovered the scalps of his father and brother who had been killed in the raid.

In 1781, while serving as an officer in the Continental Army, Van Campen and his men crept into a camp of sleeping Indians and attacked them with tomahawks. They collected a large store of plunder as well as several scalps. In April 1782, Van Campen and 25 men fought a battle with 85 Indians at Bald Eagle Creek. Nine of his men were killed, and Van Campen and most of the others were captured. Taken to Niagara, Van Campen was exchanged by the British in March 1783.

(Frederick Drimmer, ed., Scalps and Tomahawks.)

VAN CURLER, ARENT. Arent Van Curler (Corlaer) was born in the Netherlands in 1620. In 1638 he came to America to work for his relative, Kiliaen van Rensselaer, near Albany, New York. There he became supervisor of the Indian trade. In 1642 he offered the Mohawks a large reward for the release of French captives, including Father Isaac Jogues. The Indians refused his request to free the captives, but agreed to spare their lives, and Arent used the occasion to negotiate the first formal treaty between the Dutch and Iroquois.

In 1661, Van Curler purchased land from the Mohawks and founded Schenectady. He settled there the following year, and soon gained tremendous influence over the Indians. A colorful account of his diplomacy in saving the French army of Gov. Daniel de Remy de Courcelle in 1665 is provided by Cadwallader Colden:

> This Party fell in with Schenectady, a small town which Corlaer ... had then newly settled. When they appear'd near Schenectady they were almost killed with Cold and Hunger, and the Indians, who then were in that Village, had entirely finished their Ruin, if Corlaer (in Compassion

of fellow Christians) had not contriv'd their escape. He
had a mighty Influence over the Indians, and it was from him
that all the Governors of New York are call'd Corlaer to this
Day.... He perswaded the Indians that this was but a
small Party of the French Army, ... that the great Body was
gone directly towards their Castles, and that it was necessary for them immediately to go in Defence of their Wives
and Children: which they did. As soon as the Indians
were gone, he sent to the French, and supply'd them with
Provisions to carry them back.

In July 1667, Van Curler received an invitation to visit Canada
to receive the thanks of the French for his kindness. On his way,
his canoe capsized on Lake Champlain and he was drowned.
    "Arendt van Curler was one of those characters who deserve
to live in history.... He possessed feelings of the purest humanity,
and actively exerted his influence in rescuing from the savages such
Christians as had the misfortune to fall into their hands."--E. B.
O'Callaghan.
    (Cadwallader Colden, The History of the Five Indian Nations;
E. B. O'Callaghan, History of New Netherland, I; Allen W. Trelease,
Indian Affairs in Colonial New York; T. Wood Clarke, The Bloody
Mohawk.)

VAN KRIECKENBEECK, DANIEL. Daniel van Krieckenbeeck, commissary at Fort Orange, supervised Indian relations and trade. In
1626, he assisted the Mahican Indians to turn back a Mohawk invasion.
By firing their guns, the Dutch settlers put the Mohawks to flight.
Van Krieckenbeeck and his men joined the pursuit. The Mohawks
ambushed the Dutch and Mahicans, killing Van Krieckenbeeck, three
of his soldiers, and many Mahicans. The commissary or one of his
men was roasted and eaten.
    (Allen W. Trelease, Indian Affairs in Colonial New York.)

VAN SCHAICK, GOOSE, EXPEDITION. In 1779, Gen. James Clinton
ordered Col. Goose Van Schaick to attack the Onondaga Indians,
some of whom were supporting the British during the American Revolution. Most of the Onondagas received warning in time to flee, but
12 warriors were killed and 38 women and children were captured.
Three villages were burned, and cattle and crops were destroyed.
No casualties were sustained by the 558 American soldiers.
    The expedition proved to be counterproductive. The Onon-
dagas, who had been officially neutral, joined their hostile kinsmen
in raiding the frontier settlements.
    (T. Wood Clarke, The Bloody Mohawk; Dale Van Every, A
Company of Heroes.)

VAN TIENHOVEN, CORNELIS. Cornelis van Tienhoven, Secretary
of New Netherland in 1640, led 80 Dutch soldiers to Staten Island to
punish the Raritan Indians for slaughtering Dutch settlers' pigs. He
intended only to demand payment, but his men were determined to

massacre the Indians, and he finally consented. His followers tortured several Indians to death. Three years later, he played an important part in the slaughter of sleeping Indians at Pavonia and Corlaer's Hook. (See WECQUAESGEEK INDIANS; KIEFT, WILLEM.)

(Allen W. Trelease, Indian Affairs in Colonial New York.)

VENANGO. Venango, originally a Seneca settlement at the present site of Franklin, Pennsylvania, became a major Indian concentration point before 1750 when John Fraser established a trading post there. In 1753, French officers expelled the English traders, and Venango became the headquarters of the highly successful Indian diplomat Daniel de Joncaire. During the following year, Fort Machault was established there, and hundreds of Senecas, Shawnees, Wyandots, Delawares, and other Indians friendly to the French occupied the town. By the onset of the French and Indian War, Venango had become a center of Indian influence for the entire upper Allegheny area.

After Fort Duquesne fell to the English, the French reinforced Fort Machault, and more than a thousand Indians congregated there. After the loss of Niagara in 1759, however, the French burned and abandoned their facilities at Venango. The British promptly occupied the place and built Fort Venango in 1760.

At the beginning of Pontiac's War, Fort Venango was garrisoned by Lt. Francis Gordon and some 16 soldiers. About June 16, 1763, a Seneca war party approached the fort. Because they were Iroquois, Gordon assumed that they were friendly, and he opened the gates. At once the warriors slew all of the soldiers, but they saved Gordon for a worse fate, torturing him for two days before he slowly burned to death.

(Howard H. Peckham, Pontiac and the Indian Uprising; Dale Van Every, Forth to the Wilderness; F. W. Hodge, ed., Handbook of American Indians, II.)

VIELE, ARNOLD. Arnold Viele was born in New Amsterdam in 1640. As a youth he moved to Albany, engaged in the Indian trade, and became an interpreter. He was such a talented orator in the Iroquois languages that he could hold his own with the Jesuit fathers who attempted to bring the Five Nations over to the French interest. In 1687, Gov. Thomas Dongan designated him as New York's envoy to the Iroquois. He "planted the scutcheon of the Duke of York" at Onondaga, the Iroquois capital, and resided there for many years. In 1690, several members of his family were killed by Indians at Schenectady.

In addition to his diplomatic duties, Viele devoted much of his time to expanding the English fur trade. In 1692, he became the first white man to thoroughly explore the Ohio Valley. He traded along the river and its tributaries for two years, returning in 1694 with a large contingent of Indians in canoes laden with furs. His activities alarmed the French, who suspected that he was inciting the Indians against them and threatening to gain control of the Mississippi Valley.

In later life, Viele traded extensively with the Shawnees. Before his death, which occurred about 1704, he obtained land cessions on the Mohawk and Hudson rivers from the Indians.

(Solon J. Buck, The Planting of Civilization in Western Pennsylvania; Charles A. Hanna, The Wilderness Trail; Louise Phelps Kellogg, The French Régime in Wisconsin and the Northwest; Francis Parkman, Count Frontenac and New France Under Louis XIV.)

VILLIERS, COULON DE see COULON DE VILLIERS, LOUIS

VINCENNES, INDIANA. Vincennes, a major French trading post, was established about 1700. It was named for François Marie Bissot, Sieur de Vincennes, who commanded the post in 1736. Soon afterward, several Canadian families settled at Vincennes, and many of the traders married Piankashaw Indian women. During the American Revolution, George Rogers Clark seized Vincennes in 1778, lost it to Gov. Henry Hamilton's British and Indians soon afterward, and recaptured it in 1779. (See CLARK, GEORGE ROGERS, ILLINOIS CAMPAIGNS.) Afterward, American frontiersmen moved to the town, and separate French and American communities developed.

In 1786, after an attack by Kentuckians on Indian villages, the tribes on the Wabash retaliated against Vincennes. Almost 500 warriors surrounded the town, but after firing a few shots, they acceded to an appeal by the French inhabitants to spare the town and proceed to Kentucky. In 1787, Col. Josiah Harmar occupied Vincennes and held peace talks there with the Weas and Piankashaws. He left Maj. John Francis Hamtramck and a small garrison at Vincennes to maintain peace between the settlers and Indians.

In 1788, 60 Kentuckians led by Patrick Brown attacked an Indian village near Vincennes, killing 9 people. Hamtramck managed to soothe the infuriated Indians by promising to punish Brown and his men, but the garrison was too weak to bring the Kentuckians under control.

Vincennes served as the site of numerous treaty negotiations during the first two decades of the nineteenth century. In 1803, Gov. William Henry Harrison obtained large land cessions from nine tribes, and eight subsequent treaties were signed there by 1820.

(Bert Anson, The Miami Indians; Theodore Roosevelt, The Winning of the West, IV; Randolph C. Downes, Council Fires on the Upper Ohio; Charles J. Kappler, ed., Indian Affairs: Laws and Treaties, II.)

VINCENNES, JEAN BAPTISTE BISSOT, SIEUR DE. Jean Baptiste Bissot, Sieur de Vincennes, was an explorer and trader among the Indians during the late seventeenth and early eighteenth centuries. He was sent by Governor Frontenac to live with the Miamis on the St. Joseph River in 1696. Three years later, he went to the Mississippi with Henri de Tonti. In 1712, he led a force of Miami Indians to Detroit to drive away Fox warriors who were attacking the fort. The following year, he moved with the Miamis to the Maumee River.

Instructed by French officials to facilitate the fur trade by maintaining peace among the western tribes, he served an important purpose, also, in preventing the Potawatomis from trading with the English. After his death in 1719, his son François Marie Bissot, managed the Miamis until he was captured in 1736 by the Chickasaws and tortured to death.

(Bert Anson, The Miami Indians; Louise Phelps Kellogg, The French Régime in Wisconsin and the Northwest.)

VIROT, CLAUDE-FRANÇOIS-LOUIS. Father Claude-François-Louis Virot was born in France on February 15, 1722. He joined the Jesuit order in 1738, and came to Canada to serve as a missionary to the Indians. While assigned to St. Francis Mission in Canada, he undertook the task of settling Christian Abnakis in the Ohio Valley to remove them from harmful effects of French civilization, but the Delaware Indians refused to permit him to establish a Jesuit mission there.

In 1757, Father Virot served as chaplain of the French and Indian army that rushed from the Ohio to reinforce the fort at Niagara. Attacked by Iroquois when nearing the fort, the relief force was almost annihilated (see LA BELLE FAMILLE, BATTLE OF), and the priest was hacked to pieces.

(Frank H. Severance, An Old Frontier of France.)

-W-

WABAN, NIPMUC CHIEF. Waban was born at the Nipmuc town of Musketaquid, near the present site of Concord, Massachusetts, about 1604. He probably was the first chief in that colony to become a Christian, for he was converted by Rev. John Eliot in 1646. In 1651 he established a town of "praying Indians" at Natick, and he held several offices, including that of justice of the peace in that community.

In April 1675, Waban warned colonial officials that King Philip's Wampanoags were planning hostilities against the English. His listeners suspected him of dishonesty, however, and removed him with other Christian Indians to confinement on Deer Island during the ensuing conflict. He survived the war, but died shortly thereafter.

(Ola Elizabeth Winslow, John Eliot, Apostle to the Indians; Alden T. Vaughan, New England Frontier; F. W. Hodge, ed., Handbook of American Indians, II.)

WABANAKI INDIANS see ABNAKI INDIANS

WABASH, TREATIES OF THE. Several land cession treaties with tribes of the northeastern woodlands were negotiated on the Wabash River. Included were the following:

October 16, 1826, with the Potawatomis, by Lewis Cass, James B. Ray, and John Tipton.

October 23, 1826, with the Miamis, by the same negotiators.
October 23, 1834, with the Miamis, by William Marshall.
November 6, 1838, with the Miamis, by Abel C. Pepper.
November 28, 1840, with the Miamis, by Samuel Milroy and
   Allen Hamilton.

(Charles J. Kappler, ed., Indian Affairs: Laws and Treaties,
II.)

WABOKIESHIEK, WINNEBAGO PROPHET. Wabokieshiek (White Cloud,
The Light, The Winnebago Prophet) was born about 1794 and lived
near the mouth of the Rock River. He was half Sauk and he enjoyed tremendous popularity with members of both tribes. A bitter
enemy of white settlers and a supporter of Black Hawk, he claimed
to have experienced a vision that assured the Indians of support by
forces led by the Great Spirit if they waged war against white settlers.
   Wabokieshiek advised Black Hawk throughout the hostilities of
1832 and was captured with him after the defeat of the Indians at
the Battle of Bad Axe. He and Black Hawk were taken to Washington,
where they appealed to President Jackson for their freedom. After
a brief imprisonment they were released, and White Cloud moved west
of the Mississippi. He died among the Winnebagos in Kansas about
1841.
   Although White Cloud saved the life of the Indian agent Henry
Gratiot during the Black Hawk War, his reputation was that of a
cruel and cunning enemy:
   "It was he who repeatedly poured into Black Hawk's ears the
poisonous assurance of aid from the northern tribes and even from
the British.... Black Hawk was ripe for the planting of White Cloud's
dangerous seed."--Albert Britt.
   "The Prophet was a dangerously vicious individual, and it was
to such a man as this that the simple Black Hawk turned for advice."--
William T. Hagan.
   (F. W. Hodge, ed., Handbook of American Indians, II; Albert
Britt, Great Indian Chiefs; William T. Hagan, The Sac and Fox Indians; Katharine C. Turner, Red Men Calling on the Great White
Father.)

WADSWORTH, SAMUEL. Capt. Samuel Wadsworth of Boston was one
of the most active Indian fighters during King Philip's War. On
February 10, 1676, he learned of an attack on Lancaster, led 40 men
to the scene, and played an important part in compelling the Indians
to withdraw. Afterward, informed that the Indians had penetrated
almost to Boston, he patrolled the area from Hingham to Milton.
   On April 18, 1676, Wadsworth led 50 men to drive hostile Indians from Sudbury, pursued a small band into the wilderness, and
blundered into an ambush by 500 warriors. The troops took position on top of a hill and repulsed attacks throughout the afternoon.
Near nightfall, the Indians began burning the underbrush, creating
a heavy smoke that choked the soldiers and caused a disorganized

retreat. More than 30 men were pulled down, and Wadsworth was among the slain.

(Thomas Church, The History of the Great Indian War of 1675 and 1676; Douglas Edward Leach, Flintlock and Tomahawk.)

WALDRON, RICHARD, INDIAN AFFAIRS. Maj. Richard Waldron (Walderne) was born in Warwickshire, England, about 1615, and moved to Dover, New Hampshire, about the age of 25. He became an important religious, political, and military leader along the Maine-New Hampshire boundary, renowned especially for inducing the New Hampshire Indians to make peace with the colonists and to surrender their captives during King Philip's War.

In September 1676, at the conclusion of King Philip's War, a large number of Wampanoag warriors fled to supposed safety among the Abnakis. Waldron, with the approbation of colonial officials, devised a scheme to capture the Wampanoags. He invited 400 Indians to his home and induced them to participate in a sham battle with troops conducting a training exercise. During the proceedings, the entire Indian assembly was surrounded and seized without a shot being fired. The Abnakis were released, but several of the Wampanoags were hanged and the others sold into slavery.

The Indians, infuriated by this treacherous act, marked Waldron for death at the first opportunity, but he remained on his guard, and 13 years elapsed before they succeeded. During King William's War, however, they used a ruse of their own to wreak their revenge. Waldron permitted two Indian women to sleep by the fire inside his garrison house, and while the settlers slumbered, the women opened the gate to warriors who had surrounded the stockade. Jeremy Belknap described the death of the aged veteran on the night of June 27-28, 1689:

> The Indians entered, set a guard at the door, and rushed into the major's apartment.... Awakened by the noise, he jumped out of bed, and though now advanced in life ..., he retained so much vigor as to drive them with his sword, through two or three doors; but as he was returning for his other arms, they came behind him, stunned him with a hatchet, drew him into his hall, and seating him in an elbow chair on a large table ... they cut the major across the breast and belly with knives.... They then cut off his nose and ears, forcing them into his mouth; and when spent with the loss of blood, he was falling down from the table, one of them held his own sword under him, which put an end to his misery.

(Jeremy Belknap, History of New Hampshire; Edward L. Bourne, The History of Wells and Kennebunk; Thomas Church, The History of the Great Indian War of 1675 and 1676; Samuel Adams Drake, The Border Wars of New England; Herbert Milton Sylvester, Indian Wars of New England, II.)

WALK IN THE WATER, WYANDOT CHIEF. Walk in the Water
(Myeerah), a Wyandot chief, was born about 1775. In 1807 and
1808 he signed peace treaties with the Americans, but soon afterward he joined wholeheartedly in Tecumseh's movement to safeguard
Indian land from settler encroachment. He supported the British
during the War of 1812 and participated in the victory over the
Americans on the Raisin River. During the British retreat into
Canada, however, he became convinced that the Americans would win
the war and offered his services to Gen. William Henry Harrison.
After the war, he lived on a reservation near Brownstown, Michigan,
and died there about 1825.

(Frederick J. Dockstader, Great North American Indians; R.
David Edmunds, The Shawnee Prophet.)

WALKING PURCHASE. In 1737, Thomas Penn persuaded the Delaware Indians to sell him land paralleling the Delaware River from
Wrightstown along a prepared route as far as a man could walk within a day and a half. The Indians assumed that the walk would end
at the Lehigh River, the usual distance covered in that length of
time, but Penn's picked woodsmen ran much of the way, followed the
West Branch of the Delaware above Easton, and reached a point in
the Pocono Mountains. From there the line paralleled the East Branch
at a distance, taking in some 1,200 square miles. Intended by the
Indians as mere confirmation of a deed to property granted to William
Penn in 1686, the walk as conducted by his descendants was regarded
as a fraudulent land grab, especially by the Munsees, a Delaware
division forced to vacate their homeland.

When the Delawares objected, Penn persuaded the Iroquois to
order them off the land. So incensed did the Delawares become that
the Walking Purchase was a factor in their decision to raid Pennsylvania settlements during the French and Indian War.

The Walking Purchase, asserted Paul A. W. Wallace, "was a
transaction by which a small hunting territory, allegedly sold by some
Unami Delawares ... was blown up by a dishonest survey to take in
all the Munsee territory from the Delaware Water Gap to the mouth
of the Laxawaxen Creek."

(Paul A. W. Wallace, Indians in Pennsylvania; Anthony F. C.
Wallace, King of the Delawares: Teedyuscung; Sydney G. Fisher,
The Quaker Colonies.)

WAMESIT INDIANS. The Wamesit (Pawtucket) Indians, an Algonquian tribe of the Pennacook confederacy, lived along the bank of
the Merrimac River during the seventeenth century. Before the epidemic of 1620 they had a large population. Afterward, they were
so decimated that Micmac Indians and other tribes overran much of
their territory. In 1621 a band of traders from Plymouth antagonized
the tribe by persuading Wamesit women to exchange coats for
trinkets. Relations improved in 1631, however, when Wamesits took
refuge from Micmac raiders by fleeing to English settlements.

During King Philip's War of 1675, the settlers of Chelmsford
suspected the Wamesits of hostile acts. A group of citizens surrounded

a village, demanded that the Indians come out of their wigwams,
and opened fire when they complied. A Wamesit lad was killed, several men and women were wounded, and the survivors fled. The
Wamesits suffered so greatly during the war that they sold their
territory a few years later and moved to St. Francis in Canada.

(F. W. Hodge, ed., Handbook of American Indians, II; Douglas
Edward Leach, Flintlock and Tomahawk; Neal Salisbury, Manitou and
Providence.)

WAMPANOAG INDIANS. The Wampanoag (Pokanoket) Indians, a powerful Algonquian tribe, occupied much of southeastern Massachusetts
at the beginning of the seventeenth century. It is probable that
their first European contact was with Capt. Bartholomew Gosnold in
1602. Mariners must have spread the plague among them, for their
numbers were greatly reduced before European settlement began.

When the Pilgrims arrived at Plymouth in 1620, the great
Wampanoag chief Massasoit negotiated a treaty of friendship with them
which he observed as long as he lived. With the elevation of his
son Metacom in 1662, however, it had become evident that the English
soon would possess all of the Wampanoag territory. As a result, a
sanguinary war erupted with the colonies in 1675. (See KING
PHILIP'S WAR.) While Philip and his followers destroyed several
New England communities and threatened for a time to drive the
colonists into the sea, they were defeated and almost exterminated by
1677. Survivors who surrendered were sold into slavery, while others took refuge with interior tribes. A few of their descendants,
mainly mixed-bloods, survive today.

(F. W. Hodge, ed., Handbook of American Indians, II; William
C. Sturtevant, ed., Handbook of North American Indians, XV; Neal
Salisbury, Manitou and Providence; Alden T. Vaughan, New England
Frontier; Douglas Edward Leach, Flintlock and Tomahawk.)

WANNALANCET, PENNACOOK CHIEF. Wannalancet, son of Chief
Passaconaway, followed his father's instructions to maintain peace
with the English. His attempts led to much grief for himself and his
people, for the Pennacooks were imprisoned unjustly at Dover during
King Philip's War, and many of them were sold into slavery. Afterward, he and his people removed to Canada, where he died about
1700.

(Frederick J. Dockstader, Great North American Indians; Doug-
las Edward Leach, Flintlock and Tomahawk; Robert M. Utley and
Wilcomb E. Washburn, The American Heritage History of the Indian
Wars.)

WAPELLO, FOX CHIEF. Wapello, a peacefully inclined Fox chief,
was born at Prairie du Chien, in 1787. A supporter of Keokuk and
an enemy of Black Hawk, he signed the Treaty of Fort Armstrong
that ended the Black Hawk War of 1832. In 1837 he signed the
Treaty of Washington, and afterward, he toured several eastern
cities speaking about the advantages of cooperation between Indians
and whites. He died in Iowa in 1842.

(F. W. Hodge, ed., Handbook of American Indians, II.)

WAPPINGER INDIANS. The Wappinger Indians, an Algonquian confederacy consisting of nine tribes and several subtribes, occupied the east bank of the Hudson River from Manhattan to Poughkeepsie, as well as the area extending to the Connecticut River, when encountered by Henry Hudson in 1609. Less than ten years later, the Hudson River Wappingers became involved in the fur trade, and by 1643, they were at war with the Dutch, killing or capturing a dozen boatmen between New Amsterdam and Albany. They sustained 1,600 casualties in the war that lasted until 1645. The eastern Wappingers remained at peace, sold their lands to settlers, and gradually merged with other Algonquian tribes at Stockbridge, Scaticook, and the Moravian towns. A few of their descendants still live in New York and New England.

(John R. Swanton, Indian Tribes of North America; Allen W. Trelease, Indian Affairs in Colonial New York.)

WARANAWONKONG INDIANS. The Waranawonkong Indians, the most important tribe of the Esopus Munsees, lived on the west side of the Hudson River in Ulster County, New York. They were almost annihilated by the Dutch during the second Esopus War (1663–64).

(F. W. Hodge, ed., Handbook of American Indians, II.)

WARANOKE INDIANS. The Waranoke Indians, an aggressive Algonquian band, lived in Hampden County, Massachusetts, during the early eighteenth century. Between 1712 and 1723 they raided neighboring settlements, killing or capturing many English colonists. (See GRAY LOCK, WARANOKE CHIEF.)

(Herbert Milton Sylvester, Indian Wars of New England.)

WASHINGTON, D.C., TREATIES OF. More than twenty land cession treaties were negotiated at Washington by the United States Government with Indian tribes of the northeastern woodlands between 1824 and 1855. Most prominent among the negotiators were John H. Eaton, James B. Gardiner, Carey A. Harris, and George W. Manypenny.

(Charles J. Kappler, ed., Indian Affairs: Laws and Treaties, II.)

WASHINGTON, FORT, OHIO. Fort Washington was built, mainly of salvaged flatboat timbers, at Cincinnati in 1789. Intended to protect the settlements of the Miami Purchase, it became of increasing importance as the staging area of the Harmar, St. Clair, and Wayne expeditions. The fort was abandoned in 1804.

(Randolph C. Downes, Council Fires on the Upper Ohio; Dale Van Every, Ark of Empire.)

WAUMEGESAKO, CHIPPEWA CHIEF. Waumegesako (The Wampum) was born about 1789. A friend of the white settlers of Wisconsin, as head chief of a band of Chippewas, Ottawas, and Potawatomis, he signed several land cession treaties between 1827 and 1833. He died at his home at Manitowoc, Wisconsin, in 1844.

(F. W. Hodge, ed., Handbook of American Indians, II.)

WAWYACHTONOC INDIANS. The Wawyachtonoc Indians, a small
tribe of the Mahican confederacy, lived in northwestern Connecticut
and east central New York during colonial days. A majority of them
became Christians and settled at Shecomeco, New York, or Scaticook,
Connecticut. Eventually they moved with the Moravian missionaries
to Pennsylvania and Ohio.
(F. W. Hodge, ed., Handbook of American Indians, II.)

WAYMOUTH, GEORGE. In 1605, Capt. George Waymouth, employed
by English fish merchants and prospective colonists, sailed his ship,
the Archangel, along the Maine coast and into the Kennebec River.
Using trade goods as bait, he lured five Abnaki Indians aboard, kidnapped them to England, and turned them over to Sir Ferdinando
Gorges, who used them as guides in his attempts to found colonies
in North America.
(Neal Salisbury, Manitou and Providence; Alden T. Vaughan,
New England Frontier.)

WAYNE, ANTHONY, MAUMEE CAMPAIGN. As a result of the disastrous Harmar and St. Clair expeditions, President Washington appointed Gen. Anthony Wayne to lead a third army to crush the hostile
Indians of the Ohio, Wabash, and Maumee region. His army of 5,000
men, known as the American Legion, spent the winter of 1792-93 at
Fort Pitt. Early in the spring of 1793, Wayne moved the legion to
Logstown, where he assigned the men a rigorous training regime intended to toughen them up for a wilderness campaign. He advanced
to Fort Washington at the end of April and set about strengthening
existing forts and extending the road beyond Fort Jefferson.
In October 1793, Wayne established winter quarters at Fort
Greenville and continued to prepare his men for the decisive battle
that he believed would clear the way for the settlement of the Northwest Territory. In December he visited the site of St. Clair's defeat and established Fort Recovery, a post that withstood an attack
by 2,000 Indians on June 30, 1794. (See RECOVERY, FORT.)
On July 28, Wayne marched from Fort Greenville, directing his
troops straight toward the concentration of hostiles on the Auglaize
River. The Indians withdrew before his army, and he halted at
the Auglaize long enough to build Fort Defiance. Resuming his advance, he built Fort Deposit within five miles of the British Fort
Miami. On August 20, near the rapids of the Maumee, the Indians
attacked, and the legion gained the great victory that brought peace
to the region. (See FALLEN TIMBERS, BATTLE OF; GREENVILLE,
TREATY OF.)
(Dale Van Every, Ark of Empire; Clarence Walworth Alvord,
The Illinois Country; Theodore Roosevelt, The Winning of the West,
V; John Tebbel and Keith Jennison, The American Indian Wars;
Thomas Boyd, Mad Anthony Wayne.)

WAYNE, FORT, SIEGE OF. Fort Wayne was built by Gen. Anthony
Wayne in 1794 at the junction of the St. Joseph and St. Marys rivers.
In August 1812, 500 Indians, led by the Potawatomi chief Winamac,

attacked it. Garrisoned by some 70 men under the leadership of
Indian agent Benjamin Stickney, the fort withstood a siege from
August 28 to September 12, when Gen. William Henry Harrison ar-
rived with a large army and drove the Indians away.

(Freeman Cleaves, Old Tippecanoe; James A. Clifton, The
Prairie People.)

WAYNE, FORT, TREATIES OF. The first Treaty of Fort Wayne was
negotiated on June 7, 1803, by William Henry Harrison with the Delaware, Shawnee, Miami, Kaskaskia, Kickapoo, Piankashaw, Potawatomi,
and Wea Indians. The tribes ceded more than a million acres in Indiana and Illinois for an annuity of 150 bushels of salt. Boundaries
established with the Indians by the French and British around the
Vincennes area were defined.

On September 30, 1809, William Henry Harrison negotiated a
treaty at Fort Wayne with the Delaware, Miami, and Potawatomi Indians, obtaining a cession of three million acres in Indiana and Illinois in exchange for increased annuities and trade goods valued at
$5,200. The treaty infuriated Tecumseh, who insisted that the chiefs
lacked authorization to make the cession and threatened to kill any
white man who attempted to occupy the land.

(Bert Anson, The Miami Indians; Freeman Cleaves, Old Tippecanoe; R. David Edmunds, The Shawnee Prophet; Grant Foreman,
The Last Trek of the Indians.)

WEA INDIANS. The Wea Indians, a Miami subtribe, lived in Wisconsin at the time of initial European contact. By 1680 some of them
had moved to the St. Joseph River in Indiana, and by 1719, their
principal villages were located on the Wabash. Ouiatenon, near the
mouth of Wea Creek, became a rendezvous point for French traders,
and Fort Ouiatenon was established there in 1720.

During the 1750's the English trader George Croghan established friendly relations with the tribe, but Wea warriors seized Fort
Ouiatenon, then a British post, during Pontiac's War. Weas supported the British during the American Revolution until George
Rogers Clark drove them to the peace table. In 1791, Gen. Charles
Scott of the Kentucky militia attacked the Wea towns, killing 32 men
and capturing 58 women and children. Many Weas supported Tecumseh in his movement to protect Indian lands from white intrusion.

The Weas began selling their lands in 1803. In 1820 they ceded
the remainder of their homes in Indiana and removed to Missouri and
Illinois. Most of them moved to Kansas in 1832. In 1854 they joined
other remnants of Illinois tribes under the name of the Peoria and
Kaskaskia. They moved to northeastern Oklahoma in 1868, where
their descendants remain.

(Bert Anson, The Miami Indians; Randolph C. Downes, Council
Fires on the Upper Ohio; Dale Van Every, Forth to the Wilderness;
F. W. Hodge, ed., Handbook of American Indians, II.)

WECQUAESGEEK INDIANS. The Wecquaesgeek (Westchester) Indians,
a major member of the Wappinger confederacy, resided in the region

bounded by the Bronx, the Hudson, and the Pocantico rivers in Connecticut and New York. They were numerous and strong until almost annihilated by the Dutch settlers of New Netherland during the middle decades of the seventeenth century.

In 1641 a Wecquaesgeek warrior exacted revenge on the Dutch for the slaying of his uncle by murdering an elderly farmer with an axe. Director Willem Kieft sent 80 soldiers to arrest him, but he managed to make his escape. During a peace treaty signed in the spring of 1642, the tribe agreed to surrender the murderer, but failed to keep the promise. In February 1643, the Dutch, still seeking revenge, attacked the Wecquaesgeeks camped at Corlaer's Hook and Pavonia, massacring more than one hundred men, women, and children while they slept.

During the fall of 1643 the Wecquaesgeeks attacked the settlements in the area of the present New Rochelle, New York. Among the 18 settlers slain were Anne Hutchinson and most of the members of her family. A few months later, a Dutch army led by John Underhill wiped out 500 Wappingers, including some Wecquaesgeeks.

By 1663 the tribe had dwindled to 400 people. The survivors merged with other Wappinger tribes after 1689.

(F. W. Hodge, ed., Handbook of American Indians, II; E. B. O'Callaghan, History of New Netherland, I: Allen W. Trelease, Indian Affairs in Colonial New York.)

WEEQUEHELA, DELAWARE CHIEF. Weequehela, a progressive Delaware chief, lived in New Jersey during the early eighteenth century. A friend of white settlers, he adopted many of their ways, establishing a plantation on the Delaware River shore where he cultivated extensive wheat fields, lived in a substantial house with English-style furniture, and "frequently dined with Governors and great men."--Samuel Smith.

In 1728, Weequehela had a dispute with a white neighbor, Capt. John Leonard, over the ownership of a cedar swamp. Leonard refused to recognize the Indian's rights to the land, and Weequehela shot him to death. The chief surrendered to authorities, was convicted of murder, and hanged.

The Delaware Indians were infuriated by the execution of Weequehela, for, according to their beliefs, a man was justified in killing another for trespassing on his land. The chief's nearest relative, Menakihikon, attempted to incite Indian attacks on the settlements, but he was unsuccessful until the outbreak of the French and Indian War. Then, wrote Anthony F. C. Wallace, "the Munsee descendants of Menakihikon and Weequehela satisfied their honor with English scalps and prisoners in abundance."

(Samuel Smith, The History of the Colony of Nova-Caesaria, or New Jersey; Anthony F. C. Wallace, King of the Delawares: Teedyuscung.)

WEETAMOO, WAMPANOAG SACHEM. Weetamoo (Wetamo, Squaw Sachem of Pocasset) was born near the mouth of the Taunton River about 1650. The daughter of the Massachuset chief Corbitant, she became the leader of the Wampanoag town of Pocasset in Rhode Island. Sister-in-law of Metacom and daughter-in-law of Ninigret, she joined those formidable relatives in fighting the New England colonists during King Philip's War. Recognized as a formidable leader, she commanded 300 warriors during the early stages of the conflict. After the Great Swamp Fight of 1675, however, she was compelled to keep moving about to escape capture by the English. On August 6, 1676, her camp was attacked by soldiers from Taunton, Massachusetts, and she drowned while attempting to swim the Taunton River. The soldiers took her head to Taunton for display on a pole.

(Frederick J. Dockstader, Great North American Indians; Douglas Edward Leach, Flintlock and Tomahawk.)

WEISER, CONRAD, INDIAN RELATIONS. Conrad Weiser, a talented and versatile Palatine pioneer, was born in Württemberg, Germany, on November 2, 1696, and moved to the New York frontier with his parents in 1710. During the winter of 1713-14, he lived with the Mohawk Indians in order to master their language. Afterward, he moved to the Schoharie Valley, where he served as an interpreter until settling with his wife and 10 children at Tulpehocken, Pennsylvania, in 1729.

In Pennsylvania, while farming a large tract, he formed a close association with Shikellamy, the Oneida chief who served as Iroquois supervisor over the Shawnees, Delawares, and other Pennsylvania tribes. So effectively did the pair work together that Paul A. W. Wallace credits them, along with James Logan, for formulating Pennsylvania's Indian policy during the early 1730's. In 1731 Weiser was appointed the province's official interpreter, and the following year, he and Shikellamy were asked to act as agents in administering relations with the Six Nations. His influence extended, also, to tribes under Iroquois supervision.

One of Weiser's first diplomatic achievements was to bring Iroquois chiefs to Philadelphia for conferences with the Penns. In 1742 he helped negotiate a treaty that strengthened the Pennsylvania-Iroquois alliance. The following year he played an important part in preventing a war between the Iroquois and Virginia. In 1744 he served as interpreter at the Treaty of Lancaster--an important conference in which the Six Nations negotiated with Pennsylvania, Maryland, and Virginia officials, ceded lands west of the mountains, and agreed to support the English in King George's War.

Until 1748 Weiser was the man most frequently appointed by Pennsylvania officials to represent them whenever a crisis with Indians arose. After that date he usually shared such assignments with George Croghan and Andrew Montour. The three agents journeyed to the Ohio in August 1748, delivered presents to the Indians at Logstown, and negotiated a treaty, intended to counteract French influence in the area. "The Treaty of Logstown in 1748," Albert T. Volwiler asserted, "represents the zenith of English influence in the Ohio region until after 1763."

After 1748, Weiser, a sincerely religious man, shifted the emphasis of his work from diplomacy to church activities. He assisted the

Moravian missionaries, and he used his influence to curtail the liquor trade that so disrupted the life of the Indians. With the onset of the French and Indian War, however, he was called upon to serve in a military capacity. After the massacre of Pennsylvania settlers in October 1755, he organized a force of frontiersmen to deal with the emergency. Appointed colonel of the Berks County militia, he deployed his men in the Blue Mountains to guard against Indian invasions. In May 1756, he was commissioned colonel of the First Battalion of the Pennsylvania Regiment and given command of the companies east of the Susquehanna. At the Treaty of Easton in 1757 he played an important role in persuading the Delawares to make peace.

Weiser died on his farm on July 13, 1760.

(Paul A. W. Wallace, Conrad Weiser; Albert T. Volwiler, George Croghan and the Westward Movement; William A. Hunter, Forts on the Pennsylvania Frontier; Randolph C. Downes, Council Fires on the Upper Ohio; Louise Phelps Kellogg, The French Régime in Wisconsin and the Northwest.)

WELLS, MAINE, RAIDS. Wells, Maine, a settlement near the New Hampshire border, became a target of Indian attacks during King Philip's War. On September 24, 1676, Abnakis attacked the settlers as they left church, killing George Farrow and Mr. and Mrs. James Gooch. A few weeks later, led by Chief Mugg, they returned to Wells and sent Walter Gendal, a captive, to demand the surrender of the garrison house. When the settlers refused, the Indians murdered 2 men before they withdrew. In April 1677, the Abnakis struck Wells a third blow, slaying 5 settlers and sustaining the loss of 6 warriors.

During King William's War (1689-97), Wells became a place of refuge for hundreds of settlers driven from their homes in other communities. Attacks on Storer's garrison house by hundreds of Abnakis were repulsed in 1691 and 1692. (See STORER, JOSEPH, FAMILY OF.)

During Queen Anne's War (1702-13), the Indians devastated Wells on several occasions. On August 10, 1703, 500 warriors led by French officers killed or captured 39 settlers. On April 25, 1704, 2 men were killed and 1 captured, but the majority of the citizens reached safety in garrison houses. On May 11, the raiders returned, killed 2 more men and captured a third. On August 10, 1707, Indians murdered 5 men and women. On April 29, 1710, 2 farmers were slain while working in their fields. Two years later, 3 Wells men were killed and 2 captured by Indians. In September 1712, a wedding party at Wells was attacked. Two guests were killed and the bridegroom was captured. (See PLAISTED-WHEELRIGHT WEDDING.)

(Samuel Adams Drake, The Border Wars of New England; Herbert Milton Sylvester, Indian Wars of New England, II-III; Francis Parkman, A Half-Century of Conflict; Edward L. Bourne, History of Wells and Kennebunk.)

WELLS, ROBERT, FAMILY OF. During the Cherry Valley Massacre

of November 11, 1778, the Seneca chief Little Beard and his followers attacked the home of a prominent settler named Robert Wells while the family knelt in prayer in the upstairs parlor. Within minutes, Wells, his wife, his mother, his sister, three sons, his daughter, and three servants were killed and scalped.

(Barbara Graymont, The Iroquois in the American Revolution; Dale Van Every, A Company of Heroes.)

WELLS, WILLIAM. William Wells was captured in 1775 by the famous Miami chief Little Turtle during one of his raids on the Kentucky settlements. About 12 years old when taken to the Miami villages, he was adopted, became greatly assimilated, and eventually married Little Turtle's sister. They had four children, and after his wife's death, he married Little Turtle's only daughter.

Wells fought beside Little Turtle in the victories over Harmar and St. Clair, killing several soldiers, but by the time Anthony Wayne invaded the Indian country in 1794 the captive had developed a desire to return to white civilization. He parted from the chief on the friendliest terms and offered his services to Wayne's army. He proved to be an invaluable asset, for he knew the country and understood Indian warfare as did few men of his time. Commissioned captain, he served as the leader of a corps of rangers, many of whom were former captives. Wells and his men killed or captured more than forty warriors, frequently bringing in prisoners who were compelled to divulge the plans of the Indians.

After Wayne's victory and the peace he imposed on the tribes at the Treaty of Greenville, Little Turtle requested that Wells be appointed Indian agent and interpreter to the Miamis, a position that he held at Fort Wayne for many years. Hoping to set an example that would assist the Miamis adjust to white civilization, Wells built a substantial home, lived in the manner of whites, and made sure that his children received a good education. In 1797 he and Little Turtle visited President Washington at Philadelphia, and the following year he assisted Count Constantin F. S. Volney to compile a Miami vocabulary.

Wells and Gov. William Henry Harrison developed an unusual relationship during their years of service in Indiana Territory. Harrison suspected that Wells worked against him during the negotiation of land cession treaties, but considered him indispensable in keeping tribal hostilities under control. With the advent of Tecumseh's movement to unite the tribes against American expansion, Wells was in a position to influence the Miamis and other tribes. In 1808, he escorted the powerful Potawatomi chief Main Poc to Washington to meet President Jefferson, temporarily winning him away from Tecumseh's influence. Unfortunately, Wells was replaced as agent in 1809, and Harrison entertained doubts as to what course he would adopt in the event of an Indian war.

With the outbreak of the War of 1812, Wells notified American officials that several of their western posts would be attacked. Gen. William Hull sent him to help evacuate the troops and their families from Chicago, and he was killed in a valiant attempt to save the lives

of the children on August 15, 1812. (See DEARBORN, FORT, MAS-
SACRE.)

(Bert Anson, The Miami Indians; Milo M. Quaife, Checagou;
Theodore Roosevelt, The Winning of the West, V; Calvin M. Young,
Little Turtle; Harvey Lewis Carter, The Life and Times of Little
Turtle.)

WENDJIMADUB, CHIPPEWA CHIEF. Wendjimadub, a Chippewa chief
of partial French ancestry, was born at La Pointe, Wisconsin, about
1838. A friend of white settlers, and a convert to Christianity, he
served in the United States Army throughout the Civil War. He
moved to White Earth, Minnesota, in 1868 and became a successful
farmer.

(F. W. Hodge, ed., Handbook of American Indians, II.)

WENROHRONON INDIANS. The Wenrohronon Indians, an Iroquoian
tribe, lived in New York near the Neutral Nation when first encountered by Europeans. They traded with the Dutch and English
before fleeing to the Hurons to avoid annihilation by the Five Nations
in 1639. They shared the fate of the Hurons during the Iroquois
wars.

(John R. Swanton, Indian Tribes of North America; William C.
Sturtevant, ed., Handbook of North American Indians, XV.)

WEQUASH, NIANTIC CHIEF. Wequash, originally a Pequot who was
passed over for the sachemship, obtained his revenge by joining the
Niantics and guiding the New England soldiers to the Pequot stronghold at Mystic in 1637. After that massacre he became a Christian
and a friend of Roger Williams. He died in 1642, believing that he
had been poisoned by Indian enemies.

(John W. De Forest, History of the Indians of Connecticut;
Ola Elizabeth Winslow, Master Roger Williams.)

WESSAGUSSET, MASSACHUSETTS. Wessagusset, Massachusetts, was
established not far from the Plymouth settlement during the autumn
of 1622. Sixty men, most of them indentured servants, had been
sent by Thomas Weston, a London merchant, to establish a settlement
to fish and trade with the Indians. They abused the neighboring
Massachuset Indians, pilfered their corn, and planned to attack the
tribe for refusing to trade.

Plymouth officials, fearing a general Indian war, sent Miles
Standish with a small force of Pilgrims to take charge of the settlers
of Wessagusset. Standish found that some of them were living peacefully among the Indians while others were preparing to wage war to
obtain food. Standish and his followers, joined by some of the Wessagusset men, slew seven Indians and escorted most of the settlers
to safety at Plymouth. (See WITTAWAMET, MASSACHUSET CHIEF.)
Afterward, the Indians retaliated by murdering three settlers who
remained at Wessagusset.

(Neal Salisbury, Manitou and Providence.)

WETAMOO, POCASSET SACHEM   see   WEETAMOO, WAMPANOAG
SACHEM

WETHERSFIELD, CONNECTICUT, RAID. Wethersfield, Connecticut,
was founded in 1636, up the Connecticut River from Saybrook. The
colonists obtained land from the Wongunk chief Sequin with the understanding that he could live near the settlement and enjoy English
protection. Not long after the town was established, however, the
citizens drove Sequin away.
    Infuriated by his mistreatment, Sequin incited the powerful
Pequot nation to raid the new settlement. On April 23, 1637, 200
warriors attacked the colonists at work in the fields, killing 7 men,
a woman, and a child, and capturing 2 young women, hoping that they
knew how to produce gun powder. Afterward, they passed by Fort
Saybrook in canoes, hoisting the settlers' clothing on poles to resemble
a parade of English sailboats.
    The captives eventually were redeemed by a Dutch captain who
lured several warriors aboard a ship and threatened to sail out to sea
and throw them overboard unless they released the young ladies.
    (Herbert Milton Sylvester, Indian Wars of New England, I;
Alden T. Vaughan, New England Frontier; Robert M. Utley and Wilcomb E. Washburn, The American Heritage History of the Indian
Wars.)

WEWENOC INDIANS. The Wewenoc Indians, a member of the Abnaki
confederacy, lived near the mouth of the Kennebec River during the
early eighteenth century. Before 1727 most of them moved to Canada
to join the Christian Abnakis of St. Francis and Becancour.
    (F. W. Hodge, ed., Handbook of American Indians, II.)

WEYAPIERSENWAH, SHAWNEE CHIEF   see   BLUE JACKET, SHAWNEE
CHIEF

WHEELOCK, ELEAZAR. Eleazar Wheelock, minister of the Second
Congregational Church of Lebanon, Connecticut, began about 1735
to keep several children in his home to instruct them in religion and
the classics. In 1743, he took in a young Mohegan Indian, Samson
Occom, and the youth's success encouraged him to establish a school
for Indians. By 1762, he had more than twenty students, mainly
Delawares and Mohawks, but he experienced difficulty in obtaining
financial support in America because of hostility generated by recent
Indian wars. (See BRANT, JOSEPH.)
    In 1765, Wheelock sent Occom, by then a successful missionary,
to England to seek support for the school. The Mohegan succeeded
so well that Wheelock was able to move his school to a location better
suited for study at Dresden (Hanover), New Hampshire. In 1770 it
evolved into Dartmouth College.
    (John W. De Forest, History of the Indians of Connecticut;
Francis Whiting Halsey, The Old New York Frontier; Dale Van Every,
A Company of Heroes.)

WHEELRIGHT, ESTHER, CAPTIVITY OF. Esther Wheelright, the
seven-year-old daughter of a member of the Massachusetts governor's
council, was captured by Abnaki Indians during a raid on Wells,
Maine, on August 10, 1703. Adopted by an Abnaki family, she lived
with the Indians six years, learned the language, and acquired the
use of some French from the Jesuit missionary at the village on the
Kennebec River.

Finally she was redeemed by Gov. Philippe de Rigaud de Vaudreuil, taken to his home in Quebec, and educated by nuns. Within
a short time she became a Catholic, learned to love the lifestyle of
the French, and wrote to her father that she preferred to remain in
Quebec. At the age of 18 she became an Ursuline nun. She served
as mother superior of her convent from 1760 until her death in 1780.

(James Axtell, The Invasion Within; Edward L. Bourne, History
of Wells and Kennebunk.)

WHITE CHIEF, CAPTIVITY OF. White Chief, an unidentified 4-year-
old boy, was captured by Seneca Indians in the Susquehanna Valley.
Adopted into a Seneca family, he remained all of his life among the
Indians, fought against tribal enemies, married an Iroquois maiden,
and eventually became a chief. His three sons, all chiefs, were
friends of settlers of the Buffalo area. When he told his life story
to missionaries shortly before his death, he informed them that he
never regretted his decision to live out his days with the tribe.

(Harriet S. Caswell, Our Life Among the Iroquois Indians;
Frank H. Severance, An Old Frontier of France.)

WHITE CLOUD, WINNEBAGO PROPHET see WABOKIESHIEK, WIN-
NEBAGO PROPHET

WHITE EYES, DELAWARE CHIEF. White Eyes (Koquethagechton),
one of the most tragic figures in American frontier history, was born
about 1730. The place of his birth is not known, but he was living
at the mouth of Beaver River, in Pennsylvania, in 1762. By 1770
he had moved to Newcomerstown on the Tuscarawas River in Ohio,
where he served the principal Delaware chief Netawatees as a counselor.
After the death of Netawatees in 1776, White Eyes became the principal chief.

A long suffering friend of the colonists, White Eyes urged his
people to remain neutral during Dunmore's War. At the onset of the
American Revolution, he refused the Iroquois demand to fight for the
English, announcing that he had removed the petticoats draped over
his people by the Six Nations, and would do as he pleased. He kept
the Delawares neutral until 1778. Then, when his rival, Captain
Pipe, persuaded most of his people to join the British forces, White
Eyes sided with the Americans.

At the Treaty of Pittsburgh in September 1778, White Eyes was
appointed a colonel in the United States Army. He helped develop
a plan for admitting the Delaware Nation as part of the fourteenth
state of the Union, but Congress failed to ratify the treaty, and his
dreams of Indian statehood came to naught.

In November 1778, White Eyes served in Gen. Lachlan Mc-
Intosh's expedition against Sandusky. Somewhere in the wilderness
the chief died of mysterious causes. The official report indicated
that smallpox was the cause of death, but Dale Van Every asserted
that "White Eyes, the patient and endlessly persevering advocate of
a firm Delaware-American understanding, was assassinated (by the
militia) while discussing arrangements for a new conference."

    (Frederick J. Dockstader, Great North American Indians; Ran-
dolph C. Downes, Council Fires on the Upper Ohio; Dale Van Every,
A Company of Heroes; Paul A. W. Wallace, Indians in Pennsylvania;
John Heckewelder, History, Manners, and Customs of the Indian
Nations; C. A. Weslager, The Delaware Indians.)

WHITE PIGEON, POTAWATOMI CHIEF. White Pigeon (Wahbeme), a
Potawatomi chief friendly to the whites, signed the Treaty of Greenville in 1795 and the Treaty of Brownstown in 1808. In 1808 he discovered that Indians were planning to attack a Michigan town and
rushed there to warn the settlers. The grateful citizens renamed
their town White Pigeon, and he was buried there when he died at
the age of 30.

    (Dictionary of Indians of North America, III.)

WILKINSON, JAMES, WABASH CAMPAIGN. Col. James Wilkinson of
the Kentucky militia led 500 men from Fort Washington on August 1,
1791, to attack hostile Indian concentrations on the Wabash River.
Encountering little opposition, he destroyed several Miami, Wea, and
Kickapoo villages and captured 42 Indians. His success obtained for
him a commission in the regular army.

    (Bert Anson, The Miami Indians; Dale Van Every, Ark of
Empire.)

WILLETT, MARINUS. Col. Marinus Willett was born at Jamaica, New
York, on July 31, 1740. At the age of 18, he obtained a commission
as second lieutenant in a New York regiment to fight in the French
and Indian War. He was with General Abercrombie's army at Ticonderoga and with Bradstreet's expedition against Fort Frontenac. After
the war he became a merchant at New York City.

    At the onset of the American Revolution, Willett volunteered
to serve against the British. In 1775 he participated in the invasion
of Canada. He was second in command during the defense of Fort
Stanwix, and while most of the Indians were attacking Herkimer's
army, he led a sally that destroyed their camp without losing a man.
(See STANWIX, FORT.)

    In 1779, Willett served in Sullivan's invasion of the Iroquois
country and participated in Van Schaick's destruction of Onondaga.
From 1780 to 1783 he commanded the American forces in the Mohawk
Valley, fighting the British, Tories, and Indians so successfully that
he has been credited with turning the tide in that region. In October 1781, while he pursued Maj. John Ross and 500 British and Indians, one of his scouts killed the notorious partisan Walter Butler.

    After the Revolution, Willett served as New York City sheriff.

In 1792 he persuaded the Creek Indians to sign the Treaty of New York. He died on August 22, 1830.

(T. Wood Clarke, The Bloody Mohawk; Barbara Graymont, The Iroquois in the American Revolution; Dale Van Every, A Company of Heroes.)

WILLIAM HENRY, FORT, MASSACRE. Fort William Henry was built in 1755 at the southern end of Lake George. With the outbreak of the French and Indian War, Lake George became a center of military activities, the French at Crown Point and Ticonderoga controlling the northern end, and the English at Forts George and William Henry the southern end.

The first French and Indian attack on Fort William Henry occurred on March 19-22, 1757. Several assaults were repulsed before the enemy retreated, seized by panic of unidentified origin, and leaving many dead warriors and great stores of munitions on the field.

On August 2, 1757, however, Gen. Louis Joseph de Montcalm surrounded the fort with 6,200 French regulars and Canadian militia and 1,800 Indians. English defenders were greatly outnumbered and weakened by smallpox. A message was rushed to Fort Edward, only 14 miles away, requesting assistance, but Col. Daniel Webb failed to dispatch his 4,000 men to the rescue.

After holding fast for six days, the besieged Americans surrendered on August 9 upon French assurances of safe conduct. When they began their march the following morning, however, the Indians attacked, murdering many prisoners and eating several before Montcalm saved the majority by offering to become their next victim. Estimates vary as to the number of Americans who died in the massacre:

"Unable to check the chaos, Montcalm finally ... restored some order, but not before 200 of the 2,000 prisoners had been murdered."--Robert M. Utley and Wilcomb E. Washburn.

"... the Indians killed and scalped at least 50 of them, not counting the sick and wounded slain at the fort and at the first camp during the retreat. Six or seven hundred other men, women, or children were either carried off as prisoners to be tortured, or were stripped and beaten and left to die in the forest. Of these, Montcalm was able to retrieve more than 400...."--John Tebbel and Keith Jennison.

"The English, instead of showing resolution, were seized with fear and fled in confusion.... Their fear emboldened the Indians ... who started pillaging, killed some dozen soldiers, and took away five or six hundred."--Louis Antoine de Bougainville.

After the British surrender, the French and Indians destroyed Fort William Henry. In the process, they were exposed to smallpox, and as a result, an epidemic raged throughout a dozen Indian nations.

(Louis de Bougainville, Adventures in the Wilderness; T. Wood Clarke, The Bloody Mohawk; James A. Clifton, The Prairie People; Francis Parkman, Montcalm and Wolfe, II; John Tebbel and Keith Jennison, The American Indian Wars; Robert M. Utley and Wilcomb E. Washburn, The American Heritage History of the Indian Wars.)

WILLIAMS, ELEAZAR. Eleazar Williams, a mixed-blood descendant of Eunice Williams, was born on the St. Regis reservation in 1788. In 1800 he was sent to Massachusetts to be educated as a missionary. His studies were interrupted by the War of 1812, in which he served as a scout for the Americans.

After the war, Williams became a missionary to the Oneidas. An outstanding orator, he converted many of them to Christianity. He aspired to establish an Iroquois "ecclesiastical empire" by removing the Six Nations from New York to Wisconsin. With the assistance of the Ogden Land Company, holders of preemptive rights to the Iroquois homeland, he acquired land near Green Bay, and moved a portion of his followers there in 1823. The undertaking collapsed by 1830, however, when government officials rejected his dreams of empire.

Williams began to show signs of mental unbalance by 1840. In 1852 he claimed that he was the Lost Dauphin of France, kidnapped son of King Louis and Marie Antoinette, and many listeners believed him. His last years were spent as a missionary to the St. Regis Indians. He died in 1858.

(Frederick J. Dockstader, Great North American Indians; William C. Sturtevant, ed., Handbook of North American Indians, XV.)

WILLIAMS, EUNICE see **WILLIAMS, JOHN, FAMILY OF**

WILLIAMS, JOHN, FAMILY OF. The Reverend John Williams, a recent graduate of Harvard, went to Deerfield, Massachusetts, as its first pastor in 1686. He married Eunice Mather, and they had a large family. At daybreak on February 29, 1704, they were still sleeping when a Caughnawaga war party burst into their house, murdered two of their children, and captured John and his wife, Samuel (14), Esther (13), Stephen (11), Eunice (7), and Warham (4). After destroying most of the town (see DEERFIELD, MASSACHUSETTS), they marched more than a hundred captives into the wilderness on the trail to their villages in Canada. When Mrs. Williams fell on the ice while crossing Green River, her captor tomahawked her for failing to keep up the pace.

The expedition broke up on March 8, and the captives were taken to various Indian villages. Rev. Williams was redeemed by Governor Vaudreuil and lived at his mansion in Montreal. Little Warham was ransomed and taken in by a French family. In May 1704, a merchant obtained the release of the oldest boy, Samuel, and sent him to Deerfield. Esther was returned to New England during a prisoner exchange in October 1705. Then, in October 1706, the father and his children Stephen and Warham were exchanged for French citizens held prisoner in New England. (See SHELDON, JOHN.)

Eunice was held by the Caughnawaga Indians, and they refused to accept a ransom in spite of repeated efforts by her father, Governor Vaudreuil, and others to redeem her. She joined the Catholic Church and refused to consider leaving the Indians for fear, she insisted, of endangering her life in the hereafter.

In 1713, John Schuyler went to Montreal to redeem English captives and learned that Eunice had married an Indian. The following year, John Williams made a final attempt to secure his daughter, but found that "she is yet obstinately resolved to live and dye here, and will not so much as give me one pleasant look."

In later life Eunice, her Indian husband, and their children visited her brothers and sisters on several occasions, but they refused an offer of land near Deerfield if they would remain. After outliving all of her brothers and sisters, she died at Caughnawaga in 1785.

(Emma Lewis Coleman, New England Captives Carried to Canada; Francis Parkman, A Half-Century of Conflict; Howard H. Peckham, Captured by Indians; John Williams, Redeemed Captive Returning to Zion.)

WILLIAMS, ROGER, INDIAN RELATIONS. Roger Williams was born in England about 1603, educated at Cambridge, and sailed to Massachusetts in 1630 to serve as a Puritan minister. He became embroiled in religious controversy and was banished from Massachusetts in 1635, for, among other reasons, contending that the royal charter violated the land rights of the Indians.

In 1635, Williams established the settlement of Providence in the Narraganset Indian country (present Rhode Island) on land given him by the tribe. He traded with the Indians, became a student of native culture, mastered several languages, and wrote an important ethnological treatise entitled A Key into the Language of America. As his biographer Ola Elizabeth Winslow has observed, he looked upon Indians as "his equals among God's creatures," and although "some of their practices were abhorrent in his eyes ... he could respect their culture in its totality."

While Williams was unwelcome in other New England colonies, officials of Massachusetts, Connecticut, and Plymouth depended on him to use his influence among the tribes during periods of Indian hostility. He willingly risked his life for the colonists on several occasions. At the onset of the Pequot War, he persuaded the Narraganset sachem Canonicus to remain at peace: "The Lord helped me," Williams observed, "to put my life into my hand, and ... to ship myself, all alone in a poor canoe, and to cut through a strong wind, with great seas, every minute in hazard of life to the Sachem's house. Three days and nights my business forced me to lodge and mix with the bloody Pequod ambassadors, whose hands and arms, me thought wreaked with the blood of my countrymen, murdered and massacred by them on the Connecticut river, and from whom I could but nightly look for their bloody knives at my own throat also." He not only thwarted the Pequot envoys, but he established an alliance between the English and the Narragansets.

In later years, Williams was more of a trader than a preacher. He always treated Indians fairly, and he attempted to protect their lands when other Englishmen sought to defraud them. With the onset of King Philip's War, Williams urged the Narraganset chiefs to remain neutral. They agreed, but the colonists, convinced that the

tribe intended to support King Philip, attacked them in the autumn
of 1675. When Providence was threatened, Williams, then serving
as a militia captain, went forth to confer with the chiefs. They did
him no harm because of past friendship, but they destroyed his
home and most of the town on March 29, 1676. Left in near poverty,
he lived with a son until his death about the age of 80.

(Ola Elizabeth Winslow, Master Roger Williams; Neal Salisbury,
Manitou and Providence; Alden T. Vaughan, New England Frontier;
Douglas Edward Leach, Flintlock and Tomahawk.)

WILLIAMS, THOMAS, MOHAWK CHIEF   see TEHORAGWANEGEN,
CAUGHNAWAGA CHIEF

WINAMAC, POTAWATOMI CHIEF (d. 1812).   The name Winamac was
a popular one among the Winnebagos, and there were two important
chief Winamacs during the War of 1812. One of them was a staunch
supporter of Tecumseh, an instigator of the Battle of Tippecanoe,
and a leader of the Fort Dearborn massacre and the siege of Fort
Wayne. He was killed by the pro-American chief, Spemicalawba
(Captain Logan) on November 22, 1812.

(James A. Clifton, The Prairie People; F. W. Hodge, ed.,
Handbook of American Indians, II.)

WINAMAC, POTAWATOMI CHIEF (d. 1821).   Winamac, an important
Potawatomi chief during the early nineteenth century, was a friend
of the Americans. In 1805, at the Treaty of Grouseland, he helped
William Henry Harrison to obtain a cession of Indian land. An opponent of Tecumseh, he infurated that chief in 1809 by signing the
Treaty of Fort Wayne, ceding more than three million acres. He
served as Harrison's spy at Prophetstown, and he tried to warn the
Americans at Fort Dearborn to evacuate without delay in order to
forestall a Potawatomi attack. His advice was disregarded, and the
delay resulted in the Fort Dearborn Massacre.

Winamac visited Washington several times, signing land cession
treaties in 1817 and 1821. He died in 1821 at his village near the
present Winamac, Indiana.

(James A. Clifton, The Prairie People; F. W. Hodge, ed.,
Handbook of American Indians, II; Freeman Cleaves, Old Tippecanoe.)

WINNEBAGO INDIANS.   The Winnebago Indians, a powerful Siouan
tribe, lived in the area of Green Bay and Lake Winnebago, Wisconsin,
at the time of early European contact. During the early nineteenth
century their villages extended along the Rock and Wisconsin rivers.
Surrounded by Algonquian speakers, the Winnebago language was so
unique that Jean Nicolet fancied he had found the Orient when he
visited some of their villages on Green Bay in 1634. Attacked by
Algonquians and decimated by disease during the early days of the
fur trade, the Winnebagos replenished their losses by marrying members of other tribes. They resisted trade with the French until
the Ottawas compelled them to participate.

Missionary activity began among the Winnebagos in 1670, and

Father Claude Allouez established a mission among them in 1671. Afterward, many Winnebago warriors supported the French during their wars with the Fox Indians. In 1728, the tribe split into factions when a French army attacked one of their villages during a campaign against the Foxes. The pro-French division established homes near Green Bay, while those opposed to the French resided on Rock River.

The Green Bay area Winnebagos participated in most of the white men's wars between 1755 and 1815, while the Rock River warriors, by and large, remained neutral until they fought for the British in the War of 1812. During the French and Indian War, the Green Bay Winnebagos played a major role in the capture of Fort William Henry. The tribe transferred its allegiance to the British after the fall of New France. Winnebagos took little part in Pontiac's War, but they fought the Americans during the Revolution and participated in the attempt to capture St. Louis from Spanish forces. (See HESSE, EMANUEL, EXPEDITION.)

The Winnebagos, major supporters of Tecumseh and the Shawnee Prophet, were primarily responsible for the attack on Gen. William Henry Harrison's army at Tippecanoe. They participated in the assault on Fort Madison in 1813, and continued to support the British throughout the War of 1812, fighting at Mackinac and on the Miami and Raisin rivers. Although the Green Bay division signed a peace treaty afterward, the Rock River Winnebagos remained hostile.

In 1827, bloodshed resulted from white encroachment on Winnebago territory, and several settlers were slain. (See RED BIRD, WINNEBAGO CHIEF.) As usual, the tribe was divided during the Black Hawk War of 1832. The Winnebago Prophet and his followers supported Black Hawk, but most tribal elements remained at peace. Some Winnebago warriors, hoping for a reward and better terms at the conclusion of the war, captured Black Hawk for the Americans during the late summer of 1832.

In September 1832, government negotiators compelled the Winnebagos to cede much of their territory, including that belonging to bands that had not participated in the Black Hawk War. In 1837, the tribe ceded their remaining lands east of the Mississippi and began moving to Iowa, some of them forcibly transported by troops in 1840. They removed to Minnesota in 1848, but during the Sioux outbreak of 1862, they were resettled with the Omaha Indians in Nebraska and allotted lands in severalty. A few Winnebagos remained in Wisconsin and Minnesota on farms of their own, and the tribe became widely scattered.

(J. A. Jones, Winnebago Ethnology; Louise Phelps Kellogg, The British Régime in Wisconsin and the Northwest; The French Régime in Wisconsin and the Northwest; William C. Sturtevant, ed., Handbook of North American Indians, XV; John R. Swanton, Indian Tribes of North America.)

WINNEBAGO PROPHET see WABOKIESHIEK

WINSLOW, EDWARD, INDIAN RELATIONS. Edward Winslow, one of

the original Plymouth colonists, was born in Worcestershire, England, on October 18, 1595. One of the colony's leading Indian diplomats, he welcomed Massasoit to Plymouth in 1621 and cured him of an illness shortly thereafter. He studied Indian customs, asserted that some of their beliefs (especially divine sovereignty and reward or punishment after death) paralleled those of the colonists, and he made some attempts to preach about Christianity to them. In 1624 he published an account of English-Indian relations entitled Good Newes from New England.

Winslow became involved in the fur trade with the Abnaki Indians of Maine in 1625, exchanging a large cargo of corn for pelts. He explored the New England wilderness and established trading posts on the Kennebec and Connecticut rivers. In 1646 he went to England to manage affairs of the colony, and he never returned to America. He died on May 8, 1655.

(William Bradford, Of Plimoth Plantation; Neal Salisbury, Manitou and Providence; Alden T. Vaughan, New England Frontier.)

WISCONSIN HEIGHTS, BATTLE OF. The Battle of Wisconsin Heights was fought on July 21, 1832, when the Sauk chief Black Hawk led his followers to the Wisconsin River. His warriors held back the advance of Gen. James D. Henry's militia forces long enough to permit the Indian women and children to escape across the river. "In this skirmish," Black Hawk related, "with fifty braves, I defended and accomplished my passage over the Ouisconsin, with a loss of only six men; though opposed by a host of mounted militia."

(Black Hawk, Black Hawk, an Autobiography; Cecil Eby, That Disgraceful Affair, the Black Hawk War.)

WISNER, GABRIEL. Col. Gabriel Wisner of the Goshen militia participated in the pursuit of Chief Joseph Brant and his Mohawks after their Minisink raid of July 1779. The greatly outnumbered whites were ambushed by the Indians, fought until their ammunition was exhausted, and sustained many casualties when they tried to break through the Indian lines.

Mortally wounded, Wisner calmly rested his back against a tree to wait for the end. Brant believed that it would be kinder to put him out of his misery than to leave him on the field to be attacked by wolves. "With this in view," wrote William L. Stone, "he engaged Wisner in conversation, and, while diverting his attention, struck him dead in an instant, and unperceived with his hatchet."

(William L. Stone, Border Wars of the American Revolution, I.)

WITTAWAMET, MASSACHUSET CHIEF. Wittawamet, an early seventeenth-century Massachuset sachem, was a dreaded enemy of European seamen and settlers. He planned to attack Plymouth, but Chief Massasoit prevented it. In 1623, during a fight at a neighboring settlement, Miles Standish killed Wittawamet and brought his head to Plymouth to display on a pole. (See WESSAGUSSET.)

(Herbert Milton Sylvester, Indian Wars of New England, I.)

WIWASH INDIANS see NANTICOKE INDIANS

WOODWORTH, SOLOMON, EXPEDITION. During the American Revolution, Lt. Solomon Woodworth commanded a company of 50 New York rangers defending the Mohawk Valley against raids by Tories and Indians. On July 2, 1781, while scouting near Fort Herkimer, they were ambushed by a large war party. Woodworth and half of his men were killed, 10 were captured, and 15 escaped.
    (T. Wood Clarke, The Bloody Mohawk.)

WOPIGWOOIT, PEQUOT CHIEF. Wopigwooit, the principal chief of the Pequot nation, lived near the site of the present Hartford, Connecticut, when Europeans first visited the area. The Dutch negotiated a treaty with the tribe to insure peaceful relations, but in 1634, the Pequots violated its terms by slaying Indian enemies who had come to Hartford (The Hope) to trade. In retaliation, the Dutch killed Wopigwooit and several of his warriors.
    (Neal Salisbury, Manitou and Providence; Herbert Milton Sylvester, Indian Wars of New England, I.)

WUNNASHOWATUCKOOG INDIANS. The Wunnashowatuckoog Indians, a Nipmuc band, lived in Worcester County, Massachusetts, during the seventeenth century. In 1637 they permitted fugitive Pequot Indians to hide in their villages, and as a result, they were compelled to abandon their homes and flee to New York. Eventually they returned, for a remnant lived at the site in 1675.
    (F. W. Hodge, ed., Handbook of American Indians, II.)

WYALUSING. Wyalusing was a Delaware and Iroquois settlement in Bradford County, Pennsylvania (present site of Wyalusing), during the era of the French and Indian War and the American Revolution. By 1763, many of the Munsee Delawares at Wyalusing were converted to Christianity by the Moravian missionary, David Zeisberger. The mission was abandoned during Pontiac's War, reoccupied in 1765, and abandoned permanently in 1772.
    During the American Revolution, many Tories and Indian allies of the British congregated at Wyalusing to raid the Susquehanna Valley settlements. On September 28, 1778, an American army led by Col. Thomas Hartley defeated the Indians near Wyalusing. In August 1779, the village was destroyed during the Sullivan invasion of the Iroquois country.
    (F. W. Hodge, ed., Handbook of American Indians, II.)

WYANDANCH, MONTAUK CHIEF. Wyandanch, a Montauk sachem who befriended the English, was born about 1600 and lived on Long Island at Montauk Point. In 1639, he sold land to Lion Gardiner. In 1653, the Niantic chief Ninigret kidnapped Wyandanch's daughter and held her until Gardiner ransomed her. To show his appreciation, the chief gave Gardiner 7,000 acres bordering Smithtown Bay. Wyandanch died of smallpox in 1659.
    (Frederick J. Dockstader, Great North American Indians.)

WYANDOT INDIANS. The Wyandot Indians, formerly the Hurons and Tionontatis of Canada, fled to the western Great Lakes region after the destruction of their nations by the Iroquois in 1648-49. About the end of the century, some of them settled at Sandusky Bay and Detroit. By 1750, they had established villages along the White River in Indiana. (See NICOLAS, WYANDOT CHIEF.)

The Wyandots were never numerous, but they claimed a vast territory along the Ohio and near the Great Lakes, and they gained tremendous influence over their Indian neighbors. Considered to be endowed with superior wisdom, they formed tribal alliances that assisted them to profit in the fur trade and to become a power to be reckoned with during European rivalry for control of the region. About 1750, a Wyandot band settled in western Pennsylvania and became allies of the French.

The Wyandots fought against the English in the French and Indian War and in Pontiac's War, participating in Braddock's defeat, the siege of Detroit, and the capture of Fort Sandusky. During the American Revolution, they raided Kentucky, attacked Wheeling, besieged Fort Laurens, invaded St. Louis, seized the Moravian missions in Ohio, and helped defeat William Crawford's expedition.

Wyandot warriors participated in the battles against Harmar, St. Clair, and Wayne. After their defeat at Fallen Timbers, they signed the Treaty of Greenville, ceding much of their land. A decade later, many of them supported Tecumseh, and they fought for the British in the War of 1812.

After 1815, most milestones in Wyandot history consisted of land cessions and removals. In 1817 they ceded most of northwestern Ohio. (See MEIGS, FORT, TREATY OF.) In 1831 they ceded the remainder of their Ohio lands except for a reservation at Upper Sandusky. In 1842 the reservation was ceded and they removed to the present Wyandot County, Kansas. In 1855 they became U.S. citizens, and soon afterward, they were allotted lands in severalty. Most of them sold their property to whites and moved in 1867 to lands given them by the Seneca Indians in northwestern Oklahoma. Their descendants live there today.

(Randolph C. Downes, Council Fires on the Upper Ohio; Grant Foreman, Last Trek of the Indians; F. W. Hodge, ed., Handbook of American Indians, I; Theodore Roosevelt, The Winning of the West; William C. Sturtevant, ed., Handbook of North American Indians, XV; John R. Swanton, Indian Tribes of North America; Dale Van Every, A Company of Heroes.)

WYANDOT VILLAGE, INDIANA, TREATY OF. The Treaty of Wyandot Village was negotiated with the Eel River band of the Miami Indians by John Tipton on February 11, 1828. In exchange for goods valued at $10,000, the Indians ceded lands on Sugartree Creek and agreed to remove to a reservation on Eel River.

(Charles J. Kappler, ed., Indian Affairs: Laws and Treaties, II.)

WYOMING, INDIAN VILLAGE. Wyoming, located at the present site

of Wilkes-Barre, Pennsylvania, was an important Shawnee and Mahican village until 1744. From that time until the outbreak of the
French and Indian War, many Munsees, Nanticokes, and Iroquois settled at Wyoming, and it became the headquarters of the Delaware
chief Tedyuscung. During the Revolution it was the site of some of
the most famous Indian battles in American history. (See WYOMING
MASSACRES.)

(F. W. Hodge, ed., Handbook of American Indians, II.)

WYOMING MASSACRES. The fertile Wyoming Valley of Pennsylvania
was a major battleground during Pontiac's War and the American
Revolution. The Iroquois ordered the Delawares and other dispos-
sessed tribes to occupy the valley between 1742 and 1753 to protect
Six Nations territory from encroachment by white frontiersmen. In
1754 the Susquehanna Company of Connecticut purchased the valley
from a few intoxicated Iroquois chiefs without the sanction of the Six
Nations council.

Connecticut settlers arrived at Wyoming in 1762, but they were
driven away by the Delaware Indians. On April 19, 1763, the Delaware village was burned, and their chief, Tedyuscung, died in the
flames. Soon afterward, the settlers returned. The first Wyoming
Massacre occurred on October 15, 1763, when Tedyuscung's son, Captain Bull, led a Delaware war party through the valley, killing or
capturing every settler. Some of the 20 captives were tortured to
death, but a few managed to escape.

After the Treaty of Fort Stanwix of 1768, settlers flocked to
the Wyoming Valley. At the outbreak of the American Revolution
some 5,000 citizens congregated in several forts to resist an expected British and Indian onslaught. Most of their effective fighting
men were away in the Continental Army, however, and Col. Zebulon
Butler had only 450 old men and youths at Forty Fort when a Tory
and Indian force, led by Col. John Butler, and estimated at between
600 and 1,100 men, invaded the valley. On July 1, 1778, Forts
Wintermoot and Jenkins surrendered. On July 3, Zebulon Butler determined to lead his militia out of Forty Fort to stop the destruction
of homes and farms. The enemy retreated, drawing the Americans
into a trap. Iroquois warriors concealed in a swamp attacked their
left flank, threw the militia into confusion, and pursued the fleeing
men and boys with lances and tomahawks. Perhaps as many as 400
Americans were killed or captured.

Forty Fort surrendered on July 4, and the Indians and Tories
destroyed the remaining homes in the valley. Most modern historians
assert that no massacre of the inhabitants occurred, but the Battle
of Wyoming is known in frontier tradition as the Wyoming Massacre.
(See MONTOUR, LOUIS, FAMILY OF.) John Tebbel and Keith Jennison have noted that "the surviving inhabitants who escaped fled
to the mountains or to the great swamp of the Poconos, gloomily
known as 'The Shades of Death' thereafter. Most of them perished
of starvation and exhaustion."

(Barbara Graymont, The Iroquois in the American Revolution;
John Tebbel and Keith Jennison, The American Indian Wars; Dale

Van Every, A Company of Heroes; Anthony F. C. Wallace, King of the Delawares: Teedyuscung; Paul A. W. Wallace, Indians in Pennsylvania.)

-Y-

YELLOW RIVER, INDIANA, TREATY OF. Abel C. Pepper negotiated a treaty on August 5, 1836, with the Potawatomi Indians near Yellow River, Indiana. In exchange for payment of $14,080, the Potawatomis ceded the land that they had obtained by treaty three years earlier and agreed to remove beyond the Mississippi River.
(Charles J. Kappler, ed., Indian Affairs: Laws and Treaties, II.)

YELLOW THUNDER, WINNEBAGO CHIEF. Yellow Thunder was born about 1774 in Wisconsin near Lake Winnebago. In 1837, while visiting Washington, he was induced to sign a treaty requiring the Winnebagos to cede their lands east of the Mississippi and to remove beyond that river. He believed that the tribe had eight years in which to remove, and he was dismayed when informed that the treaty required the Winnebagos to vacate their homes within eight months. They remained in Wisconsin until 1840, when troops were sent to remove them. Expecting Yellow Thunder to lead an uprising, they confined him in chains, but the old chief offered no resistance, and they permitted him to remain on his homestead. He died at the age of 100.
(Frederick J. Dockstader, Great North American Indians.)

YORK, MAINE, RAID. York, Maine, was attacked before dawn on January 25, 1692, by the Abnaki chief Madockawando and 150 warriors. More than 50 settlers were killed and 80 were carried into captivity in Canada. Homes were burned and cattle slaughtered for five miles in all directions.
(Edward L. Bourne, History of Wells and Kennebunk; Herbert Milton Sylvester, Indian Wars of New England, II.)

YOUNG, JACOB see CLAESON, JACOB

-Z-

ZEISBERGER, DAVID. David Zeisberger was born in Moravia on April 11, 1721. His parents emigrated to Georgia in 1736, and he followed them four years later to become a missionary to the Indians. He labored among the Creeks of Georgia three years, then went to the Moravian headquarters at Bethlehem, Pennsylvania, to prepare for an Iroquois mission.
In 1745, Zeisberger lived with the Mohawk chief Hendrick and mastered several Indian languages. Soon afterward, he assisted Conrad Weiser to arrange a treaty with the Six Nations. He served the

Iroquois for many years, attempting to teach them skills needed for survival among the white people.

Beginning in 1763, Zeisberger left the Iroquois and began his career as a missionary to the Delawares, living first in their Wyoming Valley villages, and moving with them to the Ohio. In 1771 he established the Christian Delaware village of Schoenbrunn, and similar communities named Salem, Lichtenau, and Gnadenhutten were constructed nearby.

With the onset of the American Revolution, Zeisberger tried to safeguard the Moravian villages by maintaining neutrality, but the Christian Delawares were suspected by both the British and Americans of hostile activities. In a position to observe the movement of war parties, Zeisberger sent warnings to Fort Pitt for Wheeling and other settlements to be on their guard.

In 1781, British partisans and Indians seized the Moravian settlements. In vain, Zeisberger pleaded with the Wyandot Half King to permit the Christian Indians to harvest their crops. He and the other Moravian missionaries were marched to Detroit, while the Indian converts were removed to the Wyandot village at Sandusky. Afterward, some of the Indians who returned to their villages to harvest their crops were slain by a band of the Pennsylvania militia. (See GNADENHUTTEN; MORAVIAN INDIANS.)

After the destruction of the Moravian towns in Ohio, Zeisberger determined to establish missions in Canada. New Gnadenhutten was established near Detroit in 1782. When the Revolution ended, he established the New Salem, Ohio, mission, but he returned to Canada during the Indian wars of the 1790's, founding the Fairfield mission in 1792. In 1798, peace having been restored in the Indian country, he returned to Ohio and founded the mission of Goshen. He died there in 1808.

"As regards the frequency of his journeys among the Indians and the privations which he endured in his efforts to convert them, no one is his equal except the Jesuit Fathers of the seventeenth century."--Edmund De Schweinitz.

(Edmund De Schweinitz, The Life and Times of David Zeisberger; Reuben Gold Thwaites and Louise Phelps Kellogg, eds., Frontier Defense on the Upper Ohio; The Revolution on the Upper Ohio; C. A. Weslager, The Delaware Indian Westward Migration.)

ZWAANENDAEL COLONY MASSACRE. Zwaanendael (Swaanendael), a Dutch colony, was established at the present site of Lewes, Delaware, in 1631. Capt. Pieter Heyes delivered 28 men to the shore of Delaware Bay and sailed back to Holland to report to his employer, David DeVries. The settlers constructed a palisaded trading post, planted crops, and prepared to engage in whaling activities, but a misunderstanding arose with the neighboring Indians over the theft of a metal emblem erected by the colonists as a symbol of Dutch sovereignty. As a result, the Indians massacred 26 men at work in the fields and two in the fort. (See DEVRIES, DAVID.)

(Albert Cook Myers, ed., Narratives of Early Pennsylvania, West New Jersey, and Delaware; E. B. O'Callaghan, History of New

Netherland, I; C. A. Weslager, Dutch Explorers, Traders, and Settlers in the Delaware Valley.)